King Cotton's Advocate

LAWRENCE J. NELSON

# King Cotton's Advocate

*Oscar G. Johnston and the New Deal*

The University of Tennessee Press / Knoxville

F
341
.J64
N45
1999

Library of Congress Cataloging-in-Publication Data

Nelson, Lawrence J., 1944–
     King Cotton's advocate : Oscar G. Johnston and the New Deal /
Lawrence J. Nelson. — 1st ed.
          p. cm.
     Includes bibliographical references (p. ) and index.
     ISBN 1-57233-025-2 (cloth: alk. paper)
1. Johnston, Oscar G. (Oscar Goodbar), 1880–1955. 2. Politicians—Mississippi—
Biography. 3. Cotton farmers—Mississippi—Biography. 4. Cotton growing—Mississippi—History—20th century. 5. Mississippi—Politics and government—1865–1950.
6. Mississippi—Economic conditions. 7. New Deal, 1933–1939. 8. United States—
Economic conditions—1918–1945. I. Title.
F341.J64 N45 1998
976.2'06'092—ddc21                                                98-19739

# To Verlie

*and to the memory of our first son*

# Contents

# Illustrations

# Preface

*Fortune* magazine used to advertise that within its pages one could find ideas that presumably might be turned into profit. I discovered not profit but at least an idea. For years a pleasant habit of mine was routing through old bookshops in search of printed treasures of one vintage or another. As an undergraduate in the mid-1960s I encountered the big, bold, lavishly illustrated, and originally pricey magazines named for the Wheel of Fortune. In the back room of a decrepit bookshop lay unclaimed treasures of art dating from the Great Depression. By the time I found them their original lavish one-dollar cover price had shrunk to a quarter or fifty cents. I gathered several. Before most of them went into a closet I often browsed their beautiful pages. A few years later, on the eve of declaring a subject for a doctoral dissertation, I idled through the pages once again. There it was in the March 1937 issue. The story of an anomaly, a successful cotton planter in the Great Depression, Oscar Goodbar Johnston of Mississippi. *Fortune* called him "freakishly successful," and he ran, or so the magazine said in its title, the "Biggest Cotton Plantation." The subject pleaded for further inquiry. Though I was originally more interested in the sprawling thirty-eight-thousand-acre plantation in the fertile soil of the Mississippi Delta—what a historian of the Delta has recently called "the most southern place on earth"—this allegedly freakish planter demanded attention in his own right. That inquiry led into a complex and deeply troubled industry.

Around the time I stumbled onto *Fortune*'s story about Oscar Johnston and his plantation, the historical profession's love affair with the New Deal was being severely tested. Fulfilling the dictum attributed to the late Professor Carl Becker that the present influences ideas of the past, some historians on the left, a generation after Franklin Roosevelt's administration, found the sometimes pale liberalism of the New Deal wanting. Nowhere was this criticism more pronounced than in the assessment of Roosevelt's agricultural policies, notably in the South, where big planters ran the political economy and dominated that part of the New Deal. Left out, said the critics, were the hapless sharecroppers, trapped in a sort of modern serfdom.[1]

The criticism seemed alluring in those days. But the case of Oscar Johnston and his massive plantation commanded reexamination. It turns out that there was more here than had originally met the eye. The very personable Johnston possessed perhaps the most brilliant legal and financial mind in the entire South, with oratorical skills to match. In the New Deal years, this erstwhile politician, banker, and barrister—and now big-time Mississippi planter—held a series of federal appointments, chiefly in the Department of Agriculture. His activities provide a window to King Cotton in the New Deal, including conflict over methods of cotton control; development of cotton loans, notably one that led to the creation of the Commodity Credit Corporation; the infamous "purge" of the Agricultural Adjustment Administration liberals in the mid-thirties; and the impact of welfare capitalism and the New Deal on his cotton plantation. That plantation was home to a relative handful of whites amid thousands of blacks. In the face of impending social and technological change—a "transformation," according to one historian of southern plantations—those blacks worked the land on shares, following mules and dragging sacks across the flat, sun-scorched Mississippi Delta. Johnston and his tens of thousands of acres defied (and defy now) the monochromatic caricature of the southern planter. In 1935, Franklin Roosevelt asked Johnston to go abroad to seek possibilities for cotton stabilization; he did so, all the while lambasting U.S. economic nationalism. Through his management of the federal cotton pool, Johnston artfully, though not without controversy, disposed of the old Federal Farm Board's bearish cotton holdings left over from the Hoover administration.[2] In so doing he kept one eye on the ticker tape, outwitted the speculators, and never once broke the market. He also weathered public disclosure of huge government subsidies to his largely British-owned plantation, disclosures that, accompanied by demagoguery, returned like periodic locusts. Successfully he advocated and defended the New Deal in his native South. But Oscar Johnston knew there were two New Deals, and eventually concluded that cotton's salvation had to originate in the South, not in Washington. In 1939, at his zenith, he successfully united the disparate cotton industry into the National Cotton Council of America, and held its presidency for nearly a decade.

Oscar Johnston did none of these things for Franklin Roosevelt or the New Deal. As in Isaiah Berlin's analogy of the ancient Greek poet's musings about the hedgehog and the fox, Johnston was clearly the hedgehog. Unlike the fox, who knew lots of things, the hedgehog knew only one big thing.[3] For Johnston, that big thing was King Cotton and his position in the American economy. Johnston was a pragmatist whose commitment to New Deal solutions to cotton's problems waned as the New Deal shifted leftward. During World War II he publicly opposed the agricultural collectivism of the Farm Security Administration and its perceived alliance with northern labor unions. Then as blacks left the land for war and war work, his plantation eagerly embraced the technological changes that came to dominate the postwar South. During King Cotton's greatest crisis, in depression, peace, and war, in shrinking markets and threats from synthetics, Oscar Johnston became His Majesty's greatest advocate.

# Acknowledgments

The development of this book benefited from the assistance of many individuals and institutions. Some assistance proved essential, including that provided by Mr. Minor S. Gray, then president of the Delta and Pine Land Company in Scott, Mississippi. Mr. Gray might well have been wary of a northerner wanting to pick through the activities of his predecessor as president, Oscar G. Johnston, and the records of the gigantic plantation over which each, in their time, presided. After all, the often-visible and largely British-owned Mississippi plantation had been an easy mark for assaults by both the politically motivated and the well meaning. During a preliminary tour of possible source material many years ago, Mr. Gray informed my wife and me that no papers survived from the period I wanted to investigate.

But the subject was not closed. A few months later we again visited the plantation. This time Mr. Gray told me that after our previous visit he had routed around in the attic of one of the company's buildings. Were the records he had discovered, he wanted to know, of any value to my investigation? Such scenarios are likely to produce euphoria in any scholar's heart, and this one did in mine. He led us to file after file of material—correspondence and other records of the plantation and its one-time highly visible late president, Oscar Johnston. True, much was missing, and quite a bit of what remained was mouse chewed, but here was the stuff of history! He gave us a key to the building, some scissors to trim the mouse chewings, and let us have at it. His generosity even allowed us to retain and categorize a substantial portion of the material for a lengthy period, with only minor restriction. He later claimed that had we not come along, someday the material would have been burned up; in fact, he had the fires stoked with material from his own tenure, claiming that he wasn't "as important as Mr. Johnston." Regardless of his own self-deprecation, his importance to this project proved crucial. Over the years, Minor and his kind wife, Helen, became friends of mine. Her sweet spirit stood in contrast to his false gruff exterior, which was a facade hiding—not very well—a wonderful person. My deep and sincere thanks to him.

Many others provided important assistance at various junctures. Helen Fineran Ulibari, Gladys Baker, and J. Douglas Helms of the National Archives all provided research assistance. During one lengthy visit Doug proved particularly adept at coming up with box after box of relevant agricultural materials. Since in another, long-ago phase of my life this subject formed the basis for a doctoral dissertation at the University of Missouri–Columbia (though it bears faint resemblance to the present volume), I acknowledge the courtesies of Paul Nagel, Richard Kirkendall, David Thelen, the late Robert Karsch, and especially my mentor, the late Lewis E. Atherton. Atherton's contributions to my work, to my education, and to my life are profound.

At some stage or another, this work benefited from research grants through the Department of History at the University of Missouri–Columbia and from direct or indirect assistance from Evangel College in Springfield, Missouri. Sue Cooper of California's Pasadena City College library acquired important interlibrary loan material, as did the library staff at the University of Missouri–Columbia. Sue Nazworth of Collier Library at the University of North Alabama has, with good humor, done the same. Others at the university were also helpful in one way or another, including President Robert Potts, Kenneth Johnson, Peter Barty, Gary Green, and the late John Powers. For generously giving their time and talent, I am grateful to photographer Shannon Wells and map maker Lisa Keys-Mathews. Also, various research and release-time grants furthered progress on the manuscript. More recently, Arts and Sciences Dean Jack Moore made funds available to obtain permissions for numerous photographs. I am grateful for such assistance and encouragement. Even more important, I am thankful for my colleagues and students, who make the university such a very pleasant place to work.

The staffs of many libraries and archives have proved helpful. Such includes those at the Mississippi Department of Archives and History, Jackson; the Alabama Department of Archives and History, Montgomery; the State Historical Society of Wisconsin, Madison; the University of Iowa library, Iowa City; the Joint Collection of the Western Historical Manuscripts Collection at the University of Missouri–Columbia and the State Historical Society of Missouri, Ellis Library, Columbia; the Mitchell Library of Mississippi State University, Starkville; the late Sammy Cranford of Delta State University archives, Cleveland, Mississippi; the Southern Collection at the University of North Carolina in Chapel Hill; the Oral History Collection at Butler Library, Columbia University, New York; the National Cotton Council of America, Memphis; the Memphis Public Library; the University of Memphis library; the Carnegie Library, Clarksdale, Mississippi; Coahoma County Courthouse, Clarksdale, Mississippi; the

Franklin D. Roosevelt Library, Hyde Park, New York; and, of course, the National Archives in Washington, D.C., and College Park, Maryland, the latter facility receiving the National Archives Record Groups cited in this volume. More recently, by telephone, James Rush provided assistance from College Park.

In addition to those already mentioned, particular individuals who assisted in one way or another, whether by comment or with an idea or whatever, include the late William Rhea Blake, Read P. Dunn Jr. (a former National Cotton Council official whose own work on Johnston was published by the council in 1991), Alger Hiss (who was very generous with his time and thoughts), Chester Morgan, Roy Scott, Rodney Olsen, Larry Balsamo, JoeAnn Fava, the late Harry L. Mitchell, Robert Brandfon, John Kuhlman, H. Wesley Ward, Stanley Parsons, Bruce Pencek, Russell and Janet Tyson (for kind hospitality), Julia S. Nelson, the late J. C. Johnston and the late Paul M. Johnston (both of whom generously provided privately held material regarding their family), and the numerous people named in the interview section, who took time to communicate with me in person, by telephone, and/or by correspondence. Also, thanks to three special friends and former students: Laura Leigh Parker and Amy Michelle Owens for editing and proofreading and Rick M. Gilliam for encouragement. I am further grateful to John B. Boles, managing editor of the *Journal of Southern History*; Ann Toplovich, executive director of the Tennessee Historical Society, which publishes the *Tennessee Historical Quarterly*; and Douglas Hurt, editor of *Agricultural History,* for permission to use material in chapters 6, 7, 10, and 11 that originally appeared in one form or another in those journals. My gratitude also to those scholars and editors who took the time and offered comments while these articles were being considered for publication. The talented folk at the University of Tennessee Press were delightfully personable and professional. Director Jennifer Siler and acquisitions editor Joyce Harrison facilitated and encouraged this project (as did Meredith Morris-Babb, now associate director of the University Press of Florida), while Scot Danforth and Monica Phillips performed beautifully in the copyediting process. They, along with marketing manager Gene Adair, treated me with courtesy and kindness, and I am grateful to them all. And then thanks to those scholars whose words or work have provided me with ideas and understanding, whether specifically acknowledged in the endnotes or not. Of course, while so many have helped, the author alone bears responsibility for remaining errors of fact and interpretation.

The best is last. For their support in so many ways, and over so many years, I am indebted to my mother and father, the late Hannah R. Nelson and Lawrence P. Nelson. I want also to mention my second son, Pete, and my only daughter,

Julia, who adjusted nicely to research trips for a number of projects. Most of all, however, and for so many reasons, my debt is to Verlie M. Nelson, whose maturity and strength of character are but two of her many virtues. She has, for the more than thirty years I have known her, supported every worthy thing I have ever tried. Her husband's dedication of this volume to her cannot repay that debt, of course, but then some debts cannot be repaid, only acknowledged.

# 1

## Oscar

Since I was 18 years of age I have "worked" for every penny I have had.
—Oscar G. Johnston, 1943

He wears no man's "collar." —*Friars Point Coahomian*, 1915

**T**he manager of the Memphis bureau of the United Press wire service was upset. His local correspondent in Greenville, Mississippi, about 140 miles to the south, in the heart of the Yazoo–Mississippi Delta, persisted in dispatching trivial stories to the Memphis office. Eventually, so the story goes, a new manager took over the Memphis office, promptly sending new instructions to the troublesome correspondent. "The United Press," admonished the new chief, "is interested in stories from your territory of more than local interest. Protect us on murders, unusual and fatal auto accidents, airplane crashes, lynchings, floods, large fires, cotton research and Oscar Johnston." Hodding Carter, the Mississippi news editor and eventual Pulitzer-prize winner who related this anecdote in the 1930s, added that Johnston's neighbors in the Delta would approve of his inclusion in the wire service list. "They think he is the state's smartest man," said Carter, "and the South's."[1]

The anecdote, true or not, provides an appropriate statement about Oscar Johnston's public and private career: Johnston had long been a man to watch, even in his relatively youthful days in Friars Point, Mississippi, where he began the practice of law at the turn of the century. Young Oscar got his ambition and abilities honestly. Family tradition had it that Oscar's great great grandfather, of Ulster County, Ireland, had crossed the Atlantic at the start of the American Revolution, had fought with Cornwallis, then settled briefly in Virginia after the war. His son, Leonard B. Johnstone, born in 1792 in either Kentucky or Tennessee, fathered a daughter and three or four sons, all of whom wound up in west-central Mississippi before the Civil War. One of the boys, Oliver, Oscar's grandfather, born in Kentucky in 1827, and the only one survived by sons, arrived in the flush days of Mississippi in the 1840s. Marrying Medora Peyton and fathering two sons, John Calvin and Oscar H., Oliver eventually taught school in Copiah County in southwest Mississippi and became a pioneer druggist in

Hazlehurst. After the start of the Civil War, he enlisted as a second lieutenant in Company K of the Third Mississippi Infantry, gaining captain's rank early in 1862. More than two years later, serving under Gen. Joseph E. Johnston in the path of William T. Sherman's juggernaut through Georgia, Oliver was seriously wounded while advancing on a Yankee fortification at New Hope Church. Detained briefly and paroled at war's end, he soon swore allegiance to the Union and apparently returned to Hazlehurst. Languishing with his wound, he spent his latter years reading and studying—"thoroughly posted on business affairs." In 1879, "in the full triumphs of the Christian faith," he succumbed.[2]

Oliver's oldest son, John Calvin Johnston, Oscar's father, carried on the family tradition in business. Raised on a farm, he later studied law but entered the newspaper business in Hazlehurst following graduation from Tennessee's Cumberland University in 1872. Active in Democratic politics and public service, J.C. served, among other positions, as mayor of Hazlehurst and later as Mississippi deputy auditor in Jackson. Along the way he married Emma Goodbar of Lebanon, Tennessee, in 1878, and the first of their two sons, Oscar Goodbar Johnston, was born in Jackson on January 27, 1880. Forced by ill health to quit the auditor's office, J.C. traveled for a year and a half, recovered, and, in the fall of 1889, helped organize a bank in Friars Point, a Mississippi River town in the Yazoo–Mississippi Delta. Two years later, Goodspeed's *Biographical and Historical Memoirs of Mississippi* touted him as "a man of superior business capacity" and proclaimed the Bank of Friars Point "one of the soundest institutions in the state."[3] In public service and private business, Johnston helped advance Mississippi's transition from the Old South to the New.

Oscar and his younger brother, Alvan, grew into adolescence in Friars Point, the small but busy river community about seventy land miles south of Memphis. The seat of Coahoma County, which flourished in population and cotton before the Civil War, Friars Point became a rendezvous during the war for Generals Grant and Sherman. If that was not bad enough, postwar carpetbaggers soon "infested" the place, providing a base for Mississippi's Whig-turned-Republican governor and senator, James Lusk Alcorn. Alcorn had paid his dues: before the Civil War he had cajoled Congress into passing a levee bill. The Delta needed miles and miles of levees if the place were ever to become truly civilized. In any case, strategically situated near a bend where the big river slowed, Friars Point had become a cotton-shipping center, the lower terminal for Memphis and Friars Point river packets. It didn't last. Neighboring Clarksdale, a ballooning interior community a few miles south, soon challenged the town's hold on county government. The state legislature compromised in 1892 by dividing Coahoma into two jurisdictions, awarding one to Friars Point and one to Clarksdale. That failed to end the haggling, but by the time the legislature abolished the separate districts in 1930 and gave the seat of government exclusively to Clarksdale, Friars Point had receded into a sleepy river community.[4]

Oscar Johnston was there during the transition days. He went to school in Friars Point for a time, but, nurtured as he was in a family that valued education and achievement, he also attended schools in Jackson, Memphis, and Kansas City before taking three years of literary preparation at the new Kentucky Military Institute in Lyndon, Kentucky. Class salutatorian, Oscar graduated in June 1899 with first honors; that fall he entered the University of Mississippi to study law. There, combining academics with alcohol, young Oscar, in league with other lads, shot out some lightbulbs on campus and had to leave after only one semester. (When he ran for governor two decades later, his reason for leaving Ole Miss had become his father's "financial reverses.") He resumed his law studies at Cumberland University in Lebanon, Tennessee, his father's alma mater. To support himself Oscar worked on a farm near Lebanon, earning his keep and fifteen dollars a month. Criticized years later as a big planter with no appreciation for small farmers, Johnston pointed to his earthy youthful experiences and his allegedly humble land beginnings. It was a thin argument. Still, what he called his "natural love for the land and for farming" persisted after he graduated as class orator—a signal of things to come—and returned to Friars Point to practice law in 1901. From his savings he acquired farmland, starting with forty acres near Friars Point. County tax rolls in the 1910s show his increased landholdings, some of them improved. By the 1920s, "Through many successes and failures and trials and tribulations," he said later, he was president of and a major investor in a medium-sized plantation in the cotton-laden Delta.[5]

If young Oscar aspired to planter status, he gave much early attention to his career at the bar. His decision to set up shop in the small river community seemed to suggest no big ambition. Still, the plantation system attaching itself to rich, newly cleared land provided abundant opportunities for a diligent lawyer. Ironically, the first case for which Oscar received a fee, at age twenty-one, had nothing to do with land development. Instead he defended a black man charged with murdering another black man on a Coahoma County plantation. Respecting the abilities of an experienced colleague and fearing injustice, "or perhaps to avoid the doing of justice," Oscar shared both the case and the fee. But young Johnston required little tutelage. His skill at the bar soon became evident. Courthouse trials provided local entertainment, and young boys awaited the opening of the doors and crowded toward the front seats to hear the debates. Johnston, recalled one of the lads, "was a crackerjack lawyer," and everyone liked to hear him. His practice also took him throughout the Delta and to Jackson, where he argued cases before the Mississippi Supreme Court. In one legislative battle over a courthouse bill in 1904, when Johnston was only twenty-four, his skill-ful performance in the capital promised a bright career. "Mr. Johnston made a most creditable fight—a fight that would have reflected credit upon one much older in years and experience than he," said the Clarksdale paper. "We are justly proud of our talented young barrister," echoed the *Friars Point Coahomian;* local ladies, properly impressed, gave him "a handsome cane" for his efforts.[6]

The legal profession showcased Johnston's skills and wit. He fashioned argu-ments only after studying his cases from his opponents' perspective. Some of his court appearances even became grist for legend. According to one story, one day in the state supreme court Oscar was reading aloud from a Mississippi report when one of the judges, a political opponent, said, "Why Mr. Johnston, you know that's not the law." Oscar retorted, "Very well, then, I have no need for this," whereupon he ripped the page from the book and threw it on the floor. Johnston confirmed the story years later, adding that "it was probably a damn fool thing to do because it cost me $50 for contempt and $25 for another Mississippi re-port." Then there was the time in Friars Point when the telephone company hired him as defense counsel against an overweight plaintiff who sued for defamation after a provoked but short-tempered relief operator called him a "pot-bellied son-of-a-bitch." Since the epithet was delivered on a party line, it constituted legal publication and circulation. The telephone company wanted to settle out of court, but Johnston decided "to plead truth as justification." The judge asked him on what he relied. Oscar referred to some case he had unearthed where the term "SOB," cited as provocation for homicide, could not be taken literally but, for legal purposes, had to conform to local usage. Among sailors, for example, it could be endearing, not provocative. Oscar then got qualified medical opin-ion to affirm that the plaintiff was indeed pot bellied according to local usage of the term. "Oscar," said the plaintiff's attorney, "you don't intend to go through with it?" Said Oscar, "I've got about 50 witnesses out here that are ready to testify under oath that your client is a 'son-of-a-bitch' as we understand the term in Fri-ars Point." The telephone company settled with a nonsuit, but Oscar claimed his client was the real SOB. He sent them a bill and they paid only half.[7]

Johnston represented less flamboyantly a range of clients in his nearly two-decade legal practice. There was the Coahoma County sheriff ousted by Gov. Theodore G. Bilbo, champion of the piney woods rednecks. Then there were landowners whose Mississippi River property was grabbed for levee work. In one such case, *McKee v. Yazoo–Mississippi Delta Levee Commissioners,* Johnston skillfully established an involved but equitable basis for the value of his client's land. His views were sustained on appeal by the Mississippi Supreme Court. Years later, as president of Delta and Pine Land Company, which had miles of riverfront property, he repeatedly used the same argument.[8]

Johnston's considerable professional skills won him an enviable reputation at the bar. Such traits complemented his infectious wit, humor, and "magnetic personality." A consensus developed among his friends and even among those who saw him at greater distance: Oscar was a likable fellow, possessing an exceptionally agile mind. Most said he was brilliant. He commanded the language, dictated "like a damn machine gun," and dominated every meeting he attended. He was lusty and gregarious, a genial host, an imbiber who held his whiskey well, and a raconteur whose stories came only from real life. They said he worked hard and played hard. Always active, Oscar liked boating, camping, and hunting. In speech he combined oratory with persuasion, wooing a crowd with logic and wit. He learned scriptures as a youngster in the Methodist church, where his mother taught an adult class for years, and he read them aloud to his family; in his later years he could impress a congregation with a sermon. A man of the New South, as was his father, Oscar could eulogize the Lost Cause in the style of the nineteenth-century orators. As a young bachelor, he once boldly addressed the United Daughters of the Confederacy on "Southern Womanhood," a subject likely to produce knowing smiles among those who really knew him; but the ladies "listened . . . with wrapt [*sic*] attention."[9]

If any of the young belles of Friars Point had eyes for the rising young barrister, they were disappointed when, in February 1905, he married Miss Martha Motley Anderson, who, like Oscar's mother, hailed from Lebanon, Tennessee. The *Coahomian* pronounced Miss Martha "one of the season's loveliest brides," and she long enjoyed a reputation for intelligence and beauty. The union was of equals, as much as society would allow. Martha matched her husband in mental ability. One youngster even recalled her asserting to Oscar, "I'm smarter than you are and you know it." (One fellow recalled having been smitten with Martha—"desperately in love," he called it, when he was nine. "She was and is so pretty and profoundly impressed me at the time with the fact that she smelled exactly like a duchess and drove a very 'yachty' looking car.") But there was a "magic circle" for southern women, as political activist Virginia Foster Durr of Alabama has recently pointed out, and few females in the early twentieth century stepped outside. Martha was tempted. She plied the ladies' social circuit of Friars Point but delighted in transgressing community decorum with her shorter hemlines and impulsive behavior. Once, according to legend, she fired a pistol into the night air because it was "too damned quiet in Friars Point."[10]

The Johnstons' half-century childless marriage proved less than idyllic. Martha, aloof, enjoyed her role as Mrs. Oscar Johnston but may have been envious of her husband's rising career and the lack of her own. His notorious philandering did not help, and it persisted for years. She also spent considerable time away from home, victimized over the years by malaria, pneumonia, and tuberculosis, which Oscar called "throat trouble." In the 1920s Martha sought a drier climate in Texas and Colorado, finally winding up in Asheville, North Carolina, where the climate, said Oscar, "seemed to agree with her wonderfully." The mountain community became her home, more or less, for more than a decade. Oscar visited her there occasionally and she reciprocated two or three times a year. His infidelity was well known and there were rumors about hers. When Johnston worked in the New Deal, one woman, in a letter to Secretary of Agriculture Henry Wallace claiming Oscar had victimized her, threatened public exposure if he didn't provide material assistance for her and her niece. And in one quite believable story, Martha once returned from Asheville and was asked at a Greenville beauty parlor how she had found things. She announced, evidently for the benefit of some of the ladies present, that Oscar had entertained "all these damned Greenville bitches," and she was going to have the house "fumigated." But there is no evidence they ever contemplated divorce. Said a friend who knew them in later years, "They were made for each other but not for anyone else." Theirs was a convenient marriage, with wide latitude and independence; yet, for all the distance, they also enjoyed a certain closeness, an admiration, a mutual respect. Once, in a light moment in 1922, when Rotarian wives were called on to characterize their spouses, Martha responded, "model husband." There is also something telling about her keeping scrapbooks of Oscar's long career and then, after his death, destroying them. When serious illness laid her low, and later, when she was painfully afflicted by arthritis, Oscar's devotion was deep and sincere. When it was his turn, her devotion proved the same, whether with his tormenting eye disorders or later as he lay incapacitated in his twilight years.[11]

By the time Oscar and Martha settled into married life in Friars Point, he was ready for a political career. The leap from popular lawyer to popular politician was not far. After serving on the local board of aldermen, Johnston, at twenty-seven, easily won a four-year term in the state legislature in 1907. He won again in 1911 and 1915. Unfortunately, Johnston's political career intersected "the revolt of the rednecks," the political ascendancy of the hills and piney woods over the Bourbon-tinged Delta. Years of agitation had culminated in the primary law of 1902, a key which unlocked political doors for Mississippi's white bottom rail. Awakening the underclass with populist rhetoric and demands for political and economic justice for poor whites, a new class of politicians rode to power in Mississippi and across the South. Chief among them in Mississippi were James Kimble Vardaman, elected governor in 1903, and his wily protégé, Theodore G. "The Man" Bilbo, who followed him to the executive mansion a dozen years later. In between stood the progressive terms of Edmund F. Noel and the Delta's Earl Brewer. The progressive agenda in the first two decades of the twentieth century resulted in improved roads, literacy, public health, and greater economic and social justice including a fairer tax structure.[12]

In more than a decade in the Mississippi House, Oscar Johnston stood chiefly in the minority, even labeled "a conservative leader" by a historian of the 1908 session. But the term is slightly misleading. In some respects Johnston's legislative career anticipated what historian George B. Tindall has called "business progressivism," an advocacy of efficiency and public services if not necessarily increased democracy and social justice. Early in the century, Mississippi and the South, wallowing in poverty and cultural inertia, cried out for reform; it was a rare politician, and there were some, who could not be called a progressive of some sort. While a conservative, Johnston fought to raise the age of consent for females and advocated agricultural high schools, safe grade-crossing improvements largely at railroad expense, and public aid for a state-highway program. Amid much publicity in 1918 he doggedly pursued impeachment of Robert M. Butler, the allegedly corrupt superintendent of the state mental hospital, and demanded formal assurance that Governor Bilbo would not appoint him to any other public post. He supported the infamous "secret caucus" vote in 1910 that elected his conservative friend Leroy Percy of Greenville to the U.S. Senate to succeed the late A. J. McLaurin; the following year he worked futilely for Percy's doomed bid for a full term against Vardaman. ("My whole fight," Percy said privately six days after his defeat, "was made to redeem the state from Vardamanism.") No Bourbon, Johnston was uncommitted to fiscal retrenchment, spoke against the "tax dodger," and, in 1912, opposed Governor Brewer, his friend and fellow Coahomian, in supporting a populist statute that limited corporate landownership to ten thousand acres while totally banning corporate landownership of any farmland. That same year, however, he ably represented the Delta's agenda by achieving his main goal of his second term, passage of complicated drainage bills designed to secure about five million acres of swamp and flood lands.[13]

Undoubtedly, the 1916 session proved to be Johnston's worst year in the legislature. In January, he miscalculated badly in a contest for House Speaker, losing in a three-way race to freshman Martin "Mike" Sennett Conner of Covington County. Some saw the race as a test of strength for incoming Gov. Theodore Bilbo, known to favor Conner. True, the Vardaman-Bilbo faction dominated all Johnston's years in the legislature, but in this case the votes failed to match the factional pattern. Levee-board squabbling damaged Delta unity, and Conner got a boost from fellow Ole Miss alumni, forty of whom sat in the new House. Later in the session, Johnston also lost a battle with Bilbo over his rural credits bill, which authorized the incorporation and operation of farm-loan banks. Johnston long held a passion for agricultural finance, a subject he mastered. His carefully crafted bill, which would help farmers secure long-term, low-interest loans, reflected successful measures enacted in New York and Massachusetts and was similar to pending federal legislation. Johnston, "the ablest lawyer" in the legislature, shepherded the bill to a 114–8 passage in the House; the Senate, inviting him to direct passage of the bill in that chamber, passed it unanimously. When it got to Bilbo's desk, however, the governor boldly vetoed it, claiming outside corporations could grab huge tracts during a depression ("The surest way to acquire land," said Bilbo, "is to lend money on it.") To the anti-Bilbo *Jackson Daily News,* that was "wholly erroneous," mere "demagogic rant" reminiscent of Vardaman days. Vardaman's newspaper, *The Issue,* in fact, thought it saw lurking beneath "a garb of benevolence a sinister and insidious" motive potentially beneficial to syndicates and corporations. Johnston got the House to repass the bill over Bilbo's veto, but it lost in the Senate by a single vote.[14]

More significant than the loss of the rural credits bill was a proposal to create a tax-equalization commission. The proposed commission stood to replace the unfair and antiquated methods of land taxation wherein local property assessments rested with county boards of supervisors. In the past, if the legislature hiked the tax rate, county officials could simply lower property assessments while state indebtedness rose. The worst offenders were Delta counties, the wealthiest in the state, where local officials repeatedly underassessed land values. Resentment paralleled the ballooning state debt, up 300 percent since Reconstruction. Over the Delta's loud protest, the legislature created a centralized three-man commission to be appointed by the governor and empowered to revalue what it regarded as inappropriate land assessments. Johnston opposed the governor's appointive power, arguing instead that the commission be elected from the state's congressional districts with the governor serving as ex-officio member. He told the House that "nobody has ever dared to place in one man's hand the power to tax the people, and this is at least a step in that direction." (Bilbo soon appointed his cousin, H. K. Rouse, of Poplarville, to the new commission.) In March, Johnston joined nine other Delta representatives in explaining their votes in a bill of particulars against the measure. The Delta had reason to oppose the new commission. Under the agency, assessments fell in sixty-five poor counties, while they shot up more than 433 percent in Johnston's Coahoma County and more than 463 percent in Bolivar, another wealthy river county. Although the issue remained hot for years—emerging in 1919 as a point of contention in the gubernatorial race—when the difficulties were finally resolved the commission helped modernize Mississippi's financial apparatus.[15]

If Johnston frequently stood among the anti–Vardaman-Bilbo minority, he captured the attention of friend and foe alike. His commanding presence formed a staple of his life. That became evident in his first legislative session in

1908, when young Oscar caught the eye of former Governor Vardaman. With a heavy complement of Vardamanites in the House, the former governor's presence loomed large, the more so when he began publishing his weekly paper, *The Issue* (later *Vardaman's Weekly*), in the capital. The new paper took note of the newcomer in state politics, claiming that the legislature revealed a man's mettle. The recent session bristled with "a great many very capable and worthy young men," said *The Issue*. "A few of them possess the elements of leadership and the ability to distinguish themselves in the world. I know of no one in that body who gives more promise of success than Hon. Oscar Johns[t]on. . . . As a lawyer, he is learned, accurate in thought and tireless of work—he is a debater of grace and cogency—often eloquent and persuasive." The paper predicted Johnston's constituents would give him "every opportunity" for greater service.[16]

Oscar's political fortunes rose. Named alternate delegate to the Democratic National Convention in Denver in 1908, and as a delegate in 1912 and 1916, he later served on the Democratic National Committee. Dunbar Rowland's *Official and Statistical Register* claimed Johnston distinguished "himself as one of the ablest and strongest men in the public service of Mississippi" for his work in the legislative sessions of 1912 and 1914. The *Greenville Daily Democrat* declared him "one of the strongest men in the state" and, not surprisingly, talk arose of a gubernatorial race, something Johnston rejected, at least for the moment.[17]

Politics benefited Johnston's legal career, likely expanding opportunities and fattening fees. By 1912 he was "one of the best known young attorney[s] in the State of Mississippi," his career having outgrown Friars Point, now on its economic downside. In April, the legislative session over, Oscar and Martha moved to Clarksdale, where Johnston formed a partnership with John W. Cutrer, a planter and senior Delta criminal attorney who legend claimed lost but one case in his entire career. Cutrer had long been a Delta powerhouse. The son-in-law of Clarksdale's founder, he had sat in both houses of the Mississippi legislature, had been a delegate to the state's constitutional convention in 1890, and had served as president of the Yazoo-Mississippi Delta Levee Board. Cutrer and Johnston promised to be a formidable law firm.[18]

Johnston integrated easily into Delta society. He and Martha eventually built a spacious, two-storied home, with disconnected servants' quarters, on a corner in a fashionable Clarksdale neighborhood. Built within a year or so of each other, neighboring homes included Earl Brewer's imposing columned residence, finished after he retired from the governorship in 1916, and Jack Cutrer's sprawling Italian Renaissance showplace. The Johnstons delighted in a good time, and their new home, with its massive fireplace, saw many parties. The good citizen, Johnston found time for the local Red Cross and the Progressive Club of Clarksdale, a city betterment group. Oscar enjoyed young people—

he and Martha had even chaperoned young folk back in Friars Point. Characteristically, in 1917, "when no one else would," he organized one of the first
Boy Scout troops, perhaps the first, in the Delta. He long held a loyal place in
his heart for scouting and spent considerable time with the boys. Perhaps the
lads became surrogate sons; he inspired them in the principles of scouting, one
youngster recalling his "exceedingly strong personality." Oscar delighted in the
achievements of their adult years. One lad, who had moved to Illinois, reported
to Johnston that his son was also a Scout, now sporting the badge Oscar had pinned
on the father a quarter century earlier. Another, who became the district clerk
of Willacy County, Texas, told Johnston in 1942, "I attribute most of my success in life to the Scout training I receive[d] under you as my scoutmaster."[19]

Speculation about Johnston's political future persisted. About the time the
legislature adjourned in 1918, the vehemently anti-Bilbo *Jackson Daily News*
claimed Johnston "has been recognized by friend and foe alike as the ablest member of the House, both as a parliamentarian, in legal knowledge, and as a strat-
egist in handling legislation. Incidentally," added the paper with delight, "he
has been a veritable thorn in the side of the administration, having stirred up
several of the notable investigations of the session." Talk of his making the race
for governor in 1919 now mingled briefly with talk of a mayor's contest back in
Clarksdale. In May he was elected vice president of the state bar association.[20]

The Great War soon intruded. In June 1918, at age 38, with a lucrative law
practice and a high-profile political career, Johnston placed his property in
Martha's name and, with hopes of fighting in the war then raging in Europe,
joined the U.S. Army. Though a commission could have been his virtually for
the asking, Oscar chose instead to enlist as a private, selecting the rugged tank
corps (motto: "treat 'em rough"). His motives are open to speculation: new
challenge, boredom, patriotism, something a later culture would call "mid-life
crisis," a complement to his political ambitions, or perhaps some combination.
Membership in the state legislature exempted him from the draft, and if politics motivated him, his eye could hardly have been on the governor's chair in
1919. When he boarded the train in Clarksdale on June 19, bound for Jackson, then on to Fort Oglethorpe, Georgia, he could have had few expectations
that the war would end before Thanksgiving. That summer, news from the front
looked "very good indeed," he wrote his father, but he added that "I only pray
we may keep the 'dutch' on the run back to their own lines this fall, then let
next years fighting be on their territory." Even his marriage seemed content.
"Martha is here," he told his father, "I don't know what I would do with out
her here to help along." Though he saw her only an hour each evening at the
camp entrance, Martha proved the loyal camp follower, working as a volunteer nurse and taking a room in Gettysburg, Pennsylvania, near Camp Colt,

where the tank corps trained under the command of young Col. Dwight D. Eisenhower.[21] If Johnston designed his military service to complement his political prospects, and such is quite possible, those prospects lay beyond 1919.

Oscar liked the military. He endured the rigors of camp life—"you count for nothing, just one of millions"—drilling in foul weather, doing "'K.P.'—'wood pile' and sentry duty" as well as schooling and examinations. Influenza felled others but did not touch him. He boasted of his improved physique, reveled in his honed mental agility, and worked hard for an earned commission as a second lieutenant. Assigned to the 339th Tank Battalion, he was apparently slated to disembark for Europe when the armistice in November ended the fighting. His unit quickly demobilized; Oscar, honorably discharged but disheartened, was back in Mississippi in December.[22]

Johnston's homecoming revived talk of his candidacy for the governorship. Within a week of his return to Mississippi, he was in Jackson, ostensibly for business at the Supreme Court, but also perhaps to sample opinion and encourage speculation. Friends crowded around him in the courtroom, shaking his hand. In the capital and later in Vicksburg, where the *Evening Post* declared him "Bronzed, hard as iron and looking every way physically fit," Johnston told soldier stories and talked politics. Friends and a number of newspapers touted his candidacy; by the end of the month each mail brought encouragement from around the state. Earl Brewer would not make the race if Johnston did, thus clearing the way for anti-administration unity in the Delta. Doubtless Johnston also had been encouraged by the turn of political events. At Camp Colt he had eagerly but sporadically followed political news back home. He delighted in Bilbo's loss to Hattiesburg judge Paul B. Johnson in a race for a U.S. House seat in the August primary. "The old state has now redeemed herself," he exulted to his father at the time, "and is now worth fighting for as in the days when my grandfather gave his life for her." Senator Vardaman's defeat by Congressman Byron Patten Harrison of Gulfport may have also encouraged Johnston to think—factionalism and demagoguery had loosened their grip on Mississippi politics. Writing to the late Sen. A. J. McLaurin's son, Harris Dickson, a Johnston supporter, said he thought people wanted "to get away from the cheap politics that have nauseated us all. I believe that a straightforward decent man can now be elected Governor of Mississippi." To Dickson that meant Johnston, whose name, he said, was "being widely suggested." The iron felt hot. Promising "fair, just, economical and business-like" government, Johnston announced his candidacy for governor through the press in January 1919 and formally opened his campaign at the Tupelo courthouse on March 21.[23]

Johnston's anti-Vardaman candidacy proved to be the greatest challenge to Bilbo's heir apparent, Lt. Gov. Lee M. Russell. Atty. Gen. Ross Collins, a

Vardamanite now fallen from Bilbo's favor, complicated factional unity by also throwing his hat in the ring. Unfortunately, the anti-administration faction likewise split when former Gov. A. H. Longino, attempting a political revival, soon entered the race.[24]

Retention of the state-tax equalization commission and the pardon board formed two of the leading issues of the campaign, aside, of course, from the perpetuation of Bilbonic politics. Collins and Longino opposed the tax commission, as did Johnston, who promised some sort of tax reform. Russell, in lockstep with Bilbo, argued for the commission's retention. Johnston seemed to waffle. Before the second primary, *Vardaman's Weekly* displayed two pictures of Johnston billboards, one allegedly in north Mississippi, showing his opposition to the commission, while the other, in the south, made no mention of it. Johnston's claim to progressive legislation was all but lost amid the political mudslinging. He failed to shake the image of the conservative candidate of the corporations and the wealthy Delta crowd. Russell wrapped himself in Jeffersonian robes, labeling Johnston a Hamiltonian Democrat. One paper linked Johnston's candidacy to an alleged attempt by Earl Brewer and Jack Cutrer to grab control of the Yazoo–Mississippi Delta Levee Board. *Vardaman's Weekly* denied Johnston's progressivism, charging instead that he had "been the right hand man of Earl Brewer, 'Oily Jack' Cutrer, and Ex-Senator Leroy Percy. The people, that is the great mass of common people," said the paper shortly before the second primary, "can expect nothing at the hands of Oscar Johnston." (Percy, again maligned nearly a decade after his defeat, thought that Johnston understood Mississippi's needs better than anyone and that the state had "few men as able." He privately campaigned for him and was willing to make his support public in the local press if and when Johnston thought it helpful. Unfortunately, any statewide identity with the former senator would likely play into populist strategy.)[25]

If nothing else, Johnston's packed campaign schedule showcased his oratorical skills. Southwest Mississippi's *Woodville Republican* said his address there "was declared by those who heard it to have been one of the best political speeches delivered in this town in many years." In June the *Jackson Clarion-Ledger* noted that in his two-hour speech at the Century Theatre "he held his audience as few speakers could have done, for he is both interesting and informing." He "warmed to his subject," said the paper, "and was soon speaking at such a rapid rate that no ordinary stenographer could report him, though his voice was good and sentences clear, and easily understood. His language was chaste, his manner composed, and his speech was loaded with valuable information, about which the public knows little." Johnston soon won the support of the fence-sitting *Gloster Record*, whose editor heard "his clean-cut, straightforward speech" in Amite County on June 20. "His strongest opponents," said the *Record*, "acknowledge his marked ability, brilliant mind, force as a speaker, and that as a law maker he has a record for constructive legislation surpassed by none." The scene was repeated in Sunflower County in July when the self-proclaimed unbiased editor of the *Indianola Enterprise* heard Johnston in Inverness and "came away an Oscar Johnston supporter, as enthusiastically as any man that has rallied to his cause." The *Yazoo County News* was more succinct: "All one has to do to become a supporter of Oscar Johnston is to go and hear him speak."[26]

Despite Johnston's formidable skill on the stump, Russell supporters dredged up insidious allegations about Johnston's military record. Some thought Russell, with no military service, feared the soldier bloc, if there was such a thing. Many veterans arrived home too late to pay their poll taxes and, with dubious legality, state party officials ordered waivers. Some county committees, purportedly loyal to Russell, slowed the process. Allegations surfaced about Johnston's unpopularity among his men, that he had mistreated those in his unit. A Tank Corps sergeant publicly denied the charges, citing an instance—"one of a number"— of Johnston's self-sacrifice, and testifying to his high standing among his men. That was complemented by nine former Camp Colt soldiers, all Mississippians, who signed a letter declaring that Johnston was "at all times . . . a good soldier and a fair and square officer and that any statements to the contrary" were "absolutely false" and politically motivated.[27]

Worse were the "slurs," which surfaced even before Johnston announced his candidacy in January, about his "near soldier" status, that he had never made it to the front. The *Oxford Eagle*, a Russell paper, claimed that the "great importance" of the uniform could not hide "the many sins of the wearer." Although such an issue could easily backfire, it remained near the surface during the campaign. Fred Sullens's *Jackson Daily News* called the tactics of the Russell camp "cowardly and contemptible," and asked rhetorically what Russell did in the war. Other than work for himself and Vardaman ("that other demagogue") he did nothing. "And while Lee Russell was touring the state for 'me and Jim,' trying to secure for himself a bomb-proof job in the Governor's office," said Sullens, "Oscar Johnston was serving as a humble private in the Tank Corps at Gettysburg, peeling potatoes in the kitchen, drilling ten hours per day under a blistering sun, and learning the bloody but necessary art of killing Germans." Russell, in good physical shape and still young enough, simply chose not to serve. "One wanted to make the world safe for democracy," said the paper, "and the other didn't care a tinker's damn about what was happening in Europe, but was interested only in getting a strangle hold on the public teat in Mississippi." Other Johnston defenders were more subdued, one claiming that the speedy end to the war "should not detract from the patriotism of the young man who showed a willingness to fight." Yet it was the *Daily News* that, near the end of the campaign, blamed the kaiser, who "quit like a dog," preventing Johnston from getting to Europe.[28]

In the first primary on August 5, Johnston forced Russell into a runoff, placing second in the four-man field. Victory seemed within reach when both Collins and Longino supporters began lining up behind Johnston. In a complete break with the Bilbo faction Collins endorsed Johnston, publicly hailing him as superior to Russell in morals and ability and claiming that Johnston would "not be dominated by a dirty rascal like Theodore Bilbo." Pat Harrison, who had beaten Vardaman for a Senate seat a year earlier, also announced he would return from Washington to vote for Johnston. To the rabidly anti–Vardaman-Bilbo *Jackson Daily News* the issue was clear: "We have a choice between decent government and the perpetuation of Bilboism."[29]

Despite the first flush of hope, problems dogged Johnston's campaign. Former Governor Longino, upset by reports that Johnston supporters would have gone for Russell if Longino had been in the runoff, damaged Johnston's hopes by declaring his neutrality; sulking in his tent, he scarcely veiled his opposition. The Vardaman-Bilbo faction mounted its own assault. Johnston, portrayed as an antilabor and anti-yeoman farmer whose campaign allegedly cost three hundred thousand dollars, was linked to timber corporations and purportedly backed by wealthy Delta planters. *Vardaman's Weekly* declared that "[n]o man who has not known the hardships of the poor people is able to sympathize with them." In the piney woods, Russell's campaign charged that "[a] vote for O.G. Johnston is a vote against South Mississippi and every honest Tax-Payer."[30]

Ironically, before the first primary, one large timber executive in south Mississippi, who publicly vouched for Johnston to his employees, told Johnston he feared Russell's election. The executive thought Russell a crook and a demagogue but contributed substantially to his campaign as a hedge, "a string on him," as he called it, in case Russell won. As far as Johnston knew, the timberman contributed nothing to his campaign. His race, he said later, was financed by his own funds, some borrowed and some generated by a campaign committee. Especially rankling were Russell's repeated charges that Johnston had the backing of a huge "slush fund." Johnston offered full campaign financial disclosure if Russell would do likewise. The challenge fell on deaf ears. The charge that selfish tax dodgers were expending huge amounts to defeat Russell and abolish the tax commission was, Johnston's campaign manager admitted, "the hardest proposition I have to meet."[31]

The obstacles proved too great. In defeat, Johnston captured more than 47 percent of the vote, carrying thirty-seven of Mississippi's eighty-two counties, most in the Delta and in the western part of the state. He also carried the gulf coast and several counties in the hills and piney woods, where Russell dominated. The lieutenant governor ran an able campaign, though after the election he gloated in an Oxford speech that his triumph came in the face of huge sums spent by the opposition, a dubious if not specious charge. His victory demonstrated once more the viability of the Vardaman-Bilbo faction, apparently aided by Longino defections from the conservative camp. Bilbo had taken little active part in the campaign, though he had publicly attacked Johnston's character, roguishly urging voters to decide on the issues and not to hold against Johnston his alleged gambling, womanizing (regardless of color), swindling, and drinking. The Russell campaign had warned "Christian people everywhere" that Johnston had voted against prohibition. Friends told a story about a time during one of Johnston's speeches when a heckler asked, "Mr. Johnston, do you take a drink?" Oscar replied, "Is that an inquiry sir, or an invitation? If it's an inquiry the answer is in the affirmative. If it's an invitation, I'll see you in the grove here as soon as the speaking is over." Johnston reportedly later liked to recall that Bilbo had boasted, "I told you I could take the worst man in the state and beat the best one with him." Bilbo's remark, however, was probably closer to "[I] wanted to show Oscar Johnston that I could beat him with nothing, so I took Lee Russell and did it."[32]

Not all accepted Russell's triumph with dignity. Russell, said the *Jackson Daily News,* was elected not by Democrats but "by the Bolshevists, the Socialists, the I.W.W.'s, the Sovietists, and the ignorant and illiterate," along with "[t]he riff-raff, the rag-tag and the bob-tail of creation, aided by the large element of our population that always allowed demagogues and scoundrels to do their thinking for them." The election also meant, "[a]mong other things . . . that a shameless liar and contemptible slanderer can go on the stump in Mississippi, spew his slime on decent, honorable, high-minded gentlemen and get away with it." While Johnston admitted that it was sometimes "difficult to submit to slanderous misrepresentations," he disavowed the bitterness of the *Daily News,* congratulated Russell, and accepted defeat graciously. Pledging to continue the fight for good government, he announced he would return to the practice of law.[33]

Had Johnston been elected, he might well have exemplified something of Tindall's business progressivism, heading a progressive yet fiscally responsible and businesslike administration. Even at age thirty-nine, Johnston might have joined that cadre of politicians whose names surfaced and resurfaced, some for a generation (Mike Conner ran for governor five times, won once). Persistence in Mississippi politics often produced checkered success of some sort, especially if getting and holding public office defined success. As it developed, elements of the old factionalism lingered. The Vardaman-Russell crowd, spurning national

Democratic issues such as the League of Nations, was squeezed out of the state convention in 1920, with Johnston even being elected Democratic National Committeeman. Angered, Governor Russell launched a personal attack on Johnston, Brewer, and Cutrer, even dredging up the old charge that corporations had financed Johnston's losing gubernatorial bid. Johnston publicly denounced the personal attack, but the bitterness remained. Early in 1922, a former government stenographer, Frances Birkhead of New Orleans, sued the governor for $100,000, charging that Russell had repeatedly seduced her in 1918 with a promise of marriage. She claimed that an abortion, allegedly arranged by Russell, had left her an invalid. Incredibly, before the sensational charges and trial dragged through the press, to the outrage of Mississippians, Birkhead had tried to get Johnston, Brewer, and Cutrer to represent her. The three heard her out but refused to touch the case. Acquitted in December, Russell later publicly charged that Johnston, with others, had tried to disgrace his administration. The governor soon retracted the charge against Johnston, telling him he had had erroneous information. Johnston's businesslike reply gave little quarter: "I am definitely out of the political arena, and shall expect and demand, as a private citizen of the State, immunity from misrepresentation of any sort."[34]

Had he been passionately interested, Johnston might have again stood for office. He could have positioned himself for the U.S. Senate seat given up by John Sharp Williams in 1922 or perhaps the governorship the next year. In the Senate race, he introduced candidate Belle Kearney when she came to Clarksdale for a courthouse speech, rejecting the idea that women would not help purify politics. In the end, both he and Kearney wound up supporting the colorless conservative Hubert Stephens, who in the runoff squelched a pathetic comeback by Vardaman, by then a shadow of his former self. Other victories lay ahead for Bilbo, but he too went down to defeat, losing the gubernatorial nomination in 1923 to Henry Whitfield. Despite a tobacco-juiced old-timer's prediction, affirmed sadly by poet William Alexander Percy, that "the bottom rail's on top and its gwinner stay thar," the redneck's revolt had about run its course.[35] Though interested in politics, Johnston never really hungered for public office. No political juices flowed in the primary season; he caught no election fever.

Back in Clarksdale, Johnston threw himself into the affairs of the Delta. Aside from practicing law (his partnership with Cutrer had dissolved), Johnston, with Cutrer and a pair of local investors, Oscar Carr and W. A. Ritchie, bought Lombardy Planting Company, a moderate-sized cotton plantation near town. Oscar became president. In league with several others, including Ritchie and Cutrer, he also soon bought the Union Seed and Fertilizer Company, turning it into the Clarksdale Cotton Oil Company. Capitalized at half a million dollars, it soon boasted a lucrative ginning business. When 138 fire insurance companies in

Mississippi suspended operations in 1920–21 in the wake of a controversy with the state revenue agent, Johnston joined fifteen others in incorporating the Mississippi Fire Insurance Company in Jackson.[36]

Johnston's cotton-related investments reflected his business interests and the bullish postwar cotton economy. Not since the eve of the Civil War had cotton producers enjoyed such prosperity. Delta land values rocketed upward, commanding up to $350 an acre, paralleling escalating cotton prices. Bankers fueled the financial orgy, borrowing from other banks and liberally showering money on cotton lands and crops. The proliferate symbol of wealth, the automobile, with smiling planters behind the wheel, appeared in ever-greater numbers on Coahoma County streets and roads. (Oscar had bought a Ford in 1911 but later took a liking to Cadillacs.) Lured by the siren call of higher prices, planters held their postwar crop; in April 1920 prices climbed over forty cents a pound, and there was giddy talk of dollar cotton by July. In fact, in the spring of 1920, Oscar sold 150 long-staple bales of fall futures for ninety-three cents a pound. Clarksdale enjoyed wealth and prestige. Said one observer later, the town "was to Mississippi what Tulsa is to Oklahoma."[37]

Reality soon punctured the balloon. Depreciated European currency closed export markets and, with expanded production, glutted warehouses; prices collapsed in the summer, falling to about a third of their April quotations by the end of the year. Corn, wheat, and tobacco prices likewise fell, plunging American agriculture into severe depression. Panic and violence swept the South, flames dancing against the night sky from Texas to the Carolinas as vigilantes torched gins and mercantile businesses whose owners had not heeded advance warnings. Such attempts to halt the picking and sale of cotton were a crude substitute for rational organization among farmers. Some cotton fields lay unpicked, while in Georgia farm workers were "begging for work at any price." Although Mississippi's guaranty law quieted some fears, banks also ran into trouble, some closing their doors forever. The state's lost cotton revenues in 1920 plunged $110 million under that of the previous year. From the perspective of two decades, Oscar Johnston thought the cotton farmers' suffering after the 1929–30 collapse "was nothing compared with the suffering during the market debacle" of 1920. The whole business taught Johnston the dangers of single commodity inflation.[38]

Like the sickly patient who grabs for every cure, farmers across the South clamored for a variety of old nostrums, among them credit and acreage reduction. In the Mississippi Delta, remedies included the organization of a low-grade cotton exporting company by prominent Clarksdale attorney Gerald Fitzgerald. The company eventually exported some Delta cotton to Europe, but it is unlikely the meticulous plan ever realized the high hopes of its founders.

Probably more influential was the creation in late 1920 of the Yazoo Delta Mortgage Company, capitalized at half a million dollars and affiliated with the financially troubled Planters Bank of Clarksdale. Johnston was an organizer of the mortgage company and legal counsel for the bank, headed by the able and respected W. P. Holland, an original founder who now appealed to big-city investors to bale out his sinking bank. Whether Johnston's efforts to save Planters Bank so impressed the investors that they required his leadership, as *Fortune* magazine later claimed, is unclear; yet when the bank's directors met in December 1920 they made him chairman of the board, apparently with a mandate to assume active management. Johnston voluntarily reorganized it as the Planters National Bank in 1922—making it the largest national bank in Mississippi— and became president the following year; when he left it in 1925, it stood as one of the soundest financial institutions in the state.[39]

Helpful as such enterprises were, nothing promoted economic health in the Delta more than the Staple Cotton Cooperative Association, created in the crucible of depression and panic of 1920–21. The association was part of a wave of marketing cooperatives that swept the farm belt after the First World War. The idea was not new. Agricultural cooperatives had a checkered history that reached back to the Grange days of the nineteenth century, when farmers, trying to fight a middleman system rigged against them, began servicing and marketing commodities for their own benefit. In the early twenties, southern cotton and tobacco associations received a major impetus from a dynamic young California attorney, Aaron Sapiro, who had successfully promoted marketing cooperatives in eggs, raisins, and other products. Sapiro saw huge potential among producers of nonperishables, and his spellbinding enthusiasm supercharged delegates at a meeting of the infant American Cotton Association in Montgomery, Alabama, in 1920. The cooperative fever burned across the land, infecting the Mississippi Delta, laden with long-staple cotton. Within seventy-five to one hundred miles of Clarksdale grew most of the world's supply of long-staple varieties, cotton which always commanded premium prices over middling grade.[40]

Most of the credit for the Staple Cooperative idea has gone to a prominent young LeFlore County planter and freshman state legislator, Oscar F. Bledsoe III. Both Bledsoe and Oscar Johnston, among others, had been impressed with the result of Sapiro's work among California producers and believed deeply in the cooperative idea. With the cotton economy collapsing around them, the two Oscars, infected with the association virus, headed east in the summer of 1920, calling on banks, mills, spinners, and others, looking for solutions to the producers' problems. They returned to the Delta to help spearhead the drive for a cooperative association for long-staple growers.[41]

Bledsoe's cooperative plan struggled in its organizational birth pangs. Falling prices in 1920 tempted planters to quickly market their cotton, something that would depress prices even further. Growers were repeatedly counseled to hold their harvest, the *Clarksdale Daily Register* even running a series of articles to that effect. But an effort to pool three hundred thousand bales of the Delta's 1920 crop, endorsed by Delta planters, including Johnston, who chaired the bankers' committee designed to pool the remaining 1920 bales, apparently miscarried. Efforts to create a cooperative association intensified. Johnston became one of several evangelists of the gospel of cooperative marketing, traversing the Delta urging planters to sign contractual pledges on their 1921 crop. By late 1920, efforts to organize had faltered. Critics said the organizers shared blame for depressed prices, claiming the 1920 crop should have been marketed promptly before prices slid further. Delta bankers, keys to success, generally lined up in support, though some balked. Planters proved more recalcitrant. One prominent Delta attorney and planter remained convinced the operation would succeed if foot-dragging planters would just sign the cooperative contract. It was a sure thing, he thought. "We have men with brains, integrity, ability and grit to make a success of the association," he pleaded to the editor of the *Bolivar Commercial*, "if the growers will only sign up and cooperate with them. If they don't do it, to my mind, their actions will be tantamount to criminal." Another able organizer of the proposed cooperative, Alex Y. Scott of Bolivar County, feared what would happen in 1921 since planters had bid against one another on the 1920 crop, thereby plunging prices from ninety-five cents a pound to fifteen. Do that again, predicted Scott, and the 1921 price would be a nickel. Already in 1920 rumblings from Oklahoma and Texas told of efforts to organize a cooperative to market short-staple cotton, varieties of which totaled about fourteen million bales annually. Long staple varieties, such as that grown in the Delta, numbered a mere six hundred thousand bales per year. Those valuable bales formed the target of the Delta organizers.

The process proved tedious. In February, Lombardy Planting Company, of which Johnston was president, signed up for one thousand bales. Others signed up too; but despite publicity and the enthusiasm of the plan's backers, they did so slowly. Finally, after a series of meetings in the spring of 1921, the Staple Cotton Cooperative Association was formally organized in June at the Hotel Gayoso in Memphis. The board of directors, selected by mailed ballot of the membership, included twenty-one of the Delta's most prominent planters and economic leaders. Bledsoe became the uncontested president and was joined on the board by such Delta heavyweights as Leroy Percy, Alfred H. Stone, M. P. Sturdivant, J. H. Sherard, J. M. Yeager, E. P. Peacock, and others. Johnston joined Bledsoe and Percy on the executive committee, along with Alex Scott and Ben F. Saunders.[42]

The Staple Cotton Cooperative Association, headquartered in Greenwood, Mississippi, displayed aspects of "business agrarianism," a fiscally rational agricultural business operation. The directors soon displayed such acumen by hiring William M. Garrard as its general manager, agreeing to pay him twenty-five cents per bale marketed; such remuneration for such service amounted to one of the highest in the South and was, said one director later, "the wisest thing we ever did," both for Garrard's value and for the image it projected. Illinois-born and Mississippi-reared, Garrard had studied textiles at Mississippi A & M and at age forty had already demonstrated astute business ability. A gifted cotton trader, Garrard skillfully directed the association for thirty-seven years, steering it through good times and bad. The cooperative secured a $5 million loan for cotton exports through the federal War Finance Corporation, even before Garrard became manager, and yearly fought to maintain its pledges. It also overcame numerous early obstacles, including skepticism, ridicule, and virtual blacklisting among several cotton mills. Rumors surfaced that Johnston and Percy were getting huge salaries, when in the early days they had actually paid their expenses out of their own pockets. Selling its first bale at auction at the New Orleans Cotton Exchange, the cooperative soon proved highly successful in challenging the ancient system of cotton marketing that was both chaotic and discriminatory. The agency handled more than a half million bales in its first four years. Johnston estimated that it generated $2 million more in member profits in 1921 alone than otherwise would have been the case. The cooperative could legitimately claim at least part of the credit for the advance in prices that year; independent sellers also fixed their prices close to that of the association. From its very beginning, the Staple Cotton Cooperative took its place among the best-run institutions in American agriculture.[43]

Johnston's role in the founding and success of the Staple Cotton Cooperative Association typified his views of community service. He understood, of course, that such economy-boosting enterprises were good for everyone, including himself. But Oscar believed deeply in personal obligation, commitment, and community cooperation. He actively pursued efficiency, uplift, and community advancement. At a joint civic club meeting in 1922, he was introduced as a living definition of "service." In 1923–24, as president of the local chamber of commerce, he pumped new life into that moribund body, which in turn tried to ease the Delta's labor shortage occasioned by black exodus. At the end of 1924, one Memphis observer noted that "Clarksdale is coming back rapidly, if it has not already come back. There are larger towns in Mississippi, but none more progressive." There is also something telling about perceptions of Oscar's moral standing in the community when Gypsy Smith Jr., the popular Christian evangelist, came to Clarksdale for a three-week revival crusade in early 1924. After the town quickly erected a heated tabernacle seating about four thousand, Smith packed them in, railing against sin while calling for repentance and new birth. ("The Delta has had its fling, has made its money," declared the evangelist, "and what it needs today is not more cotton but God.") "He Christianized the whole town," recalled one resident. After three weeks Clarksdale's moral tone had improved and seven hundred men met in the local Marion Theatre and elected Oscar Johnston president of the Laymen's League, newly organized to further the work begun by Smith.[44]

But 1924 and 1925 witnessed Johnston's retreat from several demanding obligations. At the state Democratic convention in May 1924, he declined to seek reelection as national committeeman; a week later he rotated out of the presidency of the chamber of commerce, and at the end of the year he and his business associates sold their interests in Lombardy Plantation and dissolved the corporation. No longer a planter, he soon resigned from the board of the Staple Cotton Cooperative Association. Finally, at the end of 1925 he also quit as head of the Planters National Bank, one of the strongest such institutions in Mississippi. He stayed on a while longer as general counsel and board member of Tchula Cooperative Stores, but even gave that up in September 1926. It was a time of transition, not at all illogical, but a transition nonetheless. By the end of 1925, Oscar saw new vistas. A dozen years later *Fortune* magazine claimed Johnston had accepted a position with the giant Guaranty Bank of Chicago. Before he embarked for Illinois, according to *Fortune,* Johnston took a purportedly temporary assignment to work up a financial deal for a Memphis planter and promoter, Lant K. Salsbury. The dubious assertion cannot be confirmed. What is clear is that Johnston accepted the new challenge in Memphis as general counsel for Salsbury's Delta and Pine Land Company, a largely British-owned cotton plantation sprawling over tens of thousands of acres in the Mississippi Delta. The plantation, one of the largest in the South, had a high profile; Johnston, in fact, knew the company's resident manager, Professor Jesse Fox, formerly of Mississippi's agricultural experiment station. Johnston also knew Salsbury, the pair having worked closely on a land deal several years earlier through New York's Guaranty Bank, a deal involving a different group of British investors and unrelated to the present scheme. Both also knew Frank O. Lowden, a former Illinois governor who in the 1920s devoted himself to cooperative marketing among farmers. Salsbury contemplated the sale of Delta and Pine Land Company and other properties—in which Governor Lowden had interest—spread over three states; Johnston's legal and financial genius seemed aptly suited for the complex scheme.[45]

Johnston's decision to leave Clarksdale proved life-changing. He needed challenges, thrived on them, and perhaps even grew bored in their absence.

Then too, with no children and Martha off in Asheville, the decision was likely easier. One might also reasonably imagine that Salsbury's offer bore highly lucrative possibilities. In January 1926, Oscar was in Memphis, unaware that circumstances beyond his control would scuttle the proposed land deal. Instead of handling the huge sale, he would soon become one of the largest cotton planters in America.

# 2

# Corporate Planter

> Laymen who take a brief glance at the cotton belt are apt to return saying that anyone can grow cotton. That is one of the reasons why the cotton business generally is so poor—just about anybody can.     —*Fortune*, 1937

> Personally I should hate to be beaten by a business of this sort, and I have no doubt Mr. Salsbury and you both feel the same way.
> —Herbert W. Lee to Oscar Johnston, 1926

**I**n May 1926, Oscar Johnston, the new general counsel for Delta and Pine Land Company of Mississippi, sailed from New York for a meeting with the company's majority stockholders, the Fine Cotton Spinners' and Doublers' Association, Ltd., in Manchester, England. Johnston's briefcase held a complex offer to buy options on British-owned American plantations, including the mammoth Delta and Pine Land Company in the Mississippi Delta. The English bondholders were in a receptive mood, even though the deal represented a financial book loss and a tacit admission of faded profits and lost hopes.[1]

It had not always been so. Organized in 1898, the Fine Cotton Spinners' and Doublers' Association brought together spinners of sea island cotton, joined by yarn doublers who used the fine sea island staple and other varieties. Within little more than a decade, thirty-one original British affiliated firms had blossomed into fifty, employing thirty thousand workers and four million spindles. Each affiliate retained its own identity, and many such firms were prestigious, some having been organized in the eighteenth and early nineteenth centuries. Housed on St. James Square in Manchester, the association was headed by able and distinguished men of commerce. The first chairman served Manchester in parliament for two decades; the second was also a member of parliament and, in the past, was president of the Associated Chambers of Commerce of the United Kingdom. The spinning and doubling association signaled new maturity in an ancient industry.[2]

Early in the new century, events in Europe and Africa conspired to interest British cottonmen in American real estate. Such interest was not new, but by 1910 imports of fine staple cotton from Egypt had fallen in volume and quality.

Satisfactory experiments with upland grades which, it was thought, could be grown in America, destroyed the Egyptian monopoly. At the Seventh International Congress of the International Federation of Cotton Spinners and Manufacturers in Brussels, Belgium, in June 1910, a paper read by an American delegate apparently caught the attention of officials of the Manchester association. The paper, "The Causes of the Present Shortage of American Cotton and the Means to Adopt to Prevent a Recurrence," was presented by Professor Jesse W. Fox, head of the agricultural experiment station in Greenville, Mississippi. Fox had credibility; in 1909, eighty-three Delta acres at Fox's experiment station had produced ninety-four bales. Early British contact with Fox is unclear. He may have returned to America via Manchester; at some point, in Belgium or England, the Fine Spinners, apparently thinking of producing American upland long-staple cotton, reportedly told the professor that any acquisition of Mississippi real estate to supply their hungry mills hinged on his employment.[3]

The linchpin in the British acquisition of American property was an aggressive Memphis businessman, Lant K. Salsbury. A Michigan native, Salsbury took a law degree at Ann Arbor in 1890 and practiced at the bar in Grand Rapids for several years before turning his creative eye southward. He possessed vision and unusual abilities, but his talent was never more clear than as a business promoter. Having seen Michigan timber disappear, Salsbury grew interested in the southern forest industry. With little means he headed south, where he began dealing in Mississippi timber and sawmills around the turn of the century. From there he moved to New Orleans, then to Memphis, where he settled in 1903. Memphis stood strategically above the Mississippi Delta, that vast elliptically shaped alluvial tract stretching south to Vicksburg, bounded by the Mississippi and Yazoo Rivers. With soil so naturally fertile from thousands of years of deposits it could grow anything and grow it better than anywhere else in America. Slowly being developed, it seemed an American Nile. Eager and hardworking men wrestled it away from the swamps that it once was. Great levees defied the Father of Waters.[4]

Lant Salsbury, the erstwhile Yankee, saw its huge potential. Soon he had organized and financed—and then managed—an eight-thousand-acre plot in Mississippi just south of Memphis. But Mary Mac Plantation, as it was called, stood as a small scale of Salsbury's dream, a mere tease of his real ambition: a huge, highly developed super cotton plantation in the Delta. His eyes grew big. For help, Salsbury linked up with the person who could help fulfill the dream—Charles Scott of Rosedale, Mississippi. A lawyer, banker, hunter, world traveler, and big-time planter, Scott, who as a youth in the Civil War rode with Nathan Bedford Forrest, had risen to prominence in postwar cotton circles. He put on exhibits at the Cotton Exposition in New Orleans and the World's

Fair in St. Louis. He amassed several fortunes and in the process became one of Mississippi's leading citizens. In 1910, Scott, who already owned about eleven thousand acres, obtained options on an adjacent block of about twenty-one thousand more, some of which comprised several sizable and well-known plantations. To promote their sale, he solicited Lant Salsbury, who, with six associates—including A. S. Buchanan of the Tennessee Supreme Court—formed a syndicate to buy the lands. In early 1911, after futile appeals to southern and eastern financiers, Salsbury turned up in England seeking capital from the giant spinning conglomerate in Manchester.[5]

The American proposition he carried soon lured a team of Fine Spinner heavyweights to Mississippi. The delegation included John McConnel of Edinburgh, board chairman Herbert Dixon, and other directors. (The bearded McConnel, whom Oscar Johnston later called "a canny Scot," was noted for his ever-present slide rule and whiskey flask. On a later visit to America during the World War, he calculated his odds of being torpedoed on the trip home at 1 in 189,000. The *Lusitania* went down, but he was saved, and the flask was put to use.) Accompanied by Salsbury, the English guests toured the properties in Bolivar and Washington Counties proximate to Scott Station, the railroad stop named after the Mississippi planter. It all totaled more than thirty thousand acres, most in cultivation but much covered by timber. Well treated and generally well pleased, the English hunted wild geese in pre-dug pits along the Mississippi River, part of the selling job that Johnston later called "high pressure promotion." Their American visit, bolstered by legal and financial advice relative to the properties, lasted several weeks and led to a favorable report to the full executive board back in Manchester. On April 12, 1911, the Fine Spinners agreed, the secretary cabling Salsbury of their acceptance. Apparently to hurdle a Mississippi law limiting the size of cultivable acreage owned by any one corporation, the British created two giant holding companies, Triumph Plantation Company and Lake Vista Plantation Company. These plantations, each possessing $1.5 million in capital stock, acquired title to all the properties, with deeds recorded in Bolivar and Washington Counties on May 17. Now within legal limits, the holding companies leased their lands to a newly chartered operating corporation, the Mississippi Delta Planting Company, by which the whole enterprise was officially known.[6]

The huge sale coincided with two paradoxical developments in the Delta: the rising tide of boosterism and the arrival of the boll weevil, the small destructive pest that had been munching its way across the South since leaping the Rio Grande in the 1890s. A lot of weevil talk appeared in the press, including possible solutions, but no such threat could dampen the booster spirit. The Mississippi Delta was the American Nile, it was "Beulah Land," or close to it.

It was the land of milk and honey. An untapped treasure stood on the verge of discovery. Each acre cleared and drained trumpeted its coming development; each land sale signaled that finally the secret was out. The sale to the Fine Spinners was simply the most dramatic of many. Outside capital, much of it foreign, was bullish on the Delta, bullish on the South. Tangibly, the same month the British Fine Spinners voted to buy American real estate, a group of boosters met in the Peabody Hotel in Memphis and created the Delta Publicity and Improvement Association, an agency dedicated to making the dream come true.[7]

One man's hope was another man's fear. Clearly, the British spinners alone could not grow sufficient cotton on their new American properties to supply their voracious mills. But some planters feared that profits would be plowed into more land, and that prices on the cotton export market would eventually fall. Also, the British reportedly made the purchase to stop American monopolization of long-staple production. Worse, the rush on land sales, particularly to foreign capital, stirred latent populism in the Mississippi legislature. Apparently, Mississippi statute already placed a ceiling on the size of single agricultural corporations. New proposals, introduced in 1912 and supported by numerous Farmers' Union members in both houses, would prohibit corporate agricultural landownership altogether. The House passed one such bill over stiff but decidedly minority opposition, with Oscar Johnston ironically voting with the majority. Former Gov. James Vardaman also weighed in with his support. ("When the land shall be owned by the few," he said, "the many will become hewers of wood and drawers of water.") The prohibition, not effective until November 1912, eventually passed both houses, setting off a surge of incorporations to beat the deadline. Gov. Earl Brewer, who had been cool to the anticorporation statute, went to Europe in the late summer of 1912, prompting speculation about possible land sales. A bit closed-mouth with the press, Brewer hinted his trades were small. The governor returned to New York in October on Cunard's *Lusitania,* sharing the trip with Charles Scott, whose presence only heightened speculation. Referring to his land sale to the British Fine Spinners the previous year, Scott told the press, "I sold all the land I wanted and this year I have been over simply on pleasure." In any case, populism had it limits. An attempt in 1914 to force divestiture of corporate-held agricultural lands suffered defeat in the House, indicating, said the Delta's *Greenville Daily Democrat,* "a return to sanity by that body after many of its members had wandered long in the narrow paths of demagogic politics."[8]

Land sales suggested confidence among investors, but the anticorporate tone of Mississippi politics produced anxiety among the British Fine Spinners. Fortunately, a new possibility for corporate insulation from political volatility soon emerged. An old land sales corporation chartered by realtors and lawyers in

Jackson in 1886 was "winding up" its affairs in 1917. The corporation, the Delta and Pine Land Company of Mississippi, had been organized with northern capital as a speculative enterprise to dispose of timber and farmlands, which for want of back taxes, had fallen to the state. For decades it parceled off huge tracts, stimulating Mississippi's development, particularly that of the Delta. By World War I, Delta Pine's purpose stood largely complete, with more than half a million acres having passed through its hands. Its charter might have been voluntarily forfeited and canceled had that charter not acquired a special value. Signed and validated by Mississippi Atty. Gen. T. M. Miller in 1886, the charter stood in perpetuity, possessing unlimited capacity in capital stock and, among other powers, unlimited capacity in value and size of landholdings. Probably by accident, the Mississippi legislature in the 1880s failed to preserve its own rights for controlling corporations under the prevailing incorporation statute and amendments. The lawmakers eventually closed the gap, but the new legislation was not retroactive; Delta and Pine Land's charter had slipped through the loophole, as had similar charters of three other corporations. Mississippi's Constitution of 1890 slammed the door on future exemptions, subjecting corporations to the will of the legislature and mandating a fifty-year renewable life cycle.[9]

The latitude of Delta Pine's charter had never been judicially tested, but in 1917 that of one of its sister corporations found itself in front of the Mississippi Supreme Court. One of the four exceptional charters, Tchula Cooperative Stores, had been organized in Hinds County, Mississippi, in 1888, and possessed powers similar to those of Delta and Pine Land Company. The litigation developed after the Southern Realty Company refused to deed a small parcel of land to Tchula Stores, already a large landowner, after having contracted to do so in 1914. Southern Realty contended that to execute the transaction would violate Chapter 162 of Mississippi's Laws of 1912, the anticorporation statute that prevented corporate agricultural landownership. Irony built upon irony when Oscar Johnston, who, in the legislature had voted for the 1912 statute, now represented Tchula Stores before the Mississippi Supreme Court in 1917. In *Southern Realty Co. v. Tchula Cooperative Stores,* Johnston argued that his client's charter, issued in 1888, allowed wide prerogatives and that the 1912 statute was inapplicable since incorporation occurred prior to the 1890 constitution. Further, citing *Dartmouth College v. Woodward* and other cases, Johnston contended that the 1912 law, if applied to Tchula Stores, would impair their contractual obligations, a violation of Article I, Section 10 of the Constitution of the United States. Mississippi's high court agreed. Though itself not tested, Delta Pine's charter now basked in the warm glow of Tchula Stores' victory. On the strength of the court's ruling, the British Fine Spinners, never dreaming that the thirty-seven-year-old barrister who had secured the favorable rendering would eventually lead their American plantations for more than two decades, moved to acquire the charter of Delta and Pine Land Company. In 1919, in league with minority stockholders, it did so, Delta Pine then acquiring the holdings of Triumph, Lake Vista, and Mississippi Delta Planting Company. With the transplant of this new heart, the old charter, without missing a beat, began a new life as one of the largest cotton plantations in America.[10]

Once purchased, the British properties required huge expenditures for physical development, including drainage, roads, and improvements in ginning and storage facilities. Valuable timber was cleared. Scott Station soon became a habitable village with the construction of new homes, eventually boasting service and recreational amenities for the white management and visitors. In time, said Vernon Bellhouse, a director of the Fine Spinners who first visited the properties in 1912, "it became a happy white community." Out from Scott the expansive plantations were divided into units, many bearing their former names, each headed by a white resident manager overseeing scores of black tenant families tilling the soil and picking the cotton on a sharecrop basis. As general manager, Professor Jesse W. Fox oversaw the whole operation, worthy of the publicly reported $7,500 salary it took to woo him away from the experiment station; he was, Oscar Johnston later claimed, "the best husbandman in the U.S." The Scott plantation added new contiguous lands, and eventually British and other capital also went into two smaller and separate Delta plantations, Empire Plantation at Estill, Mississippi, and Delta Farms Company at Deeson, Mississippi, about forty miles from Scott.[11]

Salsbury's dream, and British intent, had been the creation of a scientific super plantation—a plan advanced with the arrival in 1915 of Early C. Ewing, a plant geneticist with the Mississippi Agricultural Experiment Station. A graduate of Mississippi A & M, Ewing had taken advanced work at Cornell University, where the eminent botanist Herbert J. Webber emphasized Mendelian principles of selective breeding. After Ewing's graduation, a stint with the U.S. Department of Agriculture, with fieldwork in Texas, preceded his service in Mississippi. A talented pioneer in cotton breeding, Ewing came to Scott "with great expectations," undeterred by dirt roads and lack of electric lights, seeking professional fulfillment and lucrative possibilities. He stayed for the rest of his long life. His work placed the British plantation on the leading edge of scientific development of hybrid cotton varieties, which paid healthy white dividends, despite the complaint in his memoir that early management failed to fully appreciate the value of such development.[12]

Despite scientific management, pioneering breakthroughs, and wide public exposure, not all was well. Troubles plagued the plantations from their start in 1911. Fronting the Mississippi River for about twenty miles, Delta Pine's monotonously flat fields cowered behind earthen levees—levees violated in 1912 and 1913. The 1911 crop was virtually a complete loss; the following year the big plantation with the big plan produced a pathetically tiny crop. Then there was the weevil and the armyworm. Even as the British had been routing around the property before they bought it, there had been a lot of public discussion about the weevil's potential threat. Early Ewing thought the hazard induced the Americans to sell; the British apparently thought they could handle it, and the sale stood as a testimony of confidence, perhaps even helping stabilize land values.[13]

Unfortunately for the British, the original plan for an American cotton supply for their mills miscarried. The staple proved unsuitable. But that was only the half of it. After plowing an original $3 million into the real estate, and throwing in another $1.5 million in additional acquisitions and improvements, the British had a largely unprofitable showplace. It eventually sucked up several million more, paying only one dividend in Salsbury's sixteen-year tenure. Flooding, weevils, and slipping cotton prospects conspired against profitability. The holding companies, Triumph and Lake Vista, failed to show a profit until 1917. They did so that year partly because the leasing company, Mississippi Delta Planting Company, had its rent doubled to reflect newly cleared acreage and increased land values. Optimism flourished until the debacle of 1920, "one of the most disappointing years we have ever experienced since we have been in business," complained Salsbury in his annual report. While postwar prices shot skyward, Salsbury held the company's share of the 1919 crop, salivating over a projected major windfall. But like many others, he held on too long. The commodity collapse that had ruined Clarksdale's economy in 1920 and had given birth to the Staple Cotton Cooperative Association also turned a potential $3 million Delta Pine profit into a million dollar loss. A tryout of more than a thousand bales of Delta Pine's 1925 crop, if not more, in the Fine Spinners' mills prompted a flurry of optimism that large parts of future crops might find their way to England and that the Scott plantation might yet fulfill British ambitions. It didn't happen. The British had made a mistake in their American venture and they knew it. Herbert W. Lee, eventually elevated to the chairmanship of the Fine Cotton Spinners' and Doublers' Association, had opposed the purchase in the first place. Outvoted at the time, Lee later found grim satisfaction in declaring, reminiscent of the American salesmanship, "they dug some goose pits and we fell into them."[14] Talented businessmen had become innocents abroad.

There was a positive side. The much-celebrated giant plantation won public plaudits, standing as a scientific agricultural laboratory. It was a factory, an agribusiness before there was such a term; yet it also stood as a curiosity, a throwback to the mythical plantation of old, with allegedly happy blacks cared for by paternalistic whites. The considerable achievements of Salsbury's leadership, including Ewing's prolific seed varieties, Jesse Fox's land husbandry, and a well-organized sharecropper labor force, presented a happy and prosperous facade. Eventually even weevils were scientifically and chemically repelled, whether by truck-mounted tanks or by newly retrofitted biplanes, an innovative and promising feature of the coming air age. For conservative businessmen, however, all of that was small compensation, if that was nearly all the compensation there was. There was no romance in red ink. Cotton growing in the 1910s and 1920s was rough business, as ruthless as the aberrations of the marketplace could make it, with weevils, weather, and periodic flooding all part of the mix. About this period metaphors abound. The British had a white elephant, an albatross, or as *Fortune* said later, "a severe transatlantic headache." They were open to offers.[15]

Opportunities for sale arose in the early twenties. Ford Motor Company seemed a likely prospect, then Mitsui Bussan Kaisha, Ltd., of Tokyo, through the offices of Mitsui and Company in New York. With no idea of ever involving himself with Salsbury's properties, Oscar Johnston met with the Memphis magnate several times relative to at least one of the potential sales. In any case, both deals collapsed. A Memphis realtor intimately involved in both prospects told Oscar years later that Salsbury overzealously rushed the Ford deal, while the falling silk market ruined any hope of completing the sale to the Japanese. Salsbury's subsequent attempt to sell the properties to an American syndicate also fell through. A later plan, the one that brought Johnston to Memphis in 1926, was no doubt Salsbury's biggest scheme yet. With former Illinois Gov. Frank O. Lowden and Listerine's Gerard B. Lambert, Salsbury looked for the creation of "Cotton Estates," a mammoth multistate corporation engulfing sizable lands in Arkansas, including Lowden's and Lambert's sprawling properties in that state, Salsbury's holdings in Louisiana, and the Fine Spinners' properties in Mississippi. Together, the real estate exceeded 130,000 acres. Johnston's task: secure options from the British.[16]

Johnston sailed for Manchester in May for his first meeting with the British. Despite a book loss, the proposed deal left the Britishers' gold bonds secure, lifted burdensome liabilities, and unencumbered cash that might find more profitable returns elsewhere. Though the complicated arrangements were struck on May 21, the Fine Spinners' solicitors balked after Johnston's departure. An altered plan involving debentures and a reduction in the American syndicate's acreage was soon substituted, winning approval on both sides of the Atlantic. Before the arrangements could be consummated, however, a new and fatal problem intruded. In October 1926, cotton prices fell sharply on the exchanges, lenders got skittish, and the British got impatient. The Fine Spin-

ners, looking to dump the properties, were unwilling to finance farming operations for 1927. In a move Johnston thought hopeless, Salsbury, hat in hand,
headed to Chicago to find operating revenues. Johnston told the British that
he could "not conceive of any banking house or financial institution agreeing
to finance the proposed new corporation for crop operations where such financing would have to start from the very beginning, and where the entire
benefit from the intended crop would go to the holders of mortgage bonds
held by others not participating in the financing."[17]

Salsbury's plans for taking up the options on the British properties dimmed.
Impatient, the Fine Spinners cabled Johnston brusquely: "Think it time your
end found some capital and carried out agreement made with us." Johnston
refused to be bullied. He appreciated neither "the tone" nor "the implication"
of the British cable. He replied:

> I do not understand that I had any agreement concerning which I am in the least
> in default. Employed by you and representing you, and in an effort to relieve you
> from a situation which I know you would like to be rid of, I evolved the scheme
> submitted. Under conditions existing when I was in England this scheme appeared
> to you, as well as to me, to be feasible and practicable, under present conditions it
> is impossible; accordingly, must be discarded, but I repeat when it is discarded, I
> do not conceive that I am in the least in default in the consummation of any agree-
> ment ever entered into by me.[18]

Oscar was right. Factors over which he and Salsbury had control had been
favorable, but the deal rested on a healthy market, and late 1926 was no time
for bulls. The big promotion stalled, victim of a slipping market. That, Johnston
told the British, was beyond his and Salsbury's control. The price decline that
torpedoed Salsbury's deal sent near panic throughout the cotton belt, rever-
berating through the boardrooms where big-money schemes were made. Too
many farmers picked too much cotton. Swelling acreage, scientific methods,
and improved weevil control hiked production dramatically. More than 47.6
million white acres in 1926—up 10.5 million since 1923—nearly doubled
American production in four years. Add good weather in 1926 and the cotton
market was in trouble. In the fall of that year prices on the New York and New
Orleans exchanges plunged deeply. Average futures closings fell from 17.15
cents for August to 12.82 cents for October. December was even lower. Average prices stood more than 7 cents under that of 1925 and more than 16 cents
under that of the poor crop year of 1923. The result, Johnston told Herbert
Lee in November, "has been to deter outside investments in anything that looks
like a cotton proposition."[19]

Delta Pine paralleled the trend. The huge company had never planted less
than twelve thousand acres to cotton at Scott; that ballooned, according to

company records, to more than eighteen thousand by the mid-twenties. Early Ewing's breeding and fertilizing efforts at Scott saw production leap from 4,680 bales in 1923 (admittedly a bad crop year) to 10,104 in 1924 and then 15,198 in 1925 before dipping a bit to nearly 12,500 in 1926. Yields jumped from a dismal 152 pounds per acre in 1923 to a phenomenal 406 in 1925.[20]

As the market spun downward in 1926, government response was belated and modest. In early October the Federal Farm Loan Board extended $30 million credit to marketing cooperatives through the Intermediate Credit Banks scattered throughout the South. U.S. Secretary of Agriculture William M. Jardine gloomily reported to President Calvin Coolidge that it would take an average price of eighteen cents a pound for cotton states to equal their 1925 income. Though Jardine thought the market dip was transient, he admitted that the cotton belt was a blotch on the nation's agricultural picture and that marketing prospects were unsatisfactory. To make matters worse, 5.6 million carryover bales from 1925 piled on top of the record-breaking volume of 1926. McNary-Haugen bills, calling for government purchase and storage of farm products, tried to pressure the administration to do more. However, early on, the proposed legislation discriminated against cotton, earning Johnston's opposition—a disaster for cotton planters, he told Sen. Pat Harrison and Congressman Will M. Whittington in February 1927. Congress eventually passed a new and improved version, with special benefits for cotton, but it fell victim to a Coolidge veto. The president did, in the midst of the market slide of 1926, appoint the Cotton Aid Board to examine cotton's ailments. Eugene Meyer Jr., manager of the War Finance Corporation, chaired the board, which also included cabinet secretaries Jardine from Agriculture, Herbert Hoover from Commerce, and Andrew Mellon from Treasury. Charged with supplementing the efforts of existing cooperative associations and Federal Intermediate Credit Banks, the new board invited Johnston to Washington to discuss cotton's woes. The administration confidently thought that given sufficient credit, cotton producers could store their crops in warehouses and then dispose of them when the market allowed.[21]

The problem was not merely credit, but the need to suppress cotton's growth. The South reached into its own quiver for the old broken arrow of voluntary acreage restriction. Despite the pathetic inadequacy of such schemes dating from the nineteenth century, a new and intensive campaign was launched in the fall of 1926. The movement centered around the South-Wide Cotton Conference at the Peabody Hotel in Memphis in mid-October. Called by Gov. Henry L. Whitfield of Mississippi, the conference attracted senators, governors, bankers, cooperative leaders and others. Oscar Johnston was there, along with Delta Pine's general manager, Jesse Fox, who, until his death in 1944, was the fellow heavily responsible for the plantation's success. The debates dragged on for hours. The conference decided that four million bales from the current crop would be held off the market and pooled in state cooperative associations. Farmers, urged to sign up for 25 percent acreage reduction for 1927, would draw operating funds from Federal Intermediate Credit Banks until the pooled cotton was sold. Despite the desperate market condition, the conference followed a mild course, spurning what Johnston called "many wild and radical plans" for cotton reduction. Calls for vigilantism and a one-year ban on all production got nowhere; there would be no enforcement. One indigenous group, the Knights of Cotton, issued a proclamation later in October calling for crop rotation, 50 percent cotton reduction, and removal "forever from the world's visible supply the annual estimated surplus production of cotton and cotton seed produced during any cotton season by plowing it under, thereby enriching the soil and promptly restoring the market prices of these products to their rightful place." It was all understandably desperate talk from understandably desperate men. Johnston and Fox wound up on the cotton conference's executive committee and the Central Acreage Committee, which soon witnessed the creation of state and local organizations across the cotton belt to bring about acreage reduction.[22]

Across the Atlantic, the British bondholders of Delta and Pine Land Company had other ideas. Herbert Lee, the Fine Spinners' executive director, had put the failed land deal behind him and looked "to make these plantations a successful and paying proposition." He thought it best to plant "the utmost possible acreage" for 1927, from his perspective a suggestion not wholly unreasonable. Of course, Johnston's ideas ran in other directions. Since the company lost money on every bale, except for keeping the whole operation together and in good shape, there was, he thought, "no conceivable excuse or reason for planting any cotton at all." Sensitive to latent populism, Oscar also knew that noncooperation by his and other large-scale plantations "would . . . invite adverse legislation and provoke the hostility of public officials as well as private citizens, thus seriously handicapping profitable operation in the future."[23]

Actually, what Johnston wanted was reduction and cotton too. Dark figures following mules across Delta Pine's monotonous expanse belied the scientific quality of the plantation's management. Diversion of marginal cotton land to feed production and intensive cultivation of reduced and culled tenant allotments would lower overhead while raising yield. In January 1927, Johnston was in Mississippi going over the properties like a bloodhound, inspecting them thoroughly for the first time. He talked with Professor Fox; he talked with unit managers. Impressed and emboldened—even the labor shortage had apparently eased—Johnston backed off from 25 percent reduction. Nevertheless, as he told Herbert Lee, "I am more interested in quantity of production than in number of acres planted."[24]

Johnston became a familiar figure on the three plantations, spending increasing amounts of time out of the Memphis office. He looked more like an executive director than a general counsel. Never fitting the traditional image of a remote absentee landlord, he preferred to see things for himself, even tenants. At a managers' meeting in Scott on January 4, 1927, he outlined his plan to revitalize the company. The shareholders had not given up on the plantation, he said, but full cooperation by everyone was required for success. Rigid austerity was also required, including intensive cultivation, no new equipment save for emergencies, repairs at home if possible, and carefully apportioned stock feed. Every cash purchase would be scrutinized and a budget system adopted. Farming was risky business; it always had been. But through austerity and economies on feed and fertilizer Oscar looked to slash operating costs at Scott by more than $100,000 for 1927. The British were impressed. "The more I see of your methods," Lee told him, "the more I have hope of these places being very quickly made into a paying proposition."[25]

Not content to school himself in Delta Pine's operations alone, Johnston soon investigated cotton growing in the West. In the cotton farming business, no one was an island. Cotton production had bloomed of late in Texas, new lands falling under the plow. Predictions about acreage reduction out west proved conflicting. Then there were intriguing reports about inexpensive harvesting of low-grade cotton by a process known as "sledding." Johnston decided to investigate firsthand. By rail and automobile, he toured Texas cotton lands for a week in February, talking with agricultural agents and others while noting topography, demography, rainfall, and other conditions bearing on future cotton production. From the Arkansas line to Dallas, Sweetwater, Lubbock, and the New Mexico border, he saw it all; then it was back to Wichita Falls and a brush through southwest Oklahoma. All the while he pondered the significance for cotton growers east of the Mississippi.

The Texas trip was no junket, but it confirmed much of what Johnston already knew, including the need for intensive farming, careful land management, and reduced acreage allotments per tenant. He dismissed the "sledding" process—a method by which an apparatus was dragged through the field to pick up low-grades. It was too impractical, he thought, for the heavy cotton stalks of the Mississippi Delta. The developing cotton region of northwest Texas, however, provided a sobering potential threat to eastern growers—what Johnston called "a serious problem." He estimated Texas would cut acreage about 15 percent in 1927. Oscar's report recommended elimination of marginal lands incapable of generating three hundred pounds per acre. Labor should be treated fairly, for pragmatic reasons if for no other, and should be encouraged to live at home by gardening and caring for a few animals for staples. If Texas provided a threat, the Delta, "properly, intensively cultivated," would in time, he said, generate more profit than cotton fields anywhere out west.[26]

Despite such optimism, there were other problems closer to home. Even as the market slid downward in the fall of 1926, the federal government claimed Delta Pine owed back taxes for the fiscal years ending 1918–20. Johnston's perusal of plantation accounts confirmed more than a third of a million dollars in unpaid taxes. Credits for a standing deposit plus overpayment in 1923 reduced that figure, but the debt still exceeded $270,000. Audaciously, Johnston offered $35,000 cash as full settlement, a proposal the Bureau of Internal Revenue refused, all the while hinting it might look kindly on a more favorable offer. Confident they would soon unload their American properties, along with the tax burden, the British refused to hike the offer; they had, however, empowered Johnston as general counsel to act as their agent. He occupied the battlefield between the government and the implacable British, who had thought the government's claim "outrageous."[27]

Johnston proved worthy of his hire. Warehouse receipts covering Delta Pine's cotton went into a safe-deposit box under his own name, protecting the crop against a potential distress warrant. Johnston hurried to Washington to haggle with the Federal Income Revenue commissioner and the assistant solicitor general. The British would not raise their offer, he said. Also, the market looked dim, and execution of the government's warrant would end in foreclosure. But he also sweetened the pot. Delta Pine would kick in an additional $5,000 and forfeit a $10,000 counterclaim dating back to 1923. Johnston also stood ready, or so he hinted, to foreclose the British mortgage on the Scott property, arguing that the Fine Spinners might hold priority over the government's claim. In that scenario, the government might line up to get hold of the plantation's relatively paltry store merchandise. It was all a bit of bluff; litigation, resulting in receivership, would be fruitless, as Johnston confided to the British, since Delta and Pine Land Company could not make bond for the whole tax claim. Fortunately for the hapless company, the government, for whatever reason, caved in. The solicitor general advised Johnston in April 1927 that he would recommend taking Delta Pine's offer. He instructed federal collectors at Nashville and Jackson to relinquish all tax liens. "It is I think really a very good settlement," exulted the once-skeptical Herbert Lee, "and we certainly have to thank you for your prompt and skilful attention to the matter because there is no doubt that if you had allowed it to get into the Courts we should have had no end of trouble and expense."[28]

Tax problems were only symptomatic of Delta Pine's poor financial ledgers. Low yields and low prices had added to the plantation's debt, and assets stood embarrassingly high, inflated by Salsbury, who anticipated sale of the properties in 1926. Accounts and the balance sheet demanded reorganization. Johnston aimed to increase first-mortgage debt and offer second-mortgage gold bonds. The company's unwieldy current account, including more than $4 million owed the Fine Spinners and secured by a general mortgage, had seriously devalued its $3 million capital stock, which Johnston now cut two-thirds. Ghosting for Salsbury, he called a stockholders' meeting in Scott for April 16, 1927, advising that approval of reorganization would put the operation in good shape for the 1927 season "and relieve it of the enormous interest burden under which it is now laboring." The thirteen minority American investors, holding 6,600 shares, supported the plan, as did the majority Fine Spinners. On April 16 all stock was represented, mostly by proxies, as other obligations and heavy rains limited attendance. Johnston's reorganization won unanimous approval; legally clothed, he planned to sail for England to finalize details. On April 18, he advised the Fine Spinners by letter that "Unless delayed by some unforseen contingency, I shall doubtless be en route to Manchester when you receive this."[29]

Then it happened. When the British did receive his letter, Oscar was not on the Atlantic but back in Mississippi. Unusually heavy rains in the Mississippi Valley swelled the great river, softening the levee fronting Delta Pine and flooding ditches and canals on the plantation. Hundreds of men filled bags, trying desperately to shore up ten miles of levee. The rising water approached the old 1913 record. Then, on April 21, 1927, the Father of Waters broke the eastern levees near Scott at Mound Landing, Mississippi, sending the flood across the Delta's flatland for more than a hundred miles. It was the worst flood in the Mississippi's recorded past, with water covering acreage equivalent to the entire state of Rhode Island. In the whole valley, three-quarters of a million people fled their homes; property damage totaled $220 million.[30]

Water totally covered Delta and Pine Land's plantation. The break in the levee fronting the plantation had given little immediate warning. Efforts to restrain the river in the middle of the night failed. Water had come within two feet of cresting, and when the levee collapsed the floods crashed over the plantation, gushing up Lake Bolivar and destroying a long bridge by the sawmill. Early Ewing, watching the overflow from a powerboat, thought it "strange, fantastic . . . like Niagra Falls," the water splashing a half-mile gash in the levee. Nearly every cotton house rose off the ground, derelicts in a muddy sea. Jesse Fox's house took several inches of water, but at the plantation store in Scott the flood rose to the countertops. The growing crop was totally destroyed, and about seven hundred tons of seed were damaged or ruined, as were tenant houses and other structures. Fortunately, no one died. Mules, however, didn't fair so well. Many drowned, the company losing about 250, and the tenants nearly all of theirs. Some of the beasts were led to the levees, others suffered both exposure and indignity on cabin porches awaiting rescue.[31]

In Memphis, Johnston got word a half hour after the break. Like a general heading for the front, he left immediately for Scott to assume command. The biggest problem was keeping the tenants together. About 1,700 quickly relocated to a camp established at Delta Farms at Deeson, unaffected by the flood. Hundreds more got to the levee or walked or were carried by boats to Greenville. When Greenville's levee collapsed, they joined other refugees in a camp down the river at Vicksburg. There, demoralized, they began to scatter; the company stood to lose its valuable labor, most or all of whom owed on their accounts. Johnston went to Vicksburg, gathered the tenants into a nine-coach train provided gratis by Illinois Central, and escorted them to the main camp at Deeson, about 260 miles to the north. At stations along the way, the Red Cross provided food and, at Deeson, housing as well. The Deeson camp, policed by the National Guard, remained under Delta Pine's management. Johnston hovered about the flooded area, anxious about tenant morale, looking to quickly relocate tenants back to their homes. According to figures Johnston provided the Red Cross, wholesale costs to furnish clothes and household equipment to tenants totaled about seventy-five dollars per family.[32]

Adding to the problem, new rains and flooding halted replanting and dashed hopes for another crop. By the end of June it was clear Scott would grow no cotton at all. At best, some hay could be substituted. To save maintenance costs, Delta Pine loaned mules to farmers farther north. Meanwhile, Johnston feared tenants would not return when the water receded. Since planters in unflooded areas tried to lure Delta Pine's tenants with offers of housing and employment— free of debt—Johnston had to write off old and new tenant accounts, starting fresh when they reoccupied their homes. Tenants momentarily enjoyed the luxury of free agency, and for Delta and Pine Land Company it did not come cheap. When it was all over, the plantation had lost crops, seed, land, mules, buildings, including more than a hundred houses, and money. Erosion and relocation of levees destroyed more than a thousand acres, while sand deposits, some six feet deep, ruined about three thousand more. Not counting the loss of the 1927 crop, some of which was insured, company losses approached half a million dollars. *Fortune,* without theological precision, later claimed, "It was as though the gods had finally appointed the river to give the coup de grace to the Britishers' already prostrate scheme."[33]

Amid the press of events, Johnston kept the British minutely abreast of flood developments and financial transactions. He even sent flood-story clippings from the *Memphis Commercial Appeal.* He knew it was going to take "considerable expenditure" to put the place back in top shape. For that the conservative Britishers would have to come stateside to see for themselves. Unfortunately, the flood had done more than damage buildings and ruin young cotton plants. It also washed away Johnston's reorganization scheme. In June he lamented that the plan was no longer as practical as it had been in April. Still, conditions required financial reorganization of some sort. Now Johnston argued that the Fine Spinners should eliminate American shareholders, placing British investment and earnings against the company's cost. To add to the flux, Lant Salsbury, having already essentially retreated from company management, looked to depart the sinking ship. Johnston, he thought, should succeed him as president, effective July 1, 1927. The flood crisis and Salsbury's diminished health helped persuade Johnston to agree, albeit temporarily. (Salsbury, ever the optimist, had fought back from an automobile accident in 1925 that injured him severely and killed his wife of thirty-five years. After leaving Delta Pine he eventually turned up in Texas, where, in the early thirties, while the rest of the nation wallowed in the Depression, he amassed another fortune, this time in the oil fields.)[34]

Before taking the helm for the indefinite future, Oscar wanted to sit down across the table from the British and chart a new course for the three plantations. There was no false modesty or gamesmanship in the relationship. This was a matter of business and economics. "A singular fatality seems to have attached to the operation of this property for the last few years," Johnston told Lee frankly in June. "Fluctuating prices in the cotton market and the overflow have balked every plan devised for putting these properties on a sound basis." For his part, Lee had already placed great confidence in Johnston. In fact, Oscar's two visits to Manchester in 1926 had so impressed the British that they figured if their American properties could be turned around, Johnston would be the main ingredient in doing so. Now, in 1927, with water still covering most of the Scott plantation, Lee said he was "more grateful than I can tell you" about Johnston assuming command on July 1. He was certain all matters of negotiation could be worked out face to face. "We are starting with you under circumstances that are most depressing for us all, and are specially depressing for you," he told Johnston in June, "but I feel sure that we shall see prosperous times together, and probably in the not distant future."[35]

The British arrived in Scott in the dog days of late August 1927. The water was gone, but the wreckage remained. Erosion, sand deposits, levee relocation, and wrecked barns and warehouses bore mute witness to the spring havoc. They were fortunate to have Johnston's services, soon ratifying his election as top man. Together they also reorganized Delta Pine's financial basis. It was the kind of thing that, save for bankers and accountants, makes the eyes glaze over. Among the changes were sophisticated accounting procedures, including delay of first-mortgage gold bond redemption and drastic reduction of capital stock, something Johnston thought overvalued. The British also agreed to write off nearly $1 million on their books and shift the fiscal year from January to March 31 to accommodate the sale of the year's crop. Accompanying Johnston's elevation to the presidency were Memphis personnel and salary changes. Everyone got a salary hike, Johnston's to $40,000 ($10,000 more than Salsbury's); with a leaner staff, Oscar still hoped to substantially reduce front-office expenses in the first year.[36]

There were other negotiating items. Johnston wanted to quit sending Delta Pine cotton to Manchester. He and Salsbury had studied marketing possibilities in America in 1926; the British at that time agreed only to the sale of poorer grades in Memphis. Also, Johnston wanted to give up trying to produce extra-long staple varieties, planting instead seed adapted to the rain areas of America. The British agreed that future cotton would sell on the open market, stipulating, however, that they could purchase on the basis of samples sent to England. Even this was soon abandoned. In 1928, Delta and Pine Land Company committed its cotton to the Staple Cotton Cooperative Association, the agency Johnston had helped establish in the early twenties.[37]

Aside from negotiations with the British, one major triumph of 1927 lay in the cotton futures market. The flood that year affected 75 percent of American acreage planted to long-staple cotton, boosting premiums for seed. Fortunately, Delta Pine recovered sufficient seed for the 1928 season and long-staple futures appeared bullish. After the levee break, Johnston had purchased futures contracts for all three plantations. He told the British he hoped futures profits would generate sufficient funds to operate throughout the season without calling on them for assistance. Less sanguine, Herbert Lee, while impressed with Johnston's handling of the 1926 crop—so much so that he did "not feel disposed to give you more than my opinion"—anxiously pressured him to bail out of the market. Oscar took his own counsel. He enjoyed playing the market, was skilled at it, and was convinced the market would advance. Six weeks after the flood his futures account showed a profit of about $100,000; bullishly he held on through the summer, looking for a smaller crop and maybe twenty-cent cotton. The gamble worked. By fall, prices topped out at 18–22 cents. Johnston liquidated his futures, and Delta and Pine Land Company had $200,000 with which to rebuild.[38]

Having failed to unload their American properties, the British Fine Spinners, following Johnston's suggestion, slowly acquired control of minority-held stock. In 1928, Johnston seized the opportunity to dump Delta Pine's troublesome

Red Bud plantation—"a very unfortunate investment," he called it—to former president Lant Salsbury. Delta Pine took a loss but in the deal grabbed Salsbury's sizable stocks in all three plantations. While the British added Vice President Robert Lynes's stock in the three companies when he left in 1929, they never got total control of all Delta Pine's stock until 1950.[39]

Johnston's financial retrenchment in the late twenties included closing down Delta and Pine Land's Memphis office and moving most of the staff to Scott. The move in 1929 was momentarily delayed by an attack of pleurisy; Johnston claimed the fluid in his lungs receded at the same rate as Mississippi's flood-waters. It was quite a change, from the bustling center of the mid-South to the sunbaked little village, a cluster of white faces amid a sea of black ones. Three round-trip passenger trains broke Scott's isolation in the early days; a Pullman departing in the afternoon arrived in Chicago the next morning. Early Ewing, who had already lived at Scott for fourteen years when the headquarters moved there, recalled that "[i]f one had the money, one could go to a show in Memphis and then board the sleeper at the station. It would in due time be picked up by the 'Pea Vine' and stop at Scott about 7:00 A.M. en route to Green-ville." When he married in 1920, Ewing said, "civilization was definitely emerg-ing in the countryside."[40]

For his part, Johnston had been no absentee landlord, commuting between Memphis and Scott by airplane, flying the contraption himself. Had the move not been dictated by economy and convenience, let alone the improved mo-rale of the resident staff, he might have kept it up. Oscar loved flying; during the war he would have preferred the air corps over tanks. Poor eyesight pre-vented that. Legend had it that to get in the army, he had memorized the eye chart. Faulty vision failed to ground him after the war, and stories about his air exploits became legend: as a banker he traded credit for flying lessons; he was shot at over Kentucky (probably by moonshiners); and he patched a leaky gas tank with soap. These were rickety barnstorming days. When he flew ("in an aeroplane") in fifty-three minutes from Clarksdale to Greenwood for a Staple Cotton Cooperative directors' meeting in 1923, even as a passenger, it was front-page news in both towns.[41]

In Scott the plantation offices were housed in a two-storied brick building. The small village out from Greenville was pleasant enough, sporting several amenities dating from Salsbury's presidency, including a hotel and recreational facilities for white management. Martha was in Asheville, but Johnston built twin unpretentious clapboard houses, one for himself and Martha and one for his and the plantation's secretary, Archibald F. Toler, and Toler's wife, Mary Ann. Johnston's paneled sunporch eventually housed assorted fowl and beast—most bagged nearby—now stuffed and mounted; a combination radio-bar sported Oscar's aged bourbon, his specialty. In time the frame house on the big plantation became a required port of call for King Cotton's students and retainers. Across the way stood Toler's house. Capable and loyal, Arch Toler had been with Oscar since his banking days in Clarksdale. Johnston, having seen quality in him, plucked him from automobile sales. Oscar thought highly of Arch, the pair enjoying an excellent working relationship right up until Toler left for military service in World War II. Their mirror houses bore witness to Johnston's secure unconcern for pretense, as did his unpresidential office, complete with unimpressive desk, on the second floor of the headquarters building (whiskey could be found in a closet). In the New Deal days, autographed pictures of Franklin Roosevelt and Secretary of Agriculture Henry A. Wallace adorned the drab wall. One story had it that the big shots' portraits flanked that of Dave Alexander, an elderly black sharecropper. The caption under the cropper's picture read, "This man knows his business."[42]

Johnston's return to his native state placed him in line for another flyer at public office, should he have wanted it. The public spotlight did capture him briefly the next year when he served as legal counsel to the state legislative committee in its prosecution of the so-called Warrenite scandal. The scandal apparently involved Mississippi's attorney general George T. Mitchell and tax commission chairman Lester Franklin, also a gubernatorial candidate, along with a Gulfport attorney and a Jackson law firm. Allegedly to prevent an antitrust suit against the Warren Brothers paving materials company of Boston, Massachusetts, $80,000 got passed under the table, touching or implicating a number of hands in the process. In late February 1930, Johnston first publicly appeared with the House committee, "although," said the *Jackson Daily News*, "he has been quietly working with the body for some time, and is accredited with developing a number of the important phases of the case." The day before, the *Memphis Commercial Appeal* had reported that Johnston "has had a hand in the development of all the testimony and information in [the committee's] possession." The fallout led to Franklin's impeachment—though he was acquitted in the state Senate—presumably the derailment of his gubernatorial plans, and the disbarment of several Mississippi attorneys.[43]

Johnston's resurfacing in public service proved fleeting. If public office crossed his mind, his greater thoughts rested on his plantations. At first it appeared that the flood of 1927 had purged Delta and Pine Land Company of its checkered past. New leadership, financial reorganization, austerity, good weather, and a reviving business economy helped produce more than a quarter-million-dollar profit in 1928. The next year profits topped $200,000. When the market dropped sharply in 1930, however, the plantation's recovery sputtered. The problem was endemic. Banks and other lending agencies failed, foreclosures spread, optimism evaporated, and America headed into the Great Depression. In 1931 Johnston told the shareholders that "the accompanying report of the Treasurer is like the 'Annals of the Poor,' short and simple."[44]

It would get a lot worse before it ever got better. A severe hailstorm accompanied by nearly nine inches of rain in May 1930 destroyed part of the crop. Then a summer drought baked the Delta until September; cotton planted after the storm did not develop, the quality of what remained was poor. Yield fell from nearly 477 pounds an acre in 1929 to a dismal 276 in 1930, producing less than a dime a pound. Feed crops suffered from the drought, forcing the company to import a greater quantity for its livestock. Johnston cut salaries, laid off some management, and altered the tenant credit system. The 1930 loss, including mortgage interest, approached $360,000.[45]

With the American investments slipping back into fiscal ruin, restructuring was again in order. The British agreed that Delta Pine should replace its original gold bonds with a new issue of first-mortgage amortization bonds for $3 million. These new bonds, carrying 5 percent interest, reflected increased property and value since 1911. A second mortgage, to mature in ten years, represented current obligations to the Fine Spinners. The British controlled both mortgages, allowing the Bank of Commerce and Trust in Memphis to hold the first mortgage bonds as trustee, empowering it to lend up to half a million dollars to Delta and Pine Land Company.[46]

Adjustments were also necessary in Delta Pine's incestuous economic relationship with Delta Farms and Empire Plantation, the two smaller noncontiguous plantations. Delta Farms was indebted to Delta Pine, Empire was indebted to both. Hard hit by flood, drought, and depression, Empire was an albatross, paying no dividend since 1920 while incurring losses of $117,000 between 1923 and 1931. Bankruptcy stalked Empire, threatening to drag Delta Farms with it. Johnston proposed that Delta Pine acquire Empire outright by canceling Empire's debt to both companies. The British agreed. In October 1931, the shareholders ratified the arrangement, adding five thousand noncontiguous acres to Delta Pine's holdings. Three companies became two.[47]

Financial overhauls failed to solve all problems. So did a good crop and further rationalization. In 1931 Delta Pine suffered another "disappointing and discouraging" year. Increased interest payments explained some of the loss, but the biggest problem was the sagging market, reflected in the 6.41 cents a pound for the 1931 crop. Seed sales plunged further, down more than $20 a ton from 1930. The plantation had furnished its sharecroppers on an 8-cent-a-pound basis; now it had to absorb an $83,000 loss on its tenant accounts. Even the futures market proved unfriendly. The market failed to recover and Johnston tried to protect the company's contracts with margins solicited from the British. As trustee, the Bank of Commerce and Trust could lend funds for farming operations but refused to authorize such funds for the futures market. Too risky. By April 1932 Delta and Pine Land Company still held July contracts on 7,700 bales at about 12.5 cents a pound. Admitting it would take a market rebound of nearly 6 cents to offset the loss and that such a prospect was dim, Johnston wrote what could have been the epitaph for every cotton producer in the South: "Under existing conditions I do not believe it possible for us to produce cotton at a profit on a six cent basis."[48]

As in the agricultural crisis of 1926, government's response proved wholly inadequate. The Federal Farm Board, established under the Agricultural Marketing Act of 1929, was supposed to promote price stability and orderly marketing, primarily through cooperative associations. The board funded these cooperatives, but in 1930 the cooperatives claimed less than 9 percent of the nation's 2.5 million cotton growers. The Farm Board also bankrolled the newly established stabilization corporations with nearly half a billion dollars to purchase surplus commodities, chiefly wheat and cotton. Despite board purchases, prices failed to respond. By 1931, its price-support funds exhausted, gone into the bottomless pit of overproduction and shrinking markets, the Farm Board held nearly 3.5 million bales of unsold cotton. When it tried to unload some of it, prices fell further, adding to the Depression. As Johnston wrote later in the *Cotton Trade Journal*, "The efforts of the Farm Board had proven worse than futile." In 1932, Johnston wanted the Democratic Party to call for its elimination. In fact, he hoped his party would oppose the "present system of governmental interference and intermeddling with private business enterprise," ironic talk on the threshold of the New Deal.[49]

The Hoover administration rejected mandatory reduction. "Even indirect purchase and sale of commodities is absolutely opposed to my theory of government," said the president. The Farm Board asked the governors of fourteen cotton states to foster crop reduction; renewed schemes, promising higher prices, swept the South. None proved successful; agricultural and political leadership languished. The Farm Board did approve $12 million in loans on the Staple Cotton Coop's 150,000 residual bales in March 1930, and a year later such loans to various southern associations totaled more than $136 million. Still, low prices reduced acreage as no encouragement from the Farm Board ever did; the farm program of the Hoover administration fell, as one scholar observed, "into self-inflicted impotence."[50]

Oscar Johnston campaigned for no reduction in the early thirties, as he had in 1926. In fact, he looked to expand acreage and production for 1933. Delta Pine had long since abandoned long-staple production, finding shorter varieties more profitable, among them Early Ewing's prolific "No. 10" seed variety, which produced cotton up to an inch and one-sixteenth in length. Demand for No. 10 was strong; one Tennessee youngster using the seed won both county and state cotton contests in 1931, producing a bit more than three bales on one acre. Seed triumphs, however, could not solve all the company's problems. While Delta Pine's 1932 crop year proved "less disappointing" than the year before, the plantation again fell into the red. Delta Pine's Bank of Commerce and Trust in Memphis, propped up by Reconstruction Finance Corporation loans, had weathered a run precipitated by official misuse of funds, but eventually, like so many others, fell into liquidation. After miles of red tape, Johnston's plantation, desperate for cash, got a loan for its 1933 operations from the Regional Agricultural Credit Corporation, an RFC subsidiary.[51]

Strained by adversity, Delta and Pine Land Company possessed superior management, efficient operation, and access to financial resources. Yet it teetered on financial ruin, a commentary on the poor health of American agriculture in the early thirties. It was small consolation that, in its misery, the mammoth plantation had lots of company. Better days lay ahead, but who could see them? As 1933 dawned, Oscar Johnston could not know that hundreds of thousands of bales of Farm Board cotton would soon become *his* responsibility, that *he* would become King Cotton's greatest advocate, and that *he* would help steer his beleaguered industry through the Great Depression.

# 3

## Golden Egg

A plague of young lawyers settled on Washington. They all claimed to be friends of somebody or other and mostly of Felix Frankfurter and Jerome Frank. They floated airily into offices, took desks, asked for papers and found no end of things to be busy about. I never found out why they came, what they did or why they left.  —George N. Peek, 1936

Let's not muff it, for otherwise we may get 5-cent cotton and disaster.
 —"Let the Goose Lay," *Memphis Press-Scimitar*, 1933

As Andrew H. Brown would say, the whole thing in a couple of nut shells is if the farmers of the South will join in this more or less radical plan, something will be done for them; otherwise, I am afraid they will have to be treated like the little boy's billy goat whose objection to being baptized led the little boy to exclaim: "Well, let's just sprinkle him and let him go to hell."
 —Oscar G. Johnston, 1933

**I**n the spring and summer of 1933 scores of young lawyers and other professionals migrated to Washington to join Franklin Roosevelt's New Deal in reshaping America. Aggressive and bright, many were also urban, liberal, and Ivy League. When the president, in his inaugural, likened the Depression to war, the liberal zealots took him seriously. They believed, as one of them said later, that "we were enlisted as a citizen army . . . for the duration of the Depression." They personified much of the enthusiastic idealism of those days and left their mark on the New Deal. Their goal was not recovery alone, but a new America. They had somehow gotten the word, observed one conservative cynic, "that a new dispensation had been given and for the first time the nation was looking to its great, serious, but hitherto unknown army of real thinkers. They came in prepared to brush aside the musty old dodos who had ruined the nation."[1]

Not all who crowded into the capital that spring and summer fit the celebrated pattern. At fifty-three, Oscar Johnston was no longer a young lawyer, nor was he urban, liberal, or Ivy League. He was a conservative from the rural South, a pragmatist whose ideals were those of King Cotton. The new Democratic administration, embraced by the South, offered hope in confronting the problems of plantation and farm after a dozen years of Republican leadership. Amid an air of expectancy, Johnston did share something with the idealistic Ivy Leaguers with whom he would jostle in the New Deal: all believed they could help shape public policy in their image.[2]

Johnston's New Deal odyssey began late one afternoon near the close of the infamous "Hundred Days" of the new administration. On May 23, 1933, Johnston got a telephone call from—according to Johnston's secretary, Arch Toler—"cohorts of President Franklin D. Roosevelt" who "urged him to come to Washington at once, and discuss the possibility of his accepting a very high position in official circles." Johnston promptly left for Memphis, where he caught an airplane the next morning. Toler doubted his boss would accept a government position—the pay was too low. Toler was wrong. Money was not the issue. Washington provided an opportunity to mold policy for Johnston's prostrate industry. He accepted the offer of finance director of the infant Agricultural Adjustment Administration (AAA), if only on a temporary basis. Henry Wallace, the new secretary of agriculture, and AAA administrator George N. Peek cabled the British Fine Spinners (FCSDA) in Manchester for permission "to borrow" Johnston for "[w]ork most important and urgent." Johnston followed with his own cable the next day. He assured the British that his acceptance would in no way prejudice their mutual concern at Scott; on the contrary, he hoped to aid the "general situation as well as our interests."[3]

The British agreed, but reluctantly. Herbert Lee told Wallace that it would be "rather a blow to us" to have Johnston's time diverted from the plantations, which had, he said, "passed through two very dreadful years, and are still by no means out of the difficulties which beset them, but from our experience of Mr. Johnston we should say that there is no man in the cotton growing world that is better calculated to help in the national work you have in hand." Also, as executive director Herbert Stowell told Johnston later, FCSDA officials assured their board of directors "that it would be a great mistake to stand in your way of getting into such close touch with cotton control."[4]

The "dreadful years" at Delta and Pine Land Company mirrored an industry in deep trouble. The economic fluctuations growing out of the World War and the intermittent agricultural depressions of the twenties and thirties had impoverished many cotton farmers. In 1930, farmers earned just half of their 1924–29 average income for their cotton and seed. The 1931 crop earned little more than a third of that average; the 1932 crop earned even less. In April 1933, cotton brought just over six cents a pound, about half of its parity price and about a third of its eighteen-cent high during April 1929. World carryover of American cotton was expected to exceed twelve million bales in 1933 compared with an average five million during the previous decade. Also, cotton was expected to jump in 1933 to 7 percent over 1932. Southern agriculture reflected the bearish statistics. In the cotton belt, millions of farm acres already had been foreclosed and millions more had gone off the tax rolls, reverting to the states for delinquency. As Oscar Johnston described it later, "The patient was indeed critically ill; drastic action was necessary if his life was to be saved."[5]

Johnston's recommendation for the finance division probably came from George N. Peek, the new AAA administrator who for more than a decade had led the crusade for farm parity. They had known each other for years, dating at least to the old McNary-Haugen days. Most likely Johnston had no personal contact with Henry Wallace before March 1933, when he offered the new secretary written proposals for revamping agricultural credit. That letter reached Wallace's desk by way of Sen. Pat Harrison, who held Johnston's abilities in "high regard." Peek also tapped Chester C. Davis to head AAA production, and W. I. Westervelt to direct processing and marketing. He thought himself "lucky enough to get" such men and claimed that "Messrs. Davis and Johnston were old-timers in farm activities and thoroughly experienced," while Westervelt "knew processing and marketing from every angle." Alfred Stedman managed publicity, and Peek's old McNary-Haugen associate, Charles Brand, came on as co-administrator. None of these men, claimed Peek's biographer, were "dreamy idealists."[6]

Peek's choice of Johnston for finance was a good one. His prominence in the cotton belt and his exceptional understanding of cotton marketing complemented his shrewdness in banking and finance and his knowledge of the law. Oscar always saw the big picture, never shrinking from proposing or implementing vigorous and complicated ideas for assisting agriculture. The *Memphis Commercial Appeal* pronounced his appointment "a happy inspiration," claiming that "[n]o man knows the cotton business from the ground up better than Oscar Johnston. The choice will inspire confidence throughout the cotton belt in the success of the new measure." The rival *Press-Scimitar* agreed, claiming Johnston was "regarded as one of the South's most practical and scientific farmers." Closer to home, Greenville's *Delta Democrat-Times* declared that "the South will be greatly benefitted" by the appointment. The paper doubted "if there is a man anywhere better qualified."[7]

Those entering the AAA jungle in the flush days of 1933 had to pick their way among various philosophies and economic positions. The discretionary features of the legislation made the selection of personnel even more significant. Ironically, Johnston's appointment ran counter to Peek's opposition to crop control. With Wallace and Davis, Johnston emphasized acreage reduction; Peek favored marketing agreements. Johnston agreed with Peek's desire for revived foreign trade and later worked for passage of Secretary of State Cordell Hull's reciprocal trade agreements. Further, ideological and policy rifts soon emerged within the AAA; talk of a cabal and bureaucratic intrigue characterized the agency for nearly two years. The major split pitted the AAA's legal division, along with others in and out of Wallace's office, against more conservative policymakers and functionaries within the agency. The legal division, headed by the brilliant and liberal New Yorker Jerome Frank, was staffed by an able group of socially conscious lawyers who wanted to promote social reform. These were part of the army of young lawyers who had come to town "dangling Phi Beta Kappa keys," said George Peek later, all of them "enveloped in the delusion that they carried with them the tablets containing a new dispensation. They were going to inform the established lawyers and the Supreme Court what the law really was." On the other side stood the AAA conservatives, including Johnston. They wanted to elevate commodity prices. The different agendas produced subliminal antagonism at first, emerging prominently in 1935 over an issue involving treatment of tenant farmers in the cotton belt. Peek was long gone by then, ousted in December 1933. He and Wallace never got along, owing as much, perhaps, to Peek having been passed over for secretary of agriculture as to their repeated clashes over procedure.[8]

Oscar presented a suspicious profile to the liberals. He fell squarely in the conservative camp and proved an effective landlord spokesman. Ideologically compatible with Peek, Davis, and Cully Cobb, head of the AAA's cotton section, he also got along very well with Wallace, the reflective and sometimes mystical Iowan who had the task of overseeing the whole operation. The AAA liberals under Frank collegially accepted one on the basis of either ability or compatible politics. In Oscar's case that meant ability. Controversies between Johnston and his liberal colleagues usually remained professional. Frank found Oscar both "delightful" and frustrating, possessing "a quick, brilliant, imaginative mind, butting into everything and particularly cotton." No one in the AAA failed to respect his extraordinarily agile mind. His disarming personal demeanor even allowed social interaction over cocktails. Alger Hiss, one of Frank's extremely able young lawyers, recalled Oscar as brilliant, witty, amusing, and very personable.[9] To the liberals who might have distrusted anyone west of New Haven and Cambridge, Johnston was clearly their match.

After accepting the AAA post, Johnston quickly divested himself of his conflict-of-interest encumbrances, including Delta Pine capital stock. Back in Washington by June 1, he stayed briefly at the Washington Hotel but soon took an apartment in the Alban Towers above Embassy Row, in the fashionable northwest section. There he avoided the noise and distractions of the office, but neither there, nor anywhere, could he escape the capital's legendary summer heat. Martha, still in Asheville, visited occasionally. Toler, in charge of the Scott office, repeatedly briefed the boss on everything at the plantations, from weevils and weather to his cabin cruiser and young geese.[10]

Johnston's finance division controlled the departments of the budget, commodity credit, and ways and means. The whole portfolio encompassed the financial aspects of the AAA's numerous commodity programs, including processing taxes and loans. Johnston wrestled with beans, peas, peanuts, and the problems of Puerto Rican coffee growing. Requests to bring new commodities under federal loans, whether grapefruit or hay, usually landed on his desk. He also conferred on pork, butter, and eggs, and even analyzed the inadequacy of refrigeration facilities in the Soviet Union, a nation many hoped would consume perishable American products.[11]

Beans and grapefruit, however, had not lured Johnston to Washington. Before him lay the prostrate cotton industry and its forty million dependents. He soon attacked the enormous problems of federally funded cotton, a tangible legacy of Herbert Hoover's aborted New Era. When the Federal Farm Board ceased operations in 1933, Uncle Sam fell reluctant heir to its huge white holdings. By Roosevelt's Executive Order on March 27, 1933, the Farm Credit Administration, the Farm Board's chief successor, acquired title to or liens on the old Hoover cotton, both spot and futures, including stocks of the defunct Federal Stabilization Corporation and the Seed and Crop Production Loan Agencies. Johnston prepared a contract, required by the Agricultural Adjustment Act of May 12, for the transfer of the consolidated federal cotton to the secretary of agriculture. On June 7 he met with President Roosevelt to win approval for the plan. It was Oscar's first meeting with FDR since the 1924 Democratic National Convention in New York City, at which Johnston had been a delegate and Roosevelt had nominated Gov. Al Smith of New York for the presidency. Oscar found the president "in a particularly good humor," he said, and very agreeable to Johnston's contract providing for the transfer of more than two million bales of federally financed cotton. The procedure included Johnston's complicated and drawn-out negotiations with Farm Credit Gov. Henry J. Morgenthau Jr. It also brought the cotton under his own supervision in the AAA's finance division.[12]

Nearly 70 percent of the bales that eventually came under Johnston's supervision stood in hundreds of warehouses in New England and the South. The remainder lay in futures contracts. Johnston's early hope to market the actual bales and replace them with futures quickly faded. Rising prices in early summer slumped in July, the worst since 1927. Attempts to dump the cotton would invite charges that the sales depressed the market as the old Farm Board had done. Meanwhile, the very existence of the cotton could be bearish in a jittery market. The Farm Board disaster had dramatized the futility of cotton storage and loans through marketing cooperatives without authority to either control production or provide rental payments. The AAA did both but also authorized the secretary of agriculture to offer option contracts to cooperating cotton producers who agreed to eliminate the percentage of their cotton acreage specified in the agreement. Fathered by Ellison D. "Cotton Ed" Smith, the aging Democratic senator from South Carolina, the option plan had been pocket vetoed by President Hoover before Roosevelt's inaugural but revived by the new Congress as Sections 3–7 of the Agricultural Adjustment Act of May 1933. Under the option idea, producers could elect to purchase government cotton now being brought under Johnston's supervision at market prices equal to that which they took out of production. By limiting production, farm costs would fall, the market would rise, and producers who elected the option contract would profit.[13]

All of this came too late to prevent cotton producers from planting a big crop in 1933. The South could not afford another winter of six-cent cotton. To prevent a disastrous bumper harvest on what Johnston predicted would be about forty million acres, a substantial portion of the growing crop would have to be destroyed. Like the slaughter of millions of piglets in a burdened hog market, the unprecedented decision to plow up millions of cotton acres in a land of need seemed to mirror a world gone mad. The emergency cotton measure was "a shocking commentary on our civilization," said Henry Wallace later. "I could tolerate it only as a cleaning up of the wreckage from the old days of unbalanced production."[14]

In early June, Johnston drafted a cotton reduction plan, and, with Cully Cobb, head of the cotton section, drew up proposed contracts for producers. Oscar opposed draconian reduction. He apparently favored a producer option range of 10–40 percent but argued that Wallace could make a final determination in July, when better harvest projections became available. The government's hastily assembled cotton program was announced on June 19. The final contract allowed for 25–40 percent acreage reduction. The sign-up campaign was scheduled for "Cotton Week" beginning June 26. Federal and state farm extension workers, vocational teachers, and volunteer committees were authorized to gauge planter willingness to enter into reduction contracts with the secretary of agriculture. Those willing to do so had to agree to destroy a representative acreage already planted to cotton. As compensation, producers would receive between seven and twenty dollars cash per acre if they elected a cash contract only, or between six and twelve dollars if they chose a cash-plus-option contract. In either case, the exact amount per acre would be determined by former productivity. Once Wallace accepted the contracts, planters had to submit to inspection both before and after plow-up to ensure compliance. Land taken out of production could be planted with soil-improvement or erosion-preventing crops or for feed and food crops for home consumption only.[15]

Although the AAA believed most cotton growers would sign contracts, the sheer enormity of the task loomed as a great obstacle. Clear explanation of the program and confidence in its administration remained vital to success. In Memphis, the mid-South cotton capital, the *Commercial Appeal* reported early in June that many planters remained hesitant about the contracts. Cotton prices were advancing to their highest levels since 1930, tempting many planters to produce a large crop. But the fickleness of the market was an old and cruel story. George Peek warned that the price rise failed to accurately reflect the market. He argued that while demand partly explained the increase, speculation, dollar devaluation, and bullish prospects over the new cotton program were also responsible. Johnston believed the AAA program stood between the producers and disaster. If planters cooperated, he thought the economy would move toward recovery. "If they refuse, and the crop now indicated is harvested," he said privately on June 10, "I fear the cotton growers' plight will be most unfortunate."[16]

Before the opening of "Cotton Week" Oscar flew to Memphis to promote the AAA's recovery plan. The mid-South's cotton capital since before the Civil War, Memphis remained important to the New Deal. A pervasive cotton culture had grown up in the city. One saw it everywhere, in the elegant lobby of the Peabody Hotel, in Beale Street's jive joints, and in the cotton offices on Front Street. Searching for the South in 1937, Jonathan Daniels deemed Memphis "the Paris of the plantation country," sitting "above a gambling land, the Cotton Kingdom." The New Deal needed support for its cotton plan and it looked to Memphis to give it. Fortunately, Oscar was at home in Memphis. Long a respected figure in the banks and factors' offices of the city, he explained or defended the New Deal for cotton many times in Memphis in the thirties. Within minutes of his arrival by plane in June 1933, he was at the Peabody speaking to an overflow crowd of newsmen, planters, bankers, and other leaders. (He talked fast, 225 words a minute, enough to confound a court reporter.) He told the sympathetic crowd that the administration was "laying a golden egg" for the cotton planter and that "[t]he economic structure and lives of 40,000,000 persons in the cotton belt depend on the success of this plan." The program was economically sound, practical, and necessary for a nationwide return to prosperity. He warned against being guiled by a temporary market rise occasioned by dollar devaluation and speculation. If planters raised fourteen million bales and were forced to dump them at a nickel or less, he said, "your blood will be on your own head, or rather it will be on the head of the nation, because it will affect us all." Johnston declared the program "justifiably sound" and announced that Delta and Pine Land Company would join up.[17]

The New Deal had found not only a policymaker, but also an effective salesman. The *Memphis Press-Scimitar* claimed Johnston "spoke as an official of the Department of Agriculture" but "used the language and terms of the Mid-South cotton farmer." One Arkansas planter who had read the plan and heard it explained in Little Rock wired George Peek that he "had no intention of joining but after hearing Oscar Johnston whom I had never met and getting his prompt and intelligent answers to the questions that had been bothering me I am entering whole heartedly and am serving on our local committee." He called for Johnston to spend the remainder of the week explaining the plan to farmers and government agents.[18]

Oscar put his heart into selling the program. During the summer he logged many miles on King Cotton's behalf, occasionally slipping into Scott for a respite, whether on his cabin cruiser or some other diversion. In late June he spoke from Washington over Columbia Broadcasting's Dixie radio network. In a July 5 address, also delivered in the capital but carried in the South on the National Broadcasting Corporation's network, he attacked those who had not signed reduction contracts. Failure to sign contracts, he warned, threatened "poverty and chaos"; he urged use of "moral suasion" and the fostering of community spirit. "Go after the objectors," he said. "Convince them that they are slackers, enemies of society and a menace to the economic welfare of the nation, if they fail to cooperate."[19]

Achieving requisite compliance took longer than anticipated. Criticism arose as far removed as North Carolina and Texas. At the end of June the *Memphis Press-Scimitar*, which favored the plan, noted that the reduction idea "isn't going over as well as it should." Policy changes occurring daily, or so it seemed to confused county agents, required changes in applications, which delayed the process. Local foot-dragging added to the delay. Arch Toler reported in late June that the Greenville newspaper wanted to photograph somebody actually signing a reduction contract. Toler thought of trying to persuade Delta and Pine Land's general manager Jesse Fox to appear for the picture, "though I am afraid," he confessed, "he is not one hundred percent in favor of the program. He advised me yesterday that he was not going to plow up any of his own 500 acres of cotton in the hills." The operation was also without precedent on such a scale. In a publicized letter to Wallace in July, President Roosevelt appealed for farmer compliance, citing both "patriotic duty" and self-interest. Slow sign-ups forced Wallace to extend the closing date from July 8 to July 12, then to July 19. Only by mid-July had producers pledged the necessary 25 percent beltwide reduction. But permits for plow-up could not be issued prior to inspection, and the paper volume forced further delay. By mid-July about a million contracts covering a potential 3.5–4 million bales had flooded the AAA. The agency was processing thirty-five thousand a day and the AAA apparently paid the salaries of additional clerks in county agents' offices.[20]

Delta and Pine Land Company stood to benefit from the New Deal. Johnston had been committed to acreage reduction for years, but he knew that back home an excellent crop was in progress. Good weather and scientific management made a good team. Toler reported that two visitors declared "that we had the prettiest crop in the entire territory." In early July he projected a possible company record—an average bale an acre. On one unit that same month, he said he had never seen more bolls per stalk; later, a crop inspector pronounced Delta Pine's crop superior to any he had seen. By leasing 25 percent of its cultivated cotton acreage, the minimum allowed, Delta and Pine Land Company could wallow in a bumper crop while benefiting from both the general reduction and the New Deal subsidy and option plan.[21] It was a planter's dream come true.

Problems persisted. Toler informed Johnston at the end of June of rumors that some producers were "padding the hell out of their production record" as a means of increasing their returns. A member of the local compliance committee, Toler figured 25 percent of cotton acreage would be pledged for reduction—padded by not less than 20 percent. The *New York Times* reported that some planters had apparently overestimated past crop yields by as much as 250 percent. Johnston had warned over CBS radio on June 28 that greed and cheating could ruin the AAA plan, a theme also sounded by the cotton section chief, Cully Cobb. No padding occurred at Delta and Pine Land Company, but for the first time the plantation, like other producers, made official surveys of cultivated acreage. Nationally, cotton acreage had topped out at well over forty million acres in 1926, but such statistics were notoriously defective, including, as they did, roads, gardens, houses, ditches, and the like. Rigorous checking of actual acreage, including use of aerial photographs and on-site measurements at Delta and Pine Land, was a by-product of the New Deal. Yields per acre naturally jumped after 1933. Johnston later figured, rather carefully, that pre-1934 cotton-belt acreage assessments suffered a minimum 12 percent inflation, while at Scott, the high of 18,711 acres planted to cotton in 1925, yielding 406 pounds each, was actually 10 percent or more off, producing a more accurate 447 pounds per acre. In 1933, Delta Pine leased the government carefully selected acreage, Toler buying sorghum and whip peas as substitutes for plowed-up cotton. The company planted, on land with adequate moisture, corn between cotton rows slated for destruction. When grasshoppers appeared on the plantation in July, Toler remarked that he hoped they would remain where they were, on acreage proposed for government lease.[22]

After a short delay, reduction plans for both Delta Pine and Delta Farms were approved in late July. The destruction finally began. "We have all hands busily engaged cutting down and plowing up the cotton here at Scott," Toler announced on July 31. "Some of the cotton is so large you can't do a thing with it except with hoes and scythes." Seasoned company mules, like those throughout the South, became so confused with the plow-up that at first they balked at treading on the maturing cotton.[23]

The plow-up was a boon to Delta and Pine Land Company. Of 13,800 acres of cotton at Scott, about 1,800 had produced low-quality staple. These acres felt the plow, as did about 1,650 others, leaving Scott with nearly 10,338 high-yield acres in cotton. On these, management spared no effort to secure a bountiful harvest. Tons of poison spread by aerial crop dusters repelled a weevil attack, while sufficient rainfall in August and tons of fertilizer helped produce impressive results. Erratic weather was offset by intensive cultivation and Ewing's prolific cottonseed, which produced beautiful white fields. On nearly 4,000 fewer acres, Delta Pine exceeded its 1932 harvest; the average 530 pounds per acre established a company record.[24]

In achieving its high yield, Delta and Pine Land Company broke the spirit and letter of the 1933 contract. The AAA plan specified reduction of "a fair average" of a normal crop. Participating producers agreed not to fertilize more than they had in 1932. While it was unlikely that the Scott plantation stood alone, increasing yields on reduced tracts only added to cotton's problems. It generated support for a baleage tax rather than acreage reduction and likely contributed to the August price decline. The early-summer balloon burst and cotton slipped below a dime. The road to recovery proved treacherous. Banks were still failing, and as one Mississippian put it later, "a vast crop of mortgages was ready for the trustees."[25]

To shore up support for the AAA program, Johnston persuaded Henry Wallace to make an appearance in Mississippi, where he also talked with farm leaders. Delta Day at the Mississippi Agricultural Experiment Station in Stoneville, a hamlet a few miles east of Greenville, provided the public stage for the secretary's visit on August 8. Wallace and Johnston spent the night at Johnston's home in Scott and drove to Stoneville the following morning. Wallace's presence in the heart of the cotton belt was no small matter. Toler's early estimate that "everybody in this part of the country" would be on hand was fairly accurate. "Being the first cotton report date," he told Johnston, "the occasion may be quite auspicious." Mississippi Gov. Mike Sennett Conner and Senators Pat Harrison and Hubert Stephens showed up, as did other dignitaries. So also did seven thousand other people from eight states. As one Mississippian recalled it later:

All the Delta was there, from DeSoto Island to the Peabody. The most of the Little Fellows and a lot of the Big Boys had to hitch-hike, but by hook or crook we got there. . . . The new Secretary was to speak, and the Delta's own Oscar Johnston was there to introduce him. When Oscar cut his galluses and began to fly, as only he can do, I said to some companions, "the secretary is in a trap." After a great ovation, belonging as much to Oscar as to his hero, Henry Wallace began speaking. At first he talked about changing the human heart and nobody understood him. But when he laid down the program and promised cotton a New Deal we rang the welkin and shook the ground. Who does not remember that day![26]

Actually, Johnston reiterated his old plea for community action and moral suasion in carrying out the government plan, and Wallace emphasized that only crop reduction could avert complete disaster in the cotton belt. He also assured farmers that cotton would be controlled for the next two years. Such remarks were all the more pointed since that same day the government forecast a bumper harvest for 1933. The following day, the Wallace-Johnston duo was in Memphis, this time speaking under the sponsorship of the local chamber of commerce. But talk was cheap. The delay in getting plow-up checks to cooperating farmers needing cash confounded the AAA's best intentions. Even though the bureaucracy processed the checks rapidly, double-checking and inspections meant that most producers, like Delta Pine, could not complete crop destruction until August. By late August, Johnston was "decidedly disappointed at the slowness" in getting plow-up checks to producers. Worse, completion of the task remained weeks away. Pressed for cash, Delta and Pine Land Company secured an interim loan from the federally sponsored Regional Agricultural Credit Corporation; not all producers could do as well.[27]

The check delay accentuated the problem of slipping prices in late summer and early fall. Prices stood considerably above what they had been at the beginning of the year, and several million potential bales had been destroyed. Still, the USDA's August crop forecast predicted a harvest only about seven hundred thousand bales under the thirteen million bales of 1932. As summer turned into fall, policy formulation on the 1933 cotton loan and the 1933–34 cotton contract demanded Johnston's attention. So did, of course, the Farm Board cotton and option contracts. When Oscar came to Washington in the spring he briefly harbored the idea of staying only three months. Those three months had come and gone, but his work had just begun.[28]

# 4

# Ten-Cent Rescue

I am told that Oscar Johnston of Mississippi put the 10 cent cotton loan
idea in the President's head.                                    —Jesse Jones, 1951

The plow-up checks, options and 10-cent loans changed the whole complex-
ion of business thruout the cotton belt this year.
                                        —*Memphis Press-Scimitar,* January 1934

I have often said that if we went to war again between the North and South,
the South could well afford to lose the war if they would send to the peace
conference Clay Williams, Oscar Johnston, and Will Clayton.
                                                        —Jerome Frank, 1952

**O**scar Johnston could hardly have been surprised by the slump in
cotton prices in the late summer of 1933. No one close to the market should
have been. Too many temporarily bullish factors had prevailed during the economic boomlet in the late spring and early summer. Johnston and AAA chief
George N. Peek had warned farmers against being deceived by early market
advances. Now, as fall approached, a large crop stood ready to pass from gin
house to marketplace.[1]

Declining commodity prices had political implications for the new administration in Washington. Renewed pressure for inflation came from Franklin
Roosevelt's own party. Facing reporters as he left the White House, Mississippi
Sen. Pat Harrison, chairman of the Senate Finance Committee, declared that
commodity prices had to rise. "I favor some form of rational inflation," he said.
"We've got to do more than we are doing. . . . If commodity prices don't rise, I
don't know when we are going to get out of this depression." Frustrated by his
failure to get some commitment from Roosevelt, Harrison warned that the next
Congress would mandate inflation and that "[t]he success of the President's
program may be in doubt."[2]

Others also pressured the White House. Sen. Cotton Ed Smith of South
Carolina wired FDR on September 11: "The price of cotton has created a des-
perate situation in the cotton belt." The following day, while Harrison met with
Roosevelt, cotton producers from several southern states meeting in South

Carolina called on the government to, among other things, fix cotton at fifteen cents and inflate the economy. Alabama Sen. John Bankhead told Roosevelt as early as August that the cotton situation looked bleak and that inflation or, better, a baleage restriction on the 1933 crop remained the only solutions. Georgia Gov. Eugene Talmadge even made the exotic suggestion that government-printed ten- and twenty-dollar bills be distributed over the country from airplanes.[3]

Though Congress was out of session until January 3, several cotton senators—including Bankhead; Oklahoma's Elmer Thomas, the most strident inflation proponent; and Cotton Ed Smith, who had returned to the capital—demanded twenty-cent cotton and inflation. *Time* reported that Thomas "was loosely threatening a march of 1,000,000 men on Washington unless there was a great outpouring of printing-press money."[4]

Much of the southern pressure for inflation sprang more from the decline in cotton prices than from ideological commitment to currency expansion. Even this demand might have been at least partially muted had the AAA gotten plow-up checks to producers more quickly. The South needed cash. Southern demands now linked cotton loans and prices with currency expansion and repeal of the AAA's processing tax. Despite such pressure, the government showed no panic. Prices declined, but the general trend was favorable. Loans against growing crops, on the security of negotiable warehouse receipts, would allow participating producers to hold their cotton until prices rose, instead of glutting the market in the fall and winter, thus allowing the speculators to reap the financial harvest. Above-market loans demanded by some southerners could move the 1933 crop into warehouses for too long, blocking trade channels.[5]

No southerner wanted to aid cotton more than Oscar Johnston. Joining no chorus for inflation, he instead recommended a reasonable loan on the 1933 crop. According to Jerome Frank, who as AAA general counsel tried to monitor Johnston's financial activities in cotton, Oscar "butted into" the discussion over the loan. "He was from the South," recalled Frank. "He knew cotton. It wasn't his province at all, but he just kind of took charge and was over at the White House." Actually, Secretary Henry Wallace had authorized Johnston to negotiate AAA loans as early as August. Though amenable to a loan at market levels, Johnston apparently sold President Roosevelt on a price-supporting ten-cent loan, at that time a penny or more below spot prices. Such loans, Johnston told Peek in September, would be nonrecourse—that is, the borrower would assume no liability if prices dropped, other than forfeiture of the actual commodity itself. Repayment of the loans depended wholly on the market. While the idea was a huge governmental gamble, Johnston argued that the plan, including financial and other details, would "enable producers to liquidate existing crop mortgages, to market their crop in an orderly fashion and to obtain the benefits which we believe will be derived from the success of the National Recovery program." Jerome Frank, often frustrated by Oscar's aggressiveness, had a jaundiced view of the nonrecourse feature. Johnston, he said later, "pushed himself into the middle of this situation and he got up an agreement which the President, without much reflection, approved. It was a 'heads I win, tails you lose' thing."[6]

The demand for action climaxed in September 1933. Roosevelt deftly side-stepped the inflation issue by agreeing to receive a southern delegation headed by Senator Bankhead on condition that they quiet their demand for currency expansion and talk only of cotton. Bankhead unrealistically urged the president to pledge the government to buy five million bales of the 1933 crop at fifteen cents a pound. Though the delegation left the White House without specific price figures, the next day, with prices on the ten-spot markets averaging a dime, Roosevelt announced Johnston's ten-cent loan on all unsold 1933 cotton; only producers signing a 1934–35 acreage-reduction contract could participate. The effect was immediate. The futures market rose and the cry for inflation subsided.[7]

If Johnston's dime loan pleased the South and let the air out of the inflationist balloon, not everyone in the New Deal was happy with the nonrecourse aspect. Wallace initially opposed it but changed his mind. In his *New Frontiers*, published the next year, Wallace argued that the gamble was "abundantly justified . . . by the special conditions prevailing at that time." In the AAA's legal division, Frank thought the nonrecourse plan "was the most shocking idea" he had ever heard. He told George Peek, who favored the plan, and Wallace, who initially did not, that it monetized cotton; later he recalled, "If there was any virtue in the gold system, it was that your average Congressman couldn't understand it and therefore couldn't monkey with it. But anybody could understand this." Frank feared more commodities would come under the loan programs. "Next you'd monetize coal, lumber and whatnot. God knows where you'd stop. You'd just have logrolling over monetizing commodities the way you did over the tariff." James P. Warburg, an economist in the Treasury Department, had similar disquietude over the idea. After talking it over with Johnston, Warburg wrote in his diary that he "should not be surprised if this quiet little step was the beginning of a very important movement which I fear will not be good."[8]

Whatever merit in the fears, wholesale logrolling over commodity loans did not materialize. While corn did come under federal loans and the government later considered a program for burley tobacco and other commodities, that was about all. For cotton, the biggest problem was to quickly establish the machinery to handle the loans. Roosevelt instructed the chairman of the Reconstruction

Finance Corporation, Jesse Jones, to provide for the loans. Stanley Reed was the RFC general counsel and erstwhile Farm Board lawyer, who Roosevelt later put on the Supreme Court. Reed decided, after some persuasive work by Johnston and a pair of able USDA economists, Louis Bean and Mordecai Ezekiel, that the loan cotton constituted sufficient security required by the RFC. Johnston argued, mistakenly as it developed, that crop limitation and continued consumption at the current rate would drive cotton to fifteen cents in a year, even if business and prices generally rose no higher. The loans would pump hundreds of millions of dollars into circulation and result in debt liquidation and increased national purchasing power. He had thought the RFC could provide the loans through the dozen Regional Agricultural Credit Corporations, but an entirely new agency, the quasi-public Commodity Credit Corporation, was created instead. Several people helped formulate the corporation's wide-ranging charter, including Johnston, members of the AAA's legal division, and Paul A. Porter, a young lawyer who had been working closely with Johnston in the Department of Agriculture. Originally conceived as an agency to funnel federal money to cotton farmers and underwrite regular lending agencies, the CCC was broadened for possible use by other commodities. Its charter was so liberal that Porter joked that the agency could do everything except "print money." Jerome Frank replied sarcastically that that was in its implied powers.[9]

With Congress out of session until January, Roosevelt created the new corporation by executive order. The CCC received dubious capitalization from the president's discretionary emergency fund, which had been authorized by the Bankhead amendment to the National Industrial Recovery Act of June 1933. Dictated by the emergency confronting the South, the whole activity constituted an imaginative hodgepodge of questionable authority. To Henry Wallace, only the crisis justified the "radical and seemingly unbusinesslike procedure" of nonrecourse loans on cotton and corn. In the cotton belt, crisis followed crisis in the late summer and early fall of 1933. The delay of more than two weeks between Roosevelt's announcement of the ten-cent loan and the actual dispersal of funds demoralized the cotton trade and prompted complaints from the South. Although some cotton was held back from trade channels in anticipation of the loan, part of the 1933 crop flowed out of producer hands at prices below the loan rate.[10]

Several last-minute obstacles remained before Roosevelt could sign the executive order and the massive influx of cash into the South could begin. For two days Johnston and Paul Porter, who had been involved in the cotton and tobacco programs and had helped draft the CCC charter, wound their way through the Washington bureaucratic maze trying to get "all the necessary clearances and approvals" for Roosevelt's executive order creating the CCC. Young

Porter, only twenty-nine, stood on the threshold of a brilliant legal career. Among other things, he later became Washington counsel for Columbia Broadcasting System and served in the Office of Price Administration, War Food Administration, and the Office of Economic Stabilization. He also chaired the Federal Communications Commission, then headed the Office of Price Administration. In 1947, with Roosevelt's trustbuster, Thurman Arnold, and Abraham Fortas, who President Lyndon Johnson later put on the Supreme Court, Porter founded a prestigious law firm. He became a "superlawyer," a Washington insider, a mover and shaker with a pleasing personality and a well-developed sense of humor. In the fall of 1933, of course, all that lay ahead. The youthful Porter was, he said at the end of his long career, in for an experience he would "never forget." He regarded Oscar Johnston highly, recalling him as "one of the most able, colorful and brilliant individuals that it has ever been my pleasure to know."

Porter had ample doses of brilliance and color himself. In fact, he proved to be quite a noted storyteller. Despite the blurring that great stories develop in the telling and retelling over decades, the essence of one of his best remained. Porter and Johnston, in Oscar's chauffeur-driven Cadillac, with the executive order in tow, embarked on their two-day odyssey. At their first stop they called at the office of the comptroller general of the United States, John R. McCarl. A Nebraska Republican who had served as the first and only comptroller general since the Harding administration, McCarl had a by-the-book reputation; he might prove obstinate.[11]

McCarl initially refused to see the pair, referring them to his general counsel. The general counsel "took the usual, typical position of a long-term public official that it would be inappropriate for the general accounting office to rule on any matter in an informal advisory basis—that the Comptroller General would be prepared to rule on this matter when it came before him." Porter said, "We tried to explain the depth of the emergency and the nature of the crisis; that the South was on fire, that civil insurrection would result unless we obtained some relief." That did little good. Oscar wondered aloud whether there really was a man named McCarl. "Well, finally by our persistence," said Porter, "we got in to see the Comptroller General. We explained the problem to him and after a great deal of discussion, he finally gave a typical general accounting office response; that when and if the matter was presented to him, he would not find cause to object. He didn't give any affirmative approval or blessing. He merely indicated . . . that he would not find any cause to object."

The document also needed approval by the Bureau of the Budget. "Well, again we were greeted with the usual routine procedures at the Bureau of the Budget and Oscar Johnston was not a man to take no, or even maybe, for an answer and he said, 'look, I want to see my old friend Lew Douglas. We served on the board of the Illinois Central Railway together.' We got in to see Douglas and explained the critical nature of the emergency and Douglas promptly gave his okay."

That did not end it. The executive order needed endorsement of the attorney general. Ahead lay "more barbed wire" before they could see Homer Cummings and obtain his approval. Johnston and Porter were told to leave the document and it would be presented to the attorney general "in due course." "Oscar . . . said 'look, Homer Cummings and I have served on the Democratic National Committee together . . . and I insist on seeing the Attorney General.'" They saw him and got his approval.

Last came the secretary of state. Porter figured later that he "had to approve it as to form and as to protocol." The traveling pair thought this would be routine. The "protocol officer . . . looked at our document," by now "a little sweaty and worn," recalled Porter, "and much to our consternation he said that the Secretary of State could not possibly approve this Executive Order." Since it had all the initials, they asked why. The protocol officer claimed the margin on the order was insufficient, that it required one-and-a-half inches; Porter's margin fell short by half an inch. Porter continued, "Oscar started pleading and asked him if he would give us a memorandum saying that he approved the Executive Order except for the margin." He refused. Porter said he would make up the margin deficiency on the next order, that he would give him two inches next time. However, as Porter vividly recalled "that didn't persuade him, and so with great impatience Oscar said, 'I've got to see Cordell Hull—I'm from Mississippi, and he is a neighbor from Tennessee. We both went to Cumberland Law School and I know him well.'"

They saw the secretary, who understood the situation facing the South. He spoke sympathetically. He was new and did not want to break departmental rules. He inquired of the young protocol officer if he, as secretary of state, had the authority "to waive the margin requirements . . . and the protocol officer allowed as how the Secretary, in his discretion, did have the authority, whereupon Secretary Hull very graciously said that in the future we must comply with the formal requirements laid down by the Department of State as to the form of Executive Orders."

The second day of adventure was drawing to a close, and Johnston and Porter now had all the requisites. They had already told Marvin McIntyre, Roosevelt's secretary, to expect them, so that the president could sign it immediately. Telegrams would soon shower the South; the very next day banks could start lending cash to farmers.

One unexpected hurdle remained. At the White House, Johnston and Porter handed over the executive order, a bit "dog-eared" by now, recalled Porter.

McIntyre told them to wait, that the president wanted to see them. "So we cooled our heels for twenty or twenty-five minutes and finally were ushered into the executive office, and the President was there with his cigarette holder at the usual rakish angle and very solemnly he said, 'Oscar, I can not sign this Executive Order.'" Taken aback, Johnston asked why. Porter remembered, "He said, 'the margin. You should know that an Executive Order must have a margin of at least an inch and a half and I have just measured this.'" They weren't sure he was serious, "but finally Oscar said, 'Mr. President, as far as I am concerned there is one of two things that you can do with this order and the other one is to sign it.' Whereupon President Roosevelt leaned back and roared. He was pulling our leg," said Porter, "and he signed it and obviously what had happened was that Secretary Hull was so amused when we left that he couldn't resist calling the President and telling him of our consternation—that we had taken over all the hurdles except half an inch on the margin of this Order, so the Order was signed."

Presidential playfulness aside, Roosevelt's signature now graced Executive Order 6340. The Commodity Credit Corporation was duly incorporated on October 17, 1933, under the liberal laws of Delaware. Porter said he drove to Wilmington to file the charter. The next day, as one of the three incorporators with Wallace and Treasury Secretary Morgenthau, Johnston was elected first vice president at the initial meeting of the board of directors. Under the CCC's program, cash flowed into the waiting hands of cotton growers who, like Johnston, needed money. About 2.5 million bales of the 1933 crop came under the loan and the producers obtained tens of millions of dollars, which enabled them to dispose of their crop in an orderly manner. After another late-season slump, the predicted rise in prices materialized; by mid-January 1934 market levels surpassed loan values and a month later hovered around twelve cents. Porter deemed the loan "probably the most economical and sensible loan the Commodity Credit Corporation ever made . . . because it immediately stabilized the market, prices rose . . . and very little of the 1933 crop stayed in the Government warehouses but went into the market place and was consumed." The agency received legislative ratification in 1935 and, said Porter, took "its position among the noblest institutions of our time."[12]

If producers had been saved by the ten-cent net placed under the 1933 crop, the cotton trade and the government still faced the burdensome problem of the old Farm Board holdings. More than 2.4 million bales of spot and futures cotton threatened price stabilization, even though, as part of the plow-up campaign more than 570,000 producers had taken options on these bales. By an incredible coincidence, producers' options covered all the available Farm Board cotton, save for about 10,000 bales. It remained clear that if the participating producers promptly demanded sale of their optioned cotton, the American and world markets might collapse, along with the price objectives of the plow-up campaign. Preventing the dumping of the regular 1933 crop on the market provided only half the victory in the battle for price stabilization. Prices simply had to be permitted to rise.[13]

Since the market dipped below nine cents from September through early December 1933, Johnston saw no need to push for rapid distribution of the option contracts to participating producers. He processed checks for producers of tobacco, wheat, and other commodities. He also developed a plan to keep most of the old Farm Board cotton off the market. He proposed that the optioned cotton, against which the secretary of agriculture held six-cent-per-pound liens, be brought to a par with the ten-cent 1933 crop by loaning an additional four cents to producers. Instead of exercising their options for sale, producers would instead take participating trust certificates in a government cotton pool. The plan was both ingenious and fiscally complicated. Aside from achieving parity with the 1933 crop, the plan required pool members to sign an acreage-reduction contract for 1934–35. Pool members would also profit when the old optioned cotton was ultimately marketed at the discretion of a pool manager to be named by Secretary Wallace. The plan received formal approval in November, first by Peek and Wallace, then by Roosevelt, who requested the necessary supplemental appropriation from the CCC. In mid-November Johnston persuaded hesitant New York bankers to loan part of the funds to the CCC, the rest to come from the Reconstruction Finance Corporation. A subsequent objection by the AAA's legal division over the financial arrangements was soon overcome; option contracts went in the mail to more than 575,000 producers in December.[14]

The envelopes that cotton farmers found in their mailboxes contained three alternatives. Before May 1, 1934, producers were told, the option holder could call for the sale and profits of his cotton, less the six cents a pound it had originally cost; or, he could ask to extend the cotton option from May 1, 1934, to May 1, 1935, by assuming interest charges after May 1, 1934. He would then be free to call his option; or, he could call the option by giving, in effect, power of attorney to the secretary of agriculture to establish and deliver the producers' cotton equity covered by the options to a cotton pool, to be directed by a pool manager. Wallace would then retain the original six-cent lien and the pool manager would borrow four cents a pound to be distributed to pool members. In exchange for the option, the manager would also issue a participating trust certificate as evidence of the producer's equity in the new cotton pool. Since the old Farm Board cotton was scattered in numerous locations, and of uneven quality and bale weight, the cotton pool would actually hold no cotton at all, only the producer's equity in the standard seven-eighths-inch middling variety of five-hundred-pound bales with prices quoted in New Orleans and New York.[15]

In arguing for the establishment of the producers' pool, Johnston had told Roosevelt in November 1933 that if four cents were advanced, growers would yield their options and join a pool. He expected the market to rise, with the participating growers reaping the profit when their equity in the pool was gradually liquidated. As an added inducement, the farmers had hardly taken their option contracts out of their mailboxes when Chester Davis, the new AAA chief who replaced Peek, announced to the press on December 20, to no one's surprise, that Oscar Johnston would head the proposed cotton pool. Davis denied rumors that the option cotton "might be recklessly or indiscriminately dumped upon the market." He said Johnston had "developed this entire transaction and set up the organization to handle this cotton," and added, "I am certain that those engaged in the cotton trade, knowing Mr. Johnston as they do, have full confidence that the interests of all parties concerned will be fully protected in the handling of this cotton. We feel that the Administration is fortunate to have Mr. Johnston's services available to do this job."[16]

The pool plan proved so attractive to farmers that more than three-quarters of the approximately 575,000 option holders, whose equity covered nearly two million bales, surrendered their options and joined Johnston's cotton pool. Except for a small number who neglected their options, the remaining producers elected the first two options and had their equity liquidated, earning profits totaling more than $12 million. To monitor the delicate market workings, Johnston had a ticker-tape machine installed in his office; in its last issue of 1933, *Newsweek* showed him reading it. If the prices that clacked through that ticker failed to rise, or worse, if they dropped, the government would be left holding the bag while the agricultural depression worsened.[17]

By the time Davis publicized Johnston's appointment as pool manager, Oscar had already returned to the South. Aside from promoting the AAA reduction program in Memphis, he wanted some time out to hunt ducks in Arkansas. The reviving economy preceded him. In early December, a *New York Times* story reported that not only had the CCC loans on the 1933 crop aided in recovery but that in the next month cotton farmers in the Memphis area would receive six to eight million dollars from the four-cent advance. Also, cotton prices stood nearly twice that of the previous year. "Today the government no longer looks on hunger as a personal crime," proclaimed the *Memphis Press-Scimitar.* The paper added that "[d]espair and fear and smug cruelty are gradually giving way to hope and achievement."[18]

No ticker-tape parade awaited him, but Johnston's return to Memphis had an element of a hero's welcome. He had successfully formulated the ten-cent loan (monetized cotton, grumbled Jerome Frank), and soon tens of millions of dollars would flow into the hands of pool participants and other former option holders. He had also won the respect of colleagues in the Department of Agriculture. Wallace told a Federal Land Bank official in December that Oscar's "services to the Administration have been invaluable and his leadership in the cotton programs has meant much to the South." The work was neither glamorous nor particularly flashy to the public eye, but it proved effective nonetheless. In an editorial promoting Johnston's impending speech at the Memphis Auditorium, the *Press-Scimitar* trumpeted, "No man has done more to bring cotton prosperity to the South than Oscar Johnston." Shelby County agent W. M. Landress asked area clergymen to publicize in their churches that Johnston's Monday morning speech was open to all. In the arena on December 11, Johnston, whose speech carried on radio, urged the packed house of three thousand, including extension agents from four hundred counties, to join the new AAA reduction, to execute their contracts, and to prevent dislocation of tenant labor.[19]

The following month, the AAA mailed thousands of checks to pool participants and other farmers or their assignees who had called their options for immediate sale. The old Farm Board cotton—nearly two million bales—left the control of Johnston's finance division and became the responsibility of Johnston's cotton pool. Oscar followed the cotton, or rather, he led it. Chester Davis assured him that he would retain authority over the pool and loan transactions. Johnston now resigned as head of the finance division effective February 1, 1934, and was succeeded by Ward Buckles, a farm-financing expert who came in from the RFC. Oscar would keep modest offices in the Department of Agriculture, where he would be on long-distance telephone calls with brokers and bankers, often in the evening after the New York exchange closed, and he would keep his ticker-tape machine; others in the AAA could grapple with the problems of grapefruit, pinto beans, and other commodities. He had to attend to personal and plantation business back home.[20] Meanwhile, whether or not he could drain the cotton pool without breaking the market remained to be seen.

# 5

# Acres, Not Bales

Johnston is "not looking at the bill from the standpoint of the farmer, but from the interests of a great British syndicate." —William B. Bankhead, 1934

I am very firmly of the opinion that no living human being can administer the Bankhead bill in such a manner as not to be detrimental to the interest of the cotton growers and of the industry as a whole. —Oscar G. Johnston, 1934

**D**espite the success of the plow-up campaign in aborting production of several million cotton bales, farmers produced slightly more cotton in 1933 than they had the year before. By limiting output through acreage reduction alone, the AAA rewarded intensive cultivation, a fact appreciated by Oscar Johnston and other scientific farmers whose shrunken fields yielded record blooms. The healthy crop of 1933 prompted a search for other methods of production control, and Washington was showered with proposals from the cotton belt. All such plans were dutifully analyzed, whether they seemed, as Johnston said, "utterly absurd" or not.

The chief alternative to acreage reduction rested on some form of bale control—that is, limiting production to a specified number of bales for a given season. Prospects for a bumper crop in 1934 further boosted the plan. When early that year the Southern Railway reported that fertilizer shipments quadrupled over the same period in 1933, *Time* declared that "John Cotton Farmer seemed determined to raise by intensive cultivation of his reduced acreage as much cotton as he could in 1934, and thus make a double profit out of the Government's attempt to bribe him into cutting down his output."[1]

The agitation for bale control was not new. Several plans had been discussed and rejected before the plow-up. Still, bale control enjoyed wide support. William B. Bankhead, a nine-term congressman from Alabama's seventh district who later became House Speaker, and his older brother, John H. Jr., freshman Alabama senator, stood among its chief proponents. Members of a southern political dynasty that began before the turn of the century, the Bankhead brothers, from Jasper, Alabama, proved influential advocates, though neither had achieved veteran status in cotton affairs. The fields around their hometown were coal, not cotton. John, capable and industrious, dabbled a bit in coal while brother Will dabbled—only twenty-four acres worth—in cotton. Still, they represented a significant cotton constituency, especially Senator John, whose political fortunes rose even as those of his rival, South Carolina's Cotton Ed Smith, fell. Chester Davis thought Bankhead wanted to oust the aging Smith from cotton's political leadership, making it "Cotton John" rather than "Cotton Ed."[2] Perhaps hanging the Bankhead name on a significant piece of legislation would be a good start.

Whatever motivated advocates of bale control, few could fail to see a need for some way to close the loophole in the acreage-reduction program. Senator Bankhead's investigation of cotton's prospects in the South, including personal inspections of several southeastern states in August 1933, caused him some concern. "Increased acreage, increased fertilizer and ideal weather," he lamented to President Roosevelt, "have ruined us." Predicting that cotton production would top that of 1932, he suggested a severe and compulsory limitation on the number of bales that could be ginned at picking time.[3]

Even though some in the administration thought productivity was too high, Bankhead's idea got a cool reception in the Department of Agriculture. The plan probably needed new legislation; it might conceivably worsen the position of southern tenants; and it would certainly encounter hostility among cotton ginners. Regulating private gins would be difficult; compulsory ginning limitations might encounter legal challenge. While the department successfully brushed off last-minute tampering with the size of the 1933 crop, more flexibility remained for 1934–35. Though skeptical, Henry Wallace could be swayed—as could, apparently, Cully Cobb, chief of the cotton section. Those opposed to bale control included Chester Davis, AAA production chief soon to replace George Peek as AAA administrator, and Oscar Johnston, who in August 1933 drafted a tentative plan for cotton acreage reduction for 1934–35, which made no mention of bale control. Johnston's plan, which eventually won bureaucratic and White House approval, called for a 40 percent acreage cutback for 1934, coupled with handsome incentives for farmers who complied.[4]

To sample producers' opinions for the next season, the Department of Agriculture convened simultaneous meetings in Dallas, Atlanta, and Memphis early in September 1933. The bale control idea enjoyed considerable grassroots support, a fact reaffirmed to Johnston when he arrived in Memphis to chair the public meeting at the Peabody Hotel. Very likely, only his intensive pre-conference lobbying prevented the meeting from endorsing bale control despite its support from, among others, Harry Wilson, Louisiana's commissioner of agriculture, and Dr. Tait Butler, mid-South editor and farm leader. "The general consensus at the Memphis meeting," said a Brookings Institution study later, "was that the baleage plan was defeated by the opposition of Oscar Johnston of the AAA and because additional legislation might be needed to put it into effect." The vote was 96–70. But there were not enough Oscar Johnstons to go around. The meetings in Atlanta and Dallas also revealed some sentiment for bale control, and the issue remained a matter of concern in both the South and the administration. In January 1934, the USDA dispatched forty thousand questionnaires to crop reporters, county agents, and committeemen to determine sentiment on bale control and mandatory producer participation.[5]

Rebuffed in his attempt to limit the ginning of the 1933 crop, Senator Bankhead meanwhile prepared legislation to mandate some form of bale regulation. After Congress reconvened in January 1934 he dropped it in the legislative hopper and the issue was thrashed out in Ellison Smith's Senate agriculture and forestry committee. Will Bankhead introduced a different version in the House in February, about the time the results of the department's poll were being tabulated. More than half of the 22,123 responses favored some form of bale regulation, but nearly all wanted a compulsory control program of some sort. Secretary Wallace pragmatically pledged that if the South really wanted it, he and his department would support it. With assistance from the AAA, the Bankhead bill underwent changes, with the latest version introduced on February 12, 1934, the same day Chairman Marvin Jones of Texas opened hearings before the House agriculture committee.[6]

Johnston followed Cobb and Wallace to the witness table and livened up the session. Cobb had been sympathetic to the proposal, Wallace helpful, lukewarm at best, but Johnston proved decidedly unfriendly. Speaking as a cotton farmer, he said, and not as an agriculture department official, he argued that the House bill provided for control of the market, not production. As such, it was no help in the AAA effort to control output. As he had told Wallace, as well as the Senate agriculture committee, excess cotton could be stored without payment of the bale tax but would remain visible and have a bearish influence on the market. He also found the Bankhead plan unnecessary, impractical, and loaded with administrative problems. With spot cotton running 12.5 cents and October futures higher yet, he claimed there was no emergency—a term Wallace had suggested be hung on the plan's title to make it more judicially palatable if legally challenged. The bill called for a central marketplace but none existed. It provided for collection of a 75 percent tax on excess cotton at the gin, but that the tax be based on weight and grade. "You cannot pay the tax until it is graded," Johnston argued, "and you cannot grade it until it has been ginned and you cannot gin it until the tax has been paid." He also pointed out that during the five- to six-month ginning season, knowledgeable tax collectors would have to be stationed at more than fifteen thousand gins.[7]

Other problems remained. Johnston expressed concern about the bill's effect on tenants who owned neither gins nor storage facilities to house cotton produced in excess of their Bankhead allotments. Small producers, as he had told Wallace earlier, might fall victim to speculators by being forced to sell their excess cotton. Planters with gins and warehouses could wait until marketing prospects improved. Johnston also doubted the bill's legality. Taxing processed cotton the farmer planned to use or store lay beyond federal authority, similar to taxing the threshing of wheat or the shucking of corn. Further, he deemed a 75 percent market value tax on surplus cotton "confiscatory," clearly not designed to generate revenue. Such a tax exceeded the government's police powers, he said, and was instead "the exercise of the taxing power of the Government to prohibit the doing of an act that is lawful and legal and that is not injurious to the public health and morals. Assuming that the purpose of the tax is to effectuate reduction in production, Congress is without authority, under the Constitution, to levy such a tax."[8]

Johnston even challenged the assumption that the South wanted a baleage tax. He claimed he "had a great many letters asking me to support a measure that would compel the 'slacker' . . . to come into the voluntary program . . . but no request to support a measure of the character of the bill that is now pending before the committee." He said he had reviewed some of the returned questionnaires and that the great majority indicated a willingness to accept any program the department might embrace, but "in none of them have we found any expression, nor have we found any advocates of a direct bill to control the emergency production by the marketing of cotton." At that moment, Will Bankhead interrupted, engaging Johnston in a brisk exchange:

Mr. Bankhead: [*interposing*]. Of course you know that the ordinary farmer is not a student in matters of legislation.

Mr. Johnston: But the man who prepared this questionnaire was.

Mr. Bankhead: That was prepared in your Department?

Mr. Johnston: It may have been; I do not know.

Mr. Bankhead: You do not know who prepared it?

Mr. Johnston: No, I do not know.

Mr. Bankhead: Did you take any occasion to inquire about that?

Mr. Johnston: No; I did not.

Mr. Bankhead: Do you know that it was prepared under the direction of the Secretary of Agriculture?

Mr. Johnston: I have no idea under whose direction it was prepared, but I know that it asks the farmer this question:

"Do you favor a plan of compulsory control of cotton production to compel all farmers to cooperate in cotton adjustment program?" And the answer to that question does not apply to this bill.

Mr. Bankhead: It applies to the principle contained in this bill.

Mr. Johnston: I think not.

Mr. Bankhead: That is the effect of it.

Mr. Johnston: I do not so consider it.

Mr. Bankhead: But a lot of intelligent students of cotton production would so consider it, would they not?

Mr. Johnston: Well, I am about as intelligent as the average southern farmer; I have spent most of my life on the farm, and I know that if I signed that I should not have in mind, that its application would be made to a bill of this kind, but the purpose was to get the man on the outside who was not willing to come into the program, to compel him to come in.

Likely irritated by Johnston's intransigence, Bankhead engaged in a few more moments of repartee, then asked, "Now about this farm you are operating in Mississippi."[9]

When the hearing adjourned for the day, the Bankheads accompanied Cotton Ed Smith to the White House, perhaps in part to head off any effect of Johnston's testimony. President Roosevelt soon endorsed the bill's principle in a letter to committee chairman Marvin Jones; released to the press, the letter was incorporated into the House Bankhead hearings. But Will Bankhead added the crowning blow. Johnston "was not looking at the bill from the standpoint of the farmer," he charged, "but from the interests of a great British syndicate."[10]

Johnston left Washington by plane soon after his testimony. Roosevelt's letter had been published and he had clearly lost the skirmish. After arriving in Memphis he told newsmen that no real harm would come from the Bankhead bill. "Since the president has voiced his approval of the principle," Johnston said, "it is my hope that Congress will perfect the bill, first squaring it with the federal constitution and second making it administratively possible."[11]

Back home, Johnston began guerrilla warfare against the Bankhead bill. Two days after Bankhead's personal attack appeared in the press, he wrote to Wallace from Scott. Dismayed at Roosevelt's public support of the tax he told the secretary, "At the risk of seeming persistent I take the liberty of submitting a brief statement of facts, which I fear have not been called to the attention of the President." He systematically outlined his views and, to counter charges that he suffered the myopia of a large-scale planter, argued that exemption certificates under the Bankhead proposal would work to the detriment of tenants. Since certificates would be issued to landowners, most of whom did not reside on their farms, they would keep sufficient certificates to gin their share—whether a fourth or a half—of the plantation's cotton. The tenants would get the short end of the deal, winding up with the heavily-taxed surplus. About 75 percent of American cotton was produced on a share basis, and if up to a million tenants produced a bale each above their allotments, Johnston believed "nothing short of armed force would prevent these tenants from ginning their surplus, and no political organization on earth would be able to withstand the pressure of a million families . . . demanding the privilege of marketing the fruits of their labor." Johnston pointed out such things, he concluded, "particularly in answer to charges made since I testified, that it is the large producer or the plantation owner, who is complaining. On the contrary, my interest is in the general economic condition. The large plantation owner will, I predict, not be hurt by the bill."

Wallace respected Johnston deeply, and remained a bit ambivalent toward the Bankhead idea. He sent Johnston's letter to Roosevelt, saying he did so at Johnston's "request"; he noted to the president that Johnston was "a very intelligent and earnest man" and strongly believed his letter "is worth your reading."[12]

Johnston's testimony in the House Bankhead hearings had not been wholly constructive. Many of his objections were correctable. In fact, Bankhead's personal attack may have possessed an element of truth. Johnston had known for years that Delta and Pine Land Company could produce a very substantial number of bales on reduced acreage through intensive cultivation of Early Ewing's prolific seed varieties. That is what the plantation had done in 1933. The federal government used the average acreage recorded for the years 1928–32 to determine how much acreage could be included in the New Deal's reduction campaign. But Johnston knew that such old acreage figures had included ditches, gardens, roads, and the like. The New Deal required more accurate measurements, but the inflated base would result in less reduction than imagined. The Bankhead proposal would sabotage efficient farm management. Yet, a few days before he appeared before Jones's committee, he told Arch Toler that the Bankhead bill "will not do any particular harm and . . . we must farm just as intensively as is humanly possible on our curtailed acreage and take our chances on being able to market what we produce." To an Arkansas farmer he repeated the claim that the bill would not hurt his operation, but he argued, "If production can be controlled in this way, the government will *discontinue the payment of rentals and benefits under a voluntary plan after this year, and will force control by law.* The result will be a serious labor displacement."[13]

Johnston returned to Washington at the end of February amid speculation that Congress would pass the Bankhead bill in one form or another. "The latest edition is so ridiculous," he told Toler, "that I do not believe it will ever be put into effect even if it is passed." In March, Mississippi congressman Wall Doxey told his colleagues that after Johnston's "very able and forceful statement before our committee," some objectionable features had been excised from the bill reported to the full House. Although Toler had earlier warned the British Fine Spinners that passage of the measure would be detrimental to Delta and Pine Land Company, he and Johnston later reassured them that the proposal would be ineffective if passed, although Johnston thought it might influence the futures market. Before it passed its version, the Senate loaded the bill with amendments, one of them a killing proviso by Josiah Bailey of North Carolina that exempted six bales above each farmer's quota. Some senators voted for the bill reluctantly, Kentucky Democrat Alben Barkley claiming he had "all my fingers and toes crossed." One opponent claimed, "If this measure is constitutional anything is constitutional." When Congress finally enacted the measure in April 1934, Johnston assured the British Fine Spinners that it would neither achieve its intended purpose nor hamper the company's operations.[14]

Despite his private assurances, Johnston's public sniping at the Bankhead plan received wide publicity. Highlights of one critical speech before the Greenville Rotary Club appeared in the local press and the *Staple Cotton Review,* the house organ of the Staple Cotton Cooperative Association. Thousands of specially printed copies were strategically distributed in Washington by the Greenville Chamber of Commerce. Some of Johnston's public opposition aroused resentment and criticism. After an interview Johnston gave to the *Memphis Commercial Appeal,* during which he called the Bankhead bill "Socialistic legislation," one critic told Senator Bankhead that he hoped "Secretary Wallace and yourself can control this gentleman in some way." Another critic, the president of the Mississippi Farm Bureau Federation, wired Cully Cobb to "[a]sk for Oscar Johnston's Resignation. His Position Ruinous." A southeast Missouri planter, who ironically was soon suspected of unfair tenant practice by an AAA field representative, complained to Wallace that Johnston's "stand on the Bankhead Bill does not set well." He also suggested, incredibly, that Johnston was "working against your cotton program," trying to keep prices low to benefit European interests. "Naturally," he said, "he is following the directions of the English company that retains him as manager of their Scott Plantation."[15]

Perhaps influenced by Johnston's protracted hostility to the legislation, Wallace wavered, sometimes publicly, much to Senator Bankhead's consternation. Wallace's and Johnston's comments affected prices and had some "weight," declared another critic. Bankhead told Wallace, "With the criticism of two outstanding members of the Department of Agriculture, namely you and Mr. Oscar Johns[t]on, I fear that there will be a growing tendency in the cotton belt to disregard the law in the matter of excessive production." He even complained to Roosevelt about "Johnston's continued hostility." Bankhead charged, "It seems strange to me that one holding a responsible position with the A.A.A. should persist in opposing the plans of the Administration."[16]

The administration hardly viewed the Bankhead plan as its own, but a watered-down version was now the law. The new Cotton Control Act allowed the tax-exempt sale of ten million bales from the 1934 crop, about 70 percent of the five-year production average. Johnston figured Delta and Pine Land Company could slightly increase its productivity over its own average and still be within its Bankhead exemption. More important, the law permitted cotton to be ginned without taxation, which simply meant that Johnston, like other efficient planters with warehouse facilities, could do basically what he had candidly suggested he would do: produce a sizable harvest, gin it, store the excess, and wait one year for the offensive statute to expire. He doubted that the plantation would ever have to pay the tax. He also reasoned that even counting new lands planted to cotton, the 40 percent acreage reduction throughout the cotton belt would approximate 28,637,000 acres, down from the five-year average of 41,000,000. From those shrunken lands he saw no possibility of production exceeding 11,500,000 bales.[17]

Neither Johnston nor the Bankheads could foresee the change in climate from the previous year. A severe drought in Texas, Oklahoma, Arkansas, and Louisiana during the summer of 1934 dropped production in those states to almost a million and a half bales beneath their Bankhead allotments. Other cotton states, including Mississippi, generally exceeded their allotments but the total production for the season still fell below nine and a half million bales. That remained below the ten and a half million bales Johnston earlier publicly warned would prove disastrous for the South. Aside from scaring recalcitrants into AAA compliance, the Bankhead Act failed to demonstrate its value in controlling production, partly because of the drought. Still, Johnston called for its repeal, perhaps because of the limited threat it posed to acreage reduction as a means of cotton control.[18]

Despite the Bankhead threat, Delta and Pine Land Company prepared for a bumper harvest. Around planting time an unfounded rumor circulated in Arkansas that the company had purchased nearly twice as much fertilizer as it had in 1933. With reduced acreage, the plantation actually purchased less in 1934, when it bought five hundred tons each of cyanamid and sulfate of ammonia, but Johnston still planned "the most intensive cultivation possible." Following his return from England, during which he and the Fine Spinners hashed out financial plans, Johnston inspected the whole plantation, finding it "in excellent condition, in fact the best in its history." Delta Pine concentrated on ten thousand acres of its "safest and best land," well prepared and fertilized. Jesse Fox, the plantation's veteran general manager, agreed that he had never been off to a better start. Similar conditions obtained at Delta Farms, where tenants planted three thousand acres to cotton. Aerial crop dusters repelled an early weevil attack and, except for a brief interim in August, the weather proved ideal.[19]

As in 1933, the efforts produced a white bounty. Tenants at Scott produced 8,309 bales, or 488 pounds per acre, an average second only to that of 1933. The bumper harvest pushed each of Johnston's plantations above its allotments, with the highest yield at Scott, where ginned bales totaled nearly 1,300 bales above the tax exemption. Fortunately for Delta Pine, producers in Bolivar County fell below their designated allotments and offered excess exemption certificates for ten to fifteen dollars per bale, all of which was legal if the certificates were bought and sold within their county of origin. Plantations that spilled across county borders, as did Delta and Pine Land Company, could use certificates for bales produced in either county. Holding to a maximum of ten dollars per certificate, Johnston acquired the requisite number for each plantation.[20]

As Johnston had repeatedly warned, the Bankhead tax worked a hardship on tenants. Paul Appleby, a fair-minded Wallace assistant in the Department of Agriculture, scored the cotton section for its landlord bias and its failure to work for the protection of tenants. "The worst indictment made of the Bankhead Bill has been its effect on the share-cropper and tenant farmer," he told Cully Cobb at the end of 1934. "You will recall that Oscar Johnston pointed out at the Senate Hearings on the Bill that its passage would result in tenants and share-croppers paying the tax on the portion of the crop paid to the land-owner as rent. Much thought was given to the possible methods of preventing this practice by regulations but the Legal Division has held that this is a matter of contractual relationship between land-owner and tenant or share-cropper; therefore, it could not be controlled by regulations."[21]

Landlords might try to justify what Appleby thought was "a vicious practice"— if they justified it at all—as a means of evening up previously uncollectable tenant accounts. At Delta Pine, improved prices and an abundant crop virtually assured collection of all tenant accounts, but the cost of tax exemption fell wholly on the sharecroppers. In the landlord-dominated Delta, tenants had little power to challenge such practices, nor did federal machinery effectively intervene on their behalf. It was an old story. The South's land problem forever confounded well-intentioned liberals in and out of government. Secretary Wallace, dubious about the Bankhead plan, confessed in the summer of 1934 that even though the possibility for success looked better, "there will be some very real difficulties in certain localities where the big planter-tenant relationship is on a basis which we in the North don't understand very well." He added, "Oscar Johnston is a big planter."[22]

Congress had given the Bankhead Act a year's trial, but it could be extended. In a popular referendum at the end of the year, farmers voted heavily to keep it for 1935, albeit in amended form. Before the vote, Johnston grumbled that local agriculture officials were campaigning for its retention and that farmers were intimidated because those officials controlled future allotment certificates. Also, ten days before the canvass, President Roosevelt announced he would ask Congress to exempt growers whose base production totaled two bales or less, which included about two hundred thousand farmers. The nine-to-one margin in favor of continuation could leave little doubt as to farmer preference. Johnston had lost again. Highlighting his bitter experience with the tax, the *Memphis Press-Scimitar,* in its report of the referendum's outcome, headed a brief wire-service story, "In Enemy Country," which pointed out that even in Johnston's own Bolivar County the vote for the tax had been overwhelming.[23]

Johnston conceded that the Bankhead tax increased producer compliance with the AAA reduction program, but he looked to the Supreme Court to strike it down. "I have not at any time thought that this law was constitutional," he told the Fine Spinners in the middle of 1935, "and now am more confident than ever that when it is brought before the Court, it will be held void." Constitutional challenges to New Deal legislation increased dramatically in 1935; marketing allotment acts such as the Cotton Control Act, the Potato Act, and the Kerr-Smith Tobacco Act provided ready targets. In 1935, as before, Johnston's plantations exceeded their Bankhead allotments; this time he held off purchasing exemption certificates for excess bales pending the outcome of a test suit challenging the tax. At the end of 1935, he advised the British bondholders that Delta Pine would make no further mortgage payments until after the court's decision. After that, he noted with optimism, "we may sell our taxable cotton and make available the proceeds."[24]

Johnston also monitored litigation against the Bankhead tax and, in the Hoosac Mills case, the AAA itself. He thought the AAA would be sustained, perhaps in a 5–4 vote, but that if it was not, Congress would quickly offer substitute legislation. He expected unanimous court rejection in the Bankhead case, producing only a "temporarily bearish" market influence. In fact, he suspected the futures market had already absorbed the possibility of Bankhead's demise. As it developed, the court did not get the chance to rule on the bale tax. In January 1936 it struck down the AAA processing tax. Toler wrote the Fine Spinners that "[c]onditions in this country pertaining to agriculture are in an utter state of chaos." Johnston, more sanguine, later told them that new legislation would soon be forthcoming and that he had no fear that cotton acreage would swell to pre-1933 levels. "Unquestionably," he wrote, "the situation challenges our ingenuity but I do not regard it as hopeless."[25]

In the wake of the AAA decision, Justice Owen Roberts forecast the invalidation of the Bankhead tax. Johnston, however, thought the litigation suffered procedural flaw. He even entertained late fears that the tax would be sustained. At his behest, and under his ghosted supervision, two of his lawyer friends from

Mississippi filed suit in Washington on January 25, 1936, directly challenging the legality of the Bankhead Cotton Control Act. It proved unnecessary. Within two weeks Congress yielded to President Roosevelt's request by repealing the act; Johnston's running battle with the Bankhead tax finally ended.[26]

Johnston wasted no time gloating over the repeal. He quickly began marketing his plantations' liberated cotton. Within ten days he had sold almost half of the nearly 2,800 excess bales. Producers throughout the cotton belt rapidly released most of their old Bankhead cotton "without creating even a ripple in the market." Johnston's sales apparently enabled him to pay the remaining interest owed to the British on some old amortization bonds, thus helping to end the crop year with "gratifying and satisfactory" results. It had been a good year indeed. Delta Pine also repaid the British Fine Spinners all the funds which had been advanced for any purpose since implementing financial restructuring in 1927.[27]

The denouement also produced a more significant result. Whatever hardships fell on tenants because of the Bankhead tax, it chiefly threatened efficient, scientific agricultural management. The act had not been the nightmare Johnston feared, partly because of technical and other changes. But its fundamental principle had represented a formidable challenge to acreage reduction as a method of cotton control. Had it been successful, as Johnston had privately warned, rental payments might have evaporated. It proved to be a major juncture in the history of government's relationship with American agriculture.[28]

Fortunately for Johnston, his uphill battle against the Bankhead tax left no visible scars, and the repeal may have mitigated some lost prestige. The controversy had demonstrated his independence within the New Deal. Meanwhile, even as he fought the Bankhead tax, he had been busy with the cotton pool, AAA loans, landlord-tenant politics, and lost foreign markets for cotton. How these problems were resolved had implications not only for the New Deal, but also for the health of a vital American industry in the Great Depression.

# 6

## An Ounce of Remedy, a Pound of Reform

I know the South and we've got to be patient.
—Franklin D. Roosevelt to Norman Thomas, 1935

**O**n the afternoon of February 5, 1935, Secretary of Agriculture Henry A. Wallace and Agricultural Adjustment Administrator Chester C. Davis looked out into a hostile press conference. With Wallace's approval, Davis had just fired several lawyers from the AAA's legal division and consumer's counsel following months of administrative infighting. Many in the audience were now ready with hard and embarrassing questions. "I never saw at any press conference so many plainly hostile representatives of public opinion, with barbed questions prepared, planted," recalled Russell Lord, who was there taking notes. "It was not a pleasant occasion." James LeCron, a Wallace aide, also sensed the heavy air. "This afternoon the Secretary's press conference boiled with pointed and hostile questions," he confided to his diary, "because most of the newswriters are liberals and were trying to get the reason for Henry's ruthless repudiation of what appeared to be his best friends."[1]

The specific and acute transgression of the legal division, headed by its able chief counsel, Jerome Frank, had been the attempt to interpret a controversial paragraph in the 1934 and 1935 Cotton Acreage Reduction Contract in favor of sharecroppers and other tenants over the objection of the planter-landlord establishment of the cotton South. The socially conscious liberals wished to stop southern landlords from evicting tenants either for union membership or because of the landlord's own greed in the distribution of government benefit checks from acreage reduction. Engaged in what they perceived as mortal combat, the conservatives prevailed and a number of liberals were ousted from the AAA.[2]

In the Great Depression the landlord-tenant system constituted a regional as well as national problem. A shelf of published literature on the subject pointed to the impoverished character of farm tenancy. In a society burdened and complicated by race and caste, this often debilitating labor system served as a means of social control. While the frequently maligned acreage-reduction program worked a hardship on some tenants, the New Deal did call attention to economic and social conditions that had long existed in the rural South.[3]

Some of those conditions were particularly noticeable in the cotton counties of northeastern Arkansas. As a critic of New Deal agricultural policy, American Socialist Party leader Norman Thomas drew further attention to the tenant problem when he toured the area in 1934. He had been invited to Tyronza, Arkansas, by two local socialists, Harry L. Mitchell and Clay East. Shocked by human misery among Arkansas sharecroppers, Thomas charged that working conditions on the plantations constituted "peonage—worse than peonage," and that the government's reduction program had driven hundreds of farmers from the land, leaving many near starvation. "I've seen the worst housing conditions in the slums of the cities and the abject conditions in some mining camps," he later charged, "but none of them compare with the deplorable condition of the sharecroppers in Arkansas."[4]

Thomas's earlier charges provoked a public retort from Oscar Johnston, a formulator of AAA cotton policy. While admitting ignorance about the situation around Tyronza, Johnston told the Associated Press: "I am intimately familiar with the labor conditions in the delta of Mississippi and I know that the condition which he [Thomas] describes does not prevail generally." While Johnston did not doubt the existence of "unscrupulous and dishonest landlords," he argued that labor had been victimized in other sections "but such treatment is the exception and not the rule." Johnston did promise that landlords who violated their 1934–35 cotton contract stood to lose their subsidies, but added, "The sharecropper system is the fairest system that can be devised for labor engaged in the production of cotton."[5]

Johnston's public reply in turn evoked a private charge from East and Mitchell that the plantation conditions described by Thomas probably existed in Mississippi and even at Delta and Pine Land Company. The "damnable system" of farm tenancy, they said, combined "the worst features of fuedalism [sic] with capitalistic exploitation," and had been made worse by the New Deal reduction programs. The pair further charged that local committees had been dominated by conservative landlords and that the sharecropper possessed no redress for grievances. Johnston denied that such conditions existed on his plantation and invited Mitchell and East to drive down to see for themselves. Norman Thomas later added that no matter how "conscientious an official Mr. Johnston may be, his enthusiastic support of the old system does not argue much of a New Deal in cotton growing."[6]

Thomas's characterization was overdrawn. Johnston's support of the tenant system was more rational and defensive than "enthusiastic." He told East and

Mitchell that he would "gladly exchange the share crop system for a wages system and pay a daily wage." There would, however, be "no work with which to employ the labor during a large part of the time when it is not necessary for him to work in the cotton field." The farmer could not support his family even at subsistence levels.[7]

The publicity generated by Norman Thomas placed added pressure on the AAA to probe the sharecroppers' problem in Arkansas. At issue was the eviction of many sharecroppers from their homes by landlords who had agreed to reduce their planted acreage in accordance with the AAA's 1934–35 cotton contract. Planters who coveted a larger portion of AAA rental benefits had reduced the number of sharecroppers on their plantations or had reduced the status of the sharecroppers to that of day laborers, freeing the planter from providing housing and other necessities.[8]

As such practices continued throughout 1934, some critics took action. They deluged the AAA with letters and telegrams protesting unfair tenant practices. Appalling conditions in several northeastern Arkansas counties probably reflected the misery of tenant life in some other areas of the South, but activities in Arkansas attracted particular national attention. The alleged eviction of about forty sharecropper families from Fairview Farms, an Arkansas plantation owned by a St. Louis attorney, Hiram Norcross, served as a catalyst in the formation of the Southern Tenant Farmers' Union (STFU) in July 1934. A biracial organization, the union aroused strong feelings in northeastern Arkansas; the open hostility of planters and some law enforcement officials contributed to beatings, night riding, and other forms of violence and intimidation between 1934 and 1936. To Norman Thomas it was, as he said on NBC radio, "a reign of terror" which, he warned, would "end either in the establishment of complete slavish submission to the vilest exploitation in America or in bloodshed, or in both."[9]

Although the STFU had been formed to enable tenants to deal effectively with the planter establishment, it also tried to pressure the AAA into halting the eviction of more sharecroppers. Legal basis—such as it was—was found in the soon-to-be-familiar "Section 7" of the 1934–35 Cotton Acreage Reduction Contract. "The producer shall endeavor in good faith," declared the controversial paragraph, "to bring about a reduction of acreage" with minimum labor displacement and "shall, insofar as possible, maintain on this farm the *normal number* of tenants and other employees . . . [and] shall permit *all tenants to continue* the occupancy of their houses."[10]

During 1934, this paragraph became a serious point of contention between the urban liberals in the AAA's legal division and consumer counsel and the conservatives and pragmatists among the landlord-oriented administrators, including both Johnston and Cully Cobb, head of the cotton section. The liberals, under Chief Counsel Jerome Frank, attempted to interpret Section 7 in order to force Hiram Norcross—and thus, cotton landlords generally—to retain the *same* tenants under the new contract rather than merely a *"normal number"* of tenants. The move to implement this liberal interpretation came in early 1935 while Davis was out of town. A liberal subordinate authorized publication of this reinterpretation, sending shock waves through the cotton belt. Upon his return, an angry Davis called for a showdown. The forced resignation of several liberals and subsequent voluntary departure of others soon followed.[11]

Did Section 7, or technically, Section I, Paragraph 7, require the landlord to not only maintain the "normal number" but also allow any tenant not making a crop to remain on the plantation during the contract period? Chester Davis thought so. He told Wallace soon after his return to Washington that such was the administrative intent when the contract was drafted in 1933 and, further, that no alternate legal interpretation "was expressed in any quarter at that time."[12] Such a contention, it seemed, rested on firm ground.

The authorship of the paragraph might reflect on intent. At least one scholar has identified Oscar Johnston as "the man who had drafted" the paragraph.[13] But the issue needs proper context. The origins of the 1934–35 cotton contract in which the paragraph appeared reached back to the summer and fall of 1933 when then AAA Administrator George Peek called on Johnston, then the AAA financial chief, for assistance in its preparation. In late August 1933 Johnston submitted his tentative plan for cotton acreage reduction, even confidentially sharing it with his company's officials back in Mississippi. After winning essential endorsement within the AAA, Johnston's outline was broadly sustained by producers' meetings held simultaneously in Atlanta, Dallas, and Memphis on September 3, with Johnston chairing the session at the Peabody Hotel in Memphis. While landlord-tenant relationships received little or no attention at these on-site gatherings—at least at Memphis—they did arouse controversy within the AAA back in Washington. The issue was joined by Alger Hiss, the legal division's representative to numerous internal AAA meetings regarding the actual drafting of the contract. Although Hiss's boss, Jerome Frank, would argue that matters of policy and law might not readily be separated, evidently Hiss's objections to potential unfair treatment of tenants related more to matters of policy than to law. By the end of September, meanwhile, Cully Cobb proposed that the landlord "be requested to keep the same number of tenants in 1934 as he had in 1933." There the issue bogged down through much of October when Johnston told Peek that several questions had to find resolution before the 1934 reduction program could mature. Among them, he said, was the landlord-tenant problem.[14]

Both Johnston and Davis seemed to credit Hiss with assistance in the formulation of the significant paragraph. Davis told Peek on November 11, 1933, that he believed the tenant section of the 1934–35 contract "would be improved if the first sentence were restated *as suggested* by Mr. Hiss as follows: '. . . shall insofar as possible, maintain on this farm the normal number of tenants and other employees; shall permit all tenants to continue the occupancy of their houses on this farm. . . .'" Prior to formal adoption of the language, Johnston and Hiss "discussed at length the proposed" paragraph, reaching "an agreement as to the phraseology." According to Johnston, "the paragraph *as prepared* by Mr. Hiss and submitted by Mr. Davis, was adopted." That is what Johnston said he remembered in January 1935 about the events of the summer and fall of 1933. Curiously, however, two months earlier he had told William R. Amberson, a tenant sympathizer, "My recollection is that *I wrote* Section 7 of the contract." Was Johnston playing fast and loose with the authorship of the paragraph? For his part, Hiss later claimed no authorship of Paragraph 7 as he had earlier claimed for at least the wording of Paragraph 9: "The determination of the Secretary that any such violation or misstatement has occurred shall be final and conclusive." Such power lodged in the secretary's hands might easily have produced confidence in the rest of the document. In any event, the language of Paragraph 7 is quite compatible with Johnston's style, and a possible explanation is that Johnston drafted the paragraph with Hiss suggesting some alteration, the identity of which remains unclear. While both apparently agreed to the ultimate phraseology, it is also apparent that both later recalled different impressions as to meaning. Hiss did not regard the legal division's interpretation of the paragraph a revision at all, while Johnston argued, "Never, at any time, insofar as I knew was there any thought or suggestion of arbitrarily requiring the owner of a farm to maintain on that farm, the identical tenants who had occupied the farm in 1933."[15]

Whoever originated the phrasing of Paragraph 7, the liberals' interpretation received support outside the AAA. Dr. William R. Amberson, a physiology professor at the University of Tennessee at Memphis, thought about testing the government's position over tenant evictions as early as February 1934. Later that year, Hiram Norcross, the apparent target of the proposed litigation, seemingly denied the allegations against him. He cited the standard interpretation of the AAA contract and claimed he had more tenants under contract for 1935 than he had in 1934; further, he told Amberson he was constructing "eight to ten new houses as well as using those houses which during the past year I gave rent free to families without crops." About the same time, Amberson, a tireless and optimistic socialist who had little faith in any help from the federal government, got some advice from one southern liberal, sociology professor

Rupert B. Vance of the Institute for Research in Social Science at Chapel Hill, to not muddy the waters. If Amberson and his crowd wanted to legally stop tenant evictions they needed to "pick an issue and a group of clients divested of extraneous issues," said Vance. "If you can prevent the opposing counsel from hanging 'communism,' 'socialism,' 'atheism,' 'race prejudice' etc., around your neck, figuratively speaking, I believe something may be done to halt by legal means the dispossession of tenants from plantations. If you allow some wiley lawyer to play with prejudices of a southern jury, as is often done in these cases, I fear you are lost."[16]

Amberson's brooding over a court case even had a role for Oscar Johnston. Incredibly, he believed Johnston would support a liberal interpretation and considered calling him as a prosecution witness if a case was litigated. In conversation with Amberson, Johnston was perhaps evasive, claiming later by letter that "I do not know that I can employ language in interpreting the section which is clearer than the language of the section," but repeating the operating phrase "normal number" while still calling for tenants "to continue" on the plantation. All that surprised Professor Vance. Although sympathetic, Vance told Amberson privately in late November 1934, "It may be gossip, but more than once I have heard him [Johnston] classified as reactionary. . . [who] dominates the actions of the Cotton Section of the AAA."[17]

Those rumors about Johnston's views were distorted, but he did possess definite ideas about what the New Deal for cotton should and should not do. In fact, with his emphasis on controlling production, raising cotton prices, and reviving cotton exports, Johnston had no interest in using the AAA as an instrument of social experimentation, as he thought others were trying to do. That Johnston's latter view was rather widely shared with those whose jobs governed the day-to-day operations of the AAA only increased the possibility of conflict with the liberals who staffed Jerome Frank's legal division. And Johnston's legal mind matched those of the liberals, a fact overlooked by one scholar who argued that Wallace's view that the reinterpretation constituted "bad law" "can be met by comparing the relative merits of Jerome Frank's legal training with that of Henry Wallace and the Cotton Section."[18]

The February 1935 purge of the liberals was presaged by months of infighting and tension. Such tension was often near the surface and reflected ideological division. Peek learned early, he said, that Frank and his lawyers "were more concerned with matters of policy than with questions of law. They appeared to be proponents of the puppet system of government and very anxious to extend government control as a prelude to government ownership." Peek also learned of ideological departmental intrigue. He remembered a subordinate coming to see him late one afternoon early in the administration:

"Do you know what's going on around here?" he asked at once.

"In a general way, I hope I do," I answered, "but what have you particularly in mind?"

"Well," he went on, "it seems crazy and maybe it is crazy, or maybe I'm crazy, but I have been to several parties now of [Rexford] Tugwell's and Jerome Frank's and they have a very different idea of this Administration from what we have. They are all talking social revolution and they have the idea that it is the mission of the Roosevelt Administration to turn us into some new kind of socialist state. They think the place to start is with the farmers because it is the farmers who in other countries have formed the chief obstacle to socialism."

Peek regarded some of the left-wing talk as "foolish stuff," "chatter," and "absurd," the talk of "prattlers." "They blame all ills on capitalism and were for abolishing it, either by degrees or at once," he said. "Since few of them, as far as I could find out, had ever employed anyone, they saw no difficulties in regulating the affairs of millions. They thought charts would do that." He added, "They deeply admired everything Russian."

But Peek understood collectivism when he saw it, including using the new farm legislation and its amendments to regiment American agriculture and destroy the farmers' independence. "There is no use in mincing words," he wrote later. "The A.A.A. became a means of buying the farmer's birthright as a preliminary to breaking down the whole individualistic system of the country."[19]

Frank was in fact a proponent of "legal realism" of the 1930s, a sort of "sociological jurisprudence" that emphasized the changing character of law. In passing on one or another AAA proposal, Frank might jot on the legal opinion from his division, "okay as to law, no comment as to policy," to which Chester Davis would reply, "your comment as to policy was not solicited." For Christmas one year, Paul Porter, the young USDA lawyer with friends on both sides of the ideological line, remembered that he "gave Jerome Frank a rubber stamp, 'okay as to law, no comment as to policy.'" More serious, Johnston and Frank clashed, for example, over legal and record-keeping procedures. On one occasion, a month before the purge, Frank sat mostly in restrained and gentlemanly silence at a meeting in Wallace's office while Johnston criticized the legal division over a matter relative to Johnston's cotton pool activities, an area Oscar regarded as his own. "I was much embarrassed at the conference in your office yesterday," Frank told Wallace the following day. Johnston "made it appear that I and my assistants were being captious and obstructive. I had to choose between remaining silent as to most of what he said or precipitating an unpleasant altercation; I preferred the former course."[20]

The truth is that Johnston's freewheeling style in handling government cotton pool transactions created a bureaucratic legal nightmare for Frank and his extremely able group of young lawyers. That the financial and bureaucratic

workings of the multimillion-dollar cotton pool were clear to Johnston is beyond question. But everything was not clear to the legal division. Johnston
evidently struck fear into the hearts of junior-level legal division lawyers. Frank
remembered that until he got an effective lawyer who could keep pace with
Johnston, he "used to wake up in the middle of the night wondering whether
we were going to have some financial disaster" because of Johnston's operations. "I tried to find out what Oscar was u[p] to because I wanted to see that
he was staying inside his authority and wasn't going to put the whole credit of
the United States behind his [government] operations. I didn't know what he
was doing. So I put some lawyer on it with him. They couldn't get along because the lawyer annoyed Oscar and Oscar's mind moved forty times as fast as
the lawyer's. By the time the lawyer understood wha[t] had happened yesterday it was all changed. I got another lawyer and he couldn't do it." Frank finally hit on the right lawyer, a young Austrian fresh out of Columbia Law School
named Bruno Schachner, "very Viennese," said Frank later, and "still in the
heel-clicking stage. He was urbane and very polite," and got along with Oscar
beautifully. "From that time I could sleep nights about Oscar. I suppose," said
Frank, "Oscar's operations were really legitimate."[21]

If time pointed up the amusing element in Johnston's relationship with the
legal division, it was a frustrated Jerome Frank who lamented to Secretary
Wallace in January 1935: "Mr. Johnston is a brilliant man, one of the most brilliant I have ever met; *it may be that his services have been of immense importance*. But that does not mean that he ought not, like any ordinary man, be required to see that records are adequately kept or that the other persons who are
required to pass upon Cotton Pool transactions are sufficiently informed about
what is involved therein so that they can pass upon them with intelligence."[22]

Frank was probably right about Johnston's modus operandi and he was certainly right about his importance. Henry Wallace, a master of hybrid corn, had
come to depend on Johnston's knowledge of cotton and his leadership in the
cotton belt. From selling the program to the cotton South in 1933 to playing
the complicated spot and futures market with pooled cotton, Johnston was
crucial to the AAA.[23]

If Johnston had been even remotely evasive with Amberson about Paragraph
7 in late 1934 he certainly was more direct with Chester Davis in early 1935.
While the legal aspects of Paragraph 7 were being hotly debated both in the
AAA and out, Johnston told Davis that he envisioned the controversial section
as a "morally obligating" provision to encourage landlords to avoid labor displacement because of acreage reduction. "To my mind," he argued, "Section
7 of the contract is clear, free of ambiguity and does not by any remote stretch
of the imagination, confer upon the Secretary of Agriculture as a party to that

contract, any right to appear as a party interested in any legal proceeding either between a landlord and a tenant or in his own right against a landlord, to enforce any provision of that Section." Johnston drew a distinction. He admitted that Secretary Wallace could cancel an offending planter's contract, but pointed out that the question of whether a tenant constituted a "menace" was "essentially a question of fact and not one of law." More important, in a veiled warning Johnston told Davis that interference in private landlord-tenant disputes "would be absolutely fatal to the success of the cotton program and would, in my judgment, be a serious political blunder."[24]

For the legal division's part, Alger Hiss understood at least some of the difficulty. He had, in fact, "recognized from the outset the impracticality of enforcing the paragraph as written," he remembered later. But he believed that "with the addition of a clause [Paragraph 9] that gave the Secretary the power to determine violations, the threat of non-payment to a landlord *might* give some more weight to the pressure on the landlord not to evict tenants no longer needed for cotton production." That view was consistent with his argument to Frank the day before the purge. He made a legal judgment based on the language of the contract but never deluded himself as to the practicality of enforcement. He wanted Wallace to seize the initiative not with an injunction, which would very likely not be sustained, but rather by stopping AAA payments to offending landlords, thus forcing their hand, in this case Norcross, by bringing suit against the secretary where "the chances of a successful outcome for the Secretary would be substantially greater."[25]

Johnston and Hiss stood united on the idea of the lack of enforceability of Paragraph 7, but Johnston deplored the stopping of benefit payments as a strong-arm tactic that was apparently having a negative reception among cotton planters. One Arkansas landlord, Clarence Twist, had complained to Johnston about allegedly unfair treatment, and Johnston in turn complained to Wallace. In fact, it was for the secretary that Johnston reserved his most strident objection and warning. Back in Mississippi when the liberals were dispatched, Johnston complained to Wallace "entirely unofficially and as a cotton producer, vitally interested in the success of *your* program." Written the day after the purge— obviously too late to bear on Wallace's decision—Johnston's warning nonetheless reflects the planter attitude. He had found back home, he told Wallace, "considerable hesitancy on the part of farm owners to go ahead with the 1935 contract unless they can be assured by you that if they withhold from cotton the acreage stipulated in their contracts they will be paid their rental without unreasonable delay and will not be penalized because of technical violations." Johnston had always thought that the 1934 plan was to avoid significant labor dislocation "and that in this effort the Department was interested in labor as a whole and not in individual cases." According to him, socialists had blown the labor problem way out of proportion "in an effort to discredit the agricultural program." While he believed in fair play for tenants, Johnston rejected the notion "that our agricultural program should be distorted into or used as a weapon to bring about so-called 'social reform', or to revolutionize the social and economic life of the cotton belt." "So serious is this situation," Johnston warned darkly, "that I take the liberty of suggesting that you personally examine this picture, [and] ascertain just what is being done by those for whose actions *you will be held responsible.*"[26]

Wallace, of course, had already acted. The secretary had, however, stood above the controversy until just a few days prior to the purge. On February 1, 1935, Democratic congressman William J. Driver of Arkansas and a delegation of his state's planters descended on Wallace's office to talk over what they believed was a reinterpretation of Paragraph 7. Wallace and his staff apparently quieted the landlords' fears, but the secretary subsequently wavered over the contract's interpretation, if not over what action should be taken. Chester Davis, Wallace recorded in his diary the day before the purge, "was much disturbed at the legal point of view" advanced by Frank and Hiss. "I don't blame him," conceded Wallace. "I have no doubt that Frank and Hiss were animated by the highest of motives but their lack of an agricultural background apparently exposes them to the danger of going to absurd lengths." Wallace, in fact, was convinced that Davis's view of the paragraph was consistent with the view the department had publicized in May 1934. "This interpretation," he reflected, "is also an interpretation of common sense." The next day, however, just hours after the purge was publicized, Frank and Hiss met with Wallace and presented their view of Paragraph 7, which, according to Wallace, "sounds just as good as that presented by Chester Davis." Even though Frank argued that the paragraph's interpretation did not constitute the real dispute between Davis and himself, Wallace pointed out that he had to solve an administrative problem, and that meant siding with Davis.[27]

Frank may have been right about the conflict with Davis, but Paragraph 7 nonetheless reflected an ideological division. Davis, a conservative but not a landlord, had scuffled with the liberals in and out of the legal division in the past and, if he had learned of it, would very likely have been pleased with Johnston's strong memo of January 26. He had been upset by the personnel troubles that had plagued his agency for some time, believing he was the object of a bureaucratic conspiracy perpetuated by Frank and Wallace aide Paul Appleby, both liberals.[28]

Davis was able to survive administrative infighting partly because Wallace believed him to be the best man to head the agency at that point; though Davis argued that his resignation was not discussed, it seems fairly clear he would have resigned if the Paragraph 7 interpretation had gone against him. "The middle-western semi-enlightened selfishness of Chester Davis simply is not understood by the left wingers of city background," Wallace reflected nearly a week after the purge. "Their attitudes in some respects are of perhaps a higher nature than Chester's but their sense of time seems to me to be wrong. They want to move too fast."[29]

Whether the planters for whom much of the cotton program had been developed and which, to that point anyway, had boosted operating revenues, would have played their trump card of noncompliance if their interpretation had been reversed is debatable. It was a card fingered more than once during the New Deal but never collectively played. Though Johnston's warning to that effect was scarcely veiled, could he seriously have contemplated withdrawing from a program for which he could claim some paternity? He had sold the program vigorously back in 1933, logging many miles to convince otherwise reluctant planters that the New Deal agricultural program meant salvation for the cotton belt. And, in fairness to the planters, the liberal interpretation of Paragraph 7 did reflect a change of operation during the life of the contract.[30]

If Johnston's reaction appeared harsh, he correctly assessed the liberals' intent. The early New Deal exuded "the reforming zeal of the Young Turks," of whom Alger Hiss was one. "We did take Roosevelt's analogy in his Inaugural to war seriously," Hiss recalled.

> We felt we were enlisted as a citizen army . . . for the duration of the Depression. But while recovery was the goal of the war, we felt, like all American troops, that we were fighting also for longer-range goals. Wilson's war was to end all wars. We believed we could, in [Rexford] Tugwell's terms, "make America over" so that there would be no more depressions. We had no blue-prints for a "made-over" America (*that* was rhetoric like Wilson's), but we knew that the farmer needed structural changes to prevent constant gluts and investors needed to drive the money changers from the temple and unions should be encouraged [and] not treated in the 19th century pattern as if they were illegal conspiracies.

According to Hiss, so intimately involved in the dispute and yet spared in the purge,

> the legal division's interpretation of par. 7 of the 1934–35 cotton contract has to be looked at in terms of the dynamics of the New Deal. We young fellows were well aware of the varied crew that manned the New Deal ship of state and that some of our crusading efforts had to be directed inwards. For example, Peek was out of step with what we believed was the "true" spirit of the New Deal; Wallace and Roosevelt, our leaders and our champions, of course exemplified the "true" spirit. So Peek's discomfiture and exit seemed to us part of the script. In regard to the cotton program, while bringing about higher cotton prices, we wanted also to aid the "forgotten

men," the tenants and sharecroppers at the bottom of the structure, at least as much proportionately as we aided the landlord. . . . We believed politically, as apparently Wallace initially did, too, that the New Deal's strength was sufficient to sustain our initial phrasing and our later interpretation of par. 7. On that score we were wrong. . . . It did seem possible and not utopian in the summer and fall of 1933— the first flush of the New Deal—to force the "economic royalists" of the cotton plantations to agree in return for large payments to keep the same tenants. . . . I believe that the strongly liberal personnel in the AAA disagreed with Oscar's concepts that the program should not be used to bring about social reform. We *did* believe in reform as well as recovery. . . . [Several of the liberals, including Hiss, believed they] were asserting legal justification for an interpretation of par. 7 which we had been led to believe (and reasonably led to believe) the Administration wanted. But we were highly conscious of our professional duties and regarded the opinion as a legal effort of which we were proud as lawyers and which we were prepared to stand behind fully. So the denouement was a surprise to all of us.[31]

Such zeal was not lost on the AAA conservatives. And Johnston had become sensitized to attacks on the plantation's labor system. That system, he complained to Chester Davis in 1934, "has even been likened to a form of peonage, serfdom or slavery. These criticisms come from persons wholly ignorant of the system or the economic situation." He contended the South would happily shift to a day-labor system if such was feasible. More than three years later he told Cully Cobb, then chief of the AAA's southern division:

This whole idea of having tenants participate in the so-called "benefit payments," made to persons participating in the Soil Conservation programs, was conceived by persons unfamiliar with the plantation system and desirous of bringing about some social and economic change in the sharecropping system. The result of the application of this policy has been unfortunate for the sharecroppers as a whole, since those plantation owners who are situated near cities, towns and villages immediately shifted from the sharecropper system to a day wage system, thus eliminating the tenant. Any person familiar with the operation realizes that the sharecropper system is more favorable to the tenant than the cash wage system.[32]

Despite such sensitivity to criticism from those who they believed did not understand the South, Johnston and the conservatives objected not at all to the mandatory retention of a "normal number" of tenants as required in the 1934–35 contract. No one in the whole debate advocated less than that. Johnston wanted to protect the tenant from planter abuse, perhaps less for humanitarian reasons than for fear of arousing public wrath. For the first time, furthermore, the landlords were encouraged to maintain at least a normal plantation census and avoid labor displacement. And at Delta and Pine Land Company acreage reduction may have even retarded mechanization—a signal of coming displacement—already in its beginning stages.[33]

Many planters may well have been selfish and petty in the whole debate over Paragraph 7. But it does not follow that they would have vindictively torpedoed an otherwise favorable program for merely having, as one scholar suggested, "to show cause for evicting tenants."[34] Doubtless that is not how the issue was perceived in the crossroads stores and plantation offices of the cotton South. Evictions, it is true, might have been employed to break unionization of tenant labor and maintain social control. Further, federal intervention in landlord-tenant relationships would—and did—encounter stiff resistance in the South until the impact of World War II, not government regulation alone, changed the South altogether. Had the Paragraph 7 issue not been resolved to his liking, there is no clear evidence that Johnston would have abandoned his leadership of the cotton pool, an agency more removed from the controversy. His own sense of obligation would have proved too strong. Still, Johnston's loyalty, pragmatic to the core, had its limits. In 1934, for example, his plantations became embroiled in a dispute with the local compliance committee on a matter totally unrelated to landlord-tenant relationships. If the committee forced the issue, he told Arch Toler privately—removed from public grandstanding—the plantations would withdraw from the program and plant full acreage. Whether he would have actually followed through on the threat remains extremely doubtful. Johnston was no fool. But the issue of bureaucratic intrusion in landlord-tenant affairs was far more sensitive and volatile. That same year, 1934, after Toler reported learning of an evidently legal mandate requiring minimum wages for unskilled nonagricultural labor, Johnston told him to ignore the order regardless of its source. He replied defiantly, "We will still run our plantation somewhat as we damn please."[35]

Aside from all other considerations, and there were several, Henry Wallace would not have wished to alienate Davis, Johnston, or their constituencies. Reflecting those constituencies, one southern newspaper hailed the purge as a "victory over radicals and agitators who were organizing sharecroppers and tenants." Wallace knew the real issue did not hinge on some legal rendering of an otherwise obscure passage in a cotton contract. The New Deal could function without the socially conscious lawyers but risked paralysis without the support of conservatives in and out of the AAA. Davis recalled that he told Wallace that allowing the liberal interpretation to stand would "'set off forces that will drive you right out of the Cabinet. You won't be able to stay.' I think Henry, at that time, agreed with me." Years later, James LeCron remembered, "We thought that Henry had acted badly. None of us in his office approved of that 'purge' at the time. I later began to see the point a little more, when the thing cooled down. I still think Wallace made a mistake on that deal, with this quick 'purge' and all. But from the standpoint of administration, it was probably the only choice he had." As it turned out, if for no other reason, the pragmatic answer would be the final solution to the conflicting personnel and purposes of the AAA.[36]

The need for cooperation at the local level, where the landlord establishment wielded economic and political power, complicated the tenancy issue. While Norman Thomas's later complaint that the government "could have done better" may be valid, what the planters, including Johnston, would have accepted from Washington remains an important consideration. "The Federal Government could not superimpose by the administration of any law a new social order upon the South," Alfred Stedman, the old AAA administrator, told Secretary Wallace in 1936. "That is one way of saying that the march of social and economic progress of the share croppers can not be forced by the Federal Government to proceed much faster than the rate that Southern opinion and Southern leadership will heartily support. To try to force a faster pace would merely be to insure violent controversy, lack of local cooperation in administration, evasion and ineffectiveness for the plan. We have found from long and hard work and gruelling experience in the AAA that there are limits beyond which we could not go."[37]

Even Rexford Tugwell knew that. "What would you do," he once asked Norman Thomas, "if you had to deal with [Senators] Joe Robinson, Cotton Ed Smith, and Pat Harrison?" Thomas replied: "That's why I'm not a Democrat." Of course, Thomas knew that Tugwell "was right." He knew that administrative timidity rested on the southerners' claim to "all the important political chairmanships. That was the price they had to pay." During one White House meeting after the purge, Thomas got around Franklin Roosevelt's disarming evasiveness long enough to ask the president to read portions of the cotton contract. Roosevelt had been so removed from the elbowing and jockeying that he had not even read the controversial contract, or at least that is what he told Thomas. "Roosevelt handed it back to me, half laughing and said, 'That can mean everything or nothing, can't it?' I said, 'In this case, Mr. President, nothing.'" Later in the conversation, Roosevelt told Thomas, "I know the South and we've got to be patient."[38]

The issue of local power remains crucial to proper perceptions of the New Deal and the purge of the liberals. Referring to the general failure of left historians to focus on this issue, historian Richard Kirkendall accurately suggested that "[t]he left . . . fails to recognize that Roosevelt had only a limited amount of power that he could use to produce social and economic change. The historian should, I assume, have realistic expectations, but historians who have viewed the New Deal from the left have not. They have assumed that the opportunities for change were much greater than they actually were." In the whole debate, Johnston effectively represented the views of his time, place, and class.

The AAA would be no vehicle for social change if he had anything to say about it. As he told a friend years later, "Unfortunately in its administration AAA as well as many other Federal Agencies saw original purposes aborted to meet the aims of social reformers and economic crack-pots. With every ounce of remedy . . . there was also inflicted a pound of 'reform.'"[39] In that, of course, Johnston's assessment seems unfairly harsh. In contrast to the millions of federal dollars expended on subsidies to producers, including Johnston's plantations, the amount diverted to "crackpot" ideas was pathetically small. As it developed, however, the resolution of the Paragraph 7 dispute turned less on what the liberals wanted than on what was possible.

# Welfare Capitalist

Many crocodile tears have been shed in the North by the Uncle Tom's Cabin type critics about the Southern sharecroppers, overlooking the pathetic hovels and sweatshops in their midst.   —Oscar G. Johnston, 1935

If the Delta planters were mostly cheats, the results of the share-cropper system would be as grievous as reported. But, strange as it may seem to the sainted East, we have quite a sprinkling of decent folk down our way.
—William Alexander Percy, 1941

The most important things we've done here are human.
—Oscar G. Johnston, 1937

**O**ne morning in the fall of 1938, while on his way to his plantation office at Scott, Oscar Johnston met a black sharecropper new to Delta and Pine Land Company. The newcomer, a clear victim of past exploitation which had left him destitute, nearly naked, and cheated out of his few worldly goods, told Johnston "a pathetic tale" of hardship and woe. Johnston, not easily fooled, thought the circumstances leading to his new tenant's status were "indefensible." Fortunately, the sharecropper had arrived, if not at the Promised Land, at least at a place of fair treatment and relative dignity. Johnston's sympathy for the new tenant was consistent with his informed view of the South's land problem. His activities in the purge of the AAA liberals marked him as a Tory in the land-lord-tenant debates of the 1930s. But if he was no liberal on the issue, neither was he reactionary. Fully cognizant of planters' dishonesty to their tenants, he confessed that he sometimes feared "that such practices are the rule rather than the exception." "I once heard a 'planter' say," he told fellow Mississippi planter Will Percy in 1938, "that the most difficult problem he had to solve in connection with his farming operations was to determine the difference between his money and his tenants' money. He frequently found it impossible to make the distinction, and I feel usually erred in his own favor." "Labor," Johnston lamented, "has been, and will probably continue to be, exploited and cheated from time immemorial, and probably will be as long as man is made in his present image."[1]

Despite such dilemmas, Johnston still lodged faith in large-scale operations such as Delta and Pine Land Company. The growth of farm tenancy reinforced that view. During the Great Depression the ranks of tenant farmers swelled by tens of thousands annually. "It does not seem to have occurred to the [government] officials," he observed in 1936, "that this very fact probably in itself condemns the idea of independent small farm units as being uneconomic and unprofitable." Johnston disagreed with the recommendation of an Arkansas state tenancy commission—convened in response to tenant unrest in that state—that various restrictions and penalties be imposed to retard the growth of large-scale corporate and individually owned plantations. Although Johnston feared no such action by the Mississippi legislature, he remained concerned about potential labor unrest that resulted from tenants noting better living conditions on government projects such as those sponsored by the New Deal's Resettlement Administration. "The government is putting rather elaborate houses and other improvements on these properties and is moving on to them poverty stricken tenant farmers," he complained in 1936. "The tendency of this is to dissatisfy tenants on privately owned properties, whose owners cannot, from normally anticipated revenues, afford the character of improvements that are built on government owned farms."[2]

At the southeastern hearings of the president's special committee on farm tenancy in Montgomery, Alabama, in January 1937, Johnston, on behalf of the Delta Chamber of Commerce, endorsed a federal loan program to enable tenants to purchase farms on a long-term basis. Johnston was cheered by lots of other planters, grumbled Tulane University historian Herman Clarence Nixon, who was there, as was Sam Franklin, who headed a socialist cooperative at Hillhouse, Mississippi, and tenant activists Howard Kester and Harry L. Mitchell. Nixon expected "something to be done on account of the campaign for rural reconstruction," as he told William Amberson after the Montgomery hearings, "but I am frankly disturbed lest the voting planters, so dominant in the Black Belt and Delta regions, control public affairs to such an extent that inarticulate tenants realize minimum benefits from the reconstruction program." Johnston acknowledged the necessity of some reforms, as he told a chamber of commerce meeting in Jackson two months later. But he opposed federal purchase of southern cotton lands for the purpose of setting up government-sponsored tenants in competition with "free farmers." The federal government, he said, "is not a proper landlord." "Every shoe clerk cannot become a store owner, every worker cannot become a factory owner," he argued, "and not all tenants can become farm owners or farm successfully by themselves." While Johnston always opposed excessive federal interference in landlord-tenant affairs, he warned fellow planters in a 1935 speech, carried over radio in the cotton belt, to deal fairly with tenants under the AAA program and avoid development of an intolerable social situation.[3]

The landlord and tenant system of the American cotton belt in the Great Depression formed an easy target for social critics. A traditional image of the system suggested a culture defined by race and caste, landless people bound to the land, impoverished minds and bodies, the sort of obscene culture discovered—and eventually exposed—by James Agee's prose and Walker Evans's lens in *Let Us Now Praise Famous Men*. Their 1941 book about three Alabama tenant families in the 1930s joined a host of contemporary studies, novels, government reports, and other descriptive accounts of the human degradation and economic deprivation suffered by tenants in the American South. Said the *Memphis Press-Scimitar* in 1935, "If ever there was a forgotten man it is the tenant farmer."[4]

The very wealth of literature on the subject assured that they would not be forgotten, but it was true that AAA acreage reduction worked a hardship on some tenants. Alger Hiss recalled that in addition to boosting cotton prices, the AAA liberals "wanted also to aid the 'forgotten man,' the tenants and sharecroppers at the bottom of the structure, at least as much proportionately as we aided the landlord." "Especially," he added, "we did not want a program of ours to *worsen* the lot of tenants and croppers." But the purge of the AAA liberals had demonstrated that that agency had not been created for social experimentation. Though it took some heat for its treatment of tenants, the New Deal in fact called attention to economic and social conditions under which the South had languished for generations. *Fortune* perceptively observed in 1935 that "The share cropper is a New Deal figure only because the New Deal discovered him. He existed before. He was a product of a system under which the cotton planter sold his cotton on a free market and bought his food and machinery and clothing on a closed market. But though the present age did not create him the present age will change him into something else. Unless the [mechanical] cotton picker does it first." That same year, AAA Administrator Chester Davis reminded Franklin Roosevelt that southern tenant "conditions . . . as you know, are of long standing and are not the result of the AAA cotton programs."[5]

The long-standing deprivation characteristic of the cotton belt's sharecrop system was mitigated at Delta and Pine Land Company. Johnston once claimed that the plantation's operation rested on a principle that "imposes upon each human being the obligation of fair and honest dealings, as between one another, a just and charitable recognition of rights and privileges of others, and a willingness on the part of each individual to render such assistance as he can to each other individual along life's pathway." Johnston knew, of course, and frankly acknowledged, that such a principle was good business. He confessed in the late 1930s:

Our efforts at improving living standards, living conditions and improving the mental, physical and moral condition of the people employed in the operation of our properties is probably partially prompted by humanitarian motives, but is primarily based upon the rather selfish idea that a happy, well provided for, reasonably moral and healthy group of tenants are more productive than a similarly sized group of under fed, dissatisfied, diseased and immoral group. Our operation is largely through the instrumentality of the "sharecropper system", a system recently much maligned and grossly misunderstood. It is nothing more nor less than a cooperative effort.[6]

Actually, Johnston enhanced a paternalistic system at Delta and Pine Land Company that had characterized the plantation and the cotton belt for years. After assuming the presidency in 1927 he eventually changed tenant contracts to a "half" basis, destroying the fragmented system that had allowed some of the tenants to provide mules and work equipment. Under the half system, the most prevalent in the cotton belt, the company furnished cottonseed, mules, tools, houses, access to woodland for fuel, credit for food, clothing, and other necessities, and half the cost of insect control and fertilizer. The cropper supplied only his labor.

By supplying all work equipment, notably mules, Johnston sacrificed some tenant independence for organizational efficiency. The company concentrated its mules in ten barns that dotted the plantation and required that tenants return them there at days' end. That alone prevented the beasts from being overworked by nocturnal riding and also permitted close supervision by the company's veterinarian, Dr. A. J. Royal, and by the doting Scotsman from Missouri, J. W. McClure. Johnston claimed that under this system, about 75 mules could do the work of 100 owned by tenants. Efficiency reduced feeding costs and no sharecropper suffered delay when a mule died or became incapacitated. During the 1930s Delta Pine's mule acquisitions averaged about 150 annually at a delivered cost of about $230 each; Johnston applied similar efficiency to other work equipment, including planters, threshers, and mowing machines. Mules formed the basis of the company's prewar agricultural equipment, and Johnston economized by inaugurating, in 1939, the annual purchase of young mule colts at about $78 apiece in sufficient numbers so as to eliminate the purchase of older and more expensive animals. The following year he outlined strict procedures for their treatment; their feed, furthermore, came from land taken out of cultivation in compliance with government restriction programs.[7]

Delta and Pine Land Company's labor force essentially comprised about eight or nine hundred black tenant families totaling several thousand workers. Each working tenant cultivated six to eight acres, and a husband-and-wife team working twelve to sixteen acres could plant another six to eight acres for each working family member. A few large families planted as much as fifty to sixty acres, but the plantation average was much less. Credit was closely tied to acreage. Between planting and picking, tenants charged against a "crop account" on which the company advanced an average of fifty cents per month. During the cotton season the company paternalistically guarded tenant health by providing credit coupons every two weeks for tenant acquisitions at plantation stores, but during most of the Great Depression such coupons were redeemable only for food staples during that two weeks. Thereafter, purchases were at tenant discretion. By the early 1940s, however, lavish amounts of cured, smoked, and canned food in most tenant pantries led to a mild relaxation of the two-week policy. Tenants also possessed a ticket book or "TB account," which permitted them to buy from the company stores beyond their regular furnish. The tenants paid their "TB accounts" by working for wages on, for example, feed crops independent of their planted acreage. Like many southern plantations, Delta Pine employed scrip in the lean years of the Great Depression but shifted to a cash-furnish system by World War II.[8]

The company's tenants worked a land characteristic of the Mississippi Delta's monotonously flat but fertile terrain. The big plantation hugging the winding Mississippi River for several miles sat in the far west-central section of the Yazoo–Mississippi Delta—an alluvial four million acres so fertile that one historian called it one of a "few rich enclaves" in a region often cited for poverty. "Outside the Scott office, a few minutes down the dusty roads," wrote *Fortune* graphically in 1937, "the big plantation begins to spread away flatly toward the horizon: the long level fields, which add up to 10,000 acres of cotton and 7,200 acres of feed and forage crops, the clumps and groves of woods— 9,000 acres of fuel—the 7,300 acres of mule lots and idle lands, all networked with creeks and drainage ditches seeping into swampland and dotted with the sharecroppers' cabins about a half a mile apart."[9]

Although operating plans were issued from the unassuming two-storied brick headquarters in the village of Scott, the rambling tens of thousands of acres were decentralized into twelve smaller units, including the noncontiguous Empire Plantation about an hour's drive south of town. Each unit sported a name, some as pedestrian as Fox, Carson, and Young, some as exotic as Lake Vista, Triumph, and Isole. Each unit or subplantation—sizable even by Delta standards—was directed by a resident "unit manager" who got $150 a month and enjoyed such perquisites as a house, telephone, electricity, fuel, running water, and a bonus for a profitable year.[10]

The company also provided incentives for ambitious tenants. When not engaged in his own plot, a sharecropper could cultivate feed and forage crops on company lands for cash wages. Aside from supplying feed for Delta Pine's work stock, tenants thus participated in soil conservation and improvement programs. Day-labor projects in 1937 earned adult males a dollar a day, women and children, seventy-five cents. These tenants, meanwhile, continued to reside in company housing and to have free access to plantation fuel and pasturage. Most families planted a small acreage in corn for which privilege they paid $12.50 per acre and, in return, owned half the corn they cultivated and harvested. In 1937, for example, four thousand acres planted in corn yielded two hundred thousand bushels, half of which belonged to the tenants. Having paid for the rent of their corn acres in cash or the equivalent in corn, Delta Pine sharecroppers could use their remaining produce as they wished. Surpluses were sometimes marketed locally but were generally purchased by the company; more often than not, however, little remained after the croppers fed themselves and their cows, chickens, and hogs. A little might be brewed for home consumption. Meanwhile, the plantation's corn provided meal for company stores and feed for the plantation's thousand or so horses and mules.[11]

Delta and Pine Land Company's sharecroppers also received furnish for their cottonseed when it was ginned in the late summer or fall. They bore half the cost of ginning at one of the company's three gins and sold their half of the seed and lint to the company at prevailing market prices. Further, tenants enjoyed economies of scale generally unavailable to renters or small farmers. For example, the plantation purchased heavy quantities of insecticide and fertilizer at wholesale costs. Both materials were applied intensively, but poisons fell only where indicated and never on the entire plantation. Costs, including that for the Delta Air Corporation, were borne evenly by the company and, on an acreage basis, by all tenants. *Fortune* claimed that calcium arsenate, developed in 1918 to combat the boll weevil, was too costly for most cotton farmers and that a lot of folk in the Bible Belt disapproved of its use because they believed the weevil was God's punishment for sin. "Mr. Johnston," said *Fortune,* "approves of calcium arsenate and can afford it." Plantation and tenant also realized other such benefits in the handling of livestock and work equipment. For tenant and landlord alike, the "half" system was economically superior to working the land on "thirds" or "fourths." All accrued debts were deducted from the tenant's share of the total income, and accounts were balanced near season's end, on "settlement day," usually before Christmas. A second "settlement" followed after all picking was complete, ostensibly leaving the tenants sufficient funds to carry them until a new "furnish" at the start of the next season in March. Delta and Pine Land Company had no written tenant contracts. Such a contract, Johnston told a Resettlement Administration official in 1937, "would be binding only on the Company, the tenant being free to abandon his contract, or to violate it at will, and having no financial responsibility cannot

be either made to observe the terms of the contract or penalized for violation."
Still, without having any contract, 862 families began the 1936 crop year at Scott
in the winter, 862 families picked that same crop in the summer and fall, and
all settled with the company at the end of the year. Even though 1936 was an
outstanding year, 114 families left for whatever reasons, some to Deeson or
Estill, others to new horizons elsewhere.

Tales of planters' dishonesty at settlement time were well known, and croppers often suffered excessive deductions from their accounts. Evidence sug-
gests that such dishonesty did not prevail at Delta and Pine Land Company.
Management did wage a frequently losing battle against those who tried to grab
the tenants' hard-earned cash on settlement day. Croppers eagerly purchased
long-delayed candies and cakes; more serious temptations awaited outside the
paymaster's office, where vendors displayed their wares. Arch Toler watched
the goings-on on settlement day in 1933. "We have so many automobile sales-
men and secondhand automobiles scattered around out front," he observed,
"that it reminds one of a dead mule with a lot of buzzards coming in for a feast."
Despite the company's efforts to the contrary, tenants frequently bought cars
of some description, usually of ancient vintage.[12]

There were other temptations. A nearby community lured tenants to town
by providing bus transportation. Toler could halt access to company property,
and might even rid the plantation of vendors, but there were no guarantees
beyond the company's borders. The company even pursued a pistol salesman,
intending to put him behind bars. And, of course, the lustful siren call of a Greenville prostitute and the potential indulgence in a bootlegger's wares remained
threats to social and economic health. *Fortune* observed in 1937 that, despite
such alluring temptations, "[m]any of D.P.L.'s croppers live what might be called
stable lives, if the word were not totally absurd on their economic level."[13]

Regulations imposed by plantation management constituted only one form
of control. Johnston denied that the system was in any way feudal but readily
acknowledged its paternalism. His management, he said, was *"in loco parentis."*
Such a relationship reflected the South's centuries'-old commitment to standards based on race and caste or what historian Ulrich B. Phillips in 1928 called
"The Central Theme of Southern History." It could stunt development and
human potential, perpetuating dependency. If planters ever doubted the system, they could bolster both their arguments and conscience by pointing to
the dependency of the croppers. They argued that blacks, for example, were
sexually careless or that they would dismantle outhouses for fuel instead of going
to the trouble of getting free firewood from the plantation woodland. Even if
the tenant proved sufficiently thrifty to acquire land himself, he was likely to
appear later seeking tenant status. "Who besides a southern farmer will share

equally in a partnership the proceeds of his business and put up everything, and that in advance?" an official of the Mississippi State Experiment Station asked rhetorically. "What other class of employer furnishes free shelter, fuel, water, garden, and pasture space?"[14]

Paternalism served as an effective and pacifying method of social control. Perhaps this partially explained why landlord-tenant conflict in northeastern Arkansas failed to plague the Yazoo–Mississippi Delta. Northeastern Arkansas sharecroppers were often white, some of whom had migrated to the area as lumbermen before the timber played out and the land and those on it fell victim to the vicissitudes of the cotton culture. With a tradition of greater economic and social independence than black sharecroppers in other areas of the South, these tenants seemingly had more in common with industrial labor in the North. By contrast, cotton tenancy such as found in the Mississippi Delta constituted, suggested Oscar Bledsoe, an influential planter, "a system of paternal guardianship which has existed for generations and is predicated on the existence of a race which requires management and in turn presents a responsibility."[15]

Such guardianship meant disputes could be settled and censorship imposed. Delta and Pine Land Company had its own policeman, who "isn't bothered very often," said *Fortune* cryptically, "but when he is the bother is apt to be violent." The plantation had "four or five homicides annually." Less seriously, if a tenant absconded with his furnish and belongings, leaving an outstanding debt, other planters might cooperate in locating the offender. In one instance, a planter from Drew, Mississippi, J. M. Yeager, wanted to apprehend a tenant who had left a large debt; he was more concerned, he told Johnston, about "the effect that it may have on others with the same notion," than about the debt. Legal infractions were essentially an internal matter.

Although paternalism imposed restraints on tenants' lives, it could also prove highly beneficial. In one case, when an Illinois Central System's Yazoo and Mississippi Valley passenger train struck and killed a milk cow owned by a Delta Pine sharecropper, the company intervened to obtain a partial settlement from the railroad. True, the tenant had owed a balance to the company for the purchase of the cow, but since the tenant may have been at fault, he might have received nothing without company intervention. Since tenants often moved from place to place, from one season to another—"with or without reason," according to Johnston—many failed to receive their share of federal subsidy benefits for which they had to make formal application. In early 1937, Johnston, who believed he treated tenants fairly, but regarded most as "utterly irresponsible," lent his support to an attempt to get USDA to try to smooth the procedure for tenants' just compensation. Such was all the more necessary since tenants kept no records and often left no forwarding address but might later make claim for benefits. AAA counsel figured the suggestion was not feasible under prevailing law, but the agency did plan on getting all benefit claims in 1937 "signed and acted upon" in advance of seasonal tenant migration. Whatever its faults, and there were many, the sharecrop system also provided the necessities of life on a year-round basis, despite the fact that cotton production required only about 125 days of labor per year.[16]

Paternalism even emanated from sources other than plantation management. An active religious life had long marked the black experience—slave and free—in the American South. Delta and Pine Land Company encouraged religious activity by financially bolstering at least some of its black churches until they became self-supporting. More than thirty such churches dotted the plantation by the mid-1920s. The Reverend Ad Wimbs, a leading black minister who edited the plantation's well-circulated weekly newspaper, the *Cotton Farmer,* was very likely quite proud of his people's social advance. "Under the persuasive influence of white people," he declared with unwitting irony in 1923, "peace among my people has been so improved that now serious disagreements are but few."[17]

A conservative attitude also seemed to prevail during the Great Depression. In 1937 nonresident black clergymen, representing nearly twenty churches on various units of Delta and Pine Land Company, organized a nondenominational pastoral conference. Aside from promoting "the Christian Religion and its activities," the ministers viewed themselves as a liaison between tenants and management in "perpetuating a spirit of true fellowship that has always existed among the white and black races all these years." These clergymen were very likely disturbed by tenant problems in Arkansas and, as a group, pledged themselves to "watch for and guard against all agitators or foreign elements who attempt to use the weak of our group as a gate way into this community with far-fetched organizations to unionize our people in such organizations that will disturb the peace and harmony of the two races in this Mississippi Delta." The pastors petitioned the plantation management "to close up all places on Sunday"—presumably business and pleasure establishments—and to vest the conference with authority to censor all periodicals distributed on the property. Management found little need to intervene directly in the moral life of the tenants and, probably because of the frequency of common law unions, required no marriage licenses of prospective tenant families.[18]

If the lifestyle promoted by black spiritual leaders served the traditions of the South, it also contributed to social health and stability. Church activities included attendance rivalry between various preachers and congregations and a committee assignment for most tenant women. While Sunday school attendance was slack, tenant families crowded the plantation's crude frame churches on Sunday nights. "Naturally," wrote George F. Paul in the *Southern Work-*

*man* in 1925, "the churches play an important part in the life of the entire community: It would be difficult to suppress the Negro's craving for spiritual expression." The choirs of Delta and Pine Land's black churches frequently met "for a big sing," Paul said.

> All up and down the broad Mississippi River at the plantation landings on Sunday afternoons in certain seasons of the year great throngs can be seen down at the water's edge. A hush comes over them. The choir leader starts some time-honored song such as "Yes, we shall gather at the river," and the strong and harmonious voices take up the soul-stirring melody. Then comes prayer and the pastor takes by the hand one of the waiting candidates for baptism and leads him out into the silent water until the chosen spot is reached. Following the rite of baptism another spiritual is sung such as "Hallelujah, 'tis done." It is a special occasion for the Negro workers, a time when old acquaintances are renewed and new friendships are formed, a time when the heart chords are tuched [*sic* ] by the spiritual significance of the rites of baptism and of the promise of being born again.[19]

A dozen years later, *Fortune* found that Delta and Pine Land's black tenants perceived God as "white-skinned," a contrast to Broadway's Depression-era hit, *Green Pastures*, in which "De Lawd" was black.[20]

Delta Pine's welfare capitalism rested on the conviction, as Oscar Johnston pointed out, that a healthy and well-cared-for tenant was a productive tenant. Referring to a specific health program, George Paul in 1925 wrote, "The increased cotton production of a few families repays many times the expense." Business pragmatism seemed to require such programs. Lant Salsbury, the plantation's president for sixteen years, believed that during his initial season about 80 percent of the sharecroppers suffered the debilitating effects of malaria. Swamp clearance, annual cabin-to-cabin inspections for stagnant water, and instructions for proper use of mosquito netting supplied by the management reduced the incidence of the disease. But poor sanitation and poor health facilities plagued the entire cotton belt, crippling Mississippi's rural black population. Most serious were social diseases, especially syphilis and gonorrhea, but pellagra and typhoid also posed significant health problems. In fact, before the mid-1930s, plantation deaths exceeded births.[21]

An epidemic of any of these diseases could destroy a labor force. Johnston attacked the problem of syphilis and gonorrhea shortly after he became responsible for Delta Pine's sharecroppers. According to O. C. Wenger, acting assistant surgeon of the U.S. Public Health Service in Hot Springs, Arkansas, Johnston was "well informed regarding problems of public health in rural communities," tutored as he was as an army officer and by experience with Mississippi Valley floods. He understood, said Wenger in 1929, that health protection and maintenance in a labor force were more cost-effective than throwing money at illness. Over the opposition of the plantation's general manager, Jesse Fox, a shrewd cotton man himself, and that of the unit managers, Johnston announced a full-scale assault on the disease in the late 1920s. He ordered the managers to gather their sharecroppers in their plantation churches at an appointed time. Such health issues require "great tact and persuasion," said Dr. Wenger. "Any measures of compulsion might mean the desertion of entire family groups from the plantation." Johnston could persuade. On each unit, in well-measured phrases, Johnston patronizingly explained their relationship. "When you make money, I make money," he told them. "When you don't, I don't; when I don't, you don't." The croppers agreed. "Yassah." "Dat's so." "Dat's de truf." "Ain't no doubt about dat." The company's mules were healthy and well fed, Johnston explained; he did not propose, he said, "to have a $250 mule at one end of a plow and a syphilitic nigra at the other." "You ought," he told them, "to want to be as good as a mule."[22]

Initial testing for gonorrhea was abandoned, but Wassermann tests administered in May 1929 proved positive on nearly a quarter of the plantation's black residents. Plantation officers and several medical professionals, including Dr. Wenger of the U.S. Public Health Service, Dr. H. C. Ricks, Mississippi's state epidemiologist, Dr. I. I. Pogue, Delta Pine's resident physician, and state and county health officials, along with nurses involved in the survey, held a conference to determine the next step. Illiteracy ruled out educational films and brochures; health professionals and plantation officials would have to persuade afflicted tenants of needed treatment. Also a budget was discussed and therapies proposed. It was understood that treatment would be free to tenants, that it could not hamper plantation work schedules, and that no tenant would be compelled to undergo therapy. In fact, local doctors reported that no tenants returned for a second shot of mercury, a painful injection in the hip. The medical team resorted to two hundred abdominal mercury rubs per patient, so that while following mules or chopping cotton, sufficient mercury would be absorbed through the skin. The so-called "sock method" was rejected because most tenants went barefoot. Dr. Wenger concluded that syphilis might have been a greater southern public health issue than pellagra, hookworm, or malaria.

Between 1930 and 1932 alone, Delta Pine's medical staff treated nearly a thousand syphilis cases, the expense borne equally by the company and by a grant from the Julius Rosenwald Fund. Under the program, the company acquired the service of a registered nurse, Pauline Hendricks, who joined the medical staff in 1928. With federal funds the Mississippi State Health Department subsequently held clinics from time to time. Unfortunately, such efforts failed to materially reduce the incidence or percentage of social disease, primarily because of infection from external sources, notably Greenville prostitutes. The anti-syphilis campaign did, however, uncover other treatable diseases, improve the general health of the labor force, and establish the company as a national leader in the fight for better health standards in an industrial organization. According to Jonathan Daniels, the North Carolina newspaper editor who visited Scott in 1937, "Mr. Johnston is entitled to almost all the credit for the first large private campaign in the United States to eliminate syphillis from a group."[23]

Efforts to improve the health of the plantation's sharecroppers found even greater success in other areas. For example, the company experimented with Atabrine and quinine for treatment of malaria, and Atabrine for its prevention, and with typhoid prophylaxis for immunization against typhoid. The latter effort enjoyed particular success, with the last typhoid death recorded in the early 1930s. At least by 1925 each tenant house possessed an uncontaminated water source, and by 1937 tenant cabins boasted outhouses—which *Fortune* termed "a luxury in much of the cotton belt"—sufficiently removed from water sources. Furthermore, in 1936 alone, three thousand tenants received typhoid vaccinations; eight cases of the disease developed, but none proved fatal. Meanwhile, measles, diphtheria, and scarlet fever were also eliminated as causes of death among the company's labor force.[24]

Since diseases such as pellagra resulted from diet deficiencies, Delta and Pine Land Company encouraged production of vitamin-laden crops for home consumption. Dr. Wenger was surprised to find poor diets among Delta Pine's sharecroppers during his Wasserman survey in 1929. Yet in tenant cabins he found phonograph players "and other nonessentials." Management efforts at diet improvement had failed, he said. Wenger also found that much of the tenants' monthly cash allowance wound up not on their tables but in old cars. Fortunately, things improved in the thirties. Each cropper family had opportunity to cultivate its own rent-free vegetable garden, and the company carried on an educational program designed to eradicate pellagra. Home-grown potatoes, string beans, turnip greens, green corn, cabbage, and sweet potatoes from the sharecroppers' quarter-acre or half-acre gardens supplemented other staples such as eggs, milk, poultry, and occasional veal and fresh pork. From company stores croppers obtained self-rising flour, macaroni, molasses, salt pork, and canned salmon. The company ground cornmeal from the tenants' own crops at the plantation's gristmill, charging only a small portion of the meal for the service. In the 1930s the company installed a meat-curing and cold-storage facility for tenant use. While the company charged a small fee, Johnston did not envision the facility as a revenue producer but simply as an encouragement to tenant self-sufficiency. Declining to purchase a large quantity of dried sweet potatoes for tenant use, Johnston declared in 1932 that "we are learning in the school of necessity to live at home."[25]

In cooperation with an outside agency, the plantation employed two black graduates of Alcorn A & M College to instruct tenants in home economics, farm mechanics, and poultry and livestock production. Under the supervision of these teachers, the tenants "put up" thousands of quarts of foodstuff and several thousand jars of preserved meat. The company provided a substantial number of the quart jars.[26]

The company inaugurated vocational education and sought to hire a full-time teacher to instruct both adults and children in domestic science. The plantation got a federally funded "Smith-Hughes" man in 1939 who, with a female assistant, taught how to preserve food. Management encouraged tenants to cultivate gardens and to improve their diet, and freely provided a substantial quantity of brewers' yeast as a means of reducing the incidence of pellagra, a plague of the South. That disease peaked at Delta Pine in the late twenties or early thirties, averaging about 365 cases a year. A decade later the disease had been virtually eradicated. Such results were impressive. To a northern flour mill representative the plantation's program stood as "the first and most outstanding example of diet-education and its benefits in connection with large groups that I have seen."[27]

To provide competent health care for the labor force, the plantation long employed a resident physician and several nurses to staff the company's thirty-bed hospital. The wooden facility remained rather crude by modern standards. In fact, to Jonathan Daniels, the editor of the *Raleigh News & Observer* who visited the area in 1937 gathering material for *A Southerner Discovers the South,* Delta and Pine Land's hospital "seemed of another world from the tiny gleaming hospital" established at a Tennessee Valley Authority construction camp he had visited. Still, the plantation hospital "seemed comfortable and it smelled antiseptic," he decided. "And it was a great deal nearer TVA's hospital than to the medical and obstetric practices which too generally prevail among the rural black folk of Mississippi." The annual cost for the medical facilities totaled about twenty thousand dollars, the cost shared by the company, tenants, and wage laborers. Each tenant family contributed approximately one dollar per cotton acre, and medical services included periodic physical examinations. The company purchased an ambulance and contracted with Greenville physicians for optometric, dental, and surgical services.[28]

Improvements in medical services and diets between 1929 and 1939 accompanied an increase in the plantation's birthrate. In that decade annual births surpassed annual deaths, with the birthrate jumping about 25 percent—a rate substantially above that of the surrounding county. The resident physician, Dr. I. I. Pogue, encouraged black sharecropper women to have their babies in the company's hospital by charging twenty dollars for delivery in the home. In 1936,

Pogue delivered ninety-seven babies; others were probably born at home, assisted by midwives who charged ten dollars for their services. All this oversight added up to good business, of course, and Johnston knew it. Observing medical advances in the tenants' behalf, Johnston's Washington colleague, Paul Porter, on a visit to the plantation, "accused Oscar of having a social conscience." Porter remembered Johnston's reply: "Social conscience, hell, . . . this is just sound economics."[29]

In addition to health services, the company maintained a recreation center for tenant use. In 1940 the plantation built a recreational facility, along with a lodge and theater where tenants could enjoy movies and stage plays and other performances. For five months each year the sharecroppers' children attended seven county schools scattered about the plantation. With black advice, the white county superintendent hired black teachers to staff the relatively crude structures.[30]

Delta and Pine Land Company's welfare capitalism extended to tenant housing. The plantation's housing was superior to the usual sharecroppers' shacks that blighted the land during the Great Depression and pre-Depression eras. Better housing apparently preceded Johnston's presidency; log structures had yielded to more accommodating houses that sported windowpanes and substantial roofs and floors. In 1937 *Fortune* deemed the company housing "better than average . . . with tight-fitting walls, grooved and tongued floors. Screening isn't provided because the croppers normally punch holes in the screens to let the dogs in or throw the slops out." Actually, the off-ground cypress structures were crowded, their architecture usually of the "shot-gun" variety—two rooms in a row with a door at each end, or four-room type for larger families. Jonathan Daniels found Delta Pine's cabins much less attractive than those on the government cooperative at Dyess, Arkansas, though more substantial than those at the socialist cooperative up the road at Hillhouse, Mississippi.[31]

Delta and Pine Land Company had long attracted national and even international attention. Many agriculturists and others made the pilgrimage to Scott to observe the company's operations. Stories featuring the plantation or research on its tenants appeared in such diverse publications as the *Progressive Farmer* and the *American Journal of Tropical Medicine.* Though it often focused on industrial organizations, Henry Luce's *Fortune* featured Johnston and his company in its March 1937 issue; the business magazine concluded that one "very important factor in Mr. Johnston's success is undoubtedly the intangible of his treatment of labor." Two months later, Jonathan Daniels stopped in Scott for a chat with America's most visible planter. In his quest of the South, the North Carolina editor evidently regarded Johnston and his sprawling enterprise worthy of discovery. Above the vast expanse of the flat Mississippi Delta, Johnston stood as a commanding figure. Daniels' research notes, however, describe him as "pot-bellied—double chin—near sighted—getting bald—merry and has, according to his friends, the gift of lucid expression—he himself says he has no prejudices." By the time *A Southerner Discovers the South* came off the press more than a year later, Johnston's balding, pot-bellied, double-chinned physique had vanished. Now he was simply "a merry man. And though near sighted, he sees the cotton South clearly in every detail. His charm lies in his conversation, wise, lively and lucid." Russell Lord, the Maryland writer who himself had visited Oscar before the New Deal, and who would later write the acclaimed *The Wallaces of Iowa*, told Daniels he liked his portrait of Johnston. Lord had been "enormously impressed," he said, "both by Oscar and by the way in which you can't even hint at the truth about a man like that in a family periodical. I saw him rather often in Washington when I was there," recalled Lord. "He was losing the sight of one eye. Said he didn't give a damn; he'd seen all he wanted to out of that eye, anyway."[32]

Johnston was a good advocate of the sharecrop system at Delta and Pine Land Company. Daniels was not totally convinced. Oscar was certain that neither the privately funded socialist Delta Cooperative Farm up at Hillhouse, Mississippi, nor the government's more elaborate experimental operation across the river at Dyess, Arkansas, would lift the sharecropper from his squalor. When Johnston had returned from Kentucky, where Martha had undergone surgery in 1936, there was dark and hostile talk among some planters about shoving the socialist cooperative "in the river." Oscar had been around long enough to know that night meetings and nightriding had a way of backfiring. A few phone calls calmed troubled waters, Johnston telling his friends to make no martyrs. "Then," he told Daniels, "I went up to see Sam Franklin [director of the Delta Cooperative] and I invited him down here. He's a nice young fellow. I think he was a little surprised. He said the other planters hadn't been so hospitable."

"Johnston laughed when he told me and said, 'I laughed then. I told him, "I want you near where people can see your failure and not far off where missionaries can make it sound like success."'"

The ingredients for success, according to Oscar, were properly mixed and blended at corporate enterprises such as Delta and Pine Land Company. There the little farmer could benefit by quality direction, management, and marketing, things normally beyond the reach of the small independent operator. "Neither the Agrarians nor the Socialists," Daniels wrote later, "would agree with such an idea. And, though neither Socialist nor Agrarian, I also disagree. Delta and Pine under Oscar Johnston proved only, it seemed to me, that Oscar Johnston is in charge at Delta and Pine. But he is man and not a system." Daniels added that "I suspect that he would be quite successful as the director of a cooperative or as papa in [a] paternalistic colony."

Sitting at the soda fountain at Delta Pine's commissary, Johnston gave his North Carolina guest a crash course in the economics and sociology of cotton culture. He told Daniels he was not so sure the tenant was "so bad off," that the tenant might be worse off as a landowner. In Friars Point, he said, independent businessmen went under more often than independent farmers. Daniels had his doubts about the sociologically scientific quality of Johnston's observations. "But isn't the farmer's insecurity growing?" he asked. "Especially in the South? What will happen to the cotton farmer in this country when the cotton picker is perfected?"

That was a question Johnston had thought about long and hard. After looking over one "ingenious contrivance" developed by the Rust brothers, John and Mack, Johnston thought that while it might have value in some places, it would not be adaptable for the Mississippi Valley. "You will understand that I do not begin to prophesy that a cotton picker will not be developed," he had told the British Fine Spinners in 1935, "but I do say with confidence that there is nothing now developed which, in my judgment, will substitute for the present method of picking." He was also on hand, along with Arch Toler and many others, at the experiment station in Stoneville on a hot day in August 1936 when the socialist Rust brothers demonstrated, with great publicity, a version of a tractor-pulled spindle picker. The results were mixed. But even if successful, while some wanted it, many did not. The *Jackson Daily News* wanted to see the picker, along with blueprints, submerged in the Mississippi River; Toler hoped it wouldn't work at all; Memphis boss Edward Crump claimed that prohibitive legislation could pass in Tennessee. *Time* noted Johnston's presence at Stoneville, claiming "He gets along well with his 3,000 Negroes, [and] wants to keep them. Newshawks . . . crowded around him last week to hear what he thought of the mechanical menace. Grower Johnston was skeptical but not scornful." If the machine is a success, said Oscar, "it will be the death knell for family-size farms and for tenants." Robert K. Straus added in *Harper's* that if successful, the Rust brothers' machines "might conceivably change the whole way of life of millions of people in the cotton belt, bringing about an economic revolution comparable to that which was brought about long ago by Eli Whitney's cotton gin." As late as 1942 Johnston thought a perfected picker would be developed, revolutionizing production and displacing workers. He also feared such a picker would enhance the politically prejudiced move to adopt tax policies aimed at breaking up big plantations.[33]

Oscar's soda-fountain discourse included his answer to the journalist's question about the picker. "Mr. Johnston took off his pince-nez glasses and rubbed them clean with the handkerchief—both the lenses that help his squinting nearsightedness and the tinted glasses above them in defense against the Mississippi sun," wrote Daniels. "Deliberately he put them back on. He regarded me through them."

Johnston said he had seen every mechanical picker in the public arena, then launched into a detailed dissertation explaining and defending the value of family-based cotton picking. He argued, among other things, that the irregular maturation of the boll lent itself to day-by-day selective harvest. Daniels persisted, "But suppose a picker should be perfected?" Daniels recorded Johnston's response:

> He shrugged his round shoulders. "The present method of farming would shortly become obsolete. The small family operators could not afford to own a picking machine. Nor could they afford the luxury of paying the owner of such a machine to pick their cotton since to do so would require either a cash outlay or a payment in kind. Land owners who now rent considerable tracts of land to millions of farm families, who rent either for cash or a share of the crop, would discontinue the renting system and proceed to farm large areas themselves using mechanized equipment including the picker. I should estimate that within five years after a successful picker was developed at least a million farmers, now engaged in the production of cotton, would be out of employment, their buying power would be destroyed with the consequent economic disturbance not only to the South but throughout the nation."
>
> And that, I thought would be freedom, freedom again for black men in the Delta, where sharecropping succeeded slavery when freedom turned out to be another name for hunger. The Yankee was ready to end slavery; but he was not ready to make freedom. And he was afraid of the only plan which might have fulfilled the purpose of his fighting: Forty acres and a mule. All my life I had heard those acres and mules referred to in derisive disdain and in all my life it was the only proposal I had ever heard which might have solved the agricultural sickness of the South. It seemed too late when I talked to Oscar Johnston. Already a new freedom threatened and men shivered at the thought of it.

As he left Scott, Daniels reflected on what he had seen and heard. "Beyond the mere counting of profits," he thought, "it seemed to me that Johnston had a sense of the integration of man and animal and earth. Definitely he had shown that cotton growing could be made profitable without dispossessing the people who had grown dependent—too dependent—on it for a sorry sustenance."[34]

That sense of the integration translated into a rapport Johnston enjoyed with the black tenants. Paul Porter rode horseback over the plantation with Johnston during a visit to Scott. One morning they stopped at a tenant cabin for breakfast. "Let's stop here at Auntie so and so's place," Porter recalled Oscar saying, "she fixes a mighty fine breakfast." Also, sometimes tenants complained about a matter directly to Johnston, and his action on their behalf stirred understandable resentment among some unit managers. Still, black suspicion lingered. Mississippi writer David Cohn thought Delta whites, indeed most white Southerners, deluded themselves into thinking their close association with blacks gave them an insight into black life. "The truth is, in my opinion," wrote Cohn, "that most Southern whites have only the faintest comprehension of the inner lives of Negroes which remain forever secret and alien to them." Oscar lamented wistfully late in his career that though he had tried hard to break down black suspicion, he had "only succeeded to a very small degree." The black, said Johnston, "has been 'gypped' so often and so consistent[l]y during the last 50 or 60 years by the white man that he has no confidence and seems to feel that the planters are constantly and consistently trying to take some advantage of him."[35]

Some of Johnston's tenants became subjects in a series of experiments conducted by a team of scientists in the spring and summer of 1939. Led by Dr. David B. Dill, professor of industrial physiology at Harvard University, the team studied the sharecroppers' health and strength under carefully controlled scientific conditions. Dill's experiments, published in the *Harvard Alumni Bulletin* and elsewhere, suggested that good diet and excellent medical care accounted for the low death rate and superior health of the black community at Delta and Pine Land Company. Picking up the story of these "Superior Sharecroppers," the *New York Times* saw added significance: "The Harvard experiments not only teach a valuable physiological lesson but [also] point the sociological moral that working for an enlightened company on a sharecropping basis need not be another form of slavery."[36]

The point was well taken. While Johnston wanted no serious challenge to prevailing conditions, welfare capitalism seemed to him the most reasonably equitable system available. "We have felt that the prejudice which we find frequently against so-called 'corporate farming' is due to lack of information," he once told the U.S. Senate Committee on Agriculture and Forestry in a prepared statement. "The corporate farm, operated as is ours, is nothing more nor less than a 'cooperative operation' indicated by reason of economy, social security, and hygiene."[37]

Such prejudice prompted suggestions in Congress that landlords be forced to rent their lands to their tenants. "As a matter of course," Johnston warned,

> the landlord can rent his land to tenants for a cash rental, and allow all of the government payments to go to the tenants. As a matter of course, the landlord will take into consideration the government payments in determining the rent which the tenant will pay. The rent being fixed as a cash rental will work a hardship upon the tenant when the cotton price is low. The rent will always be made high enough to give the landlord full returns in case the price of cotton is high. Permission to the tenant to pay his rent "in kind" automatically ties the amount of rent to the price and quantity of production, and is, we submit[,] the fairest measure.[38]

The efficient welfare capitalism at Delta and Pine Land Company may well have accounted for the relatively low annual turnover of sharecroppers. In 1928 the turnover was about 20 percent; by 1940 Johnston reported that his 821 sharecropper families at Delta and Pine Land Company for the 1939 season average 13.4 years on the plantation. Of that group, nearly three-quarters had gardens, nearly 90 percent had poultry and hogs, more than half owned their own cows, and about a third had an automobile, though the latter statistic was probably high. As Johnston told a Resettlement Administration official in 1937,

> I know from actual and intimate familiarity with the business of farming, both here in the Delta and in the hill sections of Mississippi, which are identical with farming in Georgia, Alabama and the Carolinas, that the average and reasonably thrifty or industrious tenant, farming on this property, in accordance with the system above outlined, is more comfortably housed, better provided for from the standpoint of medical attention and hygiene, better fed, better clothed and enjoys a higher percentage of luxuries, such as radios, automobiles[,] etc., than do cash renters or the average type of owner-operator, owning and operating a so-called "family size" farm.

And Johnston's declaration in his annual report for 1935 that Delta Pine's "tenants are apparently in good spirits and carrying on their work in a most satisfactory manner" was not only common, and in his mind probably true, but also in marked contrast to labor unrest in northeastern Arkansas.[39]

The Agricultural Adjustment Administration's acreage-reduction program displaced few if any tenants at Delta and Pine Land Company. Johnston curtailed the plantation's modest experiments with certain aspects of mechanized cotton production and in 1933 reverted almost wholly to traditional mule farming. The plantation remained essentially unmechanized in field implements throughout the New Deal until labor shortages occasioned by World War II forced a change not only in company practice but in American agriculture as well. Instead of "tractoring" tenants off the land, the New Deal actually retarded mechanization at the Scott plantation.[40]

In September 1933 Johnston drafted a proposal for Delta Pine's participation in the AAA's reduction plans for 1934. The document was, he told Arch Toler, "intended purely as a tentative suggestion which indicates my ideas." Under the plan no mechanization, including tractors, would be employed in cotton production. Tenants would be compensated for reduced acreage by an increased allowance at company stores and free use of company land for food production for both home consumption and local sale. Further, release time occasioned by reduced acreage would permit employment on or off the plantation. Should compliance with the acreage-reduction program idle some tenants, they would be allowed free residence in company housing, free access to plantation woods for fuel, and would receive hiring priority for company crop production on a wage basis. It was an honorable plan. Beyond the proposed schedule, Johnston thought that the inclusion of tenants in AAA subsidies, so crucial to reformers, was misplaced. In 1937, he told Cully Cobb, at the time director of the AAA's southern division, that he didn't particularly care what federal monies were funneled to tenants as long as payments to planters justified their participation in reduction programs. Johnston elaborated: "Being a landlord it would probably be worse than useless for me to undertake to point out that payments to tenants during the last three years, under the cotton program, have, in the case of sharecroppers, been nothing more nor less than mere donations, wholly without justification upon any other ground than that they were made to increase the buying power of the sharecropper. The sharecropper shifts no land from cotton to soil improving crops, he contributes nothing toward the success of the program and he sacrifices nothing."[41]

Still, Johnston's tenants who farmed reduced acreages received AAA payments, which averaged nearly $60 annually. In fact, for the period 1933 to 1942, an average of 844 tenant families farmed an average of 9,180 acres of cotton and were paid in goods, cash, and government payments averaging $571.78 annually. This total did not include free rent, fuel, kitchen gardens, and pasturage for pigs, cows, and chickens. One exemplary tenant, Lonnie Fair, was a good advertisement not only for Delta and Pine Land Company but also for welfare capitalism. The head of a family of seven, and a Delta Pine tenant since the early 1920s, Fair cultivated, with his family, more than 20 acres in cotton, 5 in corn. For approximately 125 days annually, Lonnie Fair began before dawn and ended after sundown, and the company's land and his family's labor yielded well over a bale to the acre. The Fairs tended their garden and their menagerie of cows, pigs, dogs, hens, chickens, and one horse (no automobile). They spread their dinner table with bread, stewed apples, salt pork, hog sausages, sweet potatoes, okra, molasses, and butter beans. Saturday afternoons might find them socializing in Scott, Sundays worshipping in the Jerusalem Baptist Church. In 1936 Lonnie Fair earned slightly more than $1,000 in credit and cash. If it is true, as *Fortune* admitted, "As U.S. sharecroppers go, he is a paragon of good fortune," it may also be true that he and others like him were an alternative to the crushing poverty of southern rural life in the Great Depression. "We invite a comparison of the social, physical, and economic status of the 821 families on this property," Johnston boldly told a Senate committee in 1940, "with like conditions surrounding any other group of farmers or industrial laborers in America."[42]

If Lonnie Fair was not Erskine Caldwell's Jeeter Lester of *Tobacco Road*, nor among the impoverished tenants described by James Agee and Walker Evans in *Let Us Now Praise Famous Men*, critics remained. Corporate plantations,

Delta and Pine Land Company in particular, provided "no answer to tenancy," complained one such critic in 1937. "Though the tenants on D.P.L. plantation are more prosperous than the workers on the less efficient surrounding plantations, they are, by the same token, more restricted." Another critic of the plantation system in general argued in 1934: "The normal earnings of a man and wife, if both work as tenants on a one-horse cotton farm, would probably average $260 a year in cash value. However, they pay about half of their cotton in rent, use the corn for their stock, and eat the potatoes, peas, and sorghum which they grow along with the cotton. As a result very little cash is handled. They manage to live on the advances, or by borrowing for food and clothing and permitting their crop to be taken in satisfaction of the debt. It becomes very largely a paper loss or gain." One government study found: "[E]ven when croppers and share tenants clear anything on the year's farming, they usually exhaust their resources within a few months and are destitute again at the beginning of the crop year. The landlord has to advance them credit to finance the new crop and to provide for their living expenses until the crop is sold. The average tenant in 1937 was advanced $85 for his share of crop expenses and $104 to live on while the crop was maturing. Thus the average tenant borrowed around $200."[43]

This cycle was occasionally broken, at least according to some planters. Johnston's arguments were bolstered by that of fellow Mississippi planter Will Percy who, relative to his time and place, was regarded as sort of a neighborhood liberal on matters of race and tenancy. On his Trail Lake Plantation, his unskilled 124 tenant families earned an average $427.64 in 1936, aside from other benefits such as housing, fuel, and the like. Said Percy: "Our method of earning a living seems to me to offer as humane, just, self-respecting, and cheerful a method of earning a living as human beings are likely to devise. I watch the limber-jointed, oily black, well-fed, decently clothed peasants on Trail Lake and feel sorry for the telephone girls, the clerks in chain stores, the office help, the unskilled laborers everywhere—not only for their poor and fixed wage but for their slave routine, their joyless habits of work, and their insecurity." Oscar Bledsoe, a prominent Greenwood planter and Staple Cotton Cooperative Association president, had likewise believed he enjoyed rapport with his workers. Tenant applications well exceeded his plantation's needs, he told an Arkansas planter in April 1942. "I find that the negro sharecropper reacts very favorably to any reasonable and open business management and responds efficiently in his work, which makes the plantation system a great pleasure under these conditions." Alarmed at the attacks on the plantation, Bledsoe produced a four-page tract in which he declared, "I believe in the plantation system and will fight for its preservation." Plantation tenancy was not always so idyllic, of course, and its worst elements were often muted in the arguments of its defenders. Still, Sherwood Eddy, a Christian socialist who had helped establish cooperative farms in Mississippi, including the one in the Delta at Hillhouse headed by Sam Franklin, may have said more than he intended when he claimed in 1942 that Oscar Johnston's plantations "are purely capitalistic money-making schemes *although I think his workers are well paid.*"[44]

The visibility of Johnston's gargantuan plantation invited scrutiny in the reform days of the New Deal. In the mid-1930s Delta Pine became the object of an investigation by the socialist League for Industrial Democracy and the Tyronza, Arkansas, Socialist Party. Under the leadership of Dr. William R. Amberson, a physiologist by profession and a socialist by temperament, the survey turned up numerous alleged landlord violations of AAA contracts in Arkansas. Apparently, after examining Delta and Pine Land Company settlement sheets and perhaps talking with some company sharecroppers, the Amberson committee found Johnston's administration of his AAA contracts fairer than that of other plantations examined. A government committee, investigating complaints of the Amberson committee, reported to the AAA that since "no complaints" were lodged against Delta and Pine Land Company, "this case was not investigated." Although the Southern Tenant Farmers' Union accused Johnston of contract violation, union spokesman Harry L. Mitchell in 1935 declared, "Mr. Johnston's violation was mild compared with those which have occurred elsewhere." Mitchell claimed to Wallace aide Paul Appleby that even though Johnston authored Section 7 of the contract, his own plantation violated it; Delta Pine, he said, had thirty to thirty-five fewer families in 1934 than the year before. "They evicted very few families (and may have had just cause in all cases)," said Mitchell, "but they failed to fill up the plantation when other families left voluntarily." Mitchell added, "We have no particular animus against Mr. Johnston, who has aided us in our work on several occasions."[45]

In any event, in 1936 Johnston reported to the British Fine Spinners that "[l]abor conditions with us are excellent. We have not yet been troubled by the 'professional organizers', or the socialistic agitators who have been creating more or less disturbance in other sections of the cotton belt." Johnston added that in the troubled area of northeastern Arkansas whites were plentiful. None of Delta Pine's sharecroppers had shown inclination to join the tenant union, he said, members of which were rarely black. The racial composition of the workforce was significant to Johnston. Although he preferred whites if the plantation was sufficiently small to allow personal selection, he told Jonathan Daniels in 1937 that "[t]he Negro is more amenable to discipline."[46]

In 1943 both the Delta Council, a planter-dominated betterment agency, and the National Cotton Council monitored union organizing among tenants,

including such activities across the river in Arkansas. On one Arkansas plantation, the Congress of Industrial Organizations (CIO) demanded landlord recognition, just the sort of thing feared in the Delta. Explosive social changes
involved class and economic status and meshed with civil rights for blacks, a
movement just over the horizon in the early 1940s. Such was evident when
Dorothy Lee Black, office manager of the Delta Council, attended an integrated STFU meeting in Memphis in 1942. "One particularly hysterical white
woman blamed her economic status on the 'rich planters,'" she reported to
Walter Sillers, president of the Delta Council and Mississippi state legislator,
"and remarked that everyone in the room was in the same boat 'except that
woman' (pointing very definitely at me) 'who certainly is dressed like one of those
Mississippi plutocrats.'" After another meeting later that day, Mrs. Black reported that an American Federation of Labor spokesman from Atlanta preached
civil rights and "brought down the house when he said it was because of large
scale farming operations that so many negroes were turned down by the Local
Draft Boards. He said poor health due to lack of clothes, warm and proper
housing was the result of plantation agriculture. Of course, throughout the
lecture there were many amens, hallelujahs, and praise the Lord. At the close
of his speech a negro preacher took over and we had a regular camp meeting."
Another speaker, Black said, delivered "one of the most abusive, vindictive and
profane denunciations of plantation operation and those interested in commercial agriculture that I have ever heard."[47]

Successful settlement days could blunt such talk. Some years before, when
the STFU got a foothold at Scott, at a time of year "when money was fairly
plentiful," Oscar told a friend in 1942, "organizers succeeded in setting up a
'local' here on our property," signing up nearly three hundred members. "We
paid no attention at all to it," he said. "It has died for lack of interest on the
part of its members, and an unwillingness on their part to make monthly contributions." Such behavior seemed to confirm David Cohn's observation in the
1930s. "Disturbing ideas crawl like flies around the screen of the Delta," he
said. He added, "They rarely penetrate."[48]

Johnston was endlessly rankled when critics charged that planters coerced
tenants into membership in the American Farm Bureau Federation and then
assessed their dues against their accounts. While he acknowledged that federal
subsidy checks encouraged membership, and that his company likewise encouraged such membership, he resisted all attempts at arbitrary force. "This has not
and cannot ever be our policy," he told Walter Sillers in 1947. "Every tenant on
this plantation must be left free to join or not join the church of his choice, the
lodge or lodges of his choice and the civic or economic organizations which he
may care to join. We will advise that he join an organization such as the Farm

Bureau Federation but cannot take any position which might be construed as compelling or forcing him to join." Hundreds of tenants on Johnston's plantations were members of the Farm Bureau but "became members," he told a critic in 1943, "of their own free will and accord. Neither I nor any person connected with our organization, insofar as I have any reason to believe, has made any sort of demand upon persons farming here to join the Farm Bureau. The Postmaster at the Post Office here will tell you, or anyone else, that these tenants look forward eagerly to receiving their Farm Bureau paper. They are apparently rather enthusiastic members and pay their dues voluntarily."[49]

Johnston's management of his tenants won praise from the executive secretary of the Memphis Negro Chamber of Commerce, T. J. Johnson. In a 1942 article in *Service,* an illustrated black monthly published at Tuskegee Institute in Alabama, Johnson concluded that "the future hope of the large majority of Negroes who live on the farms of the South rests in properly conducted enterprises such as the Delta and Pine Land Company, and that through the guidance of similarly conducted operations the Negro on the farm will enjoy as high a degree of social security, maintain as high a living standard, make as much progress, handle as much cash, and enjoy as many luxuries as do any group of farmers in America, regardless of race, commodity grown, or the nature of their tenure." That same year, Dr. Calvin Perkins, a black clergyman, told Johnston, "Men of your spirit have done much to lift our people to a very fine degree of self-respect and self-dependency." He added, with embarrassing hyperbole, "The Colored people regard you as the Savior of our people."[50]

Such statements highlight material benefits and ignore the debilitating aspects of a paternalistic labor system. But socialist alternatives to agricultural capitalism in the 1930s also sought to enhance the quality of life for the tenant. Also, the economic and political realities of America in the Great Depression allowed few, if any, quick and universal solutions to the South's land problems. "No sudden change could safely take place within a capitalist democracy," observed Mississippi writer David Cohn in an article on sharecropping in *Atlantic Monthly* in 1937. "Providing landownership for millions of landless and unprepared people is a vast and enormously complex problem." One scholar, Sheldon Van Auken, echoed that view more than a dozen years later, claiming the plantation system might still be "best for the South of today. It is possible," he wrote, "that, although the plantation community is undemocratic, the plantation is the best framework within which to raise the social and economic level of the Southern Negro."[51]

There remains a question in all this about Oscar Johnston and his plantation. It is the same question Jonathan Daniels asked himself as he steered his Plymouth away from Scott and across the flat Mississippi Delta in the spring of 1937: "How many Oscar Johnstons are there between Charleston and the levees? The sad answer is—the tragic thing is—that wisdom is not only rare among tenants," he concluded. "It is also rare on the piazzas." And to judge cotton production by Delta Pine standards, *Fortune* argued that same year, "would be somewhat like judging the U.S. piano business by the Steinway company, which is accustomed to selling the best pianos whether pianos in general are being bought or not." Oscar Johnston never fit the caricature of the greedy, oppressive planter. But *how unusual* were Johnston and his plantation? When convenient, Johnston might claim his operation was like many others, only larger. But then, what about Hiram Norcross, the landlord whose alleged eviction of tenants in Arkansas rippled through the South and the AAA? Was he typical? And were not the allegedly unscrupulous Twist brothers of northeastern Arkansas, who were charged with unfair, anti-tenant activities, atypical? Scholars who have focused on unethical landlords and miserable tenant conditions in northeastern Arkansas have incorrectly standardized the landlord in historical literature. A broader profile of the landlord might at least partially justify AAA chief Chester Davis's optimistic argument in 1934 that "[l]andlords as a whole have shown a desire and a willingness to be entirely fair and unselfish in connection with the cotton adjustment program. Some are reported to have voluntarily granted to their tenants a larger share of rental and parity payments than specified in the contracts. It is not fair to the great majority who have been conscientious and unselfish in these matters," he concluded, "that a small minority should be permitted to cast a cloud upon the whole program." In fact, that same year, one AAA field representative told Cully Cobb, head of the AAA's cotton section, "We are finding in running down these complaints that about 90% of them, or more, have no case for complaint whatever." "As you well know some landlords are not straight, and the same is true of tenants." In 1942, a prominent Arkansas planter lamented the "great deal of misinformation" about the plantation; he decried the Simon Legree mythology, including the notion that "we are exploiting our labor to an unbearable point." He added: "There *is* much mismanagement, and there are many kinds and cases of unfair treatment and exploitation, and we, who do appreciate that our labor must be properly handled and fairly treated, still must . . . suffer for the misdeeds of others." That same year, Johnston, who thought tenant misdeeds exceeded those of the landlord, told a friend that he knew "of no business anywhere in the United States which is conducted without abuse." In arguing with a pair of socialists about tenancy in 1934, Johnston acknowledged that they held their views as strongly as he held his, but said, "purely as a matter of abstract interest, I should like to know just what plan you would propose?"[52]

Delta and Pine Land's sharecroppers were not among the South's "forgotten farmers," nor were many of their brethren across the cotton belt. Welfare capitalism on the southern plantation masked a form of human bondage with roots deep in the soil of the slave regime. In its social control it remained repressive and exploitative. But a question remained. Had Delta and Pine Land tenants been independent owners, would they have survived the Great Depression or perhaps joined the legions who annually slid down the agricultural ladder into greater poverty? In the 1920s Oscar Johnston believed in Jeffersonian yeomanry, "that the best interest of the country would be served by having the [large-scale] properties cut up into forty, eighty or one hundred sixty acre units, owned by individuals who would occupy and actually farm the land." But the Depression had challenged the viability of the small family farm; there were, in fact, too many people on the land. Further, the coming agricultural revolution signaled by world war and developing technologies would change farming forever. Meanwhile, welfare capitalism cushioned the widespread crushing poverty of the Great Depression. Driven more by cash than compassion, that system was perhaps best exemplified at Delta and Pine Land Company. In no way, however, was it limited to Johnston's big plantation. Jonathan Daniels understood the benefits. "Here on the Mississippi Delta," he mused as he headed away from Scott in the spring of 1937, "Johnston seemed to me to be leading . . . a demonstration that mules and men, well-cared-for and well-fed, under wise direction, even in the old plantation pattern, might still together live well and happily on the rich earth of the warm South. For a little while at least."[53]

# Cotton Diplomat

> Oscar Johns[t]on, our cotton export expert wanted to sell to anyone.
> State turned thumbs down.                                    —Henry A. Wallace, 1957

**"L**ast March," wrote James Edmonds in the *Saturday Evening Post* in 1935, "Oscar Johnston was sent to Europe—to do something about cotton. Wheat growers in the Middle West and automobile factory workers in Michigan may not know Mr. Johnston, but his name is familiar in every ginhouse yard and cotton buyer's office in the North American cotton belt. And his journey was—and is—nearly as important to wheat folk and motor mechanics as to cotton people." Editor of the *Cotton Trade Journal,* Edmonds indulged in a bit of journalistic hyperbole. Even so, he had followed Oscar Johnston's foreign activities with interest and had even taken a trip of his own to South America to investigate cotton expansion in Brazil. What he found there alarmed him, and he returned home to write a trio of grim articles for the *Post.* If Johnston's "mission" failed, he warned in the last installment, "a lot of individuals down South might have to go back to the corn bread of their daddies and rediscover other means of locomotion besides internal combustion engines. And down in South America the current smiles of trans-equatorial cotton growers would persist."[1]

If there was exaggeration in such talk, it *was* true that generally slumping American cotton exports haunted agricultural policymakers throughout the New Deal. The fiber was America's leading export, with nearly half the annual crop purchased abroad. When those exports grew shaky after 1930, explanations for the decline ran the gamut. A convenient, oft-cited argument blamed the AAA's reduction program and increased domestic cotton prices for the expansion of foreign acreage and loss of American sales to cheaper foreign fiber. Even the British Fine Spinners worried about the erosion of American cotton exports to fiber from Brazil, Egypt, and East India. Cully Cobb, chief of the cotton section, criticized Edmonds as a spokesman for traders, but the indictment could apply to all such traders who were "naturally opposed to anything but volume movement of cotton." Cobb added, "We all want volume movement of cotton but we want it at a stabilized price and at a price that will enable the farmer to continue in business."[2]

One major AAA critic, William L. Clayton, of the Houston-based Anderson, Clayton and Company, repeatedly blasted the agency for causing the loss of exports. An enterprising Mississippi native, Clayton—whom Jerome Frank regarded as "completely and unmitigatedly selfish"—had risen in cotton circles to command the largest merchandising operation in the world, with offices or affiliates on five continents. Like other cotton merchants, Anderson, Clayton profits depended on volume. As the thirties wore on, volume declined. As for cotton reduction, Clayton prophesied in 1935 that "when the South arrives at the end of the present adventure, she will find she has sold her birthright for a mess of pottage."[3]

The conventional argument was tempting but seriously flawed, and some in the Department of Agriculture, including Oscar Johnston, rejected it. Relatively high cotton prices before 1930 spurred no great expansion of foreign acreage; nor did AAA practices during and after 1933 significantly affect world commerce. In the late 1920s the United States planted about half the world's acreage, which in turn produced about 54 percent of the total cotton crop. The greatest expansion of foreign cotton acreage occurred just prior to the New Deal, not after. By early 1933, when the efforts of the Federal Farm Board had collapsed, when world carryover exceeded 13 million bales, and when American cotton sold for under six cents a pound, foreign cotton plantings leaped to more than 44.5 million acres, up more than 3.5 million from the previous year. Johnston argued that the increase resulted from every nation's desire to be self-sufficient and from economic hard times, when several nations produced commodities that in good times they would have purchased abroad. More important, Johnston maintained that expanded foreign plantings were tied directly to the inability of foreign nations to buy American cotton and pay with gold. The devaluation of the dollar in 1933 brought substantial foreign purchases of American commodities, which temporarily inflated exports from the United States and also reduced the foreign dollar supply. Depreciated dollars brought fewer goods in those nations whose currency had not been likewise devalued, thus slowing international commerce. American protectionism, raised to an all-time high by the Smoot-Hawley Tariff Act of 1930, worsened exchange problems. The high tariff prohibited potential purchasers of American cotton from obtaining necessary dollar exchange by blocking their products from markets in the United States. Other measures, such as countervailing duties, antidumping legislation, and the Johnson Act of 1934, which prohibited credit to defaulting nations including the Soviet Union, also inhibited exports. "We think the trouble," Johnston told the British in 1935, "is from complications connected with international commerce, uncertain exchange rates and development in this country as well as others of the 'nationalistic policy.'"[4]

Johnston also believed that credit for the substantial boost in cotton prices—from 5.7 cents in 1933 to 12.5 cents in 1935—belonged not only to AAA reduction programs but also to dollar devaluation in international exchange. He told a Senate committee in early 1935 that without reduction and devaluation, the price would likely have been about a nickel a pound.[5]

Johnston became a bitter foe of protectionism, arguing that the tariff stood as a major deterrent to cotton exports. He thought it "inconceivable" that the South might abandon its foreign markets altogether, yet he knew that exports could not be maintained by bankrupting the industry through low prices. Johnston suffered from no illusions about an imminent downward revision in tariff rates. Agriculture had slipped into a subordinate economic status after the Civil War, but it now needed, he thought, a permanent cotton policy, not what he called congressional "narcotics, opiates, and palliatives." Agriculture needed a southern-midwestern coalition, with the South casting aside its "political inferiority complex." Johnston knew, of course, that production would have to be limited, but he justified federal subsidies to agriculture since the tariff subsidized industry. The farmer had paid his dues "from his cradle to his coffin" with every purchase he made. Now farmers needed relief from the economic burden of buying on a protected market while selling on an open one.[6]

The protected market and monetary differences caused cotton no end of trouble. In publications, letters, speeches, and before the Senate agriculture committee, Johnston argued that exchange problems retarded cotton exports. Germany stood as a prime example. Once a major importer of American staple, Germany turned increasingly to non-American cotton. Slippage in cotton exports to Germany had begun during the Hoover administration, and agents for German mills told Johnston that price was not the issue. In fact, as Johnston wrote in the *Cotton Trade Journal,* German interests were "willing to pay an appreciable premium above our prevailing price if they can be provided with American exchange by selling to America the normal quantity of merchandise heretofore imported to America from Germany. The major cause of shrinkage in exports is due to inability of foreign consumers to obtain American exchange." France, England, and Italy also shifted to non-American staple.[7]

In a decidedly pragmatic effort to move American cotton back into trade channels, Johnston joined with George Peek, the old AAA chief who was now, in name anyway, Franklin Roosevelt's foreign trade adviser, in a scheme to dispose of large quantities of American carryover cotton through a barter agreement. With a mandate from the Department of Agriculture as well as from Peek, Johnston met with German trade representatives and worked out a plan to trade up to 800,000 bales of America cotton to Germany. The burden of Johnston's effort was to circumvent American antidumping legislation, which prevented imports at prices below those of the exporting country. He added plans to trade 200,000 bales to Italy and 150,000 to France. In the German agreement, a German import company agreed to buy the 800,000 bales at the market price over twelve months. The Germans would pay 25 percent in dollars, the balance plus a fixed premium would be in reichsmarks. The reichsmarks would then be used to purchase German manufactures.[8]

The decision to negotiate the barter pact with Germany collided with State Department policy over which Secretary Cordell Hull jealously guarded his authority. A former congressman and senator from Tennessee, Hull had long been a free trader, believing that stagnation of international commerce precipitated conflict and war. Barter agreements, such as those that existed between various European states, were just what Hull was trying to eliminate through his Reciprocal Trade Agreements Act of June 1934. Emphasizing equal commercial treatment, Hull's program contrasted sharply with the barter agreements being pursued by Foreign Trade Adviser Peek. Hull later declared that Peek "wholly failed to see that such barter agreements and the trade agreements could not exist at the same time."[9]

Over at Agriculture, Henry Wallace was worried, as he frankly told Hull in September 1934, "that the State Department is beginning to lose some of its enthusiasm for any material increase in imports. If I am wrong in this," Wallace said, "please let me know. This is a matter of real concern to those who have to do with administering the Agricultural Adjustment Act because the magnitude of our job will vary almost directly with the success of your job in increasing imports." Moreover, meetings of cotton shippers throughout the South put pressure on the government to find foreign outlets for American surpluses. In the cotton belt, Johnston found "a great deal of interest" in the German deal and "[n]ot a particle" of objection. As for cotton surpluses, he told Peek in December 1934, "If we can put through the 800,000 [bales] to Germany, 100,000 or 200,000 to Italy; 100,000 to France, a little to Spain and some to Latvia, it will make all the difference in the world."[10]

While the Treasury Department studied the proposal's legality, the biggest obstacle remained the State Department. There, Roosevelt's initial approval of the deal met with strenuous opposition. The State Department argued that the proposal subsidized German exports to the United States. By giving reichsmarks at a discount to importers of German products, the importers would receive the German manufactures at lower prices than identical goods would cost from other gold standard countries. Such blatant discrimination jeopardized the integrity of the equal treatment and liberal trade ideals embodied in reciprocity negotiations. Brazil, a major cotton exporter, had already indicated that it would abandon such negotiations if the U.S.-German deal went through.

Other nations might follow suit. Also, Hull warned that favorable treatment of the Hitler regime would prove unpopular to a sizable segment of the American electorate. He added that since Germany needed cotton so badly, she would find dollar exchange somewhere.[11] Just where remained a mystery.

State apparently convinced Roosevelt to reverse himself and junk the barter deal. The decision not only destroyed long hours of negotiations but also signaled the end of Peek's influence. He eventually left government and became a critic of the administration. Johnston, meanwhile, had not been on the firing line in the controversy and remained undaunted by the setback. In fact, he was interested in fundamental reforms. No bureaucrat, he was a busy man. In November he wrote Chester Davis from Scott that he saw no point in hanging around the capital "when nothing but ordinary business is being done, and waiting on decisions and rulings from various departments." In and out of the capital while the barter issue dragged on, he stayed in Washington in January and February 1935, taking a suite at the Mayflower Hotel. Still managing the cotton pool, Oscar concentrated on the worsening problem of cotton surpluses and declining exports. At the request of the Secretary of the Treasury, Henry Morgenthau Jr., he even accepted an interim appointment in the Treasury Department "to handle all agricultural credit." Before the Treasury and Agriculture Departments agreed to share Oscar's services, Morgenthau telephoned AAA Administrator Davis and asked his opinion of Johnston. According to Morgenthau's diary, "Chester Davis said he is one of the smartest men he knew in that particular field."[12]

Johnston's failure to circumvent trade barriers were not without benefit. The barter deal highlighted the problem of international exchange and its ill effect on declining exports. It also became clear that despite those slipping exports, foreign demand for American staple remained intact. Johnston had also proven remarkably pragmatic in his attempts to loosen clogged trade channels. Neither the ideals of reciprocity nor offensive political regimes such as those in Germany or Italy prevented his efforts to benefit his troubled industry. The United States, he told one barter deal critic, who objected to dealing with Nazi Germany, could not "afford to sacrifice the markets of the world because of the political differences between citizens." On another potential deal to reduce cotton surpluses in early 1935, Gov. Angus McLean of North Carolina told George Peek that Secretary Wallace was "anxious to get rid of the surplus. It is giving him a lot of trouble. It makes it difficult to work out plans regarding reduction. He says, every time you mention it, he doesn't know anything about the technical side and therefore he has to depend on Oscar Johnston."

"I think that is true," replied Peek. "Oscar has handled the whole thing. He wants to sell cotton as badly as anybody."[13]

If the barter decision maintained American integrity in its reciprocity negotiations, it did not enhance the immediate prospects for diminishing the cotton surplus. Nor did it diminish pressure from the cotton belt to find foreign outlets. Interest groups from the South showered Washington with pleas for help. "Foreign markets once lost," lamented one southerner, "are hard to regain." Johnston also appealed to the White House on January 5, 1935, arguing that "the fate of the cotton industry in America" hinged largely on a rapid revival of cotton exports. Those exports, said Johnston, had slumped more than two million bales beneath those of the previous year, and the Department of Agriculture could do little about it; it was up to Congress and the State Department. "The demand is coming to us from every section of the Cotton Belt to do something to help the export of cotton," Johnston declared. "We, in turn, suggest that since the export of cotton involves international features, close cooperation between the State Department and the Department of Agriculture is essential."[14]

The administration thought one way to control the cotton trade might be through an international agreement. International dialogue on stabilizing wheat exports after 1933 held the hope of mild success and the United States wanted to apply a similar principle to cotton. The idea for the conference may have originated, as Henry Wallace believed, with President Roosevelt, although Johnston had recommended it to Morgenthau on January 14. In any event, Roosevelt thought the negotiations might be used as leverage against Brazil in the reciprocity talks then underway. Incredibly, he also wanted to use an international agreement to injure Japan in her war with China by cutting off Japan's cotton supply. "So far as I know," Wallace recorded in his diary, "Oscar Johnston, Henry Morgenthau and myself are the only ones who know that the President feels this way. Johnston is very skeptical as to whether anything of this sort can be made to work." The State Department rankled at the possibility of complicating the Brazilian reciprocity talks, as the German barter deal almost had, and thought the idea for an international conference was cooked up at the Department of Agriculture, despite denials from Wallace.[15]

After several White House conferences early in 1935, Roosevelt and Wallace announced in February that Johnston would go to Europe to survey the possibilities for improving American cotton exports. Ostensibly, he was to find out if price, prejudice, the tariff, or some combination, was responsible for America's declining position in the cotton market. For his part, Oscar was not interested, as he told a Senate committee investigating the export drop, in crowding American cotton onto a cheapened world market. That would negatively affect international trade and buying power. While he also believed that the old argument against the AAA's price hike was "grossly exaggerated," he still thought it was "undeniably true," as he told Henry Morgenthau, "that Brazil is rapidly increasing her acreage and becoming to that extent each year more seriously a competitor with America in world markets."[16]

In a February 16 press release, Secretary Wallace pointed out that the United States recognized its obligations to relieve world markets of the huge cotton stocks that had burdened the trade since the Hoover administration. But America wanted neither to depress world prices nor lose foreign markets for the American producer. The United States now desired "first-hand, accurate information as to the attitudes of other nations which purchase large supplies of cotton from producing countries," he said. "To this end, Mr. Johnston has been asked to go abroad and obtain such information as will be helpful in shaping our policies for the future." Wallace emphasized that although Johnston was manager of the cotton pool, the trip was not to explore new outlets for government cotton. Pool stocks, he said, would continue to flow into regular trade channels. Johnston's mission contained still another task. "Confidentially," Morgenthau told U.S. Ambassador Jesse Straus in Paris, "he is also going to make a study for the Treasury Department," though the specifics of that study remain unclear.[17]

Oscar and Martha sailed from New York in late February, arriving in London on March 6. After conferring at the American embassy, Johnston tried to learn the attitude of British cotton interests before presenting any proposals to the British government. He soon discovered that policies of the British Board of Trade followed "almost entirely" the desires of the British Cotton Growing Corporation, the Empire Cotton Growing Corporation, and of cotton associations in Liverpool and Manchester, including the Fine Cotton Spinners' and Doublers' Association.[18]

British cotton men were apparently ready and waiting for Johnston's arrival. One American official told Mordecai Ezekiel, a Department of Agriculture economist, "that there has evidently been considerable English speculation and comment about Johnston's coming over, and it is obvious that people in informed quarters here among the English are expecting unusual activity in cotton matters in the months ahead. They obviously consider us to be in a jam and appear to be waiting to see our next moves." Whatever the moves, they would have to be good ones. As an added burden, within a week of Johnston's arrival in England, the cotton market broke disastrously, sliding well below the government's twelve-cent "peg." In Liverpool at the time, Johnston later told the press that the government would not unload its loan or pool cotton below twelve cents. In fact, he quickly closed the pool. That Johnston was in England when the market broke was fortuitous, and his meeting with the press had a soothing effect. London's *Financial News* editorially hailed him as "one of the leading authorities on the world cotton situation" and, in its news column, declared that "His emphatic denial" regarding pool sales "will go a long way to dispel recent uneasiness on both the New York and Liverpool cotton exchanges." Except for what he called "the psychological effect," the importance of which Johnston fully understood, he soon regretted closing the pool, since pool stocks contained desirable staples and grades for foreign spindles.[19]

Meanwhile, there was more bad news from home. Sen. Ellison Smith and others, unsuccessfully as it turned out, proposed legislation to impound millions of bales of cotton in which the government had a financial stake. Johnston believed such legislation would prove "absolutely fatal to every hope to avoid a complete destruction of American cotton exports." From Manchester, he wrote Smith protesting "any Congressional action interfering with the rights and privileges of the pool members, and particularly against any action which would impose a burden upon those pool members, or eliminate their interests in the cotton." Congress could do something for cotton farmers if it wanted, he said, such as repealing the Johnson Act and antidumping laws. Such gestures, small in themselves, would signal congressional interest in revived commerce and boost international confidence. "The other nations," he told Smith, "have reached a conclusion that America proposes to 'go wholly Nationalistic.'" As a result, they looked to non-U.S. sources for raw materials. To Johnston, reciprocity negotiations barely made a dent. Smoot-Hawley, antidumping legislation, the Johnson Act, failure to enter the World Court, dollar devaluation, uncertain future monetary policy, and other matters had, as he told pool assistant Joe Lamkin from London, "all combined to well-nigh destroy American commerce with the world." "I am beginning to wonder" he lamented, "if America has left anything undone which could possibly be done to interfere with its export market."[20]

Oscar seemed to waver between discouragement and hope. Discussion among Europeans that the U.S. might abandon production control in favor of export subsidies injured the market, while cotton mills, anticipating another price decline, delayed their reorder of normal stocks of cotton. On the other hand, Johnston felt that if the Southern senatorial delegation diligently pressed for repeal of the antidumping statutes and for repeal or at least modification of the Johnson Act, "the effect would be almost instantaneous." If that was followed by some indication to the world that Congress would live up to the Democratic pledge of serious tariff revision he believed that "sound practical control measures and plans for the future development of agriculture" would displace temporary measures within two years.[21]

Such hopes were unfounded. Europe remained skeptical that the United States would seriously alter its tariff or trade relations. Johnston told Lamkin

that "Foreign Governments hesitate to enter into discussions with us because
of the thought that it is our major purpose to sell something to them without
in return buying something from them." Europeans also knew that the Americans stood to gain the most from international cotton stabilization, at least in
the short run. While American cotton acreage and exports had declined, foreign plantings, at least in Brazil, had increased. Johnston's problem was exac-
erbated by the British press carrying "articles from New York" suggesting that
Johnston had come seeking an agreement whereby Great Britain would limit
production and export of cotton from her colonies, including India and Egypt.
"As a result of the these articles," Johnston reported to Henry Wallace, "there is
a distinct prejudice against the mission." Highly placed Britishers told Johnston
"flatly and with much emphasis . . . that they would oppose" interference with
their colonies.[22]

Johnston attempted to mitigate the prejudice by a "frank statement" declaring that America had no thought of disturbing British development of their
colonies. In fact, there would have been little point in doing so. Cotton produced by Britain's African colonies had not only been "negligible" in quantity
but also generally low in quality, except for a small amount produced in Uganda.
Belgium developed cotton production in the Congo, but it remained small.[23]

After meetings in London, Liverpool, and Manchester, Johnston visited Paris,
Milan, Rome, and Berlin, getting European reaction to American trade policies and sounding out the desire of other nations to reach agreement on world
cotton stabilization. Since the British delicately told Johnston that India and
Egypt could speak for themselves, he flew to Delhi, returning to London via
Cairo. His overall investigation largely confirmed his earlier views, and produced few, if any, surprises. While cotton was produced in more than fifty nations, only four—India, Egypt, Brazil, and the United States—were major net
exporters. China and the Soviet Union, both large cotton producers, were nonetheless net importers. In Egypt and India, acreage and production trends had
proven reasonably stable over the previous decade, although India's estimated
cotton acreage in 1935 had actually slipped 5 million below her 1925–26 peak
of 28.4 million. Significant expansion of cotton acreage in either country seemed
improbable in the short term because of the expense of irrigation and because
available land was necessary for food crops. Nor did cotton varieties from those
countries burden world surpluses. India produced short-staple cotton inferior
in quality compared to American and Egyptian varieties; India, in fact, had to
import higher grades for her mills. As Johnston told President Roosevelt, "[I]t
is apparent that neither the price improvement which has occurred in the last
three years nor the American production control has or threatens to increase
production in either India or Egypt."[24]

The fly in the ointment was Brazil. Heavily indebted to Great Britain, she had the ability and the desire to increase both cotton production and cotton exports. England and Brazil had recently concluded negotiations on her debts wherein Britain would increase imports of Brazilian cotton to help Brazil ease her obligations. Britain was thus cool to any idea that she participate in a cotton conference that would very likely ask Brazil to cap its exports.[25] Without Brazil's active participation, an international cotton agreement would have little meaning.

Although Johnston understood Britain's position very clearly, he did not like it. "The attitude of your government toward informal suggestions, which were made by me to representatives," he wrote the British Fine Spinners from Paris, "while not unexpected, is somewhat disappointing and I frankly fear that your government will find that it has made a mistake in the long run." Calls for textile subsidies already rumbled in the U.S. Congress. If subsidized, American spinners could enter world markets and compete with the foreign textile industry.[26]

While critical of the British, Johnston was also aware that America had contributed to the export problem. The United States sat behind the highest tariff wall in its history while other nations grabbed a greater share of the cotton market. Though other factors contributed to the decline of American cotton exports, Johnston knew that Smoot-Hawley denied foreign nations the ability to acquire requisite monetary exchange to purchase American agricultural commodities. After he undiplomatically told the British press that American tariff policy and trade restrictions were responsible for 90 percent of the lost cotton trade, one British observer declared, "There Johnston has touched the sore spot. Why should men buy off those to whom they are not allowed to sell?"[27]

The consequences of economic nationalism were also evident when Johnston visited Germany in April, just about the time the State Department again scotched another attempt by George Peek to reopen German barter talks. Although Oscar spent a holiday in Berlin, his informal talks near Badenweiler on the Rhine near the Swiss border with Dr. Hjalmar Schacht, president of the Reichsbank, proved more significant. Their conversation stuck on the other thorn of American cotton exports to Germany. As the lengthy talks drew to a close, Schacht broached the idea of a bilateral conference between his country and the United States as a way to normalize trade relations. Johnston dissented, noting the political impossibility of such a move, given Adolph Hitler's attitudes toward Jews, Masons, and Catholics. Such public relations difficulties had not troubled Johnston before. Schacht, upon reflection, admitted that Johnston was right and that he too did not agree with all the Fuhrer's domestic policy. Nevertheless, referring to America's nationalist trade policies, Schacht told his guest, apparently with a certain resignation, that "when the war breaks, as it inevitably must, I am somewhat at a loss to understand how your thinking people will escape a feeling of actual responsibility for its development." This was 1935.[28]

Johnston was also told, apparently by Schacht, that Germany and Italy believed the United States was deliberately trying to undermine the Hitler and Mussolini regimes by blocking normal trade flow. Italy's failure to obtain monetary exchange reinforced her imperialist attempt to achieve a degree of independence by growing cotton in Ethiopia after 1935. Dr. Henry C. Taylor, former chief of the Bureau of Agricultural Economics, later recalled that on an overnight visit to Delta Pine's Scott plantation "Oscar Johnston told me that this highranking German [probably Schacht] told him that if the United States continued that policy of trying to suppress trade, there certainly would be another world war."[29]

George Peek might also have predicted as much. From his embittered anti–New Deal retirement in 1941 he reminded Johnston "how we threw that [German] business away by refusing to trade with them in 1934 and thereafter." It had been an American blunder. "Not only did we deny Germany access to our raw materials," said Peek, "but we singled her out as the one country to which the benefits of the Hull agreements were prohibited and in addition penalized her exports into this country under the anti-dumping provision of our tariff laws." All that happened, claimed Peek, despite written declaration by the Treasury Department that the proposed 1934 deal violated no American law. "In short," he told Johnston, more than two years after the start of World War II, "we refused her access to our raw materials and markets for her finished products, the two things she is fighting the war about. I think if we had shown a different attitude it might have had a profound effect upon the growth of Nazi-ism."[30]

Henry Taylor thought along similar lines regarding Italy's invasion of Ethiopia in 1935. Preparing a manuscript more than two decades after the aborted barter deal and Italian invasion, he told Henry Wallace, "We are trying to determine whether the failure of Italy to secure cotton through international trade was a factor in the decision to undertake the Ethiopian expedition. . . . Mussolini had the Italian people sold on the idea that Ethiopia would be a great source of gold and cotton as well as other less important items."[31]

Such views were provocative but hardly adequate as a full explanation for German and Italian aggression. So also were Schacht's grim warnings to Johnston in 1935, though they could only reinforce Johnston's own thesis about American economic nationalism. U.S. trade policy remained a source of consternation for both men, even as it did for George Peek in retirement. Years later Wallace recalled that the Department of Agriculture wanted to unload as much cotton as feasible but was dissuaded by the State Department. "In 1934 (and, I believe[,] in early 1935) I know that it was presumed to be State Department policy to look on Italy with very friendly eyes," he said. "But of course Hull had a hatred for barter deals as something utterly unholy." But that did not stop Germany. Bankruptcy in foreign exchange forced Germany to negotiate barter agreements with Brazil and Argentina in order to obtain raw cotton for her mills. Germany needed, but could not get, American raw materials, including cotton. Her accelerated commercial probes in Latin America, the Balkans, and the Orient were attempts to shore up her dollar exchange through triangular trading agreements. Cully Cobb offered a similar view in late 1935. "Brazilian cotton can compete with American cotton only with nations who cannot get credits in the United States," he said. "That is why Germany is buying in Brazil." Oscar told Henry Wallace in October 1935, in an obvious reference to the State Department, "The situation in Germany is so clear and unmistakable that it seems to me it should be apparent to every department of our government, but evidently it is not."[32]

After nearly two months abroad, Johnston returned to the United States in May 1935. His brief stint as a "cotton diplomat," as one newspaper called him, produced, at best, mixed results. Clearly an international cotton conference was neither feasible nor necessary, given foreign attitudes and the relative stability of cotton acreage in India and Egypt. Johnston did advise Roosevelt, however, that eventually some arrangement with Brazil might be warranted. The mission also failed to mollify lasting differences between the Departments of State and Agriculture over trade policies, despite their cooperation in facilitating the trip.[33] Johnston had undiplomatically criticized American trade policy while in Europe. He never defended excessive tariffs, whether they originated in the United States or in any other nation. His ultimate purpose was to unclog international trade channels for American cotton.

More positively, Johnston's roving tour provided a credible survey of cotton's international landscape and counterbalanced anti-administration criticism about the effects of domestic acreage reduction and the Brazilian threat. True, Brazil posed a danger for American cotton in the years before World War II, and in 1939 Secretary Hull even relented in his opposition to a barter deal to unload cotton. But the reasons for Brazil's encroachment on America's cotton markets by 1935 only pointed up exchange and other difficulties unrelated to the AAA. If nothing else, Johnston's own views became more sophisticated. While in Europe he advised the Department of Agriculture against talk of an American export subsidy because of its dampening effect on the European cotton market. Still, he knew that American crop reduction would probably become a permanent feature of the Cotton Kingdom and that remaining exports would have to be subsidized. Foreign markets, as he repeatedly argued, were not worth the ruin of the American cotton producer.[34]

Johnston's style and persuasive bearing had also impressed many Europeans, enhanced no doubt, by his cotton pool portfolio. After he had addressed a LeHarve luncheon group about cotton, one Frenchman told him that "the crowd here got a fairly bullish turn of mind, helped, I must say, by a 17 points rise in N.Y. the same day." The British Fine Spinners also monitored his European activities and, after his departure for America, offered an analysis in a letter to Scott. "We trust . . . that your Government Authorities will appreciate all the energy and persuasion he has been able to use whilst in this country and on the Continent," wrote Herbert Stowell. "If it has not been possible for him to obtain as much success as he would have liked from his negotiations, it will certainly not have been due to any lack of initiative on his part, as from all accounts he has used a considerable amount of driving force and argument in the interviews he has had. He will also have got into full touch with the different organisations connected with cotton and this will be of value and use to him in the future."[35]

Meanwhile, back in the United States, Johnston punctuated public pronouncements with attacks on American trade policy. In Memphis in late May to address the National Cottonseed Products Association, he told the press that he had found that other nations "were having trouble getting American dollars with which to buy American cotton. I also found a subtle prejudice growing up because of America's nationalistic policy." The next day, before an overflow crowd at the Peabody, with hundreds denied entrance, Johnston, called "the best man in America to speak on the subject of cotton," declared that American commercial policies blocked the restoration of international trade. With his speech carried on two local radio stations and the NBC network, Johnston responded to AAA critics, pleaded for tariff reduction, and argued that the "cotton farmer must have the benefit of world markets. He will not have access to world markets if America pursues a purely nationalistic policy." Johnston also warned, "America must learn that he who would sell must buy."[36]

Johnston's critique of American trade policy became a frequent staple of his speeches during and after 1935, even as it had been in 1934. In those years, in a sense, he bridged the somewhat artificial gap within the administration between the short- and long-range remedies to America's cotton export problem. He pragmatically stood with Peek on the palliative of barter deals, but he also stood with Hull on reciprocal trade and with Wallace and others in the Department of Agriculture who sought long-range solutions to the world economic order. In fact, where Johnston and cotton were concerned, as Wallace remembered decades later, he "wanted to sell to anyone." Johnston agreed with Wallace's 1934 pamphlet, *America Must Choose*, in which Wallace argued for an internationalist economic position for the United States. He also hoped to organize farmer support for the Department of Agriculture; he told Wallace in late 1935 that he believed "sooner or later a direct issue will have to be made between agriculture, on the one side, and 'those who do not view the situation as we do', on the other." That argument was akin to that of a Britisher who had expressed reservation about Johnston's trip to Europe earlier that spring. "America is still politically unwilling to make the vital and essential choice between planned economic nationalism and a restoration of the old international order," he wrote. "And until she does other countries are powerless to reverse the present economic trend."[37]

That view was overly pessimistic. In any event, although several agricultural commodities, including rice, cotton, and leaf tobacco, experienced something of a revival after the middle of 1935, all was not well.[38] Johnston's European tour had shown him to be less a diplomat than an uncompromising cotton advocate, and it had also demonstrated that the cotton industry ranked low in the American economic order.

# 9

## Outwitting the Speculators

The Cotton Pool seemed so vast and terrifying to traders that they dreaded it as a Cotton Ocean rather than a pool, for any kind of hurricane might blow up and wreck their business.　　　　—Harris Dickson, 1937

Speculators, brokers and gamblers make all sorts of demands; frankly I am not particularly interested in the wishes of these gentlemen.
　　　　—Oscar Johnston, 1934

I am a strong believer in the old adage, the substance of which is, that the time to sell anything is when others want to buy it. —Oscar Johnston, 1935

Oscar Johnston's management of the federal cotton pool might have ended before it really got started. By the time he returned to Mississippi in December 1933, there was talk of another governor's race. Such talk was not totally unreasonable. Johnston had run well in 1919, even as a Delta candidate. *Jackson Daily News* editor Fred Sullens publicly thumped for Oscar; his old campaign manager, a utilities executive, told him privately, "Really, I can't see any other man in Mississippi as its next Governor."[1]

Oscar would have made a viable candidate. Besides oratorical skills, displayed early and often, his success in the New Deal cotton programs had heightened his popularity. The biggest problem, at least in the preliminary stages, was his own lack of interest. "The political bee is not buzzing in my bonnet," he told Sullens in a letter, part of which the editor published. Oscar claimed contentment with his stint in Washington, following which, he said, he would enjoy the tranquillity of his home in Scott. To his old campaign manager he recalled with detachment his earlier race and declared that "Should the proverbial bee sting me, I can assure you it will not be upon the 'gubernatorial bump.'"[2]

The political bee was poised to strike elsewhere. During the Christmas break, Oscar found he missed "the 'strenuosity' of life in Washington." Back in the capital in January, he instructed Arch Toler to check on his taxes "so that if I should decide to get mixed up in politics, I will not be disqualified for non-payment." Johnston wanted his options open, not for the governorship, but for the U.S. Senate seat held by Hubert D. Stephens, the colorless two-term conservative who appeared highly vulnerable as the 1934 primaries approached.[3]

Oscar did his homework. He got permission from the British while in Manchester in March 1934, touched political bases around the state, and thought his support was sound and that he had a "better than even chance" of victory. One Mississippi publisher, J. B. Snider of Senatobia, who eyed the state's complicated political landscape coldly and clearly, wanted Johnston to decide if he was going to run or not. Johnston, he told Mississippi assemblyman Walter Sillers in April, could capture the grudge vote ("There are more people with grudges than those who work out of loyalty so the new comer always has a chance."). Former Governor Bilbo's hat was already in the ring, but Bilbo always had lots of political baggage. In Snider's scenario, Bilbo commanded about sixty thousand votes—about twice that of Stephens. "Both have strong opposition," he argued. "The Stephens vote to save itself will go to who ever the strong man is opposing Bilbo. You will see Stephens either withdraw from the race or go down [as] one of the worst defeated men in the states [*sic* ] history. In the second primary Johnston can win. The thing for you to do is to tell Oscar Johnston to get in this race and get in it now," he told Sillers. Snider was willing to help. "I have personally talked to more than fifty men since Saturday about this matter," he added. "Most of them admire Johnston and think he could win."[4]

The temptation proved strong but fleeting. In mid-April Johnston decided against the whole thing. Aside from the expense involved, he simply had no passion for political office and would have wanted a Senate seat only to advance the interests of business and agriculture. And while he did not say so, win or lose, a statewide race against Bilbo, the Delta's nemesis, might have revived latent populist demagoguery, something he loathed. ("We do not need hell raisers in the Senate," he said privately in September after Bilbo had promised to outdo Louisiana's Huey Long.) More important, a Senate race would have diluted Johnston's attention to cotton and reduced his effectiveness for the producer. He kept his focus. He honestly had an overriding sense of obligation to several hundred thousand cotton growers who had joined the cotton pool after the announcement of his appointment as manager; also, he would have had to turn loose of nearly two million bales of pooled cotton, including several thousand from his own plantations. And a political campaign would have cost him his foothold in the Department of Agriculture, where his influence was clearly on the rise. He considered the matter "[c]arefully and prayerfully," he told Snider, but there would be no Senate race.[5]

The decision proved crucial. Free from political temptation, he became cotton's chief advocate within the New Deal. The task of managing the federal cotton pool gave him considerable influence not only in the government but also in the commodity exchanges. The pool had been established to control the disposition of 2.4 million bales of cotton inherited chiefly from the Hoover administration's defunct Federal Farm Board. More than half of the million farmers participating in the 1933 plow-up bought options covering the government-held cotton by sacrificing part of their AAA rental benefits. Like others in the AAA, Johnston feared that sending options to the producers would, as he explained it to a House subcommittee, "create an overnight long interest of 2,400,000 bales of cotton in the hands of 572,000 people who were involuntarily in that position . . . and who wanted their money." If the producers quickly exercised their options, a market glut would likely result from the 1933 crop that was already moving into trade channels. The government offered farmers the alternative of surrendering their options, taking in turn a participating trust certificate evidencing their equity in the cotton pool headed by Johnston. For their participation the farmers received an additional four-cent per pound advance and became eligible to share in any profits from the gradual liquidation of the pool. In no event could pool members lose, since under the plan the loans were nonrecourse—to the delight of farmers and to the horror of the AAA's legal division—and any losses would be borne wholly by the government.[6]

Cotton farmers found the plan so attractive that 80 percent, or more than 443,000 of the more than 570,000 option holders, surrendered their options for a no-lose equity in the pool. About 1,950,000 bales flowed into the pool over which Johnston, in practice, exercised wide discretionary authority. Unless prices rose to fifteen cents for seven-eighths-inch middling variety, which it never did, Johnston could not sell the cotton until August 1, 1934, chiefly to allow prices to stabilize at higher levels.[7]

One problem that dogged Johnston from the beginning of the pool was the distribution of the business. Brokerage houses clamored for the privilege of handling the lucrative pool transactions on the exchanges, and their solicitation did not cease after Johnston eventually designated seven firms to receive the government business. Six of the seven—Fenner and Beane; C. D. Barney; Harris and Vose; Hubbard Brothers and Company; Weil Brothers and Dowdell; and Munds, Winslow and Potter—operated on the New York Exchange, while James L. Crump and Company served New Orleans. Johnston's arbitrary selection of the seven, all reputable agencies with proven business records, pointed up another of the discretionary powers lodged in the pool manager. An intricate financial network linked the brokers, New York banks, and the AAA. Since the brokers required a $300,000 bank deposit from the pool to guarantee margins, the amount on deposit would likely increase if additional brokers got a share of the business.[8]

Ultimately, the pressure proved too great. The monopoly enjoyed by the seven firms was broken by early 1936 when Johnston and the administration approved a plan submitted by representatives of Paine, Webber and Company, Post and Flagg, and Shearson, Hamill and Company, all members of the New York Cotton Exchange. Under the new arrangement, Paine, Webber served as an intermediary in distributing pool business to a "brokers pool" consisting of about two dozen other members of the New York Cotton Exchange. While the new arrangement failed to end resentment on Wall Street, it proved more equitable and less arbitrary than the original set-up while in the process relieving Johnston of the administrative burden of selection and the problem of dealing with multiple brokers.[9]

The arbitrary nature of handling pool accounts also reflected the potential for corruption. How the contracts were handled, who received commissions or benefits (and how much), and the potential for market manipulation for personal gain might have proven darkly tempting even for honorable men. But the New Deal, aside from later charges of harboring communists, attracted a cadre of dedicated professionals. Washington in the thirties never witnessed the plundering corruption that had, at other times, characterized public life. Johnston saw himself as a trustee for the pool participants, governed by an ethic of stewardship, personal ego, and a genuine interest in the health of the cotton industry, particularly producers.[10]

The terms of the pool contract permitted Johnston to make cotton available to the trade after July 31, 1934. Despite gradually rising prices, however, the market apparently would not readily absorb a significant flow of staple from the pool. An extended summer drought dimmed prospects of a bumper harvest, but the industry still sagged under the weight of a large carryover. By summer the cotton belt produced demands for fifteen-cent loans on the new crop, something Johnston thought out of line. Instead, he advocated a three-pronged loan program to shore up prices and maintain orderly marketing. He wanted market-level loans, or some approximation, on the new crop as well as additional advances for both pool members and farmers who still had their cotton under the 1933 loan. The latter advances, two cents a pound in each case, if the loan was twelve cents, flowed logically from the same arguments used for making the loan on the 1934 crop. Johnston believed a loan below twelve cents could break the market and that without advances on the older cotton, merchants would reap the benefits of the program instead of the producers.[11]

As in 1933, Johnston actively campaigned for a sizable loan. At a Commodity Credit Corporation board meeting on August 18, 1934, which he chaired, he failed to win the approval of Secretary Wallace, who favored eleven cents on most of the new crop and none on the old. For reasons unclear, Wallace reversed himself within forty-eight hours, joining Johnston and Chester Davis in calling for the twelve-cent loan. The motion carried at a meeting of the CCC directors on August 20, with the proxy concurrence of Wallace, who was out of town, and Stanley Reed, who also served as general counsel for the Reconstruction Finance Corporation. Reed's RFC boss, Jesse Jones, whose agency would ultimately fund the loans, also sat in on the meeting and gave his assent. The next day President Roosevelt announced the twelve-cent loan; on August 24 the AAA announced the two-cent advance for pool members.[12]

Johnston offered pool members two options. They could stay in the pool or drop out. If they stayed, they would increase their loan from 10 to 12 cents a pound with no added security and agree to deduct from the new loan carrying charges of 30 cents per bale per month from February 1 to October 1, 1934. Pool members would net 1.52 cents a pound or $7.60 a bale and, more importantly, retain both their equity in the pool and the right to share in the profits if the market advanced. Members could then surrender their certificates at their discretion. If certificate holders chose the second option, which was really not much of an option at all, they could receive a net profit based on closing prices on the New York Exchange, less the original dime lien and accrued carrying charges.[13]

To no one's surprise, the great majority of certificate holders elected to stay. Johnston had again engineered a no-lose deal for the producers. He haggled with Wallace and the AAA legal division over details of the two-cent advance, with Johnston eventually borrowing from Commodity Credit, which in turn borrowed from the RFC. The administration got Congress to amend the AAA's cotton financing operations to allow the government to refinance $100 million in commercial and commodity credit loans. That saved pool members more than $2 million per year in interest. The first checks from the two-cent advance went in the mail in mid-January 1935 and pool members ultimately pocketed more than $11 million in new loans, all of which were nonrecourse. If the market went higher, as seemed likely, members would profit, but in no case could they lose. By late summer the impending harvest looked small, the threat of a textile workers' strike neared an end (Johnston thought they were "bluffing"), and currency inflation seemed likely. For members, the pool looked like a profitable venture.[14]

Some certificate holders who dropped out of the pool were in fact pressured out through a bit of federal jawboning. Since pool membership was transferable, certificates covering about 220,000 bales of pool cotton had been bought up by several cotton merchandising companies in late 1934. Although producers had received a good return on the sales, it remained politically inexpedient to allow consolidation of large numbers of pool certificates, and to extend government benefits to large speculators, among them the American Cotton Cooperative Association, Weil Brothers, and the biggest merchandiser of them all, Anderson, Clayton and Company, of Houston, Texas. Johnston, in fact, saw the two-cent advance as a way to keep speculators from prying the certificates out of farmers' hands. He defused a potentially explosive, or at least embarrassing, situation when he met with company representatives in New Orleans in December and worked out an equitable deal to purchase the outstanding certificates on a "buyer's call." The arrangement proved beneficial for everyone, including the merchants—too favorable to the merchants as far as the AAA legal division was concerned—and caused no market disturbance. By January 8, 1935, the merchants' spot holdings had been liquidated.[15]

Although Johnston's loan plans proved beneficial to producers who needed cash, the pool did not drain very quickly. Johnston probably played the market too conservatively in the fall of 1934, when the trade might have taken more pool cotton. Ironically, pool membership proved so attractive that few if any members surrendered their certificates. To make matters worse, prices soon dipped below twelve cents, forcing an increasing quantity of the 1934 crop into government-approved warehouses. By February 1935 cotton still held under the old 1933 loan totaled only 85,000 bales, but bales held under the 1934 loan crept toward 4 million.[16]

By early 1935, as Johnston prepared to sail for Europe seeking international stabilization to counteract sagging cotton exports, domestic cotton prices moved toward a climax. Despite speculators' confidence that the government's twelve-cent loan was sufficient to "peg" prices, the market during the first trading week of March 1935 became "nervous and excited." On Monday, March 11, with Johnston in England, the market betrayed any notion of a government "peg" and, beset with selling orders, broke below twelve cents. The futures market fell 196 points, or nearly ten dollars per bale. The market rallied a bit but within another week took another precipitous drop, plunging prices to their sharpest decline since 1927.[17]

Cotton's weakness quickly spread to other commodities; anxious government officials tried to restore market confidence. In Liverpool, Johnston told the press that the government would sell no pool or loan cotton below twelve cents. In fact, he quickly closed the pool, a hasty action he soon regretted because the pool held certain scarce varieties. Still, he deemed immediate re-opening "unwise," exposing the government "to charges of vacillation and uncertainty." He weakly pointed out that prices were still twice what they had been in 1932 and that current loan contracts would be reviewed at season's end. Meanwhile, he said, administration policy would remain unchanged.[18]

Despite such assurances, the market failed to stabilize until May, and then at prices below loan rates. Immediate blame for the price drop fell on government activities in the market, along with rumors that federal loans would not be renewed. The Senate agriculture committee eventually launched a probe, during which much testimony argued that blame for the March 11 break fell heavily on public uncertainty about pool plans and whether the twelve-cent loan would be continued.[19]

In his own testimony before the committee more than a year after the market break, Johnston denied the charge of uncertainty about the pool. He had acted according to pool guidelines forbidding disturbance of the market, and the press carried notices of sales and of invitations for merchants to submit bids. In fact, Johnston repeatedly tried to allay the cotton trade's apprehension about what course he would follow. Typical was his publicly circulated letter to the president of the New York Cotton Exchange in April 1934, wherein he declared that "this cotton will not be dumped on the market, sacrificed or offered in a manner calculated to unduly disturb spot market conditions." To the point of tedium, he made similar declarations publicly and privately for two years, continually battling rumors and speculation. In 1936 an investigator for the Senate agriculture committee probing the 1935 break asked Johnston: "Rumors frequently do have as much and sometimes more effect on the market than actual facts, do they not?" Johnston replied, "Yes; and they are very often circulated with that end in view." "There is no way of preventing it?" asked the investigator. Said Johnston: "None in the world." As he told Vernon Bellhouse, executive director of the FCSDA at the end of 1935, "Much of the rumored 'uncertainties' attendant upon government activities exist only in the distorted mind of the individual who started it." And as early as August 1934 he told Sen. Ellison Smith that "More or less irresponsible individuals originate rumors and occasion the publication of so-called 'press dispatches' from day to day, with respect to the market." But Johnston was concerned about market trends, not daily fluctuations, and he refused to comment on them publicly. Nor would he jeopardize pool profits by fixing floor prices for mill buyers. In dodging the speculators Johnston continually, though not flawlessly, sought high prices and stability. Stability, he told a Senate committee in 1936, "is not what is wanted by the New York brokers."[20]

Rumors about the twelve-cent loan were undoubtedly a factor contributing to the bearish climate in March 1935. Johnston claimed that traders had concluded that a twelve-cent "floor" protected their speculation in the market, and as a consequence, mills and other buyers bought cotton but provided no hedges as insurance against a possible decline. Speculators bought futures when prices declined slightly, hoping to take advantage of expected advances. Nobody expected prices would slip below the government's "peg," which Johnston never, even before the market break, regarded as a "peg" at all. To him the twelve-cent loan was only a device to ensure orderly marketing. Chester Davis later said the AAA regarded the loans as market-supporting "but not price-fixing loans." The thin facade collapsed when those who held March futures tried to convert to May contracts, the prices of which stood considerably lower. Those with substantial March futures could only buy May futures at a loss, so many decided to sell. When prices dipped below twelve cents, mills and other buyers panicked and began selling hedges, carrying the market lower. Unable to protect their newly acquired futures, speculators sold out at a loss, completing the spiral.[21]

The market decline dispelled notions that the twelve-cent loan had been a guaranteed price fixer for the entire trade. Declaring that the break "took the whole world by surprise," Herbert Stowell may have expressed a prevalent feeling. "I must say . . . that with the large number of bales held under Government loan at 12c, it did seem as if it would be impossible for the cotton market to break below this figure. It just shows that nothing is certain in this uncertain world, and that even though you have the power of a wealthy Government behind operations in order to keep prices at a fixed level, it is not possible to control such a big commodity as cotton unless that control comes from the usual economic methods." Still, in the late spring of 1935, with distant-month futures depressed partly in anticipation of a large harvest, pressure mounted for a new loan on the growing crop. With spot prices running below twelve cents, Johnston urged Wallace and Roosevelt to resist such pressure for an immediate announcement on a new twelve-cent loan. He warned that if producers harvested twelve million bales in 1935, a distinct possibility, the government might wind up with the whole crop. And with prices below twelve cents, the RFC's legal requirements for adequate security for crop loans could not be met.[22]

Federal commodity loans in the mid-thirties brought mixed results. If the dime loan on cotton in 1933 had been a stroke of brilliance, the twelve-cent loan the following year proved disastrous. Despite the obvious virtue of government credit in facilitating orderly marketing by producers, the sagging market kept considerable quantities of American staple out of trade channels. Not counting pool cotton, by mid-1935 scattered warehouses bulged with nearly 4.5 million encumbered bales, about 40 percent of the 1934 crop. This cotton, much of it in interior warehouses, could not be released below twelve cents plus carrying charges until January 1936, when the loans matured. Johnston had found that some exports had been hampered in the spring of 1935 by the inability of American merchants to acquire scarcer grades for foreign mills. Reopening the pool in May relieved only some of that demand. He eventually came to regard the twelve-cent loan of 1934 as "an unfortunate error." Still, the culprit for the general decline in cotton exports from the 1934 crop was not the high loan but, as Johnston called it, "a disordered international trade relationship." Devalued dollars slowed U.S. purchases from industrialized gold countries, in turn shrinking their available dollars for reciprocal purchases. As a result, cotton exports declined dramatically to France, Italy, Holland, Germany, and England. England, for example, turned to India, Egypt, and Brazil, nations with which she enjoyed good trading relations, to make up her fiber deficit.[23]

By mid-1935 many in the AAA and in the cotton trade were wary of another twelve-cent loan. While powerful interests such as the Cotton Textile Institute and the American Cotton Cooperative Association lobbied for twelve cents or higher—even Johnston's friend Pat Harrison, chairman of the Senate Finance Committee, urged adoption of twelve cents—the trade was by no means united. Ironically, Johnston's Mississippi friend Walter Sillers Jr., a state legislator, wired Sen. Pat Harrison that catastrophe awaited the South if there was no twelve-cent loan. "All gains in business thus far accomplished by administration will be lost as well as hundreds of million dollars expended," he warned. "The New Deal will be as unpopular in the South as it is popular now." The early AAA walked a tightrope between supply and demand, anxious to reduce output and provide market stability, but also wanting to allow other normal market conditions to operate freely. It was all a curious mixture of federal tinkering and market factors. The AAA wanted unity in the ranks on the loan issue. While Wallace publicly favored a loan of some type, Chester Davis toyed with the idea of no loan at all. Most of the cotton section, including Davis, favored delaying a decision until the August crop report provided a clearer estimate of the size of the 1935 harvest. For Johnston, who could claim some paternity for the early New Deal loans, there was only a question of how much the new loan should be, and when it should be announced. Despite the problems of the 1934 loan, he knew that stocks of cotton held by foreign and domestic mills had dwindled. Those mills would doubtless grab up a greater supply of American staple in the 1935–36 season than they had the previous year. It was a reason to be bullish and Johnston was amenable to another twelve-cent loan. The 1933 and 1934 loans had not been designed to prop up cotton abnormally, the government never seeing them as absolute price floors. What the loans did, despite the bumpy ride of the 1934 crop, was promote orderly marketing by farmers. It was Oscar's whole point about the loans. "I well know," he told Roosevelt's secretary, Marvin McIntyre, in June 1935, "that such orderly selling by the farmer is not so profitable to brokers, that speculation is deterred; these are unfortunate consequences which will flow from orderly marketing at a fairly stable price level, a situation which, from the standpoint of the farmer and the mill, is devoutly to be desired."

Johnston's pool activities and his lobbying for reasonable loans at market or near-market levels stood out as his most important services to the cotton producer and to the stability of the industry itself. "Many communities are without banking facilities of any sort," he pointed out to Chester Davis in 1935, "and a great majority of producers are unable to obtain adequate credit. Many of them do not even know how to go about getting credit." Such financial inadequacy had led to market gluts during the harvesting season, especially in November, when the farmer, desperate for cash, unloaded his year's work at a disadvantage. Bolstered by low interest rates, small merchants preyed on the farmers' misfortunes, grabbing up small lots of cotton and selling hedges daily on the exchanges, thereby depressing the market. Lording over all, as if in the pecking order of the jungle, the merchandising giants possessed even greater advantages than the small merchant with virtually inexhaustible credit lines, storage facilities, and seats on the exchanges. What changed the whole equation, bringing equity and increased competition, argued Johnston, was a federal commodity loan, coupled, of course, with acreage reduction.

Despite the shaky cotton market in 1935, the price trend looked favorable. Weekly averages on the ten-spot markets for the forty-six weeks between August 1, 1934, and June 15, 1935, totaled 12.4 cents per pound. In that time, prices slipped below 12 cents only seven weeks—four after the market debacle on March 11 and three in the confusing wake of the Supreme Court's decision in *Schecter* v. *United States* in May, which helped destroy the National Recovery Administration. A moderate harvest in 1935, if protected by a 12-cent loan, would promote orderly consumption. It appeared the American carryover of cotton stocks would be reduced significantly in 1934, to about 9 million bales. Of that total, about 4.5 million would still be in the 1934 loan and could not be sold under 12 cents plus carrying charges. Johnston's cotton pool would hold another 800,000 bales, but many of the popular varieties had already been drained, while exports, culls, and rejected leftovers would account for much of the rest of the American carryover at the beginning of the 1935 marketing season. Popular varieties could still be had from the loan supply, but hungry textile mills, their supplies shrunken, would have to pay at least 12.75 cents in liens and carrying charges to get them.

Neither Johnston nor anyone else in the AAA wanted federal loans as a permanent fixture in the cotton belt. None wanted artificial props for American staple and all were sensitive to the political danger of setting precedents for every other agricultural commodity. Unlike prices for other commodities, however, cotton at twelve cents was only three-quarters of prewar parity; Johnston argued that publicizing loans on cotton in those terms would effectively depoliticize the issue. By August he formulated a new plan that struck a significant balance between a free and fixed market. It also offered a far superior substitute to straight loans, which he had advocated in the past and for which the South now clamored.

The idea, which won AAA approval, offered farmers below-market, nonre-course loans supplemented by adjustment subsidies. The farmer would net twelve cents and the 1935 crop would move quickly into consumption. In giving his approval for such an arrangement, President Roosevelt had to buck considerable pressure for an above-market loan. Chester Davis recalled that when he and Johnston went to the White House to outline the plan, Roosevelt "characteristically started doing the talking and our time was up . . . before we'd had a chance." Roosevelt often used the charming ploy to avoid hard issues, talking instead about one or another irrelevancy. Davis said he "loved to take the ball when you had a conference and talk your time out." Such doings prompted historian Robert Ferrell to remark that Roosevelt's "mind was a gigantic trap for any unwary visitor to the oval office; he could catch all the nuances of conversation." Johnston, always polite but immune to FDR's method, took the initiative and, recalled Davis, "really pounded the desk and said, 'Now, we've got to tell you this,' and then we went ahead and the President listened." Added Davis, "It made sense to him and he agreed."[24]

On August 22 the government announced a nine-cent loan plus subsidy plan for the 1935 crop. Congressional opposition quickly forced the administration to hike the loan to a dime, complemented by a new subsidy scale. The program—"a blend of the best features of all," Johnston claimed publicly—was the best weapon yet in the New Deal's arsenal against the enemies of agricultural stabilization in the South. Within their Bankhead allotments, eligible producers could borrow ten cents on their cotton, seven-eighths-inch middling or better, and receive a subsidy of up to two cents. The amount of the subsidy was determined by subtracting the daily average price on the ten designated spot markets from twelve cents. Funding for the subsidies, authorized by an amendment to the Agricultural Adjustment Act of 1933, came from customs receipts. Cotton prices were above a dime, and the trade stood ready to grab up the unencumbered cotton and, in fact, much of the 1935 crop moved into trade channels. The loan-subsidy idea proved so successful that a similar plan was employed in 1937; the Truman administration used the same principle in its comprehensive farm program, the Brannan Plan, more than a decade later.[25]

If the 1935 plan promoted orderly marketing, Johnston had already been trying to achieve the same result with the cotton pool. Shortly after his return from Europe in May 1935 he reopened the pool to bids from the cotton trade. Unable to find adequate supplies of certain grades of staple, merchants and textile mills repeatedly called for a resumption of sales from the pool. The market had steadied since the break in March at about 11.6 cents, and Johnston apparently wanted to take advantage of low-priced futures contracts. He pub-

licly announced on May 8 that the pool would follow normal bidding procedures and that there would be no efforts to unduly disturb the market.[26]

Merchants responded voraciously. One New York broker told Marvin McIntyre
the next day, "The market has had an excellent tone today and I believe Oscar
Johnston's policy of taking advantage of the present high basis and turning some
cotton loose will be beneficial to everyone in the cotton trade, except those
who are speculatively short, and those who have bought July and sold October
hoping there might be a squeeze in July." In the first six marketing days, Johnston
accepted satisfactory offers on 300,000 spot bales, about two-thirds of which
were in port warehouses available for export. By mid-June many of the pool's
popular varieties had been drained; sales continued until August, however, when
Johnston closed the pool to give the trade time to digest the AAA's plan for the
1935 crop. The farmers, said Johnston in an AAA press release announcing the
closing, "can with reasonable certainty calculate what his returns from the year[']s
crop will be without fear of the effect of daily market fluctuations. This will enable him to arrange his farm budget and to carry on with his operations in safety."
From May to August Johnston had marketed about 600,000–700,000 bales on
a rising market, commanding premium prices for quality grade, staple, and loca-
tion. The trade willingly paid an average 12.69 cents for the pool's stocks, a price
considerably above "free cotton" spot quotations but slightly below the price
needed to pry similar grades from loan stocks. Although Johnston hoped to quickly
resume sales, the pool remained closed until February 1936, during which time
the bulk of the 1935 harvest, free from the competition of pool sales or the
otherwise bearish impounded 1934 loan stocks, moved toward consumption.[27]

Even though the pool remained closed in the fall of 1935, changes in Johnston's
operations were underway. Before it reopened, Johnston abandoned his policy
of replacing spots with futures, the most controversial of all his pool practices.
He had obtained Wallace's permission to, upon surrender of certificates, convert spot sales into futures contracts in August 1934. He slowly began the process that fall. In 1935 he began converting spots to futures without such surrender. While critics eventually claimed that the pool was not being liquidated,
the primary purpose of such practice was to get cotton into consumption and
maintain the net holdings of the pool in anticipation of price increases. Throughout 1935 Johnston maintained futures and spots sufficient to cover outstanding participation certificates. The net pool position fell *only* after members
surrendered their equity, and low prices, particularly in the fall of 1934, kept
them from doing so. Since the pool member's equity was in the whole of the
pool rather than specific bales, Johnston sold spots and replaced them with
futures at his own discretion, without the consent or knowledge of the pool

member. While the pool contract did not mandate that he pursue this policy after August 1, 1934—that is, he could have simply sold spots covered by surrendered certificates without maintaining the net position of the pool—Johnston continued the practice for many months. In effect, he transferred the pool members' equity in spots into futures, thereby protecting the pool against the time when the membership would surrender their certificates for cancellation, possibly at a substantial profit.[28]

The practice proved beneficial for other reasons. Sales of pool cotton reduced the American surplus, while purchasing futures simultaneous with the sale of pool spots provided a hedge for the buyer. That not only helped sales but also stabilized the market. Such a practice became significant in the spring of 1935, when Johnston took advantage of a favorable "basis," the price difference between spots and futures, and bought distant-month contracts that sold for up to one hundred points below spot bales. By replacing actual cotton with futures of strictly seven-eighths-inch middling variety, he gave the pool greater uniformity while moving the actual cotton into consumption. The process eliminated not only some of the speculative nature of carrying spots but also expenses incident to spot bales, such as insurance, handling, warehousing, and carrying charges. By reducing expenses and applying earnings from distant futures discounts, Johnston shored up sizable revenues.[29]

Johnston's handling of the pool provided a responsible stabilizing influence for the cotton trade. The pool supplied needed staple varieties and compensated somewhat for seasonal market fluctuations. By selling spots in March, April, and May and replacing them with October, November, December, and January futures, Johnston eased the trade through the fall marketing season, when any glut could have proved disastrous. With sufficient notice, he might have prevented, or at least softened, the dramatic 1935 break in the cotton market. He even thought—"just within the realm of possibility"—that when the market broke on March 11, he might have been able to help stabilize prices by selling 79,000 bales of December futures and buying a like number of March contracts. As it happened, he was in Liverpool and did not learn of the price drop until he returned to his hotel that evening. Still, nobody knew, not even Johnston, what he would have done. The following January, however, while the Supreme Court was handing down its Hoosac Mills decision declaring the AAA processing tax unconstitutional, Johnston stood ready for any anxiety in the trade. He quickly placed buying orders to prevent significant market raids in the backwash of uncertainty that attended the Court's decision; as it turned out, the market advanced that day and the orders were not exercised. The pool also helped stabilize the market when the government released some of its twelve-cent loan cotton.[30]

The pool also stabilized the market in its sales to cotton merchants. Since Johnston sold through established commercial channels, merchants often submitted bids for large quantities of spot cotton for eventual resale. To protect themselves against a future price change, the merchants, when their pool bids were accepted, sold hedges on the futures market. For example, if Mitsui Company, a supplier of Japanese textile mills, bought 50,000 spot bales from the pool for export, the company insured itself by selling a like number of futures as their hedge. Johnston in turn bought the hedges as distant-month futures, intending to parcel them out in smaller quantities when the trade would absorb them. Often, he simply sold the futures back to the original spot purchaser when the cotton was consumed, and the whole transaction ended to everyone's satisfaction. Had Johnston not provided a market for the buyer's hedges, the sale might not have been made, or if it had, prices might have dropped several points on the exchange on the day of the transaction.[31]

Johnston's policy of replacing spots with futures and sometimes shifting near-month contracts forward continued in 1935. By then it was clear that substantial market increases would not be forthcoming; in fact, prices had slipped. Also, the pool's fiscal position had been maximized and the prevailing replacement policy involved additional monetary risks to the government. Political factors also surfaced. Henry Wallace intimated to Johnston that he would not likely approve continuation of the replacement practice; in fact, Johnston would not likely recommend it. Sen. John Bankhead of Alabama, whose Cotton Control Act was being litigated, talked of proposing new legislation to mandate fixed terms for liquidating all government cotton, and even the comptroller general questioned the need for the pool's continued operation.[32]

By late 1935 and early 1936 Johnston's management of the pool came under increased scrutiny. Investigators for the Senate agriculture committee probing the market break of March 1935 reached an incomplete but damaging conclusion that Johnston's futures accounts had suffered serious losses. A rumor apparently reached President Roosevelt in December that Johnston and Chester Davis might be leaving government service to reenter the private sector, not, of course, that Johnston had ever left it. Bernard Baruch, the big-time financier and confidant of presidents, advised Roosevelt that high commodity prices were crucial to his reelection in 1936; FDR wondered if he could afford to lose Davis and Johnston. Treasury Secretary Henry Morgenthau told the president that he had learned confidentially from Wallace that Johnston's pool operations were in bad shape. Wallace, said Morgenthau, thought nothing dishonest was going on but that a congressional probe could be damaging.[33]

Johnston had no intention of relinquishing management of the pool, an agency he had nurtured for two years. And Roosevelt's confidence remained unshaken. A few months later he contemplated putting Johnston in charge of Commodity Credit—an agency for which Johnston felt, he said later, "a sort of paternal interest"—if Gov. Lynn Talley's health failed to improve. Much of the criticism of Johnston's management grew out of his futures transactions, some of which confused those not versed in the intricacies of cotton marketing. The cotton market "involves the purchasing of futures and hedging the market, and things which to the ordinary layman appear more or less of a mystery and many times seem improper," Lewis Schwellenbach, a Democrat from Washington and a member of the Senate agriculture committee, confessed to Johnston in 1936. Critics also thought the pool was not draining with sufficient speed. By early 1936 the pool still held more than 642,000 spot bales and 820,000 futures contracts. The futures represented no cotton at all, of course, merely the trade's hedges Johnston had purchased for a number of reasons, not the least of which was to prevent a depression of spot prices. Since he planned to sell the futures back to the people who were short—those who had sold him the contracts in the first place—the whole transaction, when complete, would have no "marketwise effect on earth." He believed that allowing short interests to repurchase their futures, rather than requiring them to tender spot cotton when the futures matured, was not in itself a bearish influence on the market. He had no desire to short or "squeeze" the market higher, and he did not have to find new customers for his futures. Amid the hectic and often feverish tumult of the trading floors of the exchanges, pool brokers, on Johnston's instructions, could be observed casually standing around the trading ring, hands in pockets, watching and waiting for an acceptable offer. When brokers made such an offer for short interests, the pool's broker said "bought," and the futures were liquidated.[34]

Aside from pool cotton, the government still carried more than four million spot bales under the 1934 twelve-cent loan, the bulk of which had fallen under government authority because the Commodity Credit loans and carrying charges exceeded world price levels. When the nonrecourse loans matured after January 1936, producers naturally defaulted, preferring to let Uncle Sam hang on to a rather large bag of cotton, now deemed "past due paper." Johnston understood the market's psychology and had lobbied since December 1935 to extend the loans past maturity to relieve some of the market's skittishness. Meanwhile, the loan cotton remained a bearish influence, as critics charged, complemented by the market's nervousness surrounding legal challenges to the Bankhead and Agricultural Adjustment legislation.[35]

Congressional discontent surfaced in the Senate agriculture committee. Although the press had reported in the fall of 1935 that Senator Bankhead contemplated a bill to mandate fixed sales of federally financed cotton through a central selling agent, Cotton Ed Smith of South Carolina, who had toyed with the idea of impounding such cotton even before the market break of March 1935, actually introduced new legislation in February 1936. Designed to alleviate the price influence of the federal holdings, the bill, if passed, would have abolished the cotton pool and merged its remaining stocks with the millions of bales held under the twelve-cent loan. The consolidated staple would then be dispensed to the trade at the rate of 20,000–25,000 bales per week for about five years, except during the harvesting season, and would be under the supervision of a three-man board.[36]

Despite Smith's twenty-eight-year Senate seniority and chairmanship of the agriculture committee, his proposal got a cool reception in the Department of Agriculture. Johnston thought the idea was ridiculous and let officials know he would have no part of the three-man board or Smith's marketing plan. He told RFC boss Jesse Jones that the proposal was "fantastic and unworkable." Privately, and with an air of defiance, he told the British Fine Spinners, "At present I can only say that it is very certain that none of this cotton will be 'dumped' on the market and that persons who are waiting with the hope that they may buy cheap cotton from the Government, will be sadly disappointed."[37]

The possibility of dark motives hung over cotton legislation in the midthirties. Davis and Johnston both thought there might be general improper maneuvering for private gain on the part of some legislators. Davis later claimed "that some of these men in Congress had more than an altruistic interest in the price of cotton. I'm satisfied that at least three or four of them held 'long interests' in the cotton market, and were willing to use the introduction of a bill or the reporting of a bill, or a speech, for the sake of its effect on the market. That was a very complicating thing in all this period. I know that's serious, but it's true. It's true."[38] On one occasion in 1935, after President Roosevelt had agreed to Johnston's loan-plus-subsidy idea for the 1935 crop, Johnston and Paul Porter visited Cotton Ed at his residence at Washington's Wardman-Park Hotel and gave him the news. Smith protested that he had been "promised a twelve-cent loan," and they replied that the *farmers* would get twelve cents, not the futures market. Chester Davis recalled, without specifically identifying the senator, that Porter told him "that the Senator paced the floor of his hotel room and just literally seized his hair and shook it and said, 'I'm ruined, I'm *ruined!*' I don't think he was ruined," said Davis, "but I think he had to forego a profit that he thought was a certain one on cotton options he was holding." If such doings were not widely publicized in the thirties, Sen. John Bankhead suffered public humiliation a decade later. Muckraking columnist Drew Pearson charged that Bankhead had purchased cotton futures before publicly calling for an end to wartime price ceilings on cotton. Still denying the charge, the senator died in 1946.[39]

Even if such motives did not animate Smith's 1936 marketing bill, the plan seemed likely to depress the market when demand slackened, while holding prices in check when the trade expanded. By establishing a weekly quota, it would remove the discretionary powers that Johnston had employed so deftly in outwitting the speculators and generally avoiding market slides. "Markets cannot be arbitrarily created," Johnston protested in a lengthy letter to Smith. "Cotton must be sold when and if there is a market or demand. It would be unsound to force upon the market any specific quantity of cotton, however small." Robert J. Woods, of Paine, Webber and Company in New York City, told Assistant Secretary Milo Perkins in February, "Quite frankly, as I understand Senator Smith's plan, we would almost be guaranteed Government futures business for about six years, but I wholly disapprove of his plan because I think it is bad for the Government and everybody in the trade, except a few speculators. It seems to me another one of those plans which thinks of a beginning but ignores the end."[40]

When Smith opened hearings on the bill in February 1936, Johnston braced for the battle. He spent two days in executive session before the committee discussing the government's loan cotton and detailing the operations of the cotton pool. He claimed he could handle an investigation but he protested the proposed abolition of the pool, a view shared, he claimed, by certificate holders throughout the cotton belt who had wired him to that effect. He told the senators:

> The pool members, for whom I am a trustee have a stock of cotton and they think they have an equity, and I think they have an equity in it, and I protest against that equity being wiped out. They have given valuable consideration for that document. They plowed up their cotton. They took their contract in good faith. They have carried it out in good faith. They assumed that their Government was in perfect good faith when it gave them that contract, and I merely want to lodge a protest against that contract being arbitrarily canceled—and that is the effect of this bill— canceling that and take their cotton over, merging it with a lot of other people's cotton and running it through a sale that they would not have gone into.[41]

Johnston repeatedly justified the pool's futures operations. On one occasion, when Smith implied, after testimony to the contrary, that Johnston's policy of replacing spots with futures amounted to a government hedge, Johnston retorted, impatiently: "I didn't hedge. I don't seem to be able to get this thing clear to you, Senator. I never hedged a bale of that cotton. They hedged. I replaced. I tried to make that clear in the beginning, the difference between carrying cotton for my pool members and hedging cotton. I don't hedge. I have never hedged a bale in the pool." Smith had contended that Johnston should merely have sold pool stocks without replacing them, thus saving a loss on the futures market. "To be sure," Johnston quipped, "and if the market had gone the other way, probably we would have been in the penitentiary for not having protected these people. When I sold this cotton I replaced it with a like amount in futures. If I had not done that and had left them open and the market had gone up, then they would have called on me for an accounting. Suppose they had said, 'Johnston, why did you sell our cotton and fail to replace it?' I think I would have been in a very serious predicament."[42]

Although Smith used the findings of two able investigators to try to discredit the pool's futures policy, opposition to the new plan had already developed. The International Market Forecast Bureau of New York claimed the plan was bearish and feared that "all gains made since April 1933 will be lost." RFC Chairman Jesse Jones soon joined the opposition. Johnston claimed he had the support of producers, merchants, factors, and cooperative associations, the latter of which had about 700,000 bales under the twelve-cent loan. He also found support on Capitol Hill. Pat Harrison, a ranking Senate Democrat and chairman of the finance committee, publicly declared his opposition even before the hearings had concluded. "If it should be reported out of the committee I shall fight it on the floor of the Senate," he announced on February 9. "Oscar Johnston has done a remarkable job in handling the financial end of the government's cotton. His opinion, because of his fine judgment and experience, is worthwhile. In appearing before the agriculture committee he made a magnificent presentation of the objections to such a plan." Privately, Johnston got moral support from his old neighbor, Will Percy, who invoked the sentiments of his late father, Sen. Leroy Percy. "Father," said Percy, "always thought old Smith pretty much of an ass and it seems to me he is making special proof of the accusation at this time."[43]

Despite what the *New Orleans Times-Picayune* called Johnston's and Harrison's "rather formidable opposition," Smith's committee reported the bill favorably on February 14. The committee, however, had no desire to discredit Johnston; he had won even the respect of the investigators. "I think he has proceeded as rapidly as possible with respect to his spot bales," said one of them, "and the general opinion of those with whom I have talked is that Mr. Johnston has marketed his actual cotton very well indeed." Republican Sen. George Norris of Nebraska, who had been "impressed" by Johnston's "thorough understanding of the situation and his ability to handle it," told his colleagues that Johnston "was a good man." "As I understand it," he added, "nobody is dissatisfied with Johnston." Chairman Smith replied, "He did the best he could with a bad system."[44]

Johnston failed to share Smith's requiem for the system. On the very day the South Carolinian introduced his controversial bill, Johnston publicly announced that he was reopening the pool to the trade. Johnston had wanted to reopen the pool since late 1935, but its timing took some of the steam out of the new bill. Congressional discontent, however, may have goaded him. His invitation for bids was a way to test what cotton varieties the trade wanted and what price it would pay. Within a few days, the pool collected 103 sealed bids covering nearly a quarter million bales from prospective buyers, including merchants wishing to fill orders for both foreign and domestic mills. After testifying before Smith's committee, Johnston flew to New Orleans to formally accept the bids amid much fanfare, including a photograph of the event in the *New Orleans Times-Picayune.* [45]

Although Johnston could sell only 50,000 spot bales because the pool had been drained of certain popular varieties, he decided to accept new offers on the remaining stocks as long as the market remained stable. Such judgment proved successful. Against the backdrop of Smith's ominous proposal, Johnston began reducing the pool's spot holdings, which fell to 350,000 bales by March 7 and to 225,000 by the first week of April. At the same time, he reduced the pool's futures to less than 642,000 bales and planned to liquidate them as they approached maturity. If he could not get nearly spot prices for his futures, he demanded delivery. Ordinarily, a long interest would be a bearish factor in the market, but since available raw cotton was in short supply and the contracts were held by the government, which stood ready to take delivery of spot cotton if necessary, Johnston's futures position was actually bullish for the trade. In liquidating his January and March contracts he had to take up about 28,000 spot bales, but May contracts were liquidated almost wholly, save for delivery of about a thousand bales.[46]

Despite the attention paid to the pool, its holdings formed only a Sargasso Sea amid an ocean of government loan cotton. Still, favorable consumption of large stocks of pool cotton suggested the trade was hungry for more. As acting chairman of the Commodity Credit Corporation, Johnston, sanguine that the Smith bill would fail, developed a plan to release a large quantity of cotton held under the 12-cent loan. Johnston's plan, approved by Wallace in March and later by RFC Chairman Jesse Jones but not announced pending the clearing of the political waters, required no congressional approval. It provided for the return of one million bales of loan cotton to producers by September 1, 1936, at 11.25 cents per pound—a figure below the loan rate. The growers would make a profit, the government, though absorbing some loss, would be rid of some of its bearish cotton, and mills would be supplied with necessary varieties to keep pace with increased textile sales before the 1936 crop entered trade channels.[47]

To mollify Smith, the administration let him take credit for Johnston's plan, or so claimed *Newsweek* magazine. Despite the senator's long seniority and committee chairmanship, the Roosevelt administration had done little to cultivate the aging and crusty South Carolinian, whose career in the thirties was on the downside. More than once he complained bitterly to Chester Davis that the administration had ignored him and that "what they do to me they wouldn't do to a dog." Nor had Cotton Ed, whom *Time* called "the self-anointed chamberlain to King Cotton," hung his name on any significant agricultural legislation for three years—not since he had fathered the Cotton Option plan in early 1933. Sadly, Smith had already begun his slide into buffoonery. A perennial campaign race-baiter, he would in a few months gain lasting notoriety for stalking out of the Democratic National Convention in Philadelphia when a black clergyman offered the invocation. ("And as I pushed through those great doors, and walked across that vast rotunda," said Smith later, "it seemed to me that old John Calhoun leaned down from his mansion in the sky and whispered in my ear, 'You did right, Ed.'") Still, Cotton Ed was a long-time survivor, and would withstand FDR's attempted "purge" of anti–New Dealers in 1938, only to be felled in his bid for a seventh term in 1944 when the times had clearly passed him by. In any case, in the spring of 1936, Smith abandoned his marketing bill—"manifest surrender," said one reporter—and introduced another that essentially embodied the administration plan. This face-saver, quickly passed, was largely a pitiful charade since the plan required no legislative approval. Unfortunately for Smith, the embarrassment leaked to the press and, despite the administration's patronizing efforts, Senator Smith, chided *Newsweek*, "still feels very badly."[48]

More important, the favorable response from the cotton trade exceeded all expectations. Although the original CCC plan called for the sale of a million bales by September 1, at a loss borne by the government, farmers had been so enthusiastic that RFC Chairman Jones announced on May 7 that the loan cotton would be returned to producers for resale by June 1. The cotton withdrawn from government loan stocks during April and May immediately went into domestic consumption or was exported. The Hoosac Mills decision also helped the domestic textile industry by killing the processing tax, thereby lowering staple costs by about 25 percent. By late spring, mills in the United States hummed above pre-Depression levels and even a fifth or a quarter above that of 1935. In the same period, French and German mills increased consumption 25–30 percent while English mills ran about 15 percent above the previous year. A number of British mills as well as mills in New England and in the southeast ran into difficulty obtaining sufficient unencumbered staple. In June some U.S. firms warned the CCC they would have to shut down in the absence of desirable supplies. Further, it appeared the carryover of varieties grown in the Mississippi Valley would be quite small.[49]

Commodity Credit responded to the demand. At a CCC meeting on Saturday, June 27, RFC Chairman Jesse Jones asked Johnston, who had returned from the Democratic National Convention in Philadelphia, how much lien cotton the trade would take. Oscar, who had monitored developments and urged the release of additional cotton, thought about 350,000 would satisfy the demand. That same day, with spot markets at nearly 12.4 cents, the CCC announced the release of additional 1934 staple through July 20, 1936. In less than three weeks, buyers grabbed up more than a quarter million bales, with a few more days to run. At the end of the second release, growers had apparently sold a bit more than 390,000 bales. Throughout the revival period, moreover, the market advanced from about 11.5 cents in the spring to more than 13 cents in July. By the following year, producers redeemed more than 2.7 million bales of loan cotton at a loss to the government of about $14 million. As consolation, the government reduced its burdensome supply in orderly fashion. Further withdrawals reduced the total to only 1,665,000 bales under the 12-cent loan in 1937. Several weeks after the June 27 announcement, Johnston, back in Scott, told CCC general counsel John Goodloe, "Criticism and complaint from the mills was silenced. The market behaved beautifully, and, in my judgment, the whole situation fully justified the course which we pursued."[50]

Meanwhile, Johnston successfully liquidated the cotton pool in the spring and summer of 1936. Since the pool had reopened in February, sales had steadily drained available stocks, including bales warehoused in New York, New Jersey, and New England, as well as low-grade varieties for use in mattress construction. Johnston liquidated about 200,000 May futures and in June sold the pool's 317,000 July holdings on an advancing market; he then began selling the remaining 124,300 October futures. On July 7, with the bell on the New York Cotton Exchange sounding the close of the day's trading, brokers quietly bought up the last 25,000 October contracts held in the pool and the federal government went out of the cotton contract market for the first time since the old Farm Board began its futures operations in 1930. Between February and July 1936 Johnston had sold nearly a million bales of government futures on a generally advancing market. During the same period he accepted bids on the pool's last 630,000 spot bales and carefully parceled them out when the market could absorb them. By the time the futures were liquidated, only about 80,000 spot bales remained in the pool, most or all of which stood in warehouses in Galveston and Houston, where they were available for export to the Far East. Save for a mere 106 bales, title to which was being litigated, the last of the pool's stocks found buyers by the end of July 1936. Then the last tangible legacy of the Farm Board passed into trade channels. Though little or no fanfare marked the event, Harris Dickson later wrote, "The cotton trade now breathes easier, no longer panicky over two and one-half million unsold bales that would break the markets. Big operators and little operators gather round on July 31st, smiling happily when they saw the government shut up shop and take down its sign, UNCLE SAM, COTTON MERCHANT."[51]

Controversy marked Johnston's two-and-a-half year management of the pool. Given his discretion and the lack of precedent, such controversy should not have been unexpected. He took criticism from nearly every quarter, but never more than over his policy of replacing spots with futures. That policy may even have strained his working relationship with Wallace, who eventually opposed the practice. More fundamental were the nagging questions about the pool's purpose and Johnston's motives. During the hearings on the Smith bill in February 1936 a New York columnist publicly raised an oft-discussed issue: "whether the producers' pool was being conducted for the purpose of selling cotton in the interest of its members, or was being conducted as a price-controlling organization, a sort of cotton stabilization fund." Johnston clearly believed the latter flowed from the former, and his sense of stewardship for pool members is unmistakable. Jerome Frank, who often scuffled with Johnston over legal issues in the AAA, wondered about more arcane motives, namely Johnston's possible desire to play the commodity market with industry powerhouses such as Will Clayton. "Oscar's eyes grew big," recalled Frank. "He thought he was smarter than, or as smart as, Clayton, but he never had enough money to play against Clayton in the market." The pool gave him that chance. "That," said Frank, "together with this other stuff he'd done, gave him a tremendous position in the cotton market." Johnston "was a very rapid thinker," recalled Frank, "and it was very difficult to keep up with him. I had to watch him to see that he was doing these things legally. I was a little afraid. Oscar was a very able man. . . . But I was afraid that Oscar, with the United States Treasury behind him, might go haywire." Of course, no hard evidence has surfaced to support such a loose observation about Oscar's motives. Still, the control of the pool—and in some measure the market—could be heady indeed. "At once," after Johnston took over the cotton pool, said Harris Dickson later, "the amiable Mr. Johnston became a figure of fear. Big operators trembled at his power, too much power as they complained for one man to wield, and apprehended a panic whenever he might offer 'pool' cotton for sale." That did not happen, but Johnston's discretionary power, often exercised with Wallace's approval, gave enormous significance to his every pronouncement at home and abroad about federally controlled cotton. The potential for personal and corporate corruption was so vast as to make the pool unique among commodity operations. Johnston knew that no one person would wield such power again.[52]

Independent criticism also arose. In April 1936, shortly after the government announced its intention to release a million bales of loan cotton back to producers for marketing, the Brookings Institution, a Washington public policy think tank, issued one of its commodity studies, *Cotton and the AAA,* by economist I. I. Richards. Sterile in prose but able in research, the study heavily criticized federal loan practice in part because it allegedly retarded consumption of U.S. staple. Richards also suggested that the government's ten-cent loan in 1933 would have prevented option holders from breaking the market without establishing the cotton pool. Richards, whose data did not reflect the rapid developments in the spring of 1936, argued that "it is necessary to conclude that the AAA has not demonstrated its ability to dispose of government cotton."[53]

Richards's points were arguable. That the twelve-cent loan had retarded consumption of American cotton is beyond serious question. Johnston knew that. He had made a mistake. If the government had lost money on the deal, maybe the South might have told itself that it was their subsidy, like the tariff had been for northerners. But the formation of the 1933 pool seemed a logical if unique step in the disposition of cotton held by the old Farm Board and other agencies. It was a judgment call, and Johnston's management of the cotton pool embodied a string of judgment calls. The pool certainly took longer to drain than anyone would have guessed. And Johnston had no desire for an encore with the cotton under the twelve-cent loan; in the summer of 1935 he even opposed widespread reconcentration of loan cotton from interior to port warehouses partly because he feared it might lead to another pool. His own experience, he told the CCC, had exhibited the bearish influence of such amalgamation. He argued that it was best to leave the loan cotton scattered throughout the South in the hands of those who had grown it. In any case, while Richards's study was still warm from the press in 1936, the CCC's second release of loan cotton quieted complaints from textile mills, hardly disturbed the market, and in Johnston's view, exonerated the government's course.[54]

Despite controversy, Johnston's management of the cotton pool proved successful. By adhering to the specifics of the pool arrangements, he gradually fed the burdensome Hoover cotton into consumption at appropriate opportunities and generated profits for participating producers. Pool sales grossed $175 million, with the price for nearly 2 million bales, through two years of market fluctuation, averaging an astounding 12.4 cents per pound. Johnston's Pool operations pumped $67 million into the pockets of farmers, who sacrificed $23 million in plow-up benefits, leaving a handsome profit of $44 million. After deducting benefits and operating costs, including brokers' fees, commissions, administrative costs, and carrying charges, an audit showed a surplus of $1.8 million. Few New Deal agencies could boast such success, and Johnston was proud of it.[55]

The accolades began even before the pool's liquidation. The cotton trade, including the exchanges, was happy with the outcome. John Goodloe, general counsel for Commodity Credit, told Johnston, "I suppose you are receiving directly many of the congratulatory expressions being heard here with reference to the liquidation of the producers' pool and, also, to the manner in which the release of the 12 cent loan cotton has been handled." The British Fine Spinners, having loaned Johnston to the AAA with mixed feelings, also lauded him for his achievement, which undoubtedly, said Herbert Stowell, "has not only been of enormous use to the trade, but also must have added very considerably to your status in being entrusted with the management of it." He added: "It must have needed a very considerable amount of thought and arrangement in order to see that everything worked out in a suitable way without injuring too much the position of so many different interests."[56]

While the liquidation of the pool could not have been successful without the temporary revival of the worldwide cotton economy in 1936 and the impounding of the loan cotton, Johnston's patient management and healthy disdain for cumbersome bureaucracy made success more likely. His pool office counted six employees—including Johnston, an assistant, a technician, and a stenographer, messenger, and secretary—with annual salaries totaling about twenty-five thousand dollars. He shrewdly outguessed the speculators, seized numerous marketing opportunities—even if he was perhaps too conservative at times—and provided a stabilizing if sometimes bearish influence on the cotton trade. He easily vindicated Chester Davis's remark about him to relief administrator Harry Hopkins in June 1934. "I do not believe," said Davis, "there is any man in the country who understands cotton marketing better than he does."[57]

Meanwhile, Johnston withstood uneasiness within the AAA about his pool management, shrugged off a challenge from the chairman of the Senate agriculture committee, and welcomed an investigation of his transactions. In 1938 he saw his handling of the pool relative to the American Cotton Cooperative Association (ACCA) endorsed after a Senate probe of that agency. The report of the Senate agriculture committee's investigation of the ACCA, the New Orleans agency which handled the bulk of the pool cotton, cleared it of any wrongdoing. When the committee voted eleven to two in June 1938 to accept the vindicating report sponsored by Louisiana's Democratic freshman senator, Allen Ellender, the *New Orleans Times-Picayune* claimed it "took a deliberate slap at its chairman, Senator Ellison Smith of South Carolina." Reportedly Ellender and Smith nearly came to physical blows over the report.[58] For his part, Johnston had articulated the vital stake of the cotton producer in national and international commerce.

Oscar was gratified by the whole thing. He told his old exiled friend George Peek, now an administration critic, that he was "delighted with the thought that I have now about concluded the arduous task which you 'wished on me three years ago,' and notwithstanding the fact, and probably will be, fraught with many disagreeable incidents, the job has been a most interesting one."

Replied Peek: "I have had many occasions to comment upon the magnificant [*sic*] manner in which you ran away with the job in Washington." One British commodity broker had a similar reaction. "I consider you have certainly pulled the brands out of the fire," he said, "and I believe you are one of the very few men who could have done it." Referring to the economic upswing of 1936, he added, "Well, after many years of depression, it looks as if cotton is King again."[59] Unfortunately for His Majesty, the advancing market of 1936 proved only a breathing spell. The economic dislocations and loss of markets occasioned by depression, Smoot-Hawley, and World War II still lay ahead.

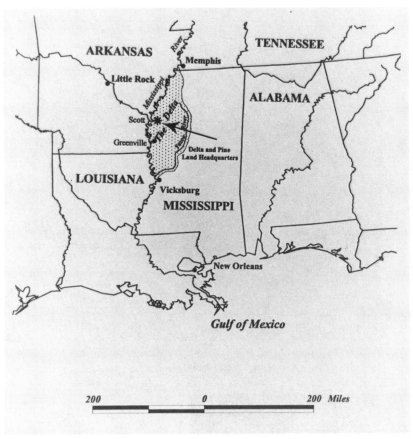

The Mississippi Delta. Adapted from *Fortune*, March 1937, by Lisa Keys-Mathews.

Johnston family photograph, ca. 1890s. Oscar is fourth from left (in chair). His father, J. C. Johnston, is third from right. Courtesy of the Johnston family.

Oscar G. Johnston, cotton's advocate, in a contemplative pose (date unknown). Courtesy of the National Cotton Council.

In Memphis, Tennessee, Oscar Johnston (right) explains the cotton acreage reduction and subsidy program to D. E. Wilson, a Nesbit, Mississippi, planter who had fifteen hundred acres in cotton in 1933. Wilson was also head of the Mississippi Farm Bureau. Johnston was in Memphis in June 1933 to sell the New Deal cotton program to planters, bankers, and others. From the *Memphis Press-Scimitar* Morgue. Courtesy of the University of Memphis Libraries.

Oscar Johnston reading ticker tape in the Department of Agriculture, 1933.

Oscar G. Johnston,
ca. 1933. Courtesy
of the National
Cotton Council.

Johnston with Harry Wilson, Louisiana commissioner of agriculture, ca. 1933. From
the *Memphis Press-Scimitar* Morgue. Courtesy of the University of Memphis Libraries.

Johnston (top right, center) with General Manager Jesse Fox (to Johnston's right) and plantation unit managers, Delta and Pine Land Company, 1930s. Alfred Eisenstaedt, Life Magazine, © Time Inc.

Johnston with Archibald Toler, his loyal assistant and Delta and Pine Land Company's secretary, 1930s. Alfred Eisenstaedt, Life Magazine, © Time Inc.

Lonnie Fair, a sharecropper at Delta and Pine Land Company, 1930s. Alfred Eisenstaedt, Life Magazine, © Time Inc.

Delta and Pine Land Company sharecropper Lonnie Fair having his cotton checked, 1930s. Alfred Eisenstaedt, Life Magazine, © Time Inc.

**DELTA & PINE LAND CO. OF MISSISSIPPI**

Scott, Miss. NOV 21 1933 ___ 193___

Bought of _Darby Leubler_

Plantation _LEE_

How Works _____ ½ With Company _____

LAWRENCE GREENWOOD 28438

| BALE No. | WEIGHT | TOTAL WEIGHT | PRICE | AMOUNT |
|---|---|---|---|---|
| 1 | | | | |
| 2 | | 2040 | 10 x | 204 00 |
| 3 | | | | |
| 4 | | | | |
| 5 | | 2860 | 9 x | 257 60 |
| 6 | | | | |
| 7 | | | | |
| 8 | | | | |
| 9 | | | | |
| 10 | | 550 | 8 x | 44 00 |
| 11 Remnant | 5000 | 10480 @ 3 ½ | | 60 7 80 |
| 12 | | | | 15 00 |

19810

| | | |
|---|---|---|
| | Total Cotton | 922 50 |
| Seed at $12.00 per Ton—Lb. 2096 0 | Amount Seed | 146 72 |
| Total Amount Cotton and Seed | | 1069 52 |
| Less Levee Tax - - - $ 20.96 | | 136 22 |
| Less Gin Charge $ 115.28 | | |
| | NET | 933 28 |

Deduct $_____ For Hauling

| | | |
|---|---|---|
| ½ To Tenant | 466 64 | 466 64 |
| To | | 287 30 |
| ½ To Company | 466 6 | 179 34 |
| Total | 933 2 | |

Prepared by _____

Checked by _____

PAID NOV 21 1933 SCOTT MISS.

Delta and Pine Land Company settlement sheet from 1933. Courtesy William R. Amberson Papers, Southern Historical Collection, Library of the University of North Carolina at Chapel Hill.

Delta and Pine Land Company, 1930s. Oscar Johnston's unpretentious office was on the second floor of the building at right. Alfred Eisenstaedt, Life Magazine, © Time Inc.

Cotton bales prepared for shipment, Delta and Pine Land Company. Alfred Eisenstaedt, Life Magazine, © Time Inc.

Oscar and Martha Johnston's home at Delta and Pine Land Company, 1930s. His dog Whoopi is in the driveway. Alfred Eisenstaedt, Life Magazine, © Time Inc.

Johnston with Senator John H. Bankhead II (D-Ala.), seeking congressional sanction of a program to protect the cotton industry during war emergency, March 7, 1941. Courtesy of AP/Wide World Photos.

Johnston at the witness table (on postwar planning for cotton), U.S. Senate, Washington, D.C., December 12, 1944. Courtesy of the National Cotton Council.

Johnston speaking at the National Cotton Picking Contest, 1946. Courtesy of the National Cotton Council.

Johnston with "Maid of Cotton" Hilma Seay of Memphis, Tennessee, May 1947. Seay's cotton attire was designed to promote cotton's use in fashion. From the *Memphis Press-Scimitar* Morgue. Courtesy of the University of Memphis Libraries.

Johnston in later days, 1948. Courtesy of the National Cotton Council.

Martha and Oscar Johnston (retired) in 1949. Courtesy of the National Cotton Council.

# When Hope Was All But Gone

Cal Alley cartoon which appeared in the *Memphis Commercial Appeal,* October 5, 1955, following Oscar Johnston's death. Courtesy of the *Commercial Appeal.*

# 10

# Tempest in a Tea Pot

BRITISH-OWNED FIRM IN MISSISSIPPI GETS HUGE A.A.A. PAYMENTS—
CONCERN HEADED BY ASSOCIATE OF WALLACE—. . .
—*Providence Journal*, 1936

The House was told that Queen Elizabeth has a financial interest in a
Mississippi farm that received $1.54-million in subsidy payments in the
last two years.                                    —*New York Times*, 1971

**I**n the vanguard of large-scale corporate agriculture in the South,
Oscar Johnston never wanted unnecessary publicity for his huge and largely
foreign-owned plantation. Corporate enterprises could easily arouse populist
passions lurking beneath the surface of southern politics. During the redneck's
revolt, Johnston had seen the Vardamans and Bilbos stir such passions. His own
bid for governor had been badly damaged by his portrayal as a representative
of planter interests.[1]

In the mid-thirties Johnston and his giant plantation found themselves in
the national limelight over the company's large New Deal subsidies. The controversies of the cotton pool had not yet cooled before he found himself embroiled in another one. Ironically, the new attention sprang not from the long
tradition of redneck passion but from investigative journalism and issue-hungry
Republicans looking for political capital in an election year. It was Oscar's nightmare come true.[2]

After the Supreme Court gutted the original AAA in early 1936, one Republican senator, Michigan's Arthur H. Vandenberg, displayed an interest in
the beneficiaries of the New Deal's crop-reduction program. Vandenberg, a
sometime-mentioned Republican presidential prospect, had his antenna tuned
for Democratic embarrassment if not scandal. In February 1936, for example,
he charged that WPA workers had to make kickbacks to Democratic campaign
coffers. Now prospects of new soil conservation legislation providing subsidies
for cooperating producers heightened curiosity in past recipients. By "a clever
bit of sleuthing," according to *Time*, Vandenberg found that Supreme Court
Justice Willis Van Devanter, who had not recused himself in the Hoosac Mills

case, had been executor and beneficiary of some AAA payments accruing from his late wife's Montana farm holdings. The checks, which Van Devanter soon returned, were pathetically small—sixty dollars and change. Aware of some very large payments to big-time producers, Vandenberg hunted larger game. "Who, he asked," wrote *Time*, "was the cotton grower who received $168,000, the hog-raiser who received $219,825, the Puerto Rican sugar producer who received $961,064?"[3]

Aware that the administration would not like to disclose AAA benefits to wealthy individuals and corporations ("They would sound bad," said *Newsweek*), Vandenberg queried Secretary Henry Wallace about payments of $10,000 or more. In fact, Vandenberg introduced a Senate resolution in March 1936 mandating such disclosure. Within two weeks Cotton Ed Smith's Senate agriculture committee endorsed the idea, dropped the disclosure ceiling to $1,000, and recommended passage by the full Senate. (Even Mississippi's junior senator, Theodore G. Bilbo, for whatever motive, quietly inquired about Delta and Pine Land Company's benefits through 1935.) Meanwhile, one enterprising journalist for Rhode Island's *Providence Journal*, Stanley Chipman, got a scoop. His prying, including information from Dun and Bradstreet, revealed that Delta and Pine Land Company of Mississippi, with tens of thousands of acres, had been a large beneficiary of the AAA cotton-reduction program. (Approximately 18 percent of the most recent benefits went to tenants, according to the AAA.) But that was only the beginning. He found that the company's president, Oscar G. Johnston, who drew more than $42,000 in salary and bonuses for 1934, was "one of the ranking officials in A.A.A.," and the corporation was "controlled by the Fine Spinners and Doublers Association of Manchester, England." He broke his story in the *Providence Journal* on April 5: "BRITISH-OWNED FIRM IN MISSISSIPPI GETS HUGE A.A.A. PAYMENTS—CONCERN HEADED BY ASSOCIATE OF WALLACE—. . ." Savoring the revelations, Vandenberg had the story reprinted in the *Congressional Record*.[4]

An apparent conflict of interest hovered about the story. Johnston, "regarded as one of the most able cotton growers in the South," ran the cotton pool and helped direct the Commodity Credit Corporation. He was "prominently associated with Secretary Wallace and Administrator Davis in the A.A.A.," and was "[v]ested with official powers which enable him to exercise vast influence over cotton growing and merchandising of raw cotton." Chipman got to the real problem: "The question also may be raised whether the financial interests held in the Delta & Pine Land Co. by the English textile firm has not aided it to compete with American textile manufacturers. Inasmuch as the English company is reported to be the principal bondholder in the Mississippi enterprise, it is assumed that it enjoyed interest payments through revenue derived in substantial measure from United States Government subsidies." "Without any reflections at all on Mr. Johnston," Senator Vandenberg said of the whole business, "the question immediately arises as to whether this is a proper practice."[5]

Vandenberg's spark—"some hot copy," *Fortune* called it later—suddenly burst into flame. While Chipman's public revelation was still on the newsstands, Secretary Wallace, who had resisted disclosure, now felt the heat and released a report to Smith's Senate committee containing some figures on the corporations that had received large AAA subsidies under the crop-reduction program. Not surprisingly, Oscar Johnston and Delta and Pine Land Company stood high on the list. Johnston, "nationally known cotton expert, manager of the Federal Cotton Pool and associated since June of 1933 with the AAA," had received the largest single payment for 1934, totaling nearly $124,000 in that year alone.[6]

This provided front-page material for both the *New York Times* and the *Washington Post.* The *Post* headlined its story on April 8: "$177,947 AAA Cash Paid to British Firm, Wallace's List Shows." The accompanying story was no better: "Close scrutiny of Secretary Wallace's list of large benefit payments under the AAA yesterday developed the fact that a British-controlled Mississippi cotton plantation received in 1933 and 1934 a total of $177,947 for not growing cotton. The president of the cotton-growing enterprise, the Delta & Pine Land Co., of Scott, Miss., is Oscar G. Johnston, manager of the cotton producers' pool for the AAA, and director and first vice-president of the Commodity Credit Corporation which lends to producers directly or through banks." In New Orleans, on April 9, the *Times-Picayune* put its story, "Link Pool Head and British Growers," on page 12, while closer to home, the *Memphis Press-Scimitar* the same day titled its wire-service story "AAA Generous to Britishers," adding the subheading, "But Checks for $178,000 To Plantation Were Deserved, Says Wallace."[7]

Actually, Johnston's name and that of his company had been the only ones specified in Wallace's preliminary report to Smith's committee. Other large recipients, still anonymous, had been listed only by locality, and the report showed a total of forty-six cotton payments over $10,000 in 1933. Wallace quickly added, "It is easy to concentrate attention on these big payments, but they are not representative." The forty-six largest cotton payments, he showed, amounted to less than 1 percent of the $112,700,000 paid to cotton growers in 1933 under the AAA. "Neither the act, nor the farmers using the act," Wallace declared, "regarded the payments as charity, but as a system of financing a practicable operation to control production and bring about improvement for the whole agricultural industry." The next day the secretary went on the radio to defend the AAA benefit payments and reaffirm that most of the federal money "went to the men who needed it most, the small producers." Vandenberg, meanwhile, kept up the attack. Wallace, he charged, had "succeeded up to now in keeping under cover·all these flagrant cases of shoveling the people's money into the coffers of the corporations, when all the time the country was laboring under the impression that the billion dollar farm benefit fund was being parceled out to individual farmers who are in financial distress."[8]

Wallace's initial reluctance to release the names of large beneficiaries proved embarrassing. Meanwhile, as *Time* reported later, "The Senate Agriculture Committee embraced the Vandenberg resolution almost as if it had been an Administration measure, [and] prepared to whip it through the Senate at the first opportunity." Trying to catch up with events, Wallace claimed he had no problem with the thrust of Vandenberg's resolution, that he too believed in public disclosure. He objected, however, to the time-consuming task involved in reporting all the names and said that the Department of Agriculture routinely rejected requests for public disclosure because the department did not wish to aid creditors or those who would exploit the recipient. "Besides," said *Time* in its paraphrase of Wallace, "the list might induce gangsters to invade the [recipient's] farm," thus placing the "farmer's daughter" in danger. Vandenberg retorted, "If the farmer who made that $298,000 for not planting so many thousands of acres of cotton has a daughter, she must be a girl without a soul. That farmer is a corporation." The tension was humorously relieved when Wallace countered, in his midwestern accent, "that he had said the 'farmer's dollar,' not the 'farmer's daughter.'" Nevertheless, in a conciliatory letter to Cotton Ed Smith, Wallace indicated he would comply with congressional wishes.[9]

Wallace's belated efforts to placate Vandenberg failed to prevent the senator's resolution, along with Johnston and Delta Pine, from being dragged through a Senate floor debate. Vandenberg claimed that Wallace made the information on Johnston available because the secretary thought Vandenberg was going to reveal it in a speech. "I didn't intend to make a speech," Vandenberg said with a laugh, "because the first I knew of the checks Johnston had received was when I read of them in the paper." But the Michigan Republican was not laughing when he called for more information. "Let's have the names and addresses of all who received the big payments," he demanded. "Maybe there still is hidden away in the up-to-now confidential files instances of other officials on the AAA pay roll, who, like Oscar Johnston of Mississippi, government cotton expert, heads a company that admittedly has drawn down $177,947 for not raising or for plowing under cotton."[10]

Majority Leader Joseph T. Robinson of Arkansas tried to play down the whole embarrassment, suggesting to his Senate colleagues that Vandenberg was politically motivated, becoming "a great champion of publicity." Vandenberg, he said, had opposed passage of the Agricultural Adjustment Act in the first place. But Robinson also pointed out that his Senate colleague had also opposed a measure in 1932 to publish the names of recipients of loans from the Reconstruction Finance Corporation, a Republican creation. "Those Senators who hear him now as the emboldened champion of publicity for political purposes," said Robinson, "will be amazed to recall what he said [in 1932] when no Presidential campaign was in prospect for him and when only a senatorial campaign in Michigan was in the offing." Robinson entered part of Vandenberg's 1932 denunciation of publicity in the RFC case in the *Congressional Record*. He did the same for some remarks of Boake Carter, a popular commentator who also criticized Vandenberg's actions: "if the snorts of indignation [over AAA payments] are because of an outraged sense of righteousness," claimed Carter, "then perhaps the snorters are engaging in a little public hypocrisy. They are snorting at nothing less than a tariff, and a tariff is a pet G.O.P. baby." For more than a century, said Carter, the tariff—"which reached a climax in the Smoot-Hawley business"—put millions of consumer dollars in manufacturers' pockets. Add them up, he said, and it "would make the Triple A benefits to agriculture look like a pink-tea party in comparison." It looked like "the pot calling the kettle black."

Vandenberg, of course, never had been after mere disclosure. He wanted payment limits to big producers. Sen. Tom Connally, Democrat of Texas, knew that. Despite the fact that production costs would very likely decrease on a large and efficient plantation, Vandenberg was vulnerable on the point of equal treatment. Vandenberg, Connally charged, "is opposed to the way in which it [the AAA] is administered on a basis of equality, on a basis of equity, on a basis of impartiality, to give to the large farmers, though few there be, the same measure of justice that is given to the small farmers."

Political hypocrisy was nothing new. Still, despite Democratic counterattacks on Republican motives, Vandenberg, who denied political motives, possessed a powerful argument. In an obvious reference to Johnston and his official role in the AAA, Vandenberg asked if it was "sound public policy to leave any share of the responsibility for the granting of the payment of these subsidies in the hands of Government officers who are themselves large beneficiaries of these subsidies being granted and paid? Can there be any two opinions upon this proposition? Does it not involve a conflict of interest which the prudent administration of public affairs cannot tolerate?"[11]

That argument proved difficult to ignore. Whatever his motives, Vandenberg had exposed potential for corruption in government bureaucracy. His resolution passed the Senate on April 27, and in June, Wallace dutifully submitted a 134-page report detailing all AAA benefit payments over $10,000. The report showed that in three seasons, 1933–35, Delta and Pine Land Company had received more than $318,000 in government subsidies, while Delta Farms Company (changed in 1934 to Delta Planting Company) at Deeson, also foreign-owned and managed by Johnston, had received nearly $78,000 during the same period. Together, the totals approached $400,000.[12]

Johnston, meanwhile, made no public statement and apparently tried to ride out the storm. No one had charged him with dishonesty; a public reply might have drawn more attention than it was worth. Stanley Chipman had written as early as April 5 that "Mr. Johnston's integrity as a Government official has never been questioned." Still, there was an apparent conflict of interest. On April 18, 1936, while the issue smoldered in the press and in the Senate, Johnston appeared before Cotton Ed Smith's agriculture committee to testify about his cotton pool activities. When one investigator asked him if he was "connected with an English cotton firm," Oscar replied, "Unfortunately, yes."[13]

On the other side of the Atlantic, the British press had picked up the story. "American Congressmen were startled to-day," reported one British daily on April 6, "by a newspaper report that a British-controlled cotton enterprise in Mississippi has been receiving large benefits in cotton subsidies from the Federal Government." Another paper headed its story in similar fashion: "£40,000 Farm Payment—U.S. Crop Plan Aids Manchester Firm." The paper claimed, "The campaign is now taking on momentum on the discovery that American farm relief has helped pay the interest of British bondholders, and possibly aided foreign textile interests in competition with American manufacturers." Herbert W. Lee, the Fine Cotton Spinners' chairman, publicly acknowledged that the British had a controlling interest in Delta and Pine Land Company but insisted that there was "nothing unusual about that." "We have no political influence of any description," he declared. "These companies are American companies under American law, and they have not participated in benefits to any greater extent than any of the other cotton plantations."[14]

Maintaining a public posture designed to play down the revelations, the British privately betrayed their irritation: "it seems rather ridiculous," wrote Herbert Stowell to the American company, "that any fuss should be made over a past effort that whatever might be said about it, appeared to have a fair amount of success, and was possibly the only way to save the situation." Still, the British bondholders declared that the controversy caused them little alarm. "The offer to put land out of action was an optional one produced for the benefit of the farmers," Stowell said with an air of indignation. "The D. & P.L. Co. agreed to support it, and it might have been foolish and would not have been loyal if they had not done so. The plan was produced in order to put prices on to a better basis and to give the owner of land some possibilities to recover from the disastrous seasons that had resulted after the big drop in prices had taken effect." He added: "It might be argued that the Plantations would have done as well, if not better, by not agreeing to that offer. It was, however, a deal that was meant to be open to all that desired to take part in it."[15]

In a private reply to the Fine Spinners, Johnston suggested that Vandenberg was politically motivated and had an eye on the Republican presidential nomination in competition with Alf Landon, Frank Knox, William E. Borah, and former president Herbert Hoover. Vandenberg had also unearthed big payments to corporations under the sugar and corn-hog programs. "Evidently," said Johnston on April 21, "Vandenburg [*sic*] felt that he might get some notoriety from developing for the public the facts in connection with these payments, at the sametime [*sic*] he felt that the making of these large payments to corporate interests would prove unpopular with the labor element in the industrial sections." He echoed British optimism: "The whole matter was somewhat of a 'tempest in a tea pot,' and appears to have blown over."[16]

Johnston was partly right, but he was mostly wrong. The great splash of publicity did subside, but AAA critics quietly began working for a restructuring of the AAA payment system. In April Vandenberg had declared publicly that he wanted a reverse sliding scale to limit payments on larger operations. On June 6, 1936, in a rare Saturday session, the Senate took action on the big-payments issue. It voted to amend the Soil Conservation Act by curtailing by 25 percent AAA payments over $2,000. Payments over $10,000 would be cut in half.[17]

The tempest grew stronger. The Delta Chamber of Commerce, a relatively new organization that occasionally served as a Washington lobby for the thousand or so large planters in the nineteen counties of northwest Mississippi, quickly approved a protest following a hastily called meeting of its agricultural committee, of which Johnston was a member. The spokesman for the Delta chamber, William Rhea Blake, fired off a letter to Secretary Wallace. "In the first place," he protested, "it certainly is not right to change the rules in the middle of the game." He also included a warning about the consequences if the Senate amendment passed the House:

> Even if the Bill is not made effective this year, we still feel that such a policy of discrimination against the large operators in this section, as set forth in the Senate Bill, is unfair, not only to the operator, but also to his renters and share croppers. *This will most certainly result in the large operators withdrawing from the Program and increasing their cotton acreage.* It is not hard to imagine the reaction that will set in when the cry goes out that "the large operator is increasing acreage while the little man is cutting acreage." Such a deplorable condition would unquestionably demoralize the entire Soil Conservation Program in this section.[18]

The Delta Chamber also planned a lobbying campaign directed at Wallace and the Delta's congressional delegation, although it was probably unnecessary. Time stood on the side of the planters; within two weeks Congress adjourned leaving the planters' interests secure, "at least for the time being."[19]

Undaunted, Senator Vandenberg renewed his investigation of AAA benefit payments when the Department of Agriculture appropriation bill for 1938 came before the Senate in the next Congress. On the Senate floor he railed against alleged bureaucratic mishandling of AAA funds and then directed his attacks at large wheat and sugar companies whose operations were heavily mechanized and required few laborers. It was only a matter of time until Delta and Pine Land Company was drawn into the fray. In May 1937 Vandenberg inquired into its participation in the government programs.[20]

Soil Conservation Administrator Howard Tolley answered Vandenberg's inquiry about Delta Pine openly and promptly, referring the senator also to Wallace's public report of June 1936. Tolley's office showed Johnston Vandenberg's letter and asked him to check the accuracy of their report. Johnston soon dispatched a lengthy letter to Tolley on June 4, 1937, explaining both details and rationale for his company's participation in the AAA program. Privately, Johnston was a bit disgusted with Secretary Wallace's recent statements to the House agriculture committee about payments to large producers. When the original issue arose in 1936 Wallace had loyally, if a bit clumsily, defended the payments. He had even suggested that critics of the system be prepared to offer "either a method of breaking up large-scale holdings or a plan of production adjustment which would have worked without their being included." Now Wallace appeared to weaken, seemingly amenable to a sliding benefit scale similar in intent to what Vandenberg had been advocating. Responding to Wallace's comments, Johnston bluntly told Cully Cobb in June 1937, "Unless it is thought that the programs can be made successful without the cooperation of the so-called plantation type cotton producer, it would be idle for Congress to set up a scale providing for reduced compensation to the large operators, for it is quite certain that they would not cooperate if so discriminated against." Johnston thought Wallace suffered a common misperception: "that the larger producers benefit disproportionately as compared with smaller producers as a result of benefit payments." In fact, Johnston claimed the opposite was the case. "The cooperation with the program for the last four years has been extremely costly to the large operators," he told Cobb. "Such operators usually have certain fixed overhead expenses, they are equipped and powered to operate their full base acreage, they have in the past produced their own food and feed crops to a considerable extent. To take out of cotton land, which is cultivated on a share basis, and to shift that land to nonmarketable crops, which are not particularly needed to the operation and which must be worked on a cash basis, is a costly procedure."[21]

Johnston's June 4 letter to Tolley provided the venue for breaking his long public silence on the big payments controversy. His letter apparently implied that Vandenberg was hypocritical in view of the tariff bounty accruing to Michigan sugar beet interests. Since AAA payments to cotton producers totaled more than $125 million annually, compared with only about $6 million to Michigan's sugar interests, Tolley thought Johnston would place himself in an embarrassing position. Before releasing Johnston's letter to the press, Assistant Administrator Alfred Stedman, wishing to protect his colleague from "an effective comeback by the Senator," telephoned Oscar in Mississippi and suggested he alter the reference to the sugar interests. Johnston agreed, and after the revised letter was forwarded to Vandenberg, copies of the fresh version were posted on the AAA's press-section bulletin board. Wire services and press correspondents gave Johnston's first public statement on the issue "a good play" in the Sunday editions of July 11, 1937.[22]

Johnston explained his company's participation in the AAA reduction programs. After detailing Delta Pine's compliance with the 1933–36 government contracts, he summed up by declaring that the company could have made more profits had it not complied with the reduction program (a fiscal possibility because of the rise in the cotton market, but politically prohibitive). He added, however, that compliance was no "sacrifice." He continued: "We feel that the active cooperation of large and small producers was essential. We cooperated in the program not because of the expectation of rentals and benefit payments, but because we believed in the economic soundness of those programs, we believed that they were essential to the restoration of any degree of prosperity to the nation, we believed that they could not succeed without the cooperation of at least eighty per cent of the producers, we believed that the burden incident to this cooperation should not be borne alone by the small producers." Johnston also claimed the tenant census at Scott had risen, while tenant credit more than doubled. Delta Pine, he said, paid more than $130,000 in direct federal and state taxes in 1935 alone. "If it is felt that these programs can be made just as effective without the cooperation of the larger producing operations, we are willing to be excused from further participation therein, and to leave the burden incident to reduction of the existing surplus of cotton upon the shoulders of the small producers, but in so doing we point out that in our judgment such a course would be grossly unfair to the small producer."

Johnston took a parting shot at Republican protectionism. Subsidies to cotton farmers, regardless of the size of their operations, he said, were "negligible when compared to the enormous bounty which the consumers of America pay annually as a subsidy to the tariff protected industries of America."[23]

The AAA thought the release of Johnston's statement would "help to correct any unfair opinions about the whole situation." In its own defense, the agency claimed that payments to Delta and Pine Land Company were required under the law; if Congress did not like the law, then Congress would have to change it. And that is what Congress did. After nearly a year of haggling over the contents of general farm legislation, Congress passed the Agricultural Adjustment Act of 1938 in February of that year. Tucked into Title I of the act was a $10,000 ceiling on soil-conservation payments, effective January 1, 1939. Although Johnston and other officials of the planter-dominated Delta Chamber of Commerce had deemed such a limitation "unfair and unconstitutional" when it was proposed in 1937, he issued no public protest at the time of its passage.[24]

He did, however, briefly consider establishing a small, noncontiguous part of Delta and Pine Land Company as a separate plantation, making it eligible for an individual soil conservation payment like its giant parent. Barring that, he privately threatened to take his company out of the government program. He had told the British Fine Spinners as early as December 1936 that the company should remain in compliance only as long as they were compensated on the same basis as all other producers. Now that the discriminatory legislation had been approved, he told the company shareholders bluntly: "If this is not changed, it is probable that we shall decline to cooperate under, and comply with, the control program for 1939."[25]

Talk was cheap. Johnston and his companies were going nowhere. For him to have taken his plantations out of the federal programs would have compounded the problem, doubtless increasing what Johnston called "narrow-minded prejudice" toward corporate planters and severely limiting his effectiveness in speaking on subsequent government programs. And by the time the payment ceiling became law, Johnston was deeply involved in the organizational work of his National Cotton Council. In reality, it is unlikely that many large planters left the program over the limitation. Even prior to its implementation many privately feared that noncooperation with the Soil Conservation and Domestic Allotment Act of 1936 might cripple the AAA and lead to a six-cent crop. Equally important, while the AAA of 1938 placed a $10,000 ceiling on soil-conservation payments, the law imposed no limitation on the more significant price-adjustment payments, which were designed to provide a percentage of parity for cotton producers. Congress further reduced soil-conservation payments later on, but the controversy after World War II centered largely on the size of price-adjustment or parity payments that, in some individual cases, exceeded a million dollars. Such payments were not limited until the Agricultural Act of 1970, when Congress imposed a $55,000 ceiling.[26]

Although the ceiling on soil-conservation payments in the AAA quieted the big-payments controversy momentarily, the affair opened the door to later reminders of the existence of large-scale agricultural operations. In 1942 Johnston was again castigated in Congress as one of several who were "getting payments far beyond what they deserve." Six years later a Republican congressman, criticizing the New Deal and referring to Delta and Pine Land Company, declared: "While the New Deal reached down and exacted a Federal tax from people making $500 per year, it used the money to give the landed aristocracy of one farm of the South over $750,000 in subsidies." In 1957, two decades after the Vandenberg affair, *Life* magazine, in an editorial on inflation, asked, "Is there any reason why the U.S. taxpayer should pay—as it does—a $1.9 million subsidy to Mississippi's Delta & Pine Co., a British stock corporation, to raise unneeded cotton?" Two years after that, Sen. John J. Williams, a Delaware Republican, told his Senate colleagues, "We cannot justify a program which will support a British-owned corporation in its farming operations in America to the amount of nearly $6 million in just 3 years." In 1970, the House voted to limit price-support payments when, according to the *New York Times*, it "was told that Queen Elizabeth has a financial interest in a Mississippi farm that received $1.54-million in subsidy payments in the last two years."[27]

Such revelations always seemed to offend republican-yeoman values in America. But if one could cut through the demagoguery—and there was lots of that—the big-payments controversy had shown something about the state of American agriculture. Despite Henry Wallace's early efforts to show how unrepresentative payments to corporate planters were, the fact remained that the big planters possessed even more power in the cotton belt than their aggregate acreage would suggest. Like the planters of the Old South, these new corporate counterparts exerted influence out of proportion to their numbers. But how was that any different from any other part of the U.S. economy? Americans had always been ambivalent about bigness. And then the big-payments fiasco was part of the national debate over government-landlord-tenant relationships. That debate achieved tangible results in 1937 with the creation of the Farm Security Administration, an agency originally designed to encourage farm ownership. Viewed in that context, federal payments to larger producer-landlords, as the *Washington Post* suggested, intensified "doubts as to the extent of the benefits conferred upon the small tenant farmers and the sharecroppers, for whose assistance some naively thought the AAA program was designed." Such thoughts *were* naive—and quite aside from the point of either practicality or equity. At the same time it was genuinely disturbing for Americans to view the decline of the family farm and the malfunctioning of the agricultural ladder, whereby the thrifty were supposed to move toward fee-simple ownership, not bankruptcy. What business, after all, one might have asked, did Connecticut General Life Insurance Company have in receiving giant federal subsidies for its 24,000-acre plantation in Mississippi? It had a perfectly legal right, of course, but what did that say about the American economy? And subsidies to a foreign-owned corporation, as the Delta and Pine Land Company issue had shown, were even more explosive.[28]

Some did see the issue in larger context. "Publicity'on the larger crop benefit checks," suggested one news editor in 1936, "should be very helpful in showing how far the process of bankruptcy had gone in concentrating land ownership in the hands of bank[s] and insurance companies." These sentiments were also expressed by Texas Sen. Tom Connally, who, while acknowledging "the alarming growth of corporation farming" in the United States, nonetheless lauded the AAA for slowing the rate of forced farm sales between 1933 and 1935. Representative Marvin Jones of Texas, like other Democrats, tried—as would Johnston—to make the publicity over the federal subsidies a two-edged sword. Jones suggested that the Tariff Commission list all corporations that annually benefited $100,000 or more from tariff laws. The *Memphis Press-Scimitar* agreed. While noting that the AAA payments and the protective tariff were basically even, the paper charged that "the protective tariff was the original sin. Out of it grew the demand that the farmer who paid protective tariff prices for what he bought be given a tariff too." "For the first time Triple A put the tariff shoe on the farmer's foot."[29]

The New Deal had been generally good for American farmers and very good for large-scale agriculture, as the Vandenberg affair had shown. In mid-1935, President Roosevelt, apparently feeling the heat from Sen. Huey Long's charges that the administration had done little for farmers, asked Johnston to come up with some evidence verifying New Deal cotton contributions. Using figures from Dr. Mordecai Ezekiel, a USDA economist, Oscar did so, telling the president that cotton's net value had, on average, leaped nearly 80 percent in 1933–34 over 1932, from about $80 million to an average $400 million in each of the latter years. If parity had not been reached, it had "been approached," said Johnston, allowing cotton farmers to pay taxes and interest debts and become consumers of American products.[30]

That was true for Delta and Pine Land Company, though the big-payments controversy marred the most productive year in its history. For nearly a decade Johnston tried to hone the plantation's efficiency in order to attract potential buyers and release the British from their American investment. But the Vandenberg affair, with its negative publicity, was only one salvo in the continuing warfare against corporate agriculture. The Farm Credit Administration halted lending by federally controlled agencies to agricultural corporations unless the borrower's majority stockholders guaranteed repayment. Johnston thought the decision "purely arbitrary" and "without the slightest economic justification." It was, he told the British, a continuation "of the general preju-

dice against agricultural corporations, and is a demagogic catering to a socialistic labor and tenant agitation." Since Delta Pine's primary bondholders were
foreign, Johnston feared the new ruling meant putting up collateral other than
the real property, and seeking operating loans from commercial banks rather
than from the agencies the plantation had used in the past. But legal ceilings
limited the amounts national banks could lend on real property as collateral
for such loans. And heavy obligations against Delta Pine's first and second
mortgages essentially precluded further credit based on the company's assets.
The growing crop would be the lone collateral for operating funds, but the crop's
value could not be properly estimated until mid-season, and the plantation
needed cash for tenants, fertilizer, seed, and new mules long before that.[31]

Johnston had a solution. He resurrected his two-year-old scheme to buy
federal securities to use for collateral for operating loans, eliminating the need
to pledge the company's first-mortgage gold bonds. In a bad year, he told the
British, the company would not have to call on them for assistance, a soothing prospect for long-suffering bondholders. The Fine Spinners, anxious to
pay off the plantation's current account, and reluctant to throw more money
at their American investment, had earlier rejected the idea. Now, in flush days,
they proved more amenable. Details were worked out when a two-man British delegation visited the plantations in October 1936. Securities were purchased the following year, and the first-mortgage gold bonds were finally dispatched to Manchester.[32]

Besides adverse publicity and discriminatory financing, Delta Pine also faced
heavy excess and undistributed profits taxes under the Federal Revenue Act
of 1936. The company was enjoying a banner year, and Johnston was loathe to
shell out about $20,000 under the new law, at least not without exploring al-
ternatives. For months, Johnston, the Fine Spinners, and the company's New
York auditors haggled over the best course to pursue. Heavy taxes in America
and Britain discouraged distributing the excess profits by way of a dividend to
the Fine Spinners, and, aside from a change in the law or its rejection by the
courts, the only remaining way to legally dodge the tax was to declare insol-
vency and file for the appointment of a receiver. Neither Johnston nor the British
wanted that; the Fine Spinners, though having downplayed the Vandenberg
business earlier in the year, noted "a feeling easy to arouse in your own political parties against any foreign owned corporations." They wished no encores
involving perceptions of tax evasion.[33]

When hope faded for a test case in the courts, Johnston finally resolved to
pay the tax, though taking the auditor's advice to do so under protest. Oscar
had already taken his case to Pat Harrison, who, as chairman of the Senate
Finance Committee, worked for tax revision. Unfortunately for Delta and Pine

Land Company, the legislative battle for revision and repeal dragged on for years; the repeal came too late to save the company nearly $33,000 in undistributed profits taxes for 1936.[34]

One development to emerge from the tax issue was further consolidation of Delta Pine stock in British hands. Johnston wanted to act unilaterally on the Fine Spinners behalf and urged their acquisition of the remaining American shares. He had begun the process of acquiring more stock for the British in the late twenties, though by 1936, Americans, including himself, still owned about 13 percent of the total. If a dividend was declared, he thought the British should have it all. In the wake of the Vandenberg publicity, the Fine Spinners were less enthusiastic, believing the minority American shareholders made for good public relations. Still, Johnston got the green light, and by early 1937 garnered all the stock, save for a few holdouts, among them Shields Abernathy, Lant Salsbury's son-in-law, who clung to his twenty shares until 1950.[35]

None of the threats to corporate agriculture in 1936 could destroy the plantation's excellent year, likely "the most satisfactory" in the company's history, Johnston told the shareholders. Much of the success was clearly visible by August and September: big, beautiful white cotton bolls as far as the eye could see. Even the weather helped check the weevil. Tenants picked a phenomenal 660 pounds an acre at Scott. That was not only a company record but also, Johnston thought, maybe the best ever on a large-scale unit in America. Delta Pine's cotton, sold through the Staple Cotton Cooperative in Greenwood, commanded premium prices. Such mills as Parkdale, Ruby, and Cannon of North Carolina, and Standard Coosa Thatcher of Chattanooga grabbed up huge quantities. Buyers also lined up for Early Ewing's trade name Deltapine seed, developed in his laboratory and on thirty-odd experimental acres at Scott. The company sold a record four thousand tons of seed, netting an average of seventy dollars per ton. Among single merchandisers, the plantation by 1937 ranked first in the world in sales volume to other planters. There was more. The company built a new cotton gin in 1936, equipping it, and an older one, with a new diesel engine. For the 1937 season, new tenant houses were constructed, others repaired. New acreage was cleared and drained, while aerial photographs, designed to show land not in cultivation, would sharpen plantation efficiency.[36]

While Johnston knew the four profitable years of the New Deal would not necessarily be repeated, the 1936 season was what he had been working toward. He had been a loyal and able steward of British interests. But would the conservative British bondholders sell, even if buyers could be found? Johnston contemplated the sale of the noncontiguous Empire unit, which lay about forty miles south of Scott in Washington County. Some irregular tracts, totaling several hundred acres, had been sold to neighboring planters, leaving a well-honed efficient plantation of about 4,500 acres. His plan was to charter a producers' association at Empire, colonize it with white tenants, and allow them to amortize their farms over as much as forty years. The producers' association would hold title to community assets, and the tenants would be rigorously screened and adequately supervised. Construction of a hundred new houses, at $1,750 apiece, would be financed by the federal government. Profits from cooperative projects would be divided ratably. Johnston spent long hours developing the charter, deed of trust, amortization, costs, housing, subdivision, insurance, and anticipated yields. He had maps and plats. The time seemed right. The place stood in excellent shape, and Johnston believed the new Congress, scheduled to convene in January 1937, would fund the promotion of family farms. He either knew or got acquainted with all the officials likely to play a significant role in the negotiations, including W. W. Alexander, Resettlement Administration director; his assistant, Milo Perkins; and regional director T. Roy Reid and his assistant E. B. Whitaker, both in Little Rock, Arkansas.

The plan, detailed though it was, soon aborted. Despite great interest, the government had no available funds, at least none at the moment. Worse, the British torpedoed the scheme. If they sold at all, it would be the entire tract, not piecemeal over decades, even though subdivision offered more lucrative possibilities and, as Johnston told them after the fact, avoidance of a variety of taxes.[37]

Of Johnston's ideas *Fortune* mused later that Oscar's "skeptical, pragmatic body" possessed little more than an ounce of socialism, that his faith lay in well-run corporate plantations such as Delta and Pine Land, but that he wanted "a cooperative experiment" at Empire. That really missed the point. His plans for Empire had nothing whatever to do with socialism and everything to do with unloading British property at a favorable return, and, secondarily, with the encouragement of agrarian yeomanry. In that regard, his ideas had not really changed since the 1920s. "It is my belief, based upon almost a life time of observation in the Mississippi Delta," he said in 1927, five months after taking the reins of the Britishers' sprawling plantations, "that it is both practicable and profitable to grow cotton in the Mississippi Delta by corporations operating large acreage, at a profit, but I believe further that the best interest of the country would be served by having the properties cut into forty, eighty or one hundred sixty acre units, owned by individuals who would occupy and actually farm the land."[38]

Johnston took the British rebuff in stride, offering alternatives only as part of his stewardship. With an eye toward federal purchase of Empire for a government-run project, Johnston kept in touch with the Resettlement Administration. The agency had no funds for such a buyout, but, in the event of future appropriations, it had Empire appraised in 1937; a year later Whitaker approached Johnston about a possible sale. In September 1938, the Farm Security Administration, Resettlement's successor, tentatively offered $140,000 for Empire, excluding personal property, a sum naively low, even insulting, for a first-class moneymaker. Johnston replied, with a hint of indignation, that nothing less than $450,000 would be considered. He acknowledged land could be purchased for the government's lowball figure, but added that he had "never seen any land at that price that I would be willing to purchase, or even to farm if it was donated." Negotiations ceased.[39]

Having found relief from their transatlantic headache, the British basked in optimism. As early as May 1936, Herbert Lee, chairman of the board of the giant conglomerate, offered a glowing report of the American properties to the thirty-ninth general stockholders meeting in Manchester. "The Cotton Plantations," he said, "have easily paid the interest on our Gold Bonds, and are now able to finance their crops without any financial aid from us, and we have today no anxiety about their management. Mr. Oscar Johnston, who is the President of these great plantations, is known to you by name, through his work for the American Government, and he and his effective staff have brought them to their highest point of efficiency. Speaking generally, the outlook from this portion of our investments is certainly more cheerful than it was some years ago."[40]

# 11

# Fence Rails
# and Graveyards

The Mississippi Delta begins in the lobby of the Peabody Hotel in Memphis
and ends on Catfish Row in Vicksburg.          —David L. Cohn, 1935

If the South was cotton's kingdom, the Peabody Hotel in Memphis was
His Majesty's palace. For decades the movers, shakers, and retainers of King Cotton
crowded the proud hotel's suites, hallways, and mezzanine meeting rooms. Mississippi's Delta, the royal ground of the realm, reportedly began in its grand lobby.
A hundred Peabody conventions reflected cotton's rising and falling fortunes.
None, however, could match the drama, emotion, and eloquence of the meeting
of the Association of Southern Commissioners of Agriculture, who convened at
the Memphis hotel in September 1937. Even as the controversy over New Deal
subsidies to big planters cooled, a new and heated debate over cotton loans
and subsidies erupted in and out of the nation's capital. Nowhere were the raw
edges of that controversy more exposed than at the Peabody. As the New Deal
receded from high tide, this two-day conference, like a political and economic
barometer, reflected failing New Deal fortunes in the South, including farmer
attitudes after several years under the Agricultural Adjustment Administration.[1]

Just prior to the opening session of the convention on September 2, the government announced details of its loan program on the 1937 cotton crop. What
the South heard it did not like. The loosely organized, "quasi-official" Association of Southern Commissioners of Agriculture wielded, according to one political observer, "considerable political weight." Their collective displeasure over
the government's plan promised trouble for the New Deal agricultural program. The commissioners believed the Roosevelt administration had betrayed
the South and were "boiling with anger" toward the president and his secretary of agriculture. Headed by the commissioners but attended by hundreds
of influential planters, merchants, brokers, and others interested in the cotton
program, the convention bristled with anger and stood ready to pass strong
resolutions denouncing Wallace and AAA policy. The Roosevelt administration was in for a severe tongue-lashing from the once-loyal cotton belt.[2]

The acute discontent of the cotton South, an important element in the New Deal's political coalition, lay in the economic developments of 1937. Sales prospects for the 1937 cotton crop appeared strongest since the Great Depression began. Average prices for the 1936 crop, even without a government loan, had been the best since 1929. Some industrial activity returned to pre-Depression levels, reflecting a general emergence from the Depression's darker days. Cotton exports remained low, but domestic consumption surged, and mills and merchants bought raw staple at premium prices, some even logging orders through the middle of 1937.[3]

Heady from the rising market, producers across the cotton belt abandoned acreage reduction, adding nearly four million acres to the 1936 total. "Last spring, the Southern planters were filled with a gambling fever," said TRB in the *New Republic* later. "They were talking of 20-cent cotton, and expecting to make ten years' profits from a summer's work." The resultant record crop of 1937 not only helped plunge the South back into recession but also prompted a new clamor for crop reduction. In fact, the temporary economic revival had actually masked fundamental problems facing the cotton industry. Lagging exports, discriminatory trade policies, and the prospect of encroaching synthetic fibers constituted formidable problems. The market downturn during the summer of 1937 only added to King Cotton's slipping fortunes.[4]

The crisis became acute in early August 1937. Prices slipped badly while Congress proved unable to produce comprehensive farm legislation to replace the gutted AAA. As Congress approached recess, pressure mounted on and off Capitol Hill for executive action. "UNLESS PRICES ARE PEGGED BY GUARANTEE BY GOVERNMENT LOAN OF FROM TWELVE TO fiFTEEN CENTS," wired one Texas congressman to President Roosevelt, "WE WILL IN THE SOUTHLAND BE IN WORSE CONDITION THAN ANY TIME SINCE THE CIVIL WAR." J. E. McDonald, Texas Commissioner of Agriculture, told Roosevelt that a "[m]ass meeting of representative farmers" in his state had called for a fifteen-cent loan, "justified," he thought, in light of the Department of Agriculture's announcement of a seventeen-cent parity price. About the same time, a delegation of Southern Commissioners of Agriculture and other planter lobbyists descended on Washington, hat in hand, looking for crop subsidies and loans. Before Sen. Cotton Ed Smith's agriculture committee the commissioners cavalierly declared, "Where the money is coming from is no concern of ours."[5]

Disaster soon struck. The cotton world's annual August ritual was about to begin. In this particular year, *Life* captured a bit of the drama: "On Aug. 9, as the clock ticked toward daylight-saving noon in the Eastern U.S., the eyes and ears of the cotton world turned eagerly toward Washington. In the great trading centres of New York, Liverpool, Alexandria, Bombay, Shanghai and Osaka, cotton men waited almost as anxiously as did growers and middlemen huddled around radios and market boards in the South. The U.S. Crop Reporting Board was about to release its first estimate of the U.S. cotton crop for the new year which began Aug. 1."

What jangled over the wires and airwaves sent already slipping prices over the edge and immediately broke the market to near a dime for 7/8-inch middling cotton: 15,593,000 bales for the harvesting season. Ten days later the price slipped below ten cents, "the lowest price," said the Associated Press, "in four years." The market might have broken even worse on August 9 had cotton men the world over known the awful truth that the Crop Reporting Board's estimate was conservative, woefully conservative. During the fall, estimates were revised upward until it really did not matter any more; when it was all over, the black and white stoop labor of the Cotton Kingdom had picked nearly 19 million bales—an all-time high.[6]

Franklin Roosevelt had relished the squirming of those southerners who petitioned him in August for a twelve-cent market "peg." At a press conference six days before the Crop Reporting Board dropped its bomb on the cotton trade, the president fielded questions about a new Supreme Court nominee to replace retiring Justice Willis Van Devanter, and other matters. But nothing dominated the conference as did the question about the clamor from the South and the possibility of new loans on the 1937 cotton crop.

"Mr. President," asked a reporter, "there is quite a bit of agitation in the South for the Commodity Credit Corporation to make a twelve cent loan to check the decline in prices of cotton. Have you any comment to make on that?"

Indeed he did. Roosevelt began a dissertation of what he had inherited from Hoover and that he needed crop reduction in return for loans or it would bankrupt the U.S. Treasury. "Everything 'hunky dory,' lovely and everybody happy" in the spring, he said. But there was no crop control. Now with a huge crop looming—FDR thought about 14.5 million bales, a pathetically low figure as it turned out—he wasn't going to ask Congress for lending authority without new crop-control legislation. When a reporter hinted that the president didn't need any new congressional authority, the president replied, "I cannot make loans until we have some solution in the future of the surplus problem."

Beyond all that, of course, the South had not only helped kill Roosevelt's court reorganization bill—a bill, aimed at the Supreme Court, which had wrecked the AAA and, with it, acreage reduction—but also had sidetracked his wages and hours bill. Roosevelt had wanted farm legislation limiting acreage, as he suggested in his August 3 press conference, but never got that either. Now came cotton lobbyists wanting big loans from Commodity Credit for a potential bumper crop. The president let the southerners dangle awhile.

There was some shadowboxing; but something had to be done, politically if not economically. By the time Congress recessed and the smiling agriculture commissioners and other cotton lobbyists trouped out of Washington, agreement was reached on a loan of either nine or ten cents—the decision on which rested with USDA—supplemented by a two- or three-cent subsidy payment. The twelve-cent total would approximate 75 percent of parity. Benefits would go only to those farmers complying with acreage restrictions for 1938, and Congress agreed to make comprehensive farm legislation priority number one when Congress reconvened.[7]

The southerners' pleasure at their apparent rescue was short lived. The details of Wallace's plan first trickled out of the Department of Agriculture, then were formally announced at the end of August. To the shock of many producers throughout the cotton belt, let alone the state agriculture commissioners, Wallace declared that the subsidy—he had decided on three cents—would not be paid on the entire 1937 crop, as the South had assumed, but only on cotton grown on about two-thirds of the South's base acreage. In other words, if a planter raised cotton on, for example, one hundred acres between 1928 and 1932 and his yield was two hundred pounds per acre, that one hundred acres represented his "base" acreage. The three-cent subsidy would apply to 65 percent of his base acreage, or, in the example, sixty-five acres, even if his yield from those sixty-five acres exceeded two hundred pounds per acre. If the planter wished, he could receive a nine-cent loan on all his cotton if he placed it in a government-approved warehouse and agreed to pay carrying charges after June 30, 1938. While the price adjustment could not exceed three cents per pound, Wallace held out the possibility that payments could be made on a larger percentage of acreage if the payments did not exceed the $130 million appropriated by Congress.[8]

A few days later, on September 3, the Association of Southern Commissioners, angry over the alleged double cross, convened at the Peabody in Memphis. Happily for Wallace and the New Deal, if not ironically as well, the featured speaker at the two-day affair was Oscar G. Johnston. Johnston had long been an effective New Deal spokesman, without ever being a New Dealer, if the New Deal was defined by the AAA lawyers, the national planners, and the social engineers. The New Deal before 1937 was a big umbrella, and pragmatists such as Oscar Johnston got under it. As Roosevelt's 1936 reelection loomed, the Democratic National Committee hoped to make use of Johnston's services. Paul Appleby, a Wallace assistant, told E. J. MacMillan, director of the Democratic National Committee's Joint Speakers Bureau, that "Mr. Johnston is a very effective speaker, and a person of national reputation and standing, and I think he can put in some good licks for the cause." After Oscar spoke to the agricultural section of the American Bankers Association in New Orleans in 1935, one banker told Henry Wallace that it was "one of the best New Deal speeches I have heard." He embodied "the careful lawyer who prepared his case thoroughly. His temperament was sympathetic, and not too emotional for a thinking audience." His topic to the bankers was cotton, "but [he] prudently wove into his subject the theory of the whole, and made its logic apply equally to meat and bread." Oscar touched all the bases—protectionism, trade, facts, and statistics. "It is my feeling that if he is not now one of the first-string New Deal speakers, it would be an oversight not to use him as such," said the banker. "Knowing the diverse sentiments of his audience and the necessity for preserving open-mindedness, he *didn't mention the New Deal,* but talked the common-sense of economics. I believe that New Dealers should so speak to non-sympathizers that they will like it and join hands." The banker added, "In my opinion Mr. Johnston is a mighty good representative to send to doubtful territory in any part of the land."[9]

In September 1937 the "doubtful territory" was the Peabody Hotel in Memphis. Oscar Johnston's views differed markedly from the southern commissioners of agriculture, angry over the 1937 cotton plan. At least some of the 1937 loan plan had been his. He had persuaded Roosevelt to loan a dime in 1933 but had been embarrassed by the straight twelve-cent-loan "peg" in 1934. That the market had broken in March 1935, in the face of such a "peg," suggested that it was not much of a "peg" after all. In 1935, however, Johnston apparently originated the idea of a ten-cent loan and two-cent subsidy. That plan had "worked beautifully," with cotton flowing into trade channels instead of government-approved warehouses.

A month before the Peabody convention, while the agriculture commissioners haggled in the capital, Johnston had been enjoying a vacation cruise. Martha had fallen "very desperately ill" in August 1936 and had undergone cancer surgery at St. Joseph's Hospital in Lexington, Kentucky, in September. She convalesced for two months in the hospital and, ever so dishearteningly slow, for several more at home after returning to Scott in mid-November. Johnston proved ever attentive, taking an apartment in Lexington during Martha's stay at the hospital. Fortunately, aside from removing him from politics in a presidential election year and preventing both of them from attending the royal coronation of George VI in London in early 1937, the illness seemed fortuitously timed. The cotton pool was essentially behind, and the rigorous schedule of the latter months of 1937 lay ahead. Further, the ordeal may well have cemented their relationship as never before. Faltering health sent Martha back to Lexington in March, but by summer 1937 she had fully recovered, appearing more healthy than she had in years. Her recovery allowed an extended

holiday aboard Johnston's newly purchased cabin cruiser, appropriately chris-
tened the *Martha J*. Taking delivery of the craft at Port Clinton, Ohio, Oscar
and Martha, with a few friends, a deckhand, and a cook, leisurely cruised Lakes
Erie, Huron, and Michigan, with an excursion into Canada's Georgian Bay.
Business, however, was never far away. On board were drafts of legislative proposals pending before the House and Senate agriculture committees.[10]

There was some cause for alarm. The depressed futures market reflected
the good weather and increased acreage throughout the cotton belt. Spot prices,
which had advanced so nicely during the 1936 season, now began to slide in
anticipation of the bountiful harvest. Then, too, slipping prospects for a good
marketing season in large measure reflected the general economic recession
itself. After his boating party docked at Chicago, Johnston made his views
known. Fearing the government contemplated a repetition of the 1934 twelve-
cent loan, he wired President Roosevelt that a loan of twelve cents or one even
approximating the current market value would be "a serious mistake." He argued that price-pegging or an above-market loan might allow foreign cotton
to undersell American staple in world markets, further retarding exports. He
had, of course, contended in 1935 that higher American prices had not prompted
expansion of foreign growths; now he argued that price-pegging could further
demoralize the domestic market during the current slump. Whether he was
being consistent or disingenuous, he preferred a lower loan rate complemented
by an adjustment subsidy—a better deal for producers. He urged both the
president and his old friend Pat Harrison to adopt the 1935 plan whereby the
government paid the producer the difference between the market price and
twelve cents, or about 75 percent of parity. Under this plan, Johnston's constant goal of orderly marketing would be assured, American cotton would be
more competitive in the world market, and producers would have to repay only
the original loan, around nine cents per pound. Of course, Johnston suggested
that the government make adjustment payments only to those producers who
agreed to limit their acreages for 1938.[11]

Roosevelt and Harrison respected Johnston's views; Harrison evidently found
them in accord with his own. The Department of Agriculture warmly received
Johnston's advice, and AAA administrator Howard Tolley was glad to have him
"on record" regarding the twelve-cent loan. "We agree entirely with your
thoughts about the loan," he wrote Johnston, "and we are giving serious consideration to what can be done in the way of a difference payment." Tolley
cautioned, however, that congressional funding was limited and that low cotton prices paralleled those of other commodities.[12]

In Memphis on August 14, his cruise nearly over, Johnston publicly declared
his opposition to "price-pegging or above-market loans." He soon exchanged

his boating attire for a business suit and returned to Washington to help shape the 1937 loan. The problem was thrashed out within the department and the Commodity Credit Corporation in the latter part of August. Declared Secretary Wallace later: Johnston's "assistance in this matter was very helpful indeed and I believe that with possibly some minor exceptions the program as announced met with Mr. Johnston's entire approval."[13]

But the nine-cent loan and the three-cent subsidy package was not what raised the ire of the southern agriculture commissioners, now assembling at the Peabody. The outrage was the 65 percent limitation. Defection from the government's policy seemed imminent. As expected, the convention opened with ringing denunciations of Wallace and his attempts to subvert the congressional will by limiting the subsidy payments to a percentage of the crop. Speaker after speaker trekked to the rostrum to lambaste the New Deal plan, and, according to one reporter, "Even the most restrained speakers contended that the Secretary had made a 'grave mistake.'" Johnston "had not cut out an easy task" when he took the floor and challenged the indictments against Wallace. Debating the secretary's move, said Johnston, was futile; the issue was "as dead as the Mississippi ordinance of secession in 1861." Wallace had to confine the three-cent adjustment to 65 percent of the 1937 base acreage, Johnston contended, because Congress had authorized only $130 million for such subsidies. Had Wallace's pledge exceeded 65 percent "he should have been impeached in twenty-four hours."[14]

Johnston took the offensive. He reminded the convention that blame for the anticipated bumper crop of 1937 fell squarely on those who had rejected soil conservation and instead had sown cotton to the fences and even in cemeteries. To "a wave of applause," he declared that "[f]or the Secretary to have . . . attempted to make price adjustment payments to those who cooperated and those who did not on an equal basis would have been a stench in the nostrils of the cotton South."[15]

After defending Wallace and the loan in the morning session of the opening day, Johnston outlined his plan for cotton's future in the afternoon. He held the rostrum late into the evening, much to the conspicuous irritation of some of the agriculture commissioners who shared the head table with him. The commissioners were trapped. In both sessions, said the *New York Times*, "Mr. Johnston was vigorously applauded." Added the *Times:* "Growers and brokers had come from considerable distance to have their problems solved and demanded that the head of the Delta and Pine Land Company remain on his feet until their questions had been answered."[16]

By late evening even the commissioners, their angry plans blunted, added their own questions. When the session recessed, said the *Times,* "the attending delegates were agreed that Mr. Johnston 'took over the meeting.'" The commissioners, perhaps a bit irritated by Johnston's aggressiveness, asked for written proposals for their overnight reflection. Johnston was way ahead of them. He had come to the convention "with ample printed copies . . . and had them distributed promptly." Of the entire affair, the *New York Times* declared that the convention had been "swept off its feet through two days of discussion by the eloquence and economic reasoning of Oscar Johnston." His defense of Wallace, said the *Jackson Daily News*, was "eloquent," and TRB in the *New Republic* claimed that only his "strenuous opposition" halted passage of angry petitions. "For two days," declared TRB, "Mr. Johnston was constantly on his feet, answering questions, admonishing, cajoling, prophesying."[17]

In the convention's executive session, limited only to the agricultural commissioners, bitter arguments over public resolutions dragged on for hours. J. C. Holton, Mississippi's agriculture commissioner and Johnston's spokesman in the executive session, walked out of the private meeting in disgust when fellow commissioners failed to endorse pro-Johnston resolutions, including a hearty endorsement of Wallace's move on the nine-cent loan and subsidy limitation. In fact, they lightly scolded Roosevelt and Wallace for the 65 percent limitation and asked that Wallace "join with this Association in presenting a petition to the Congress at its next regular or special session to provide such additional funds as may be required." They also tabled a resolution, favored by Johnston and Holton, recommending repeal of Smoot-Hawley, but passed one calling for tariff-offset payments to farmers, with such funds to be generated by the tariff itself. Still, most commissioners reportedly remained "sympathetic to his suggestions," said one correspondent. "They indicated privately that they would lend local support to his plan."[18]

Johnston had effectively parlayed his "immense prestige among planters" into a defense of government policy. But problems remained. As summer ebbed into fall, embers of discontent over several aspects of government policy smoldered in the South. Some farmers were frustrated about acreage allotments, and planter hostility to perceived federal interference in the distribution of benefit payments between landlords and tenants "was particularly intense." In the weeks following his return from Washington in late August, Johnston had been in contact with producers and farm leaders from almost every section of the South. Without exception, he warned Howard Tolley, he found them "exceedingly bitter" over certain features of the proposed cotton program. Johnston may have short-circuited some discontent in southeast Missouri in late September by promising cotton farmers, angry over what they perceived as unjust acreage allotments under past AAA programs, that the 1938 program would be an improvement. He urged a crowd of fifteen hundred to unify and make themselves heard. While the three-cent adjustment payment remained sufficiently attractive to prevent massive noncompliance with the current program, Johnston nevertheless told the administration that producers would comply "reluctantly, with a feeling of discontent and bitterness that I think will spell trouble for the Department for some time to come."[19]

There was also a larger issue at work. As Washington emphasized reform over relief, the South had second thoughts about its loyalty to the New Deal. Deeply resenting federal intrusion, the South helped stall reformist antilynching and wages and hours legislation in Congress. And Pat Harrison's public displeasure with the New Deal after his defeat in the majority leader contest—with assistance from Roosevelt to winner Alben Barkley of Kentucky—only further weakened political support. The Democrats threw a senatorial "harmony dinner" at Washington's Raleigh Hotel way back on August 10, but there was no masking the deep rift in the majority party. "As the banqueters sipped and munched, [the] biggest U.S. news was being made," observed *Life*, "by the new civil war raging between the President and the rebel Democrats, chiefly Southerners, who have now definitely seceded from the New Deal." Referring to employer and chamber of commerce opposition to wages and hours legislation, TRB concluded that the Southern Commissioners of Agriculture convention "completes the line-up of the reactionary South against Mr. Roosevelt. . . . Now a representative section of Southern planters in effect declares war to the finish on the New Deal." While "Johnston softened the Association's manners," noted TRB, "he did not soften its spirit. It departed from Memphis with its anger against Mr. Roosevelt and Secretary Wallace unabated." Rankled and perhaps looking to the formation of future policy, some commissioners talked about organizing politically. For his part, Roosevelt poked the South in the eye two days after the big "harmony" shindig by naming Alabama's Sen. Hugo Black, a lonely southern New Deal workhorse, to the Supreme Court. As *Life* saw it, "Observers who blame the Democratic split entirely on the impetuosity of the President's reform program forget that the conservatism of the South, rooted in tradition and the land, is one of the great solid facts of U.S. life. One of the surest signs that the Depression is over is the way Southern Congressmen, uprooted by hard times, are now scurrying back to cover."[20]

As a southerner himself, Oscar Johnston's defense of the administration in 1937 flowed from economic pragmatism, not ideological commitment to the New Deal. His loyalty belonged solely to King Cotton and the economic health of the South. Like many Americans, cotton producers in the spring of 1937 thought their long night of depression was over. With mandatory controls off and prices good, cotton producers thought they could make an economic killing by overplanting. But 1936 and 1937 proved to be merely an economic interlude.

When the "free" market (hardly free given government involvement and international crises), so admirable in the spring, collapsed, the South cried for federal help tailored to its liking. It was time to rethink government beneficence toward agriculture. Johnston believed the future of the American cotton industry would be determined more by world economic conditions than by federal cotton programs alone. He wanted a permanent federal cotton policy, but he also knew King Cotton needed a coherent voice. As he told the convention at the Peabody in 1937, "if the South is to be saved from economic ruin it must organize and organize and organize."[21]

# 12

# King Cotton Needs a Voice

Cotton has been whispering. Cotton can speak but its voice has been as
soft as its fiber and as low as its price.          —Oscar G. Johnston, 1937

**T**he year 1937 formed a watershed in the development of the American cotton industry. The avalanche of white bales stimulated organization in cotton's kingdom. Oscar Johnston's restless desire to organize southern cotton producers paralleled the deteriorating cotton economy in 1937 and 1938. Nearly every economic indicator carried a dim prognosis. The average price per pound slipped from 12.4 cents in July 1937 to under a dime in September. The price might have slid further had it not been for the loan program, limited as it was. But if the loan alleviated one problem, it created another: warehouses still bulged with cotton held under the disastrous 1934 loan. Although the 1938 loan stood at only 9 cents, or a dismal 53 percent of parity, it still exceeded the market. The general business recession led to a decline in domestic consumption of cotton, worsening the problem. Trade barriers and large foreign harvests sent cotton exports to low levels not seen in half a century. Prices likewise slipped, settling at 8.4 cents for the 1937–38 season, with the result that nearly a third of the devastating harvest of 1937 came under federal control. At the start of the 1938 season, private and government carryover totaled 11.5 million bales. That rose even higher, to nearly 13 million in 1939. Nearly a third of the 1938 crop came under the federal loan, with only a fraction of it redeemed. As two commodity specialists said later, "both the producers and the government were again buried under a pile of cotton."[1]

Not only were cotton producers ill affected by overproduction, low prices, and economic nationalism (synthetic materials stood on the horizon), the entire cotton industry was plagued by seemingly hopeless internal division. Though producers, handlers, and processors shared a common industry, they possessed different agendas and often worked at cross-purposes. Rational organization was thwarted. What appeared to be good for merchants, ginners, warehousemen, or cottonseed crushers, notably volume, may not have been good for producers. Will Clayton, for example, whose giant Anderson, Clayton and

Company of Houston shipped more cotton than anyone else in the world, called for abandoning crop controls despite producer demands for marketing quotas. In the fall of 1937, a "Committee for Cotton," comprising processors and handlers, hoped to defeat production controls in the fall bill of 1938. Grenville Mellon, president of the Port Commission of Gulfport, Mississippi, also a cotton warehouseman, argued against federal cotton controls and called for a meeting of representatives of the various branches of the cotton industry. For warehousemen, more cotton, whether held by producers or merchants, or under federal loan, meant more business. Even the president of the American Cotton Shippers Association, Robert Mayer of Dallas, had declared in the spring of 1937 that conditions warranted increased production.[2] Many farmers thought so too.

By 1937 most of the special interests within the cotton industry had already organized state and national associations. Among them, cotton producers, though the most numerous, remained the weakest and the least organized. Marketing cooperatives had provided some muscle, particularly in the Mississippi Delta, while organizations such as the powerful American Farm Bureau Federation, headquartered in Chicago, filled some of the gap. But for all its influence, the Farm Bureau, successful in organizing the corn belt, was ill equipped to pursue the special goals of cotton farmers. Despite strong leadership from its able president, Edward A. O'Neal, the American Farm Bureau in the South was strong only in Tennessee and in O'Neal's native Alabama. To O'Neal's dismay, southern senators and congressmen, as well as different interest groups within the trade, offered separate and occasionally conflicting cotton proposals.[3]

One agency destined to play a crucial role in the organization of the cotton industry was the Delta Chamber of Commerce, a promotional body for the nineteen or so cotton counties of northwest Mississippi. Formed in 1935 chiefly to push for flood control and highway legislation, the latter of which easily passed the state legislature in 1936, the Delta chamber might have withered and died had it not been for the vision of, among others, William T. "Billy" Wynn, an astute Greenville planter, attorney, and businessman, and a close friend of Oscar Johnston. The chamber's original manager resigned to promote highway legislation in Florida, leaving a stenographer—a widow from nearby Leland—as its only employee. Wynn, one of the agency's organizers, argued, along with others, for its retention. The chamber, in debt and humbly housed in a couple of vacant rooms of the Delta's Agricultural Experiment Station at Stoneville, needed a strong, self-starting secretary-manager to give it new life. The board of directors, representing the Delta's planter and business elite, found such a person in William Rhea Blake, a Virginia native who had married the daughter of a Greenville physician, T. B. Lewis. A 1927 history and political science graduate of the University of Virginia, Blake had logged nine years in sales promotion

and public relations at the Appalachian Power Company in Bluefield, West
Virginia. On visits to Mississippi he had met Billy Wynn, who lived in the same
neighborhood as his father-in-law. He had long since fallen in love with the
Delta, had seen its potential, and had looked for an opportunity to move south.
This was his chance. Boundless in energy, enthusiasm, and ability—and a quick
learner—young Rhea, not yet thirty, arrived in May 1936 to begin the arduous
task of financing and fully organizing the Delta Chamber of Commerce.[4]

Within weeks of his arrival, he was in the thick of the campaign to keep Congress from limiting soil-conservation payments to large planters, the chamber's
major constituents. But the big battles over farm legislation lay ahead. Armed
with letters of introduction from Johnston, including one to Farm Bureau President Ed O'Neal, Blake spent part of the summer of 1937 in Washington lobbying Congress and monitoring proceedings. The Delta chamber wanted to work
with the Farm Bureau, including the bill introduced by John W. Flannagan Jr., a
Virginia Democrat. Though the chamber's agricultural committee, chaired by
Johnston, found "fundamental features" of the bill inimical to cotton producers,
Johnston thought it was salvageable. He told Blake in July that if Congress adjourned and there were no hearings, then "nothing further" could be done until
a new Congress. He thought that in such a case they should get with the Farm
Bureau and try "to get things lined up for the next session." Despite President
Roosevelt's insistence on passage of a farm bill, the House agriculture com-
mittee balked, taking no action; Congress adjourned in August. Meanwhile,
Johnston was off on his Great Lakes cruise aboard the new *Martha J*. Aboard
was a draft of an alternate farm bill—even more objectionable than Flannagan's.
It is not too hard to imagine that the boating companions mulled over the need
for a cotton producers' organization more influential than the Delta chamber.[5]

Just *when* Oscar Johnston first contemplated creating an organization of
cotton producers is unclear. A long-time believer in organization and individual
responsibility, Johnston thought cotton's impotence could be reversed by organizing producers. He knew political and economic power had long tilted
against the South; in a speech to the American Cotton Shippers Association in
1937, he likened the tariff, Bryanesque, to "a crown of thorns pressed down
on the heads of cotton producers." At a meeting of the Commodity Club in
New York City a few weeks later, he stridently warned that cotton producers
saw no patriotic, economic, or moral duty to exist in poverty to sustain high
production. The cotton farmer, he declared, would demand from the government the same generous treatment industry had enjoyed for six and a half decades. Also, by 1937 the New Deal had almost pressed the limits of what it
could do for cotton, aside from scaling back the tariff and negotiating international reciprocal trade agreements.[6]

In the late summer that year, Rhea Blake, brimming with lots of ideas and trying to energize the chamber of commerce, linked up with a young Mississippi planter and entrepreneur named Jimmy Hand, an emerging leader in his own right from Rolling Fork in the south Delta. The pair tried to promote the chamber in the northern Delta counties of Coahoma and Tunica, where organization was weak. In the wake of the devastating crop report in August that forecast a huge harvest, Blake and Hand concluded that something had to be done to promote the consumption of cotton, that long-term crop controls were a dead end. They agreed that Blake would approach the most prominent organization man in the Delta, Billy Wynn of Greenville.

Wynn was the man. He not only possessed skills in banking, law, and business, he was also a quiet persuader, enormously respected, and one whose opinion carried great weight. The Greenville-to-Arkansas ferry across the Mississippi River stood among his enterprises. His self-effacing demeanor, genuine humility, and willingness to remain in the background belied his organizational genius. No ill was spoken of Billy Wynn. Albert Russell, nephew of Gov. Lee Russell, Johnston's opponent in 1919, had great admiration for Billy Wynn. The younger Russell, who worked for the Delta organization before World War II and for the National Cotton Council after, thought "the concept of the Council," he said later, "came from the mind and spirit of Billy Wynn." Russell regarded him as "a second father," a "perfect gentleman" who "never pushed himself out front." If you wanted something done, Billy Wynn was the man. Blake went to see him about the cotton consumption idea he and Jimmy Hand had been discussing. "Well, I had a long session with Billy about it," recalled Blake later. "We left his office, I can see it now way up there on the top . . . floor of the old Weinberg Building; a big old ceiling fan above us with no air conditioning in those days, you know, hot as the devil, and we went on out to Billy's house and had a drink. We talked more and more." Wynn was interested. But it was clear that the Delta chamber was too puny to tackle the job of promoting cotton consumption nationally. What seemed reasonable, though, was that it might be able to organize something that could do it. "At this point," said Blake, "it was Billy Wynn who said, 'You know, this just might work because you've got to build this thing around a man and we've got the man.'" The man, of course, was Oscar Goodbar Johnston.[7]

Blake and Russell were pretty sure Billy sold Oscar on the idea. If that is true, Oscar had been thinking about cotton consumption for some time. Lots of people had. The Cotton Research Foundation had been established in Memphis in 1936 with hopes of creating a laboratory in which scientists would find new uses for an old product. No lab developed, but the next year the foundation signed a contract with the Mellon Institute of Industrial Research in

Pittsburgh to do it for them. The nonprofit foundation paid no salaries and looked for and received no quick fixes to cotton's plight. But the goal was clear: increased consumption.

As one of the foundation's directors, Oscar Johnston joined other new-use evangelists, among them Everett Cook, a prominent Memphis cotton man, and William Jasspon, president of the Memphis Chamber of Commerce. Even as other scientists in other labs tinkered with synthetics—rayon would soon try to horn in on cotton's kingdom in automobile tire construction—Johnston, Jasspon, and Cook hit the circuit in the spring of 1938 in search of cash and moral support. They traveled first to New York, then to Chicago, then to New Orleans, where they wined and dined with the big shots at Antoine's in the French Quarter. Later it was off to Atlanta, where Oscar acknowledged that the South's monarch had lost much of his "kingly" status, but stressed the link with the Mellon operation.[8]

Oscar, of course, was one of the slipping monarch's strongest retainers. Increased consumption stood high on his agenda; in 1937 he blended it with an idea for a producers' organization. Hodding Carter, a Greenville journalist who · in the 1940s won a Pulitzer prize for his editorials on racial justice, remembered Johnston musing about some type of cotton organization in September that year as they drove together with Rhea Blake toward Memphis to attend the raucous convention of the Southern Commissioners of Agriculture. Johnston had been talking to his traveling companions about the ill effects for cotton farmers of high tariffs, totalitarianism, economic nationalism, the Sino-Japanese War, and the absence of organization. But it was clear to Johnston that the government could not save the farmer; he had to help himself. Then, said Carter, "unexpectedly and diffidently," Oscar told his fellow travelers about a movie he had seen, *The Life of Emile Zola,* Hollywood's Oscar-winning portrayal of the French writer's embroilment and personal sacrifice in his country's tragic Dreyfus Affair. Oscar had seen it in St. Louis while attending a board meeting of the Federal Reserve and "was much taken" by it, Rhea Blake remembered later. While the big-screen Zola, played by Oscar-nominee Paul Muni, was somewhat fictionalized, Johnston found inspiration in the Frenchman who spurned the ease of retirement for a noble cause.[9]

Oscar Johnston did not organize the National Cotton Council of America because he saw a Hollywood film, regardless of how touching the portrayal.[10] But he did begin formulating serious plans for an organization of cotton producers—and cotton producers only—soon after the agriculture commissioners meeting in September, if not before. To help in organizing, Johnston wanted to work with the American Farm Bureau, despite differences over one issue or another. He sought "a frank discussion" with Edward A. O'Neal, the Farm

Bureau chief who closely guarded his organization's turf. But O'Neal could hardly keep out a proposed organization in an area where the Farm Bureau had been ineffective. Johnston tried to assuage him: "Naturally it is our desire to effect this [cotton] organization in a manner which will insure complete accord and cooperation with the National [*sic*] Farm Bureau Federation." After a half-day conference with Johnston in Chicago, which also included Farm Bureau Vice President Earl Smith and General Counsel Donald Kirkpatrick, O'Neal told his Washington lobbyist that Johnston "promises me definitely that he wants to work with the Farm Bureau, both state and national, and have no duplication of effort. . . . He does want a strong, militant Farm Bureau organization in the South to work with the cornbelt, in the American Farm Bureau family." O'Neal thought his southern state bureaus could restrain Johnston if he got out of line.[11]

Restraining Johnston's influence in the cotton belt proved no easy task. Tension over turf soon went public. In October 1937 Drew Pearson and Robert Allen, syndicated muckrakers, reported in their "Washington Merry-Go-Round" that Farm Bureau big shots, "upset by the prospect" of a cotton organization, were trying to head off the movement. The producers, suggested the columnists, were dissatisfied with the representation they were getting from the regular farm organizations. "Back of the movement" for the organization, they declared, "is Oscar Johnston, behind-the-scenes formulator of every major cotton policy in the administration, and considered the ablest cotton man in the South." Pearson and Allen said, "Johnston and his friends say that high pressure groups in other sections of the country, such as the powerful sugar-growers' lobby, are forcing the South to form its own organization. While he [Johnston] strongly favors co-operation between Southern and Western farmers, he nevertheless points out that sometimes a sectional stand is necessary and that large farm organizations with members all over the country can't take such a stand." O'Neal had to admit that the cotton belt had been difficult to organize, but he told Johnston, "Like you, I am so anxious that we get the cotton farmers *cotton organization conscious* so we can act effectively together. There are too many ideas and too many leaders in the South, therefore we have never gotten anywhere."[12]

Publicly denying the muckrakers' allegations that cotton producers were dissatisfied with the parent Farm Bureau, Johnston claimed the organization was "an excellent medium through which farmers *throughout the nation* may express their views and ideas concerning proposed or pending legislation." Maybe so, but whose views? In any case, Oscar chose prudence. He counted on using county and state farm bureaus and agricultural associations as springboards for his proposed cotton organization. He hoped that increasing the membership of local farm bureaus would build a firm base from which cotton representatives could be chosen. Where well-established organizations existed, Johnston was careful to take up issues of membership, campaigns, financing, and other matters with state and local bureau officials. Where none existed, as in Oklahoma and Georgia, he thought producers should organize and affiliate with the national Farm Bureau Federation.[13]

Despite the cozy arrangement, Johnston, as Pearson and Allen had detected, had his own agenda. That was clear in the case of the Mississippi Farm Bureau, an organization which fell under Johnston's influence in the fall of 1937. Johnston thought his home state bureau was too shackled by the parent organization regarding such issues as the tariff, on which Farm Bureau could take no effective stand. In mid-October, Johnston sold the Mississippi Farm Bureau executive directors on a series of proposals to increase its purposes, membership, and financing. He even suggested that the name be changed to the "Mississippi Agricultural Association" and that its charter be amended to allow withdrawal from the American Farm Bureau if desired. He told the president of the Tennessee Farm Bureau, J. Francis Porter, an O'Neal friend, that the Mississippi association "will remain a member of the national organization, and will cooperate with the national organization in all matters of national importance, *but will be free to take its own attitude with respect to cotton.*" He added: "I want to assure you in advance that the movement is in no sense critical of, or antagonistic to, the American Farm Bureau Federation." About the same time, however, he told the Mississippi Bureau's secretary, H. S. Johnson, that it seemed to him "that the primary object of the State Association is for promotion of the interests of the farmers of Mississippi, and that its primary object is not merely to become a member of some other organization." Still, Johnston reiterated his allegiance to the American Farm Bureau. He was walking a tight line. With the endorsement of the state bureau's board of directors, he suggested that other cotton states be urged to follow Mississippi's example. If such efforts proved successful, his national cotton council would be adequately financed and in a position to attack some of the central problems facing the American cotton producer.[14]

Having done his homework, Johnston carried his plan to the annual convention of the Mississippi Farm Bureau Federation in November 1937. He told the delegates that dairying, industry, and manufacturing had all achieved success through organization. The rayon industry, cotton's competitor, he said, had scientific laboratories to advance the interests of synthetics. That is what cotton needed, along with political action. "Have an organization so strong in Mississippi," he urged, "as to send a delegation to the legislature stating 'we demand to be recognized.'" By the end of November, if Ed O'Neal remained confident that the southern state bureaus could check Johnston's activities, he could have forgotten about much help from the Mississippi chapter, at least for the moment. Aside from receiving endorsement to further the interest of his cotton council, he had even been elected a director and statewide vice president.[15]

Johnston's drive for a cotton council now shifted into higher gear. In late November and early December his speaking itinerary across the Delta resembled a political campaign. Within a week he spoke eight times in eight counties, including Tunica, Quitman, and Coahoma in a single day. His message was standard: "500 Hear Johnston's Impassioned Plea for Organized Crop Program," declared the local press after his December 1 speech at the courthouse in Clarksdale, his old hometown. "Cotton growers must do what industry has done for a century and what agriculture, except cotton, has done for years—organize." At a dime a bale, he said, cotton producers could finance and staff a national bureau in Washington to give voice to King Cotton's demands, to lobby Congress, and to develop and promote new uses for the fiber.[16]

Enthusiasm rose. The mail brought new requests for his appearance, and Richard O. Baumbach of the *Cotton Trade Journal* asked him for an article for the New Orleans–based weekly. One Mississippian who had heard Johnston in Clarksdale thought his speech "plain, practical and sound," while a Memphis realtor offered to urge the seventy thousand cotton farmers on his mailing list to join the new cotton council. "In my opinion," he told Johnston, "you have started the greatest movement ever commenced in the interest of cotton. . . . While you have the movement started let[']s put it over." Interest also brewed in several other states, including Texas, where the Farm Bureau affiliate, the Texas Agricultural Association, boasted around fifteen thousand members and seemed to be gaining. One report suggested that Johnston's plan "would bring in thousands of Texas cotton farmers who are not now members of the Association." Farmers in the Missouri boot heel, geographically akin to the cotton areas of northeast Arkansas, also looked with interest on a cotton organization, although the president of the state's farm bureau, R. W. Brown, was cool to the idea. He told Johnston that in states such as his "there would be as much reason for livestock councils, corn councils, etc., as cotton councils," resulting, he said, "in confusion" and "failure." But Brown did not speak for all in his state. One Missouri planter whom Johnston had wooed told him in 1938, "We, in Missouri, are very anxious to cooperate with any movement and shall be glad to have any part in regard to the association."[17]

While Johnston preached organization to cotton farmers, Congress met in special session, called by Roosevelt in November 1937 to deal with comprehensive farm legislation. Johnston and Ransom Aldrich, president of Mississippi's Farm Bureau affiliate, agreed to send to Washington the Delta Chamber's Rhea Blake to represent both groups. Blake left immediately on the *Tennessean* and, save for a Christmas break, stayed until February. Johnston later joined Blake in the capital, went to the annual Farm Bureau convention in December, and, after spending Christmas in Scott, went back to Washington. Johnston, "for many reasons," preferred a low profile for himself; he got the Mississippi Agricultural Association to have Blake, soon labeled "Oscar Johnston's man," to accompany Aldrich back to Washington. Having Blake there, Johnston told O'Neal, would reassure Delta farmers who had been joining the Mississippi association.[18]

In the new farm legislation the Delta conservatives had their own agenda. They wanted no discrimination based on farm size, no interference in land-lord-tenant relations, and no tampering with base-acreage allotments that would allow administrative reshuffling of such allotments within each state (the House bill contained such a provision, potentially damaging to the Delta). House and Senate conferees soon eliminated the latter provision; the bill, the Agricultural Adjustment Act of 1938, passed in February, provided for marketing quotas, acreage allotments by counties, and Commodity Credit loans up to 75 percent of parity. Congress added a populist sop by limiting rental subsidies to $10,000 annually to any individual or corporation, but placed no ceiling on the more significant price-adjustment payments. Lobbying a tight-fisted Congress for price-adjustment appropriations eventually became a task for Johnston's cotton council.[19]

Even as he monitored legislation, Oscar Johnston was moving away from dependence on government. Before he left the capital to resume organizational activities, he severed his official ties with the Department of Agriculture and Commodity Credit, publicly citing requirements of his election to the board of directors of the Federal Reserve Bank in St. Louis. Henry Wallace had talked him out of resigning from the CCC over a policy dispute regarding the 1934 loan stocks a year earlier. Now, however, it was time to go. His resignation, he told Henry Wallace, "in no wise lessens my loyalty to the Administration and particularly to the Department of Agriculture, nor my interest in the welfare of agriculture." Wallace replied: "It is my feeling that the government owes you a real debt of gratitude for your many services."[20] The Federal Reserve appointment provided a convenient cover for Johnston's exit. By January 1938 it was clear that if the cotton industry was to meet the challenge of emerging synthetics and contracting markets, it would have to organize or die. Johnston also knew that the organizational work would have to originate in the cotton belt, not in Washington.

In the cotton belt Johnston was not alone in thinking big thoughts about a cotton organization of some sort. Thinking and talking had been going on for some time. One who had been mulling it over was Norris Blackburn, a leader in the cotton compress and warehouse business in Memphis. Blackburn had been in the business since the 1910s, had demonstrated innovation and progressive vision, and, with others, notably C. A. Bertel of New Orleans and Francis Beatty of North Carolina, had helped form the National Cotton Compress and Warehouse Association. Oscar Johnston addressed their first convention in New Orleans. Such associations were symptomatic of the cotton industry. Organizations of one segment of the industry or another proliferated but none worked together. Blackburn got wind of the move to organize producers and assess a tax per bale to finance the promotion of cotton consumption. Why not spread the costs and involve the whole industry? Efforts to drum up support in Memphis yielded only more talk; no one really opposed the idea, but men of lesser vision—or greater realism—thought the scheme too hard or too "utopian" for success. However, Blackburn and Bertel continued to talk.

New Orleans, not Memphis, became a percolation point for cotton unity. An influential group in the port city that included not only Bertel but also Richard Baumbach of the *Cotton Trade Journal,* E. O. Jewell, president of the Spot Cotton Merchants Association, also of New Orleans, and Garner O. Tullis, president of the New Orleans Cotton Exchange, took leadership in talking up cotton unity. The New Orleans group commissioned a research survey by members of the faculty at the College of Commerce and Business Administration at Tulane University. The academic study relating to organization, not ready in preliminary form until mid-1938, was designed to provide "informational data" for cotton council founders. Meanwhile, in December 1937 several of the New Orleans group met with Louisiana Gov. Richard Leche, presenting him with the idea of an industry-wide organization. Leche liked it, and the following month obtained endorsement from fellow governors at the Southeastern Governors Conference in Washington.[21]

If support might be generated within the narrowly based segments of the cotton industry, the task was more daunting among the more numerous and independent-minded farmers. And who could bring them all together? Norris Blackburn knew that would have to be Oscar Johnston, whom he knew by more than reputation. The president of the Union Compress and Warehouse Company, where Blackburn worked, was Douglas Brooks, a Mississippi planter. He was also Billy Wynn's brother-in-law. The New Orleans group, as it became known, stood ready to yield leadership to Johnston, the most visible and respected cotton man in America. As Blackburn recalled, "I felt for such an organization—and I told this to the first meeting of the New Orleans group— for it to be a success it would take the most outstanding cotton man in the country, and I felt that that man would be Mr. Oscar Johnston. And that he should be the one to pull the groups together. Everyone that I knew had confidence in Mr. Johnston in being able to do that."[22]

Just when Johnston agreed to assume leadership of the broadened call for an industry-wide cotton council remains unclear. In October 1937 he had warned producers to "beware of entangling alliances," and as late as the end of April 1938 he still thought in terms of a producers organization only. Within a month, however, he embraced the larger vision, perhaps because of mutual safeguards, or perhaps because of the sheer pragmatic wisdom of uniting producers, processors, and handlers of a single commodity and its by-products in a common effort to increase consumption. He knew cotton was an internally competitive industry. Edward Lipscomb, a key figure in the Cotton Council later on, claimed that cotton's survival was "a miracle . . . because it is the only industry I can think of where, certainly at that time, it was to the benefit of each branch to cut the throat of the other ones." But increased consumption was something on which all could agree; permanent reduction led nowhere. All that was, of course, easier said than done. The various trade associations boasted individuals of varying abilities, but translating the dream of a united industry into reality required leadership not previously demonstrated in a divided but desperate commodity. Except, however, for the leadership of Oscar Johnston. Ed Lipscomb expressed the consensus. Oscar, he said, was "the only person on God's green earth that could have ever put it together."[23]

The third annual meeting of the Delta Chamber of Commerce provided the opportunity to test the viability of the proposed cotton council. Johnston tried hard to get Secretary of State Cordell Hull to keynote the event, enlisting Pat Harrison and Henry Wallace to urge his appearance. Not only would Hull provide a major draw, but his presence would emphasize the importance of international trade reciprocity. Tariff walls had devastated the South by shutting foreign markets for many of its commodities, including cotton. Unfortunately, Johnston met frustration; Hull begged off, citing "unusual and delicate emergency matters" that precluded accepting new engagements. Johnston now settled for Dr. Francis B. Sayre, an assistant secretary of state in charge of reciprocity, whom Hull had suggested to Senator Harrison as a replacement. It proved to be a good choice. Son-in-law of Woodrow Wilson, a former Harvard professor, and a strong advocate of reciprocal trade, Sayre enjoyed Johnston's respect, having "done excellent missionary work" speaking throughout the South. Oscar knew Sayre, had heard him speak in Cleveland, Ohio, and had read some of his speeches given elsewhere. A talk on international trade, Johnston told him, would raise the consciousness of southerners and lead to increased support from that section. "For awhile," said Johnston, "our people clamored for a repeal of our tariff laws or a drastic downward revision thereof. We realize now that, because of development of sundry complications, the desired result can only be obtained by means of international trade agreements, rather than by direct legislation on the part of our Congress."[24]

The success of the council now hinged on the events of June 15, 1938, the

date set for the Delta Chamber's annual meeting. To accommodate the anticipated crowd, the athletic stadium of Mississippi Delta State Teachers College
in Cleveland, Mississippi—in the heart of the Delta itself—provided the site.
More than 40 percent of the entire American cotton crop bloomed within two
hundred miles in any direction of the Mississippi Delta.[25] It was an appropriate, even graphic, choice. From this soil—and not from the marble halls of
Congress nor from the cavernous confines of the Department of Agriculture—
would spring survival; men from competing—even jealous—segments of the
industry would have to sit together and contemplate their shared fate.

The invitation list boasted the big shots, the very establishment, of cotton's
kingdom. Governors and other political leaders would mingle with planters,
commissioners of agriculture, news editors, leaders of interest groups, and most
important, representatives of the five major segments of the American cotton
industry—producers, merchants, warehousemen, ginners, and cottonseed crushers. Blake, Wynn, and others had worked tirelessly for the occasion; on June 15 it
began to pay off. By train and automobile, hundreds of members, delegates,
and guests converged on the little teachers' college. The chamber's annual
meeting, closed to the public, began at 9:00 A.M., although the featured attrac-
tion followed the noon luncheon held in the college dining hall. By early afternoon, as the Mississippi sun "bore down with an intensity not before reached"
that summer, a crowd numbering somewhere from one to three thousand—
depending on who did the counting—assembled in the athletic stadium. Flags,
bunting, and a concert by the local high-school band provided a festive aura,
and the "profusely decorated" speakers' platform groaned under the weight of
dignitaries and other big shots. Then Oscar was at the rostrum, his thirty-minute
declaration of purpose, call for unity, and introduction of Sayre carried over
NBC's Memphis affiliate, WMC. The former Harvard professor, his dark suit
and starchy collar proving he was no southerner, performed very ably, his speech
carefully honed to meet the thirty-minute national air time over NBC's New
York Red Network. Gracious remarks about Johnston were followed by a so-
ber plea for reciprocal trade agreements, linking them to the welfare of the
cotton farmer. Sayre urged the industry to take initiative to protect its future
when the trade agreements expired in 1940. No policy demanded more allegiance and support in the South, he said, than the reciprocal trade program.[26]

His job done, the assistant secretary wiped his face as he sat down, and the
applause faded. Other speakers trekked to the rostrum, then Oscar Johnston
called for interested parties to reassemble in the college auditorium. Here the
real work would begin; five hundred filed in, pleased, no doubt, to escape the
merciless Mississippi sun. Billy Wynn, outgoing Delta Chamber president,
called the throng to order. (Earlier that day, to escape negative bourgeois con-

notations, and reflective of the antibusiness rhetoric of the New Deal, the three-year-old Delta Chamber of Commerce renamed itself, innocuously, the Delta Council.) Soon Oscar was on his feet again, doing what he did best, persuading, orating, and commanding the respect of able and competitive men in a competitive industry. No one in the national capital spoke for all of cotton, he said. And cotton must find new uses, must be vigorously promoted, and must recapture foreign markets. It would cost money and time, he said, but the survival of the cotton belt hinged on unity.[27]

Applause, unity, and enthusiasm filled the air. Mississippi's Gov. Hugh White now pledged nine thousand dollars seed money, such appropriation to be extracted from a special legislative session soon to convene to consider other business; the governor also promised to approach his colleagues from other states. From the floor, amid waving hands, came calls for the creation of a national cotton council. Endorsements rolled in like the surf, including unanimous agreement among all branches of the industry from each of the seven cotton states represented. Joining the bandwagon were government officials; commissioners of agriculture from Tennessee, Louisiana, and Mississippi; and leaders of allied organizations, including John Pettey from the National Cottonseed Products Association, Garner Lester of the National Ginners Association, N. C. Williamson of the American Cotton Cooperative Association, Douglas Brooks of the American Cotton Shippers Association, C. A. Bertel of the National Cotton Compress and Cotton Warehouse Association, and, from the west, George Payne of the Irrigated Cotton Growers Association. Telegrams from cotton-state governors neither present nor represented unanimously endorsed the idea. By voice acclamation the throng named Johnston temporary chairman of the new council, empowering him to proceed to build a permanent organization. Rhea Blake, who had done so much of the legwork for the occasion, was named temporary secretary. According to J. C. Holton, Mississippi's agriculture commissioner, "Mr. Johnston was given an ovation and it was quite apparent that his leadership was the first prerequisite to the success of the proposed organization."[28]

The whole affair looked like an express train racing through the station. Those gathered in the hall were mostly the true believers; few had come to debate. Louisiana's agriculture commissioner, Harry D. Wilson, did urge caution against haste, fearing creation of "jealousies among various groups." But that view was easily countered and even Wilson came along. Governor White had already told the crowd, "I think we have waited longer than we should already to start this." Ed O'Neal's absence might have been noted, but no matter. The presidents of several Farm Bureau affiliates, J. F. Porter of Tennessee, Ransom Aldrich of Mississippi, and Romeo Short of Arkansas, ever a Farm Bureau loyalist, had already climbed aboard. After mimeographed copies of Johnston's prospectus for the new council had fluttered through the hall, Harold Young, vice president of the Arkansas Farm Bureau, was on his feet calling for substantial endorsement of Oscar's plans. Those plans reiterated the goals of finding new uses for cotton, promotion and advertisement, and legislative activity. Also, the new council would take no action without unity. Each state would have at least five representatives, one from each group. Approval was unanimous. Noted the *New York Times*, "Votes electing him [Johnston] came from farmers, shippers, ginners, seed crushers, warehouse men and those interested in every phase of handling the staple." And the Associated Press quoted representatives from several states who said that "if Oscar Johnston will serve as president of this organization, our people will join in."[29]

The enthusiasm of the gathering belied the fact that these were hardheaded businessmen, and giddy talk never produced dollar cotton. Cotton's valley of dry bones was rattling with new life, but the bones had no flesh. In the first flush of confidence, as King Cotton's retainers spread out across the South, everything seemed possible. Two days after Delta State Johnston told the press that he looked to call a permanent organizational meeting—more than one hundred delegates from sixteen states—sometime in mid-July. Little did he know, little did anyone know, that it would take not one month but five. The trench warfare of organizing state chapters proved more tedious and daunting than it first appeared, though Mississippi showed the way by chartering the first state chapter on July 5. For a couple of weeks the organizational work went ahead in halting fashion. Committees needed appointing; interest groups had to name delegates. But it was summer, vacation time, some people were in, others not. The fledgling operation ran up big telephone bills calling all over the cotton belt. The Delta Council carried Rhea Blake's salary and expenses, guiding its latent offspring through gestation. Help was on the way. Said Blake: "The first doggone thing that had to be done [was that] the governor had called that special session of the legislature and I had to run down to Jackson and lobby the damn bill through the legislature." "To get that nine thousand bucks." It was a tidy sum, and, suggestive of Oscar's standing and perhaps the desperation of the moment, the legislature parted with the people's cash without audit. Of course, millions of dollars of other people's money had passed before Johnston's eyes in the New Deal days; this was small but vital change. In any case, Johnston named Billy Wynn committee treasurer, and on the strength of the state's uncashed nine-thousand-dollar warrant, the Delta Council financed operations until the council's organizational meeting.[30]

Then disaster struck. The commander of the whole operation was sidelined early in the battle. The problem was Oscar's left eye, a cataract. His eyes had not been good for years, thick glasses like bottle bottoms trying to compensate for worsening vision. He had joked that he had seen everything "out of that eye he wanted to, anyway." But this was no joke. The surgery, supposedly routine, was set for July 5 in Memphis. One day earlier was the respite before the storm. A local planter in the Lake Washington community, Larry Pryor, threw his annual Independence Day party and invited everyone for a good time. The mules raced; the whiskey flowed. Oscar, Billy Wynn, Rhea Blake, everybody was there. Then Oscar left for Memphis. "Well," said Blake later, "five days after the operation the eye hemorrhaged, filled with blood, and he started suffering the torment of the damned. We didn't have air conditioning then, and I came up here [Memphis] and I never will forget that poor man lying there holding to that bed and just wringing wet. He was a profuse perspirer anyway. He was just there, in this terrible pain and they couldn't get it stopped."[31]

For nearly five weeks Oscar languished on his bed of affliction—a man of spirit and action unable to read a line, imprisoned in a darkened room. Some days were better than others, but the mid-South summer heat penetrated the gloom. In August he transferred to Michael Reese Hospital in Chicago, where he came under the care of a high-powered specialist willing to try something different. Blake recalled:

> They had some new sort of treatment . . . that they raised his temperature and induced this high fever to dissipate the blood clot in his eye. After so many of those treatments they sent Oscar home. They wanted Dr. Montgomery, Dr. Cameron Montgomery, who was the outstanding eye man in Greenville [to continue]. Greenville was quite a little medical center back in those days: The Gamble Brothers, Dr. Hugh Gamble and Dr. Paul Gamble, had the Gamble Clinic. Billy told me this; Oscar didn't tell me this. Cameron Montgomery and Billy were close friends and he told Billy that he had refused to give these treatments to Oscar because he said that they sometimes later had some effect on brain damage.[32]

But the treatments did continue in Mississippi, though without the attending optimism of the Chicago specialist. Oscar had gone home to Scott the latter half of August, the agonizing pain having subsided. For two months bandages masked both eyes, a cataract developing in the right one also. At the end of August he was still housebound, much of the time spent in bed. His recovery now depended on his absorption of the blood in the hemorrhaged eye. Eventually, medical pessimism waned, and improvement was noted. In mid-September Johnston finally, for the first time, got back to his desk at Delta and Pine Land Company. Adding to normal correspondence, he now anticipated a visit by the British bondholders in October. "I have certainly had a 'helluva time,'" he told a medical friend in November, "but am now promised that someday (if I live long enough) I will be able, with the use of an appropriate lense [*sic*], to use the injured optic normally. It s[t]ill gives me some trouble, and is so intensely sensitive to light that I am forced to keep it covered except in an absolutely dark room. There is still some swelling . . . of the eye lid." A month later he could make out headlines, though he used his eye only momentarily. Meanwhile, though Johnston was attended by a nurse, Martha's eyes became his, she doing most of the reading for him; in Chicago, a secretary, between dictations, had read him novels, preferably mysteries. He could not write, of course, and he allowed as how he had "been considerably 'slowed down.'"[33]

With Johnston sidelined, the ball bounced into Rhea Blake's and Billy Wynn's court. Referring to the cotton council business, Blake said, "all this stuff was projected and it had to be done." If Martha was Oscar's eyes, Billy and Rhea were his legs and mouth. The day of Oscar's operation, July 5, the pair, along with the state Farm Bureau chief Ransom Aldrich and his vice president, Boswell Stephens, set up the Mississippi cotton council chapter. That was appropriate, of course, since the council was a heavily Mississippi operation anyway. Richard Baumbach of New Orleans was a key figure in organizing the Louisiana chapter. Baumbach, in fact, joined Blake in a southeastern swing, organizing Alabama, Georgia, and the Carolinas; by early fall Blake was in Virginia. On October 6, Johnston, up for the occasion, organized Tennessee at the Peabody in Memphis, with Everett Cook, cotton tycoon, becoming chairman. That same day, Rhea Blake, back from the east coast, set up the Missouri unit in Sikeston with Billy Wynn. The next morning they were at the Albert Pike Hotel in Little Rock doing the same thing for Arkansas. It was all quite an adventure, enough to tire anyone. But Blake was smart, aggressive, resilient, a won't-take-no persuader of enormous tenacity. He was Oscar's man. When it was all over, Hodding Carter wrote about Blake, Wynn, and Baumbach and their odyssey. "By airliner, by train, more frequently by automobile," he said, "they have traveled separately and together, persuading dubious state groups to whom they are strangers, smoothing internal differences, bringing together clashing producers, ginners, compressors, seed crushers, merchants to whose divergent doors the name and purpose of Oscar Johnston is a ready passkey."[34]

But what about the West? Across the Mississippi, across the plains, problems lurked. In some ways, the West stood as an end in itself. Would Blake find the doors locked? Texas in particular stood as the biggest problem, requiring tact and diplomacy and, if possible, Oscar Johnston himself. So Texas would be put off while Oscar slowly convalesced. Rhea Blake now headed to California, Billy Wynn planning to join him in mid-October. A linchpin in the California set-up was William A. "Bill" Coberly of Los Angeles. A big landowner, Coberly also held a gaggle of cotton gins in the rich San Joaquin Valley. He also ran the California Cotton Oil Corporation. But Coberly, a Republican, and an especially conservative one at that, had never met Oscar, and even harbored "real misgivings about this fellow Oscar Johnston." To conservative eyes, Johnston had been a New Dealer. Coberly's daughter had married former president Herbert Hoover's son, but suspicious views of Oscar's politics were not Coberly's alone, perhaps spilling even into Texas. Oscar was no New Dealer, of course, but "a lot of people" thought so, said Blake, "because he had been up there with them, you see. It was Oscar and Henry [Wallace] and Rex [Tugwell] and all that business. . . . Everybody called everybody by their first name in the New Deal, you know." From a distance, some might have regarded Johnston's pragmatism as left-wing ideology; Oscar never made that mistake. Fortunately, Coberly's friends included Mississippi cotton oil men Fenton Guinee and John H. Pettey, both of Greenwood. They helped pave the way to California, where Blake was met by Coberly and some of his associates. Lamar Fleming Jr., a vice president of Houston's Anderson, Clayton and Company, the trading giant with heavy interests out west, also calmed fears (in Texas or California or both) about Oscar's "New Deal" past. California fell into place, as did Arizona and New Mexico. Johnston, gaining strength back in Scott, told Pettey on October 21: "Rhea has done a splendid job in the West. A wire from him tells me that he has met Mr. Coberly, who showed him every courtesy and consideration. I have a wire and a letter from Mr. Coberly, advising that it is his plan to meet me in Dallas on Thursday, the 27th, in order that he, Will Clayton, and I may discuss sundry details incident to the establishment of the National Cotton Council." That very day Blake was in Las Cruces, with plans to rendezvous with Johnston in Dallas.[35]

Texas was the land of opportunity and booby traps. Some people, including Texans, jealous over turf or prestige or both, did not want the council to work. Such criticism often sprang from nonproducers, men who feared that an industry-wide operation might "some way or other lessen the importance of *their* organization." One notable pocket of opposition centered around a dynamic Hillsboro cotton merchant, Burris C. Jackson, a politically connected (Tom Connally, Sam Rayburn) mover and shaker in the American Cotton Shippers Association. Also, Robert Mayer of Dallas, president of the shipping association in 1937, had opposed Johnston's view of acreage reduction, arguing instead for increased output. But of bigger concern was Burris Jackson. Son of a Texas cotton merchant, Jackson, to Rhea Blake's mind, "was exceedingly able, young, ambitious politically," with "more brass than Sousa's band." And he had married well. "His energy and ambitions knew no bounds," said Blake, "and he had organized a thing called the Texas Statewide Cotton Committee and he had gotten it off the ground." Further, when the AAA of 1938 authorized a USDA laboratory to seek new cotton uses, Jackson tried to get it for Texas.

Blake and others wanted it in Mississippi (it finally wound up in New Orleans, probably because of its sponsor, Sen. Allen Ellender of Louisiana). It was all a bit of rivalry, said Blake, who thought Jackson "undoubtedly looked on this [the Cotton Council] as something challenging him in his future and he gave us lots of trouble." Lamar Fleming, a Jackson mentor of sorts, stood for the council, and, though with an agenda at variance with Johnston's, helped mitigate the Texas opposition. According to Blake, Jackson "would . . . have given us a hell of a lot more trouble than he did, if it hadn't been for Lamar." In 1940 Johnston got wind of new efforts in Texas ("where lack of cooperation is so noticeable") to sidetrack his infant organization. A cotton meeting in Dallas in March that year, according to a confidential report, provided a forum for trashing the new Cotton Council. One critic claimed, said the report, "that the cotton states east of the Mississippi had always dominated the Southern agricultural picture and that if Texas' cotton problems were to be solved, Oscar Johnston and his bunch east of the river could not do it." According to the report, Burris Jackson also weighed in with his attacks, decorated with invective, arguing that the interest of Texas stood apart from the new organization. (Most southern textile mills stood east of the Mississippi, while Texas cotton producers sent 90 percent of their huge crop into foreign markets.) According to Jackson, the Cotton Council, while trying to supplant existing organizations, strengthened eastern mills. His own outfit could do more for Texas, and do it with less money.[36]

There were other problems too, and not limited to Texas. And populism, laced with bitterness, lurked just under the surface, illustrated by producer antagonism toward merchants, their "betters" perhaps. Rhea Blake remembered Reagen McCrary, a cotton producer and father of later television actor Tex McCrary. "Old man Reagen was from Calvert, Texas," recalled Blake. "He was a small farmer, weather-beaten, hard as nails, leathered skin, a glint in his eye, and thought that Will Clayton had horns!" "In those days a lot of farm leaders built their organization by attacking the business interests, and particularly attacking the cotton merchants who 'always stole their cotton, and never paid them for it,' see. No matter what the market was. 'Them damn merchants, they steal our cotton every fall'; that was their attitude." When the council was organized, cotton producers' average allotments stood at around five acres. But if King Cotton's throne was to be saved, the nobility would have to do it. "You had some large operators and some highly efficient operators and they were the people that really took the lead in organizing the Cotton Council," said Blake. "Obviously a lot of these poor fellows, they didn't even know that there was such a thing, and wouldn't have understood it if you had talked to them. A lot of them were illiterate."[37] If nothing else, such talk made it clear that there would be no institutionalized voice in the proposed organization for sharecroppers and other tenants.

Rhea Blake was glad to save the Texas meeting for Oscar Johnston. Released from his darkened imprisonment, Oscar, patched eye and all, and accompanied by Martha, headed for Dallas. There, on October 27, at the Baker Hotel, Johnston told thirty-odd Texas cotton leaders that cotton stood divided on legislation, production, and market control. Efforts to equalize supply and demand focused on the former, virtually never on the latter. But on consumption, he said, all could agree. Government could pull no "rabbit out of the hat" for them; they would have to do it themselves. He referred to the Tulane study and recounted the development of other industries now organized. Cotton's time had arrived. Johnston hoped that industry representatives, "lashed by the whip of necessity," would "lay aside personal views, ideas, individual prejudices, group interests, and unite for the purpose of developing an organization, capacitated, armed and implemented to attack the serious problem with which we are confronted."[38]

The homework in Texas had been done and it bore success, at least for the moment. J. R. McCrary, the crusty cotton farmer from Calvert, became temporary chairman of the state cotton council unit. It all captured the crucial endorsement of Will Clayton, although the *Dallas Morning News* put its own extravagant spin on the story. Said the paper the next day: "A movement launched eighteen months ago by the state-wide cotton committee for Texas, headed by Burris C. Jackson, Hillsboro, was carried along here Thursday into a national movement." According to Jackson, his organization, still trying to secure the research lab for his home state, would continue its work. With Texas in the fold, however grudgingly to some, perhaps, Oklahoma rounded out the field the very next day. Preliminary organization in more than a dozen states now stood complete. Johnston, chairman of the Committee on Organization, called for elected representatives to meet at 10:00 A.M. at the Peabody in Memphis on November 21 to establish the National Cotton Council of America.[39]

It came not a day too soon. The Memphis meeting intersected the downward skid of an industry in deep trouble. Cotton exports in the first several months of 1938 fell almost a million bales under the same time in 1937. Warehouses bulged with unsold staple, synthetics threatened, and world carryover, much of it American, ballooned. King Cotton had survived all manner of adversity, including wars, weevils, drought, disease, and social and economic dislocation. But loss of its domestic market, now threatened, would prove fatal. Said Johnston to the delegates on November 21, "I am quite certain that the plight of the industry today is more serious than ever before in its history." As cotton retainers checked into the Peabody (prompted by "ordinary animal instinct" for survival, Oscar told them) they had their work cut out for them.[40]

Then it was 10:00 A.M., November 21, 1938. After the invocation by the Reverend Robert G. Lee, pastor of one of the city's big Baptist churches, eighty-six representatives from fourteen states answered Rhea Blake's roll call, as did more than two dozen members of the Advisory Council. Then they all settled in for one of Oscar's podium performances—"a magnificent presentation," said one later. Black-patched Oscar—"a large aggressive man," claimed the *Memphis Press-Scimitar*—talked about problems and threats facing American cotton. He talked about the dodo bird, the dinosaur, and Gulliver, who was subdued by Lilliputians. He rehearsed the agony of their shared industry and about divided Democrats who fell apart in 1896 and Republicans who did the same in 1912. He talked about "forgetting differences" and hatchet burying, about coopera-tion, consumption, advertising, markets, and tariffs. He invoked Ben Franklin's dictum about hanging together or hanging separately. For years, he confessed, he had harbored the hope that the major components of cotton's kingdom would unite in a single room in a single goal. "That ambition," he said, "is realized." Hodding Carter, the Greenville editor with a flair for the dramatic, observed the goings-on. "In a mezzanine floor assembly room of Memphis' Peabody Hotel, cotton history is being written this 21st of November, 1938." "Not all of the . . . delegates have come prepared to agree fully with the chairman or his program," he noted, "but as Oscar Johnston continues speaking their gestures of approval become more frequent. These delegates whose names are business and agri-cultural talismen from California to the Carolinas are alert to possible flaws in any proposals to help cotton. Now they exchange pleased glances."[41]

Johnston's "great ovation" was followed by the real work. Resolutions, mo-tions, open and closed meetings, and bylaws filled the Peabody's air for two days. (Blake recalled watching Johnston earlier dictate the constitution and bylaws of the council: Oscar paced the floor, hands thrust deep in his pockets, getting every detail, every punctuation, never stopping, all without paper. That, of course, was Oscar's style.) In the end, Johnston got what he wanted, an or-ganization to promote "consumption of American cotton, cottonseed, and the products thereof." Fourteen state units would kick in two cents per bale for a hefty budget. Decision making was properly distributed; no general policy would arise without approval of two-thirds of the membership (an old Demo-cratic Party rule), each branch of the industry voting separately and retaining veto power. This was a time for open harmony, and no minority reports sur-faced. By voice vote, Johnston was named permanent chairman to serve until the first annual meeting, scheduled for Dallas on January 24, 1939. A presti-gious trio of cotton men filled vice chairmanships: Harold Young, of the Ar-kansas Farm Bureau, who had been present at the creation at Delta State; loyal Lamar Fleming Jr., of Houston's Anderson, Clayton; and Dr. David R. Coker, prominent South Carolina producer and cottonseed breeder. Blake and Wynn retained their now-permanent vital slots as secretary and treasurer. The Committee on Organization passed out of existence, its noble work complete. The National Cotton Council was born. "Over the meeting," said the *Memphis Commercial Appeal,* "stood the broad shadow of a man who yesterday became the No. 1 figure in American cotton by virtue of driving spirit, blunt logic and sharp interpretation of the South's problem—low cotton consumption. He is Oscar Johnston." On its editorial page the paper added that "The Memphis meeting is evidence that the jolt has awakened some of us. . . . Kid Cotton is in there fighting." Claimed the rival *Press-Scimitar,* "This is a great achievement which could not have been possible without industrial statesmanship of a high order, and that was supplied by Oscar Johnston." Said the *Dallas Morning News,* "He speaks with authority."[42]

The two months between the Memphis meeting and the Dallas convention were busy ones. Rough edges in state units needed smoothing, delegates to the first annual convention needed electing, and funds needed raising. Three hundred Arkansas cotton men, for example, voted thumbs up at Little Rock in early December to support the council, eyeing thirty thousand dollars as their share of start-up costs. After entertaining his new friend Bill Coberly and his wife for Thanksgiving at Scott (he admired Coberly's overcoat so much that he soon ordered one from Oviatt's in Los Angeles), Oscar too was on the move, now selling the council in Memphis, now talking cotton in Washington, now speaking at an agricultural forum at the University of Illinois; soon he was in Arizona, then El Paso, and finally in Dallas. He was not totally sanguine. He remained cautious about the whole operation, still tentative about a plan that in one shape or another had occupied his thoughts for well over a year. Just before Christmas 1938, halfway in time between Memphis and Dallas, Johnston confessed to his old New Deal colleague Paul Porter, by then a counsel for Columbia Broadcasting in Washington, that it was "too early to forecast the outcome of the efforts to set up the organization. There has been no trouble about 'organizing,'" he said. "The dispute arises when it comes to talking about 'financing.'" Oscar never did anything small, of course, never could be satisfied with underfunded plans. When he ran a plantation for the British, it was a big one, even if often in need of cash; when he drained the federal cotton pool, it was all done with big numbers and in ways that unnerved the AAA legal division. Now it was to be a national cotton council. "I am unwilling to proceed with any sort of organization that is not adequately financed to enable it to do a good job," he told Porter. He would nix the whole idea without $150,000 to start, without $150,000–250,000 "in sight" for the first year's operation, and without approval for at least half a million dollars for subsequent years. He told Porter about the two-cent a bale budget ($240,000) and that some states expected to have their share in Billy Wynn's hands before the Dallas meeting.

But the problem was Texas. There, he said, "[a] small group . . . has taken the position that this is too much money, and that we should not attempt to raise more than $15,000.00 or $20,000.00 at this time. The whole thing will be thrashed out at the Dallas meeting, which has been called for January 24th and 25th, and at which time we should know definitely if there is, or is not, to be a National Cotton Council." Meanwhile, Billy Wynn had established a trust fund for contributions, Mississippi's original $9,000 seed money carrying the operation thus far. But, said Johnston defiantly, "[l]ists of all contributors, showing name, address and amount of each contribution, are required, and I have made the statement that if at the Dallas meeting we find the organization inadequately financed, I shall call the 'deal' off, and refund every penny contributed."[43]

As it developed, there would be a national cotton council after all. When the first annual meeting convened at the Adolphus Hotel in Dallas in January 1939, Billy Wynn reported that $100,000 of the proposed $240,000 start-up had been paid or pledged. (In addition, apparently, the Louisiana legislature gave $5,000 and an Arkansas delegate announced that Gov. Carl Bailey would ask his legislature for $10,000.) It was not all Johnston had wanted, but still enough to prevent his abdication. He was in it for the long haul. The well-attended convention carried out its business with dispatch, endorsing the work of the Executive Committee in matters of board selection, voting procedures, and the like. By acclamation it approved a slate of candidates for the twenty-five-man board of directors (a sort of "who's who" of the cotton kingdom), a board already empowered to develop and implement council bylaws along the lines of those endorsed at Memphis in November. Among its resolutions, the convention recommended the release of large quantities of accumulated federal loan stocks, and the guarantee of market adjustment payments to raise cotton prices to 75 percent of parity. The convention also ratified Memphis as its national headquarters. The following day the new directors elected Oscar Johnston president of the council and chairman of the board; regional vice presidencies went to Lamar Fleming, Harold Young, and Daniel C. Roper, Franklin Roosevelt's erstwhile secretary of commerce, filling in for David Coker, who had died shortly after the Memphis meeting. Blake and Wynn returned to their usual slots. The board also approved the bylaws and worked out other details incident to the organization. The National Cotton Council of America became a reality.[44]

Optimism blended with reality. "The first high hurdle is behind the Cotton Council," observed Hodding Carter later, "for its ideas and ideals have been sold to the industry, and the medium for their resale to the nation has been perfected." This was "a campaign," said the *Memphis Commercial Appeal*, "to put King Cotton back on his throne." The whole industry, "from producer to exporter," claimed the *Dallas Morning News* soberly, "girded its loins for a war to restore the staple and its products to its former place of glory."[45] If there was optimism, maybe that was part of the rite of passage for a new and ambitious undertaking. But men of ability and leadership, pressed by desperation, had come too far to turn back now.

Facing cotton's problems head-on, Oscar Johnston steered his new organization into unsettling days when markets were shrinking and the world teetered on the edge of war. The whole business was a "herculean task," said the Dallas daily, one that would challenge his leadership. Countless controversies lay ahead. And then there was the ever-present problem of money, a problem Rhea Blake deemed priority number one.[46]

As His Majesty's retainers fanned out from Dallas in the bleak days of 1939, King Cotton, in the twilight of his reign, at last had found a voice. None could know at the time, of course, that the infant cotton council would have to do much more than its stated purposes of finding new uses for cotton and cottonseed. Nor could they know that such new uses would not fundamentally increase consumption relative to competitive "manmades" or that a world soon at war would shut down international markets. They also did not know that their budget would be pitifully small for all that needed doing and that haggling with Congress over legislation, in ways never imagined in 1939, would become a major council activity. And who could envision that in time spin-off operations such as the Institute for Cotton International and Cotton Incorporated, itself requiring legislation, would independently assume major goals of promotion, research, and development, and that fights within and without, including defections and collisions with the Farm Bureau, would both discourage and energize?

But, boarding their trains out of Dallas in 1939, neither could these men realize fully what they had done, that from these origins would spring an organization that, despite failures, would boldly take on challenges, conquer some, and work on others, and that textile mills and cotton cooperatives would eventually join the family. The men who ran the council, lobbied Congress, and took their efforts worldwide were men who could run anything—gifted executives such as William Rhea Blake, who guided the organization for decades after the Johnston era. And who could know that the council, representing disparate elements that seemed to defy unity, would be the instrument that would organize cotton—an industry touted decades later by a secretary of agriculture as a model of such commodity organization, and that, ultimately, they had created an organization that would save cotton's industry, if not its crown, in the process enhancing millions of lives?[47] The National Cotton Council of America—now triumphant, now defeated, now triumphant again—was Oscar Goodbar Johnston's crowning achievement. An old and major American industry had finally come of age.

# 13

## I Have Never Liked the Term "New Deal"

A group of starry eyed "do gooders" in 1932 took advantage of the political situation resulting from the debacle of 1929 and rode into power.
—Oscar G. Johnston, 1942

I know of no place, except possibly Hell, that I would not prefer to Washington, but unfortunately now it has become necessary to go there for everything, including almost the right to live.    —Oscar G. Johnston, 1942

The City is a veritable madhouse—hotels crowded, with half the people there trying to do something and the other half trying to keep them from it. My sympathies are with the latter half in most instances.
—Oscar G. Johnston, 1943

**E**ight months after Dallas, the infant National Cotton Council was baptized into a world at war. International markets for cotton shut down, compounding the problem facing a new organization that proposed simply but profoundly to find new uses for cotton and cottonseed. Fortunately, no one really knew the real threat of synthetics just on the horizon, or, as Rhea Blake recalled, "it might have just made us quit before we started." Oscar Johnston devoted every minute to his offspring, save that demanded by his plantations, all without compensation. He had to adjust to the political confinement of his new identity as president of a wide-ranging organization, no longer free to speak his own mind. To Oscar it was his "alter ego," to Rhea Blake it was "that box." Little triumphs in the early years were matched by underfunding and maverickism within the industry, so much so that Johnston privately confessed to the possibility of calling the whole thing off. He didn't, of course, and the council survived to hold the industry together during the war; the really big contributions would come in the following decades. The idea of unity was compelling; the structure of the council was sound, and it was headed by Oscar Johnston, whose leadership, when it really counted, never flagged.[1]

In the early council years Johnston was often away from Scott on organization business. He eventually tried to devote more time to his Mississippi plantations and even had a chance to take the British "out 'whole'" through the sale of their properties. But a new regime in Manchester was pleased with the success of their investments and refused to budge on the huge Scott plantation, quite a turnaround from the time Johnston had joined the company in the 1920s. Around the same time, Johnston began purchasing properties for himself, named Bolivar Farms, adjacent to Delta Planting Company, in which he eventually held about 30 percent interest. He hoped to buy out the British holdings at the Deeson plantation and amalgamate it with Bolivar Farms. But the British didn't like the Bolivar Farms idea, and they refused his personal offer, made more than once, to buy out their interest in Delta Planting Company, expanded to about ten thousand finely honed acres; at first they likewise refused to buy out his 30 percent, finally relenting, then selling the whole Deeson operation at the end of World War II. Oscar likewise sold Bolivar Farms. In a separate deal in the spring of 1946, the British also sold Delta Pine's noncontiguous Empire Plantation at Estill, Mississippi.[2]

Meanwhile, of further concern was Martha's health, suffering as she did with exceptionally painful arthritis. Seeking some relief for her affliction in the spring of 1941, they sought a climate change aboard their cabin cruiser off Florida. Yachting was something of a passion with Oscar, causing a man rather tightfisted with his money to splurge on an expensive indulgence. Oscar had always liked pleasure boats and loved racing on Moon Lake when he lived in Clarksdale. Paul Porter remembered his own outings with Johnston: "It used to scare the hell out of me. He would stand up in that boat and at reasonably full power, would go up and down the Mississippi." Oscar's tastes ran to cabin cruisers, one of which, *Lady Luck*, blew up in July 1932, nearly costing him his life. Martha was living in Asheville in those days and there were women aboard, which stirred local gossip. But by the time he bought a new thirty-eight-footer in 1937 and named it *Martha J*, his marriage was on more settled ground. The pair would head off for the Gulf of Mexico when they could, which was not often, usually with a complement of servants and friends. Oscar apparently liked fiddling with his boats as much as sailing them. His 1937 craft, protected in a nice boathouse at the Greenville Yacht Club, was featured in an advertisement in *Yachting* magazine in January 1938, and his personally designed interior apparently became the "standard" on new models. Always on the lookout for larger craft, Oscar bought a slightly used fifty-foot cruiser in 1940. The boat was built in Ohio in 1939 and sailed to Memphis in September that year, its owner arrested on criminal charges of some sort. Under the watchful eye of a caretaker, it remained at the Memphis Yacht Club until Johnston bought it the following spring, picking up a virtually new teak-decked boat for about $20,000, which when built had listed for more than $32,000. (Even then Oscar was open to a deal, which never materialized, on a sixty-footer for $30,000.) A three-week vacation to the Gulf soon followed; a five-week cruise, the one seeking relief for Martha's arthritis, took them to Key West a year later. At the time, J. R. McCrary, a prominent Texas producer and state Cotton Council board member, told Johnston that he hoped Martha's health would improve in Florida and that the trip would, he said, "strengthen you for the strenuous days ahead. Unless I miss my guess, America will have overtime work for men of your ability, in the very near future."[3]

Indeed it did. Before and during World War II, Johnston was in and out of Washington. As president of the National Cotton Council of America, he dealt with Agriculture Secretary Claude Wickard, Wallace's successor, over one issue or another; he argued with Leon Henderson of the Office of Price Administration over federal "price fixing"; and he haggled, as a Mississippi farmer, with government bureaucrats over Delta Pine's wheat allotments or priority for wire fencing—hard to get during the war—without which the plantation's new cattle herd, slowly being developed in lieu of the cropland taken out of production under the AAA of 1938, might have to be sold. Even before Pearl Harbor, the Cotton Council, seeing no future in deeper acreage cuts, got Wickard to reverse himself on the issue. Though Johnston still spent much of his time on council business, he continued to serve on the board of directors of the Illinois Central Railroad, to which he had been elected in 1940, and the Federal Reserve Board of St. Louis, where he was also deputy chairman. He accepted board membership on the Farm Foundation of Chicago and appointment as consultant on the War Manpower Commission's Regional War Manpower Committee for Region VII in October 1942. Though he regarded the latter as his patriotic duty, he found that time pressures prevented him from serving, and he quickly resigned. Adding to the burdens was another bout with cataracts in 1941. His 1938 eye operation had been a miserable failure and for three years he languished more or less "in a 'fog,'" with little hope of improvement. In the spring of 1941, however, the damaged eye rather spontaneously improved to 20/50 vision; unfortunately the right one also needed surgery. After getting the best specialist he could find, Dr. J. H. Dunnington of New York City, he submitted to cataract surgery in mid-September 1941—but not before slipping over to Quincy, Massachusetts, to lambaste American trade protectionism at a *Fortune*-sponsored roundtable. With Blake in Memphis and Toler in Scott, for six weeks or so Oscar languished in New York. Martha stayed at his hospital bed the whole while, sleeping for several weeks in a room across from his until the rising hospital census forced her to give it up. Undaunted, she took an apartment at the Stanhope, but was there only to sleep, usually returning to the hospital during breakfast and remaining all day; she stopped reading to Oscar only when the nurse chased her out late at night. Oscar endlessly worried about her own health, but his protests fell on deaf ears.

Oscar was determined to follow medical orders this time. He was told that failure to follow the rules, and exerting himself, had delayed recovery after the 1938 operation. This time there could be no physical or mental exertion. Still, despite precautions, the left eye soon hemorrhaged, and Johnston again plunged into the agonizing torture that followed, though it proved less severe than before. After six weeks in the hospital in New York, Dunnington allowed him to board a Pullman for Memphis, where his car and driver met them. For several days he lay in a darkened room, facing general convalescence for weeks more. He did manage to get to his plantation office in early November, the first time since August. Though he could dictate, he could not read, and strenuous activity was out of the question. All the while, Martha stayed at his side, neglecting her own growing invalidism from arthritis, making Oscar all the more restless at his own malady. Their mutual doting was characteristic of their revived relationship, made all the more poignant by their afflictions. They were together constantly, two fiercely independent people now depending on each other. He rarely took a trip without her, and he always worried about her health. By Christmas 1941 she could hardly hold a pen to carry on correspondence, and she suffered great pain in the back of her head. Oscar was deeply troubled by it all, and for the first time since he had come home from the army in 1918, he anticipated a Christmas without a house full of dinner guests. By early 1942 he could read, drive, and be somewhat normal again for the first time since 1938. Looking for some rest, he told a friend, "We both appear to need some little physical overhaul."[4]

Neither rest nor leisurely attention to his plantations greeted his return to work. In addition, there were rumors, always rumors, that the huge Scott plantation overplanted its AAA cotton allotments. One such rumor in 1941 gained wide currency, generating bureaucratic checking and paperwork, finding only that the company slightly underplanted for the three years after implementation of the AAA of 1938. "About the only report we can make regarding the 'basis' for the rumor is that seemingly someone simply told a damn lie," said an exasperated county agent. He added, "This looks a good bit like some more 'Fifth Column' stuff." The same rumor arose the following year, the AAA checked, and again Delta Pine was officially shown to have underplanted. "Annually critics start some sort of rumor," Johnston told I. W. Duggan, AAA southern regional director in Washington, "and annually the check-up shows that in an effort to comply strictly with the regulations, we have usually not planted the full permitted acreage." According to Johnston, in ten seasons, 1933–42, the plantation was found in excess of its cotton allotments only twice, in such cases under 2 percent; eight times the plantation was underplanted. After discounting the 1941 rumor, the Bolivar County agent told his superior, "These people get the same consideration given others, no more, no less."[5]

Other problems lay beyond the plantation and the petty rumors. The outbreak of the war disrupted international trade, including crucial markets for cotton, the results of which had serious economic and political implications around the world. Seeking a hedge against the threat of Nazism in the American hemisphere, the United States soon proposed buying up, if necessary, surplus cotton from a number of Latin American nations, including Peru, whose port of Lima stood a relatively short bomber's flight from the Panama Canal Zone. The word was that cotton purchases might also be slated for Nicaragua, Paraguay, and even Brazil. For its part, Peru had lately expanded its cotton production, exporting much of its crop to Europe and the Orient. The National Cotton Council had supported renewed reciprocity in 1940, though the world war destroyed its effectiveness. Still, in early 1942 the council opposed such reciprocity if it would be used to poke a hole in the Smoot-Hawley Tariff to admit long-staple cotton—unless, of course, war exigencies required it. What the United States proposed to do was quite different. The economic and political consequences of closed markets dictated cementing as many nations to the Allied cause as possible.

The Commodity Credit Corporation, the point agency in the proposed cotton purchase, tapped Oscar Johnston to fly to South America as part of the small U.S. delegation to handle some of the arrangements. Johnston again donned government garb, creating a mini-flurry in the media. Drew Pearson and Robert S. Allen's syndicated "Washington Merry-Go-Round" suggested that Johnston's choice for the purchase ensured southern congressional support. In fact, cotton prices dropped sharply on the exchange after the announcement of Johnston's CCC appointment. The *New York Times* pointed to "trade sources," which saw the announcement as an influence in the price slide. Five days later, the *Times* claimed Johnston's appointment "was of widespread market interest," the cotton trade thinking the CCC "was preparing to call 1941 loan cotton." The appointment even landed Johnston in the "People of the Week" section of *United States News.* For his part, Johnston thought the South American trip would consummate the Peruvian deal, and that he could look into a like arrangement with Brazil for 1943. While in South America, he wanted to size up the situation in Argentina as well, albeit unofficially, since that country retained diplomatic ties with the Axis. The details were quite complicated, but such proposed international arrangements were part of what Johnston called his "rather ambitious" plans for cotton after the war. In fact, *Time* later reported that the Peruvian deal "was not just another U.S. subsidy to a Good Neighbor. It was a step, in Claude Wickard's words, toward 'the working out of world cotton production and marketing problems after the war.'" The Latin American talk even sparked speculation of "a World Cotton Pool."

Martha got medical clearance to accompany Oscar and by late April 1942 all was set. Then, very quickly, the trip was off. Martha fell ill, and the deal was quickly negotiated. Johnston, for his part, met with a Peruvian delegation in Washington. With pressing details involving establishing an office in Peru and arranging with brokers and others to facilitate the deal, Oscar had his long-time personal friend, Everett Cook, a Memphis cotton merchant and chairman of the National Cotton Council's Foreign Relations Division, join the U.S. delegation in his stead. "So," said *Time,* "Oscar stayed in Washington and meditated on cotton's war and post-war worlds." The Peruvian deal, lasting until 1945, worked out very satisfactorily, and the United States also arranged to buy up relatively small cotton crops in Haiti and Puerto Rico.[6]

Meanwhile, Johnston was already involving himself in an issue closer to home. He had a growing unease with the New Deal. King Cotton's conservative retainers had scarcely tolerated liberals when the New Deal was young, but the world war altered the American agenda, shrinking possibilities for reform. Industrialist "dollar-a-year men" now assumed center stage in Washington's wartime bureaucracy. Liberals might be found in Vice President Henry Wallace's Board of Economic Warfare or the Office of Price Administration, both wartime agencies, or in the older National Labor Relations Board and the Farm Security Administration. For the latter agency, with its perceived threat to the plantation regime and to fee-simple landownership in general, Oscar Johnston reserved his most strident opposition. While Johnston had kept rank with the administration when the South began to abandon the New Deal as it tilted leftward in 1937, his loyalty always had been pragmatic. His independence within the government machinery had a long history. Rarely reticent, he resisted pressure for the Bankhead tax in the mid-thirties and had fought the liberals in the AAA's legal division to the bitter end. His biggest concern over the direction of federal programs by the early forties was the operation of the Farm Security Administration (FSA), a successor of Rexford G. Tugwell's old short-lived Resettlement Administration (RA). Sponsored by a pair of conservative southern Democrats, John Bankhead of Alabama and Marvin Jones of Texas, the Bankhead-Jones Farm Tenant Act of 1937 attempted to shore up the family-size farm in the Great Depression and halt the epidemic of mortgage foreclosures. FSA's ambitious and eclectic projects included resettlement communities, some carried over from Tugwell's RA days. Johnston disliked such projects because the federal government could put up more elaborate housing and amenities than normally available to average independent farmers. The result, he groused privately in 1936, was to lower morale among tenants on private plantations, the owners of which could not afford to compete with federal resources.[7]

By 1940 Johnston became convinced that the FSA had shifted toward socialized agriculture, a not unrealistic perception, and soon voiced his concern within the Department of Agriculture to FSA officials. Since the early New Deal he had known and had enjoyed friendly relations with C. B. "Beanie" Baldwin, the Henry Wallace associate who now headed the agency. Also, with no desire to be quoted or engage the matter publicly, he told his friend, Edward Meeman, editor of the *Memphis Press-Scimitar*, that "I do have my 'fingers crossed' when I say that I am not in accord with, nor approve, the present program of the Farm Security Administration in its 'rehabilitation work'. The efforts are well meant," he said, "but I fear are misguided and misdirected. This is, of course, a mere expression of misgivings."[8]

Those misgivings became deeper and his words more strident. Though his "attitudes toward 'socialistic agriculture'" put him on the outs with some in the administration—"in the 'dog house,'" he called it in 1941—he made no public break with the administration over FSA until 1942. The administration, he thought, had shifted toward labor advocacy, a trend likely to continue, and toward socialization of agriculture as evidenced in the FSA-sponsored communal projects. He was also privately critical of the Southern Tenant Farmers Union, "a purely socialistic or communistic movement intended primarily," he said, "to provide revenue for communists too lazy to do manual work, and too ignorant to do any worthwhile 'brain work,' but shrewd enough to prey upon the ignorant 'Parlor Reds' of New York. Such suckers as Mayor [Fiorello] LaGuardia, Mrs. [Eleanor] Roosevelt, and others have aided these leeches in earning a livelihood by preying upon the credulity of ignorant farm people." The STFU posed no threat in itself, he thought. "It is a straw indicating the direction in which the wind is blowing, and when we find people of prominence and education being victims to the extent of supporting these grafters, we must realize that there is a serious trend or drift which if not stopped, will ultimately seriously and adversely affect our national economy."[9]

In Johnston's view, northern labor radicals such as Phillip Murray, head of the Congress of Industrial Organizations (CIO), had formed something of an unholy alliance with the FSA socialists. Their agendas meshed. In February 1942, Murray, claiming the FSA like numerous other "more progressive agencies of the New Deal" was being attacked by "reactionary forces," called for union support of that agency. Indeed, he called for its expansion. For its part, the FSA's "long term objectives," according to well-circulated documents that Johnston acquired, included minimum wages for agricultural workers, subdivision of and graduated taxes and eminent-domain proceedings against large

landholdings, and acquisition of "government title *to as much land as possible.*"
As Johnston's friend and Staple Cotton Cooperative Association president Oscar
Bledsoe told Walter Sillers, "There is no doubt that the F.S.A. and the C.I.O.
intend to break up the plantation system here in the Delta, and [they] have
the support of the Federal Government."[10]

In March 1942, even though his criticism had been fairly muted, Johnston
was attacked in Congress during a payment-limitation debate and linked with
the Farm Bureau Federation's criticism of the FSA, all demonstrating that
the demagogic politics of class envy was not limited to Mississippi. Representative Frank E. Hook, a Michigan Democrat, told his colleagues that a limitation would save money and affect only "men like—well, you boys from the
South know Oscar Johns[t]on with his $1,300,000, and those who are getting
payments far beyond what they deserve. I mention Oscar Johns[t]on because
of the large Government check he received before we limited the payments
to $10,000." Johnston was naturally indignant. Though he admitted to Hook
that "I may be flattering myself in assuming that you had reference to me,"
he concluded that he must be the Oscar Johnston in question. "It would be
interesting for me to know what you mean by 'Oscar Johnston with his
$1,300,000.00,'" he said. "I certainly do not have any such sum of money, have
never had any such amount, in fact have never even wanted that much money.
The statement was evidently made for the purpose of arousing prejudice in
the minds of small calibre men who, because of ignorance, envy, and jealousy,
entertain a personal dislike of, or animosity toward, men who, even through
ability and hard work, have accumulated a substantial amount of money. I have
never received one penny from the Government either for Soil Conservation
or Price Adjustment."[11]

Aware of the risks, Johnston soon went public with his criticism of the FSA,
though he first did so—extemporaneously—in the friendly atmosphere of a
meeting of the Mississippi Farm Bureau Federation at Leroy Percy State Park in
July 1942. He argued that the agency, aiming to grab huge tracts of farmland,
was acting in bad faith by so framing its tenant-purchase contracts to eliminate any chance of fee-simple ownership. In subsequent speeches in Mississippi, Arkansas, and Tennessee, and in private correspondence, Johnston developed a litany of allegations against the FSA, charging it with wasting public
money, violating congressional intent, and building a giant clientele among its
tenants so as to support its sovietization of American agriculture. Among its
several allies stood the CIO and the leftist National Farmers Union. In his early
attacks neither Johnston nor the Farm Bureau had any desire to destroy the
agency, merely to force it back to the purpose for which Congress intended it:
the financial restoration of the family farm through private ownership.[12]

Johnston's attacks stirred considerable support in Mississippi and Arkansas. One law firm in Indianola, in the Delta's Sunflower County, which had "heard a great deal" regarding Johnston's Percy Park speech, wanted more information (including "Red and Communistic Tendencies of the FSA") because they expected litigation against local FSA projects and wanted to be prepared to serve the agency's disgruntled tenants. Since much of Johnston's criticism was framed as part of a larger assault on the New Deal and left-wing bureaucracy, so also was much of the support it generated. One planter said he had his eyes opened by Johnston's speech in Greenville, adding that he felt "many of us realize that something is vitally wrong with our Government Administration and your talk cleared up a lot of things for me." Another Mississippian, agreeing with Johnston and watching the growth of bureaucratic intrusion "under the guise of our war effort" wondered "where a Southern Democrat, grounded in the faith, will have to go to vote?" Others exhibited greater passion which, after a decade of the New Deal, lurked beneath the surface. "My father rebelled in 1861 and his grandfather in 1776," said one supporter. "Despite my eighties," he said, "I can still carry a gun and may have to revolt against a socialistic dictatorship in Washington, run by Harry Hopkins and C.I.O. Hope our old South rises up for its rights." And one old friend from Friars Point, a Spanish-American War veteran, told Oscar, "I am for you as far as giving you my full support with a winchester. When do we start[?]" He added: "I think we should call for a divorcement of the New Dealers from our party or better still a kicking out of them in the same way a white man would kick out a woman who he had found laying up with a nigger." More calmly, Mississippi Congressman Will M. Whittington, who agreed with Johnston about the FSA, told him, "The chickens are coming home to roost."[13]

If the public attacks on FSA by the head of the National Cotton Council generated public support, they also invited counterattacks. The debate was joined in late November 1942 when C. B. Baldwin appeared in Little Rock to attend a Food for Freedom meeting. When the press reminded Baldwin of Johnston's remark about FSA contracts, Baldwin retorted, angrily, "Did Mr. Johnston ever sign a contract with one of his tenants?"[14]

Ironically, within a few days Johnston himself appeared in Little Rock at the annual meeting of the Arkansas Farm Bureau. He denied Baldwin's charges that he and the Farm Bureau wanted to destroy the FSA. But he reiterated the agency's many sins, waved the red flag of communism, and claimed that FSA's policies, unless reversed, would turn American farmers into "'glorified peasants' of the Government." The CIO, the Farmers Union, and the FSA, he said, all conspired to "drive a wedge into agriculture." That same day, the FSA's regional director in Little Rock, A. D. Stewart, joined the fight. Johnston's charges were "serious," he said, and publicly called on Johnston to prove his allegations and name those in the agency who were guilty of subversive activities.[15]

Within two weeks Johnston, hoping news accounts would publicize the controversy nationally—an unusual stance for the big planter who coveted a low profile—replied to Stewart, first by mail, then, the following day, through the press. Inviting Stewart to demonstrate errors in his charges, Johnston rehashed old allegations about violating congressional intent, unfair tenant contracts, collectivization of American agriculture, discriminatory taxes against large operators, the CIO connection, and the like. He even dragged in the director of FSA's forebear, Rexford Tugwell—long since stamped "Rex the Red"—who, said Johnston, promoted land socialism as governor of Puerto Rico. He also charged the FSA with fostering cotton picking on an hourly basis, something Johnston regarded as "utterly unsound and impractical," but a pathetic idea likely to spread.[16]

The debate had consequences. His attacks, Johnston told a friend in December, "have brought down upon me an avalanche of criticism and protest from administration people," or, as another friend put it, "the paid heads of the uplift bureaus," all of which he was quite willing to endure to see the FSA brought back within congressional intent. "I am definitely of the opinion," he said privately a year after Pearl Harbor, "that unless 'we the people' assert ourselves and insist upon a return to truly democratic principles, and the abandonment of a lot of socialistic or communistic ideas and 'isms,' we are going to have cause, when the war is won, to wonder if the victory was worth the price."[17]

In its defense, FSA issued a trio of press releases, each announcing a yeoman farmer success story. In each of three states a farmer was getting, or about to get, a deed to his property. In Alabama, one not on a cooperative would publicly get deed to his 171-acre tract from Sen. John Bankhead himself; another, a black farmer in Rankin County, Mississippi, was slated to get his in a celebration in February 1943. One Louisiana newspaper saw that as an invitation to attack. "While one prominent Mississippian, Oscar Johnston, big Delta cotton planter, was lambasting FSA a few days ago," it said, "announcement came from Jackson, the state capital, of plans for honoring a hill country negro farmer who had made good as a result of help given him under the Bankhead-Jones farm purchase act administered by the Federal [*sic* ] Security Administration." Johnston headed a national cotton group and "doesn't believe the FSA has accomplished anything for the farming interests of the South," declared the editor. "The case of the negro farmer in Rankin county appears to furnish convincing evidence that Mr. Johnston's appraisal has missed the mark in a big way."[18]

A few days later, another paper, Alabama's *Birmingham News,* thought the FSA farmers' buyout in Limestone County was news indeed. It called the FSA a "constructive agency" and attacks on it "insidious," and it claimed that Johnston's

Scott plantation was "cooperatively owned, even if the term is spelled corporation rather than cooperation." "We do not see that the FSA cooperative enterprise is any less desirable than Mr. Johnston's corporation-owned plantation," the *News* announced. According to the paper, "The plan is working better than we fear Mr. Johnston wants it to work. He is afraid that the FSA, by helping small farmers get on their feet, may somehow upset the established cotton-growing system."[19]

Hard work and landownership were always worthy achievements. But the original forty-year, 3 percent loan to the forty-one-year black farmer in Rankin County was $1,495 on 120 acres, timber from which he sold for $600, enabling him to reduce the lien to $895. With a wife and nine children, at least two of whom could work, he further reduced his indebtedness over five years an average $179 annually, plus interest and, presumably, taxes, Johnston reasoned. To Johnston that was not remarkable. "It would indeed be strange if at least three out of some 80,000 FSA 'clients' in Mississippi and Arkansas had not been able to 'pay out,'" he told a critic privately. "For each of these three, I can point you to 50 so-called 'clients' who have been evicted. I can also point you to several who are ready, willing, and able to 'pay out,' and have been denied that right and had deeds refused them." He had, he said, received "innumerable letters from FSA 'clients'" and had talked personally "with a great many" who painted a less than pretty picture.

Johnston's numbers about evictions may have been suspect, but his point was well taken. In fact, in praising the farmer's payout as an "amazing accomplishment," the Louisiana editor may have said more than he intended. Johnston said he had "personally inspected some of the large plantations which have been acquired here in the Delta by FSA, and find that even last year, 1942, when all through this area exceptionally good crops were made, the production on these FSA-operated plantations were substantially below normal. I have seen this Winter FSA 'clients' buying hay, corn, and oats with which to feed live stock because their barns were empty, while privately-owned farms immediately adjacent had their cribs and barns full of corn, hay, and oats." *The Delta Leader*, a conservative black paper run by a Greenville clergyman and editor, H. H. Humes, said, "If the government wants to know the truth, we can furnish a long list of names of Negroes who have bought and paid for farms within four years time and who are not connected with the FSA." The *Leader*, one of the few black voices allowed to speak in the Delta, admired thrift but argued long-term FSA indebtedness would produce indolence instead. "When FSA starts playing up a Negro paying for FSA land, we want to ask, what about the hosts who have paid for their plots long before the FSA started? What about the others who have bought farms? Can we find some national publicity for them?"[20]

Though Johnston's tenants did not move toward ownership, sharecroppers at Scott picked nearly 14,500 cotton bales in 1942, yielding 18.8 cents a pound and $53 a ton from its seed. The tenant share, $812,049.76, less advance of $5 a bale during picking time, left them well over half a million dollars. From that, nearly $75,000 was deducted for war savings bonds purchased by the croppers, leaving them $455,771.56 in cash. That figure probably did not include an average $35–$40 USDA subsidy payment that the tenants kept. Johnston had met three times with groups of tenants to talk up the Series E war savings bonds, "at which I have sought to impress on them the seriousness of the war situation," he told a Treasury Department official, "the necessity for cooperation of individual citizens, and their obligations to contribute to the cause by the purchase of bonds. I do not know just what we can do toward inducing them to buy bonds other than 'moral suasion.' We, of course, cannot coerce them or demand that they purchase." Johnston held off purchasing Series F bonds allocated to his two plantations pending the outcome of corporate income tax legislation, but Delta Pine employees, all the whites and some of the blacks, authorized a 5 percent paycheck deduction for war bonds. Some bought their full quota.[21]

That many tenants bought war bonds demonstrated economic and community stability. Such stability was also displayed in Delta Pine's relatively low annual turnover, their tenure averaging fourteen or fifteen years. After the 1942 cash settlement, Johnston told Chester Davis, the old AAA warhorse now president of the St. Louis Federal Reserve, that a few tenants bought milk cows and used cars and that "all of them have laid in a few weeks' supply of groceries and bought quite a bit of furniture and clothing." He added, "There is an old adage in this area to the effect that the more money a negro clears from his crop, the more miles he will travel away from the farm. This has not been our experience in the past, nor is it the case this year." As Johnston said bluntly at the end of 1942: "Both our company and our tenants have made a lot of money."[22]

As the public criticism of Johnston spilled into 1943 he got the green light from the National Cotton Council to carry on the anti-FSA campaign. The council's fifth annual convention in January condemned FSA's socialism while commending their president's "efforts to expose the subversive program of that Administration." Further, a council staffer, L. T. Stone, operating out of Memphis, provided legwork in researching FSA activities in Mississippi, Arkansas, and southeast Missouri. Stone got fairly good cooperation from area planters, officials, and local farm bureaus. Hardly impartial, his investigations in January, February, and March 1943 confirmed notions of FSA waste, mismanagement, intimidation, shiftlessness, and low production. One planter and cattle-yard operator from Cleveland, Mississippi, told him that FSA tenants believed that regardless of their production record, the federal government guaranteed their living. Confronted with FSA waste, one FSA employee told the planter he feared losing his job if he lost his clients. And when the planter was trading for livestock with an FSA client, the client sweetened the deal by offering several spools of wire because the federal agency, he said, had provided more than he could use anyway. Another planter told Stone that FSA farms provided the best hunting because game birds liked the overgrown trash and weeds. In still another case, an equipment dealer who also served as a member of the board of supervisors for Humphreys County, Mississippi, told Stone that in his district FSA held 85 of 150 voters. The supervisor claimed FSA had bought three excellent plantations, dispossessed the tenants, and contracted for forty thousand dollars in new farm equipment, even though the plantations already had sufficient machinery and wartime shortages inhibited ordinary farmers from getting repairs for old equipment. According to another supervisor in the same county, FSA tried, unsuccessfully, to force sale of his land by intimidation. And in the Delta's Bolivar County, one planter whose land adjoined a large FSA project testified that after the agency acquired the land, fine cypress housing was destroyed, replaced with houses of uncured sap pine, structures unable to withstand the Delta's climate. The stories became routine. "Production gone to ———," reported Stone. "Gross mismanagement and waste. Shiftlessness, irresponsible attitude being encouraged in tenants."[23]

More serious, Stone reported that Portageville Farms in southeast Missouri, an FSA project, was well run, individualistic, and profitable, but that FSA officials would not allow the tenants and the farm association to pay off their indebtedness to the government and thus become self-sufficient. "The complaint now," said Stone, "is similar to what we have heard before; that is, that FSA never intended to relinquish control of either the individual or the land." A similar argument was made by Ronnie Greenwell, a ginner from Hayti, Missouri. Stone reported that Greenwell, apparently an early FSA supporter, found that FSA always wanted more and more clients without attending to those they had. Indebted to the government, the client would always fall short of independence. In Arkansas, Stone heard more stories of FSA corruption, entrapment in debt, Big Brotherism, intimidation, and fraud.[24]

Johnston had no confidence in the New Deal uplifters. Rexford Tugwell—an academic from Columbia University, brain truster, original Resettlement Administration director, governor of Puerto Rico, and no believer in fee-simple ownership—had told Johnston numerous times that since the soil constituted "a natural resource," the federal government should hold its title, allowing individuals to cultivate it only in conformity with government regulations. Johnston argued that Tugwell's policies, including luring farmers into becoming clients of the government, were carried forward into the FSA, first under Dr. Will Alexander, "a theorist with no practical business experience of any sort, no familiarity with farming, and distinctly Liberal if not outright Radical in his thinking," and then under C. B. Baldwin, "a young man with not the slightest agricultural experience."[25]

Even more outrageous to Johnston was the FSA's practice of land acquisition. Although agricultural appropriation legislation for 1942 forbade FSA land purchases, a practice in effect for years, the agency still managed to acquire holdings indirectly. Johnston's classic and oft-cited example was that of the well-known Phillipston Plantation in Leflore County, Mississippi. When Connecticut General Life Insurance Company acquired the half-century-old plantation in the Great Depression, it retained Phillipston's black and white tenants, some of whom had resided there for forty or more years. Approached by FSA in 1942, however, Connecticut General sold out, not to FSA—because of the legislative prohibition—but to fifty or so FSA-acquired families to whom FSA loaned the requisite funds to purchase the tract. Phillipston's sixty-seven-year-old manager was let go as was the entire roster of seventy-six tenant families. Invited to the property by neighbors, Johnston said he heard pathetic and heartrending stories from evicted tenants who had to be off the property by the end of 1942. The new farmers, Johnston complained to Congressman Will Whittington, had no latitude. All matters relative to farming operations were dictated by FSA. Taxpayers would pick up the financing tab, which would go on indefinitely, during which time the client would make a decent living but never possess "a 'Chinaman's chance'" to become an independent landowner or "a fit citizen of democratic government." According to Johnston, Phillipston was no isolated example. Johnston claimed FSA owned or controlled hundreds of thousands of acres in the Mississippi Valley, much of it fallow, and had a clientele of hundreds of thousands of families. The political potential was enormous, with FSA having ability to shape public policy in ways Johnston deemed unwise.[26]

Johnston's assaults on the FSA generated more than criticism and support. His mailbox, he said, filled up with "pathetic letters" from FSA clients in several southern states. Apparently, some of the clients feared eviction and begged Johnston for help. One letter that caught Johnston's eye was from Booker M. McDade, a white FSA client on the Plum Bayou Project near Wright, Arkansas, about eighty miles or so from Scott. Johnston, along with Henry Wallace, Rexford Tugwell, and other agriculture dignitaries had been at Plum Bayou's dedication back in the heady days of 1936; of late, however, Johnston had lost track of its development. McDade and his family, already successful farmers when FSA solicited them, moved on the project in 1937, among its original clients. After five years of diligence McDade wanted to buy his tract, something he believed FSA had promised when he joined the project. FSA refused, but said it would sell the next year. Then, in 1942, McDade, financially self-sustaining, got an eviction notice that claimed he had been an unsatisfactory and uncooperative client. The FSA regional director claimed he was in arrears on two loans and had not yet paid his current rent. McDade looked to Johnston for advice.[27]

After initial contacts between Johnston and McDade by mail and telephone, the Cotton Council's field representative, L. T. Stone, rented a car in Little Rock and drove to Plum Bayou in early January 1943 for an on-site investigation. The McDades, still on the property, had decided to give in to the FSA eviction and had found new lodgings. Stone, impressed with the family, reported that they were out of debt and that FSA had used McDade's project as a publicity model. McDade even showed Stone a thousand-dollar war bond. Stone got them to agree to stay on their unit and to cooperate in helping to stop FSA abuse, something Stone found in abundance at Plum Bayou. Within a day or two the McDades—Booker, his wife, and daughter Laverne—met again with Stone in Little Rock, the party then driving to nearby Hot Springs for a conference with Oscar Johnston, who had been vacationing at the resort in hopes of alleviating Martha's neuritis. Oscar told them what he had advised from the beginning—that is, to sit tight. He even said to tell the other tenants the same thing. He wanted to force the FSA to take action, seeing the McDade case as an effective weapon against the troublesome agency.[28]

Accompanied by Martha and her mother—a woman Oscar greatly admired—Johnston soon drove to Plum Bayou for his own inspection. He lunched with McDade and his wife, toured much of the project, and talked with dozens of clients, who like McDade, wanted deeds to their units but faced possible eviction. Oscar was quite impressed with the McDades, including Laverne, a young woman of remarkable intelligence who had been high-school valedictorian and had completed two years of college. As Stone earlier advised, she had been preparing a written report of their experience at Plum Bayou and was drafting a list of those who might provide affidavits for the Cotton Council's use.[29]

Meanwhile, the FSA renewed its pressure for eviction in January 1943, threatening forcible removal if necessary. Rumors flew around Plum Bayou that U.S. marshals would carry out the orders. A dozen or so families vacated; others, including McDade and two other families, Manning and Priest, held on, encouraged no doubt by Johnston's pledge of legal assistance, word of which had reached Plum Bayou's supervisor. Johnston's visit, in fact, set off quite a stir at the project, something he generally wished to avoid, knowing that publicity of his personal involvement could be exploited by FSA. But if he was going to use McDade and others as a weapon against the agency, then he was prepared to do so completely and ethically. He hired Arch F. House of the Little

Rock law firm Rose, Loughborough, Dobyns and House to work with Edward Brockman, a Pine Bluff attorney already retained by the Plum Bayou cooperative association. Further, he contracted with the United States Fidelity and Guaranty Company in Meridian, Mississippi, to provide bonds in case of liability against McDade and Manning. His commitment did not end there. At Delta and Pine Land plantation, he set aside acreages comparable to those worked by McDade and Priest in the event all else failed and the pair was actually convicted. Day labor worked that land in the meantime.[30]

Johnston also broadened the base of involvement. He worked cooperatively with the Arkansas Farm Bureau, which did some investigative work, as well as with his good legal friend Billy Wynn of Greenville. As in a chess game each side eyed the other warily. For his part, Johnston's on-site attorney, A. F. House, kept in contact with the assistant U.S. attorney in Little Rock as to government intentions, but was decidedly pessimistic that his clients could be successfully defended. Government promises regarding purchase agreements were hazy and, in any case, as the Supreme Court in *Wickard* v. *Filburn* (1942) had declared, the federal government was not legally bound by unwarranted statements of its employees.[31]

Meanwhile, the biggest threat to the Farm Security Administration was not in its real or imagined failures in Arkansas or elsewhere. It was in Washington, where conservative pressure mounted to slash the FSA's budget or kill it altogether. The attack on the FSA stood as a logical outcome of the conservative trend in Congress witnessed during Roosevelt's second term, as well as the economic shift occasioned by World War II. Defense plants, like the Pine Bluff Arsenal near Plum Bayou, lured increasing numbers off the farm, and the returning prosperity they represented signaled trouble for some New Deal agencies. The New Deal, battle scarred, had run its course; its proponents gained no ground and were instead reduced to staving off budget cuts to at least stay in business. Numerous agencies, including the old Work Progress Administration, the Civilian Conservation Corps, and the National Youth Administration, possibly valuable in their day, simply could not survive World War II, nor, given the new national agenda, should they have. Though the Farm Security Administration had a range of liberal supporters such as the Southern Tenant Farmers' Union, church groups, and organized labor, they proved no match for powerful congressional conservatives, emboldened all the more by FDR's failure in 1938 to "purge" conservatives from the Democratic ranks and by dramatic Republican gains in the 1942 elections. House conservatives such as Missouri's Clarence Cannon, Georgia's Malcolm Tarver, and Illinois's Republican Everett Dirksen sharpened their budget knives even as Ed O'Neal's American Farm Bureau Federation, increasingly alienated by the leftward shift of the New Deal, weighed in against the FSA. The new kid on the block, Oscar Johnston's National Cotton Council, soon followed. The opposition all dovetailed with the Joint Committee on Reduction of Nonessential Federal Expenditures, chaired by Sen. Harry F. Byrd of Virginia. Within weeks of America's entry into World War II the FSA wound up on the committee's hit list.[32]

When the Agricultural Appropriations Subcommittee opened hearings in 1943, the conservatives were ready. Appropriations for FSA had slipped in the early forties; this would be the critical year, and recent events in the agency's Region VI, which embraced Arkansas, Mississippi, and Louisiana, and included the troubled Lake Dick and Plum Bayou projects, would command center stage. On March 15, in a lengthy appearance before the subcommittee chaired by the fair-minded Malcolm Tarver of Georgia, Oscar Johnston, speaking as president of the National Cotton Council, wasted little time before attacking the FSA. He read the council's recent resolutions damning the agency's conduct in the cotton belt, rehashed many of its alleged sins, and praised the original intent of Congress in passing the Bankhead-Jones Farm Tenant Act, which, unfortunately, had been subverted. He charged that FSA activities stood opposed to fee-simple ownership and dragged in his favorite enemy of that principle, Rexford Guy Tugwell.[33]

Before he could fully develop the Plum Bayou case, Johnston inadvertently aroused the subcommittee's curiosity about possible FSA land purchases in 1943, something outlawed under existing statute. Johnston tried to show an insidious connection between the FSA and the Congress of Industrial Organizations. According to Johnston, a large landlord in northeastern Arkansas— a man named Chapin—had recently complained to him that the CIO had organized tenants on an adjacent plantation. He then got a letter informing him that it had also organized 70 percent of his own tenants. Hereafter, he was advised, labor contracts would be negotiated through the CIO. If that was not enough, within a few days an FSA agent showed up at his plantation claiming he had heard that some of Chapin's acreage was available and that the FSA would be pleased to relieve him of it under a ten-year lease. The turn of events in the Chapin case may have been pure coincidence, said Johnston, but he thought he could convince the subcommittee of a CIO-FSA "direct tie-up," and produced the old Phillip Murray letter as evidence.[34]

At Plum Bayou, according to Johnston, the FSA method of operation was in no sense isolated. Solicitors selected potential clients, holding out the hope of farm ownership in five years under certain conditions. After five years, Booker McDade, Johnston's star exhibit, stood ready to buy, but was denied; the next year he faced eviction. Johnston's investigation of the project, he told Tarver's subcommittee, had not only revealed a score or more empty houses, but a nearly complete turnover of the families on the property—129 in all since the project began. FSA's selective treatment overlooked some families who were heavily indebted, while others, like McDade, faced eviction. "I found," said Johnston, "that their lease contract is nothing more or less than a share-crop contract." And though the appropriation statute for 1943 had mandated liquidation of FSA's cooperative projects, Johnston had failed to see evidence of that at Plum Bayou.[35]

One possible violation of at least the spirit of that statute was the Phillipston Plantation in Mississippi, where scores of black residents had been ousted by FSA in favor of a lesser number of white families. It was one of Johnston's favorite FSA outrages. Johnston rehearsed for the subcommittee some of the sadness and cruelty inflicted on the elderly blacks, and was himself at Phillipston on eviction day in November 1942. A stenographic record of the entire goings-on, which Johnston held up to the subcommittee, included "the final prayer" of an elderly black preacher. "His prayer was taken down," said Johnston, "and it is interesting and pathetic."

"Has it been answered yet?" Chairman Tarver interjected.

"No sir; it evidently was not heard."

Everett Dirksen offered his own view. "I am not so sure it was not heard," he said.

"It may have been heard," replied Johnston. "I am hopeful that it is now going to be answered."[36]

There were other stories of FSA inefficiency. "I am naming you specific cases that I saw," Johnston told the congressmen, "and I am telling you that I have in my files innumerable letters from clients and from neighbors of the F.S.A., but primarily I am basing it on clients, people themselves who were hurt and who are suffering and are being unjustly treated, and who are being evicted and not being permitted to buy their land."[37]

Bureaucracies die hard. FSA Administrator Beanie Baldwin followed Johnston to the witness table. For two days the subcommittee grilled him on Johnston's charges, Baldwin stoutly but futilely rebutting his testimony. Dragging Tugwell into the record, he said, was "nothing but an appeal to passion and prejudice, . . . cheap demagoguery and another example of the smear technique." While it was true that 129 families had left Plum Bayou, 114 original families remained. Many of those who had left took jobs at the Pine Bluff Arsenal. As for McDade, the FSA had its own version. McDade, claimed Baldwin, proved uncooperative, had neglected his operation, and worked increasingly off his project. His payments fell in arrears. Then there was the Chapin issue, which Baldwin defended as part of the leasing project; he denied he had had anything to do with CIO organizing efforts and that if there was any evidence to the contrary, he would seek to halt such activity. As for Phillipston, FSA had not purchased the land, simply financed the venture; and as for the pathetic cases cited by Johnston, well, they had been relocated by FSA to happier surroundings.[38]

Tarver's subcommittee was not satisfied, and neither were the folks back in Arkansas, where the press mounted increasing attacks on the FSA. Booker McDade became something of a local hero. A feature story, complete with photographs, in Little Rock's *Arkansas Democrat* in late March celebrated the McDades as model farmers unfairly ordered off their farm, where they had faithfully labored for six years. McDade denied he had neglected his unit, and the pictures of the homestead, along with the menagerie of livestock and well-stocked pantry, seemed difficult to refute. They cowered in fear of every vehicle that approached, scared it might contain a constable empowered to evict them. Said McDade: "I simply can't believe it has happened to me and my family. Why? You'd never be able to figure it out unless you lived with it a long time. Probably I know all the reasons behind it only too well."[39]

Those reasons, according to McDade, included his own thrift. His troubles, he thought, "resulted from refusal to borrow and borrow, and to stay in debt to the government. I've paid off and don't owe one cent on the few hundred dollars advanced to me the first couple of years I was here. And, too, I've been pressing in my demands that the government keep its original promise to me to let me buy my place after I'd operated it on a rental basis for five long, hard years to prove my worth. The fellow who owes the government the most money is the fellow who stays the longest, it seems."[40]

Public reaction seemed to be running in favor of McDade and his colleagues. After the press reported that House and Brockman were defending the Plum Bayou tenants, House noted that people repeatedly stopped him on the street to complain about the FSA and express sympathy for the tenants. "It seems to be generally felt," he told Johnston in April, "that there is something wrong with F.S.A. when it would try to evict those who are industrious and successful. The public criticism is the same as yours; the F.S.A. plan is fundamentally wrong." Indeed, almost daily, Little Rock papers carried ill stories of FSA woes and, beginning in April, an *Arkansas Gazette* staffer, in four installments, mercilessly lambasted the agency, including two scathing reviews of Plum Bayou. The great promise of 1936 simply failed to match the reality of 1943.[41]

Still, the attorney was ever cautious. Concerned about his clients' welfare, he believed the best course was to get the government to allow the tenants to stay through 1943 with a promise to vacate at the end of the year. He thought that filing liability bonds would be detrimental because the paper trail would inevitably lead to Oscar Johnston, something the FSA could publicly exploit. Johnston agreed that McDade's defense in a lower court would probably fail, but was more sanguine if the case could be transferred to an equity court, something House thought impossible. House believed there was simply no hope of defending against the government lawsuits if they were ever filed. And that was the catch. Despite the FSA's dire eviction threats, Johnston thought the agency was bluffing.[42]

Apparently they were. Although the eviction chess game continued through the spring—Johnston constantly mulling over strategy with attorney House—no marshal's car ever came up the road to evict the McDades. The FSA still had friends, but its days were numbered, and it directed its efforts elsewhere. Congressional appropriations for fiscal 1944, approved in the spring of 1943, gutted the agency, prohibiting its cooperative and land-lease activities and slashing its budget. The House bill provided enough funds, said Johnston in June, for "a reasonably economic funeral." As early as April, Region VI director A. D. Stewart announced the liquidation of twenty-three projects and the elimination of several hundred FSA positions in the mid-South. All that presaged the demise of the agency; it died with an anticlimactic whimper. An ad hoc House committee gathered testimony and documents for more than a year, in the end damning the FSA for subverting the Bankhead-Jones legislation and for defiance of Congress. The committee charged the agency—"an experiment station in un-American ideas"—with promoting "communistic resettlement projects, where families could never own homes" and where life was regimented. What was left of the agency was quietly absorbed into the new Farmers Home Administration after World War II.[43]

Even so, the break-up carried no guarantee that McDade would get to purchase his unit, despite a lobbying effort on his behalf by Arkansas Sen. John McClellan. The word was that another Plum Bayou client, reportedly a favorite of Project Manager Stanley Rhodes, wanted the McDade unit—well farmed and boasting a fine orchard—for himself. As late as June 1943 Johnston hoped to stave off McDade's eviction long enough for FSA's reorganization; in the backwash he thought McDade stood a good chance of getting his deed. Johnston was reluctant to write McDade directly, fearing that his mail, which had to go through a central post office at Plum Bayou, "might get into wrong hands or might stir up some further trouble." Still, House kept a watchful eye, ready to alert Johnston to any new activity. In August, Laverne McDade, having taken a teaching job near Manilla, Arkansas, some distance north of Plum Bayou, reported to Johnston that they were still in the fight and that it appeared that FSA had caved in. "Frankly I think they are afraid they will lose," she said. "The publicity was to [*sic*] much for them."[44]

Perhaps the ordeal proved too much for McDade as well. That fall he packed up and headed for California; whether he finally would have been allowed to purchase his unit remains unclear, but the beleaguered FSA never did forc-

ibly evict anyone from Plum Bayou. Johnston thought that once the fall harvest was finished his obligations to the Plum Bayou trio would be discharged;
he remained grateful for their courage and stamina. He paid House's $200 fee
in September, accepting the Little Rock attorney's offer to keep an eye on the
goings-on at Plum Bayou.[45]

The whole fight with the Farm Security Administration both reflected and
deepened Johnston's disillusionment with the direction of government. "From
the beginning I have never liked the term 'New Deal,'" he said in late 1942.
"In my judgment the Democratic and Republican parties offered opportunities for every American to express himself with respect to political and economic principles. A group of starry eyed 'do-gooders' in 1932 took advantage
of the political situation resulting from the debacle of 1929 and rode into power."
Johnston hoped one of the parties, preferably his own, would overcome the
challenges of the zealots and restore "two-party government" based on democratic principles.[46]

His hope that the Democratic party would purge the "starry eyed 'do gooders'"
led him to join the southern delegation against his old friend Henry Wallace
at the Democratic convention in Chicago in July 1944. Oscar had long held
Wallace in high regard. But the vice president, fast becoming a darling of the
left, had offended the South, among others, and gave ammunition to his southern enemies at the convention by calling for racial equality and abolition of the
poll tax. The South's opposition to Wallace wrote a certain postscript to the
death of the New Deal. A Mississippi delegate, Johnston would have preferred
former senator and Supreme Court Justice Jimmy Byrnes of South Carolina
or Sen. John Bankhead of Alabama, or so he told Bankhead after the fact. For
his part, Senator Bankhead had told Oscar two weeks before the convention
that while he had "no illusions about being nominated," he thought he could
serve as a focal point for the dump-Wallace movement. A divided Mississippi
delegation, in fact, voted for Bankhead on the first ballot, Walter Sillers standing in for Johnston in a seconding speech. Robert Hannegan of St. Louis, open
to the nomination of Sen. Harry S. Truman of Missouri, but above all hoping
to eliminate Wallace, warned that without a major switch on the second ballot
the nomination could go to Supreme Court Justice William O. Douglas or back
to Henry Wallace. A bitter fight ensued in Mississippi's caucus, Truman finally
winding up with the delegation's divided second ballot and the ballots of other
delegations as well. Johnston was "highly pleased" over Truman's selection, previous encounters having impressed him with the Missourian's "very genuine interest in agriculture." Rhea Blake later recalled that as head of the senate committee investigating defense industries, Truman had been friendly to the Cotton
Council regarding cotton use in tire production instead of the exclusive use of

rayon. Johnston knew cotton was virtually king in eight southeastern Missouri counties. He much preferred Truman to Sam Rayburn of Texas or Alben Barkley of Kentucky, or the incumbent—whom Bankhead called "that dangerous Red by the name of Wallace." "Truman understands our problems," Oscar told Bankhead after the convention, "and will I am very certain be sympathetic."[47]

If Johnston was sanguine about Truman, he had been less so about the outcome of the world war. His concerns were not about eventual Allied victory, which he never really doubted, but about the shape of its aftermath. He feared the ascendancy of anticapitalist labor unions in the CIO mold. In fact, strikes and shortages awaited postwar America; Johnston publicly attacked Teamster's president Daniel Tobin after *The International Teamster* in 1946 called for a cotton boycott to break the power of congressional conservatives. Regardless, government both during and, at least for a time, thereafter would have a key role in cotton loans and acreage regulation and would, in general, prevent an encore of the economic disaster that befell American agriculture after World War I. For all his criticism of the federal government, Johnston was no advocate of laissez-faire. Also, fashioning a sound postwar world, something Johnston thought about constantly, would be a daunting task. Johnston knew that international trade had never been "normal" between the wars and that, very possibly, the trading relationships of the pre-1914 world were gone forever. Still, though cognizant of human nature, he hoped for a better world, where international commerce was devoid of economic nationalism and trade barriers. "At the risk of appearing disloyal," he said privately, six months after the United States entered the war, "I presume to hazard the opinion that the people of Germany did not precipitate the present war insofar as they are concerned because of the desire to dominate the world." The Versailles Treaty, complemented by French, English, and U.S. trade policies, created "an impossible situation, and one that developed Hitler—had it not been Hitler it would have been some other man who would have arisen as a product of his environment." It was an old theme. For Japan, Johnston had no sympathy at all—calling them "cocky little devils" twelve days after Pearl Harbor. He saw the war as a culmination of a half century of sinister ambitions. In any case, he knew a peaceful postwar world depended on commerce that produced higher living standards for all people, not merely the few; otherwise, he said, "we will have done nothing except bring about an enforced and wholly temporary cessation of hostilities." But as he had told George Peek on the eve of America's entry into the war, "Unless you and I are as fortunate, or as unfortunate, depending on the point of view, as was old man Methuselah, neither of us will be on hand to see just how the whole thing turns out."[48]

# Epilogue

I'm not here to preach the funeral for King Cotton.
                                                    —Oscar G. Johnston, 1945

He wore no man's collar.                             —Paul A. Porter

In the early 1940s cotton's kingdom teetered on the threshold of a technological and social revolution. Nonetheless, a Work Projects Administration study in 1940 concluded that King Cotton still reigned in the South and that the ante- and postbellum plantation remained—complete with its money crops, cheap labor, landlord system, and the like. Such plantation characteristics could apply to small units as well as large. For most of Oscar Johnston's tenure, Delta and Pine Land Company characterized much of what the government study concluded about plantations generally, as well as what one sociologist that same year termed an "old" plantation: a relatively large labor force of black sharecroppers steeped in the plantation tradition, reluctance to mechanize cotton production, and paternalism of whites. Delta and Pine Land Company now stood on the edge of becoming what one geographer has called a "neoplantation," part of what he deemed the "Renaissance of the Southern Plantation." Such neoplantations were characterized by mechanization, centralized management, and a shift toward a capital- rather than labor-intensive basis. Another student of the plantation argued in 1950 that "in an age of corporate as well as governmental giganticism the possibility exists that the cotton South may assume the pattern of the corporate farm."[1]

By the early 1940s, prospects of change loomed, including massive labor displacement resulting from the mechanical cotton picker. The pessimism associated with such prospects seemed warranted in the Depression, but World War II, along with a shifting national political agenda, including civil rights, changed everything. An out-migration of farm labor, dwarfing that of the 1910s and 1920s, hastened the death of the oft-maligned sharecrop system, achieving in the process what no reformer or social engineer had ever been able to do. Threatened also by the erosion of their hegemony, the Delta's planter establishment braced for the transition. Delta and Pine Land Company's annual reports virtually mirrored the pattern of labor losses. Though Johnston told the stockholders in April 1941 that the company's labor supply was contented and "adequate," a year later, just a few months after Pearl Harbor, he noted that labor lost to military service was "fairly substantial" and likely to worsen. While mechanization of crops other than cotton would ease the problem, picking the cotton would pose a more serious challenge and likely extend the harvesting season. As it turned out, the opposite was true. The company did not have to hire outsiders during the 1942 harvest, since the tenants did so themselves at a dollar per hundred pounds.[2]

The manpower drain soon hit the front office. Arch Toler, for years Johnston's trusted assistant at Scott, and at Clarksdale before that, enlisted in the army in late 1942, his work now picked up by David Gavin. Gavin had, for several years, carried heavy secretarial duties, including that for the National Cotton Council. Three women joined the headquarters staff at Scott; another female handled warehouse seed shipments, while yet another managed and ran a company gin. "If this thing keeps on much longer," said Oscar a year after Pearl Harbor, "the plantation will probably be operated by 'petticoats.'"[3]

By early 1944 the general labor problem was "rather uncomfortable," Johnston told the stockholders. Many workers were in uniform and others would follow, along with some loss to defense plants, which offered attractive wages and hours. Further, when the men left for war, their wives and children usually followed, living in town and sustained by government stipend, with the women sometimes seeking domestic work or other employment. Johnston believed Delta Pine's housing and better pay would attract a greater share of available farm labor in the Delta, but he remained uneasy about the whole problem, hinting that cotton production might be reduced if the war dragged on and labor needs remained constant.[4]

It all got worse before it got better. A wholesale wartime exodus created a huge labor gap on southern plantations and farms. A survey of twelve counties of the Mississippi Delta in July 1944 revealed that the area fell more than 48 percent below its labor needs for agricultural production. Similarly, according to the same survey, Delta Pine's Bolivar County, a national leader in cotton production, could muster only about half of the more than 3.5 million man-hours required for agriculture. Estimates predicted the shortfall would worsen. That same year, on one plantation with 700 acres in cotton, a like number of bales should have passed through the gin house by December 1; unfortunately, on New Year's Day, 1945, about 250–300 acres, laden with cotton, still sat idle.[5]

Looking to mechanize cotton production as much as possible, Delta Pine bought a Graham Paige Motor Company "sizz weeder," a flame-throwing contraption designed to replace the time-honored but laborious chopping and

hoeing of weeds and grasses around the young cotton plants. Though it ac-
quitted itself well in experiment station trials and became a familiar implement
in mechanized cotton production, Johnston remained a bit skeptical. His long-
held doubts about a perfected picker—and he had seen lots of failures—vanished
after International Harvester successfully demonstrated its new machine on
the Hopson Brothers plantation outside Clarksdale in 1944. Delta Pine promptly
placed an order. Johnston discounted earlier calamitous predictions about labor
displacement, telling a House subcommittee six months before V-E Day that "too
many people have been growing cotton for all of them to make a decent living
out of it," and predicting that former cotton growers would produce alternative
commodities or be absorbed by new industries. At one time leery of exploitative
"fly-by-night" small industries wringing the South dry of cheap labor, as he confessed in 1937, Johnston now eagerly anticipated the arrival of new industries.
They "are turning their eyes southward," he said with approval in December 1944.
"This is a great boon to our southern economy and is coming just at the right time."[6]

Soon the Scott plantation boasted two pickers and looked to get four more
for 1946. Insufficient labor and severely unfavorable weather at key moments
in the crop season resulted in a bad cotton harvest for 1945. But mechanization of all aspects of cotton production had passed out of its experimentation
phase, retarded now only by the inability of planters to acquire equipment with
sufficient speed. Production of mechanical pickers proceeded on an ad hoc
basis throughout the war. International Harvester built only a hundred or so
from 1941 to 1945. That changed after the company opened a $20 million fa-
cility outside Memphis in the summer of 1948, turning out eleven hundred
pickers that year alone, many of them headed for California and the Yazoo–
Mississippi Delta. By early 1947 Delta Pine had five pickers in place and anticipated the delivery of ten more, all of which would complement a healthy
stable of four-row planters and cultivators, two- and four-row flamethrowers,
and other mechanical equipment. By 1951 the Scott plantation had increased
its inventory to twenty-five pickers and fourteen flamethrowers. Even though
it seemed appropriate in the early days to handpick bottom bolls, the old tenant system died slowly. Some tenants remained well into the 1950s—a handful of mules competing with two hundred tractors—but Johnston had signaled
the end by starting to sell off the company's mules as early as 1945. Across the
cotton belt, it took more than two decades to completely mechanize cotton
production. Such mechanization required much more than hulking, odd-looking
machines lumbering across the flat fields. Methods of planting, control of weeds
and pests, new plant varieties, and assorted other issues had to be resolved to
achieve greatest efficiency. Along the way farm size grew, while the number of
commercial farms fell precipitously.[7]

Meanwhile, Johnston knew production costs would have to fall if cotton was to successfully compete with synthetics and other materials. Mechanization, necessary because of labor shortage, was the key. After the war he spun off a series of articles touting the virtues of mechanization, promising it would not drive out the small producer who merely supplemented his diversified farm income with only one or, at the most, a few bales of cotton annually. According to Johnston, this small farmer, not dependent on cotton alone, would see no rise in capital or operating costs, allowing him to compete with both mechanical and standard labor.[8] Despite such optimism, Johnston could not have been more wrong. In fact, the small farmers' flight from the land characterized the next generation.

In "Mechanization, Cotton's Shot in the Arm," in the *Cotton Trade Journal,* Johnston prophesied cheerily, "Wives will be liberated from the fields to devote their energies to home improvement. Children will spend more time in school. Farm income will increase, spelling greater comfort and more advantages for the entire family." Later, in "Mechanization—A Key to Progress," in the *Georgia Review,* he pointed to the dramatic drop in labor man-hours when cotton production was mechanized. Men and mules in North Carolina's coastal plains required 118 such hours per cotton acre, 141.1 in his own Mississippi Delta. Mechanization, even with two-row equipment, dropped those hour figures to 19.7 and 43.7, respectively. Out west in the high plains the mule system had virtually disappeared. Various devices plummeted man-hours per acre under 7. At Scott, said Johnston, 525 families did the same work after the war that 850 families did from 1935 to 1944. In 1947, in the *Saturday Evening Post,* he answered in the negative his own question, "Will the Machine Ruin the South?" He argued that "[m]echanization is not the cause, but the result of economic change in the area."[9]

Even as Oscar Johnston directed his giant company's transition to a mechanized agribusiness, he faced his most formidable obstacle yet, one he would not master. His health began to decline. His eyes, always a problem, again deteriorated, and Martha now drove the car when they went out together. More insidious, more tragic, was the slippage of his mental agility, the great gift he had employed so skillfully and creatively for half a century. Characteristically subtle at first, then progressively worse—noted in the late 1940s even though Johnston could still carry on correspondence—the loss of mental faculties forced the British, a new generation now in ascendancy, to demand his resignation in 1950. Having steered Delta and Pine Land Company through depression, war, and into a technological transformation, it was a necessary yet ignominious end to a remarkable career. He had left the helm of the National Cotton Council two years before, but that organization had long been viable without him. Rhea

Blake's executive leadership further ensured its stability and success. The board of directors, to raise funds, established the Oscar Johnston Cotton Foundation in 1948; five years later they named Johnston founder and honorary chairman of the board. Meanwhile, Oscar's deterioration proved inexorable. He remained mobile into the early 1950s. If met on the street, he could talk about the crop, but he wasn't the old talkative, gregarious Oscar. The light was gone. Instead of dignified retirement to his own plantation, or long elder statesmanship in an industry which he left in much better shape than he had found it, he was relegated to a small, unpretentious house in nearby Greenville. He fell victim to a scourge of old age: a fall, a broken hip, and immobility. It was inoperable. Oscar was also diagnosed with myasthenia gravis, a debilitating muscular disease. Martha proved passionate in her watchful care. Devoted, proud, and protective, she barred the door of the small house to virtually all but the closest friends. She was unable to bear having her husband's condition displayed. Those admitted included Minor Gray, the son of Oscar's cousin, and his wife, Helen. Gray had managed both Bolivar Farms and Delta Planting Company and would become Delta Pine's president in 1959. For at least the last two years of his life, Oscar apparently had no recognition of Minor or his Greenville visits. Martha, assisted by a registered nurse and various servants, was faithful to the end. The nurse, Bessie Taylor, in more than a year caring for him, never heard him utter a word. As he lay prostrate he knew nothing about the construction on North Parkway in Memphis of the new headquarters of the National Cotton Council of America and the Oscar Johnston Cotton Foundation. Even as plans went forward for the facility's dedication on October 19, 1955, Johnston, stricken with pneumonia, entered King's Daughters' Hospital in Greenville on September 23. Ten days later, on October 3, 1955, he succumbed. He was seventy-five.[10]

Eulogies from across the South were unanimous in their recognition of Johnston's importance to the cotton industry. Leaders of one cotton interest or another piled praise on their hero. The *Memphis Commercial Appeal* said "Oscar Johnston's contribution to the South's economic progress and to modernization of the cotton industry were of such magnitude as to almost beggar evaluation." His hometown paper said his death removed "a giant among Mississippians and a peer of any American whom we can measure in terms of creative force. . . .And for those who take joy in a magnificent intellect, the performance of his incisive, penetrating mind, so scornful of sham and fuzziness, was a wondrous and memorable thing." To another observer, cotton had "lost its greatest leader." Of course, Oscar's position had long been secure. When he retired from the council presidency in 1948, the *Commercial Appeal* claimed Oscar had made Scott "the center of the cotton universe." Even earlier, Hodding

Carter, always lavish, thought one could partially judge Johnston's significance by sitting along "the dusty gravel road which follows the river, and count[ing] the automobiles of investigators of the left and right, foreign agricultural experts, writers, social workers, fellow planters, economists, politicians and financiers who travel to Scott plantation for information and observation."[11]

Decades later the memories of those who had known and worked with Johnston remained vivid. "Well, I thought Mr. Oscar was a very big man," said McDonald Horne Jr., a 1940 Chapel Hill Ph.D. who worked for years as an economist for the National Cotton Council. "I never really saw any flaws in Mr. Oscar. He was such a big man in my time that I just sort of worshipped him. He was a very approachable down-to-earth man, a big man, a smart man." Albert Russell, longtime council staffer and eventual executive vice president and secretary, thought that Johnston had an ego characteristic of great achievers. "Yes, I saw some ego in him," recalled Russell, "but I also saw a great deal of humility in him. He was smart enough to use his power when he needed to use it; he was smart enough to keep his mouth shut when he should have. He dominated every meeting that he participated in." Added Russell, "Well, when Mr. Oscar sat down, the board was in session."

Both Horne and Russell had similar recollections about Johnston's speech making. Horne said he "had the experience of writing a speech for him and having him get up to a podium before a big audience, lay the speech in front of him, forget all about it, and make a much better speech than I could have written. He was a brilliant and a resourceful man, equal to any occasion." Russell recalled that press requirements meant they wrote speeches "he never made. He always talked extemporaneously. He could hold any audience almost better than anybody I've ever seen." Public Relations Director Edward Lipscomb had his own experience. He said:

> Oscar Johnston is one of the few men, he is the only man really, that I've ever seen who could . . . come in on the afternoon before his annual address to the convention and pace the floor and dictate an hour and fifteen minute annual address, just right off the top of his head, and it would be great. I would grab it and keep folks up all night getting it mimeographed and ready for the press the next day. The next day he would get up on the platform, deliver an hour and fifteen minute address just as good, and bearing no relationship to what I had given the press. I mean it might not even cover the same points, but it was great.

Added Lipscomb: "He could hold an audience in the palm of his hand for an hour and fifteen minutes and still be saving souls, where a preacher would be shot at after twenty minutes, you know. He was great on that. This way he spoke all across this [Cotton] Belt." One Mississippi ginner, Garner Lester, active in the council, recalled he had been in Washington one time when

Johnston testified on some cotton measure. Johnston, he said, "really made a wonderful impression. In fact, I heard one of the senators say, 'Well, I never heard a man testify like that man.'"

Col. Francis Beatty, a Carolina warehouseman and one of the council's original directors, recalled that, despite his eyesight problem, Oscar "always knew what was going on. He could take four, or five, or half a dozen drinks and that only added to his eloquence." Johnston was down to earth, but, according to Beatty, "[n]ot the patting on the back type. When he saw you, he knew you and that sort of thing, but his goal was always right there. He wanted everybody to work with him, but he wasn't going to give you a lot of blarney about . . . 'you're a good guy' and all that sort of thing. His idea was that 'This is just the goal; this is what we've got to work for and it's just as much your interest as it is mine. Let's pitch in and get it done.'" Norris Blackburn, another organizer present at the creation of the council, claimed "you could just almost look at [Johnston] and tell that he was an outstanding leader. He had a brilliant mind, and he could bring people together. He could explain things so clearly to anyone and secure their cooperation."[12]

In time, Mississippi officials named an eighteen-mile stretch of highway in Johnston's honor, one such official even citing Oscar's efforts in 1912, futile at the time, to get the legislature to pass the state's first highway department bill. And there was the Oscar Johnston Cotton Foundation and of course a plaque that graced the new National Cotton Council headquarters in Memphis, eventually moved inside to make way for one for Rhea Blake. "A Memorial Dedicated with Grateful Appreciation to Oscar Johnston," it said, "Whose Works Contributed to the Welfare of Millions and Whose Genius United the Great American Cotton Industry." Such gestures were sincere testimonials of honorable men, and in the case of the foundation, a worthy method of fundraising. Johnston was what his fellows said he was. He was an organizer, a motivator, and a gentle commander, one who could look into a tenant's problem, yet pound a president's desk. Johnston's predictions did not always prove true, and he was locked in his time and place on issues of race and class. Yet he was a planter who eluded caricature during his life and eludes it now. Where once there was Oscar Johnston and a desperate and divided cotton industry run by leaders of varying talents, there is now the Foundation and the National Cotton Council of America, Cotton Incorporated, and other spin-off operations. Eventually dethroned, King Cotton would no longer exact tribute from his retainers. Instead, His Majesty would have to settle for becoming "King of Fibers" or "The Fabric of Our Lives," a consolation made possible by His chief advocate, Oscar Johnston.[13]

# Notes

## Abbreviations

| | |
|---|---|
| AAA | Agricultural Adjustment Administration |
| ACCA | American Cotton Cooperative Association |
| CCC | Commodity Credit Corp. |
| CL | Carnegie Library, Clarksdale, Miss. |
| CLD | Correspondence of the Legal Division |
| COHC | Columbia Oral History Collection, Butler Library, Columbia Univ., New York |
| DPLC | Delta and Pine Land Company |
| DPLCR | Delta and Pine Land Company Records, Mitchell Library, Mississippi State Univ., Starkville |
| FCSDA | Fine Cotton Spinners' and Doublers' Association, Ltd. |
| FDRL | Franklin D. Roosevelt Library, Hyde Park, N.Y. |
| FSA | Farm Security Administration |
| GC | General Correspondence |
| JFM | Johnston Family Material |
| LTF | Landlord-Tenant File |
| MDAH | Mississippi Dept. of Archives and History, Jackson |
| MOHP | Mississippi Oral History Program, Univ. of Southern Mississippi, Hattiesburg |
| MPSM | *Memphis Press-Scimitar* Morgue, Univ. of Memphis Library |
| NA | National Archives, Washington, D.C., College Park, Md. |
| NCCA | National Cotton Council of America |
| OF | Official File |
| OJ | Oscar Goodbar Johnston |
| OJSF | Oscar Johnston Subject File |
| PCP | Production Control Program |
| PPF | President's Personal Files (FDRL) |
| RFC | Reconstruction Finance Corp. |
| RG 16 | Records of the Office of the Secretary of Agriculture, National Archives |
| RG 29 | Records of the Land Roll for Coahoma County, Miss., MDAH |
| RG 83 | Records of the Bureau of Agricultural Economics, National Archives |
| RG 96 | Records of the Farmers' Home Administration, National Archives |
| RG 145 | Records of the Agricultural Stabilization and Conservation Service, National Archives |
| RG 161 | Records of the Commodity Credit Corp., National Archives |
| USDA | U.S. Dept. of Agriculture |
| WPA | Works Projects Administration |

## *Preface*

1. "Biggest Cotton Plantation," Fortune 15 (Mar. 1937): 160 (quotation); James Cobb, *The Most Southern Place on Earth: The Mississippi Delta and the Roots of Regional Identity* (New York and Oxford, 1992); Anthony Badger, *The New Deal: The Depression Years, 1933–40* (New York, 1989), 2–4. If DPLC was ever the largest cotton plantation in the United States, it evidently lost that distinction to one or another plantation, but probably to the Wilson Plantation in Arkansas, whose founder, Lee Wilson, reportedly amassed more than sixty thousand acres by 1933. A subdivision of the Wilson property occurred after World War II. Michael E. Wilson to Minor Gray, Mar. 17, 1989, with enclosures, including a partial reproduction of Seymour Freedgood, "The Man Who Has Everything—in Wilson, Ark.," *Fortune* (Aug. 1964): 143–44. These materials were given to the author. See also, among other public sources, *Memphis Press-Scimitar,* June 20, 1936, 3; *Time,* Apr. 20, 1936, 18. Delta Pine's letterhead once boasted "Largest Cotton Plantation in the World"; that boast was abandoned, returning as "Largest *Staple* Cotton Plantation in the World" (italics added; the "staple" designation may have referred to long-staple varieties, distinguishing the plantation in that manner). That was replaced by "Originator of Deltapine Cotton" later in the 1930s. The Wilson letterhead claims plantation origins in 1886. In any case, DPL's designation as the largest or the biggest took root in the media and probably in the public perception as well. Regardless of its ranking, DPLC of Mississippi became the most *visible* such agricultural enterprise in the United States.

2. Robert Brandfon of Holy Cross College called my attention to some of these possibilities in a reply letter to me, Dec. 12, 1969. On the transformation of cotton production, see Jack Temple Kirby, "The Transformation of Southern Plantations, c. 1920–1960," *Agricultural History* 57 (July 1983): 257–76; see also Kirby, *Rural Worlds Lost: The American South, 1920–1960* (Baton Rouge and London, 1987), especially 1–79, 334–60; Gilbert Fite, *Cotton Fields No More: Southern Agriculture, 1865–1980* (Lexington, Ky., 1984); Pete Daniel, *Breaking the Land: The Transformation of Cotton, Tobacco, and Rice Cultures Since 1880* (Urbana and Chicago, 1985), 239–55; Gavin Wright, *Old South, New South: Revolutions in the Southern Economy Since the Civil War* (New York, 1986), 239–74; see also Pete Daniel, "The Transformation of the Rural South, 1930 to the Present," *Agricultural History* 55 (July 1981): 231–48.

3. See Isaiah Berlin, *The Hedgehog and the Fox: An Essay on Tolstoy's View of History* (New York, 1953, 1986).

## *1. Oscar*

1. Hodding Carter, "Cotton Fights Back! The Story of the National Cotton Council," a four-part 1939 document evidently reprinted by the National Cotton Council, perhaps from a news article. Given to the author by the council. In the author's possession (other copies are presumably at the National Cotton Council, Memphis).

2. OJ to Mrs. D. R. Pope, Apr. 20, 1939; D. R. Gavin (citing Johnston) to Mrs. George L. Patton, Sept. 4, 1941, DPLCR; OJ to Oscar B. Johnston (no kin), Feb. 27, 1942, original copy in possession of Minor S. Gray (copy placed by author, with Gray's permission, in DPLCR); *Biographical and Historical Memoirs of Mississippi, Embracing an Authentic and Comprehensive Account of the Chief Events in the History of the State, and a Record of the Lives of Many of the Most Worthy and Illustrious Families*

*and Individuals*, 2 vols. (Chicago, 1891), 1:1044 (first quotation); Lutz Wahl to Eula Lee Rehfeld, July 28, 1928; allegiance affidavit, July 13, 1865; unidentified newspaper clipping (Apr. 1879) (second quotation); handwritten genealogical material, JFM; James M. McPherson, *Ordeal By Fire: The Civil War and Reconstruction* (New York, 1982), 431–32; see also *The War of the Rebellion: A Compilation of the Official Records of the Union and Confederate Armies*, 69 vols. in 128 books plus index (Washington, D.C., 1880–1901), 45:665. The Goodbar genealogy apparently extended from England to Virginia to Tennessee. Oscar's maternal great-grandfather migrated from Rockbridge County, Virginia, to Overton County, Tennessee, where a son, James Madison Goodbar, Oscar's grandfather, was born. OJ to Mrs. E. P. Patterson, Jan. 17, 1938, DPLCR.

3. *Biographical and Historical Memoirs of Mississippi*, 1:1043–4 (quotations); unidentified newspaper clipping (probably *Friars Point Coahomian*, Dec. 1919), JFM; *One Hundred Years of Progress in the Mississippi Delta, Centennial Edition* (Clarksdale, Miss., 1936), 32, copies in MDAH and CL; see also *Jackson Weekly Clarion*, Nov. 6, 1878, 3; *Greenville Daily Democrat*, Apr. 29, 1914, 2; *Tennessee: A Guide of the State* (New York, 1939), 446.

4. Lillian A. Pereyra, *James Lusk Alcorn: Persistent Whig* (Baton Rouge, 1966), 37, 60, 73; see Herbert C. Weaver, *Mississippi Farmers, 1850–1860* (Chapel Hill, 1947), 21, 25; Linton Weeks, *Clarksdale and Coahoma County: A History* (Clarksdale, Miss., 1982), 24, 26; *One Hundred Years of Progress*, 30, 32, 34; Dunbar Rowland, ed., *Mississippi, Comprising Sketches of Counties, Towns, Events, Institutions, and Persons, Arranged in Cyclopedic Form*, 3 vols. (Atlanta, 1907), 3:449, 757 ("infested" quotation); Dunbar Rowland, *History of Mississippi: The Heart of the South*, 2 vols. (Chicago and Jackson, Miss., 1925), 2:710–11; William C. Harris, "The Reconstruction of the Commonwealth, 1865–1879," and David G. Sansing, "Congressional Reconstruction," both in Richard A. McLemore, ed., *A History of Mississippi*, 2 vols. (Jackson, Miss., 1973), 1:548, 569–70, 571; James F. Brieger, comp., "Hometown Mississippi," 4 pts., n.d., 1:188, copy in MDAH; see also *Jackson Daily News*, Nov. 25, 1925, pt. 1, Nov. 27, 1925, 12. For a more recent view of Friars Point, see feature story in *Jackson Clarion Ledger/Daily News*, Feb. 5, 1984, 1H, 3H.

5. Dunbar Rowland, *The Official and Statistical Register of the State of Mississippi* (Nashville, 1908), 1045; (Nashville, 1912), 414–15; (Madison, Wisc., 1917), 847; biographical material in OJSF (includes copies of some published material), MDAH; RG 29; OJ to Lewis Henderson, Nov. 30, 1937; OJ to Robert L. Myers, Oct. 15, 1940; OJ to John J. Sparkman, Apr. 19, 1943 (last two quotations), DPLCR; "Biggest Cotton Plantation," *Fortune* 15 (Mar. 1937): 131; Gray Interviews (including comment by Mrs. O. D. Johnston Gray); *Clarksdale Daily Register*, Apr. 16, 1919, 1 (article by C. N. Harris, editor of *Madison County Herald*); *Memphis Commercial Appeal*, May 16, 1919, 51 (advertisement, including "financial reverses" quotation).

6. Harris Dickson, "*Oscar Johnston* of Scott, Mississippi," in "Magnolia Sketches," 6 vols. (3 vols. draft, 3 vols. finished) of radio program typescripts, WJDX, Jackson, Miss., Apr. 5, 1939–May 15, 1942 (WPA of Mississippi), ser. 6, no. 16, Sept. 19, 1940, 9:15 A.M. (six pages), 451, Dickson (Harris) Collection, MDAH (hereinafter cited as Dickson, "Oscar Johnston—Magnolia Sketches," Dickson (Harris) Collection); OJ to Mattie Maynard, Dec. 5, 1941 (second quotation), DPLCR; Frank Robinson interview (third quotation); *Clarksdale Daily Register* in *Friars Point Coahomian*, Mar. 19, 1904, 3 (fourth quotation); Apr. 16, 1904, 3 (last two quotations).

7. Paul Porter interview; WPA Historical Research Project, Coahoma County, the Bar (project 2984, assignment 27), May 7, 1937 (including interview with Mary Flynn Johnston), 23, CL.

8. *Jackson Daily News,* Feb. 15, 1916, 8; Feb. 20, 1916, 4, 5; OJ to Lowell W. Taylor, Nov. 5, 1942, DPLCR; unidentified newspaper clipping, "In the Public Eye (Hon. O. G. Johnston)" (probably *Clarksdale Daily Register*), May 26, 1922, Scrapbook— Clarksdale, vol. 1, CL (all citations hereinafter to this scrapbook are from vol. 1 and will be cited as Clarksdale Scrapbook, CL).

9. Daisy Wells Mancill to OJ, Feb. 7, 1934 (first quotation); William Rhea Blake interview (second quotation); *Friars Point Coahomian,* June 25, 1904, 3 (third quotation); see also John K. Bettersworth, *Mississippi: A History* (Austin, 1959), 451; confidential interview 1; Gray interviews; see various oral histories relative to the National Cotton Council of America in MOHP.

10. Rowland, *Official and Statistical Register* (1908), 1045; (1912), 414–15; (1917), 845; biographical material in OJSF, MDAH; *Friars Point Coahomian,* Mar. 18, 1905, 3 (first quotation); see also *Memphis News,* Aug. 15, 1904; in *Friars Point Coahomian,* Aug. 20, 1904, 3; confidential interview 2 (second quotation); Sam Houston Northcross to OJ, June 3, 1941 (third quotation), DPLCR; see also *Friars Point Coahomian,* Mar. 4, 1905, 3; Mar. 25, 1905, 3; Sept. 2, 1905, 3; Mar. 30, 1907, 4; June 1, 1907, 4; Apr. 24, 1909, 5; Oct. 8, 1910, 5; Mar. 30, 1912, 5. In the 1970s elderly ladies of Friars Point could still recall Martha stories (last quotation); Virginia Foster Durr, *Outside the Magic Circle: The Autobiography of Virginia Foster Durr,* ed. Hollinger F. Barnard, foreword by Studs Terkel (Tuscaloosa, Ala., 1985), xi; Tom Ross interview; "Biggest Cotton Plantation," 131; see Martha Johnston's obituary in *Greenville Delta Democrat-Times,* Oct. 27, 1965, 2.

11. *Friars Point Coahomian,* Aug. 8, 1908, 3; Aug. 15, 1908, 3; Robinson interview; Minor Gray interviews; William Rhea Blake interviews ("made for each other" quotation and beauty parlor story); Pauline Hendricks interview; confidential interview 1; OJ to Charles Matthews, Mar. 18, 1927 (first and second quotations); OJ to Alvin J. Goodbar, June 29, 1927; OJ to Walter Sillers, July 5, 1927; OJ to Frank K. Houston, July 7, 1927, DPLCR. The precise nature of Johnston's involvement with the woman remains unclear. J. D. LeCron, a Wallace assistant, told her, "This is a matter between you and Mr. Johnston and one with which the Secretary of Agriculture has no connection." Woman to Wallace, Nov. 15 [1937]; LeCron to Woman, Nov. 20, 1937 (quotation); see also Woman to Wallace, n.d., and LeCron to Woman, Nov. 23, 1937, GC, RG 16, NA. See also *Clarksdale Daily Register,* Mar. 18, 1921, 1; Aug. 25, 1925, 2; and Dec. 28, 1925, 1 (the latter piece also quotes extensively from an unidentified Memphis newspaper); Oct. 11, 1922, 1 ("model husband" quotation); *Memphis Commercial Appeal,* May 16, 1919, 51 (advertisement). For more on health issues, see below and other relevant correspondence in DPLCR.

12. Albert D. Kirwan, *The Revolt of the Rednecks: Mississippi Politics: 1876–1925* (Lexington, Ky., 1951; reprint, New York, 1965); William F. Holmes, *The White Chief: James Kimble Vardaman* (Baton Rouge, 1970); Chester M. Morgan, *Redneck Liberal: Theodore G. Bilbo and the New Deal* (Baton Rouge, 1985); Larry T. Balsamo, "Theodore G. Bilbo and Mississippi Politics, 1877–1932," Ph.D. diss., Univ. of Missouri–Columbia, 1967; Charles G. Hamilton, *Progressive Mississippi* (Aberdeen, Miss., 1978); Charles G. Hamilton, "Mississippi Politics During the Progressive Period, 1904–1920," Ph.D.

diss., Vanderbilt Univ., 1958; see also Dewey W. Grantham, *Southern Progressivism: The Reconciliation of Progress and Tradition* (Knoxville, 1983), and William Alexander Percy, *Lanterns on the Levee: Recollections of a Planter's Son* (New York, 1941, 1967).

13. Charles G. Hamilton, "The Turning Point: The Legislative Session of 1908," *Journal of Mississippi History* 25 (Apr. 1963): 104 (first quotation); Hamilton, "Mississippi Politics," 338–39; George B. Tindall, "Business Progressivism: Southern Politics in the Twenties," *South Atlantic Quarterly* 62 (winter 1963): 92–106, especially 94; George B. Tindall, *The Emergence of the New South, 1913–1945* (Baton Rouge, 1967), 219–53, cited by Morgan, *Redneck Liberal*, 16–18; Holmes, *White Chief*, 195, 254; Kirwan, *Revolt of the Rednecks*, 269–70; *Memphis Commercial Appeal*, Jan. 3, 1912, 11; Jan. 19, 1912, 16; Jan. 30, 1912, 9; Feb. 14, 1912, 16; Feb. 23, 1912, 9; Feb. 28, 1912, 8; Mar. 12, 1912, 18; Mar. 15, 1912, 14 (for example of Johnston's House leadership); Sept. 26, 1912, 1; May 16, 1919, 51 (advertisement); *Clarksdale Daily Register,* Apr. 16, 1919, 5 (article by C. N. Harris, editor of *Madison County Herald); Greenville Delta Democrat-Times,* July 9, 1919, 4 (advertisement; see same in *Tunica Times,* Aug. 2, 1919, 1); Nov. 14, 1958 (clipping in NCCA); *Jackson Daily News,* Jan. 12, 1916, 6 (including "tax dodger" quotation); Mar. 21, 1916, 1; Aug. 3, 1919, 3; Aug. 11, 1919, 4; see also David Holt, "One Wise Man in the State Legislature," *Jackson Daily News,* Mar. 12, 1916, 14; *Journal of the House of Representatives of the State of Mississippi* (Nashville, 1912), 1125; (Memphis, 1914), 998–99. Remarks of Judge J. Q. Robins Introducing Honorable Oscar Johnston at Tupelo, Mississippi, Scrapbook—Clarksdale, CL. Percy to John R. Gage, Aug. 7, 1911, Percy Family Papers, MDAH (Percy quotation; "With Vardaman elected," Percy added, "I consider Bilbo's election fortunate for the state. The more nauseous the dose, the sooner the vomiting will relieve the patient"). Johnston was criticized in 1919 for having voted against the child labor law, presumably in 1908, a charge his campaign advertisement did not deny. Yet Johnston supported child labor legislation in 1912 and 1914. *Memphis Commercial Appeal,* Aug. 22, 1919, 4 (advertisement); *House Journal* (1912), 1125; (1914), 998; Hamilton, *Progressive Mississippi,* 66–68; Hamilton, "The Turning Point," 104–6. Nannie Pitts McLemore, "The Progressive Era," in *History of Mississippi,* ed. Richard J. McLemore, 2:45–46, ·58. For the progressive era in Mississippi and the South, see also works cited in note 12 and the Mississippi *House Journal* during these years.

14. Kirwan, *Revolt of the Rednecks,* 259; Hamilton, "Mississippi Politics," 330–31; Hamilton, *Progressive Mississippi,* 166 (Johnston opposed prohibition); *Jackson Daily News,* Jan. 3, 1916, 2; Jan. 4, 1916, 1; Jan. 6, 1916, 2; Jan. 9, 1916, 10; Jan. 26, 1916, 1; Feb. 13, 1916, 5; Feb. 23, 1916, 1; Mar. 7, 1916, 2; Mar. 11, 1916, 4, 8; Mar. 17, 1916, 4; Mar. 28, 1916, 4 ("wholly erroneous," "demagogic rant," "ablest lawyer," and "acquire land" quotations), 8 (including "acquire land" quotation). *Greenville Daily Democrat,* Jan. 5, 1916, 1; Jan. 6, 1916, 1, 2. *Yazoo Sentinel,* Jan. 6, 1916, 1. *The Issue,* Mar. 30, 1916, 8 ("garb" quotation); Apr. 6, 1916, 3. Balsamo, "Theodore G. Bilbo and Mississippi Politics," 108–9.

15. Kirwan, *Revolt of the Rednecks,* 260–64, 292, 295; Balsamo, "Theodore G. Bilbo and Mississippi Politics," 109–15; *House Journal* (Memphis, 1916), 1239–42; *Jackson Daily News,* Feb. 25, 1916, 1 (quotation); Apr. 8, 1916, 2; see also *Clarksdale Daily Register,* Feb. 2, 1922, 1.

16. *The Issue,* Mar. 28, 1908, 4; also reprinted in *Friars Point Coahomian,* Apr. 4, 1908, 1.

17. *Memphis Commercial Appeal*, May 16, 1912, 9; June 8, 1932, 2; biographical material in OJSF, MDAH; *Clarksdale Daily Register*, June 15, 1920, 1, 2; June 16, 1920, 1; June 17, 1920, 8; *Greenville Daily Democrat*, Mar. 31, 1914, 2; Rowland, *Official and Statistical Register* (1917), 847.

18. Weeks, *Clarksdale and Coahoma County*, 90, 116, 171; *Friars Point Coahomian*, Mar. 30, 1912, 5; Apr. 13, 1912, 5 (quotation); Apr. 20, 1912, 5; Cutrer biographical material, including that of WPA, in John Cutrer Subject File, MDAH.

19. Weeks, *Clarksdale and Coahoma County*, 112, 114, 117–18; *Clarksdale Daily Register*, Jan. 16, 1916, 1; Jan. 19, 1916, 1; Dec. 31, 1918, 6 (first quotation); May 20, 1918, 3; *Jackson Daily News*, Jan. 31, 1916, 5; *Friars Point Coahomian*, Sept. 28, 1907, 4; unidentified newspaper clipping, JFM; confidential interview 2 (second quotation); OJ to L. C. Parrish, Dec. 8, 1926; OJ to Wheeler McMillen, June 3, 1941, Sept. 3, 1942; OJ to E. W. Palmer, Dec. 11, 1939; S. E. Smith to OJ, Apr. 30, 1942 (third quotation); OJ to Smith, May 2, 1942, DPLCR; *Memphis Commercial Appeal*, May 16, 1919, 51 (advertisement). Johnston's home in Clarksdale cost $26,000 "when material was extremely cheap." OJ to Parrish, Dec. 8, 1926, DPLCR. Public records in the Clarksdale courthouse indicate that Johnston incurred some indebtedness to his mother-in-law. The house still stands, converted, appropriately, into a law firm.

20. *Jackson Daily News*, reprinted in unidentified newspaper clipping (probably *Clarksdale Daily Register*), Mar. 29, 1918, Scrapbook—Clarksdale, CL; Dunbar Rowland, *Courts, Judges, and Lawyers of Mississippi* (Jackson, Miss., 1935), 265.

21. "Biggest Cotton Plantation," 131; Dickson, "Oscar Johnston—Magnolia Sketches," 451–52, Dickson (Harris) Collection; *Clarksdale Daily Register*, June 19, 1918, 3; *Memphis Commercial Appeal*, May 16, 1919, 51 (advertisement); OJ to Regional Manager, U.S. Veterans' Bureau, Mar. 22, 1927; OJ to Demaree Bess, July 21, 1942; see also George R. Neblett to OJ, June 11, 1942, DPLCR; OJ to J. C. Johnston, n.d. ("Monday night" 1918), JFM.

22. OJ to J. C. Johnston, five letters, n.d., "Monday night" (1918) (first quotation); Sept. 19, 1918 (second quotation); n.d., "Saturday Afternoon" (1918); n.d., "Saturday Night" (envelope postmarked Oct. 6, 1918); n.d., "Saturday" (envelope postmarked Sept. 15, 1918), JFM; OJ to Regional Manager, U.S. Veterans' Bureau, Mar. 22, 1927, DPLCR; "Biggest Cotton Plantation," 131; Dickson, "Oscar Johnston—Magnolia Sketches," 451–52, Dickson (Harris) Collection; biographical material in OJSF, MDAH; *Jackson Clarion-Ledger*, reprinted in unidentified newspaper clipping (probably *Clarksdale Daily Register*), Dec. 18, 1918, Scrapbook—Clarksdale, CL; *Clarksdale Daily Register*, Dec. 12, 1918, 3.

23. *Jackson Clarion-Ledger* in *Greenville Daily Democrat-Times*, Dec. 13, 1918, 2; *Greenville Daily Democrat-Times*, Jan. 6, 1919, 2; *Vicksburg Post* in *Clarksdale Daily Register*, Dec. 21, 1918, 5; Dec. 31, 1918, 1, 6; Jan. 24, 1919, 1, 6 (third quotation); *Jackson Clarion-Ledger* in unidentified newspaper clipping (probably *Clarksdale Daily Register*), Dec. 18, 1918, Scrapbook—Clarksdale, CL; *Vicksburg Post*, Dec. 18, 1918 (first quotation), in *Clarksdale Daily Register*, Dec. 18 (?), 1918; unidentified newspaper clippings, Dec. 20, 27, 1918; see Remarks of Judge J. Q. Robins Introducing Honorable Oscar Johnston at Tupelo, Mississippi, Scrapbook—Clarksdale, CL; unidentified newspaper clipping containing Johnston's announcement statement, n.d. (1919); *Memphis Commercial Appeal*, Mar. 22, 1919, 8, clipping; OJ to J. C. Johnston, n.d. (envelope postmarked Sept. 15, 1918; second quotation), clippings and letter in JFM;

Johnston's announcement statement appears in *Clarksdale Daily Register,* Jan. 23, 1919, 1, 6; Charles G. Hamilton, *Mississippi, Mirror of the 1920s* (Fulton, Miss., 1979), 10–11; Harris Dickson to A. J. McLaurin, Dec. 18, 1918, Dickson (Harris) letter, MDAH.

24. Unidentified newspaper clipping (probably *Clarksdale Daily Register*), Dec. 20, 1918, Scrapbook—Clarksdale, CL; Kirwan, *Revolt of the Rednecks,* 292; Holmes, *White Chief,* 371.

25. *Greenville Daily Democrat-Times,* July 9, 1919, 4 (advertisement); *Jackson Clarion-Ledger,* in same paper, Aug. 9, 1919, 2; *Jackson Daily News,* Aug. 3, 1919, 3; *Tunica Times,* June 14, 1919, 1; June 28, 1919, 1; July 6, 1919, 1; July 19, 1919, 1; Aug. 2, 1919, 1; *Memphis Commercial Appeal,* May 16, 1919, 51 (advertisement); July 28, 1919, 5; Remarks of Judge J. Q. Robins Introducing Honorable Oscar Johnston at Tupelo, Mississippi, Scrapbook—Clarksdale, CL; *Clarksdale Daily Register,* Apr. 16, 1919, 1, 5 (by C. N. Harris, editor of *Madison County Herald*); *Vardaman's Weekly,* July 24, 1919, 11 (quotation); Aug. 21, 1919, 16; *Carroll News,* in same paper, June 26, 1919, 4; Kirwan, *Revolt of the Rednecks,* 292–96; Holmes, *White Chief,* 372; Percy to Mr. Cato, June 27, 1919 (quotation); Percy to OJ, June 27, 1919, Percy Family Papers.

26. All five newspapers' comments were reprinted in the *Greenville Daily Democrat-Times* (in order), Apr. 16, 1919, 2; June 12, 1919, 1; July 2, 1919, 2; July 16, 1919, 2 (last two); *Clarksdale Daily Register,* May 17, 1919, 3; *Jackson Daily News,* Mar. 30, 1919, 8; see also *Jackson Clarion-Ledger* in *Greenville Daily Democrat-Times,* Aug. 9, 1919, 2.

27. Kirwan, *Revolt of the Rednecks,* 294; Clark F. Gross to J. O. Prude Jr., n.d., printed in a paid section in the *Memphis Commercial Appeal,* July 26, 1919, 8 (first quotation); letter by nine soldiers to the soldiers of Mississippi, printed in *Greenville Delta Democrat-Times,* Aug. 21, 1919, 1 (last quotations); see also *Jackson Daily News,* Aug. 21, 1919, 8; Aug. 24, 1919, 8.

28. Johnston's statement in *Clarksdale Daily Register,* Jan. 23, 1919, 2; *Oxford Eagle* in *Jackson Daily News,* Jan. 15, 1919, 4; *Vicksburg Evening Post* in *Greenville Daily Democrat-Times,* Jan. 28, 1919, 2 (next to last quotation); *Jackson Daily News,* Aug. 14, 1919, 4. The *Lexington Advertiser* also ridiculed Russell, "who was unknown in connection with the war, other than in filling out, as did every other lawyer, some questionnaires." Reprinted in *Greenville Daily Democrat-Times,* Aug. 22, 1919, 2.

29. *Jackson Daily News,* Aug. 6, 1919, 1; Aug. 7, 1919, 1; Aug. 8, 1919, 1; Aug. 9, 1919, 6; Aug. 10, 1919, 1; Aug. 14, 1919, 6; Aug. 17, 1919, 1 (Collins's quotations); Aug. 24, 1919, 12 (last quotation); *Greenville Daily Democrat-Times,* Aug. 7, 1919, 1; Aug. 11, 1919, 2; Aug. 16, 1919, 2; see Aug. 21, 1919, 2; and Sept. 8, 1919, 2; *Tunica Times,* Aug. 9, 1919, 1; Aug. 16, 1919, 1; *Memphis Commercial Appeal,* Aug. 8, 1919, 1; Collins to J. N. Flowers, n.d., printed in *Memphis Commercial Appeal,* Aug. 16, 1919, 20; Aug. 18, 1919, 8; Aug. 24, 1919, 19; Aug. 25, 1919, 8.

30. *Vardaman's Weekly,* Aug. 7, 1919, 4 (first quotation); Longino to editor of *Jackson Clarion-Ledger,* Aug. 18, 1919, printed in *Vardaman's Weekly,* Aug. 21, 1919, 5; see also June 26, 1919, 7; July 10, 1919, 14; Aug. 21, 1919, 15; see also *Jackson Daily News,* Aug. 22, 1919, 4; *Poplarville Free Press,* Aug. 22, 1919, 1 (advertisement; second quotation); Kirwan, *Revolt of the Rednecks,* 294–95.

31. OJ to J. B. Murphy, May 15, 1940, DPLCR (first quotation); see a distorted and factually flawed version of the campaign in Allan A. Michie and Frank Ryhlick, *Dixie Demagogues* (New York, 1939), 8; Johnston statement in *Clarksdale Daily Register,* June 21, 1920, 1 ("slush fund" quotation); Kirwan, *Revolt of the Rednecks,* 295 (last quotation).

32. Hamilton, *Mississippi, Mirror of the 1920's*, 12–13 (the runoff map fails to include Noxubee among Johnston counties); Rowland, *Official and Statistical Register, 1920–1924* (Jackson, Miss., 1923), 378; *Jackson Daily News*, Sept. 4, 1923, 3; Kirwan, *Revolt of the Rednecks*, 295–96; Holmes, *White Chief*, 272–73; *Greenville Daily Democrat-Times*, Sept. 8, 1919, 2; *Memphis Commercial Appeal*, Aug. 28, 1919, 1, 5; Feb. 26, 1930, 2 (last quotation); Johnston statement in *Clarksdale Daily Register*, June 21, 1919, 1; campaign advertisement (?) in *Vardaman's Weekly*, Aug. 21, 1919, 15 (first quotation); Porter interview (campaign speech quotations); "Biggest Cotton Plantation," 131. Johnston apparently picked up some Longino supporters. *Greenwood Commonwealth* (weekly edition), Aug. 13, 1919, 1 (and *Greenville Democrat-Times*, apparently *Daily Democrat-Times*, therein); see also *Greenwood Commonwealth*, Aug. 20, 1919, 3, 7.

33. *Jackson Daily News*, Aug. 28, 1919, 4 (quotations); Aug. 29, 1919, 8; *Greenville Daily Democrat-Times*, Aug. 29, 1919, 1; see also *Tunica Times*, Aug. 29, 1919, 1; *Greenwood Commonwealth*, Sept. 3, 1919, 4 (last quotation). According to Harris Dickson, Johnston "showed no genius as a rabble-rouser, and was defeated." Dickson, "Oscar Johnston—Magnolia Sketches," 451, Dickson (Harris) Collection.

34. Hamilton, *Progressive Mississippi*, 161; Kirwan, *Revolt of the Rednecks*, 297–99; *Clarksdale Daily Register*, June 15, 1920, 1, 2; June 16, 1920, 1; June 17, 1920, 8; *Memphis Commercial Appeal*, in same paper, June 18, 1920, 1; *Clarksdale Daily Register*, June 21, 1920, 1–2; Feb. 6, 1922, 1; Feb. 7, 1922, 4–5; Dec. 13, 1922, 1; Russell to OJ, July 19, 1923; OJ to Russell, July 30 (probably July 20), 1923 (quotation), both printed in *Clarksdale Daily Register*, July 21, 1923, 1; see also Brewer to Russell, printed in *Clarksdale Daily Register*, Feb. 8, 1922, 1; *Jackson Daily News*, Feb. 6, 1923, 1; Feb. 8, 1922, 1; July 29, 1922, 1; see *Greenwood Commonwealth* (weekly edition), Aug. 20, 1919, 1 (and *Lexington Advertiser* quoted therein); *Memphis Commercial Appeal*, June 20, 1920, I, 12.

35. Morgan, *Redneck Liberal*, 39–40; for Vardaman, see Holmes, *White Chief*, 374–79; Percy, *Lanterns on the Levee*, 153 (quotation); Kirwan, *Revolt of the Rednecks*, vii, 297–314; *Clarksdale Daily Register*, June 27, 1922, 1; Aug. 19, 1922, 1; Aug. 23, 1922, 1; *Jackson Daily News*, Sept. 3, 1922, I, 1; Belle Kearney to OJ, Apr. 13, 1938, DPLCR; for Bilbo and Whitfield, see also Vincent A. Giroux Jr., "The Rise of Theodore G. Bilbo (1908–1932)," *Journal of Mississippi History* 43 (Aug. 1981), 200–202; and Bill R. Baker, *Catch the Vision: The Life of Henry L. Whitfield of Mississippi* (Jackson, Miss., 1974), 78–98.

36. *Clarksdale Daily Register*, Feb. 20, 1920, 3; May 8, 1920, 1; Dec. 15, 1920, 1; Dec. 21, 1920, 1; Dec. 23, 1920, 2; Dec. 30, 1920, 1; Jan. 12, 1921, 1; Mar. 30, 1921, 4; unidentified newspaper clipping (probably *Clarksdale Daily Register*), Dec. 28, 1918, Scrapbook—Clarksdale, CL; Lombardy Planting Company financial reports, Dec. 31, 1923 and Mar. 31, 1925; capital stock certificates, Apr. 3, 1920, DPLCR.

37. *Memphis News-Scimitar* in *Clarksdale Daily Register*, Dec. 22, 1924, 1 (quotation); *Clarksdale Daily Register*, Sept. 7, 1920, 1; Dec. 9, 1920, 2; *Friars Point Coahomian*, Feb. 11, 1911, 5; OJ to J. H. McCormick, July 15, 1941, DPLCR; William L. Giles, "Agricultural Revolution, 1890–1970," in McLemore, *History of Mississippi*, 2:197; George B. Tindall, *The Emergence of the New South, 1913–1945* (Baton Rouge, 1967), 111–12.

38. Tindall, *Emergence of the New South*, 111–12 (including first quotation); James Shideler, *Farm Crisis, 1919–1923* (Berkeley and Los Angeles, 1957), 49–51; *Clarksdale Daily Register*, Oct. 6, 1920, 1; Nov. 16, 1920, 5; Dec. 4, 1920, 1; Jan. 6, 1921, 1; Mar. 17, 1921, 1; Mar. 18, 1921, 1 (Johnston statement); Mar. 19, 1921, 1, 6; Mar. 30, 1921, 6; Apr. 27, 1921, 3; Apr. 29, 1921, 3; Apr. 30, 1921, 3; Aug. 5, 1921, 1; Jackson

*Daily News,* Apr. 7, 1921, 1; Cully Cobb to OJ, Oct. 1, 1926; OJ to Cobb, Oct. 7, 1926; OJ to J. H. McCormick, July 15, 21 (last quotation), 1941; see OJ to John E. Mitchell Jr., Jan. 23, 1942, DPLCR; Ben B. McNew, "Banking, 1890–1970," in McLemore, *History of Mississippi,* 2:318–20.

39. Tindall, *Emergence of the New South,* 113–14; Shideler, *Farm Crisis,* 50–51, 85; Weeks, *Clarksdale and Coahoma County,* 120, 171, 173; *Clarksdale Daily Register,* Dec. 2, 1920, 1; Dec. 6, 1920, 3; Dec. 7, 1920, 1; see also Nov. 17, 1920, 1; June 12, 1922, 1; June 17, 1922, 3; June 19, 1922, 1 (advertisement); Jan. 30, 1923, 1, 3; Dec. 23, 1924, 1; Dec. 10, 1925, 1; *Jackson Daily News,* Jan. 31, 1923, 2; for coverage of Fitzgerald's exporting company, see *Clarksdale Daily Register,* Oct. 1920–Feb. 1921, July and Dec. 1921; "Biggest Cotton Plantation," 131–32. Harris Dickson, perhaps repeating the *Fortune* claim, also, in 1940, said Johnston's services were a condition to the bank bailout. Dickson, "Oscar Johnston—Magnolia Sketches," 452, Dickson (Harris) Collection.

40. Tindall, *Emergence of the New South,* 116; Shideler, *Farm Crisis,* 99–104; *Clarksdale Daily Register,* Sept. 9, 1920, 1, 3; Feb. 28, 1928, 1921, 4; Mar. 22, 1921, 4 (latter two are articles on cotton marketing); *New York Evening Post* in *Jackson Daily News,* Dec. 6, 1922, 10.

41. *Clarksdale Daily Register,* Sept. 7, 1920, 1; Sept. 22, 1920, 4; Oct. 16, 1920, 4; Oct. 18, 1920, 4; Oct. 19, 1920, 1; Dec. 3, 1920, 1; Dec. 15, 1920, 1, 6; see also Oct. 15, 1920, 1; Oct. 21, 1920, 2; and Oct. 28, 1920, 1; eulogies to Bledsoe in *Staple Cotton Review* 32 (Feb. 1954): 1–2. Bledsoe had been working on the cooperative idea before Sapiro appeared on the scene. "*The Dearborn* and the Staple Cotton Cooperative Association," *Staple Cotton Review* 2 (Oct. 1, 1924): 11 (signed by nineteen SCCA board members, including Oscar Johnston).

42. *Clarksdale Daily Register,* Dec. 15, 1920, 1; Feb. 9, 1921, 1; Feb. 12, 1921, 1; Feb. 15, 1921, 1; Feb. 21, 1921, 1; Mar. 1, 1921, 1; Mar. 22, 1921, 4 ("The Marketing of Your Cotton Crop"); Mar. 25, 1921, 2; Apr. 16, 1921, 3; Apr. 26, 1921, 6; Apr. 28, 1921, 3; May 14, 1921, 3; May 26, 1921, 1; June 15, 1921, 1; *Jackson Daily News,* May 28, 1921, 1; June 15, 1921, 1; June 28, 1921, 7; Walter Sillers Jr. to Oscar Bledsoe, Nov. 20, 1920; Walter Sillers (Jr?) to William F. Gray, Mar. 2, 1921; see Bledsoe statement, with copied quotations, Oct. 4, 1921, Walter Sillers Jr. Papers, Delta State Univ. archives, Cleveland, Mississippi; see statements of bankers' support also in Sillers Papers.

43. See relevant material in *Clarksdale Daily Register,* July 9, 1921, 1; July 13, 1921, 3; July 14, 1921, 1; Aug. 24, 1921, 1; Aug. 26, 1921, 1; Sept. 17, 1921, 1, 2; Sept. 28, 1921, 4; Oct. 13, 1921, 1 (including material reprinted from *New Bedford [South Carolina] Sunday Standard*), Nov. 16, 1921, 1; Aug. 15, 1922, 1; Oct. 8, 1922, 1; Oct. 28, 1921, 1; June 2, 1925, 3 (advertisement); June 9, 1925, 6 (advertisement containing auditors' statement); June 25, 1925, 5; *Greenwood Commonwealth* in same paper, Aug. 12, 1921, 3; *Jackson Daily News,* Aug. 7, 1922, 4; Aug. 13, 1922, I, 8; Oct. 2, 1922, 2; Nov. 27, 1922, II, 2; Dec. 8, 1922, 6; Mar. 13, 1923, 6; Nov. 9, 1923, 4; "The Delta and the Association," *Staple Cotton Review* 1 (Oct. 15, 1923): 1; "Back to the Fundamentals: The Origin, Purposes, Plans, and Operations of the Staple Cotton Cooperative Association," *Staple Cotton Review* 12 (Apr. 1934): 1; Mabelle White, Mary Jane Whittington, and W. M. Garrard Jr., "William Mountjoy Garrard IV, 1881–1958," *Staple Cotton Review* 36 (Sept. 1958): 1; OJ to J. Howard Ardrey, Mar. 24, 1924, DPLCR. For business agrarianism, see Tindall, *Emergence of the New South,* 114; Grant McConnell, *The Decline of Agrarian Democracy* (Berkeley and Los Angeles, 1959); and Richard Hofstadter, *The Age of Reform: From Bryan to F.D.R.* (New York, 1955).

44. *Memphis News-Scimitar* in *Clarksdale Daily Register,* May 24, 1923, 1; *Clarksdale Daily Register,* Aug. 3, 1921, 4; Aug. 31, 1921, 4; Nov. 30, 1921, 1, 2; Feb. 22, 1922, 1, 2 ("Service" quotation); May 12, 1923, 1, 4; Sept. 26, 1923, 1; June 6, 1924, 1; Dec. 22, 1924, 1 (Clarksdale quotations); Ross interview (resident quotation). When Smith returned to Clarksdale in March to address the league, Johnston presided. See extensive coverage of Smith's crusade and its planning and relevant related matters in *Clarksdale Daily Register,* Jan.–Feb. 1924, particularly Jan. 31, 1924, 1; Feb. 4, 1924, 1; Feb. 8, 1924, 1 (quotation); Feb. 23, 1924, 1; Mar. 6, 1924, 1; Mar. 7, 1924, 1; "Gypsy Smith and the Delta," *Staple Cotton Review* 2 (Apr. 1924): 1. On black migration, see Neil R. McMillen, *Dark Journey: Black Mississippians in the Age of Jim Crow* (Urbana and Chicago, 1989), 257–81; and James R. Grossman, *Land of Hope: Chicago, Black Southerners, and the Great Migration* (Chicago and London, 1989).

45. OJ to Bledsoe, May 13, 1925, printed in *Staple Cotton Review* 3 (July 1, 1925): 1–2; *Clarksdale Daily Register,* Feb. 22, 1922, 1; May 30, 1924, 1; June 6, 1924, 1; May 22, 1925, 1; June 20, 1925, 1 (including OJ's printed letter); June 30, 1925, 1; July 6, 1925, 1; Dec. 10, 1925, 1; *Jackson Daily News,* May 29, 1924, 1; "Biggest Cotton Plantation," 132; OJ to Tchula Cooperative Store[s], Sept. 29, 1926; OJ to George T. Rives, Sept. 29, 1926; OJ to Earl Brewer, Sept. 29, 1926; and other relevant correspondence in DPLCR.

## 2. Corporate Planter

1. "Biggest Cotton Plantation," 131–32; *Sydney(Australia) Daily Telegraph,* June 18, 1926, clipping in DPLCR; A. C. Wild, "History of Delta and Pine Land Company," typed copy, n.d. (ca. 1960s), DPLCR.

2. *The Fine Cotton Spinners' and Doublers' Association, Limited* (Manchester, 1909), 12–15, 49–51, copy in DPLCR; see "Biggest Cotton Plantation," 127.

3. Early C. Ewing, "History of the Delta and Pine Land Company," typed manuscript, 1967, DPLCR; A. C. Wild to George Patterson, Dec. 22, 1965, and extracts of FCSDA minutes, DPLCR; Arthur Foster and Arno S. Pearse, "Delta and Pine Land Company of Mississippi, Scott, Miss.," *International Cotton Bulletin* 2 (Sept. 1923), 18; W. Lawrence Balls, *The Cotton Plant in Egypt, Studies in Physiology and Genetics* (London, 1912), ix, 178; see *Memphis Commercial Appeal,* May 14, 1911, II, 5. News accounts call the early Fox offer into question. W. D. Davis became the first resident general manager at Scott in 1911. A farming manager would be employed, but as of May 1911 had not been. *Memphis Commercial Appeal,* May 26, 1911, 4; see also *Meridian Star,* in *Greenville Weekly Democrat,* Oct. 17, 1912, 4 (also in *Greenville Daily Democrat,* Oct. 16, 1912, 2).

4. On Salsbury, see *Tennessee: The Volunteer State, 1769–1923,* 5 vols. (Chicago and Nashville, 1923), 3:197–99; C. P. J. Mooney, ed., *The Mid-South and Its Builders, Being the Story of the Development and a Forecast of the Future of the Richest Agricultural Region in the World* (Memphis, 1920), 260; Marion G. Evans, "Our New President," *Memphis Chamber of Commerce Journal* 1 (June 1918): 111 (see comments on Salsbury by C. H. Williamson on page 110), copy in Memphis Public Library, Memphis, Tennessee. *Memphis Commercial Appeal,* June 19, 1932, I, 2; "Biggest Cotton Plantation," 128. On the Delta, see Robert Brandfon, *Cotton Kingdom of the New South: A History of the Yazoo Mississippi Delta from Reconstruction to the Twentieth Century* (Cambridge, Mass., 1967); Cobb, *The Most Southern Place on Earth*; E. L. Langsford and B. H. Thibodeaux, *Plantation Organization and Operation in the Yazoo–Mississippi*

*Delta Area,* U.S. Dept. of Agriculture Technical Bulletin No. 682 (May 1939); Fern E. Dorris, "The Yazoo Basin in Mississippi," *Journal of Geography* 28 (Feb. 1929), 72–79; Robert W. Harrison, *Alluvial Empire,* vol. 1 of *A Study of State and Local Efforts Toward Land Development in the Alluvial Valley of the Lower Mississippi River,* 2 vols. (Little Rock, 1961).

5. For Salsbury, see appropriate references in note 4 above; also see *Memphis Commercial Appeal,* Feb. 9, 1912, 29, and managers' meeting minutes, Jan. 15, 1926; Vernon Bellhouse, Delta and Pine Land Company (five double-spaced legal-size pages memoir), Sept. 30, 1948; Minor S. Gray to "Whom It May Concern," Mar. 2, 1962, memorandum; Gray to W. T. Winterbottom, n.d. (ca. 1962) (two memorandums; the first of these memorandums contains copies of letters, OJ to Alexander Fitzhugh, June 30, 1948, and OJ to Martel McNeely, July 16, 1945; at least the latter letter stands independently in DPLCR); Gray to Winterbottom, Nov. 1, 1962; Oscar Johnston, Delta and Pine Land Company of Mississippi (six double-spaced typed pages), n.d. (1947); Wild, "History"; Ewing, "History" (Ewing included Johnston's and Wild's manuscripts as appendices to his own); extracts from minutes of executive directors meetings in 1910–11 by Wild contained in his letter to George Patterson, Dec. 22, 1965, copied in Ewing, "History," DPLCR. Salsbury had been preceded to Manchester by Isaac Reese, an American who may have been a representative of Scott but who, in any case, became a stockholding colleague of Salsbury in the Mississippi properties. Minutes extracts in Wild to Patterson, Dec. 22, 1965, in Ewing, "History"; *Memphis Commercial Appeal,* May 18, 1911, 1; Oscar Johnston, "Industrial Plan of the Delta and Pine Land Company of Mississippi," *Journal of Social Hygiene* 26 (Feb. 1940): 73–74; Brandfon, *Cotton Kingdom,* 128, 150; "Biggest Cotton Plantation," 128. On Scott, see published and unpublished (apparently WPA) material in Charles Scott, Subject File, MDAH; *Memphis Commercial Appeal,* Apr. 29, 1913, 12; Oct. 27, 1916, 7 (obituary). See also Scott to Leroy Percy, Jan. 20, 1909, Percy Family Papers, MDAH. On both Salsbury and Scott, see "Biggest Cotton Plantation," 128.

6. "Biggest Cotton Plantation," 127–29; Ewing, "History"; Wild, "History"; OJ to Fitzhugh, June 30, 1948 (first quotation), copied in Gray memorandum, Mar. 2, 1962; see OJ to Richard Winborne, Jan. 30, 1939, DPLCR; Committee on Agriculture, *Hearings Before the Senate Committee on Agriculture and Forestry, A Resolution to Investigate Certain Activities of the American Cotton Cooperative Association in Connection with the Marketing of Cotton Financed by the Federal Government,* 75th Cong., 3d sess. on S. Res. 137, 1938, 97 (second quotation; hereinafter cited as *Senate ACCA Hearing*); minutes extracts in Wild to Patterson, Dec. 22, 1965, in Ewing, "History"; Bellhouse, Delta and Pine Land Company, DPLCR; *Memphis Commercial Appeal,* Apr. 1, 1911, 4; May 18, 1911, 1; May 26, 1911, 4; *Memphis News-Scimitar* in *Greenville Weekly Democrat,* Apr. 13, 1911, 5; see also in *Greenville Daily Democrat,* Apr. 12, 1911, 10; and other relevant sources cited in note 5 above.

7. For boosterism, boll weevils, and land sales, see *Memphis Commercial Appeal, Greenville Weekly Democrat,* and *Daily Democrat* in these years. See for example, *Memphis Commercial Appeal,* Apr. 27, 1911, 4; May 14, 1911, II, 5; June 1, 1911, 6; July 2, 1911, I, 1, 2, 12; July 27, 1911, 4; Dec. 6, 1911, 9; *Greenville Daily Democrat,* July 11, 1912, 10; July 21, 1912, 1; Aug. 22, 1912, 1; and others; see also J. G. Jones to Leroy Percy, Dec. 1, 1908, Percy Family Papers, MDAH. For a history of the boll weevil, see Douglas Helms, "Just Lookin' For a Home: The Cotton Boll Weevil and the South," Ph.D. diss., Florida State Univ., 1977.

8. *Memphis News-Scimitar* in *Greenville Weekly Democrat,* Apr. 13, 1911, 5; also in *Greenville Daily Democrat,* Apr. 12, 1911, 10; *Memphis Commercial Appeal,* June 10, 1911, 16; Jan. 13, 1912, 9; Feb. 14, 1912, 16; Feb. 23, 1912, 9 (first quotation); Mar. 3, 1912, I, 18; Oct. 16, 1912, 9; *Greenville Daily Democrat,* Sept. 25, 1912, 1 (also in *Greenville Weekly Democrat,* Sept. 26, 1912, 1); Mar. 20, 1914, 2 (second quotation); (also *Greenville Weekly Democrat,* Mar. 17, 1914, 2); Wild, "History"; see also Gray memorandums, Mississippi *House Journal,* and other relevant sources cited in note 5 above; *Memphis Commercial Appeal,* Oct. 6, 1912, I, 17 (Scott quotation); Oct. 9, 1912, 3; see also Oct. 16, 1912, 9.

9. "Biggest Cotton Plantation," 129; Brandfon, *Cotton Kingdom,* 61–62, 129; Johnston, "Industrial Plan," 73–74; Wild, "History"; Gray memorandums and OJ letters therein (OJ to McNeely, July 16, 1945, also stands independently in DPLCR); Johnston, Delta and Pine Land Company of Mississippi; resolution in DPLC Minute Book, Jan. 3, 1917 ("winding up" quotation); contract between FCSDA, DPL, et al., June 19, 1919; The Charter of Incorporation of the Delta and Pine Land Company of Mississippi (Apr. 1886), memorandum, p. 2, box 26, DPLCR. On Delta Pine's charter, T. M. Miller, Mississippi's attorney general in 1886, wrote "There is nothing in the foregoing charter of incorporation violative of the Constitution of this State." See quotation also in Gray to Winterbottom (first of two memorandums; n.d., 1962), DPLCR. See photoduplicated advertisements of the old DPLC, including map of about 350,000 acres of Delta real estate owned by the enterprise, 1886–1919. For a brief description of the early activities of this land speculation company, see Brandfon, *Cotton Kingdom,* 61–63.

10. *Memphis Commercial Appeal,* Oct. 16, 1912, 9; contract between FCSDA, DPL, et al., June 10, 1919; The Charter of Incorporation of The Delta and Pine Land Company of Mississippi (Apr. 1886), p. 2 of memorandum, box 26; DPLC, Minute Book, July 31, 1919, 147–49; Johnston, Delta and Pine Land Company of Mississippi, DPLCR; see *Southern Realty Co. v. Tchula Cooperative Stores* in *Cases Argued and Decided in the Supreme Court of Mississippi at the March Term, 1917,* reported by Robert Powell (Columbia, Mo., 1917), 114. Johnston advised the British in 1943 that "[t]he charter under which Delta & Pine Land Company operates will protect it unless the Supreme Court of the United States should see fit to reverse the position which has been maintained by it for more than 100 years, but this is an exceptional and peculiar charter containing privileges and immunities not now contained in any other charter in the State of Mississippi, and insofar as I know, any other charter of an agricultural corporation in America." OJ to FCSDA, May 17, 1943, JFM.

11. Bellhouse, Delta and Pine Land Company; Ewing, "History"; Wild, "History"; see "Acreage of Lands in the Different Estates (1920–1926)," DPLCR; *Memphis Commercial Appeal,* May 26, 1911, 4; *Meridian Star* in *Greenville Weekly Democrat,* Oct. 17, 1912, 4 (also in *Greenville Daily Democrat,* Oct. 16, 1912, 2); Clarence J. Owens, "Biggest Cotton Plantation in the World," *Jackson Daily News,* Mar. 14, 1922, 5; "Biggest Cotton Plantation," 126, 130, 156 (Johnston quotation).

12. Ewing, "History," DPLCR; "Does It Pay the Delta Farmer to Grow Long Staple Cotton?" *International Cotton Bulletin* 3 (Mar. 1926): 419–20; "Biggest Cotton Plantation," 126, 156, 158; see Ewing to E. W. Allen, Feb. 19, 1919; see Ewing résumé, Oct. 3, 1928. For some of his debate with Johnston over his remuneration, see Ewing to OJ, June 15, Sept. 17, 28, 1928; OJ to Ewing, Sept. 24, 1928, DPLCR.

13. "Biggest Cotton Plantation," 127–30; Ewing, "History"; see annual reports in DPLCR; unidentified newspaper clipping; "The Greatest Cotton Plantation, Scott, Miss., The Story of Salsbury Cotton," Aug. 18, 1922, DPLCR.

14. Annual Statement and President's Report for the Year Ending January 31, 1921 (first quotation); Mississippi Delta Planting Company, Lake Vista Planting Company, Triumph Planting Company Statement and President's Report for the Year Ending January 31, 1918; Wild, "History"; Herbert Lee to Early Ewing, Oct. 8, Dec. 1, 1925; see OJ to Lee, Oct. 7, Nov. 4, 1926; and D. R. Gavin to Allan W. Leftwich, Sept. 5, 1940, DPLCR; "Biggest Cotton Plantation," 127–30 (last quotation on 129). Numerous sources, some of those cited in note 5, may be consulted for the miscarriage of the Britishers' original plans; long-held assumptions that the Fine Spinners never used any DPL cotton are inaccurate.

15. "Biggest Cotton Plantation," 127; Owens, "The Biggest Cotton Plantation in the World"; Foster and Pearse, "Delta and Pine Land Company of Mississippi, Scott, Miss.," 18–22; *Sydney Daily Telegraph,* June 18, 1926, clipping in DPLCR; Ewing, "History"; Wild, "History"; annual reports; DPLC, Cotton Production Record (1912–1969); see extracts of various letters in DPLC advertisement during the 1920s, DPLCR.

16. W. W. Fariss to OJ, Feb. 2, 16, 1943; OJ to Fariss, Feb. 3, 12, 1943; OJ to Alexander Fitzhugh, June 30, 1948, copied in Gray memorandum; Wild, "History," DPLCR; "Biggest Cotton Plantation," 132.

17. Wild, "History"; Ewing, "History"; OJ to Fitzhugh, June 30, 1948, copied in Gray memorandum; agreements, FCSDA, and OJ; Herbert William Lee and OJ, both May 21, 1926; OJ to Lee, June 1, 2, Oct. 5 (quotation), 6 (five-page letter), 1926; OJ (?) to Lee, June 18, 1926; Lee to OJ, June 15, 1926; Addleshaw, Sons and Latham to OJ, May 20, 1926; cablegrams, Distaff (FCSDA) to OJ, June 14, 1926; Lee to OJ, June 29, 1926; A. F. Toler to OJ, June 28, 1926, telegram; *Sydney Daily Telegraph,* June 18, 1926, clipping, DPLCR; "Biggest Cotton Plantation," 132.

18. OJ to Lee, Oct. 6, 1926 (five-page letter; contains British quotation); see also Distaff to OJ, n.d. (cablegram), DPLCR.

19. OJ to Lee, Nov. 4, 1926 (five-page letter; quotations); Wild, "History," DPLCR; USDA, *Yearbook of Agriculture, 1926* (Washington, D.C., 1927), 262–63, 975; USDA, *Yearbook of Agriculture, 1927* (Washington, D.C., 1928), 920; "Biggest Cotton Plantation," 132.

20. DPLC Cotton Production Record, DPLCR. While 1923 was not a representative year because of unusually calamitous weather, the trend in production was upward.

21. *New York Times,* Oct. 8, 1926, 25; Oct. 10, 1926, I, 17; Oct. 15, 1926, 33; see also Oct. 11, 1926, 35; *Jackson Daily News,* Oct. 11, 1926, 11; *New Orleans Times-Picayune,* Oct. 13, 1926, 1; William Jardine, "The Secretary's Report to the President" (Nov. 1, 1926), in *Yearbook of Agriculture, 1926,* 1–2; Gilbert Fite, "Voluntary Attempts to Reduce Cotton Acreage in the South, 1914–1933," *Journal of Southern History* 14 (Nov. 1948), 485; Theodore Saloutos, *Farmer Movements in the South, 1965–1933* (Berkeley, 1960), 267–71; OJ to S. L. Gwin, Oct. 16, 1926; OJ to Harrison, Feb. 7, 1927, telegram; see OJ to Whittington, Feb. 7, 1927; see Whittington to OJ, Feb. 9, 1927; OJ to A. Y. Scott, Nov. 17, 1926, DPLCR.

22. Fite, "Voluntary Attempts," 481–99; Theodore Saloutos, "The Southern Cotton Association, 1905–1908," *Journal of Southern History* 13 (Nov. 1947), 492–510; Saloutos, *Farmer Movements in the South,* 152–54, 278–81; *New York Times,* Oct. 13,

1926, 9; Oct. 14, 1926, 22; *New Orleans Times-Picayune,* Oct. 14, 1926, 1; *Jackson Daily News,* Oct. 13, 1926, 1; OJ to Lee, Dec. 6, 1926 (first two quotations); Cotton Proclamation Issued by the Executive Committee of the Knights of Cotton Assembled in Extraordinary Session, Oct. 23, 1926 (and abstract), Memphis; Report of the Executive Committee of the South-Wide Cotton Conference (Memphis, 1926), DPLCR; statement of B. J. Young in *Memphis Press-Scimitar,* n.d. (dateline Mar. 20 [1950]), MPSM; see also Leroy Percy to J. W. McGrath, Feb. 13, 1922, Percy Family Papers, MDAH.

    23. Lee to OJ, Nov. 23, 1926; OJ to Lee, Dec. 7, 1926; see OJ to A. Y. Scott, Nov. 17, 1926, DPLCR.

    24. OJ to Lee, Dec. 7, 1926; Jan. 8 (quotation), 22, 1927; Minutes of a Special Meeting of the Managers of the Delta and Pine Land Co., of Miss., held at Scott, Miss., Tuesday, Jan. 4, 1927, DPLCR.

    25. Hatcher interview; Minutes of a Special Meeting of the Managers, Jan. 4, 1927; OJ to Lee, Dec. 27, 1926; Jan. 8, 15, 1927; Lee to OJ, Feb. 15, 1927 (quotation), DPLCR.

    26. OJ to DPLC, Feb. 26, 1927 (unsigned report of trip); OJ to Lee, Feb. 5, 1927; OJ to J. R. Nail, Feb. 18, 1927; OJ to Robert Rheinstrom, Feb. 18, 1927; see also OJ to E. L. Anderson, Feb. 22, 1927; and Jesse Fox (?) to Victor N. Schoffelmayer, Feb. 4, 1927; OJ to Lee, Mar. 19, 1927, DPLCR.

    27. Lee to OJ, Oct. 1 (and quotations of cables therein), 5 (quotation), 1926; OJ to Lee, Oct. 5 (quotation), 6 (two-page letter), 1926; OJ to Distaff (FSCDA), Sept. 29, 1926; A. W. Gregg to OJ, Oct. 9, 1926, telegram, DPLCR.

    28. OJ to General Counsel, Bureau of Internal Revenue, Oct. 11, 1926, telegram; OJ to A. W. Gregg, Oct. 22, 1926, Apr. 4, 1926; OJ to Lee, Oct. 6 (two-page letter), 22, 1926; Gregg to OJ, Apr. 14, 1927; Lee to OJ, Oct. 5, 1926; Nov. 5, 1926 (quotation); Apr. 5, 1927; OJ to Distaff, Apr. 4, 1927 (cablegram); see other relevant correspondence, DPLCR.

    29. Wild, "History"; Salsbury to the Shareholders of the Delta and Pine Land Company, Inc., Apr. 1, 1927, memorandum (first quotation); OJ to Lee, Apr. 1, 18, 1927; OJ to Distaff, Apr. 14, 1927, telegram; OJ to Harry M. Bryan, Apr. 12, 18, 1927; Wild, "History"; see OJ to Dennis Murphree, Apr. 18, 1927, DPLCR. American shareholders were few: Mr. and Mrs. Harry Bryan (714); Lant Salsbury (3,292); Frank O. Lowden (250); Shields Abernathy (100); Mrs. Helen Abernathy (100); George Tucker (357); Mrs. Ione M. Tucker (357); George Bell (713); Mrs. (probably A. S.) Buchanan (714); J. S. Shortle (1); Robert Lynes (1); a Mr. Harris (1). OJ to Lee, Apr. 12, 1927, DPLCR. Note irregularity in handling of one American proxy in OJ to George Bell, Apr. 18, 1927, DPLCR.

    30. OJ to Lee, Apr. 18, 1927, DPLCR; "Biggest Cotton Plantation," 130–31; National Emergency Council, *Report to the President on the Economic Conditions of the South* (Washington, D.C., 1938), 15; *Greenville Delta Democrat-Times,* Apr. 21, 1927, 1; Wild, "History"; Ewing, "History," DPLCR; Pete Daniel, *Deep'N As It Come: The 1927 Mississippi River Flood* (New York, 1977), 7, 9, 10, 14, 15, 16, 17; Percy, *Lanterns on the Levee,* 249; J. L. Hatcher interview; see *Memphis Commercial Appeal,* Apr. 22, 1927, 15; Apr. 23, 1927, 4, 13; for a general flood story, including pictures, see "The Great Mississippi River Flood of 1927," *National Geographic* 53 (Sept. 1927): 243–89.

    31. "Biggest Cotton Plantation," 130–31; Percy, *Lanterns on the Levee,* 24; Daniel, *Deep'N As It Come,* 14–17; OJ to Lee, Apr. 26, May 2, 6, 14, 1927; OJ to Harry Bryan, May 4, 1927; Ewing, "History," DPLCR. Ewing claimed he heard of two drownings; he also said company losses reached around $750,000.

32. OJ to Lee, Apr. 26, 1927; OJ to Bryan, May 4, 1927; see also OJ to Mrs. Earl Brewer, May 4, 1927; and OJ to Mrs. Harry Dukes, May 4, 1927; OJ to Mr. Bondy, May 9, 1927, DPLCR.

33. OJ to Lee, Apr. 26, May 2, 3, 6, 14, 24 (two-page letter), 31, June 11, 1927; OJ to Reuben Sledge, June 7, 1927; R. F. Cartledge to DPLC, Apr. 29, 1927, telegram; see Lee to OJ, June 24, 1927; OJ to F. R. Mays, May (?) 1927; Wild, "History," DPLCR; "Biggest Cotton Plantation," 131.

34. OJ to Lee, Apr. 26, May 2, 1927; OJ to J. J. Sample, July 2, 1927 (quotation); OJ to Lee, May 24 (one-page letter), June 11, 1927; OJ to Bryan, June 28, 1927; see also other relevant correspondence; managers' meeting minutes, Jan. 15, 1926, DPLCR; *Memphis Commercial Appeal*, June 19, 1932, I, 2; see Salsbury's obituary in *Memphis Press-Scimitar*, July 12, 1938, 1, 2.

35. OJ to Lee, May 24 (one-page letter), June 11 (quotation), 15, 1927; Lee to OJ, Dec. 13, 1926; June 2, 24 (quotation), 1927; OJ to Bryan, June 28, 1927; OJ to J. J. Sample, July 2, 1927, DPLCR.

36. Wild, "History"; OJ to Bryan, June 28, 1927; OJ to Sample, July 2, 10, 1927; OJ to Lee, June 30, July 6 (and attached salary schedule), 1927, DPLCR. Wild incorrectly noted Salsbury's salary at $50,000. There seems some discrepancy in Johnston's statement to the British in 1942. There he reported a salary of $32,000 plus 5 percent bonus on net profits for the fiscal year ending in March 1929, his first full fiscal year as president. That fell by nearly a quarter, to $24,600 annually for 1930–32. After he joined the New Deal with its per diem remuneration, he requested no increase in his plantation salary; he established the National Cotton Council without salary and served as its president without salary, taking only travel expenses. Not until 1941–42 did he begin redevoting his full energies to his plantations, that year participating again in the employee bonus plan. Head office salaries increased less than $3,000 in the dozen years after 1930, that increase primarily occasioned by the company's new Planting Seed Division, with Toler as manager getting 25 cents per ton commission, assistant David Gavin 12.5 cents, and agronomist Early Ewing, the fellow really responsible for it all, getting a dollar, in each case beyond their regular salaries. OJ to FCSDA, Feb. 19, 1942, DPLCR.

37. Wild, "History"; Johnston, Delta and Pine Land Company of Mississippi; D. R. Gavin to Allan W. Leftwich, Sept. 5, 1940, DPLCR; *Staple Cotton Review* 6 (Oct. 1928), 3; W. Fred Stout interview.

38. OJ to Lee, Nov. 4 (five-page letter), Dec. 27, 1926; May 2, 6, 24 (two-page letter), 31, 1927; Lee to OJ, May 20 (quotation), June 1, 14, 1927, DPLCR; "Biggest Cotton Plantation," 131.

39. OJ to Fitzhugh, June 30, 1948; OJ to McNeely, July 16, 1945, both copied in Gray memorandum (McNeely letter also stands independently in DPLCR); OJ to Lee, Dec. 29, 1928 (quotation); Wild, "History"; see OJ to Lee, June 11, 1927, DPLCR. Lynes possessed only one share of DPLC stock, but he had one hundred shares of Empire and seventy-one of Delta Farms. Wild, "History"; minutes of a company meeting, Mar. 20, 1929; Gray to Winterbottom, Nov. 1, 1962, memorandum, DPLCR.

40. Ewing, "History," DPLCR.

41. Ibid.; Gray interviews; Conn interview; confidential interview 1; J. C. Johnston Jr. to author, July 17, 1979; OJ to J. C. Johnston, July 18, 1918, JFM; "Biggest Cotton Plantation," 127; *Clarksdale Daily Register*, Mar. 14, 1923, 1 (quotation); *Greenwood Commonwealth* (weekly edition), Mar. 14, 1923, 1; *Greenville Daily Democrat-Times*, Jan. 31, 1929, 1.

42. Conn interview (quotation); confidential interview 1; Gray interviews; "Biggest Cot-ton Plantation," 127, 156; Bellhouse, Delta and Pine Land Company; Ewing, "History," DPLCR; Jonathan Daniels, *A Southerner Discovers the South* (New York, 1938), 182.

43. OJ to S. P. Knut, Nov. 22, 1934, DPLCR; coverage of the scandal by the *Jackson Daily News* begins on Feb. 12, 1930 (quotation from Feb. 27, 1930, 18; issues of Feb. 24–26 are missing); coverage in *Memphis Commercial Appeal* begins Feb. 13, 1930 (quotation from Feb. 26, 1930, 1; for Warren Brothers' explanation of the alleged payoff, see Mar. 4, 1930, 1, 4); *Jackson Daily News,* May 27, 1933, 8; James Eastland interview.

44. Wild, "History"; Statement and President's Report (1930), Apr. 1, 1931 (quotation), DPLCR.

45. Statement and President's Report (1930); DPLC, Cotton Production Record; Wild, "History", DPLCR.

46. DPLC, Amortization Deed of Trust, Dec. 1, 1931; Wild, "History"; Statement and President's Report, 1931 (Apr. 1, 1932); FCSDA to Bank of Commerce and Trust Co., n.d. (1932?); Herbert Stowell to Bank of Commerce and Trust Co., Jan. 26, Mar. 22, 1932 (latter two are copies); J. L. Ross to OJ, Apr. 2, 1932, DPLCR.

47. Lee to OJ, Apr. 12, 1927; OJ to Lee, Apr. 18, 1927; OJ to Walter Sillers Jr., Feb. 24, 1933; OJ to Empire Shareholders, Oct. 12, 1931 (form letter); OJ to T. H. McNeill, Apr. 20, 1932; Stowell to OJ, Oct. 28, 1931; shareholder and proxy list and proxies; Notice of Special Shareholders Meeting of Empire Plantation Company, Oct. 12, 1931; Statement and President's Report (1931), Apr. 1, 1932; Wild, "History," DPLCR.

48. Statement and President's Report (1931); DPLC, Cotton Production Record; Wild, "History," DPLCR.

49. For discussions of the Farm Board's activities, see David E. Hamilton, *From New Day to New Deal: American Farm Policy From Hoover to Roosevelt, 1928–1933* (Chapel Hill, 1991); Saloutos, *Farmer Movements in the South,* 272–76; Tindall, *Emergence of the New South,* 256–57; Murray R. Benedict, *Farm Policies of the United States, 1790–1950: A Study of Their Origins and Development* (New York, 1953), 257–67; Arthur Schlesinger Jr., *The Crisis of the Old Order, 1919–1933* (Boston, 1957, 1964), 240; Van L. Perkins, *Crisis in Agriculture: The Agricultural Adjustment Administration and the New Deal* (Berkeley, 1969), 25; John Moloney, *Cotton in Peace and War, Papers of the Institute of Research and Training in the Social Sciences* (Nashville, 1944), 15–16; "Government's Biggest Business Venture," *Fortune* 2 (Nov. 1931), 37–38, 40–41, 123–24; Herbert C. Hoover, *State Papers, and Other Public Writings,* ed. William Myers, 2 vols. (Garden City, New York, 1934), 2:312; Oscar Johnston, "What Happened? and What Next?" *Cotton Trade Journal* 15 (International Edition, 1934–35): 13; Walter Parker to OJ, June 20, 1932, telegram; OJ to Parker, June 21, 1932 ("intermeddling" quotation), DPLCR. For a sympathetic contemporary analysis, see Joseph Davis, "The Program of the Federal Farm Board," *American Economic Review* 21 (Mar. 1931, supplement): 104–13. Actually, as David Hamilton, in *From New Day to New Deal* (236), argues, "the debate over farm legislation [in early 1933] was not one clearly dividing the devout defenders of laissez-faire from the proponents of the modern liberal state. Rather, it focused on what types of governmental action to undertake and on how to reconcile the need for new systems of economic control with older values that had shaped the American past."

50. Schlesinger, *Crisis of the Old Order,* 240 (quotations); *Memphis Commercial Appeal,* Mar. 13, 1930, 1; Theodore Saloutos, *The American Farmer and the New Deal* (Ames, Iowa, 1981), 274–75.

51. Johnston, "What Happened? and What Next?" 13; Statement and President's Report (1932), Apr. 1, 1933 (first quotation); OJ to Sillers and Roberts, Mar. 17, 1933 (second quotation); OJ to Stowell, Dec. 14, 1933; OJ to Sillers, Feb. 24, 25, 27, 28, 1933; Sillers to OJ, Feb. 23 (with attached waiver notice), 24, 1933; OJ to C. H. Johnston, Jan. 12, 1933; press release attached to Harvey Couch to OJ, Oct. 3, 1932; Wild, "History"; OJ to E. McLallen Jr. (Nickey Bros., Inc.), Jan. 4, 1933; see call for DPL board of directors notice, Feb. 1933; OJ to C. L. Wortham, Mar. 20, 1933; Arch Toler to Mississippi State Tax Commission, June 27, 1933, DPLCR; Perkins, *Crisis in Agriculture,* 25; Benedict, *Farm Policies of the United States,* 274.

## 3. Golden Egg

1. Alger Hiss to author, Aug. 21, 1979 (first quotation); Peek, with Crowther, *Why Quit Our Own?* 112 (second quotation). Rexford G. Tugwell, one of Franklin Roosevelt's "brain trusters," later argued that "[t]he magnitude of the problem put it beyond the limits of any traditional solution." Tugwell, *Roosevelt's Revolution: The First Year—A Personal Perspective* (New York, 1977), xv.

2. See Henry A. Wallace, *New Frontiers* (New York, 1934), 169–70.

3. Toler to C. H. Johnston, May 24, 1933; text of Johnston's cable (OJ to H. C. Stowell, May 26, 1933) in OJ to Herbert Stowell, Apr. 19, 1934; Stowell to OJ, May 8, 1934; Wild, "History"; see OJ to Mary Oglesby, May 29, 1933, DPLCR; Wallace and Peek to Distaff, FCSDA, May 25, 1933 (cable), GC, RG 16, NA.

4. Lee to Wallace, May 26, 1933 (cable); Lee to Wallace, May 26, 1933 (first two quotations), both in GC, RG 16, NA; Stowell to OJ, May 8, 1934; see OJ to FCSDA, Apr. 18, 1934, DPLCR. Johnston's compensation would be adjusted.

5. Henry I. Richards, *Cotton Under the Agricultural Adjustment Administration, Developments Up to July 1934,* Brookings Institute Pamphlet No. 15 (Washington, D.C., 1934), 4–5; Richards, *Cotton and the AAA,* Brookings Institute Publication No. 66 (Washington, D.C., 1936), 10–12; Johnston, "What Happened? and What Next?" 13; Oscar Johnston, speech to U.S. Chamber of Commerce (southeastern regional meeting, Birmingham, Ala.), Nov. 20, 1934, reprinted by Sen. John Bankhead (D-Ala.) in *Congressional Record, Senate,* 74th Cong., 1st sess., 79, pt. 1:147 (quotation). Cotton prices generally refer to middling grade 7/8-inch staple.

6. OJ to Wallace, Mar. 9, 1933; Harrison to Wallace, Mar. 23, 1933; Wallace to Harrison, Mar. 28, 1933, GC, RG 16, NA; Peek, with Crowther, *Why Quit Our Own?* 106; Gilbert Fite, *George N. Peek and the Fight for Farm Parity* (Norman, Okla., 1954), 254; see Peek to J. R. Leavell, May 26, 1933, telegram, George N. Peek Papers, Joint Collection, Univ. of Missouri Western Historical Manuscript Collection, Columbia, and State Historical Society of Missouri Manuscripts, Ellis Library, Univ. of Missouri–Columbia; Porter interview; Jerome Frank, AAA general counsel, recalled that "Johnston had been brought in by Peek to handle fiscal operations." Frank, COHC; see also Theodore Saloutos, *The American Farmer and the New Deal,* 56–58.

7. Unidentified newspaper clipping (probably *Memphis Commercial Appeal*), n.d. (1933); see also Associated Press story in unidentified newspaper clipping, May 27, 1933,

JFM; *Memphis Commercial Appeal,* May 28, 1933, I, 6 ("A Happy Selection"); *Memphis Press-Scimitar,* May 27, 1933, 2; *Greenville Daily Democrat-Times,* May 27, 1933, 2. The *Clarksdale Daily Register* said Johnston was regarded as "one of the most brilliant lawyers ever to belong to the Mississippi Bar and one of the shrewdest financiers ever to direct a financial institution." *Clarksdale Daily Register,* May 27, 1933, 1. See also *Jackson Daily News,* May 27, 1933, 1, 8.

8. Peek, with Crowther, *Why Quit Our Own?* 21 (quotation), 112–23; Donald Grubbs, *Cry from the Cotton: The Southern Tenant Farmers Union and the New Deal* (Chapel Hill, 1971), 17–61; David Conrad, *The Forgotten Farmers: The Story of Sharecroppers in the New Deal* (Urbana, Ill., 1965), 105–19, see 136–53; Fite, *George N. Peek,* 243–46; Russell Lord, *The Wallaces of Iowa* (Boston, 1947), 326–69; Perkins, *Crisis in Agriculture,* 50–97; Hiss to author, Aug. 21, 1979; Wallace to Roosevelt, May 15, 1933, OF 1, FDRL; see also Wallace to Peek, May 12, 1933, Peek Papers.

9. Frank, COHC (second quotation); Hiss interview. Hiss used those terms in describing Johnston and claimed Frank found him "delightful" (as quoted); Bledsoe interviews.

10. OJ to DPLC, May 27, 1933; see OJ–Toler correspondence during Johnston's absence in 1933, DPLCR. In 1936 Johnston held more than one hundred shares of Delta Pine stock, about 3 percent of the total. OJ to FCSDA, Aug. 7, 1936, DPLCR.

11. For a flowchart of the new AAA, see Schuyler C. Wallace, *The New Deal in Action* (New York, 1934), 81; see also Perkins, *Crisis in Agriculture,* 91, 94; *Memphis Press-Scimitar,* Dec. 9, 1933, 12; OJ to Jesse Jones, Sept. 22, 1933, memorandum, OF 1K, FDRL.

12. Executive Order No. 6084, Mar. 27, 1933, in Samuel Rosenman, ed., *The Public Papers and Addresses of Franklin D. Roosevelt,* 13 vols. (New York, 1938–50), 2:85–89; Oscar Johnston, "Origin and Operation of the 1933 Cotton Producers' Pool to Dec. 15 in 1934," *Cotton Trade Journal* 15, no. 8 (International Edition, 1934–1935): 116–17; see also *New York Times,* Mar. 27, 1933, 1; OJ to Toler, June 10, 1933, DPLCR; *Senate ACCA Hearing,* 73–79; OJ to Wallace, June 21, 1933, memorandum, and attached agreement between the FCA and Secretary Wallace, June 20, 1933, GC, RG 16, NA; OJ to Frank, June 13, 1933; OJ Wallace, July 10, 1933, memorandum, AAA, CLD, RG 16, NA (copy of OJ to Frank also in PCP, RG 145, NA); OJ to Peek, July 17, 1933, memorandum, PCP, RG 145, NA. Since a majority of this cotton was from the old Farm Board, it will hereinafter, where appropriate, be referred to as the Farm Board cotton.

13. Edwin Nourse, Joseph Davis, and John Black, *Three Years of the Agricultural Adjustment Administration,* Brookings Institute Publication No. 73 (Washington, D.C., 1937), 295; OJ to Toler, June 10, 1933, DPLCR; *Senate ACCA Hearing,* 74–75, 77, 88; Earnest Brown to Frank, May 23, 1933, memorandum; see OJ to Frank, June 13, 1933, AAA, CLD, RG 16, NA (latter also in PCP, RG 145, NA); and *Memphis Press-Scimitar,* Mar. 11, 1935, 1; Perkins, *Crisis in Agriculture,* 44–45, 49; *New York Times,* Mar. 1, 1933, 25; Mar. 5, 1933, 10; Mar. 8, 1933, 30; Mar. 17, 1933, 1, 2. The negotiations to acquire the cotton from the FCA continued into the fall of 1933. See OJ to Guaranty Trust Co. of New York and Chase National Bank, Nov. 15, 1933, AAA, CLD, RG 16, NA.

14. Tentative Plan for Controlling the Production of Cotton for the Crop Year of 1933, June 4, 1933, memorandum, PCP, RG 145, NA; *Senate ACCA Hearing,* 76; Wallace, *New Frontiers,* 174–75, 200.

15. Tentative Plan, memorandum, PCP, RG 145, NA; Mordecai Ezekiel to Wallace, June 15, 1933, memorandum, GC, RG 145, NA; *New York Times,* June 20, 1933, 34; Richards, *Cotton Under the AAA,* 7. Compensation averaged about $12.95 per acre in the cash-only contract and about $9.25 per acre in the cash-and-option contract. *Senate ACCA Hearing,* 77; see also Conrad, *Forgotten Farmers,* 44–47.

16. *Memphis Commercial Appeal,* June 3, 1933, 9; Richards, *Cotton Under the AAA,* 20–21; see also Perkins, *Crisis in Agriculture,* 106; OJ to Toler, June 10, 1933 (quotation), DPLCR.

17. *Memphis Commercial Appeal,* June 24, 1933, 1–2 (first, second, and fourth OJ quotations); *Memphis Press-Scimitar,* June 24, 1933, 1–2 (third Johnston quotation); OJ to Toler, June 10, 1933, DPLCR; David L. Cohn, *The Life and Times of King Cotton* (New York, 1956), 185; Daniels, *A Southerner Discovers the South,* 125.

18. *Memphis Press-Scimitar,* June 24, 1933, 1–2; P. W. Wilson to Peek, June 27, 1933, telegram, GC, RG 145, NA; see also Peek to R. E. Lee Wilson, June 29, 1933, GC, RG 145, NA.

19. *Memphis Commercial Appeal,* July 6, 1933, 1; OJ to Toler, June 28, 1933, telegram, DPLCR. See also *New York Times,* June 29, 1933, 5. Night riding and illicit plow-ups were rare. Public pressure likely helped, but a rumor that federal credit would be unavailable to uncooperative farmers stimulated compliance. Richards, *Cotton Under the AAA,* 44.

20. *Memphis Press-Scimitar,* June 30, 1933, 6; *New York Times,* July 9, 1933, 1 (FDR quotation); Toler to OJ, June 28, 1933; OJ to Toler, July 17, 1933; T. Y. Williford to OJ, Aug. 26, 1933, DPLCR; see Richards, *Cotton Under the AAA,* 18.

21. Toler to OJ, July 3, 19, 25, 1933, DPLCR. Johnston's manager at Delta Farms Company at Deeson reported in July that despite the plow-up, the plantation's yield would equal that of 1932. Toler to OJ, July 14, 1933, DPLCR.

22. Toler to OJ, June 27, 28, 30 (quotation), July 17, 1933, DPLCR; *New York Times,* June 29, 1933, 5; Richards, *Cotton and the AAA,* 110–15; *Memphis Press-Scimitar,* June 30, 1933, 6. The *Press-Scimitar* warned that "[b]eing too 'optimistic' as to the price of cotton this fall, may kill the goose before she lays the golden eggs for the South." June 30, 1933, 6. OJ to Herbert Stowell, Dec. 3, 1936; OJ to FCSDA, Apr. 20, 1942, DPLCR.

23. Toler to OJ, July 25, 31, 1933; see also Statement and Annual Report (1933), Apr. 19, 1934, DPLCR; Gray interviews; *New York Times,* Aug. 10, 1933, 3; Aug. 11, 1933, 14. Not every mule could be persuaded. See Harris Dickson, *The Story of King Cotton* (New York and London, 1937), 281.

24. Statement and President's Report, 1933 (Apr. 19, 1934); Wild, "History"; DPLC, Cotton Production Record; Toler to OJ, July 19, Aug. 10, 17, 18, 25, 29, 30, Oct. 14, 1933, and others in 1933, DPLCR. Empire Plantation at Estill leased 600 acres to the government, leaving 1,800 in cotton; Delta Farms at Deeson leased 1,100 acres out of 4,500.

25. For a facsimile of the 1933 contract, see *Agricultural Adjustment, A Report of Administration of the Agricultural Adjustment Act, May 1933 to Feb. 1934* (Washington, D.C., 1934), 328–29. Increasing fertilization after the 1933 plan was announced did not significantly affect the size of the 1933 crop. Perkins, *Crisis in Agriculture,* 111–12; *Memphis Commercial Appeal,* Aug. 16, 1933, 3; Peter Stubblefield to the editor of the *Memphis Commercial Appeal,* n.d. (1943) (Mississippian quotation), clipping in DPLCR. This letter was published in the *Commercial Appeal,* May 24, 1943, and was essentially reprinted in the *Jackson Clarion-Ledger.* See relevant materials and correspondence in the Henry A. Wallace Papers (FDRL), microfilm in the Univ. of Iowa Library, Iowa City.

26. Toler to OJ, July 26 (quotation), Aug. 18, 1933, DPLCR; *Memphis Commercial Appeal*, Aug. 9, 1933, 1, 2; *Greenville Daily Democrat-Times*, July 20, 1933, 1; Aug. 8, 1933, 1; *Memphis Press-Scimitar*, Aug. 8, 1933, 1; Stubblefield letter in *Memphis Commercial Appeal*, clipping in DPLCR and in Wallace Papers (FDRL), microfilm in Univ. of Iowa Library (descriptive quotations). See also Martha Swain, *Pat Harrison: The New Deal Years* (Jackson, Miss., 1978), 54.

27. *Memphis Commercial Appeal*, Aug. 9, 1933, 1, 12; *Memphis Press-Scimitar*, Aug. 8, 1933, 1; Aug. 9, 1933, 1, 2; *Greenville Daily Democrat-Times*, Aug. 8, 1933, 1; OJ to Toler, Aug. 26 (quotation), 28, 1933; Toler to OJ, Aug. 18, 26, Sept. 27, Oct. 14, 1933; Wild, "History," DPLCR.

28. *New York Times*, Aug. 9, 1933, 27; *Senate ACCA Hearings*, 97–98; see also C. A. Cobb to Chester Davis, Aug. 25, 1933, memorandum; OJ to Herman Oliphant, Aug. 25, 1933; Alger Hiss, Nov. 1, 1933, memorandum, PCP, RG 145, NA; *Memphis Commercial Appeal*, June 24, 1933, 2; OJ to Mary Oglesby, May 29, 1933, DPLCR.

## 4. Ten-Cent Rescue

1. *New York Times*, July 4, 1933, 20; *Memphis Commercial Appeal*, June 24, 1933, 1–2; Richards, *Cotton Under the AAA*, 20–21; see also Perkins, *Crisis in Agriculture*, 106.

2. *Time*, Sept. 25, 1933, 9; *New York Times*, Sept. 13, 1933, 3; Sept. 15, 1933, 5; Arthur M. Schlesinger Jr., *The Coming of the New Deal* (Boston, 1958), 236–37 (Harrison quoted in Schlesinger, 236, and *Time*; partially quoted in Swain, *Pat Harrison*, 59).

3. Smith to Roosevelt, Sept. 11, 1933, telegram, GC, RG 16, NA; *New York Times*, Sept. 13, 1933, 34; Bankhead to Roosevelt, Aug. 21, 1933, OF 258, FDRL; *Time*, Sept. 25, 1933, 9.

4. *Time*, Sept. 25, 1933, 9; Oct. 2, 1933, 9 (quotation); see also Schlesinger, *The Coming of the New Deal*, 236; Porter interview.

5. *Time*, Sept. 25, 1933, 9; Oct. 2, 1933, 9; OJ to Peek, Sept. 22, 1933, memorandum, OF 258, FDRL; *Memphis Commercial Appeal*, Sept. 23, 1933, 1; *New York Times*, Sept. 13, 1933, 34; Sept. 19, 1933, 1; Schlesinger, *The Coming of the New Deal*, 236–37.

6. Wallace to C. R. Cooksey, Aug. 23, 1933, Loans, RG 16, NA; *Memphis Commercial Appeal*, Sept. 23, 1933, 1; Jesse Jones, with Edward Angly, *Fifty Billion Dollars: My Thirteen Years with the RFC* [1932–45] (New York, 1951), 89; Schlesinger, *The Coming of the New Deal*, 61; OJ to Peek, Sept. 22, 1933, memorandum (Johnston quotation), OF 258, FDRL; Frank, COHC; see Johnston, Memorandum on Ten Cent Cotton Loan, n.d. (Oct. 1933), and working draft, Oct. 12, 1933 (originally prepared for Louis Bean), attached to Mordecai Ezekiel to Stanley Reed, Oct. 17, 1933, GC, RG 16, NA.

7. *Time*, Oct. 2, 1933, 9; see Johnston, Memorandum on the Ten Cent Cotton Loan, n.d. (Oct. 1933), and working draft, Oct. 12, 1933 (originally prepared to Louis Bean), attached to Ezekiel to Reed, Oct. 17, 1933, GC, RG 16, NA; *New York Times*, Sept. 22, 1933, 27; Sept. 23, 1933, 1; see also Sept. 21, 1933, 1; Richards, *Cotton and the AAA*, 213–14; Wallace, *New Frontiers*, 58.

8. Frank, COHC; Wallace, *New Frontiers*, 59; Paul Warburg, COHC.

9. Jones, with Angly, *Fifty Billion Dollars*, 88–89; *Memphis Press-Scimitar*, Oct. 17, 1933, 1; Richards, *Cotton and the AAA*, 214–15; Frank, COHC, Paul A. Porter interview with James Ward, Feb. 2, 1968 (at the time of this interview, Ward was assistant to the administrator of the Agricultural Stabilization and Conservation Service. The author wishes to acknowledge Mr. Ward's generosity in giving the author a copy of

that transcript as well as permission to use it. In the interview with the author in 1975, Porter recounted incidents covered in the Ward interview, there being some differences in Porter's recollection. In the exchange between Frank and Porter over the CCC charter, the thrust of the statements are reversed but the issue of the breadth of the charter remains the essential point. The Ward version is employed in this instance.); see Wallace and Morgenthau to Roosevelt, Oct. 10, 1933, GC, RG 145, NA; Frank to Glenn McHugh, Oct. 2, 1933, memorandum, PCP, RG 145, NA; Johnston, memorandum on ten-cent cotton loan, n.d. (Oct. 1933), and working draft (originally prepared for Louis Bean), Oct. 12, 1933, attached to Ezekiel to Reed, Oct. 17, 1933, GC, RG 16, NA. During his 1968 interview with James Ward, Paul Porter had "no explicit recollection" of the broadening of the title of CCC but did "have a vague recollection that Oscar Johnston, with whom I was working very intimately . . . at this time, did say after a White House meeting, let's make this broad enough so it will cover the spectrum and I would not be surprised if that suggestion did not come from President Roosevelt, although I have no hard evidence or recollections that this was true."

10. Porter interview; Porter interview with Ward; Jones, with Angly, *Fifty Billion Dollars*, 88–89; Wallace, *New Frontiers*, 59 (quotation); Wallace and Morgenthau to Roosevelt, Oct. 10, 1933, GC, RG 145, NA; *Memphis Press-Scimitar*, Oct. 17, 1933, 1; Richards, *Cotton and the AAA*, 214; Kenneth McKellar to Roosevelt, Oct. 16, 1933, telegram, OF 258, FDRL; N. C. Williamson and E. F. Creekmore to Roosevelt, Oct. 16, 1933, transcribed telegram; notations regarding McKellar telegram, OF 736, FDRL. See copy of Executive Order 6340, Oct. 16, 1933, OF 736, FDRL, and RG RFC 161, NA; and in Rosenman, *The Public Papers and Addresses of Franklin D. Roosevelt*, 2:404–07.

11. Porter interview with Ward (first and third quotations); Porter interview (second quotation); Richard Lowitt, *George W. Norris: The Triumph of a Progressive* (Chicago and London, 1978), 115; Joseph Goulden, *The Superlawyers: The Small and Powerful World of the Great Washington Law Firms* (New York, 1971), 110–43; *Washington Post*, Nov. 27, 1975, B, 18; *Los Angeles Times*, Nov. 27, 1975, II, 4; see OJ to Toler, Oct. 6, 1933, DPLCR. The account is from the typed transcript of Porter's interview with Ward in 1968. As before, differences exist between Porter's 1968 and 1975 interviews, but in this story they are both understandable and nonessential. Porter possessed a pleasant humor that enhanced his ability at recounting anecdotes. After his death in 1975, *Time* called him an "eminent Washington lawyer and raconteur," *Time*, Dec. 8, 1975, 86. Porter liked to quote his old friend and law partner, Thurmond Arnold, who once said, "I'm now an old man and I've been asked to reminisce, but . . . please don't check up on me too carefully, because perhaps the things I remember the best never happened at all." But of his trip with Johnston, Porter declared to the author that he would "never forget it." Porter interview (as in many anecdotes, errors of fact may creep in, as in Johnston's alleged service with Lew Douglas on the board of Illinois Central Railroad; Johnston's service on the board came later than the incident described); see also Arnold anecdote in Porter interview with Ward. Joseph Goulden had a rather jaundiced view: "Arnold and Porter's founding partners are a classic case of New Dealism gone sour: reformers who defected to climb over the battlements and join the 'economic royalists' they had fought so vigorously for FDR," Goulden, *The Superlawyers*, 110.

12. Executive Order No. 6340, Oct. 16, 1933, in Rosenman, *The Public Papers and Addresses of Franklin D. Roosevelt*, 2:404–6; Oscar Johnston, "Pool and Loan Holdings Are Explained by Oscar Johnston," *Cotton Digest*, May 23, 1936, 5; Richards, *Cotton*

*Under the AAA,* 95n; Richards, *Cotton and the AAA,* 214, 216; Wallace, *New Frontiers,* 59; Porter interview; Porter interview with Ward (quotations); Saloutos, *The American Farmer and the New Deal,* 69; CCC Minutes (Incorporators), Oct. 18, 1933, 1–2, 7; CCC Minutes (Board of Directors), Oct. 18, 1933, 1–2, RG 161, NA; Peek and Wallace to Roosevelt, Oct. 19, 1933; Roosevelt to CCC, Nov. 8, 1933, OF 736, FDRL; draft of letter prepared by OJ for Marvin McIntyre, to be sent to Jed Johnson, n.d. (Dec. 1934), OF 258, FDRL. The reference to the Illinois Central Railroad is erroneous. Johnston did not become a member of the board of directors of the rail line until 1940. *New York Times,* Apr. 19, 1940, 34.

13. House Committee on Appropriations, *Hearing Before the Subcommittee of the House Committee on Appropriations (Agriculture Department Appropriation Bill for 1935),* 73d Cong., 2d sess., 1934, 1039–40 (hereinafter cited as *House Subcommittee Appropriations Hearing, 1935*); OJ to Roosevelt, Nov. 8, 1933, OF 736, FDRL; *Senate ACCA Hearings,* 77, 81–82; Johnston, "Origin and Operation," 116–17; memorandum by Francis Shea, n.d., OJ to Frank, Oct. 31, 1933, memorandum; Nov. 16, 1933, memorandum, PCP, RG 145, NA; see *Time,* Nov. 20, 1933, 16.

14. *Time,* Nov. 20, 1933, 16; *House Subcommittee Appropriations Hearing, 1935,* 1039–40; Johnston, "Origin and Operation," 117, 138; *Senate ACCA Hearing,* 81–82; OJ to Roosevelt, Nov. 8, 1933; FDR to CCC, Oct. 20, 1933; Nov. 8, 1933; Wallace and Peek to FDR, Oct. 19, 1933, OF 738, FDRL (copy also in Minutes, Special Meeting of the Executive Committee, Nov. 16, 1933, RG 161, NA); *Memphis Press-Scimitar,* Nov. 13, 1933, 2; OJ to Guaranty Trust Co. of New York, and Chase National Bank, Nov. 13, 1933, AAA, CLD, RG 16, NA; A. W. McCain to Wallace, Nov. 23, 1933 (copy); Z. B. Curtis to Wallace, Nov. 23, 1933 (copy), GC, RG 16, GC, NA; OJ to Frank, Oct. 31, Nov. 6, (two), 11 (and eight-page attachment), 16, 20, 1933, memorandums, PCP, RG 145, NA (for memorandum of Nov. 16, 1933, see also in AAA, CLD, RG 16, NA); OJ to Peek, Nov. 2, 4, 1933, memorandums; OJ to Wallace, Nov. 3, Dec. 4, 1933, memorandums; OJ to Glenn McHugh, Nov. 9, 10, 16, 17, 1933, memorandums, PCP, RG 145, NA; (OJ to Wallace, Nov. 3 and Dec. 4, 1933, memorandums, and OJ to McHugh, Nov. 10, 1933, memorandum, also in GC, RG 16, NA); OJ to Lynn Talley, Nov. 7, 1933, PCP, RG 145, NA; OJ to Robert A. Cooper, Dec. 7, 1933; OJ to Cooper, Dec. 7, 1933, memorandum, AAA, CLD, RG 16, NA; OJ, Nov. 7, 1933, memorandum, PCP, RG 145, NA; Frank to OJ, Nov. 16, 17, 1933, memorandums, PCP, RG 145, NA (memorandum of Nov. 16, 1933, also in AAA, CLD, RG 16, NA); OJ to Toler, Nov. 6, 9, 16, 20, 27, 1933, DPLCR; AAA press releases, Nov. 20, Dec. 18, 1933, PCP, RG 145, NA; and Dec. 20, 1933, AAA, CLD, RG 16, NA; *Washington Post,* Dec. 12, 1933, clipping in PCP, RG 145, NA. For copy of option and pool agreement, and other relevant documents, see PCP, RG 145, NA.

15. Johnston, "Origin and Operation," 117, 138; *Senate ACCA Hearing,* 77–78, 82–83.

16. OJ to Roosevelt, Nov. 8, 1933, OF 736, FDRL; AAA press release, Dec. 20, 1933, AAA, CLD, RG 16, NA.

17. Johnston, "Origin and Operation," 138; OJ to Toler, Jan. 12, 1934, DPLCR; see Alston Garside, "Government Activities in Cotton—Part 2(a)," *Cotton Digest* Jan. 11, 1936, 5–7; Dan Ring to Marvin McIntyre, Nov. 24, 1933, GC, RG 16, NA; Charles H. Hyde, New England Cotton Industry Request for Storage, n.d., enclosed with Charles Hyde to Roosevelt, Nov. 1, 1933, OF 258, FDRL; *Newsweek,* Dec. 30, 1933, 9; see OJ to FCSDA, Dec. 26, 1933, DPLCR.

18. *Memphis Press-Scimitar,* Dec. 9, 1933, 12; Dec. 11, 1933, 6 (quotation); *New York Times,* Dec. 3, 1933, IV, 1 (story by Thomas Fauntleroy); Johnston, "What Hap-

pened? and What Next?" 13; see OJ to Toler, Nov. 27, 1933, DPLCR; see also OJ to Peek, Dec. 28, 1933; OJ to Cully Cobb, Dec. 28, 1933, telegram; and Cobb to OJ, Dec. 28, 1933, GC, RG 145, NA.

19. Johnston, "Origin and Operation," 138; *Senate ACCA Hearing,* 85; Wallace to E. J. Bodman, Dec. 22, 1933, GC, RG 145, NA (copy also in GC, RG 16, NA); *Memphis Press-Scimitar,* Dec. 8, 1933, 8 (quotation); see also Dec. 9, 1933, 12; Dec. 11, 1933, 1; Dec. 12, 1933, 8.

20. OJ to Toler, Jan. 17, 1934, DPLCR; *Senate ACCA Hearing,* 83; W. A. Jump, Dec. 7, 1933, memorandum; Wallace to Peek, Dec. 2, 1933, memorandum, GC, RG 145, NA; Davis to OJ, Feb. 5, 1934, memorandum; Davis to Buckles, Feb. 5, 1934, memorandum, GC, RG 145, NA; OJ to Chester Davis, July 20, 1934; William E. Byrd Jr. to OJ, July 25, 1934; OJ to Byrd, July 31, 1934, GC, RG 145, NA.

## 5. Acres, Not Bales

1. OJ to Wallace, Sept. 7, 1933, DPLCR; Report of proceedings at conference held in Memphis, Tenn., Sept. 5, 1933, to consider control of cotton production for the years 1934 and 1935, 8, PCP, RG 145, NA; *Memphis Commercial Appeal,* Aug. 16, 1933, 3; *Time,* Feb. 19, 1934, 13.

2. Richards, *Cotton and the AAA,* 186n; John Bankhead to Roosevelt, Aug. 21, 1933, OF 258, FDRL; Evans C. Johnson, "Bankhead Family," and Selden K. Smith, "Smith, Ellison Durant 'Cotton Ed,'" in *The Encyclopedia of Southern History,* ed. David C. Roller and Robert W. Twyman, 100–101, 1119 (Baton Rouge, 1979); *Time,* Feb. 19, 1934, 14; Walter J. Heacock, "William B. Bankhead and the New Deal," *Journal of Southern History* 21 (Aug. 1955): 347–49; report of the proceedings of conference held in Memphis; see also Dickson, *The Story of King Cotton,* 282–83; Evans C. Johnson, "John H. Bankhead 2d: Advocate of Cotton," *Alabama Review* 41 (Jan. 1988): 30–58.

3. Bankhead to Roosevelt, Aug. 21, 1933, OF 258, FDRL.

4. Roosevelt to Bankhead, Sept. 18, 1933, OF 258, FDRL; Wallace to Bankhead, Aug. 29, 1933, PCP, RG 145, NA; Wallace to William Danforth, July 17, 1934, GC, RG 16, NA; Cobb (to OJ), Nov. 27, 1934, memorandum, GC, RG 145, NA; OJ to Davis, Jan. 26, 1935, memorandum, LTF, RG 145, NA; Davis, COHC; OJ to Toler, Aug. 26, 1933, DPLCR; *Memphis Commercial Appeal,* Aug. 16, 1933, 3; Sept. 23, 1933, 11.

5. E. A. Miller to Chester Davis, Aug. 29, 1933, memorandum (with attached mutual drafts by Miller, Johnston, and Paul Porter), PCP, RG 145, NA; *Memphis Commercial Appeal,* Aug. 16, 1933, 3; Aug. 3, 1933, 21; Sept. 5, 1933, 1, 8; *Memphis Press-Scimitar,* Sept. 5, 1933, 1; OJ to Wallace, Sept. 6, 1933, DPLCR; OJ to Wallace, Sept. 6, 1933, telegram, PCP, RG 145, NA; *New York Times,* Sept. 10, 1933, IV, 8 (story by Thomas Fauntleroy); report of proceedings at conference held in Memphis, Tenn., PCP, RG 145, NA; OJ to Davis, Jan. 26, 1935, memorandum, LTF, RG 145, NA; Richards, *Cotton Under the AAA,* appendix, 121n; OJ to Davis, Nov. 23, 1934, GC, RG 145, NA; AAA press release, Jan. 26, 1934, OF 1K, FDRL; see also OJ to secretary of the treasury, Sept. 15, 1933, PCP, RG 145, NA; Richards, *Cotton and the AAA,* 355 (quotation); Committee on Agriculture, *Hearing on the Bankhead Cotton Control Bill,* 73d Cong., 2d sess., 1934, H.R. 8402 (and earlier drafts), serial 1 (hereinafter cited as *House Bankhead Hearing*).

6. Heacock, "William B. Bankhead and the New Deal," 351; Porter to Appleby, Jan. 15, 1934, memorandum, GC, RG 16, NA; AAA press release, Feb. 7, 1934, PCP, RG 145, NA; Richards, *Cotton Under the AAA,* appendix, 121n; OJ to Davis, Nov. 23, 1934, memorandum, GC, RG 145, NA; *House Bankhead Hearing.*

7. *House Bankhead Hearing,* 32, 45–49 (quotation on 49), 57, 69, 75 (Cobb's testimony and exhibit, 1–27; Wallace's testimony, 29–45); OJ to Wallace, Sept. 7, 1933, DPLCR; Committee on Agriculture and Forestry, *Hearings to Regulate the Production and Ginning of Cotton,* 73d Cong. 3d sess., 1934, 74–75.

8. *House Bankhead Hearing,* 46, 48, 49 (quotations), 57, 68; OJ to Wallace, Sept. 7, 1933, DPLCR.

9. *House Bankhead Hearing,* 46–47, 53, 77–78.

10. *Memphis Press-Scimitar,* Feb. 17, 1934, 1, 2 (quotation). For full text of Roosevelt's letter to Jones, Feb. 16, 1934, see *House Bankhead Hearing,* 139; *Time,* Feb. 26, 1934, 9. Congressman Bankhead was not totally wrong when he told Jones's committee that Johnston's criticism amounted to "matters of detail in effectuating the principle of compulsory control," *House Bankhead Hearing,* 143.

11. *Memphis Press-Scimitar,* Feb. 17, 1934, 2.

12. OJ to Wallace, Feb. 19, 1934; Wallace to Roosevelt, Feb. 26, 1934, OF 258, FDRL. On his letter Wallace scribbled a note to White House secretary Marvin MacIntyre: "Mac—Please pass this on HAW."

13. Bankhead to Roosevelt, Apr. 19, 1934, OF 258, FDRL; OJ to Stowell, Sept. 20, 1935; Jan. 14, 1936; Dec. 3, 1936; OJ to FCSDA, Dec. 28, 1936; OJ to Carlos Garcia-Mata, July 6, 1936; OJ to Toler, Feb. 10, 1934; OJ to C. G. Mears, Feb. 23, 1934 (last quotation, emphasis added), DPLCR; OJ to Wallace, Jan. 31, 1935, PCP, RG 145, NA; *House Bankhead Hearing,* 143; Mordecai Ezekiel to Henry Wallace, June 15, 1933, memorandum, GC, RG 145, NA.

14. OJ to Toler, Mar. 1, 1934; OJ to FCSDA, Apr. 12, 1934 (one of two); May 1, 1934; Toler to Stowell, Feb. 1, 1934; Toler to FCSDA, Apr. 3, 1934, DPLCR; *Congressional Record,* 73d Cong., 2d sess., 1934, 78, pt. 4:4195 (Doxey quotation); *Time,* Apr. 9, 1934, 16 (last two quotations); see also *Memphis Commercial Appeal,* Apr. 12, 1934, clipping in OF 258, FDRL.

15. High Lights from an Address Delivered by Hon. Oscar Johnston before the Greenville, Miss., Rotary Club on Feb. 22, 1934—From the *Daily Democrat-Times,* Greenville, Miss. (Preamble and resolutions adopted by the Board of Directors of The Chamber of Commerce, of Greenville, Washington County, Mississippi, on the 26th day of Feb., 1934), copy included with a letter from Will M. Whittington to Wallace, Mar. 2, 1934, GC, RG 16, NA; Oscar Johnston, "The Bankhead Bill," *Staple Cotton Review* 12 (Mar. 1934): 1–4; B. L. Mallory to Bankhead, Apr. 14, 1934; *Memphis Commercial Appeal,* Apr. 12, 1934, clipping in OF 258, FDRL; Southeast Missouri Planter to Wallace, Apr. 23, 1934, GC, RG 145, NA; see also relevant notation in GC, RG 145, NA. For the suggestion of unfair landlord-tenant practice, see C. C. Smith to Cobb, June 10, 1934, GC, RG 145, NA. Replying to the planter for Wallace, C. B. Baldwin pointed out Johnston's interest in higher American cotton prices, and added: "The Secretary of Agriculture and the officials of the Agricultural Adjustment Administration have every confidence not only in the integrity and sincerity of the purposes of Mr. Johnston but also highly respect his ability and knowledge of the cotton situation." Baldwin to Southeast Missouri Planter, May 3, 1934, GC, RG 145, NA.

16. S. W. Haaga to Bankhead, Apr. 20, 1934; J. J. Gunn to Bankhead, Apr. 12, 1934 ("weight" quotation); Bankhead to Wallace, Apr. 24, 1934, GC, RG 16, NA; Bankhead to Roosevelt, Apr. 19, 1934, OF 258, FDRL.

17. OJ to FCSDA, May 1, 1934, DPLCR. Nonexempt ginned cotton, stored in warehouses, remained subject to government liens in the amount of the tax. Richards, *Cotton Under the AAA,* 167, 185.

18. USDA, *Yearbook of Agriculture, 1935* (Washington, D.C., 1936), 696; OJ to FCSDA, July 17, 1934; June 14, 1935 (six-page letter); Stowell to OJ, Aug. 14, 21, 1934; see OJ to Stowell, June 11, 1934; Aug. 29, 1934, DPLCR; *Memphis Press-Scimitar,* Feb. 2, 1934, 14; George Bishop to Wallace, May 15, 1934; see OJ to Wallace, Jan. 31, 1935, memorandum, PCP, RG 145, NA; Franklin D. Roosevelt, Press Conferences, 14 (Sept. 21, 1934), 87, FDRL.

19. In 1931 Delta Pine purchased 1,345 tons of fertilizer; in 1932, 1,285 tons. Apparently, the pounds per acre ratio in 1934 was slightly higher than in either of those years. Toler to Mrs. A. H. Parks, Mar. 12, 1934; Parks to Toler, Mar. 15, 1934; OJ to FCSDA, Apr. 12 (one of two; quotations), 18, May 1, 1934; July 17, 1934; OJ to Stowell, Aug. 29, 1934; OJ to Herbert Lee, Sept. 10, 1934; see also OJ to FCSDA, July 6, 1934; OJ to Stowell, Nov. 16, 1934, DPLCR.

20. DPLC Production Record; OJ to Stowell, Nov. 16, 1934; OJ to Lee, Nov. 16, 1934, DPLCR.

21. Memorandum, Appleby to Cobb, Dec. 27, 1934, PCP, RG 145, NA.

22. Ibid.; Wallace to William Danforth, July 17, 1934, GC, RG 16, NA; Richards, *Cotton Under the AAA,* 174, 175n; OJ to FCSDA, May 1, 1934; Nov. 14, 1934; OJ to Stowell, Nov. 16, 1934; OJ to Lee, Nov. 16, 1934, DPLCR.

23. OJ to FCSDA, Dec. 11, 1934; OJ to Stowell, Dec. 21, 1934; see also Stowell to OJ, Dec. 7, 1934, DPLCR; *Time,* Dec. 10, 1934, 15; Dec. 24, 1934, 12; OJ to Cobb, Nov. 23, 1934; Cobb (to OJ), Nov. 27, 1934, memorandum, GC, RG 145, NA; Richards, *Cotton Under the AAA,* 188–93; *Memphis Press-Scimitar,* Dec. 15, 1934, 1 (quotation), 2.

24. OJ to FCSDA, June 14, 1934 (six-page letter; first quotation); OJ to Stowell, Sept. 20, 1935; Dec. 12, 1935; Dec. 16, 1935 (last quotation); see also Dec. 2, 13, 1935; OJ to FCSDA, Oct. 14, 1935; Jan. 1, 1936, DPLCR; OJ to Wallace, Jan. 31, 1935, memorandum, PCP, RG 145, NA; Saloutos, *The American Farmer and the New Deal,* 126.

25. OJ to Stowell, Dec. 12, 1935; OJ to Vernon Bellhouse, Dec. 26, 1935 (first quotation); OJ to Stowell, Feb. 6, 1936 (third quotation); Toler to Stowell, Jan. 15, 1936 (second quotation), DPLCR; see *Memphis Commercial Appeal,* Jan. 7, 1935, 1; *Memphis Press-Scimitar,* Jan. 6, 1936, 1; see *Senate Disposition of Cotton Hearings,* 15.

26. Ironically, if litigation proved too late for quick disposition, Johnston planned to momentarily absorb the defeat by paying the tax and marketing the surplus cotton from the 1935 crop. OJ to Stowell, Dec. 12, 1935; Jan. 14, 30, 1936; Feb. 6, 1936, DPLCR; *New York Times,* Jan. 7, 1936, 12; Feb. 4, 1936, 1; Feb. 5, 1936, 1, 6; Feb. 6, 1936, 4. The market slipped in February of the release of former Bankhead cotton. Committee on Agriculture and Forestry, *Hearings Before the Committee on Agriculture and Forestry, on Senate Joint Resolution 205, A Joint Resolution Providing for the Disposition of Certain Cotton Held by the United States,* 74th Cong., 2d sess., 1936, 15 (hereinafter cited as *Senate Disposition of Cotton Hearings*).

27. OJ to Stowell, Feb. 6, 15, 20 (first quotation), 1936; Statement and President's Report (1935), Apr. 27, 1936 (second quotation), DPLCR.

28. Blake Interviews; OJ to Wallace, Jan. 31, 1935, memorandum, PCP, RG 145, NA; OJ to Mears, Feb. 23, 1934, DPLCR.

## 6. An Ounce of Remedy, a Pound of Reform

1. Lord, *The Wallaces of Iowa,* 406; LeCron's diary entry is contained in James LeCron, COHC.

2. See Grubbs, *Cry from the Cotton,* 30–61; Conrad, *Forgotten Farmers,* 136–53; Saloutos, *The American Farmer and the New Deal,* 105–6; Lord, *The Wallaces of Iowa,* 393–409; Bernard Sternsher, *Rexford Tugwell and the New Deal* (New Brunswick, N.J., 1964), 198–207; Schlesinger, *The Coming of the New Deal,* 77–81; Richard S. Kirkendall, *Social Scientists and Farm Politics in the Age of Roosevelt* (Columbia, Mo., 1966), 98–103; Edward L. and Frederick H. Shapsmeier, *Henry A. Wallace of Iowa: The Agrarian Years* (Ames, Iowa, 1968), 202–4; Irons, *New Deal Lawyers,* 157–80; M. S. Venkataramni, "Arkansas Sharecroppers," 225–46; and Gladys Baker, "'And to Act for the Secretary': Paul Appleby and the Department of Agriculture, 1933–1940," *Agricultural History* 45 (Oct. 1971): 235–58. Richard Lowitt has published significant excerpts from Wallace's diary, as well as other materials, in "Henry A. Wallace and the 1935 Purge in the Department of Agriculture," *Agricultural History* 53 (July 1979): 607–21. These materials, where appropriate, may be compared with Wallace, COHC. For LeCron's view see his COHC. For a helpful review of Grubbs's volume, see that by Thomas A. Krueger in the *Journal of Southern History* 37 (Nov. 1971): 667–68.

3. *Memphis Commercial Appeal,* July 22, 1934, II, 3. For a discussion of southern social and economic conditions, see Gunnar Myrdal, *An American Dilemma: The Negro Problem and Modern Democracy* (New York, 1944), 230–78; and John Dollard, *Caste and Class in a Southern Town* (New Haven, 1937).

4. *Memphis Press-Scimitar,* Feb. 19, 1934, 12 (first quotation); Feb. 20, 1934, 8 (second quotation).

5. *Memphis Press-Scimitar,* Feb. 19, 1934, 12.

6. East and Mitchell to OJ, Feb. 19, 1934; OJ to East and Mitchell, Feb. 20, 1934, DPLCR; Norman Thomas, *The Plight of the Share-Cropper* (New York, 1934), 11.

7. OJ to East and Mitchell, Feb. 20, 1934, DPLCR.

8. *Memphis Press-Scimitar,* Mar. 12, 1934, 8; see Grubbs, *Cry from the Cotton,* 28–29; Conrad, *Forgotten Farmers,* 82; Venkataramni, "Arkansas Sharecroppers," 225–46.

9. Howard Kester, *Revolt Among the Sharecroppers* (New York, 1936), 70 (quotation); see Grubbs, *Cry from the Cotton,* and Conrad, *Forgotten Farmers,* for discussions of the Norcross case and related developments. But also see what appears to be a denial of the charges in Hiram Norcross to William R. Amberson, Nov. 28, 1934, William R. Amberson Papers, Southern Historical Collection, Univ. of North Carolina Library, Chapel Hill. Thomas later claimed "that the Western Union Company in Arkansas turned over copies of all my telegrams to [Sen.] Joseph Robinson [D-Ark.], so that he would know what was going on. That's the way things are done down there. Lawyers were intimidated from taking cases. It was quite a small reign of terror. You never knew when a meeting was going to be broken up," Thomas COHC; see also Thomas to Roosevelt, Mar. 15, 1936, telegram (copy), OF 1K, FDRL.

10. See Grubbs, *Cry from the Cotton*; Conrad, *Forgotten Farmers*; USDA, 1934 and 1935 Cotton Acreage Reduction Contract, copy in Amberson Papers; see also copy in *Memphis Commercial Appeal,* Nov. 30, 1933, 4.

11. For the particulars of the case one may consult several secondary works includ-

ing those by Lord, Conrad, and Grubbs. For context, primary sources such as, but not limited to, Davis, COHC, Wallace, COHC, and primary materials in Lowitt, "Wallace and the 1935 Purge," may also be consulted.

12. Davis to Wallace, Feb. 4, 1935, memorandum (quotation), LTF, RG 145, NA; see also Davis, COHC, and Conrad, *Forgotten Farmers,* 152–53.

13. Grubbs, *Cry from the Cotton,* 42.

14. OJ to Davis, Jan. 26, 1935, memorandum (including quoted excerpt of Cobb to Davis, Sept. 28, 1933, memorandum, quoted there; "requested" quotation), LTF, RG 145, NA; OJ to Toler, Aug. 26, 1933, DPLCR; Frank to Peek, Sept. 8, 1933, memorandum, in Lowitt, "Wallace and the 1935 Purge," 620; OJ to Peek, Oct. 26, 1933, memorandum, PCP, RG 145, NA (also quoted in OJ to Davis, Jan. 26, 1935, memorandum, LTF, RG 145, NA).

15. OJ to Davis, Jan. 26, 1935, memorandum, LTF, RG 145, NA (first two and last quotations, including excerpt of Davis to Peek, Nov. 11, 1933, memorandum [emphasis added]); OJ to Amberson, quoted in Amberson to Paul Appleby, Nov. 21, 1934, PCP, RG 145, NA (emphasis added); USDA, 1934 and 1935 Cotton Acreage Reduction Contract, copy in Amberson Papers; Hiss interview (telephone); Hiss to author, Aug. 21, 1979; Hiss to Frank, Jan. 26, 1935, memorandum, LTF, RG 145, NA; see also *Memphis Commercial Appeal,* Nov. 30, 1933, 4. In a letter apparently by Amberson, he declared "Section 7 of this contract was written by Mr. Oscar Johnston, of Scott, Miss.," Amberson (?) to "Bob," Nov. 18, 1934, Amberson Papers.

16. Thomas, COHC; Amberson to Harry Mitchell, Feb. 22, 1934; Amberson to Thomas, Feb. 22, 1934; Amberson to OJ, Oct. 21, 1934, Nov. 23, 1934; Amberson to Norcross, Nov. 23, 1934; Norcross to Amberson, Nov. 28, 1934; Vance to Amberson, Nov. 9 (quotation), 29, 1934, Amberson Papers; see also "Rough draft of letter sent to Mr. Jerome Frank in the summer of 1934 by William R. Amberson," Amberson Papers.

17. Amberson to OJ, Oct. 21, 1934, Amberson Papers. Johnston quoted by Amberson in latter's letter to Paul Appleby, Nov. 21, 1934, PCP, RG 145, NA; Vance to Amberson, Nov. 29, 1934, Amberson Papers.

18. Grubbs, *Cry from the Cotton,* 60; see Porter interview; Hiss interview; confidential interview 3.

19. For developments, see Conrad, *Forgotten Farmers;* Porter interview; Frank to Wallace, Jan. 10, 1935, memorandum, GC, RG 16, NA. Peek, with Crowther, *Why Quit Our Own?* 22, 113–21.

20. Frank to Wallace, Jan. 10, 1935, memorandum, GC, RG 16, NA; Porter interview (anecdote quotations). On legal realism and sociological jurisprudence, see Alfred Kelly, Winfred Harbison, and Herman Belz, *The American Constitution: Its History and Development,* 7th ed., 2 vols. (New York and London, 1991), 2:454–55.

21. See Porter interview; confidential interview 3; Frank, COHC.

22. Frank to Wallace, Jan. 10, 1935, memorandum, GC, RG 16, NA (italics added).

23. Porter interview; Dunn interview. Johnston told Paul Porter: "one of the two of us has got to survive," since nobody else knew about the cotton pool program; Porter interview. See also Wallace to Roosevelt, Feb. 26, 1934 (including Wallace's handwritten note to Marvin McIntyre on the letter), OF 258, FDRL. Wallace was also concerned about the southern congressional delegation if the liberals prevailed. Conrad, *Forgotten Farmers,* 146–47.

24. OJ to Davis, Jan. 26, 1935, memorandum, LTF, RG 145, NA. In his *Forgotten Farmers,* Conrad may be hinting at hidden motives of at least some of the liberals: "The influence of [Lee] Pressman and Hiss was strong in the Legal Division. Although the official correspondence of these two, plus that of [Nathan] Witt and [John] Abt, seems to reflect no particular political viewpoints, nonetheless, they played an important part in the division in early 1935 to make a rash and dangerous move on behalf of the Southern tenant farmers. It was an action *well calculated* to disrupt the entire cotton program, cause trouble in the plantation areas, and tear AAA apart" (109; italics added). It is unclear what is meant by "well calculated," and, in fairness, this passage is found in the context of communism within the AAA. But any implication that disruption formed a motive for a variant interpretation of Paragraph 7 remains dubious. Pressman, Witt, and Abt "had nothing to do with the reduction program and were fully occupied with their own responsibilities," Hiss argued later. "There was certainly no intent on anyone's part to disrupt the cotton programs, etc. On the contrary, the fear of Chester (and I now see Oscar, too) and Cully Cobb that vigorous attempts to enforce the retention of tenants obligation would disrupt the program is what led to the purge and to the acquiescence in nullification of par. 7 however interpreted." Hiss to author, Aug. 21, 1979. Conrad seems to believe that after the contract was issued, any liberal interpretation was hopeless, even calling the liberals' move to side with tenants "rash and dangerous" (109); see *Forgotten Farmers.*

25. Hiss to author, Aug. 21, 1979 (first two quotations); Hiss to Frank, Jan. 26, 1935, memorandum (last quotation); see also Francis Shea to Robert McConnaughey, Feb. 4, 1935, memorandum, LTF, RG 145, NA.

26. OJ to Wallace, Feb. 6, 1935, GC, RG 16, NA (italics added). Curiously, Johnston complained to Wallace that "a requirement that identical labor be maintained on the plantation is almost impossible of compliance. It would be utterly one-sided regulation, since the tenant may move at will. . . . If the laborer sees fit to move he may do so, and the landowner who attempts to restrain him subjects himself to prosecution for 'peonage.'" The legal division did not argue for such a regulation (see Hiss to author, Aug. 21, 1979); no one did. If Johnston was reacting to such a nonexistent threat, perhaps an opportunity for accommodation on both sides was missed. Johnston may have used the argument as a red herring.

27. Wallace diary, Feb. 4–6, 1935, in Lowitt, "Wallace and the 1935 Purge," 614–16; see also Wallace, COHC; and C. H. Alvord to Cobb, Apr. 17, 1934, memorandum, LTF, RG 145, NA; see Grubbs, *Cry from the Cotton,* 57. A problem of interpretation arises over Wallace's view of the firing of Jerome Frank a few days after the purge. He evidently came to believe that Frank's "connection with the interpretation of Section 7 is quite remote indeed," and that Frank may have been a victim of an "injustice." Had Wallace believed that before the purge, would he have allowed Frank's dismissal? Given the deep personality and ideological rift, it seems quite likely that he would have. See Wallace, Feb. 9, 11, 1935, in Lowitt, "Wallace and the 1935 Purge," 617–19; Wallace, COHC.

28. Wallace diary, Feb. 2, 1935; see J. D. Black to Wallace, Feb. 2, 1935, Lowitt, "Wallace and the 1935 Purge," 612–13; Wallace, COHC; Davis, COHC.

29. Wallace diary, Feb. 11, 1935, in Lowitt, "Wallace and the 1935 Purge," 619; Wallace, COHC.

30. *Memphis Commercial Appeal,* June 23, 1933, 1; Conrad, *Forgotten Farmers,* 152–53; and P. W. Wilson to Peek, June 27, 1933, telegram; GC, RG 145, NA. What planters would have done or not done if the liberals had won is a matter of informed speculation.

What is clear is that a scholar who critiques the purge essentially from the perspective of another generation risks methodological error. One such scholar compared New Deal reform of Wall Street and the old competitive ideal—for which there was much popular support—with potential reform of the cotton system. He argues that "the AAA liberals were not trying to overhaul the entire plantation system. In the controversy over Section 7, they were not even trying to improve it. *They were merely trying to make sure that AAA crop reduction did not worsen the situation and for this they were fired.*" All the liberals would have demanded of the planter, he argues, was "not that they keep exactly the same tenants; only that they show cause for any evictions. Are we to assume that planters would sabotage a program so overwhelmingly favorable to them, so heartily approved by them, simply out of anger at being made to show cause for evicting tenants? The author cannot believe that Southern landlords were quite that selfish and vindictive." Grubbs, *Cry from the Cotton*, 60–61 (emphasis in original). The fact remains that the liberals' rendering of Paragraph 7 was seen as a change during the life of the contract. And it is simply not true that the liberals did not wish to use Paragraph 7 as an instrument of reform, although it is difficult to know precisely what is meant by not overhauling "the entire plantation system" or "not even trying to improve it."

31. Hiss to author, Aug. 21, 1979 (first emphasis added); Porter interview; see Schlesinger, *The Coming of the New Deal*, 79.

32. OJ to Davis, Feb. 14, 1934, memorandum, PCP, RG 145, NA; OJ to Cobb, June 4, 1937, GC, RG 145, NA.

33. *Memphis Press-Scimitar,* Dec. 9, 1933, 12; OJ to Progress Manufacturing Co., Mar. 14, 26, 1931; OJ to Minneapolis-Moline Implement Co., May 3, 1933; see V. (?) J. Dannreuther to OJ, Apr. 29, 1933; see also Statement(s) and President's Report(s) during the 1940s; "Johnston, Operating Schedule, Delta and Pine Land Company, Under Proposed Agricultural Adjustment Program for 1934" (typed three-page manuscript, Sept. 23, 1933), DPLCR; Gray interviews; Johnston's statement in *House Bankhead Hearing*, 71; Betty Carter, "Mules in the Delta," in *Mules and Mississippi* (Jackson, Miss., 1980), 37–38.

34. Grubbs, *Cry from the Cotton*, 60.

35. OJ to Toler, Mar. 2, May 2 (quotation), 1934, DPLCR.

36. *Memphis Commercial Appeal,* Feb. 12, 1935, 1. The pragmatic view of the purge has long been recognized by scholars (see those cited in note 2). Davis, COHC; LeCron, COHC. It has also been suggested that Wallace's response reflected his "presidential ambitions," Lowitt, "Wallace and the 1935 Purge," 609–10; Tugwell, *Roosevelt's Revolution*, 198–99, 206, 298–99; see also Saloutos, *The American Farmer and the New Deal*, 251–52. For Wallace's public view nineteen years later, see *U.S. News & World Report,* Jan. 8, 1954, 42.

37. Thomas, COHC; Stedman to Wallace, Feb. 25, 1936, memorandum, PCP, RG 145, NA; see the implications of Grubbs's argument in *Cry from the Cotton*, 59–61. Conrad seems clear that the liberals missed their opportunity when the contract was drafted and that nothing could be done after the fact. See Conrad, *Forgotten Farmers*, 109, 152–53.

38. Tugwell's question is in Norman Thomas, *After the New Deal, What?* (New York, 1936), 36; Thomas's reply, and the identification of Tugwell as the questioner, is in Thomas, COHC. The question in COHC varies from that in Thomas's 1936 book, but the thrust is the same. Thomas, COHC ("was right" quotation and FDR anecdote). See also Frank Friedel, *FDR and the South* (Baton Rouge, 1965), 65–66.

39. Richard S. Kirkendall, *The United States, 1929–1945: Years of Crisis and Change* (New York, 1974), 155; OJ to Lamar Fleming Jr., Apr. 6, 1943, DPLCR.

## 7. Welfare Capitalist

1. OJ to Percy, Nov. 10, 1938 (quotations), DPLCR; see also Bledsoe interviews. Percy had thought Johnston underrated "the amount of dishonesty practiced by land-lords in this section in their settlements with their tenants," Percy to OJ, Nov. 8, 1938, DPLCR. In his memoirs, Percy pointed to the black tenant's vulnerability: "Share-crop-ping is one of the best systems ever devised to give security and a chance for profit to the simple and the unskilled. It has but one drawback—it must be administered by human beings to whom it offers an unusual opportunity to rob without detection or punishment. The failure is not in the system itself—the failure is in not living up to the contractual obligations of the system—the failure is in human nature. The Negro is no more on an equality with the white man in plantation matters than in any other deal-ings between the two. The white planter may charge an exorbitant rate of interest, he may cheat him in a thousand different ways, and the Negro's redress is merely theo-retical. If the white planter happens to be a crook, the share-cropper system on that plantation is bad for Negroes, as any other system would be. They are prey for the dis-honest and temptation for the honest." Still, Percy thought there were lots of honest landlords; Percy, *Lanterns on the Levee*, 282. In 1942 Johnston told an attorney friend in Mississippi, "I have had occasion, unofficially, to review the record in a good many tenant-landlord controversies that have arisen in connection with the agricultural pro-gram, and frankly I have found very flagrant cases of abuse. In some instances the abuse was from the landlord to the tenant; in others, from the tenant to the landlord. I have also found that usually the sympathy of the Department [of Agriculture] has been with the tenant, just as I have frequently found the sympathies of our courts to be with what the courts have seen fit to term 'the weaker party' to the proceeding," OJ to Forrest Cooper, July 11, 1942, DPLCR.

2. OJ to Stowell, Dec. 17, 1936 (six-page letter), DPLCR.

3. *New York Times*, Dec. 14, 1935, 2; Jan. 7, 1937, 28; *Clarksdale Register and Daily News*, Mar. 10, 1937, 4; *Memphis Press-Scimitar*, Mar. 9, 1937, 7 (Johnston quo-tation; these two latter newspapers contain slightly different quotations from Johnston); Herman Clarence Nixon to William R. Amberson, Jan. 9, 1937, Amberson Papers; see Johnston et al., *A Review of the Special Farm Tenancy Committee's Report, House Document No. 149, by The Committee on Agriculture, Delta Chamber of Commerce*, Mar. 29, 1937 (Stoneville, Miss.), 4, copy in DPLCR; and Rhea Blake to L. C. Gray, Jan. 11, 1937, and accompanying preamble and resolutions to the National Tenancy Commission from the Delta Chamber of Commerce, Jan. 11, 1937; Gray to Blake, Jan. 18, 1937, President's Commission on Farm Tenancy, RG 83, NA. Johnston served as chairman of Delta Chamber of Commerce Subcommittee on Tenancy. OJ to Percy, Nov. 10, 1938, DPLCR.

4. *Memphis Press-Scimitar*, May 21, 1935, 6; for discussions of tenancy, see Conrad, *Forgotten Farmers*; Grubbs, *Cry from the Cotton*; Louis Cantor, "A Prologue to the Protest Movement: The Missouri Sharecropper Roadside Demonstration of 1939," *Journal of American History* 55 (Mar. 1969): 804–22; Cantor, *A Prologue to the Protest Movement: The Missouri Sharecropper Roadside Demonstration of 1939* (Durham, N.C., 1969); Harry L. Mitchell, *Mean Things Happening in This Land: The Life and Times of H. L. Mitchell, Co-Founder of the Southern Tenant Farmers Union* (Montclair, N.J., 1979); T. J. Woofter Jr. and A. E. Fisher, *The Plantation South Today*, WPA, Social Prob-

lems Series Number 5 (Washington, D.C., 1940); T. J. Woofter Jr., William C. Holley, and Ellen Winston, *The Plantation South, 1934–1937,* WPA, Research Monograph 5 (Washington, D.C., 1940); E. L. Langsford and B. H. Thibodeaux, *Plantation Organization and Operation in the Yazoo–Mississippi Delta Area,* USDA Technical Bulletin 682 (Washington, D.C., 1939); Charles S. Johnson, Edwin R. Embree, and W. W. Alexander, *The Collapse of Cotton Tenancy: Summary of Field Studies and Statistical Surveys, 1933–35* (Chapel Hill, 1935); Charles S. Johnson, *Shadow of the Plantation* (Chicago, 1934); National Emergency Council, *Report on the Economic Conditions of the South*; Kester, *Revolt Among the Sharecroppers*; Thomas, *The Plight of the Share-Croppers*; James Agee and Walker Evans, *Let Us Now Praise Famous Men* (Boston, 1941); and others.

5. Hiss to author, Aug. 21, 1979; "Cotton's in the Well," *Fortune* 12 (July 1935): 41; Davis to Roosevelt, Mar. 19, 1935, memorandum, OF 1K, FDRL.

6. OJ to Frank A. Palen, May 15, 1937, DPLCR.

7. "Biggest Cotton Plantation," 132, 156; OJ to D. C. Trent, June 14, 1937, Region VI File, RG 96, NA; OJ to unit managers, Dec. 9, 1940, memorandum; Statement and President's Report (1939), Apr. 20, 1940; OJ to D. S. Lantrip, Nov. 15, 1937, DPLCR. See Betty W. Carter, "Mules in the Delta," William R. Ferris, "Mules in the South," and additional material in *Mules and Mississippi,* especially 37–38; also, Ralph Shlomowitz, "The Origins of Southern Sharecropping," *Agricultural History* 53 (July 1979): 557–75.

8. "Biggest Cotton Plantation," 126; Statement and President's Report (1942), Apr. 17, 1943; OJ to A. H. Ramsay, Apr. 16, 1942, OJ to B. M. McGriff, Jan. 29, 1943 (last quotation), DPLCR; *Senate ACCA Hearing,* 99; Minor Gray to author, Feb. 25, 1971; Gray interviews; Hatcher interview (Hatcher served as plantation store manager at Scott, Miss.); Johnston, Operating Schedule, DPLCR. See also "The World's Largest Cotton Plantation," *Manufacturers Record* 98 (Aug. 28, 1930), 50 (reprinted from *Staple Cotton Review*) A very small number of white tenants had been employed in tractor operations on the plantation; *House Bankhead Hearing,* 71, 78.

9. Brandfon, *Cotton Kingdom of the New South,* viii (first quotation). For geographical discussions of the Delta, see Langsford and Thibodeaux, *Plantation Operation and Organization in the Yazoo–Mississippi Delta Area*; Dorris, "The Yazoo Basin in Mississippi," 72–79; Harrison, *Alluvial Empire*; "Biggest Cotton Plantation," 156 (see map of Delta on 158); and Cobb, *The Most Southern Place on Earth,* 3–5.

10. "Biggest Cotton Plantation," 156 (see photograph of headquarters building on 126); OJ to Ralph Sitton, July 3, 1937; see also OJ to W. G. Henley, Sept. 7, 1940, DPLCR.

11. OJ to Alexander Fitzhugh, Nov. 29, 1937; OJ to Lantrip, Nov. 15, 1937, DPLCR; OJ to Trent, June 14, 1937, Region VI File, RG 96, NA; "Biggest Cotton Plantation," 156.

12. OJ to Lantrip, Nov. 15, 1937; OJ to Will Percy, Nov. 10, 1938; Toler to OJ, Nov. 22 ("buzzards" quotation), 25, 1933, DPLCR; OJ to D. C. Trent, June 14, 1937 (contracts quotation), Region VI File, RG 96, NA; see *St. Louis Post-Dispatch,* Jan. 25, 1933 (?), clipping in Amberson Papers; Hatcher interview; Gray interviews; Gray to author, Feb. 25, 1971; DPL, plantation census material, DPLCR. *Fortune's* declaration in 1937 that "about 28 percent of the cropper families manage to have some sort of automobile" is perhaps excessive, as was Johnston's claim that about a third of the tenants owned cars in 1939. Statement of Oscar Johnston Re Legislation Limiting Soil Conservation Payments (to the Senate Committee on Agriculture and Forestry, mimeographed, n.d., probably 1940), with OJ to I. W. Duggan, Feb. 19, 1940, LTF, RG 145, NA; "Biggest Cotton Plantation," 156 (text quotation), 160, see also 130; see DPLC settlement sheets

in Amberson Papers. It has also been suggested that blacks on the plantation owned cars "ranging from new cars to Model T's and other museum pieces," J. R. Hildebrand, "Machines Come to Mississippi," *National Geographic* 71 (Sept. 1937): 287. In 1937 one person who felt cheated by DPLC complained to Howard Tolley, AAA administrator, that "I do not think I have been paid according to the agreement and I have been charged with many things that I was not supposed to pay. . . . I do not think they have paid me near enough," farmer to Tolley, May 11, 1937 (copy); R. F. Croom to T. Y. Williford, May 14, 1937; Croom to farmer, May 14, 1937, GC, RG 145, NA.

13. Toler to OJ, Nov. 25, 1933, DPLCR; Hildebrand, "Machines Come to Mississippi," 287; "Biggest Cotton Plantation," 160; Hatcher interview; Gray interviews.

14. "Biggest Cotton Plantation," 156 (first quotation), 160 (last quotation); see also Daniels, *A Southerner Discovers the South,* 182; *Senate ACCA Hearing,* 99; U. B. Phillips, "The Central Theme of Southern History," *American Historical Review* 34 (Oct. 1928): 30–43; see Toler to OJ, July 25, 1937, DPLCR.

15. *St. Louis Post-Dispatch,* Jan. 28, 1935 (?), 1, 3 (quotation), clipping in Amberson Papers; see OJ to Stowell, Dec. 17, 1936 (six-page letter), DPLCR.

16. See "Biggest Cotton Plantation," 127, 128; Yeager to OJ, Apr. 21, 1937; David Gavin to Virgil Adkins, Aug. 22, Sept. 3, 20, and Oct. 10, 1940; Adkins to Gavin, Sept. 2 and Oct. 9, 1940, DPLCR; OJ to Chester Davis, Feb. 14, 1934, memorandum, PCP, RG 145, NA; OJ to Paul Porter, Jan. 11, 1937 ("with or without" and "irresponsible" quotations); Cully Cobb to E. H. White, Jan. 16, 29, 1937; White to Cobb, Jan. 21, 1937; Cobb to OJ, Jan. 27, Mar. 8 ("signed" quotation), 1937; OJ to Cobb, Feb. 6, 1937, GC, RG 145, NA; see also Sheldon Van Auken, "A Century of the Southern Plantation," *Virginia Magazine of History and Biography* 58 (July 1950): 377–78.

17. See Thomas L. Webber, *Deep Like the Rivers: Education in the Slave Quarter Community, 1831–1865* (New York, 1978): 43–58; see "Biggest Cotton Plantation," 130; "Negro Workers on the World's Largest Cotton Plantation," *Manufacturers Record,* Oct. 25, 1923, 105–6 (quotation, 106); George F. Paul, "Welfare Work on a Delta Plantation," *Southern Workman* 54 (July 1925): 317.

18. Untitled typed statement regarding the pastor's conference, Scott, Miss., May 4, 1937, DPLCR; Hendricks interview.

19. "Biggest Cotton Plantation," 130; Paul, "Welfare Work," 317–18.

20. "Biggest Cotton Plantation," 130.

21. Paul, "Welfare Work," 316–17; see Wimbs in "Negro Workers," 106; see also OJ to Palen, May 15, 1937, DPLCR; "Biggest Cotton Plantation," 158; and Daniels, *A Southerner Discovers the South,* 189–90.

22. Daniels, *A Southerner Discovers the South,* 189–90 (Johnston and sharecropper quotations from 190); "Biggest Cotton Plantation," 158; see O. C. Wenger, "A Wasserman Survey of the Negroes on a Cotton Plantation in Mississippi," *Venereal Disease Information* 10 (July 20, 1929): 281–88 (quotations on 282, 284); Porter interview; see also Oscar Johnston, "Industrial Plan," 76. Tenants unable to appear had tests administered in their homes; Wenger, "Wasserman Survey," 283.

23. OJ to I. I. Pogue, Mar. 20, 1937; see also H. C. Ricks to OJ, Nov. 7, 1931, DPLCR; Johnston, "Industrial Plan," 76–77; Pauline Hendricks, untitled and unpublished address (1962), copy in DPLCR; Hendricks interview; Wenger, "Wasserman Survey," 283–85 (quotation on 284); see "Biggest Cotton Plantation," 158; Daniels, *A Southerner Discovers the South,* 189. "Much is said of the fertility and productivity of the soil of our southern states," Johnston told Delta Pine's physician in 1937.

Millions dollars are annually spent for training the minds of our boys and girls, for building roads, schools, courthouses and jails. Comparatively little is expended in protecting and preserving the greatest asset we have; viz., the health of the people. Likewise, we have in the past spent hundreds of thousands of dollars in the effort to eradicate smallpox, yellow fever, typhoid fever, meningitis and other contagious diseases, but comparatively little has been expended in an effort to eradicate social diseases which annually exact an enormous toll of human life, and which is responsible to a very great extent for much of our crime, our insanity and our incurable diseases. The effort to prevent crime, the care and custody of our criminals, care and treatment of our blind, our insane, our deaf and our incurable indigents, cost the taxpayers of the state hundreds of thousands of dollars annually. Much of this could be eliminated by an eradication of the fundamental causes of social diseases. (OJ to I. I. Pogue, Nov. 4, 1937, DPLCR)

24. Johnston, "Industrial Plan," 76; T. J. Johnson, "Delta and Pine Land Company," *Service* 6 (Apr. 1942): 12; see also Paul, "Welfare Work," 316; "Biggest Cotton Plantation," 158.

25. OJ to Max Buckingham, Oct. 20, 1939; OJ to Myron L. McNeil, Apr. 27, 1932 (quotation); McNeil to OJ, Apr. 23, 1932; OJ to Lantrip, Nov. 15, 1937, DPLCR; David B. Dill, "Fatigue Studies Among Mississippi Sharecroppers," *Harvard Alumni Bulletin* 42 (Oct. 20, 1939): 116; OJ to Trent, June 14, 1937, Region VI File, RG 96, NA; see "Biggest Cotton Plantation," 158.

26. Johnson, "Delta and Pine Land Company," 12; F. J. Hurst, "Mississippi's Largest Cotton Farm," *Progressive Farmer* 55 (Feb. 1940): 8.

27. OJ to Lydia Kastor, Aug. 8, 1939; OJ to Buckingham, Oct. 20, 1939; Buckingham to OJ, Oct. 24, 1939 (quotation), DPLCR; Johnston, "Industrial Plan," 76; "Biggest Cotton Plantation," 158.

28. Daniels, *A Southerner Discovers the South*, 189; "Biggest Cotton Plantation," 158; Johnson, "Delta and Pine Land Company," 12; Johnston, "Industrial Plan," 75–76; OJ to Lantrip, Nov. 15, 1937, DPLCR; OJ to Trent, June 14, 1937, Region VI File, RG 96, NA. Primary causes of death remained heart disease and tuberculosis, accounting for 28 percent of all plantation deaths. "Biggest Cotton Plantation," 131.

29. Dill, "Fatigue Studies Among Mississippi Sharecroppers," 118; "Biggest Cotton Plantation," 158; Porter interview. For general comparison, see D. Clayton Brown, "Health of Farm Children of the South, 1900–1950," *Agricultural History* 53 (Jan. 1979): 170–87.

30. Hurst, "Mississippi's Largest Cotton Farm," 30; "Biggest Cotton Plantation," 131.

31. Paul, "Welfare Work," 316; "Biggest Cotton Plantation," 158; Gray interviews; Daniels, *A Southerner Discovers the South*, 183; see also "Negro Workers," 103.

32. Foster and Pearse, "Delta and Pine Land Company of Mississippi, Scott, Miss.," 18; unidentified newspaper clipping, "The Greatest Cotton Plantation, Scott, Miss., The Story of Salsbury Cotton," Aug. 18, 1922, DPLCR. See Sid Robinson, David Dill, J. W. Wilson, and Malus Nielsen, "Adaptations of White Men and Negroes to Prolonged Work in Humid Heat," *American Journal of Tropical Medicine* 21 (Mar. 1941): 261–87; Hurst, "Mississippi's Largest Cotton Farm," 8, 30; J. R. McLaren, "La Hacienda algodonera mas grande de los Estados Unidos," *La Hacienda* 32 (Oct. 1937): 238–51; M. E. Lobo to DPLC, Oct. 18, 1937, DPLCR; "Biggest Cotton Plantation," 158; Jonathan Daniels, "Notes Made on Southern Tour," typed transcript of handwritten notes (May 20, 1937), 53; Daniels to Jim [Putnam], n.d. (1938), apparently a draft of a letter; Lord to Daniels, Oct. 12, 1938, Jonathan Daniels Papers, Southern Historical Collection, Univ. of North Carolina Library, Chapel Hill, North Carolina; Daniels, *A Southerner*

268 _Notes to Pages 107–11_

_Discovers the South,_ 191; Lord, _The Wallaces of Iowa._ Paul Porter also recalled Oscar saying that he had "seen everything out of that eye I want to anyway," Porter interview; see also, _United States News,_ Apr. 17, 1942, 49.

33. Daniels, _A Southerner Discovers the South,_ 181–85; OJ to S. T. Hubbard, Dec. 22, 1942, DPLCR; Gilbert Fite, "Mechanization of Cotton Production Since World War II," _Agricultural History_ 54 (Jan. 1980): 198; OJ to FCSDA, Nov. 25, 1935, DPLCR; _Time,_ Sept. 14, 1936, 47–48, 50 (quotation); see also "Oscar Johnston Doubts Value to Farmer of Machine Picker," _Memphis Press-Scimitar,_ Sept. 1, 1936, 1, 2; Straus, "Enter the Cotton Picker: The Story of the Rust Brothers' Invention," _Harper's_ 173 (Sept. 1936): 386; see _New York Times,_ Sept. 1, 1936, 1, 2; see also "Biggest Cotton Plantation," 160.

34. Daniels, _A Southerner Discovers the South,_ 185–87, 192.

35. Hatcher interview; Gray interviews; Porter interview; OJ to Denton Manufacturing Co., Jan. 21, 1943, DPLCR (latter quotations); see Henry Gaston to OJ, Sept. 7, 1942; OJ to Gaston, Sept. 21, 1942, DPLCR; David Cohn, _Where I Was Born and Raised_ (Boston, 1948), 276–77 (partially quoted in McMillen, _Dark Journey,_ 282).

36. Dill, "Fatigue Studies Among Mississippi's Sharecroppers," 116–18; see also Robinson et al., "Adaptations of White Men and Negroes to Prolonged Work in Humid Heat," 261–87; David Dill, J. W. Wilson, F. G. Hall, and Sid Robinson, "Properties of the Blood of Negroes and Whites in Relation to Climate and Season," _Journal of Biological Chemistry_ 136 (Nov. 1940): 449–60; Sid Robinson, David Dill, P. M. Harmon, F. G. Hall, and J. W. Wilson, "Adaptations to Exercise of Negro and White Sharecroppers in Comparison with Northern Whites," _Human Biology: A Record of Research_ 13 (May 1941): 139–58; _New York Times,_ Nov. 19, 1939, II, 7; the story in the _Times_ is included in "Science in the News," by Waldemar Kaempffert.

37. Statement of Oscar Johnston Re Legislation Limiting Individual Soil Conservation Payments, LTF, RG 145, NA. See Daniels, _A Southerner Discovers the South,_ 182.

38. Statement of Oscar Johnston Re Legislation Limiting Individual Soil Conservation Payments, LTF, RG 145, NA.

39. OJ to Trent, June 14, 1937, Region VI File, RG 96, NA (first quotation). Statement and President's Report, 1935 (Apr. 27, 1936), DPLCR. See "Biggest Cotton Plantation," 158. Wenger, "Wassermann Survey," 282. Statement of Oscar Johnston Re Legislation Limiting Individual Soil Conservation Payments, LTF, RG 145, NA; DPL, plantation census material, DPLCR; plantation census figures suggest there were 820, not 821 cropper families in 1939 and that more than 1 in 5 had automobiles, not 1 in 3.

40. OJ to Progress Manufacturing Company, Mar. 14, 16, 1931; OJ to Minneapolis-Moline Power Implement Co., May 3, 1933; see V.(?) J. Dannreuther to OJ, Apr. 29, 1933; Johnston, Statement and President's Report for the years of World War II, DPLCR; Gray interviews; see Johnston, Operating Schedule, DPLCR; also Johnston's testimony regarding Delta Pine's retreat from mechanization in _Bankhead Hearing,_ 71; see also Carter, "Mules in the Delta," 37–38.

41. OJ to Toler, Nov. 27, 1933; Johnston, Operating Schedule, DPLCR; OJ to Cobb, June 4, 1937, GC, RG 145, NA.

42. Statement and President's Report (1942), Apr. 17, 1943, DPLCR; "Biggest Cotton Plantation," 128–29; Statement of Oscar Johnston Re Legislation Limiting Individual Soil Conservation Payments, LTF, RG 145, NA.

43. Nicholas Reed, "The South: A Middle Way," *Carolina Magazine* 66 (Mar. 1937): 4 (first critic); Johnson, *Shadow of the Plantation,* 111 (second critic); Woofter and Fisher, *The Plantation South Today,* 11 (last quotation); see Erskine Caldwell, *Tobacco Road* (New York, 1932).

44. Percy, *Lanterns on the Levee,* 280; Bledsoe to R. B. Snowden Jr., Apr. 22, 1942, Sillers Papers; Bledsoe, Sharecropping with the Government and Private Individuals, copy in Sillers Papers; Sherwood Eddy to Clement Biddle, Jan. 13, 1943, Delta and Providence Farms Papers, Southern Historical Collection, Univ. of North Carolina Library, Chapel Hill.

45. William R. Amberson, et al., "Report of a Survey Made by Memphis Chaper L.I.D. and the Tyronza Socialist Party under Direction of Wm. R. Amberson," in Thomas, *Plight of the Share-Cropper,* 19–34; see a few DPLC settlement sheets in Amberson Papers. According to Norman Thomas, the committee "found a reduction in the number of families employed" at DPLC; Thomas, *Plight of the Share-Cropper,* 11. H. L. Mitchell, a member of the Amberson committee who did not visit DPLC on that occasion, claimed that "No one but Amberson thought much of a man . . . whom Amberson sent down to do some checking of various plantations, including Delta Pine and Land [*sic* ] Co.," Mitchell to author, Aug. 20, 1973; J. Phil Campbell, E. A. Miller, and W. J. Green, Report of Adjustment Committee on Investigation of Landlord-Tenant Contracts (Sept. 1, 1934), Supplement (Investigation of cases mentioned in the report of the Memphis Chapter, League for Industrial Democracy), 76, LTF, RG 145, NA; Mitchell to Paul Porter, Mar. 27, 1935, PCP, RG 145, NA (quotation). In *Mean Things Happening in This Land,* 46, Mitchell claimed that a "survey party found that conditions on Johnston's plantation in Mississippi were about the same as they were on plantations in eastern Arkansas." For Johnston's independence, see his letter to Toler, Aug. 26, 1933, DPLCR. The number of tenant families operating at Scott did drop according to the plantation census of April 1934 but returned to what might be considered a normal figure by 1936. Census material, DPLCR; see "Biggest Cotton Plantation," 158.

46. OJ to FCSDA, Apr. 6, 1936, DPLCR; Daniels, *A Southerner Discovers the South,* 184.

47. Dorothy Lee Black to Walter Sillers, Feb. 12, 1943; Black to Sillers, Nov. 12, 1942, Sillers Papers.

48. OJ to Caswell P. Ellis Jr., Mar. 13, 1942, DPLCR; Cohn, *Where I Was Born and Raised,* 41 (quoted, with slight variation, in Cobb, *The Most Southern Place on Earth,* 209).

49. OJ to Sillers, Apr. 24, 1947; see Sillers to OJ, Apr. 23, 1947, Sillers Papers; see OJ to Frank Hook, Mar. 16, 1942, OJ to B. M. McGriff, Jan. 29, 1943 (last quotation), DPLCR. In a provocative article, "Mississippi Delta Planters and Debates Over Mechanization, Labor, and Civil Rights in the 1940s," Nan Elizabeth Woodruff properly injects the discussion of civil rights into the 1940s issue of mechanization and argues that Delta planters tried "to reform the plantation without changing the power relations that defined it" (263). She argues further that such planters "joined with the AFBF [American Farm Bureau Federation] in opposing legislation to improve the lives of plantation workers" (265). But there is little warrant for the planter malice implicit in the comment and, more important, there is likewise little evidence that sharecroppers' lives would improve more by the efforts of the socialist or even nonsocialist labor unions than from the enhanced benefits, admittedly pragmatic, which the planters tried to offer, benefits demonstrated in the article. The article also notes that Johnston believed

that Farm Bureau tenant sign-ups were more readily obtained if such tenants believed parity checks came from Farm Bureau efforts (though not actually *"from the bureau"*) which is true as far as it goes. But Johnston was resistant, as his letter to Sillers shows, to any strong tactics to entice tenant sign-ups. Claims that "[m]any planters" bought tenant subscriptions for *The Delta Leader* (279), a pro-plantation black paper edited by a conservative black minister, Rev. H. H. Humes, and that tenants "preferred to earn cash wages and to escape the planters' credit system, which withheld their earnings," and which forced them "to buy at the plantation commissary" (265), are countered by the experience of Oscar Johnston, who refused Humes's offer to have DPLC match one hundred free subscriptions (which would leave the company open to charges of favoritism; besides, Johnston thought they had enough money to buy their own), and by the fact that, at Delta Planting Company at least, the plantation store operated independently on a cash basis. See OJ to B. M. McGriff, Jan. 29, 1943; Humes to OJ, Feb. 18, 1942; OJ to Humes, Feb. 19, 1942, DPLCR.

50. Johnson, "Delta and Pine Land Company," 12; Calvin Perkins to OJ, June 19, 1942 (clergy quotation); see also T. J. Johnson to OJ, Feb. 12, 1942, DPLCR.

51. David L. Cohn, "Share-Cropping in the Delta," *Atlantic Monthly* 159 (May 1937): 588; Van Auken, "A Century of the Southern Plantation," 387.

52. Daniels, *A Southerner Discovers the South,* 192; "Biggest Cotton Plantation," 192; see Statement of Oscar Johnston Re Legislation Limiting Individual Soil Conservation Payments, LTF, RG 145, NA; *Senate ACCA Hearing,* 100; OJ to Henry Wallace, June 7, 1938, GC, RG 145, NA; OJ to John Sparkman, Apr. 19, 1943, DPLCR. But see a different focus in OJ to W. W. Fariss, Feb. 16, 1943, DPLCR; see also *Memphis Press-Scimitar,* Apr. 16, 1936, 1. For discussions of the cases of Norcross and the Twist brothers, see Conrad, *Forgotten Farmers;* Grubbs, *Cry from the Cotton;* Mitchell, *Mean Things Happening in This Land;* Mitchell to Porter, Mar. 27, 1935, PCP, RG 145, NA. In his letter to Porter, Mitchell called the Twist problem "a really bad case for immediate legal action." See also Amberson to Hiram Norcross, Nov. 23, 1934, and Norcross to Amberson, Nov. 28, 1934, Amberson Papers. Davis to District Agents and Others Who are to Assist with Landlord-Tenant Problem, May 5, 1934, LTF, RG 145, NA; C. C. Smith to Cully Cobb, June 10, 1934, GC, RG 145, NA; R. B. Snowden Jr. to Oscar F. Bledsoe, Apr. 20, 1942 (next to last quotation), Sillers Papers; OJ to Forrest Cooper, July 15, 1942; OJ to Clay East and H. L. Mitchell, Feb. 20, 1934 (last quotation), DPLCR.

53. OJ to Howard Doane, Dec. 2, 1927, D. Howard Doane Papers, Joint Collection, Univ. of Missouri, Western Historical Manuscript Collection–State Historical Society of Missouri Manuscripts, Ellis Library, Univ. of Missouri–Columbia; Daniels, *A Southerner Discovers the South,* 192.

## 8. Cotton Diplomat

1. James Edmonds, "High Prices and Ten Years?" *Saturday Evening Post,* Sept. 7, 1935, 14; *Memphis Press-Scimitar,* Dec. 18, 1935, 7 (Cobb quotation); Wallace to Henry Taylor, Aug. 11, 1957, Taylor Papers; see also Edmonds's two other articles in the *Saturday Evening Post:* "'Much Obliged!' Bows Brazil to Uncle Sam's AAA," Aug. 10, 1935, 5–7, 72–74, and "Amending the Brazilian Weather?" Aug. 31, 1935, 18–19, 49–50, 52.

2. *Statistical History of the United States from Colonial Times to the Present* (Stamford, Conn., 1965), 546; Stowell to OJ, July 6, 1934; OJ to FCSDA, May 21, 1934; see Toler to OJ, Oct. 18, 1933, DPLCR; *Time,* Aug. 17, 1936, 57–58, 60, 62; W. L. Clayton,

"Farm Relief," *Cotton Digest,* Mar. 25, 1933, 9; article by Clayton in *Memphis Press-Scimitar,* Dec. 18, 1933, 2; *Memphis Press-Scimitar,* Dec. 18, 1935, 7 (Cobb quotation); Committee on Agriculture and Forestry, *Hearings Before the Committee on Agriculture and Forestry on the Loss of Export Trade and the Means of Recovery,* 74th Cong., 1st sess., 1935 (hereinafter cited as *Senate Loss of Export Trade Hearings*); Johnston's speech to U.S. Chamber of Commerce (southeastern regional meeting), Birmingham, Ala., Nov. 20, 1934, reprinted by Sen. John Bankhead in *Congressional Record,* 74th Cong., 1st sess., 1935, 79, pt. 1:147; Murray R. Benedict, *Farm Policies of the United States, 1790–1950: A Study of Their Origins and Development* (New York, 1953), 311. For a review of the New Deal and foreign agricultural markets, see Saloutos, *The American Farmer and the New Deal,* 137–49.

3. *Time,* Aug. 17, 1936, 57–58, 60, 62; Frank, COHC; Toler to OJ, Oct. 18, 1933, DPLCR; article by Clayton in *Memphis Press-Scimitar,* May 5, 1935, 2 (quotation). See also *Memphis Press-Scimitar,* Dec. 18, 1935, 7; see "Cotton's in the Well," 36, 38–39, 41.

4. *Memphis Commercial Appeal,* June 5, 1933, 1; OJ to FCSDA, May 21, 1934, June 14, 1935 (quotation); OJ to Stowell, May 28, 1934, DPLCR; Johnston, "What Happened? and What Next?" 13, 122; see similar arguments in Henry A. Wallace, "Cotton Control and Exports," *Cotton Digest,* Feb. 9, 1935, 6–8; Henry A. Wallace, "The Cotton Program Carries On," *Cotton Digest,* Apr. 20, 1935, 7–10; Cully Cobb, "Cotton and the AAA," *Cotton Digest,* Oct. 20, 1934, 17–18; *Senate Loss of Export Trade Hearings,* 90, 103; *New York Times,* Feb. 1, 1935, 4; Johnston speech to Chamber of Commerce, Nov. 20, 1934, reprinted in *Congressional Record,* 147–50.

5. *Senate Loss of Export Trade Hearings,* 103; John Kenneth Galbraith, *Money: Whence It Came, Where It Went* (Boston, 1975), 93–94n, 200, 210–12.

6. OJ to Stowell, May 28, 1934; OJ to FCSDA, May 21, 1934, DPLCR; *Memphis Press-Scimitar,* Aug. 30, 1934, 1; Johnston speech to Chamber of Commerce, Nov. 20, 1934, reprinted in *Congressional Record,* 149–50 (quotations); *Senate Loss of Export Trade Hearings,* 107–8; Benedict, *Farm Policies of the United States,* 267.

7. Johnston, "What Happened? and What Next?" 112; Cobb, "Cotton and the AAA," 18; *Memphis Press-Scimitar,* Aug. 3, 1936, 1; Peter Molyneaux, *The Cotton South and the American Trade Policy* (New York, 1936), 58–59; *Senate Loss of Export Trade Hearings,* 95. USDA, *Report of the Secretary of Agriculture, 1937* (Washington, D.C., 1937), 50, 52.

8. Telephone conversations, OJ to Peek, Nov. 10, 1934; OJ to Judge Moore, Dec. 3, 1934; Peek to Bankhead, Dec. 5, 1934; Peek to Angus McLean, Jan. 14, 1935, transcripts in Peek Papers; OJ to Wallace, Nov. 2, 1934, memorandum; OJ to Davis, Nov. 10, 1934, memorandum, GC, RG 16, NA; OJ to Davis, Nov. 23, 1934, GC, RG 145, NA; Memorandum on the agreement between the United States and Deutsche-Baumwoll Tausch of Bremen, Germany, Dec. 10, 1934, Peek Papers; Francis B. Sayre to Roosevelt, Feb. 6, 1935, OF 614-A, FDRL; *New York Times,* Nov. 3, 1934, 21; Stowell to OJ, Sept. 14, 1934; OJ to FCSDA, Dec. 11, 1934, DPLCR.

9. Cordell Hull, *The Memoirs of Cordell Hull,* 2 vols. (New York, 1948): 1:371.

10. Wallace to Hull, Sept. 21, 1934; see also OJ to Wallace, Sept. 19, 1934, memorandum (copy), GC, RG 16, NA. See also Henry Taylor to Wallace, Aug. 19, 1957, Taylor Papers. Telephone conversations, Peek to Bankhead, Dec. 7, 1934; OJ to Peek, Dec. 11, 1934 (Johnston quotations), transcripts in Peek Papers. Peek suggested that Johnston consider selling cotton to Russia and Germany by way of England. Although the British Fine Spinners had told Johnston that their efforts to collect several hundred thousand

dollars from German debtors for yarns and cotton textiles had been unsuccessful, he knew German importers could "find pound exchange easier than dollar exchange," telephone conversation, OJ to Peek, Nov. 10, 1934, transcript, Peek Papers; Stowell to OJ, Sept. 14, 1934, DPLCR.

11. Hull, *Memoirs*, 1:371–74; telephone conversation, Moore to Peek, Dec. 3, 1934, transcript, Peek Papers; Hull to Roosevelt, Dec. 14, 1934 (and enclosure), President's Secretary's File, FDRL. For brief accounts of the deal, see Fite, *George N. Peek*, 277; Lloyd Gardner, *Economic Aspects of New Deal Diplomacy* (Madison, Wisc., 1964), 103; Dick Steward, "In Search of Markets: The New Deal, Latin America, and Reciprocal Trade," Ph.D. diss., Univ. of Missouri–Columbia, 1969, 144–46. None of these accounts mention Johnston's role in the arrangement, but all discuss the climax and ramifications of the Peek to Hull controversy.

12. Hull, *Memoirs*, 1:374; see also Fite, *George N. Peek*, 277; *Memphis Commercial Appeal*, Jan. 1, 1935, 13, Jan. 10, 1935, 1; *Memphis Press-Scimitar*, Jan. 9, 1935, 1; Morgenthau Diaries, Dec. 7, 1934, 2:252 (last two quotations; see also Jan. 8, 1935, 3:57), FDRL; press release, Jan. 8, 1935, GC, RG 16, NA; OJ to Davis, Nov. 23, 1934, GC, RG 145, NA; OJ to Toler, Jan. 4, 1935, DPLCR; see Wallace to Henry Taylor, Aug. 29, 1957, Taylor Papers.

13. Telephone conversations, Peek to Ellison Smith, Jan. 24, 1935; see also Peek to McLean, Jan. 14, 1935, transcripts in Peek Papers; OJ to Emanuel Licht, Nov. 9, 1934, quoted in Licht to OJ, Nov. 13, 1934, OF 258, FDRL.

14. C. L. Merritt to Roosevelt, Jan. 2, 1935, telegram (first quotation); OJ to Louis Howe, Jan. 5, 1935, OF 258, FDRL. One attempt to bridge the gap between State and Agriculture was contained in Johnston's attempt to get a modification of the antidumping statute in order to increase imports. Johnston rightly believed that the antidumping law had not been formulated to meet the problems of gold countries clamoring to increase their exports to the United States. The proposal got Roosevelt's attention but had to run the bureaucratic gauntlet. While the State Department might sympathize with Johnston's general idea of increasing imports, especially from gold countries, it objected to his method of tampering with the protectionist antidumping law. According to Assistant Secretary of State Francis B. Sayre, it would invite other nations to unload goods in the United States at the low rates that Japan, for example, because of her deflated currency, could sell them. Since American commerce rested on triangular trade, bilaterals, reasoned Sayre, "inevitably involve preferential treatment which we are struggling hard to combat in our general trade relations." Still, Johnston's proposal got a hearing in an ad hoc interdepartmental committee in February 1935, but because the issue was, according to Sayre, "bristling with difficulties," it apparently suffered the same fate as the German barter deal. Sayre to Roosevelt, Feb. 6, 1935 (first quotation); Sayre to Marvin McIntyre, Feb. 20, 1935 (second quotation); see also Roosevelt to Sayre, Feb. 4, 1935, memorandum, including added notations; Roosevelt to McIntyre, Feb. 12, 1935; McIntyre to Sayre, Feb. 13, 1935, OF 614-A, FDRL. The author is indebted here to Edgar B. Nixon, ed., *Franklin D. Roosevelt and Foreign Affairs*, 3 vols. (Cambridge, Mass., 1969), 2:398–400.

15. Wallace Diary, Jan. 19, 1935, Univ. of Iowa Library, Iowa City; Wallace, COHC; OJ to Morgenthau, Jan. 14, 1935, memorandum, Morgenthau Correspondence, FDRL; Mordecai Ezekiel to Loyd Steere, Mar. 22, 1935, GC, RG 16, NA; Henry Taylor, COHC; see Taylor to Wallace, July 10, 1958, Taylor Papers; President's Press Conferences (White

House), Jan. 16, 1935, FDRL (also in Nixon, *Franklin D. Roosevelt and Foreign Affairs,* 2:364–65; see Nixon's notes on 365); *Memphis Commercial Appeal,* Jan. 16, 1935, 1; Feb. 16, 1935, 1; OJ to Toler, Jan. 22, 1935 (two), DPLCR; see Hull, *Memoirs,* 1:373.

16. Presidential Press Conferences (White House), Jan. 16, 1935, FDRL (also in Nixon, *Franklin D. Roosevelt and Foreign Affairs,* 2:364–65); AAA press release, Feb. 16, 1935, GC, RG 145, NA; *Memphis Commercial Appeal,* Jan. 16, 1935, 1; Feb. 16, 1935, 1; OJ to Toler, Jan. 22, 1935 (two), DPLCR; Wallace, COHC; Wallace Diary, Jan. 19, 22, 1935, HAW Papers, Univ. of Iowa Library; *Senate Loss of Export Trade Hearings,* 90, 98–99, 103; *New York Times,* Feb. 1, 1935, 4; OJ to Morgenthau, Jan. 14, 1935, memorandum, Morgenthau Correspondence, FDRL. Regarding the possibility of an international cotton conference, Wallace told his diary: "The President urged Oscar to remember that the British are strictly selfish and cold blooded in handling matters of this sort," Wallace Diary, Jan. 22, 1935, HAW Papers, Univ. of Iowa Library. In a letter introducing Johnston to British Prime Minister J. Ramsay MacDonald, Roosevelt referred to Johnston as "My good friend," and told MacDonald, "This whole subject is still in the exploratory stage, but I hope that general agreement can be had on some plan which will more greatly stabilize the world raw cotton situation, even if such stabilization is only in experimental form at the beginning." Whether Johnston presented the letter to the prime minister is unclear, owing to MacDonald's illness. Roosevelt to MacDonald, Feb. 14, 1935; see also Roosevelt to Ray Atherton, Feb. 14, 1935, PPF 2221, FDRL (and in Nixon, *Franklin D. Roosevelt and Foreign Affairs,* 2:405–6); Atherton to Hull, Mar. 13, 1935 (cable), GC, RG 16, NA.

17. AAA press release ("Oscar Johnston to Make Survey of Foreign Markets"), Feb. 16, 1935, GC, RG 145, NA; Morgenthau to Straus, Feb. 16, 1935, Morgenthau Correspondence, FDRL.

18. OJ to Wallace, Apr. 2, 1935 (quotation); Atherton to Hull, Mar. 13, 1935; Hull to Wallace, Mar. 12, 1935, GC, RG 16, NA.

19. Steere to Ezekiel, Mar. 7, 1935 (first quotation); *London Financial News,* Mar. 21, 1935, clippings; OJ to Lamkin, Mar. 25, 1935 (last quotation); see also cable, OJ to Lamkin, Mar. 25, 1935, GC, RG 16, NA; *New Orleans Times-Picayune,* Mar. 12, 1935, 1, 3; Mar. 13, 1935, 25; Mar. 15, 1935, 33; Mar. 17, 1935, 18; *Senate Disposition of Cotton Hearings,* 10–11; Lancashire Statistical Service (Manchester, Eng.), Mar. 23, 1935, typed copy in DPLCR.

20. OJ to Lamkin, Mar. 25, 1935 (first, fourth, and fifth quotations); OJ to Smith, Mar. 12, 1935 (second and third quotations), GC, RG 16, NA.

21. OJ to Lamkin, Mar. 25, 1935, GC, RG 16, NA.

22. Ibid. (first quotation); OJ to Wallace, Apr. 2, 1935 (remaining quotations), GC, RG 16, NA.

23. OJ to Wallace, Apr. 2, 1935, GC, RG 16, NA (quotations); OJ to Roosevelt, May 15, 1935, OF 1K, FDRL.

24. Obviously, neither of those countries would see much value in their participation in an international cotton conference designed to control either production or the world market. OJ to Roosevelt, May 15, 1935, OF 1K, FDRL; OJ to Wallace, Apr. 2, 1935; Johnston, Memorandum of Conferences held with Sir Frederick Leith-Ross et als [*sic* ] on Monday, Mar. 18th, and on Thursday, Mar. 21st, 1935, GC, RG 16, NA; see OJ to Stowell, Apr. 11, 1935; OJ to Sydnor Odem, May 20, 1935, DPLCR.

25. OJ to Stowell, Apr. 11, 1935, DPLCR. See James Edmonds' articles cited in note 1 above; on Brazil, see also "Cotton's in the Well," 38–39, 41.

26. OJ to Stowell, Apr. 11, 1935, DPLCR.

27. Johnston also blamed the national desires to buy raw materials from others who took industrial commodities in exchange, resultant prejudice against buying U.S. goods, bartering among Europeans, synthetic material, especially in Italy, and lower prices of Brazilian fiber. He later added America's creditor status and other factors. *Memphis Commercial Appeal,* May 28, 1935, 11 (see also Mar. 20, 1935, 2); OJ to John Bankhead, June 20, 1935, printed in *Congressional Record,* 74th Cong., 1st sess., 1935, 79, pt. 10:11374; Lancashire Statistical Service, Mar. 23, 1935 (quotation), typed copy in DPLCR; see also *London Financial News,* Mar. 21, 1935, news item and editorial, clippings in GC, RG 16, NA; and *Memphis Press-Scimitar,* May 28, 1935, 1, 2.

28. Johnston recounted his conference with Schacht several years later in "On Demobilizing the War Economy," *Fortune* 24 (Nov. 1941): 15–16. Telephone conversation, OJ to Peek, May 7, 1935, transcript, Peek Papers; Francis B. Sayre to Roosevelt, Apr. 6, 1935, OF 971, FDRL; see also cross-reference notations, State Dept., Apr. 6, 1935, OF 1K, FDRL; see also OJ to Peek, Nov. 13, 1941, DPLCR.

29. Taylor, COHC (quotation); Taylor to Wallace, June 2, 1958; see also July 19, 1958, Wallace Papers; see also Taylor to Wallace, July 28, 1957; Aug. 19, 1957, Taylor Papers. On Taylor, see Kirkendall, *Social Scientists and Farm Politics,* and Saloutos, *The American Farmer and the New Deal.*

30. Peek to Johnston, Nov. 6, 1941, DPLCR.

31. Taylor to Wallace, Aug. 19, 1957, Taylor Papers.

32. Of course, as *Newsweek* pointed out in 1936, exchange could also help Germany re-arm. *Newsweek,* May 9, 1936, 20; Wallace to Taylor, Aug. 29, 1957 (Wallace quotation), Taylor Papers; *New York Times,* June 15, 1936, 9; TRB, "Washington Notes," *New Republic,* Sept. 22, 1937, 186; *Memphis Press-Scimitar,* Dec. 18, 1935, 7 (Cobb quotation); OJ to Wallace, Oct. 31, 1935, GC, RG 16, NA (Johnston quotation).

33. *Memphis Press-Scimitar,* May 27, 1935, 1 (quotation); OJ to Roosevelt, May 15, 1935, OF 1K, FDRL; OJ to Wallace, Oct. 31, 1935, GC, RG 16, NA.

34. *Memphis Commercial Appeal,* Jan. 24, 1939, 2; Feb. 9, 1939, 1, 2; Feb. 15, 1939, 4 (but see editorial, "Brazil Has Troubles, Too," *Memphis Press-Scimitar,* May 24, 1935, 10); OJ to FCSDA, Aug. 19, 1935, DPLCR; see also OJ to Bankhead, June 1935, printed in *Congressional Record,* 11373–75; OJ to Wallace, Mar. 21, 1935 (cable), Morgenthau Correspondence, FDRL; telephone conversation, OJ to Peek, May 7, 1935, transcript, Peek Papers; *Memphis Press-Scimitar,* May 28, 1935, 2.

35. S. Palle to OJ, Apr. 15, 1935; Stowell to DPL, Apr. 26, 1935, DPLCR.

36. *Memphis Press-Scimitar,* May 27, 1935, 1 (first quotation); May 28, 1935, 1, 2 (remaining quotations).

37. OJ to Bankhead, June 20, 1935, printed in *Congressional Record,* 11374; OJ to Wallace, Oct. 31, 1935, GC, RG 16, NA; see Saloutos, *The American Farmer and the New Deal,* 137–40, 149; Derek Clayton, untitled document (typed copy; last quotation), n.d. (handwritten "4/6/35," filed Apr. 8, 1935), GC, RG 16, NA.

38. See *Statistical History of the United States,* 546; Saloutos, *The American Farmer and the New Deal,* 147–48.

## 9. Outwitting the Speculators

1. "Johnston Won't Run" (editorial), *Jackson Daily News,* Dec. 26, 1933, 6; J. O. Prude Jr. to OJ, Dec. 15, 1933, DPLCR.

2. OJ to Sullens, in *Jackson Daily News,* Dec. 16, 1933, 6. In his editorial, Sullens claimed that "several of the actual aspirants for the Governorship will probably breathe easier. The possibility of Oscar Johnston entering the race was not at all to their liking." With Johnston out of the gubernatorial race, other candidates sought his support, including Lt. Gov. Dennis Murphree and Jackson attorney Paul Johnson. Privately, he supported Murphree. Johnson to OJ, July 12, 25, 1934; OJ to Johnson, July 17, 1934; Murphree to OJ, May 31, 1934; OJ to Prude, Dec. 22, 1933, DPLCR.

3. OJ to Lynn Talley, Dec. 14, 1933, Tray 44, RG 161, NA (first quotation); OJ to Toler, Jan. 17, 1934 (second quotation); OJ to FCSDA, Apr. 18, 1934, DPLCR.

4. OJ to FCSDA, Apr. 18, 1934, DPLCR; Snider to Sillers, Apr. 12, 1934, Sillers Papers.

5. OJ to FCSDA, Apr. 18, 1934, DPLCR; OJ to Snider, Apr. 18, 1934; see also OJ to Sillers, Apr. 18, 1934; Sillers to OJ, Apr. 20, 1934, Sillers Papers; OJ to A. J. Pentecost, Sept. 11, 1934, DPLCR ("hell raisers" quotation). Johnston quietly supported Stephens who lost to Bilbo; later he apparently declined to participate in an abortive attempt to prevent Bilbo from taking his seat; OJ to Pentecost, Sept. 11, 1934; S. P. Knut to OJ, Nov. 19, 1934; OJ to Knut, Nov. 22, 1934, DPLCR. Years later, in 1942, a friend claimed he would "die unsatisfied" if Oscar didn't become governor of Mississippi, a position for which Johnston had not the slightest ambition; indeed, he believably had had no ambition in that regard since 1919. Johnston thought the same thing in 1942 as he had thought about a possible Senate race in 1934, that he was doing more good where he was. Frank W. Williams to OJ, Jan. 14, 1942; OJ to Williams, Jan. 16, 1942, DPLCR.

6. Carrying charges would be deducted from the gross profits. Committee on Appropriations, *Hearing Before the Subcommittee of the House Committee on Appropriations on the Agricultural Department Appropriation Bill for 1935,* 73d Cong., 2d sess., 1934, 1040 (first quotation). See also OJ to Roosevelt, Nov. 11, 1933, OF 736. FDRL; *Agricultural Adjustment in 1934, A Report of Administration of the Agricultural Adjustment Act, Feb. 15, 1934, to Dec. 31, 1934* (Washington, D.C., 1935), 63; *Senate ACCA Hearing,* 85; Johnston, "Origin and Operation," 138; OJ to Peek, Sept. 22, 1933, memorandum, OF 258, FDRL; *Memphis Commercial Appeal,* Sept. 23, 1933, 1.

7. OJ to Ellison Smith, Aug. 6, 1934, GC, RG 16, NA. Of the more than 130,000 who held options but rejected the invitation to join the pool, most chose to authorize the sale of the nearly 500,000 bales covered by their options by May 1, 1934. Johnston disposed of the nonpooled cotton on a steadily rising market. Marvin McIntyre to Jed Johnson, n.d. (Dec. 1934), letter prepared by Johnston (see OJ to McIntyre, Dec. 3, 1934), OF 258, FDRL. See also AAA press release, Jan. 24, 1934, PCP, RG 145, NA. Among Johnston's rehearsals of the cotton pool's history, see *Senate ACCA Hearing,* especially 73–89.

8. OJ to Wallace, Sept. 17, 1934, GC, RG 16, NA; Paul Porter to OJ, May 27, June 13, 1935, GC, RG 145, NA; Porter to Milo Perkins, May 15, 1935, GC, RG 16, NA; OJ to Wallace, Oct. 29, 1935, GC, RG 145, NA (copy also in GC, RG 16, NA; quotations); *Senate Disposition of Cotton Hearings,* 18; Robert J. Woods to Perkins, July 13, 1935; Wallace to John McFadden, Oct. 11, 1935; Perkins to Woods, Nov. 27, 1935, GC, RG 16, NA; OJ to Wallace, Nov. 19, 1935, GC, RG 145, NA. Cotton pool files reportedly

bulged with hundreds of letters calling for a more equitable distribution of government business. Paul Porter, who had worked closely with Johnston, and was now executive assistant to Chester Davis, told Wallace's assistant that "all sorts of political pressure" had been applied to boost the requests. In one case Postmaster General James A. Farley had apparently appealed directly to Wallace on behalf of a New York brokerage house. Porter to Perkins, May 15, 1935, GC, RG 16, NA; see also, OJ to Wallace, Oct. 29, 1935, GC, RG 145, NA (copy also in GC, RG 16, NA); Wallace to McFadden, Oct. 11, 1935, GC, RG 16, NA.

9. *Senate Disposition of Cotton Hearings,* 18; OJ to Wallace, Oct. 29, 1935, GC, RG 145, NA (copy also in GC, RG 16, NA); Wallace to McFadden, Oct. 11, 1935, GC, RG 16, NA; see also Perkins to Woods, Nov. 27, 1935, GC, RG 16, NA; OJ to Wallace, Nov. 10, 1935, GC, RG 145, NA.

10. *Senate Disposition of Cotton Hearings,* 19; see OJ to Smith, Aug. 6, 1934, GC, RG 16, NA. During the Hoover administration, the American Cotton Cooperative Association, custodian of the government's cotton, resisted pressure from New England's congressional delegation and others, including Sen. Ellison Smith of South Carolina, on behalf of New England warehousemen, who wanted some of the action. When pressure was renewed in 1933 Johnston likewise resisted, raising the ire of Charles H. Hyde, representing New England warehouse interests. After getting nowhere with Johnston, Hyde took the issue up with President Roosevelt, who referred it to Secretary Wallace. "Now what is Mr. Johnston's interest?" asked Hyde. "He is the owner or controller of 23,000 acres of cotton growing land. He is known to have been intimately associated with the cooperative managers and the great cotton dealers; and that he has full confidence in them is evidenced by the contract he has made putting them in full control of the government's cotton. That he is keenly interested in the speculation is also manifest for he has had a ticker installed in his office." Wallace supported Johnston fully, including his signing a contract with the American Cotton Cooperative Association to handle nearly all of the government cotton. Once cotton was stored in New England warehouses, Wallace contended, its owners fell "under a considerable bargaining handicap" because of added shipping costs out of New England in the event of a failure to reach an acceptable selling price. Johnston's recommendations, unlike those of Hyde's client, said Wallace, "appears to me to be fully in accord with the best interests of the cotton farmer and of the Government." (He added: "The numerous allegations you make in your letter bearing on the manner in which Mr. Johnston has conducted the cotton operations of the Department of Agriculture are without foundation in fact.") Charles H. Hyde to Roosevelt, Nov. 1, 1933, with Hyde's New England Cotton Industry Request for Storage, n.d. (1933); Wallace to Hyde, Dec. 6, 1933; see also Louis McHenry Howe to Hyde, Nov. 20, 1933, OF 258, FDRL.

11. *Senate ACCA Hearing,* 85; OJ to CCC, Aug. 20, 1934, memorandum, OF 258, FDRL; OJ to FCSDA, July 6, 1934, DPLCR; Alston Garside, "Government Activities in Cotton—Part 2(b)," *Cotton Digest,* Jan. 18, 1936, 6; unsigned memorandum to Wallace, Dec. 7, 1934, PCP, RG 145, NA.

12. Garside, "Government Activities in Cotton—Part 2(b)," 5; OJ to CCC, Aug. 20, 1934, OF 258, FDRL; unsigned memorandum to Wallace, Dec. 7, 1934, PCP, RG 145, NA; Wallace and Davis to Roosevelt, Sept. 10, 1934; Roosevelt to Talley, Sept. 12, 1934; Wallace to Roosevelt, Nov. 24, 1934, OF 736, FDRL; AAA press release, Aug. 24, 1934, PCP, RG 145, NA.

13. Johnston agreed to purchase surrendered certificates only if he believed he could sell cotton equal to that covered by the certificates without disturbing the market. When accepted, such certificates were canceled, along with the member's equity. Johnston, "Origin and Operation," 138; *Senate ACCA Hearing,* 85; Committee on Appropriations, *Subcommittee of House Committee on Appropriations (Agricultural Appropriations Hearing for 1936),* 74th Cong., 1st sess., 1935, 1328; *Agricultural Adjustment in 1934, A Report,* 63; OJ to Stowell, Aug. 29, 1934; OJ to Stowell, Oct. 16, 1934, memorandum, DPLCR. See also Garside, "Government Activities in Cotton—Part 2(b)," 6; OJ to Wallace, July 9, 1934, memorandum, GC, RG 16, NA (copy also in PCP, RG 145, NA); OJ to Wallace, July 26, 1934, AAA, CLD, RG 16, NA; AAA press release, Aug. 24, 1934, PCP, RG 145, NA; Wallace to Roosevelt, Nov. 24, 1934, OF 736, FDRL.

14. AAA press release, Jan. 17, 1935, AAA, CLD, RG 16, NA; *Senate ACCA Hearing,* 85; OJ to Stowell, Aug. 29, 1934 ("bluffing" quotation), DPLCR; OJ to Wallace, July 26, 1934, AAA, CLD, RG 16, NA; OJ to Smith, Aug. 6, 1934, GC, RG 16, NA. The chief controversy centered on whether Johnston should borrow the requisite money for the two-cent pool advance from Commodity Credit, or whether Wallace should borrow from the RFC. Wallace eventually decided on the former course, justifiably wishing to avoid individually debiting his account. Unsigned memorandum, Nov. 23, 1934, PCP, RG 145, NA; see also Jerome Frank to J. Warren Smith, July 21, 1934, memorandum; Frank, Nov. 10, 1934, file memorandum and added notation; Wallace to OJ, Nov. 10, 1934, memorandum; Frank to Chester Davis, Nov. 9, 1934, confidential memorandum, PCP, RG 145, NA; Wallace to Lynn Talley, Nov. 24, 1934; unsigned to Wallace, Dec. 7, 1934, memorandum; unsigned, Dec. 13, 1934, file memorandum; Frank and Francis Shea to Davis, Dec. 22, 1934, memorandum; Frank to Davis, Dec. 29, 1934, memorandum; Frank, Dec. 29, 1934, policy memorandum; Frank to Paul Appleby, Jan. 2, 1935, memorandum, AAA, CLD, RG 16, NA (copies of some of these documents also in PCP, RG 145, NA). Over the mild reluctance of the conservative British Fine Spinners, who would have been very likely pleased to cash in their certificates held by DPLC, Johnston chose to accept the two-cent advance. The company held certificates totaling 2,400 bales in the pool, and by retaining equity it received a government check for $18,240, signifying a net advance of $7.60 per bale. If the market went higher, as Johnston expected, Delta Pine could substantially increase its profits. OJ to Stowell, Aug. 29, 1934; Stowell to OJ, Sept. 14, 1934, DPLCR. Although Delta Pine's participation in the pool might have appeared as a conflict of interest, it might have suggested a lack of confidence had Johnston kept the company out of the pool. As a gesture designed to mitigate conflict of interest charges, Johnston arranged for Delta Pine's futures sales to be handled by the Staple Cotton Cooperation Association of Greenwood, Mississippi, of which Johnston was a director. OJ to Stowell, May 28, 1934, DPLCR.

15. One published report claimed Johnston threatened to resign if the Treasury refused to pay the merchants, a claim without documentary support and in any event highly dubious. J. L. Severance, *Journal of Commerce* (New York), column, typed copy in AAA, CLD, RG 16, NA; Richards, *Cotton and the AAA,* 208–9; *Senate Disposition of Cotton Hearings,* 7–8; Frank to Appleby, Dec. 14, 1934, memorandum; OJ to Frierson and Co., Dec. 6, 1934, PCP, RG 145, NA; Wade Armstrong to Roosevelt, Dec. 14, 1934, OF 258, FDRL; OJ to Wallace, July 9, 1934, GC, RG 16, NA.

16. Richards, *Cotton and the AAA,* 208–9n; OJ to Richard Harriss, Feb. 21, 1935, GC, RG 16, NA.

17. *New Orleans Times-Picayune,* Mar. 12, 1935, 1, 3; Mar. 17, 1935, 18; Mar. 18, 1935, 17 ("nervous and excited" quotation); *Senate Disposition of Cotton Hearings,* 10–11; OJ to Joe Lamkin, Mar. 25, 1935, GC, RG 16, NA.

18. *New Orleans Times-Picayune,* Mar. 12, 1935, 3; Mar. 13, 1935, 23; Mar. 15, 1935, 33; Lancashire Statistical Service (Manchester, Eng.), Mar. 23, 1935 (typed copy), DPLCR; *Senate Disposition of Cotton Hearings,* 10.

19. *New Orleans Times-Picayune,* Mar. 12, 1935, 1, 3; Committee on Agriculture and Forestry, *Hearings Before the Committee on Agriculture and Forestry Pursuant to Senate Resolutions 103,125, 172, and 182; Resolutions to Investigate the Causes of the Rapid Decline in the Price of Cotton on the Cotton Exchanges Before, On, or Subsequent to Mar. 11, 1935, Part 2,* 74th Cong., 2d sess., 1936, 1276 (hereinafter cited as *Senate Price Decline Hearings); Senate Disposition of Cotton Hearings,* 11.

20. *Senate Price Decline Hearings,* 1277, 1278 ("None in the world" quotation); Johnston letter quoted in *New York Times,* Apr. 6, 1934, 35; see also AAA press release, Jan. 24, 1934, PCP, RG 145, NA; OJ to Smith, Aug. 6, 1934; Mar. 12, 1935, GC, RG 16, NA; OJ to Vernon Bellhouse, Dec. 26, 1935, DPLCR; *Senate Disposition of Cotton Hearings,* 74 (last quotation); see also OJ to Richard Harriss, Feb. 21, 1935, GC, RG 16, NA.

21. *Senate Disposition of Cotton Hearings,* 11; OJ to Harriss, Feb. 21, 1935, GC, RG 16, NA; Davis, COHC (quotation); see also CCC Board of Directors (signed by Wallace, Davis, Buckles, Johnston, W. I. Myers, J. E. Wells Jr.) to Roosevelt, Aug. 9, 1935, OF 736, FDRL. A "hedge" is a form of "trade insurance" and is one aspect of futures trading, used by producers to protect themselves against a market decline. For a full discussion of hedging, see W. H. Hubbard, *Cotton and the Cotton Market* (New York, 1928), 309–46.

22. OJ to Marvin McIntyre, May 31, 1935, and attached OJ to Wallace, May 31, 1935, memorandum, OF 1K, FDRL; OJ to Roosevelt through Herbert Feis, Mar. 22, 1935, or before (memorandum, résumé of cable), OF 258; OJ to Chester Davis, May 31, 1935, memorandum (Johnston's memorandum to Wallace attached), PCP, RG 145, NA; see also OJ to Johnston Bankhead, June 20, 1935, reprinted in *Congressional Record,* 74th Cong., 1st sess., 1935, 79, pt. 10:11373–75; Stowell to Toler, Apr. 15, 1935 (quotation), DPLCR. By early August there was very little "free" cotton outside federal control; OJ to FCSDA, Aug. 3, 1935.

23. *Senate Price Decline Hearings,* 1271; *Senate ACCA Hearing,* 92 ("unfortunate error" quotation); see Richards, *Cotton and the AAA,* 223. OJ to Wallace, May 31, 1935, memorandum, OF 1K; OJ to Roosevelt through Herbert Feis, Mar. 22, 1935, or before (memorandum, résumé of cable), OF 258, FDRL; OJ to McIntyre, May 31, June 15 ("disordered" quotation), 1935, OF 1K, FDRL; OJ to FCSDA, June 14, 1935, DPLCR. Port warehouses suffered a decline in business because of increased transportation costs to coastal facilities. The CCC reconcentrated about one-third of the cotton held under the twelve-cent loan, with the government assuming the costs. Richards, *Cotton and the AAA,* 223; Samuel Satin to James F. Byrnes, Apr. 15, 1936; V. M. Carothers to OJ, Oct. 15, 1935; OJ to Carothers, Nov. 20, 1935, Information and Inquiry, RG 161, NA; see also other relevant correspondence in the same place; Jesse Jones to Roosevelt, Aug. 30, 1935; Roosevelt to Richard B. Russell Jr., Aug. 31, Sept. 21, 1935; Russell to Roosevelt, Sept. 10, 1935, OF 736, FDRL; see also G. C. Rathell to CCC Executive Committee, July 11, 1935, memorandum, in Minutes of the CCC Executive Committee, July 12, 1935, and other minutes of that date, Minutes, vol. 2, RG 161, NA.

24. OJ to Wallace, May 31, 1935, memorandum; OJ to McIntyre, June 15, 1935, OF 1K, FDRL; OJ to Davis, June 27, 1935, GC, RG 16, NA; Richards, *Cotton and the AAA,* 224–25; Porter interview; Davis, COHC (quotations); *Memphis Press-Scimitar,* Aug. 30, 1935, 7; OJ to FCSDA, June 14, 1935, and other relevant correspondence with the British; CCC Board of Directors to Roosevelt, Aug. 9, 1935, memorandum, OF 736, FDRL; Robert H. Ferrell, *Choosing Truman: The Democratic Convention of 1944* (Columbia, Mo., and London, 1994), 2; Sillers to Harrison, Aug. 5, 1935, telegram (copy); Harrison to Sillers, Aug. 14, 1935, telegram; see Harrison to Sillers, Aug. 27, 1935, Sillers Papers. Paul Porter later hinted that "Oscar and I" developed the loan and adjustment payment idea (whether referring to the 1933 loan or the 1935 idea, or both, is unclear); Porter interview.

25. Richards, *Cotton and the AAA,* 225–26; see also Porter interview; Davis, COHC; OJ to Stowell, Aug. 17, 1935, DPLCR; AAA press releases, Aug. 22, Sept. 11, 1935, PCP, RG 145, NA (copy of Aug. 22 also in AAA, CLD, RG 16, NA); *Memphis Commercial Appeal,* Aug. 25, 1935, I, 1, 4; *Memphis Press-Scimitar,* Aug. 24, 1935, 1; Murray Benedict, *Farm Policies of the United States,* 484–85. A twelve-cent loan would have brought every bale under federal control, requiring $700 million, Johnston argued. There was "no comparison" between the price-pegging proposal and the loan-subsidy plan, the latter of which, he said, was "a blend of the best features of all." Board of Directors, CCC to Roosevelt, Aug. 9, 1935, memorandum, OF 736, FDRL; OJ to Wallace, Nov. 22, 1935, memorandum, GC, RG 16, NA; *Memphis Press-Scimitar,* Aug. 30, 1935, 7 ("blend" quotation); Nov. 9, 1935, 2; AAA press release, Sept. 11, 1935, PCP, RG 145, NA; Johnston, "Pool and Loan Holdings Are Explained by Oscar Johnston," *Cotton Digest,* May 23, 1936, 6.

26. *Senate Disposition of Cotton Hearings,* 11; *Senate Price Decline Hearings,* 1263; Toler to Stowell, May 10, 1935, DPLCR; *New York Times,* May 9, 1935, 31; *Memphis Commercial Appeal,* May 9, 1935, 1; AAA press release, May 8, 1935, AAA, CLD, RG 16, NA; see also OJ to Talley, May 9, 1935, in Minutes of Executive Committee of CCC, May 10, 1935, Minutes, vol. 2, RG 161, NA.

27. Philip B. Weld to McIntyre, May 9, 1935, OF 258; OJ to Roosevelt, May 15, 1935, memorandum, OF 1K, FDRL; OJ to FCSDA, June 14, 1935, DPLCR; AAA press releases, Aug. 22, 23 (Johnston "quotations"), Sept. 11, 1935, PCP, RG 145, NA (copy of Aug. 22 also in AAA, CLD, RG 16, NA); *Senate Disposition of Cotton Hearings,* 10–11, 72; *Senate Price Decline Hearings,* 1229, 1265, 1283–4; OJ to Wallace, Oct. 23, 1935, memorandum, GC, RG 145, NA; OJ to Wallace, Nov. 22, 1935, memorandum, GC, RG 16, NA; see also OJ to Milo Perkins, Nov. 29, 1935, GC, RG 145, NA; OJ to Vernon Bellhouse, Dec. 26, 1935, DPLCR.

28. OJ to Wallace, Aug. 16, 1934; Wallace to J. R. McCarl, Aug. 17, 1934, GC, RG 16, NA (copy of Aug. 16 letter also in PCP, RG 145, NA); press release, Oct. 3, 1934 (initiated by Johnston), PCP, RG 145, NA; *Senate Price Decline Hearings,* 1197–9; *Senate Disposition of Cotton Hearings,* 62–63; OJ to Wallace, Jan. 22, 1935, memorandum, PCP, RG 145, NA; Johnston, "Origin and Operation," 138; Johnston, "Pool and Loan Holdings Are Explained," 6.

29. *Senate Price Decline Hearings,* 1186–91, 1198–9, 1239; *Senate Disposition of Cotton Hearings,* 9, 10, 23–24, 62–63, 70; *Senate ACCA Hearings,* 91; "Biggest Cotton Plantation," 160; Garside, "Government Activities in Cotton—Part 2(b)," 6–7; OJ to Wallace, Jan. 22, 1935, memorandum, PCP, RG 145, NA.

30. *Senate Disposition of Cotton Hearings,* 10; *Senate Price Decline Hearings,* 1235–6, 1270–5 (quotation on 1275), 1287; Garside, "Government Activities in Cotton—Part 2 (b)," 6.

31. *Senate Disposition of Cotton Hearings,* 24–25; see also, *Senate Price Decline Hearings,* 1244–5.

32. *Senate Price Decline Hearings,* 1237–8, 1245; *Senate Disposition of Cotton Hearings,* 21, 74; OJ to Perkins, Nov. 29, 1935; OJ to Wallace, Dec. 5, 1935, GC, RG 145, NA; OJ to Wallace, Nov. 22, 1935, memorandum; Wallace to OJ, Nov. 30, 1935, GC, RG 16, NA; Robert Harriss to Marvin McIntyre, Dec. 17, 1935, OF 258, FDRL; J. R. McCarl to Wallace, Oct. 10, 1935 (copy), PCP, RG 145, NA.

33. *Senate Disposition of Cotton Hearings,* 101; Morgenthau Diaries, Dec. 13, 1935, 14:1, FDRL.

34. *Senate Disposition of Cotton Hearings,* 17 ("Bought" quotation), 59 ("marketwise" quotations), 61, 65 (Schwellenbach quotations); OJ to Wallace, Aug. 16, 1934, GC, RG 16, NA; USDA report to the secretary of the Treasury regarding CCC cotton loans and cotton pool, Feb. 10, 1936, PCP, RG 145, NA; Roosevelt to Jesse Jones, Mar. 19, 1936, memorandum, OF 736, FDRL; OJ to Carl Robbins, Aug. 26, 1939 ("paternal" quotation), miscellaneous, RG 161, NA; *Memphis Press-Scimitar,* Feb. 22, 1936, 10; OJ to Bellhouse, Dec. 26, 1935, DPLCR.

35. *New York Times,* Feb. 2, 1936, I, 28; Feb. 5, 1936, 6 ("past due paper" quotation); J. L. Severance, *Journal of Commerce* (New York), column, typed copy in AAA, CLD, RG 16, NA; OJ to Wallace and H. R. Tolley, Jan. 23, 1936, memorandum; OJ to Davis, Dec. 20, 1935, GC, RG 145, NA; OJ to Bellhouse, Dec. 26, 1935; OJ to Stowell, Feb. 6, 20, Mar. 11, 1936; OJ to FCSDA, Apr. 6, 1936, DPLCR; *Senate Disposition of Cotton Hearings,* 15, see also 48–49, and J. L. Severance, "Early Smith Bill Action Is Expected—Opposition Fears Allayed As Market Freed from Manipulation Is Seen," 148–50.

36. *New York Times,* Feb. 2, 1936, 28; Feb. 5, 1935, 1, 6; *New Orleans Times-Picayune,* Feb. 4, 1936, 5; *Senate Disposition of Cotton Hearings,* 1–2 (see also Severance, "Early Smith Bill Action Is Expected," 148–50); *Congressional Record,* 74th Cong., 2d sess., 1936, 80, pt. 2:1334; OJ to Perkins, Nov. 29, 1935, JF, RG 145, NA; Robert Harriss to McIntyre, Dec. 17, 1935, OF 258, FDRL; OJ to Smith, Mar. 12, 1935, GC, RG 16, NA; OJ to Stowell, Feb. 6, 1936, DPLCR.

37. OJ to Jesse Jones, Feb. 10, 1936, RFC Loans, RG 161, NA; *New York Times,* Feb. 5, 1936, 6; Feb. 9, 1936, III, 8; Feb. 15, 1936, 2; *Newsweek,* Apr. 18, 1936, 35; OJ to Stowell, Feb. 6, 1936, DPLCR; see OJ to Smith, Feb. 4, 1936, reprinted in *Senate Disposition of Cotton Hearings,* 44–46.

38. Davis, COHC; Conn interview; Porter interview. There were also allegedly unsavory things outside the commodities market. In 1940 Wallace learned "that Senator Smith had given a letter to a rascal who had been going around among New England warehouses offering to get business for them on a commission basis." Wallace's source believed, as Wallace recorded in his diary, that "this made Senator Smith particularly vulnerable. He said Oscar Johnston had exposed this same kind of thing several years previous when he was with the AAA by using the Washington Merry-Go-Round [a syndicated muckraking column by Drew Pearson and Robert Allen]. This was the only instance as far as I know in which anyone connected with the Department of Agriculture has used the Washington Merry-go-Round." Wallace Diary, Jan. 23, 1940, Univ. of Iowa Library.

39. Porter interview ("promised" quotation); Davis, COHC ("ruined" quotation); Johnson, "Bankhead Family," 100; Johnson, "John Bankhead, 2D," 54–58.

40. *New York Times*, Feb. 15, 1936, 2 (Johnston quotations), see also Feb. 9, 1936, III, 8, and *New Orleans Times-Picayune*, Feb. 7, 1936, 10, 25, *Newsweek*, Apr. 18, 1936, 35; OJ to Smith, Feb. 4, 1936, reprinted in *Senate Disposition of Cotton Hearings*, 44–46 (Johnston quotation also); Woods to Perkins, Feb. 14, 1936 (three-page letter), GC, RG 16, NA.

41. *Senate Disposition of Cotton Hearings*, 25 (quotation); see also *Jackson Daily News*, Feb. 22, 1936, 5.

42. *Senate Disposition of Cotton Hearings*, 23–25.

43. I.M.B.F. to OJ, Feb. 6, 1936, telegram, in *Senate Disposition of Cotton Hearings*, 41 (see OJ to Smith, Feb. 4, 1936, 45); OJ to Stowell, Feb. 20, 1936; Stowell to OJ, Feb. 26, 1936; Percy to OJ, Feb. 11, 1936, DPLCR; *Memphis Press-Scimitar*, Feb. 20, 1936, 13; see also M. E. Goode to Richard Russell, Feb. 24, 1936, Information and Inquiry, RG 161, NA; Percy to OJ, Feb. 11, 1936, DPLCR; *New Orleans Times-Picayune*, Feb. 10, 1936, 1 (Harrison quotation), 4; see also Feb. 17, 1936, 19; *New York Times*, Feb. 15, 1936, 2.

44. *New Orleans Times-Picayune*, Feb. 17, 1936, 19; *New York Times*, Feb. 15, 1936, 2; *Memphis Press-Scimitar*, Feb. 14, 1936, 24; *Senate Disposition of Cotton Hearings*, 106, 110, 119, 158–59 (passim for respect of investigators). Smith had told the committee earlier: "we don't want to mix up a bad policy with the reflection that the man [Johnston] was a bad man." *Senate Disposition of Cotton Hearings*, 158.

45. *New Orleans Times-Picayune*, Feb. 3, 1936, 5; Feb. 13, 1936, 1, 3; Feb. 14, 1936, 1, 2; *Jackson Daily News*, Feb. 14, 1936, 12; OJ to Stowell, Feb. 6, 1936, DPLCR. *Senate Disposition of Cotton Hearings*, 84; see OJ to Wallace, Dec. 5, 1935, GC, RG 145, NA; and other material relative to Johnston's desire to reopen the pool. Bids were also accepted on long-staple pool stocks at Greenwood, Mississippi. *New Orleans Times-Picayune*, Feb. 13, 1936, 3; Feb. 14, 1936, 2; *Journal of Commerce* (New York), Feb. 14, 1936, clipping included with Woods to Perkins, Feb. 14, 1936 (one-page letter), GC, RG 16, NA. Before opening the bids, Johnston told Wallace that the pool "cannot be correctly charged with 'squeezing the futures market' so long as we evince a willingness to sell our long futures at a price slightly below the price at which spot cotton's selling and since we are offering to sell 'at the market' spot cotton, we cannot correctly be charged with participating in a 'corner' of the spot market." OJ to Wallace, Feb. 10, 1936, memorandum, GC, RG 16, NA. A few days later, however, Johnston told the press that he would demand spot delivery on his March contracts, denying it was a "squeeze" because spot prices still stood higher than futures. When the following day he reversed his demand, speculators holding long March contracts were caught off guard, and the market slipped several points. *New Orleans Times-Picayune*, Feb. 14, 1936, 1; *Memphis Press-Scimitar*, Feb. 14, 1936, 24; Feb. 15, 1936, 10; *Journal of Commerce* (New York), Feb. 14, 1936, clipping included with Woods to Perkins, Feb. 14, 1936 (one-page letter), GC, RG 16, NA; *Pearsall's Market Bulletin*, Feb. 14, 1935 (attached to one of Wood's two letters to Perkins of that date).

46. *New Orleans Times-Picayune*, Feb. 14, 1936, 1; OJ to Stowell, Feb. 20, Mar. 11, 1936; OJ to FCSDA, Apr. 6, 1936, DPLCR; OJ to Wallace, Feb. 10, 1936; OJ to Wallace, Mar. 28, 1936, memorandum, GC, RG 16, NA; *Memphis Commercial Appeal*, Apr. 2, 1936, 23; *New York Times*, Apr. 5, 1936, III, 1.

47. The government would thus write off a $10 million loss; OJ to Stowell, Mar. 11, 1936; OJ to FCSDA, Apr. 6, 1936, DPLCR; *Newsweek*, Apr. 18, 1936, 35; *New York Times*, Apr. 5, 1936, III, 1; *Memphis Commercial Appeal*, Apr. 3, 1936, 23; Apr. 5, 1936, I, 1, 2; *New Orleans Times-Picayune*, Apr. 5, 1936, 1; Johnston, "Pool and Loan Holdings Are Explained By Oscar Johnston," *Cotton Digest,* May 23, 1936, 6; OJ to Wallace, Mar. 30, 1936, memorandum, RFC Loans, RG 161, NA. Johnston had offered a substitute method of selling the loan cotton as early as February. *New Orleans Times-Picayune,* Feb. 17, 1936, 19.

48. *Memphis Commercial Appeal*, Apr. 2, 1936, 23; Apr. 3, 1936, 23 ("manifest surrender" quotation); OJ to FCSDA, Apr. 6, 1936, DPLCR; *Memphis Press-Scimitar,* Apr. 2, 1936, 17; *Newsweek,* Apr. 18, 1936, 36; *New York Times,* Feb. 9, 1936, III, 8; Davis, COHC ("dog" quotation); *Time,* Apr. 20, 1936, 80; Harry Ashmore, *Civil Rights and Wrongs: A Memoir of Race and Politics, 1944–1994* (New York, 1994), 6–9 (walkout quotation on 8), 406. "Smith, Ellison DuRant," *Biographical Directory of the United States Congress, 1774–1989, Bicentennial Edition* (Washington, D.C., 1989), 1827; see also Daniel Hollis, "'Cotton Ed Smith'—Showman or Statesman?" *South Carolina Historical Magazine* 71 (Oct. 1970): 235–56.

49. *New York Times,* Apr. 5, 1936, III, 1; May 8, 1936, 43; May 25, 1936, 35; OJ to Stowell, May 11, June 1, 1936; Stowell to OJ, Feb. 25, 1936; Apr. 16, 1936; Stowell to DPL, Apr. 6, 1936, DPLCR; see Murray Benedict and Oscar Stine, *The Agricultural Commodity Progams: Two Decades of Experience* (New York, 1956), 12–13.

50. Although the second release of loan cotton was made on similar terms as the April 4 announcement, the market value stood higher. Thus, in order to withdraw cotton from the loan for resale, the producer had to pay the original loan plus part of the carrying charges. OJ to FCSDA, July 1, 1936, DPLCR; Roosevelt to OJ, July 7, 9, 1936, memorandums; OJ to Roosevelt, July 10, 1936; report (draft prepared by Johnston for Roosevelt's signature) to Ellison Smith, July 10, 1936 (copies were likely sent to several other senators), OF 258, FDRL (see also notations regarding the issue, July 7, 1936, OF 736, FDRL); OJ to Jesse Jones, May 23, 1936, reproduced in CCC Executive Committee Minutes, 3:2–7, May 29, 1936, RG 161, NA; OJ to Morris Sheppard, May 18, 1936, Information and Inquiry, RG 161, NA; OJ to Goodloe, July 22, 28 (quotation), 1936, RFC Loans, RG 161, NA; OJ to McIntyre, July 10, 1936; Murray Stewart Jr. to Roosevelt, July 8, 1936, OF 258, FDRL; Benedict and Stine, *The Agricultural Commodity Programs,* 12–13; see USDA reports to the secretary of the Treasury regarding CCC loans and cotton pool, July 13, 20; Aug. 10, 1936, PCP, RG 145, NA.

51. *Memphis Commercial Appeal,* June 11, 1935, 1, Apr. 1, 1936, 1; *Memphis Press-Scimitar,* Feb. 24, 1936, 11, Mar. 7, 1936, 10, Apr. 1, 1936, 14, July 8, 1936, 1, July 30, 1936, 4; *New York Times,* Mar. 4, 1936, 39, Apr. 1, 1936, 46, June 20, 1936, 23, July 8, 1936, 27, July 31, 1936, 30; OJ to Stowell, Mar. 11, 1936; OJ to FCSDA, Apr. 6, July 1, Aug. 7, 1936; OJ to Herbert Lee, July 9, 1936, DPLCR; OJ to Wallace, Feb. 10, Mar. 28, 30, memorandums, GC, RG 16, NA; Paul Porter to Milo Perkins, Feb. 14, 1936, memorandum, GC, RG 16, NA; Dickson, *The Story of King Cotton,* 286. After Johnston sold all of the pool's 317,000 July contracts, the market actually advanced to a season high of 12.12 cents per pound. *New York Times,* June 20, 1936, 23.

52. The column, n.d., was J. L. Severance of the *Journal of Commerce* (New York), reprinted in *Senate Disposition of Cotton Hearings,* 148–50. Frank, COHC; OJ to Smith, Aug. 6, 1934, GC, RG 16, NA; Dickson, *The Story of King Cotton,* 285; Conn inter-

view; Dunn interview; Blake interviews. For a critical view of Johnston's pool handling, see *Senate ACCA Hearing*, 128. The potential for corruption extended to government loan cotton. When in 1936 a Senate investigator, probing a possible conflict of interest, asked Johnston if he shared information about loan cotton with the British Fine Spinners, Johnston replied: "Definitely, I have not." *Senate Price Decline Hearings*, 1271. Whether the inquisitor was asking only about the 1934 loan cotton is uncertain, but Johnston's emphatic denial seemed to contradict the heavy flow of information to Manchester. See relevant correspondence in DPLCR, for example, July 6, 1934, Aug. 3, 19, 1935. But Read Dunn Jr., later a young associate of Oscar's, and still later, a Senate-confirmed commissioner on the Commodities Futures Trading Commission, reviewed relevant Johnston-to-British correspondence, 1933–36, in 1989, then offered his views: "While I agree that he [Johnston] did tell them [the British] a great deal I think that he did not cross the line of propriety as it was then drawn. I think the price information in the letters was more indications of what was being requested and what various groups were pressing the Department to adopt. Other price indications were prices the poop sheets and market letters were stating, in other words, public information. It is true that the way the line is drawn today he would have been far across it. In fact he would not have been permitted to hold office unless he divorced himself from his business." Dunn to author, Nov. 24, 1989.

53. Richards added: "The experience of the AAA with the cotton option plan used in 1933 does not demonstrate that government cotton can be disposed of effectively by giving it to producers in payment for curtailing current production." Richards, *Cotton and the AAA*, 204–5, 212 (text quotation), 228 (endnote quotation); *Memphis Commercial Appeal*, Apr. 14, 1936, 10. Issued prior to the liquidation of the cotton pool and the significant movement of loan cotton into trade channels, the Brookings study, despite its value, lacks requisite perspective.

54. Minutes of the Executive Committee of the CCC, July 12, 1935, Minutes, vol. 2, RG 161, NA; OJ to Morris Sheppard, May 18, 1936, Information and Inquiry, RG 161, NA; OJ to John Goodloe, July 22, 1936, RFC Loans, RG 161, NA; *Senate ACCA Hearing*, 92; see *Senate Price Decline Hearings*, 1239, 1260.

55. *Senate ACCA Hearings*, 85–86; *New York Times*, July 31, 1936, 30; see report (draft prepared by Johnston for Roosevelt's signature) to Smith, n.d. (July 1936) (copies also apparently sent to several other senators), OF 258, FDRL; Johnston, "Pool and Loan Holdings Are Explained," 5; OJ to FCSDA, Aug. 7, 1936, DPLCR; *Senate Disposition of Cotton Hearings*, 73. "The further liquidation of the Pool is a pure formality," Johnston told Wallace in January 1937, "involving routine detail that is being carried forward under the direction of my assistant, Mr. Lamkin, and which does not require my presence in Washington." OJ to Wallace, Jan. 20, 1937, GC, RG 16, NA. The $1.8 million in the federal Treasury remained a source of controversy long after the pool had been liquidated and even after Johnston left the government in 1938. Several senators, led by Cotton Ed Smith of South Carolina, believed the funds should have been distributed as a final payment—about a dollar per bale—to producers who had participated in the pool. Johnston, whose companies had a stake in the outcome, believed, according to law, that the federal government had claim on the surplus, a reversal of his earlier views. *Senate ACCA Hearing*, 86, 95–96, 151; see *Senate Disposition of Cotton Hearings*, 73. Title IV of the AAA of 1938 authorized making the funds available to producers. *Memphis Commercial Appeal*, Jan. 27, 1938, 1. After a round of hearings

and legislative haggling, the $1.8 million was apparently dispensed to producers in 1939. Committee on Appropriations, *Hearings Before the Subcommittee of the House Committee on Appropriations (Appropriations for Retirement of 1933 Cotton Pool Participation Trust Certificates),* 75th Cong., 3d sess., 1938; see also *Memphis Commercial Appeal,* Feb. 7, 1939, 5.

56. Billy Wynn to Robert H. Wynn, Aug. 3, 1936; Stowell to OJ, June 13, July 13, 1936, DPLCR; Goodloe to OJ, July 17, 1936, RFC Loans, RG 161. NA.

57. Davis to Hopkins, June 26, 1934, GC, RG 145, NA; see also "Biggest Cotton Plantation," 160; *Senate Price Decline Hearings,* 1280.

58. *New Orleans Times-Picayune,* June 9, 1938, 2 (quotation); see also *Memphis Commercial Appeal,* June 9, 1938, 1, 2; *Congressional Record,* 75th Cong., 5th sess., 1937, 81, pt. 7:7777; see *Senate ACCA Hearing; Time,* Apr. 20, 1936, 80, 82.

59. OJ to FCSDA, Aug. 7, 1936; OJ to Peek, July 24, 1936; Peek to OJ, July 27, 1936; Jack Little to OJ, July 16, 1936 (last quotation), DPLCR. Peek, still bitter, added: "I shall always feel that had every move not been obstructed we should have made a clean up of a good many of the problems. For example, if we had been permitted to sell cotton when we had a chance I am of the opinion there would have been no need for worry about the 12c loans."

## 10. Tempest in a Tea Pot

1. *Jackson Daily News,* Aug. 21, 1919, 4; Kirwin, *Revolt of the Rednecks,* 295; *Vardaman's Weekly,* June 26, 1919, 7; July 24, 1919, 11; Aug. 21, 1919, 5, 13. Some selected accounts of factionalism within the Mississippi Democratic Party include V. O. Key Jr., *Southern Politics in State and Nation* (New York, 1949), 229–53; Kirwin, *Revolt of the Rednecks*; Percy, *Lanterns on the Levee*; and Balsamo, "Theodore G. Bilbo and Mississippi Politics."

2. "Biggest Cotton Plantation," 125; Balsamo, "Theodore G. Bilbo and Mississippi Politics"; Balsamo to author, Mar. 1, 1972.

3. Van Devanter returned his small checks. *Time,* Apr. 20, 1936, 18 ("sleuthing" quotation and last quotation); "Biggest Cotton Plantation," 125; *Newsweek,* Apr. 18. 1936, 13; *New York Times,* Feb. 29, 1936, 8; Mar. 6, 1936, 15; Mar. 24, 1936, 16; *New York Herald-Tribune,* Apr. 9, 1936, 1, 8; *Congressional Record,* 74th Cong., 2d sess., 1936, 4150, 6175; see David Tompkins, *Senator Arthur H. Vandenberg: The Evolution of a Modern Republican, 1884–1945* (East Lansing, Mich., 1970), 122. Vandenberg opposed the AAA of 1938. Michael W. Schuyler, "The Politics of Change: The Battle for the Agricultural Adjustment Act of 1938," *Prologue: The Journal of the National Archives* 15 (fall 1983): 170.

4. *Newsweek,* Apr. 18, 1936, 13; *Congressional Record,* 74th Cong., 2d sess., 1936, 4150, 6174–75; *Memphis Commercial Appeal,* Mar. 26, 1936, 10. Bilbo to C. A. Cobb, Apr. 3, 1936; see E. A. Miller to Bilbo, Apr. 16, 1936, GC, RG 145, NA; see "Biggest Cotton Plantation," 125. Chipman's story also reprinted in *New York Herald-Tribune,* Apr. 5, 1936, 21. For Vandenberg's position in the anti–New Deal faction of the Republican Party after 1935, see James T. Patterson, *Congressional Conservatism and the New Deal: The Growth of the Conservative Coalition in Congress, 1933–1939* (Lexington, Ky., 1967), 102–3, 108; and Tompkins, *Senator Arthur H. Vandenberg,* 114–58.

5. *Congressional Record,* 74th Cong., 2d sess., 1936, 6175; *New York Herald-Tribune,* Apr. 7, 1936, 8 (Vandenberg quotation); see also *Time,* Apr. 20, 1936, 18.

6. "Biggest Cotton Plantation," 125; *New York Times,* Apr. 6, 1936, 1 (report quotation); see *Washington Post,* Apr. 5, 1936, 1, Apr. 6, 1936, 1, 7; *New Orleans Times-Picayune,* Apr. 9, 1936, 12.

7. *New York Times,* Apr. 6, 1936, 1; *Washington Post,* Apr. 8, 1936, 1; *New Orleans Times-Picayune,* Apr. 9, 1936, 12; *Memphis Press-Scimitar,* Apr. 9., 1936, 10; *Jackson Daily News,* Apr. 8, 1936, 1.

8. *Time,* Apr. 20, 1936, 18 (first quotation); *New York Times,* Apr. 6, 1936, 1 (second quotation); *New Orleans Times-Picayune,* Apr. 7, 1936, 4 (fourth quotation); Apr. 8, 1936, 7 (third quotation).

9. *New York Times,* Apr. 6, 1936, 1, 4; *Time,* Apr. 20, 1936, 18; see also *New Orleans Times-Picayune,* Apr. 8, 1936, 7; Wallace to Ellison Smith, Apr. 15, 1936, reprinted in *Congressional Record,* 74th Cong., 2d sess., 1936, 6193; see also 4996.

10. *New Orleans Times-Picayune,* Apr. 7, 1936, 4 (quotations); see also Apr. 10, 1936, 2.

11. *Congressional Record,* 74th Cong., 2d sess., 1936, 6172–73, 6175, 6190 (Connally quotation); 75th Cong., 1st sess., 1937, 4500–4501.

12. Congressional Record, 74th Cong., 2d sess., 1936, 6196; (June 18, 1936), 9836; U.S. Congress, Senate Documents, Payments Made Under Agricultural Adjustment Program, 74th Cong., 2d sess., no. 274, ser. 10016 (Washington, D.C., 1936), 34, 47, 55; *Memphis Commercial Appeal,* June 20, 1936, 1; *Jackson Daily News,* June 20, 1936, 5.

13. *Congressional Record,* 74th Cong., 2d sess., 1936, 6175 (first quotation); *Senate Price Decline Hearings,* 1270 (second quotation).

14. *Manchester Daily Dispatch* (?), Apr. 6, 1936 (first quotation, plus Lee quotations); *London News Chronicle* (?), Apr. 6, 1936 (headline and "campaign" quotation), clippings in DPLCR.

15. Stowell to DPL, Apr. 6, 1936, DPLCR.

16. OJ to Stowell, Apr. 21, 1936, DPLCR.

17. *New Orleans Times-Picayune,* Apr. 7, 1936, 4; June 7, 1936, 12; *Congressional Record,* 74th Cong., 2d Sess., 1936, 6175.

18. Blake to Wallace, June 10, 1936 (mimeographed; emphasis added); Blake to the Members and Friends of the Delta Chamber of Commerce, June 11, 1936 (mimeographed), DPLCR.

19. Blake to the Members and Friends of the Delta Chamber of Commerce, June 11, 1936 (mimeographed), DPLCR.

20. *New York Times,* May 14, 1937, 16, May 20, 1937, 15, May 22, 1937, 6, May 23, 1937, 20; Vandenberg to Howard Tolley, May 25, 1937, GC, RG 145, NA; Wild, "History," DPLCR; *Congressional Record,* 75th Cong., 1st sess., 1937, 4500–4501.

21. *New York Times,* May 30, 1937, I, 18; Tolley to Vandenberg, May 29, July 8, 1937; see J. B. Hutson (?) to Alfred Stedman (handwritten note), May 26, 1937; OJ to Tolley, June 4, 1937, GC, RG 145, NA; *Louisville Courier-Journal,* Apr. 6, 1936, 1, 2 (Wallace quotation); OJ to Cobb, June 4, 1937, GC, RG 145, NA.

22. Stedman to OJ, June 24, 1937 (first quotation); July 14, 1937 (second quotation); OJ to Stedman, June 28, 1937, GC, RG 145, NA; see also *New York Times,* July 11, 1937, 7; *Memphis Commercial Appeal,* June 11, 1937, 1, 2.

23. OJ to Tolley, June 4, 1937 (quotations and information), GC, RG 145, NA; *New York Times,* July 11, 1937, I, 7 (compare quotations where appropriate).

24. Stedman to OJ, July 14, 1937 (first quotation), GC, RG 145, NA; *New York Times,* May 30, 1937, 18; USDA, *Annotated Compilation of the Soil Conservation and Domestic*

*Allotment Act, as Amended, the Agricultural Act of 1938, as Amended, and Acts Relating Thereto* . . . (Washington, D.C., 1938), 10; *Memphis Commercial Appeal,* Jan. 26, 1938, 1; William T. Wynn, J. T. Thomas, and Johnston to Willam Rhea Blake, July 22, 1937, telegram (last quotation), DPLCR.

25. OJ to Stowell, Dec. 3, 1936; Statement and President's Report (1937), Apr. 16, 1938, DPLCR.

26. OJ to I. W. Duggan, Nov. 10, 1938 (quotation), GC, RG 145, NA; *New York Times,* Mar. 10, 1936, 4; Blake interviews; for ongoing controversy, see relevant material in note 27 below; see also *New York Times,* Feb. 4, 1970, 17, July 9, 1970, 1, 75, July 23, 1970, 1, 23, Aug. 6, 1970, 1, 19, Aug. 18, 1970, 34, Sept. 15, 1970, 15, Sept. 16, 1970, 1, 10, Oct. 8, 1970, 26, Dec. 1, 1970, 23, Apr. 9, 1971, 12, June 24, 1971, 42, Mar. 16, 1972, 15; *Congressional Record,* 91st Cong., 2d sess., 1970, 14179–83, 29092–93. See the subsidies debate in *USA Today,* May 18, 1990, 12A.

27. Rep. Frank E. Hook (D-Mich.), *Congressional Record,* 77th Cong., 2d sess., 1942, 2119; Rep. Reid F. Murray (R-Wisc.), *Congressional Record,* 80th Cong., 2d sess., 1948, A3679; *Life,* Feb. 4, 1957, 43 (see denial and defense in *Congressional Record,* 85th Cong., 1st sess., 1957, A1115–16; *Congressional Record,* 86th Cong., 1st sess., 1959, 3140, see also 3138–48; *New York Times,* June 24, 1971, 42; see also *Congressional Record,* 92d Cong., 1st sess., 1971, 21635.

28. Sidney Baldwin, *Poverty and Politics: The Rise and Decline of the Farm Security Administration* (Chapel Hill, 1968); Grant McConnell, *The Decline of Agrarian Democracy,* 84–96; *Washington Post,* Apr. 7, 1936, 8. For reference to Connecticut General's participation in the cotton programs of 1934 and 1935, see *Senate Documents,* 74th Cong., 2d sess., 1936, 47, 55; for later payments made to several life insurance companies that had acquired agricultural lands through mortgage foreclosures, see *New York Times,* Mar. 5, 1940, 39. A number of scholars have demonstrated that agricultural planning in the early years of the New Deal reflected the strong influence of the large producers. See, for example, Conrad, *Forgotten Farmers*; Kirkendall, *Social Scientists and Farm Politics in the Age of Roosevelt*; Grubbs, *Cry from the Cotton*; Perkins, *Crisis in Agriculture*; Fite, *George N. Peek*; Saloutos, *The American Farmer and the New Deal*; Venkataramni, "Arkansas Sharecroppers."

29. *Memphis Press-Scimitar,* Apr. 6, 1936, 6 (first quotation), Apr. 14, 1936, 6 (last quotations), Apr. 21, 1936, 4; *Memphis Commercial Appeal,* Apr. 21, 1936, 1; *Congressional Record,* 74th Cong., 2d sess., 1936, 6191 (Connally quotation).

30. OJ to Marvin McIntyre, June 27, 1935; OJ to Roosevelt, June 27, 1935, OF 1K, FDRL; letter notation, June 27, 1935, PPF 2221, FDRL.

31. OJ to Herbert Stowell, July 18, 1936 (quotation); OJ to FCSDA, Aug. 7, Dec. 30, 1936; see Wild, "History," DPLCR.

32. OJ to Stowell, July 18, 1936; Stowell to OJ, Aug. 7, 14, Dec. 15, 1936; OJ to FCSDA, Dec. 28, 1936; OJ to Fred Stout, Jan. 15, 1937; Stout to Credit Clearing House, May 25, 1937, DPLCR.

33. *New York Times,* June 24, 1936, 11; OJ to Stowell, July 18, Oct. 27, Dec. 18 (two two-page letters); OJ to FCSDA, Aug. 7, 1936; Stowell to OJ, Aug. 26, Nov. 24, Dec. 2 (four-page letter; quotation); Barrow, Wade, Guthrie and Company to OJ, Nov. 2, 1936; Barrow, Wade, Guthrie and Company to Stowell, Nov. 2, 1936; OJ to Barrow, Wade, Guthrie and Company, Nov. 9, 1936; OJ to Stowell and W. A. Perry, Oct. 23, 1936, memorandum, DPLCR.

34. OJ to Collector, Internal Revenue, Jackson, Miss., June 11, 1937; OJ to Stowell, Dec. 18, 1936 (two two-page letters); Frank Wisner to OJ, June 23, 1937; OJ to Wisner, June 29, 1937, DPLCR; *New York Times*, Nov. 12, 1936, 1, Nov. 30, 1936, 1, June 25, 1939, III, 1. In 1940, after the repeal, the company tried, with unclear results, to reclaim the profits on the grounds that corporations with existing deficits should not have had to pay the tax. Fred Stout to Barrow, Wade, Guthrie and Company, Mar. 25, Apr. 16, 1940; Barrow, Wade, Guthrie and Company to Stout, Apr. 9, 1940, DPLCR.

35. OJ to FCSDA, Aug. 7, 1936; Stowell to OJ, Aug. 26, 1936; OJ to Stowell, Dec. 18, 1936 (two two-page letters); Minor S. Gray to W. T. Winterbottom, Nov. 1, 1962; Wild, "History," DPLCR.

36. Statement and President's Report (1936), Apr. 19, 1937 (quotation); DPLC, Cotton Production Record; Herbert Stowell to OJ, Dec. 3, 1935; OJ to FCSDA, July 25, Aug. 3, 1935, July 1, Aug. 1, 1936; OJ to Stowell, Dec. 27, 1934, July 1, Nov. 11, Dec. 1, 3, 18 (two two-page letters), 1936; "Biggest Cotton Plantation," 158; Hubert Phelps Machine Co. to DPL, Aug. 29, 1936; OJ to Egyptian Minister of Agriculture, July 14, 1937; OJ to Jack Little, July 6, 1937; Toler to M. E. Lobo, Oct. 22, 1937; Toler to Madokoro Shoten, Dec. 19, 1936; Lumus Cotton Gin Co. to DPL, Aug. 15, 1936, telegram, DPLCR; OJ to Lawrence Myers, Apr. 27, 1937, GC, RG 145, NA; see OJ to FCSDA, May 1, 1934, Feb. 19, 1942 (five-page letter); see OJ to Lawrence Myers, Apr. 14, 1939, DPLCR; OJ to Tom Linder, Feb. 9, 1945, Sillers Papers; T. Y. Williford in *Bolivar County Democrat*, Dec. 2, 1936, 1. Never satisfied, Ewing introduced Deltapine No. 14 in 1942, jumping the yield at Scott to 814 pounds an acre. "When this occurred," recalled Ewing later, "I felt like exclaiming 'Eureka!'" Ewing's prolific and skillfully produced seed series spread across the cotton belt, sought by farmers from Arizona to the Carolinas. Deltapine varieties could claim credit for increasing average staple from the standard seven-eighths to a full inch by the end of World War II. Such increase, matched by higher yields, reduced production costs everywhere Deltapine seed was sown. Some southern counties planted Deltapine varieties exclusively. Walton County, Georgia, for example, led the whole state in yield and value per acre. See Ewing, "History," DPLCR.

37. OJ to Stowell, Dec. 14, 1935 (with attached map), Nov. 18, 21, 1936; Stowell to DPL, Dec. 30, 1935; Distaff (FCSDA) to DPL, Dec. 28, 1935, telegram; OJ to FCSDA, Nov. 21, 30, Dec. 30, 1936; Walker Wood to OJ, Nov. 30, 1936; OJ to Milo Perkins, Nov. 30, 1936; OJ to E. B. Whitaker, Nov. 24, Dec. 18, 1936; OJ to T. Roy Reid, Dec. 2, 1936; Whitaker to OJ, Dec. 1, 15, 1936, Jan. 18, 1937; Stowell to OJ, Dec. 15, 1936, DPLCR.

38. "Biggest Cotton Plantation," 160; OJ to D. Howard Doane, Dec. 2, 1927, Doane Papers.

39. Whitaker to OJ, Feb. 8, 9, 1937, June 8, July 1, Sept. 13, 22, 1938; Toler to Whitaker, Aug. 16, Sept. 5, 1938; Whitaker to Toler, Sept. 1, Oct. 1, 1938; OJ to Whitaker, Feb. 11, 12, June 10, 1937, July 5, Sept. 24, 1938 (quotation), DPLCR.

40. "The Fine Cotton Spinners' and Doublers' Association, Limited . . . Mr. Herbert W. Lee's Review of the Year's Activities" (thirty-ninth general stockholders meeting, Manchester, Eng.), May 29, 1936, reprint from *The Statist*, June 6, 1936, DPLCR.

## 11. Fence Rails and Graveyards

1. Among several scholars who have written on failing New Deal fortunes generally, see William E. Leuchtenberg, *Franklin D. Roosevelt and the New Deal, 1932–1940* (New York, 1963), 252–74; James MacGregor Burns, *Roosevelt: The Lion and*

*the Fox* (New York, 1956), 291–404; and Richard Polenberg, "The Decline of the New Deal, 1937–1940," in *The New Deal,* ed. John Braeman, Robert H. Bremmer, and David Brody (Columbus, Ohio, 1975), 1:246–66. For a brief survey, see Kirkendall, *The United States,* 124–26. For a brief history of the Peabody Hotel, see Mary Ann Connell, *The Peabody: A Living Tradition* (Oxford, Miss., 1981).

2. TRB, "Washington Notes," 186 (first two quotations); *New York Times,* Sept. 4, 1937, 21 (last two quotations). The reporter for the *Times* was Felix Belair Jr., whose reports were "Special to the New York Times." All references to the *Times* in this chapter are to reports by Belair.

3. Benedict and Stine, *The Agricultural Commodity Programs,* 17; National City Bank of New York, *Economic Conditions, Governmental Finance, United States Securities,* Dec. 1936, 170 (monthly reports).

4. *Statistical History of the United States,* 301; see nine-page review of government cotton policies (evidently drafted by Paul H. Appleby, assistant to Secretary Wallace, n.d., probably Aug. 1937), and Appleby to William Hassett, Aug. 12, 1937, OF 258, FDRL; TRB, "Washington Notes," 186; Benedict and Stine, *Agricultural Commodity Programs,* 17.

5. See *Newsweek,* Aug. 21, 1937, 10–12 (last quotation); *Time,* Aug. 16, 1937, 7; TRB, "Washington Notes," 186; Nat Patton to Roosevelt, Aug. 7, 1937, telegram (first quotation), OF 258, FDRL. Patton added: "WE IN CONGRESS IN A MEASURE ARE TO BLAME WE SHOULD HAVE FORESEEN THIS IMPENDING DISASTER AND ACTED ACCORDINGLY. J.E." McDonald to Roosevelt, Aug. 4, 1937, OF 258, FDRL; see also relevant material in OF 258 and OF 736 (notations), FDRL.

6. *Newsweek,* Aug. 14, 1937, 32, Aug. 21, 1937, 10, Sept. 20, 1937, 34, Dec. 20, 1937, 42; *Life,* Aug. 23, 1937, 20; see also *Time,* Aug. 16, 1937, 7; *Memphis Press-Scimitar,* Aug. 9, 1937, 7–8, Aug. 19, 1937, 18 (AP quotation).

7. *Newsweek,* Aug. 21, 1937, 11, Sept. 13, 1937, 29–30; *Memphis Press-Scimitar,* Aug. 18, 1937, 2; *Time,* Aug. 23, 1937, 9; *Life,* Aug. 23, 1937, 20; see TRB, "Washington Notes," 186; Rosenman, *The Public Papers and Addresses of Franklin D. Roosevelt, 1937 Volume* (New York, 1938), 5:316–18 (press conference quotations).

8. *Memphis Press-Scimitar,* Aug. 18, 1937, 2, Aug. 31, 1937, 12 (see also Sept. 5, 1937, 6); TRB, "Washington Notes," 186; USDA, Bureau of Agricultural Economics (Washington), "The Cotton Situation," Sept. 28, 1937 (first page), courtesy to author by Dr. Gladys Baker, Historian, Agricultural History Group, National Economic Analysis Division, USDA, Washington (1975); also, Baker to author, Sept. 3, 1975; AAA press release, Aug. 30, 1937, Office of Information, RG 16, NA; see also *Jackson Daily News,* Sept. 4, 1937, 9. For Sen. Tom Connally's attempt to secure a ten-cent loan, see *Memphis Press-Scimitar,* Aug. 25, 1937, 16. For an explanation of how the 1937 loan was to function, see Oscar Johnston's detailed discussion in *Memphis Commercial Appeal,* Sept. 6, 1937, 3; see *Newsweek,* Sept. 13, 1937, 30.

9. TRB, "Washington Notes," 186; Appleby to MacMillan, May 18, 1936; MacMillan to Appleby, May 19, 1936; see also Milo Perkins to OJ, May 16, 1936; F. W. Foote to Wallace, Nov. 22, 1935, GC, RG 16, NA.

10. See W. T. Wynn to Pat Harrison, Aug. 6, 1937, telegram, OF 258, FDRL; Porter interview; Jones, with Angly, *Fifty Billion Dollars,* 89; see OJ to Marvin McIntyre, June 15, 1935, memorandum, OF 1K, FDRL; OJ to John Bankhead, June 20, 1935, reprinted in *Congressional Record,* 74th Cong., 1st sess., 1935, 79, pt. 10:11373; *Senate Price Decline Hearings,* 1271; OJ to Harrison, Aug. 6, 1937, telegram ("worked

beautifully" quotation), OF 258, FDRL; see also OJ to Howard Tolley, Aug. 16, 1937, CCC, RG 16, NA; OJ to Jack Little, Aug. 7, 1937; William Rhea Blake to OJ, July 21, 1937; OJ to Blake, July 23, 1937, DPLCR; Blake interviews; Gray interviews; OJ to George Peek, June 22, 1937 ("very desperately ill" quotation); OJ to Herbert Stowell, Nov. 18, Dec. 17, 1936; OJ to George Mahan Jr., Mar. 19, 1937; Mahan to OJ, Mar. 25, 1937; OJ to Charles P. Williams, Mar. 20, 1937; OJ to Francois Lebel, May 7, 1937; OJ to W. M. Whittington, July 23, 1937; see Toler to Ed Lipscomb, Mar. 26, 1937; see return address in OJ to Messrs. Barrow, Wade, Guthrie and Company, Nov. 9, 1936, DPLCR; see also Toler to J. D. LeCron, Oct. 20, 1936, GC, RG 16, NA.

11. OJ to Roosevelt, Aug. 6, 1937, telegram, GC, RG 145, NA; OJ to Harrison, Aug. 6, 1937, telegram; see also W. T. Wynn to Harrison, Aug. 6, 1937, telegram; Will Clayton to Harrison, Aug. 6, 1937, telegram, OF 258, FDRL. Clayton sent his telegram at Wynn's "suggestion" and also urged adoption of the 1935 plan. Further, see N. C. Williamson to M. L. Wilson, Aug. 6, 1937; and Williamson to Tolley, Aug. 6, 1937 (all telegrams), GC, RG 16, NA; see also Howard Stovall to Roosevelt, Aug. 5, 1937 (synopsis of telegram); and Roosevelt to Stovall, Aug. 19, 1937 (synopsis of letter), OF 736 (notations), FDRL; see Harrison to Walter Sillers, Aug. 14, 1937, telegram, Sillers Papers.

12. Harrison to Roosevelt, Aug. 11, 1937, OF 258, FDRL; Tolley to OJ, Aug. 14, 1937, GC, RG 145, NA.

13. *Memphis Press-Scimitar,* Aug. 14, 1937, 3 (Johnston quotation); see OJ to Jack Little, Aug. 17, 28, 1937, DPLCR. Wallace to Oscar Bledsoe, Oct. 20, 1937, GC, RG 145, NA.

14. TRB, "Washington Notes," 186; *New York Times,* Sept. 4, 1937, 21, 25 (all quotations). At the convention, Johnston was Wallace's "lone defender." *Jackson Daily News,* Sept. 3, 1937, 1.

15. *New York Times,* Sept. 4, 1937, 25 (quotations); see also TRB, "Washington Notes," 186; and Cohn, *The Life and Times of King Cotton,* 257.

16. *New York Times,* Sept. 4, 1937, 21 (quotations); see also the *New Republic,* Sept. 22, 1937, 186. Conceivably, the South might have pressed for a deficiency appropriation bill to cover the total of their potential crop, but this might have encountered stiff opposition in Congress; in any event, there seems no evidence that any such approach was contemplated.

17. *New York Times,* Sept. 4, 1937, 21 (first quotation), 25 (second quotation), Sept. 5, 1937, III, 1 (third quotation); *Jackson Daily News,* Sept. 4, 1937, 1; TRB, "Washington Notes," 186.

18. *New York Times,* Sept. 5, 1937, III, 1, 6; Sept. 6, 1937, 25; "Association, The Southern Commissioners of Agriculture, Resolutions acted upon at a meeting held at Memphis, Tennessee, Sept. 3 and 4, 1937" (submitted by C. C. Hanson, secretary of the association, Memphis, Tenn., Sept. 7, 1937; quotation), mimeograph, DPLCR.

19. TRB, "Washington Notes," 186; TRB also referred to Johnston as "one of the great cotton planters of the world." *New York Times,* Sept. 5, 1937, III, 6, Oct. 2, 1937, 25, 31 ("intense" quotation). Some planters believed the South was being denied its share of federal largess and that the proposed 1938 plan was no improvement over that of 1937. *New York Times,* Oct. 2, 1937, 31 (quotation); *Memphis Commercial Appeal,* Sept. 30, 1937, 1, 4, Oct. 1, 1937, 1, 2, Oct. 2, 1937, 1, 4; *Caruthersville (Missouri) Democrat-Argus,* Oct. 1, 1937, 1; OJ to Tolley, Oct. 4, 1937, GC, RG 145, NA (Johnston quotations). For Johnston's suggestions regarding acreage allotment distribution along more equitable lines, see his letter to J. B. Hutson, Oct. 9, 1937, GC, RG 145, NA.

20. *Newsweek,* Aug. 7, 1937, 13–14; Aug. 21, 1937, 10; see July 31, 1937, 5; TRB, "Washington Notes," 186–87; Swain, *Pat Harrison,* 157–64; *Life,* Aug. 23, 1937, 23.

21. TRB, "Washington Notes," 186; *New York Times,* Sept. 4, 1937, 25 (quotation).

## 12. King Cotton Needs a Voice

1. Benedict and Stine, *The Agricultural Commodity Programs,* 17 (including footnote), 18 (quotation); *Memphis Commercial Appeal,* Feb. 5, 1939, 9, Feb. 25, 1939, 9.

2. *Clarksdale Register and Daily News,* May 25, 1937, 1; *Jackson Daily News,* Oct. 13, 1937, 12; *New York Times,* May 2, 1937, III, 8. Clayton had opposed acreage reduction in 1933. Clayton to Peek, May 7, 1933, Peek Papers; Carter, "Cotton Fights Back!"

3. Blake, MOHP; Blake interviews; Christina Campbell, *The American Farm Bureau and the New Deal: A Study of the Making of National Farm Policy, 1933–1940* (Urbana, Ill., 1962), 129.

4. Blake, MOHP; Blake interviews; Wilmer Foreman, "The History of the National Cotton Council," forty-page typed manuscript draft, n.d. (1963), provided to author by Mr. Foreman, at the time director of public relations for the NCCA; Albert Russell, "Activities of the Delta Council," *The Mississippian* (Oxford) student newspaper, May 9, 1941, 6, copy in Delta and Providence Farms Papers.

5. OJ to Blake, July 16, 17, 23 (second and third quotations), 1937; letters of introduction for Blake from Johnston to Senators J. H. Bankhead and James P. Pope, and Farm Bureau president Edward A. O'Neal, all July 16, 1937; OJ to E. H. White, July 17, 1937; W. M. Whittington to OJ, July 20, 1937; W. T. Wynn, J. Tol Thomas, and OJ to Blake, July 22, 1937, telegram; Blake to OJ, July 15, 21, Aug. 2, 1937; Unanimous Report of the Sub-Committee on Agriculture, Delta Chamber of Commerce (Stoneville, Miss.), July 5, 1937, (first quotation) (see also Supplemental Report by subcommittee to full committee, n.d.), DPLCR; Orville M. Kile, *The Farm Bureau Through Three Decades* (Baltimore, 1948), 239–40; Blake, MOHP; see also *Memphis Commercial Appeal,* July 9, 1937, 19; and Blake to OJ, Sept. 11, 1937, DPLCR. Blake wrote Johnston on July 21 that "The Farm Bureau certainly muddied the water" with the Flannagan bill. "In so doing they antagonized a big portion of the House Committee." Blake to OJ, July 21, 1937, DPLCR.

6. *New York Times,* May 2, 1937, III, 8 (first quotation); May 28, 1937, 31; Johnston, "What Happened? and What Next?" 121. In November 1937 Johnston told the National Foreign Trade Council's world trade dinner in Cleveland, Ohio, that "Agricultural America demands, and proposes to make its demands heeded, either an intelligent revision of the tariff . . . or a compensating or 'tariff offset' payment," *Memphis Commercial Appeal,* Nov. 5, 1937, clipping in DPLCR.

7. Blake, MOHP (Blake quotation); Blake interviews; Russell, MOHP; see other oral histories in MOHP relative to NCCA.

8. Blake, MOHP; Russell, MOHP; Blake Interviews; *Memphis Press-Scimitar,* June 23, 1936, 5, July 1, 1936, 11, June 3, 1937, 13, June 4, 1937, 8, Apr. 22, 1938, 20, Apr. 26, 1938, 3, May 24, 1938, 14, May 25, 1938, 14; *Memphis Commercial Appeal,* May 25, 1938, 11 (quotation; AP story nearly as in *Memphis Press-Scimitar* of same date; see also *Clarksdale Daily Register,* Apr. 26, 1938, 4); see OJ to Cotton Research Foundation, June 16, 1937 (two), and other occasional Johnston correspondence regarding the foundation in DPLCR.

9. Carter, "Cotton Fights Back!"; see Foreman, "History of the National Cotton Council"; Blake interviews (quotation); on *Zola*, see Robert Osborne, *Academy Awards Illustrated: A Complete History of Hollywood's Academy Awards in Words and Pictures* (LaHabra, Calif., 1969), 67; Leslie Halliwell, *Halliwell's Film Guide*, 2d ed. (New York, 1979), 509–10; Adam Garbicz and Jacob Klinowski, *Cinema, The Magic Vehicle: A Guide to Its Achievement, Journey One: The Cinema Through 1949* (Metuchen, N.J., 1975), 282.

10. Either journalistic liberty or naïveté had prompted Carter, apparently in 1939, to declare: "Two years ago, Oscar Johnston of Mississippi saw a motion picture about a Frenchman named Emile Zola. Had he not, it is improbable that the National Cotton Council of America would be representing today the first unification of cotton growers, ginners, warehousemen, seed crushers, and cotton merchants—the five primary cotton groups—within a sore beset industry." Carter, "Cotton Fights Back!" See also story by John A Parris Jr., a UP writer, "Cotton Council Idea Was Born During a Movie," *Memphis Press-Scimitar,* Sept. 1, 1939, MPSM: "Oscar Johnston of Mississippi saw a motion picture about a Frenchman named Emile Zola and, inspired by Actor Paul Muni's interpretation of the crusading novelist's life, began a crusade to put King Cotton back on his throne and protect the livelihood of 36,000,000 people in the mud and mule and mortgage belt."

11. See *New York Times,* Sept. 25, 1937, 25; OJ to O'Neal, Sept. 7, 1937 (first two quotations); O'Neal to OJ, Sept. 10, 1937, DPLCR; O'Neal to Chester Gray, Nov. 2, 1937, quoted in Campbell, *The Farm Bureau and the New Deal,* 131; see 129–33 for Farm Bureau-Cotton Council relations.

12. Drew Pearson and Robert S. Allen, "The Washington Merry-Go-Round" (syndicated), *(Little Rock) Arkansas Gazette,* Oct. 12, 1937, 4; see also *Memphis Commercial Appeal,* Oct. 12, 1937, 11; O'Neal to OJ, Dec. 21, 1937, DPLCR (emphasis in original; also quoted in Campbell, *The Farm Bureau and the New Deal,* 129); OJ to Charles Baker, Nov. 20, 1937; OJ to J. Mell Brooks, Dec. 22, 1937, and other correspondence relative to Johnston's desire to work with the American Farm Bureau Federation, DPLCR.

13. *Jackson Daily News,* Oct. 14, 1937, 3, clipping (italics added); OJ to J. Mell Brooks, Dec. 22, 1937; OJ to R. W. Brown, Dec. 4, 1937; OJ to W. R. Ogg, Dec. 24, 1937, DPLCR.

14. OJ to J. F. Porter, Oct. 15, 1937, 6 (quotation); OJ to Henry C. Taylor, Oct. 8, 1937; OJ to Paul Porter, Oct. 15, 1937; OJ to H. S. Johnson, Oct. 25, 1937; Lewis Henderson to OJ, Nov. 26, 1937; see Rhea Blake to George M. Cheney, Dec. 16, 1937; H. S. Johnson to County Farm Bureau Presidents, Oct. 15, 1937 (mimeographed), DPLCR. Campbell, *The Farm Bureau and the New Deal,* 145. Some of Johnston's proposals were short lived. Amendments changing the name and assessing membership dues at ten cents per bale instead of a flat two dollars were approved at the Nov. 1937 convention. Perhaps because of lagging dues, the two-dollar fee was reinstated the following September. The old name, "Mississippi Farm Bureau Federation," was also restored. Membership Report of the Mississippi Agricultural Association for the Eight Months Ending June 15, 1938 (To All County Farm Bureaus), n.d; Ransom Aldrich to OJ, Sept. 12, 1938, DPLCR; *Jackson Daily News,* Sept. 12, 1938, 1, 5.

15. *Jackson Daily News,* Nov. 29, 1937, 6; Rhea Blake to George M. Cheney, Dec. 16, 1937, DPLCR.

16. OJ to Richard Baumbach, Nov. 29, 1937; OJ to Joe Pritchard, Dec. 4, 1937;

W. C. Neill to Blake, Nov. 27, 1937 (copy); OJ to Neill, Nov. 29, 1937; Louise N. Hammond to OJ, Nov. 27, 1937, DPLCR; *Clarksdale Register and Daily News,* Dec. 2, 1937, 1, 4 (quotations).

17. J. E. Merritt to OJ, Dec. 2, 1937 (first quotation); Neely Bowen to OJ, Nov. 27, 1937 (second quotation); Baumbach to OJ, Nov. 26, 1937, telegram; Bentley B. MacKay to OJ, Dec. 13, 1937 (third quotation); see also J. Mell Brooks to OJ, Dec. 17, 1937; G. W. Woodruff to OJ, Oct. 4, 1937; OJ to R. C. Branch, Dec. 22, 1937; James K. Price to OJ, Nov. 27, 1937; R. W. Brown to OJ, Nov. 29, 1937 (fourth quotation); OJ to Brown, Dec. 4, 1937; OJ to Charles B. Baker, Nov. 20, 1937, and Jan. 26, 1937; Baker to OJ, Jan. 24, 1938 (last quotation); OJ to Edward O'Neal, Nov. 20, 1937; William Jasspon (WHJ) to Charles Baker, Nov. 17, 1937, Dec. 4, 1937, DPLCR. One Meridian businessman, less interested in a cotton council, told Johnston that the South's salvation required men of his stature in Congress. Johnston replied: "I believe that if I can succeed in perfecting a southwide organization of cotton growers along the lines upon which I am at present working, I will be in a position to accomplish a great deal more for our section than I could in the United States Senate." Frank P. Williams to OJ, Nov. 9, 18, 1937; OJ to Williams, Nov. 11, 1937, DPLCR.

18. Blake, MOHP (second quotation); Blake interviews; OJ to H. S. Johnson, Dec. 22, 1937 (first quotation); OJ to O'Neal, Dec. 23, 1937 (one of two); see also OJ to G. C. Mingee, Dec. 23, 1937; OJ to O. C. Shipp, Dec. 23, 1937; OJ to Charles Baker, Dec. 4, 1937; OJ to R. W. Brown, Dec. 4, 1937; see OJ to A. B. Stevens, Jan. 24, 1938, DPLCR. Unfortunately, in the eight months ending in mid-1938, the Mississippi Farm Bureau affiliate suffered dramatic attrition, erasing nearly 43 percent of its membership of the same period the year before. Even the Delta lost heavily, and only a few counties, including Coahoma, Holmes, and Yazoo, posted major gains. Such losses superficially challenge but do not overturn Rhea Blake's later contention that there would have been no cotton council without the huge crop of 1937. Johnston's refinancing scheme may have been at least partially to blame. Planter leadership would prove all the more crucial. Oscar was undaunted. "It occurs to me," he told Ransom Aldrich in June 1938, "that it is necessary for us to make a very determined drive to increase membership of the County Farm Bureau organizations and that the establishment of a National Cotton Council is an excellent starting point." Membership Report of Mississippi Agricultural Association for Eight Months Ending June 15, 1938 (To All County Farm Bureaus), n.d.; OJ to Ransom Aldrich, June 20, 1938, DPLCR; Blake, MOHP.

19. Kile, *The Farm Bureau Through Three Decades,* 236–43; Benedict, *Farm Policies of the United States,* 375–79; Campbell, *The American Farm Bureau and the New Deal,* 113n, 113–15. *Agricultural Adjustment, 1939–1940, A Report of the Activities of the Agricultural Adjustment Administration, July 1, 1939 Through June 30, 1940* (Washington, D.C., 1940), 125; *Memphis Commercial Appeal,* Jan. 26, 1938, 1; OJ to I. W. Duggan, Nov. 2, 1938, GC, RG 145, NA. Kile and Campbell include the Farm Bureau's role in the new legislation, as does Edward A. O'Neal, "The Farm Bureau's Day By Day Fight for a New AAA," speech given before the annual meeting of the Illinois Agricultural Association, Springfield, Ill., Jan. 28, 1938, copy in DPLCR; see also Schuyler, "The Politics of Change," 165–78; Alexander Fitzhugh to OJ, Feb. 28, 1938, DPLCR; Blake interviews; Blake, MOHP. In a 1938 article, "Is There Need of a Definite Cotton Policy for the United States?" Johnston argued that marketing quotas might be necessary to achieve price stability in fat as well as lean years. He favored acreage

restriction, soil conservation, and "tariff offset" subsidies gained from manufacturers' sales taxes. If 75 percent of cotton producers complied, the program would become compulsory for all. Johnston also called for reciprocal trade and a national cotton council. *Cotton Trade Journal* 18 (International Edition, 1938), 14–15, 154–55, 171, 173.

20. OJ to Wallace, Jan. 5, 1938; Wallace to OJ, Jan. 12, 1938; OJ to Wallace, Jan. 20, 1937, Feb. 2, 1937; OJ to Lynn P. [Talley], Jan. 20, 1937 (evidently not delivered to Talley); Wallace to OJ, Jan. 27, 1937, GC, RG 16, NA; *Memphis Commercial Appeal*, Jan. 4, 1938, 12; *Clarksdale Register and Daily News*, Jan. 14, 1938, 8; *New York Times*, Jan. 14, 1938, 33. Johnston had served since May 1937 on the Memphis branch of the Federal Reserve Board of St. Louis. In January 1938 he was elected to the overall board of directors. *Memphis Commercial Appeal*, Jan. 6, 1938, 2, Jan. 14, 1938, 12; *New York Times*, May 30, 1938, May 30, 1937, II, 12; Federal Reserve Bank of St. Louis, Report to the Stockholders for Year Ended Dec. 31, 1937 (Roster listed as of May 7, 1938), 7; and Report for Year Ended Dec. 31, 1938, 7; see also OJ to Lewis Henderson, Nov. 30, 1937, DPLCR. A. C. Wild believed Johnston resigned his federal positions because of the ten-thousand-dollar payment ceiling. Wild, "History," DPLCR. Such a contention is without foundation. Johnston even advocated mandatory compliance if 75 percent of cotton producers agreed. Aside from the fact that the New Deal was winding down, the strongest and most likely motive for his resignations was that his federal ties might hamper organizing an independent national cotton council.

21. Blackburn, MOHP ("utopian" quotation); Francis J. Beatty, MOHP; Bill Foreman, "The History of the National Cotton Council" (typed manuscript draft, 1963), in author's possession; National Cotton Council, *25th Annual Report of Activities, National Cotton Council of America* (n.p., Jan. 1, 1964); Richard Baumbach to OJ, June 10, 1938 ("informational data" quotation), DPLCR.

22. Blackburn, MOHP.

23. *Jackson Daily News*, Oct. 13, 1937, 12 (first quotation); OJ to Henry Wallace, Apr. 25, 1938; OJ to Cordell Hull, Apr. 21, 1938; OJ to Hugh White, May 21, 1938 (including draft of letter Johnston prepared for Governor White's use, n.d.); see also OJ to R. W. Hamilton, Feb. 8, 1938, DPLCR; Lipscomb, MOHP; Dunn, MOHP; Blake interviews.

24. OJ to Hull, Apr. 21, May 7, 1938; Hull to OJ, May 2, 1938 (first quotation); OJ to Harrison, Apr. 21, 1938; Harrison to OJ, Apr. 25, 1938; OJ to Wallace, Apr. 25, 1938; Blake to Harrison, Apr. 21, 1938; Blake to Sayre, May 13, 1938; Wynn to Harrison, Apr. 30, 1938; Sayre to OJ, Apr. 28, 1938; OJ to Sayre, n.d. (Apr. 1938) (second quotation); May 21, 1938 (third quotation); see also Sayre to OJ, May 27, 1938, DPLCR; *Memphis Commercial Appeal*, June 5, 1938, I, 10; *Clarksdale Register and Daily News*, June 14, 1938, 2.

25. Blake to Harrison, Apr. 21, 1938, DPLCR.

26. Foreman, "The History of the National Cotton Council"; Carter, "Cotton Fights Back!"; J. C. Holton, radio remarks, WJDX, Jackson, Miss. (typed transcript, No. 393), June 17, 1938, DPLCR (first quotation); *Bolivar Commercial*, June 17, 1938, 1 (second quotation); Francis B. Sayre, "What Trade Agreements Mean to the Cotton Grower," address before the Delta Chamber of Commerce, Cleveland, Miss., June 15, 1938, *Department of State Commercial Policy Series 52* (Washington, D.C., 1938); *Memphis Press-Scimitar*, June 15, 1938, 1, 4; June 16, 1938, 1, 2; *Memphis Commercial Appeal*, June 16, 1938, 5, 7; *Clarksdale Register and Daily News*, June 15, 1938, 1, 2, 4; *The Delta Star* (Greenville, Miss.), June 16, 1938, 1; *New York Times*, June 16, 1938, 33.

27. Carter, "Cotton Fights Back!"; Foreman, "The History of the National Cotton

Council"; Blake interviews; Johnston, untitled address, Dec. 4, 1939, copies in DPLCR and NCCA; *Memphis Commercial Appeal,* June 15, 1938, 1, 3, June 16, 1938, 1; *Bolivar Commercial,* June 17, 1938, 1; *Memphis Press-Scimitar,* June 16, 1938, 1, 2.

28. Carter, "Cotton Fights Back!"; Foreman, "The History of the National Cotton Council"; *Proceedings of the Committee on Organization, National Cotton Council,* Hotel Peabody, Memphis, Tenn., Nov. 21–22, 1938, NCCA; *Memphis Commercial Appeal,* June 16, 1938, 1, 4; *Memphis Press-Scimitar,* June 16, 1938, 1, 2; *Clarksdale Register and Daily News,* June 15, 1938, 1, 4; *Jackson Daily News,* June 15, 1938, II, 9; *New Orleans Times-Picayune,* June 16, 1938, 1, 14; *The Delta Star,* June 16, 1938, 1, 7; *New York Times,* June 16, 1938, 33; Holton, radio remarks, June 17, 1938, DPLCR.

29. *Dallas Morning News,* June 16, 1938, I, 9 (AP quotation); *New Orleans Times-Picayune,* June 16, 1938, 1 (first quotation), 14 (AP quotation); *Memphis Press-Scimitar,* June 16, 1938, 1, 2 (White quotation); Carter, "Cotton Fights Back!"; *New York Times,* June 16, 1938, 33; Blake interviews; Oscar Johnston, "Why a National Cotton Council," an address by Hon. Oscar Johnston before the organization meeting of the Texas Delegation, National Cotton Council, Dallas, Oct. 27, 1938, NCCA.

30. *Memphis Commercial Appeal,* July 6, 1938, 10; *Memphis Press-Scimitar,* June 18, 1938, 5; Blake, MOHP; Blake interviews; OJ to Paul Porter, Dec. 22, 1938, DPLCR; Carter, "Cotton Fights Back!"; *Proceedings of the Committee on Organization, National Cotton Council,* NCCA; see other oral histories relative to NCCA in MOHP.

31. Russell Lord to Jonathan Daniels, Oct. 12, 1938, Daniels Papers, Southern Historical Collection, Univ. of North Carolina Library, Chapel Hill, North Carolina (the quotation about the eye is not in quotation marks in Lord's letter; the author has noted such a comment elsewhere); Blake, MOHP.

32. Blake, MOHP; Blake interviews; see Arch Toler to J. O. Lamkin, Aug. 4, 1938, and other correspondence relative to the matter in DPLCR.

33. Blake, MOHP; Blake interviews; Toler to Lamkin, Aug. 4, 1938; OJ to George Peek, Aug. 31, 1938; OJ to James Leavell, Sept. 17, 1938; OJ to R. W. Lea, Sept. 17, 1938; OJ to Virgil Payne, Nov. 18, 1938 (first quotation); OJ to Mrs. M. Long, Dec. 1, 1938; OJ to Marion Wilkins, Dec. 20, 1938 (second quotation); OJ to Paul Porter, Dec. 22, 1938, DPLCR; Carter, "Cotton Fights Back!"; OJ to Jesse Tapp, Nov. 2, 1938, GC, RG 145, NA.

34. Blake, MOHP (first quotation); Blake interviews; Carter, "Cotton Fights Back!"; *Memphis Press-Scimitar,* Oct. 6, 1938, 1, Oct. 7, 1938, 8, Oct. 14, 1938, 13; Blake to Jonathan Daniels, Sept. 21, 1938, telegram; Delta Council to Daniels, Sept. 26, 1938, Daniels Papers, Southern Historical Collection, Univ. of North Carolina Library, Chapel Hill, North Carolina. For assessments of Blake's abilities, etc., see other oral histories relative to the NCCA in MOHP. After knowing and observing Blake for seven years, Oscar told Chester Davis, "I doubt if there is any man in America today who is more intimately familiar with the many and varied factors involved in the Raw Cotton Industry." He had become, said Johnston, "my right hand." OJ to Chester Davis, June 15, 1943, DPLCR.

35. *Memphis Press-Scimitar,* Oct. 7, 1938, 6; Blake, MOHP (Blake quotations); Blake interviews; Blake to Pettey, Oct. 21, 1938, DPLCR. For Texas problems, see relevant citations below.

36. *New York Times,* May 28, 1937, III, 8; Blake interviews (first quotation; Souza quo-

tation); Blake, MOHP (other Blake quotations); see *Dallas Morning News*, Oct. 28, 1938, II, 6, Jan. 16, 1938, I, 11; L. T. Stone to OJ, Mar. 11, 1940 (last two quotations), DPLCR.

37. Blake, MOHP.

38. OJ to J. M. Miller, Oct. 24, 1938, DPLCR; Johnston, "Why a National Cotton Council" (quotations), NCCA.

39. *Dallas Morning News*, Oct. 28, 1938, II, 6, see also 1; OJ to Paul Porter, Nov. 1, 1938, DPLCR; *Proceedings of the Committee on Organization, National Cotton Council*, NCCA; see also Blake, MOHP.

40. *Proceedings of the Committee on Organization, National Cotton Council* (quotations), NCCA; *New York Times*, Nov. 25, 1938, 22; *Memphis Press-Scimitar*, Nov. 1, 1938, 12, see also June 28, 1938, 16, Aug. 22, 1938, 16, Nov. 22, 1938, 16.

41. *Proceedings of the Committee on Organization, National Cotton Council* ("magnificent" quotation; OJ quotation); Blake interviews; *Memphis Press-Scimitar*, Nov. 21, 1938, 1; Carter, "Cotton Fights Back!" For press coverage of the meeting, see *Memphis Commercial Appeal*, Nov. 21, 1938, 1, 2, Nov. 22, 1938, 1, 10, 17, Nov. 23, 1938, 1, 4; *Memphis Press-Scimitar*, Nov. 21, 1938, 1, 2, 3, Nov. 22, 1938, 1, 2, Nov. 23, 1938, 15, Nov. 24, 1938, 14; *Dallas Morning News*, Nov. 22, 1938, II, 2; *New Orleans Times-Picayune*, Nov. 22, 1938, 1; *Atlanta Constitution*, Nov. 22, 1938, 2; *Jackson Daily News*, Nov. 21, 1938, 1, 9, Nov. 22, 1938, 1; *New York Times*, Nov. 22, 1938, 42, Nov. 23, 1938, 32. See these papers for material below as well.

42. *25th Annual Report of Activities, National Cotton Council of America* ("ovation" quotation), NCCA; *Memphis Commercial Appeal*, Nov. 22, 1938, 1, 6 (third and fourth quotations), Nov. 23, 1938, 4 (second quotation); *Memphis Press-Scimitar*, Nov. 24, 1938, 14 (see also Nov. 28, 1938, 14); *Dallas Morning News*, Nov. 22, 1938, II, 2; *Proceedings of the Committee on Organization, National Cotton Council* (including "Preamble and Resolutions Providing for the Creation, Organization and Establishment of the National Cotton Council of America"), NCCA; Johnston, untitled address, Dec. 4, 1939, copies in DPLCR and NCCA; Blake, MOHP.

43. *Memphis Press-Scimitar*, Dec. 5, 1938, 12, Dec. 10, 1938, 1, Dec. 11, 1938, 1, 2; Johnston, untitled address before the annual convention of the Southern Newspaper Publishers Association, Old Point Comfort, Va., June 16, 1939, NCCA; Johnston, untitled address, Dec. 4, 1939, copies in DPLCR and NCCA; D. R. Gavin to R. W. Lea, Jan. 24, 1939; OJ to Lea, Jan. 28, 1938; Frank Lowden to OJ, Feb. 7, 1939; Arch Toler to Harper Leech, Jan. 14, 1939; OJ to Porter, Dec. 22, 1938, DPLCR; *Bolivar Commercial*, Dec. 23, 1938, 1.

44. *Dallas Morning News*, Jan. 25, 1939, 1, 7; Jan. 28, 1939, II, 2; Resolution Adopted by Unanimous Vote by the National Cotton Council, of America, in Regular Session, Dallas, Texas, Jan. 24, 1939; Minutes of the Board of Directors of the National Cotton Council of America, Dallas, Texas, Jan. 25, 1939; Minutes of the First Annual Meeting of the National Cotton Council of America, Dallas, Texas, Jan. 24, 1939, copies of resolutions and minutes in DPLCR; *Memphis Commercial Appeal*, Jan. 26, 1939, 1; *Business Week*, Jan. 28, 1939, 15–16; Carter, "Cotton Fights Back!"; Blake, MOHP.

45. *Memphis Commercial Appeal*, Jan. 24, 1939, 1; *Dallas Morning News*, Jan. 25, 1939, 1.

46. *Dallas Morning News*, Jan. 24, 1939, II, 2; Blake, MOHP.

47. See Blake interviews; Blake, Blackburn, Russell, Lipscomb, Dunn, and numerous other oral histories relative to NCCA in MOHP.

## 13. I Have Never Liked the Term "New Deal"

1. Beatty, MOHP; Blake, MOHP (quotations); William Reid, MOHP; Blake interviews; OJ to Lamar Fleming Jr., Apr. 6, 1943 ("alter ego" quotation); OJ to N. C. Williamson, July 10, 1940; see OJ to J. L. Wilson Jr., Dec. 6, 1939; OJ to George Peek, Nov. 13, 1941, DPLCR; Blake to author, Sept. 11, 1975, including Cotton Programs, seven-page typed manuscript, Sept. 4, 1975, by Earl Sears.

2. OJ to Charles Whyte, Aug. 28, 1942; OJ to W. W. Fariss, Feb. 12, 1943 (quotation); OJ to Ione M. Allen, July 19, 1941; OJ to Henry Cook and Son (attn. John Hunter), Jan. 24, 1941, DPLCR; OJ to FCSDA, May 17, 1943, JFM; Gray interviews; W. Fred Stout to Dun and Bradstreet, Inc., Dec. 16, 1946, DPLCR; see material relative to sale of Delta Planting Company in DPLCR.

3. OJ to J. L. Wilson Jr., Dec. 6, 1939; OJ to Charles Whyte, Aug. 28, 1942; OJ to FCSDA, Feb. 19, 1942, DPLCR; biographical material in OJSF, MDAH; Patterson notes in DPLCR; Blake, MOHP; Blake interviews; Gray interviews; Hatcher interview; Porter interview; OJ to Robert Mullen, May 3, 1939; OJ to Basil Kennedy, June 12, 1939; OJ to Nelson and Almen, Sept. 4, 1939; OJ to Nelson and Almen (attn. Erik Almen), Feb. 5, 1940, and related correspondence, 1940; OJ to Billy Wynn, May 4, 1940; OJ to Mitchell Company, May 2, 1940; OJ to Lloyd's Register of American Yachts, May 4, 1940; OJ to C. M. Isenhower, May 13, 1940; OJ to N. Erik Almen, May 15, 1940; OJ to Gray Motor Marine Co., June 24, 1940; OJ to H. H. Jennings Co. (attn. Herman Jagle), July 8, 1940; OJ to Henry Grebe, Oct. 2, 1940; OJ to Francis DeArmorsolo, Apr. 10, 1941; OJ to F. W. Williams, Apr. 21, 1941; OJ to J. O. Lamkin, June 14, 1941; McCrary to OJ, Apr. 19, 1941, DPLCR; Blake, MOHP. All aboard the *Lady Luck* were blown into the water but all survived; Oscar and one of the women were the most severely injured. He was laid up for weeks. Friends quickly replaced the destroyed cabin cruiser with a used thirty-eight-footer, absent motor and other amenities. Arthur Prescott Jr. to OJ, July 21, Aug. 15, 1932; OJ to Prescott, Jan. 25, Aug. 9, 18, 1932, DPLCR. As for Johnston's 1939 cruiser, it would, unfortunately, see more action in the Gulf than anyone realized. In August 1942, nearly nine months after American entry into World War II, she was requisitioned by the government for patrol duty in the U-boat-infested waters of the Gulf, Oscar having taken the government's stingy settlement of $17,500. Still looking for other possibilities, Johnston was now reduced to taking an option on a small towboat in New Orleans and contemplating converting his boathouse into something livable; wartime inability to get necessary materials dashed those plans. Though still open to other ideas, he looked to the war's end to get back into serious boating. OJ to G. W. Ford Yacht Agency, Mar. 19, 1942; OJ to Lewis Supply Co., Aug. 28, 1942; OJ to Lawrence Salmon, Aug. 31, 1942; War Shipping Administrator (voucher approved by administrator, Nov. 17, 1942; paid Feb. 4, 1943); OJ to John W. Magill, Jan. 28, 1943, DPLCR; Gray interviews.

4. OJ to Myrtle Lindsay, Apr. 28, 1939; OJ to J. H. McCormick, July 15, 21, 1941; Ed Lipscomb to Arch Toler, Oct. 6, 1941; Alexander Fitz Hugh to M. A. Myers, Oct. 7, 1941; OJ to Lillian A. Phelan, Aug. 12, 1941; OJ to Margaret Wynn, Aug. 18, 1941; OJ to Reagen McCrary, Oct. 29, 1941; OJ to Claudius Murchison, Oct. 31, 1941; OJ to Margarite Long, Nov. 3, 1941; OJ to James B. Murphy, July 24, Nov. 10, 1941; OJ to George Peek, Nov. 13, 1941; OJ to S. R. Morison, Nov. 19, 1941; OJ to N. C. Williamson, Nov. 25, 1941; OJ to Nance McDonald, Dec. 10, 1941; OJ to Jeanne Maddox, Dec. 18,

1941 ("fog" quotation), Dec. 22, 1941; OJ to Francis DeArmorsolo, Apr. 10, 1941; OJ to Max Nahm, Jan. 12, 1942; OJ to F. P. Williams, Jan. 16, 1942 ("overhaul" quotation); OJ to Will Clayton, May 8, 1942; OJ to Forrest Black, July 13, 1942, DPLCR. On the developing cattle herd, see OJ to W. G. Henley, Sept. 7, 1940; OJ to A. J. Royal, Dec. 24, 1940; OJ to Edward Janney, Mar. 6, 1941; OJ to E. T. Woolfolk, Jan. 29, 1942; OJ to H. Stowell, Feb. 17, 1942, DPLCR; OJ to Sam B. Bledsoe, Oct. 19, 1942, GC, RG 145, NA; see also OJ to Walter Sillers, May 31, 1949, Sillers Papers. On some of Johnston's wartime assignments see OJ to B. R. Richey, Sept. 18, 1942; OJ to Chester Davis, Dec. 3, 1942; OJ to E. F. Creekmore, Dec. 4, 1942; M. S. Eccles to OJ, Dec. 15, 1943; OJ to Eccles, Jan. 11, 1944; Paul McNutt to OJ, Oct. 12, 1942, May 28, 1943; OJ to B. F. Ashe, May 8, 1943; Henry Taylor to OJ, June 4, 1943, and numerous other correspondence in DPLCR; *New York Times*, Mar. 30, 1940, 24; Apr. 19, 1940, 34. See *Memphis Press-Scimitar*, Jan. 2, 1942, MPSM.

5. T. Y. Williford to T. M. Patterson, May 20, 1941 (copy); OJ to Duggan, July 23, 1942, GC, RG 145, NA, and other relevant correspondence in the same place.

6. OJ to all members of the NCCA, Jan. 27, 1940, and attached sheet; OJ to Ben Williams, Aug. 27, 1940; OJ to E. H. Lawton, Jan. 29, 1940; OJ to Fred Rankin, Mar. 20, 1942; OJ to Chester Davis, Mar. 26, 1942; OJ to E. F. Creekmore, Apr. 13, 1942 (dictated Apr. 12; "rather ambitious" quotation); OJ to N. Mossop, Apr. 13, 29, 1942; OJ to Oscar R. Johnston, Apr. 22, 1942; OJ to Everett Cook, Apr. 22, 1942; OJ to Murray Johnston, Apr. 23, 1942; OJ to James E. Brooks, May 30, 1942; OJ to J. D. Little, June 2, 1942; OJ to J. B. Hutson, Apr. 30, 1942, memorandum; OJ to Alston H. Garside, June 16, 1942; OJ to Claude R. Wickard, Feb. 16, 1942; OJ to FCSDA, July 29, 1942; James Hand Jr., The Proposed Trade Agreement with Peru, Feb. 3, 1942, DPLCR; *United States News*, Apr. 17, 1942, 49; Pearson and Allen, "Washington Merry-Go-Round," *Memphis Commercial Appeal*, Apr. 26, 1942, IV, 4; see also Apr. 8, 1942, 13; Apr. 9, 23 ("No particular news came overnight to spur trading, but guessing was still being done as to just what the Department of Agriculture has in mind in the appointment of Oscar Johnston to the CCC."); Apr. 12, 1942, III, 5; Apr. 25, 1942, 1, 3; May 16, 1942, 1; *New York Times*, Apr. 8, 1942, 31; Apr. 13, 1942, 25; *Time*, May 4, 1942, 78 ("World Cotton Pool" quotation), 80 ("meditated" quotation); see also Grover B. Hill to Carl Hayden, Mar. 13, 1942; H. A. Nelson to Air Transport Association Representative, Apr. 8, 1942 (certificate); J. B. Hutson to W. A. Jump, Apr. 23, 24, 1942, memorandums; Claude Wickard to Sumner Welles, Mar. 23, 1942, memorandum, GC, RG 16, NA; OJ to Alben Barkley, Feb. 16, 1942 (copy); Grover Hill and Frank Walston to OJ, Apr. 8, 1942; Wickard to Cordell Hull, Apr. 14, 1942; Wickard to OJ, Mar. 4, 1942, GC, RG 16, NA; *Progress Bulletin* (General Bulletin No. 66 published by NCCA), Nov. 15, 1945, 8, copy in GC, RG 16, NA; Hull to FDR, June 18, 1942; Proposed Trade Agreement with Peru Concession of Long-Staple Cotton (typed, n.d.), OF 287, FDRL; Wickard communication with FDR, notations, filed Apr. 4, 1942, OF 736, FDRL; USDA press release, "Commodity Credit Corporation Peruvian Cotton," Apr. 24, 1942; "Memorandum of Understanding" between Sec. Wickard and the Minister of Finance of the Republic of Peru, Apr. 22, 1942, DPLCR.

7. Dean Albertson, *Roosevelt's Farmer: Claude R. Wickard in the New Deal* (New York and London, 1961), 273; OJ to Stowell, Dec. 17, 1936 (six-page letter), DPLCR; Baldwin, *Poverty and Politics*; Donald Holley, *Uncle Sam's Farmers: The New Deal Communities in the Lower Mississippi Valley* (Urbana, Ill., 1975).

8. OJ to Meeman, Sept. 18, 1940; OJ Frank Hook, Mar. 16, 1942, DPLCR; see also C. B. Baldwin to Southeast Missouri planter, May 3, 1934, GC, RG 145, NA.

9. OJ to E. S. Morris, Dec. 8, 1941 (first two quotations); OJ to Caswell P. Ellis Jr., Mar. 13, 1942 (last quotations); OJ to Forrest Black, July 13, 1942, DPLCR.

10. Phillip Murray to "All National, International Unions, Regional Directors and Local Industrial Unions and Industrial Unions Councils," Feb. 27, 1942 (copy; first quotation); accompanying FSA document which called for meetings in Columbus, Ohio, May 1941 (copy?; last quotation); see OJ to C. D. Miller, July 24, 1942, DPLCR; Bledsoe to Sillers, July 20, 1942; R. B. Snowden Jr. to Bledsoe, Apr. 20, 1942, Sillers Papers.

11. OJ to Hook, Mar. 16, 1942, DPLCR (including partial Hook quotations); *Congressional Record,* Mar. 9, 1942, 77th Cong., 2d sess. 88, pt. 2:2118–19 (Hook quotations on 2119). A year later Johnston went through similar demagoguery when, speaking of small farms, Democratic congressman John J. Sparkman of Alabama, though complementary of Johnston, nonetheless asked his colleagues, "What does Mr. Johnston know about that? His time is taken up there with this immense plantation of thousands of acres, and with tenants and day laborers working on those farms. He does not come into daily contact with individual farm families that are trying to make a living." OJ to Sparkman, Apr. 19, 1943, DPLCR (quotation); *Congressional Record,* 78th Cong., 1st sess., 1943, 89, pt. 3:3373.

12. OJ to C. D. Miller, July 24, 1942; P. W. Allen to OJ, Sept. 28, 1942; OJ to Allen (Johnson and Allen), Oct. 2, 1942; OJ to Robert Wynn, Dec. 16, 1942; see also numerous other relevant correspondence in DPLCR; and Walter Sillers to Mrs. W. M. Black, July 30, 1942, Sillers Papers; Holley, *Uncle Sam's Farmers,* 262.

13. P. W. Allen to OJ, Sept. 28, 1942; R. E. Townes to OJ, Oct. 28, 1942; Bates Tabb to OJ, Nov. 25, 1942; W. H. Rucker to OJ, Oct. 29, 1942; Tom Gibson to OJ, Nov. 26, 1942; Whittington to OJ, Nov. 28, 1942 (quotations in order), DPLCR; Said Whittington: FSA's "purpose was not to socialize or Sovietize, but its purpose was to enable worthy tenants to become land owners. I was never in sympathy with the program of the Farm Security Administration."

14. *Memphis Commercial Appeal,* Nov. 22, 1942, I, 19, Nov. 24, 1942, 20; Holley, *Uncle Sam's Farmers,* 262 (quotation).

15. *Memphis Commercial Appeal,* Nov. 24, 1942, 20 (first and third quotations); Holley, *Uncle Sam's Farmers,* 262 (second quotation).

16. OJ to Bates Tabb, Dec. 7, 1942; *Memphis Commercial Appeal,* Dec. 6, 1942, II, 7, clipping and letter in DPLCR; Holley, *Uncle Sam's Farmers,* 262; Ashmore, *Civil Rights and Wrongs,* 24 (Rex the Red quotation).

17. OJ to Robert Wynn, Dec. 16, 1942 (first quotation); Bates Tabb to OJ, Nov. 25, 1942 (second quotation); OJ to Robert Sanders, Nov. 24, 1942 (last quotation), DPLCR.

18. The USDA Summary (Washington, D.C.), Dec. 17, 1942, mimeographed copy in DPLCR; OJ to B. M. McGriff, Jan. 29, 1943; "Honor for Negro Farmer," *Shreveport Journal,* Jan. 26, 1943, clipping and letter in DPLCR.

19. "Cotton, Food and FSA," *Birmingham News,* Jan. 30, 1943, 4, clipping in DPLCR.

20. "Honor for Negro Farmer," *Shreveport Journal,* Jan. 26, 1943, clipping; OJ to McGriff, Jan. 29, 1943; "Others, Too," *The Delta Leader,* Feb. 21, 1943, clipping, DPLCR. On Humes, see, for example, Dorothy Lee Black to Walter Sillers, Feb. 9, 1943; Sillers to Black, Mar. 31, 1943, Sillers Papers; Woodruff, "Mississippi Delta Planters and Debates," 279–80; and Humes to OJ, Feb. 18, 1942; OJ to Humes, Feb. 19, 1942, DPLCR.

21. OJ to Chester Davis, Dec. 22, 1942; OJ to M. B. Swayze, Oct. 10 (quotation), 22, 1942, DPLCR.

22. OJ to Davis, Dec. 22, 1942; OJ to Paul Johnston, Dec. 30, 1942 (last quotation), DPLCR. "There is only one kind of property which my observation and experience teaches me they will acquire when they can and will hang onto until death, and that is land. In a rather long and intimate experience with negroes, particularly during some 15 or 18 years in which I was actively engaged in law practice, I do not recall a single instance of a negro having voluntarily sold a tract of land which he had acquired in any way. There are three small farms and one small home site of five acres scattered about through out the plantation which belong to negroes. These properties belonged to negroes in 1911 when the properties constituting this plantation were being assembled by Mr. Charles Scott and his associates. The negroes refused to sell and their heirs since have refused all offers. We have made some rather fantastic offers based not on intrinsic values but on 'nuisance' values for these properties but to no avail." OJ to Alexander Fitz-Hugh, Feb. 22, 1943, DPLCR.

23. See unanimous resolutions of NCCA, Jan. 26, 1943; OJ to B. S. Reed, Mar. 5, 1943; Stone to W. M. Hynds, Jan. 29, Feb. 6 (quotation), 1943, memorandums, DPLCR; see *Memphis Press-Scimitar,* Jan. 25, 1943, MPSM. Even before his Percy Park appearance in July 1942 Johnston said privately, "There were wonderful possibilities under the [FSA] legislation, but unfortunately it has been so aborted that I have been surprised at Senator Bankhead's persistence in standing by FSA rather than repudiating the Administration as it is presently conducted, and demanding that the whole thing be over-hauled and reshaped so as to aim at the original goal." OJ to C. D. Miller, July 24, 1942, DPLCR.

24. Stone to Hynds, Feb. 15, 22, and Mar. 6, 1943, memorandums, DPLCR.

25. OJ to M. L. Sigman, May 21, 1943, DPLCR. The quotation is not necessarily a reference to Tugwell's actual words.

26. OJ to Sigman, May 21, 1943; see statement relative to FSA, presumably by OJ, n.d. (ca. 1942); OJ to Will M. Whittington, Dec. 1, 1942, DPLCR.

27. Committee on Appropriations, *Hearings Before the Subcommittee of the Committee on Appropriations, House of Representatives, 78 Cong., 1 Sess., on the Agriculture Department Appropriation Bill for 1944,* 78th Cong., 1st sess., 1943, 1623–24 (quotation) (hereinafter cited as *House Appropriations Subcommittee Hearings for 1944*); Holley, *Uncle Sam's Farmers,* 261–63; see also OJ to Sigman, May 21, 1943; Laverne McDade's report; and OJ to John J. Sparkman, Apr. 19, 1943, DPLCR.

28. *House Appropriations Subcommittee Hearings for 1944,* 1624–25; Stone to Hynds, Jan. 9, 1943, memorandum; OJ to B. T. Abbott, Dec. 29, 1942, DPLCR.

29. *House Appropriations Subcommittee Hearings for 1944,* 1624–25; Stone to Hynds, Jan. 9, 1943, memorandum; OJ to Bernie L. Anderson, Dec. 30, 1942, DPLCR.

30. OJ to Gene Rutland, Mar. 3, 1943; OJ to F. W. Williams, Feb. 9, 15, 1943; Stone to Hynds, Feb. 12, 1943, memorandum; OJ to House, Apr. 7, 1943; see Stone to OJ, Feb. 1, 1943; Stone to McDade, Feb. 1, 1943; House to Billy Wynn, Apr. 5, 1943, and other relevant letters, DPLCR.

31. Waldo Frazier to OJ, Feb. 16, 18, 1943, telegrams; OJ to Frazier, Feb. 19, 1943, telegram; Frazier to OJ, Feb. 18, 1943; Mar. 13, 1943; OJ to Frazier, Feb. 19, 1943; OJ to Edward Brockman, Feb. 15, 1943; House to Brockman, Mar. 23, 1943; House to Billy Wynn, Mar. 25, 1943, and numerous other relevant correspondence, DPLCR.

32. Holley, *Uncle Sam's Farmers*, 242–45; *Arkansas Democrat*, Nov. 4, 1942, 1–2; see Wesley McCune, *The Farm Bloc* (Garden City, New York, 1943), 165–67, 177, 188–89, 266.

33. Holley, *Uncle Sam's Farmers*, 110, 250–51; *House Appropriations Subcommittee Hearings for 1944*, 1616, 1618–20, 1637, 1639.

34. *House Appropriations Subcommittee Hearings for 1944*, 1622–23 (quotation), 1630–31; Holley, *Uncle Sam's Farmers*, 263–64.

35. *House Appropriations Subcommittee Hearings for 1944*, 1622, 1625, 1627 (quotation), 1628; Holley, *Uncle Sam's Farmers*, 263.

36. *House Appropriations Subcommittee Hearings for 1944*, 1628–29 (quotations); also exchange quoted in Holley, *Uncle Sam's Farmers*, 264.

37. *House Appropriations Subcommittee Hearings for 1944*, 1630; also quoted in Holley, *Uncle Sam's Farmers*, 264.

38. Holley, *Uncle Sam's Farmers*, 265–66; *House Appropriations Subcommittee Hearings for 1944*, 1643 (quotation), 1653–54, 1657, 1691–93.

39. Holley, *Uncle Sam's Farmers*, 265–66; Helene Ward, "Model Farmer Perplexed by Eviction Order," *Arkansas Democrat*, Mar. 26, 1943, 1, 8 (quotation), clipping in DPLCR.

40. *Arkansas Democrat*, Mar. 26, 1943, 8, clipping in DPLCR; also quoted in Holley, *Uncle Sam's Farmers*, 266–67.

41. House to Wynn, Apr. 5, 1943; House to OJ, Apr. 9, 1943 (quotation); see relevant newspaper clippings in DPLCR; Holley, *Uncle Sam's Farmers*, 268.

42. House to Brockman, Mar. 25, 1943; House to Wynn, Mar. 25, 1943, Apr. 5, 1943; OJ to House, Apr. 7, 1943; House to OJ, Apr. l9, 1943, DPLCR.

43. OJ to House, June 4, 1943 (first quotation); *Memphis Commercial Appeal*, Apr. 9, 10, 1943, 13, clippings in DPLCR; and numerous other relevant correspondence in the spring of 1943 in DPLCR; Holley, *Uncle Sam's Farmers*, 271–72 (latter quotations), 280.

44. OJ to House, Aug. 4, 11 (quotation), 1943; House to OJ, May 8, 19, 29, 1943; Laverne McDade to OJ, Aug. 8, 1943 (quotation); OJ to Laverne McDade, Aug. 11, 1943; Claude Wickard to John McClellan, May 21, 1943 (with McClellan's handwritten note to Johnston at the bottom, DPLCR; see also McClellan to Wickard, May 14, 1943 (copy); see also C. B. Baldwin to McClellan, June 10, 1943; Hattie Caraway to Wickard, May 14, 1943 (copy); Baldwin to Caraway, June 10, 1943, GC, RG 16, NA.

45. With some reluctance he paid at least half of Edward Brockman's one-hundred-dollar fee, with the pledge to pay the balance if the Plum Bayou clients could not be located and if Brockman thought Johnston was still obligated. It is possible Johnston was reimbursed by the cotton council, and possibly also by the Farm Bureau. Holley, *Uncle Sam's Farmers*, 269; OJ to Waldo Frazier, Apr. 7, 1943; OJ to House, Aug. 11, Sept. 2, 1943; House to OJ, Aug. 14, 1943; Brockman to OJ, Oct. 28, Dec. 16, 1943; OJ to Brockman, Nov. 24, 1943, DPLCR.

46. OJ to Robert H. Wynn, Dec. 16, 1942, DPLCR.

47. Rhea Blake, who, like Johnston, worked closely with Bankhead, doubted Oscar really favored him for the vice-presidential nomination. Blake interviews; OJ to Milo Perkins, Sept. 23, 1943, DPLCR; Bankhead to OJ, July 5 (first Bankhead quotation), 26 (second Bankhead quotation), 1944; see also July 7, 1944; OJ to Bankhead, July 25, 1944; see also July 1, 1944 (shorter letter), John Bankhead Papers, Alabama Dept. of Archives and History, Montgomery, Alabama; Walter Sillers to James Eastland, Apr. 15, 1945, Sillers Papers; on the Truman nomination, see Robert A. Garson, *The Democratic Party and the Politics of Sectionalism, 1941–1948* (Baton Rouge, 1974), 120–22;

Eugene Roseboom, *A History of Presidential Elections* (New York, 1957, 1964), 485; Ferrell, *Choosing Truman*; and David McCullough, *Truman* (New York, 1992), 292–324.

48. OJ to Peek, Nov. 13, ("normal" quotation), Dec. 19 ("cocky little devils" quotation), Nov. 24 ("Methuselah" quotation), 1941; OJ to Will M. Whittington, Dec. 1, 1942; OJ to N. Mossop, Dec. 7, 1942; OJ to T. G. MacGowan, June 9, 1942 (other quotations), DPLCR; "How to Crack the Cotton Bloc," *The International Teamster,* June 1946, copy in Sillers Papers; OJ to the People of the Cotton Belt, June 14, 1946; William Rhea Blake to All Cotton Belt State Legislators, June 17, 1946 (mimeographed letters), Sillers Papers; *Memphis Press-Scimitar,* June 14, 1946, 22, Jan. 28, 1947, MPSM.

## Epilogue

1. Woofter and Fisher, *The Plantation South Today,* 7 (quotation); Sue Lyles, "Concepts of the Old and New Plantation Systems," *Rural Sociology* 5 (Apr. 1940): 227–29; Woodruff, "Mississippi Delta Planters and Debates over Mechanization, Labor, and Civil Rights in the 1940s," 263; Merle Prunty Jr., "The Renaissance of the Southern Plantation" (abstract of a paper presented at a meeting of the Association of American Geographers, Apr. 1954), *Annals of the American Association of American Geographers* 44 (Sept. 1954): 276; see also Merle Prunty Jr., "Changes in Settlements on the Deltapine Plantation, 1939–1954" (abstract of a paper presented at a meeting of the Association of American Geographers, Apr. 1955), *Annals of the American Association of American Geographers* 45 (Sept. 1955): 292; Merle Prunty Jr., "The Renaissance of the Southern Plantation," *Geographical Review* 45 (Oct. 1955): 459–91; especially helpful is Kirby, "The Transformation of Southern Plantations," 258, 258n; Van Auken, "A Century of the Southern Plantation," 384–85.

2. Fite, "Mechanization of Cotton Production Since World War II," 198; Woodruff, "Mississippi Delta Planters," 263–84; Cobb, *The Most Southern Place on Earth,* 198–209; Statement and President's Report (1940), Apr. 19, 1941; (1941), Apr. 18, 1942; OJ to E. F. Creekmore, Dec. 4, 1942, DPLCR. For one view of planters and labor problems during World War II, see also Nan Elizabeth Woodruff, "Pick or Fight: The Emergency Farm Labor Program in the Arkansas and Mississippi Deltas during World War II," *Agricultural History* 64 (spring 1990): 74–85.

3. OJ to Creekmore, Dec. 4, 1942, DPLCR.

4. Statement and President's Report (1943), Apr. 15, 1944, DPLCR.

5. Survey and plantation data are contained in Walter Sillers's redraft of a letter Johnston proposed to send to Tom Linder; this was not included in the letter. The seven hundred acres in question belonged to Mrs. Sillers. See drafts and relevant Sillers-to-Johnston correspondence, Feb. 1945, Sillers Papers.

6. Statement and President's Report (1944), Apr. 21, 1945, DPLCR; Nicholas Lemann, *The Promised Land: The Great Black Migration and How It Changed America* (New York, 1991), 3–6; Committee on Agriculture, *Hearings Before the Subcommittee of the Committee on Agriculture (Cotton),* 78th Cong., 2d sess., 1945, 109–10; OJ to F. W. Williams, Nov. 11, 1937 ("fly by night" quotation), DPLCR; see also J. D. Ratcliff, "Revolution in Cotton," *Collier's,* July 21, 1945, 24, 40–42.

7. Statement and President's Report (1945), Mar. 26, 1946; (1946) Apr. 19, 1947, DPLCR; Gilbert Fite, "Mechanization of Cotton Production Since World War II," 194–95, 195n, 201, 206–7; James E. Edmonds, "Around the Clock on the South's Largest Cotton Plantation," *Cotton Trade Journal* (International Edition, 1956–1957): 41. "Machines

Invade Delta-Pine Land," *Greenville Delta Democrat-Times,* Mar. 9, 1951, 1C; Fite cites "More Cotton Pickers on the Way," *Business Week,* July 10, 1948, 70, and "Six-Bale Picker: International Harvester's Mechanical Cotton Picker," *Business Week,* Nov. 27, 1943, 60–70; Charles R. Sayre, "Cotton Mechanization Since World War II," *Agricultural History* 53 (Jan. 1979): 105–24, especially 108. See also Cobb, *The Most Southern Place on Earth,* 204–6; Kirby, *Rural Worlds Lost;* Fite, *Cotton Fields No More;* Wright, *Old South, New South;* Daniel, *Breaking the Land.*

8. OJ to Tom Linder, Feb. 9, 1945 (draft, but apparently the version sent); see OJ to Walter Sillers, Feb. 16, 1945, Sillers Papers.

9. Johnston, "Mechanization, Cotton's Shot in the Arm," *Cotton Trade Journal* 15 (International Edition, 1947): 151. Johnston, "Mechanization—A Key to Progress," *Georgia Review* 2 (spring 1948): 13–14, 17–18; Johnston, "Will the Machine Ruin the South?" *Saturday Evening Post,* May 31, 1947, 36–37, 94–95, 98 (quotation on 37); see also *Memphis Press-Scimitar,* May 27, 1947, MPSM.

10. Gray interviews; Blake interviews; *Memphis Commercial Appeal,* Jan. 27, 1953, clipping in Oscar Goodbar Johnston biography, Memphis Public Library; *Memphis Commercial Appeal,* July 17, 1955, I, 4, clipping; invitation to dedication ceremony, JFM; *Memphis Press-Scimitar,* n.d. (United Press dateline Jan. 21 [1948]), Mar. 6, 1950, n.d. (dateline Mar. 20 [1950]), and Oct. 19, 1955, MPSM; Bessie Terry telephone interviews (including interviews conducted by Terry's daughter, JoeAnn Fava); *Memphis Commercial Appeal,* Oct. 4, 1955; *Cotton Oil and Gin Mill Press,* Oct. 8, 1955; unidentified obituaries, Oct. 7, 1955, clippings in NCCA.

11. *Greenville Delta Democrat-Times,* Oct. 5, 1955, 4; *Memphis Commercial Appeal,* Oct. 5, 1955; Gerald Dearing, "Cotton Comment," *Memphis Commercial Appeal,* Oct. 5, 1955 ("greatest leader" quotation), clippings in NCCA; *Memphis Commercial Appeal,* Feb. 15, 1948, clipping in OJSF, MDAH; Carter, "Cotton Fights Back!"; eulogies, NCCA; see *Time,* Oct. 17, 1955, 110.

12. Horne, Russell, Lipscomb, Lester, Beatty, Blackburn, MOHP, including biographies.

13. *Greenville Delta Democrat-Times,* Nov. 14, 1958, clipping in NCCA; Jon Thompson, with photographs by Cary Wolinsky, "King of Fibers," *National Geographic* 185 (June 1994): 60–86.

# Bibliography

*Manuscripts*

This book was possible not only because of a number of manuscript collections at various depositories and libraries but also, primarily, because of the support and generosity of spirit of Mr. Minor S. Gray, a long-time employee of Delta and Pine Land Company of Mississippi (and Delta Planting Company) and president from 1959 to 1973. Mr. Gray, whose support has already been acknowledged, made available to me a major portion of the letters and other documents, once in my possession and herein cited as Delta and Pine Land Company Records. These materials are now located in the larger collection of company records in the archives of the Mitchell Library of Mississippi State University, Starkville. Although I have not checked the presence of most of the cited documents since they have been deposited at the library, the staff of Mississippi State's archives has done a first-class job of organizing the company's materials. These papers, while crucial for this study, are checkered in their totality.

Delta and Pine Land's records, including some personal correspondence of Oscar Johnston, is supplemented by Johnston's, Delta and Pine Land Company's, and other government material in the National Archives once located in Washington, D.C., and moved during 1994 to the new National Archives facility in College Park, Maryland. Chief among such collections is Record Group 145 (Agricultural Stabilization and Conservation Service), containing memos and other material of the old Agricultural Adjustment Administration. Also very helpful were Record Group 16 (Office of the Secretary of Agriculture), Record Group 161 (Commodity Credit Corporation), containing materials relative to an arcane and sometimes overlooked New Deal agency, and, to a very small extent, Record Group 96 (Farmers Home Administration) and Record Group 83 (Bureau of Agricultural Economics).

The Franklin D. Roosevelt Library in Hyde Park, New York, contains several collections relevant to this study, as does the Mississippi Department of Archives and History in Jackson. Several manuscripts in the Southern Historical Collection at the University of North Carolina in Chapel Hill were utilized, notably, but not limited to, the William R. Amberson Papers and the Jonathan

Daniels Papers. Two important oral history collections were also exploited, namely the Columbia Oral History Collection in the Butler Library at Columbia University in New York City, and the collection of National Cotton Council of America oral histories in the Mississippi Oral History Program at the University of Southern Mississippi in Hattiesburg (the latter materials were delivered to the author). The author also conducted several interviews of those who knew and/or worked with Oscar Johnston. Some material provided the author by the generosity of the late Paul M. Johnston, and the late J. C. Johnston Jr., Oscar's half-brothers, also proved valuable. Other utilized manuscript sources, valuable in their own way, are included among those cited below.

Alabama Dept. of Archives and History, Montgomery
    Bankhead, John H. Papers.
Carnegie Library, Clarksdale, Miss.
    WPA Historical Research Project
    Scrapbook—Clarksdale
Delta State University, Cleveland, Miss.
    Sillers, Walter, Jr. Papers.
Johnston, Paul M.
Joint Collection, University of Missouri, Western Historical Manuscripts Collection-
    State Historical Society of Missouri Manuscripts, Ellis Library, University of
    Missouri–Columbia.
    Doane, D. Howard. Papers.
    Peek, George N. Papers.
Mississippi Dept. of Archives and History, Jackson
    Cutrer, John. Subject File.
    Delta and Pine Land Company. Subject File.
    Dickson (Harris) Collection
    Dickson (Harris) Letter
    Johnston, Oscar. Subject File.
    Percy Family Papers.
    RG 29 (Auditor).
    Scott, Charles. Subject File.
Mitchell Library, Mississippi State University, Starkville
    Delta and Pine Land Company Records (DPLCR).
National Archives
    Records of the Office of the Secretary of Agriculture. RG 16.
    Records of the Farmers Home Administration. RG 96.
    Records of the Bureau of Agricultural Economics. RG 83.
    Records of the Agricultural Stabilization and Conservation Service. RG 145.
    Records of the Commodity Credit Corporation. RG 161.
National Cotton Council of America, Memphis, Tenn.
Franklin D. Roosevelt Library, Hyde Park, N.Y.
    Morgenthau, Henry. Diaries.
    Morgenthau, Henry. Papers, Correspondence.
    Official Files 1K, 258, 614-A, 736.

Press Conferences.
Roosevelt's Secretary's Files.
Roosevelt's Personal Files (2221).
Southern Historical Collection, University of North Carolina Library, Chapel Hill
Amberson, William R. Papers.
Daniels, Jonathan. Papers.
Delta and Providence Farms Papers.
State Historical Society of Wisconsin, Madison
Taylor, Henry C. Papers.
University of Iowa Library, Iowa City
Wallace, Henry A. Papers (microfilm of FDRL material).
Wallace, Henry A. Diary.

## Oral History

Columbia Oral History Collection, Butler Library, Columbia University, New York
Davis, Chester C.
Frank, Jerome
Taylor, Henry C.
Wallace, Henry A.
Warburg, Paul
Mississippi Oral History Program, University of Southern Mississippi, Hattiesburg
Baker, Harry S.
Barringer, Lewis T.
Beatty, Francis J.
Billings, Earle N.
Blackburn, Norris C.
Blair, Raymond E.
Blake, William Rhea
Coberly, William B., Jr.
Coker, Robert R.
Cortright, George C.
Denton, Chauncey L., Jr.
Dunn, Read P., Jr.
Edwards, Macon
Ford, Hadley
Giffen, Russell
Horne, McDonald K., Jr.
Jackson, Robert C.
Kennedy, James R.
Kirkpatrick, Clifton
Lawson, W. D., III
Lester, Garner M.
Lipscomb, Edward L.
Lockett, Aubrey L.
Mayes, J. E.
McCabe, W. Gordon

Montgomery, Walter S.
Power, Carlton H.
Reid, William E.
Russell, Albert R.
Sayre, Charles R.
Wilson, J. Clyde
Youngker, Charles F.

**By Author**

Blake, William Rhea. 1972, 1975 (in person and telephone).
Bledsoe, Samuel. 1975 (in person and telephone).
Confidential Interview 1, 1975.
Confidential Interview 2, 1979 (telephone).
Confidential Interview 3, 1975.
Conn, Earl. 1975.
Dunn, Read, Jr., 1975.
Eastland, James, 1978.
Gray, Minor S. 1970s (in person, including comment by Mrs. O. D. Johnston Gray, and
    telephone).
Hatcher, J. L. 1975.
Hendricks, Pauline. 1972.
Hiss, Alger. 1979 (telephone).
Porter, Paul. 1975.
Robinson, Frank. 1972.
Ross, Tom. 1975 (telephone).
Stout, W. Fred. 1975.
Taylor, Bessie. 1975 (telephone), and by JoeAnn Fava, 1994 (telephone).

**Other**

Johnston, Mary Flynn. Carnegie Library, Clarksdale.
Porter, Paul A. (interview by James Ward).

*Letters*

Blake, William Rhea. 1975.
Dunn, Read Jr. 1989.
Gray, Minor S. 1971.
Hiss, Alger. 1979.
Johnston, J. C., Jr. 1979.
Johnston, Paul M. 1975.

*Congressional Hearings*

U.S. Congress. *Annotated Compilation of the Soil Conservation and Domestic Allot-
    ment Act, as Amended, the Agricultural Act of 1938, as Amended, and Acts Relat-
    ing Thereto. . . .* Washington, 1938.
————. Senate. Committee on Agriculture and Forestry. *Hearings to Regulate the Pro-
    duction and Ginning of Cotton.* 73d Cong., 3d sess., 1934.
————. House. Committee on Agriculture. *Hearing on the Bankhead Cotton Control
    Bill.* 73d Cong., 2d sess., 1934. H. R. 8402. Serial 1.

————. House. Committee on Appropriations. *Hearing Before the Subcommittee of the House Committee on Appropriations (Agriculture Department Appropriation Bill for 1935)*. 73d Cong., 2d sess., 1934.

————. House. Committee on Appropriations. *Subcommittee of House Committee on Appropriations (Agricultural Appropriations Hearing for 1936)*. 74th Cong., 1st sess., 1935.

————. Senate. Committee on Agriculture and Forestry. *Hearings Before the Committee on Agriculture and Forestry on the Loss of Export Trade and the Means of Recovery*. 74th Cong., 1st sess., 1935.

————. Senate. Committee on Agriculture and Forestry. *Hearings Before the Committee on Agriculture and Forestry, on Senate Joint Resolution 205, A Joint Resolution Providing for the Disposition of Certain Cotton Held by the United States*. 74th Cong., 2d sess., 1936.

————. Senate. Committee on Agriculture and Forestry. *Hearings Before the Committee on Agriculture and Forestry Pursuant to Senate Resolutions 103, 125, 172, and 182; Resolutions to Investigate the Causes of the Rapid Decline in the Price of Cotton on the Cotton Exchanges Before, On, or Subsequent to March 11, 1935, Part 2*. 74th Cong., 2d sess., 1936.

————. House. Committee on Appropriations. *Hearing Before the Subcommittee of the House Committee on Appropriations, Appropriations for Retirement of 1933 Cotton Pool Trust Certificates*. 75th Cong., 3d sess., 1938.

————. Senate. Committee on Agriculture and Forestry. *Hearing Before the Senate Committee on Agriculture and Forestry, A Resolution to Investigate Certain Activities of the American Cotton Cooperative Association in Connection with the Marketing of Cotton Financed by the Federal Government*. 75th Cong., 3d sess., 1938. S. R. 137.

————. House. Committee on Appropriations. *Hearings Before the Subcommittee of the Committee on Appropriations, on the Agriculture Department Appropriation Bill for 1944*. 78th Cong., 1st sess., 1943.

————. House. Committee on Agriculture. *Hearings Before the Select Committee of the House Committee on Agriculture, to Investigate the Activities of the Farm Security Administration, Pursuant to House Resolution 119, A Resolution Creating a Select Committee to Investigate the Activities of the Farm Security Administration, Adopted by the House March 18, 1943, Part 3*. 78th Cong., 1st sess., 1944.

————. House. Committee on Agriculture. *Hearings Before the Subcommittee of the Committee on Agriculture (Cotton)*. 78th Cong., 2d sess., 1945.

## Newspapers and Magazines

*Arkansas Democrat*
*Atlanta Constitution*
*Birmingham News*
*Bolivar Commercial*
*Clarksdale Daily Register/Register and Daily News*
*Delta Star*
*(Friars Point) Coahomian*
*Greenville Daily Democrat/Daily Democrat-Times*
*Greenville Weekly Democrat*
*Greenwood Commonwealth* (and *Weekly Edition*)

*Jackson Daily News; Clarion Ledger/Daily News*
*London News-Chronicle*
*London Financial News*
*Manchester Daily Dispatch*
*Memphis Commercial Appeal*
*Memphis Press-Scimitar*
*Mississippian* (Oxford student newspaper)
*New Orleans Times-Picayune*
*New York Herald-Tribune*
*New York Times*
*Newsweek*
*Poplarville Free Press*
*Saturday Evening Post*
*Shreveport Journal*
*Staple Cotton Review*
*Sydney (Australia) Daily Telegraph*
*Time*
*Tunica Times*
*United States News/U.S. News and World Report*
*Vardaman's Weekly/The Issue*
*Washington Post*
*Yazoo Sentinel*

## Books and Articles

Agee, James, and Walker Evans. *Let Us Now Praise Famous Men*. Boston, 1941.
Albertson, Dean. *Roosevelt's Farmer: Claude R. Wickard in the New Deal*. New York and London, 1961.
Ashmore, Harry S. *Civil Rights and Wrongs: A Memoir of Race and Politics, 1944–1994*. New York, 1994.
"Back to the Fundamentals: The Origin, Purposes, Plans, and Operations of the Staple Cotton Cooperative Association." *Staple Cotton Review* 12 (Apr. 1934): 1–2.
Badger, Anthony. *The New Deal: The Depression Years, 1933–40*. New York, 1989.
Baker, Bill R. *Catch the Vision: The Life of Henry L. Whitfield of Mississippi*. Jackson, Miss., 1974.
Baker, Gladys. "'And to Act for the Secretary': Paul Appleby and the Department of Agriculture, 1933–1949." *Agricultural History* 45 (Oct. 1971): 235–58.
Baldwin, Sidney. *Poverty and Politics: The Rise and Decline of the Farm Security Administration*. Chapel Hill, 1968.
Balls, W. Lawrence. *The Cotton Plant in Egypt, Studies in Physiology and Genetics*. London, 1912.
Benedict, Murray R. *Farm Policies of the United States, 1790–1950: A Study of Their Origins and Development*. New York, 1953.
Benedict, Murray, and Oscar Stine. *The Agricultural Commodity Programs: Two Decades of Experience*. New York, 1956.
Berlin, Isaiah. *The Hedgehog and the Fox: An Essay on Tolstoy's View of History*. New York, 1953; reprint, 1986.
Bettersworth, John K. *Mississippi: A History*. Austin, 1959.

"Biggest Cotton Plantation." *Fortune* 15 (Mar. 1937): 125–32, 156, 158, 160.

*Biographical and Historical Memoirs of Mississippi, Embracing an Authentic and Comprehensive Account of the Chief Events in the History of the State, and a Record of the Lives of Many of the Most Worthy and Illustrious Families and Individuals.* 2 vols. Chicago, 1891.

Braeman, John, Robert H. Bremmer, and David Brody. *The New Deal.* Vol. 1, *The National Level.* Columbus, Ohio, 1975.

Brandfon, Robert. *Cotton Kingdom of the New South: A History of the Yazoo Mississippi Delta from Reconstruction to the Twentieth Century.* Cambridge, Mass., 1967.

Brown, D. Clayton. "Health of Farm Children of the South, 1900–1950." *Agricultural History* 53 (Jan. 1979): 170–87.

Burns, James MacGregor. *Roosevelt: The Lion and the Fox.* New York, 1956.

Caldwell, Erskine. *Tobacco Road.* New York, 1932.

Campbell, Christina. *The American Farm Bureau and the New Deal: A Study of the Making of National Farm Policy, 1933–1940.* Urbana, Ill., 1962.

Cantor, Louis. "A Prologue to the Protest Movement: The Missouri Sharecropper Roadside Demonstration of 1939." *Journal of American History* 55 (Mar. 1969): 804–22.

————. *A Prologue to the Protest Movement: The Missouri Roadside Demonstration of 1939.* Durham, N.C., 1969.

Carter, Hodding. "Cotton Fights Back! The Story of the National Cotton Council." A four-part 1939 document evidently reprinted by the National Cotton Council, perhaps from a news article. Given to the author. In author's possession (other copies are presumably at the National Cotton Council, Memphis).

Clayton, W. L. "Farm Relief." *Cotton Digest,* Mar. 25, 1933, 8–9.

Cobb, Cully. "Cotton and the AAA." *Cotton Digest,* Oct. 20, 1934, 17–18.

Cobb, James. *The Most Southern Place on Earth: The Mississippi Delta and the Roots of Regional Identity.* New York and Oxford, 1992.

Cohn, David L. *God Shakes Creation.* Cambridge, Mass., 1935.

————. *The Life and Times of King Cotton.* New York, 1956.

————. *Where I Was Born and Raised.* Boston, 1948.

————. "Share-Cropping in the Delta." *Atlantic Monthly* 159 (May 1937): 579–88.

Connell, Mary Ann. *The Peabody: A Living Tradition.* Oxford, Miss., 1981.

Conrad, David. *The Forgotten Farmers: The Story of Sharecroppers in the New Deal.* Urbana, Ill., 1965.

"Cotton's in the Well." *Fortune* 12 (July 1935): 34–41, 130, 132, 134, 136.

Daniel, Pete. *Breaking the Land: The Transformation of Cotton, Tobacco, and Rice Cultures Since 1880.* Urbana and Chicago, 1985.

————. *Deep'N As It Come: The 1927 Mississippi River Flood.* New York, 1977.

Daniels, Jonathan. *A Southerner Discovers the South.* New York, 1938.

Davis, Joseph. "The Program of the Federal Farm Board." *American Economic Review* 21 (Mar. 1931), 104–13.

"The Dearborn and the Staple Cotton Cooperative Association." *Staple Cotton Review* 2 (Oct. 1, 1924): 1–12.

"The Delta and the Association." *Staple Cotton Review* 1 (Oct. 15, 1923): 1.

Dickson, Harris. *The Story of King Cotton.* New York and London, 1937.

Dill, David B. "Fatigue Studies Among Mississippi Sharecroppers." *Harvard Alumni Bulletin* 42 (Oct. 20, 1939): 113–19.

Dill, David, J. W. Wilson, F. G. Hall, and Sid Robinson. "Properties of the Blood of Negroes and Whites in Relation to Climate and Season." *Journal of Biological Chemistry* 136 (Nov. 1940): 449–60.

"Does It Pay the Delta Farmer to Grow Long Staple Cotton?" *International Cotton Bulletin* 3 (Mar. 1926): 410–20.

Dollard, John. *Caste and Class in a Southern Town.* New Haven, 1937.

Dorris, Fern E. "The Yazoo Basin in Mississippi." *Journal of Geography* 28 (Feb. 1929): 72–79.

Durr, Virginia Foster. *Outside the Magic Circle: The Autobiography of Virginia Foster Durr.* Edited by Holinger F. Barnard. Foreword by Studs Terkel. Tuscaloosa, Ala., 1985.

Edmonds, James. "'Much Obliged!' Bows Brazil to Uncle Sam's AAA." *Saturday Evening Post,* Aug. 10, 1935, 5–7, 72–74.

———. "Amending the Brazilian Weather?" *Saturday Evening Post,* Aug. 31, 1935, 18–19, 49–50, 52.

———. "Around the Clock on the South's Largest Cotton Plantation." *Cotton Trade Journal* (International Edition, 1956–1957): 40–43.

———. "High Prices and Ten Years?" *Saturday Evening Post,* Sept. 7, 1935, 14–15, 75–78, 80–82.

"Eulogies to Oscar Bledsoe." *Staple Cotton Review* 32 (Feb. 1954): 1–2.

Evans, Marion G. "Our New President." *Memphis Chamber of Commerce Journal* 1 (June 1918): 111.

Ferrell, Robert H. *Choosing Truman: The Democratic Convention of 1944.* Columbia, Mo., and London, 1994.

*The Fine Cotton Spinners' and Doublers' Association, Limited.* Introduction by Frank Whitworth, Secretary. Manchester, Eng., 1909 (copy in DPLCR).

Fite, Gilbert. "Mechanization of Cotton Production Since World War II." *Agricultural History* 54 (Jan. 1980): 190–207.

———. "Voluntary Attempts to Reduce Cotton Acreage in the South, 1914–1933." *Journal of Southern History* 14 (Nov. 1948): 481–99.

———. *Cotton Fields No More: Southern Agriculture, 1865–1980.* Lexington, Ky., 1984.

———. *George N. Peek and the Fight for Farm Parity.* Norman, Okla., 1954.

Foster, Arthur, and Arno S. Pearse. "Delta and Pine Land Company of Mississippi." *International Cotton Bulletin* 2 (Sept. 1923): 18–22.

Friedel, Frank. *FDR and the South.* Baton Rouge, 1965.

Galbraith, John Kenneth. *Money: Whence It Came, Where It Went.* Boston, 1975.

Garbicz, Adam, and Jacob Klinowski. *Cinema, The Magic Vehicle: A Guide to Its Achievement, Journey One: The Cinema Through 1949.* Metuchen, N.J., 1975.

Gardner, Lloyd. *Economic Aspects of New Deal Diplomacy.* Madison, Wis., 1964.

Garside, Alston. "Government Activities in Cotton—Part 2(a)." *Cotton Digest,* Jan. 11, 1936, 5–7.

———. "Government Activities in Cotton—Part 2(b)." *Cotton Digest,* Jan. 18, 1936, 5–7.

Garson, Robert A. *The Democratic Party and the Politics of Sectionalism, 1941–1948.* Baton Rouge, 1974.

Giroux, Vincent A., Jr. "The Rise of Theodore G. Bilbo (1908–1932)." *Journal of Mississippi History* 43 (Aug. 1981): 180–209.

Goulden, Joseph. *The Superlawyers: The Small and Powerful World of the Great Washington Law Firms.* New York, 1971.

"Government's Biggest Business Venture." *Fortune* 2 (Nov. 1931): 37–38, 40–41, 123–24.

Grantham, Dewey W. *Southern Progressivism: The Reconciliation of Progress and Tradition.* Knoxville, 1983.

"The Great Mississippi River Flood of 1927." *National Geographic* 53 (Sept. 1927): 243–89.

Grossman, James R. *Land of Hope: Chicago, Black Southerners, and the Great Migration.* Chicago and London, 1989.

Grubbs, Donald. *Cry from the Cotton: The Southern Tenant Farmers Union and the New Deal.* Chapel Hill, 1971.

"Gypsy Smith and the Delta." *Staple Cotton Review* 2 (Apr. 1924): 2.

Halliwell, Leslie. *Halliwell's Film Guide.* 2d ed. New York, 1979.

Hamilton, Charles G. *Progressive Mississippi.* Aberdeen, Miss., 1978.

———. "The Turning Point: The Legislative Session of 1908." *Journal of Mississippi History* 25 (Apr. 1963): 93–111.

———. *Mississippi, Mirror of the 1920s.* Fulton, Miss., 1979.

———. *From New Day to New Deal: American Farm Policy from Hoover to Roosevelt, 1928–1933.* Chapel Hill and London, 1991.

Harrison, Robert W. *A Study of State and Local Efforts Toward Land Development in the Alluvial Valley of the Lower Mississippi River.* Vol. 1, *Alluvial Empire.* Little Rock, 1961.

Heacock, Walter J. "William B. Bankhead and the New Deal." *Journal of Southern History* 21 (Aug. 1955): 347–59.

Hildebrand, J. R. "Machines Come to Mississippi." *National Geographic* 71 (Sept. 1937): 263–318.

Hofstadter, Richard. *The Age of Reform: From Bryan to F.D.R.* New York, 1955.

Holley, Donald. *Uncle Sam's Farmers: The New Deal Communities in the Lower Mississippi Valley.* Urbana, Ill., 1975.

Hollis, Daniel. "'Cotton Ed Smith'—Showman or Statesman?" *South Carolina Historical Magazine* 71 (Oct. 1970): 235–56.

Holmes, William F. *The White Chief: James Kimble Vardaman.* Baton Rouge, 1970.

Hoover, Herbert C. *State Papers, and Other Public Writings.* 2 vols. Edited by William Myers. Garden City, N.Y., 1934.

Hubbard, W. H. *Cotton and the Cotton Market.* New York, 1928.

Hull, Cordell. *The Memoirs of Cordell Hull.* 2 vols. New York, 1948.

Hurst, F. J. "Mississippi's Largest Cotton Farm." *Progressive Farmer* 55 (Feb. 1940): 8, 30.

Irons, Peter H. *The New Deal Lawyers.* Princeton, N.J., 1982.

Johnson, Charles S. *Shadow of the Plantation.* Chicago, 1934.

Johnson, Charles S., Edwin R. Embree, and W. W. Alexander. *The Collapse of Cotton Tenancy: Summary of Field Studies and Statistical Surveys, 1933–35.* Chapel Hill, 1935.

Johnson, Evans C. "John H. Bankhead 2d: Advocate of Cotton." *Alabama Review* 41 (Jan. 1988): 30–58.

Johnson, T. J. "Delta and Pine Land Company." *Service* 6 (Apr. 1942): 11–12.

Johnston, Oscar. "Industrial Plan of the Delta and Pine Land Company of Mississippi." *Journal of Social Hygiene* 26 (Feb. 1940): 73–77.

———. "Is There Need of a Definite Cotton Policy for the United States?" *Cotton Trade Journal* 18 (International Edition, 1938): 14–15, 154–55, 171, 173.

———. "Mechanization, Cotton's Shot in the Arm." *Cotton Trade Journal* 22 (International Edition, 1947): 150–51, 166–67.

————. "Mechanization—A Key to Progress." *Georgia Review* 2 (spring 1948): 10–19.

————. "Origin and Operation of the 1933 Cotton Producers' Pool to December 15 in 1934." *Cotton Trade Journal* 15 (International Edition, 1934–35): 116–17, 138, 161.

————. "Pool and Loan Holdings Are Explained by Oscar Johnston." *Cotton Digest,* May 23, 1936, 5–6.

————. "The Bankhead Bill." *Staple Cotton Review* 12 (Mar. 1934): 1–4.

————. "What Happened? and What Next?" *Cotton Trade Journal* 15 (International Edition, 1934–35): 13, 112, 121.

————. "Will the Machine Ruin the South?" *Saturday Evening Post,* May 31, 1947, 36–37, 94–95, 98.

Jones, Jesse, with Edward Angly. *Fifty Billion Dollars: My Thirteen Years with the RFC* [1932–45]. New York, 1951.

Kelly, Alfred, Winfred Harbison, and Herman Belz. *The American Constitution: Its History and Development.* 7th ed. 2 vols. New York and London, 1991.

Kester, Howard. *Revolt Among the Sharecroppers.* New York, 1936.

Key, V. O., Jr. *Southern Politics in State and Nation.* New York, 1949.

Kile, Orville. *The Farm Bureau Through Three Decades.* Baltimore, 1948.

Kirby, Jack Temple. *Rural Worlds Lost: The American South, 1920–1960.* Baton Rouge and London, 1987.

————. "The Transformation of Southern Plantations, c. 1920–1960." *Agricultural History* 57 (July 1983): 257–76.

Kirkendall, Richard S. *Social Scientists and Farm Politics in the Age of Roosevelt.* Columbia, Mo., 1966.

————. *The United States, 1929–1945: Years of Crisis and Change.* New York, 1974.

Kirwin, Albert D. *The Revolt of the Rednecks: Mississippi Politics: 1876–1925.* Lexington, Ky., 1951; reprint, New York, 1965.

Krueger, Thomas A., review of Donald Grubbs, *Cry From the Cotton: The Southern Tenant Farmers' Union and the New Deal* (Chapel Hill, 1971), in the *Journal of Southern History* 37 (Nov. 1971): 667–68.

Langsford, E. L., and B. H. Thibodeaux. *Plantation Operation and Organization in the Yazoo–Mississippi Delta Area.* USDA Technical Bulletin 682. Washington, 1939.

Lemann, Nicholas. *The Promised Land: The Great Black Migration and How It Changed America.* New York, 1991.

Leuchtenberg, William E. *Franklin D. Roosevelt and the New Deal, 1932–1940.* New York, 1963.

Lord, Russell. *The Wallaces of Iowa.* Boston, 1947.

Lowitt, Richard. "Henry A. Wallace and the 1935 Purge in the Department of Agriculture." *Agricultural History* 53 (July 1979): 607–21.

————. *George W. Norris: The Triumph of a Progressive.* Chicago and London, 1978.

Lyles, Sue. "Concepts of the Old and New Plantation Systems." *Rural Sociology* 5 (Apr. 1940): 227–29.

Manchester, William. *The Glory and the Dream: A Narrative History, 1932–1972.* Boston, 1974.

McConnell, Grant. *The Decline of Agrarian Democracy.* Berkeley and Los Angeles, 1959.

McCullough, David. *Truman.* New York, 1992.

McLaren, J. R. "La Hacienda algodonera mas grande de los Estados Unidos." *La Hacienda* 32 (Oct. 1937): 238–51.

McLemore, Richard A., ed. *A History of Mississippi*. 2 vols. Jackson, Miss., 1973.

McMillen, Neil R. *Dark Journey: Black Mississippians in the Age of Jim Crow*. Urbana and Chicago, 1989.

McPherson, James. *Ordeal By Fire: The Civil War and Reconstruction*. New York, 1982.

Michie, Allan A., and Frank Ryhlick. *Dixie Demagogues*. New York, 1939.

Mitchell, Harry L. *Mean Things Happening in This Land: The Life and Times of H. L. Mitchell, Co-Founder of the Southern Tenant Farmers Union*. Montclair, N.J., 1979.

Moloney, John. *Cotton in Peace and War, Papers of the Institute of Research and Training in the Social Sciences*. Nashville, 1944.

Molyneaux, Peter. *The Cotton South and the American Trade Policy*. New York, 1936.

Mooney, C. P. J., ed. *The Mid-South and Its Builders, Being the Story of the Development and Forecast of the Future of the Richest Agricultural Region in the World*. Memphis, 1920.

Morgan, Chester M. *Redneck Liberal: Theodore G. Bilbo and the New Deal*. Baton Rouge, 1985.

*Mules and Mississippi*. Jackson, Miss., 1980.

Myrdal, Gunnar. *An America Dilemma: The Negro Problem and Modern Democracy*. New York, 1944.

National City Bank of New York. Economic Conditions, Governmental Finance, United States Securities (monthly reports). New York, 1936.

National Cotton Council. *25th Annual Report of Activities, National Cotton Council of America*, n.p., 1964.

"Negro Workers on the World's Largest Cotton Plantation." *Manufacturers Record*, Oct. 25, 1923, 103–6.

Nixon, Edgar B., ed. *Franklin D. Roosevelt and Foreign Affairs*. 3 vols. Cambridge, Mass., 1969.

Nourse, Edwin, Joseph Davis, and John Black. *Three Years of the Agricultural Adjustment Administration*. Brookings Institute Publication No. 73. Washington, 1937.

"On Demobilizing the War Economy." *Fortune* 24 (Nov. 1941): 15–16.

*One Hundred Years of Progress in the Mississippi Delta, Centennial Edition*. Clarksdale, Miss., 1936 (copies in MDAH and CL).

Osborne, Robert. *Academy Awards Illustrated: A Complete History of Hollywood's Academy Awards in Words and Pictures*. LaHabra, Calif., 1969.

Owens, Clarence J. "Biggest Cotton Plantation in the World." *Jackson Daily News*, Mar. 14, 1922, 5.

Patterson, James T. *Congressional Conservatism and the New Deal: The Growth of the Conservative Coalition in Congress, 1933–1939*. Lexington, Ky., 1967.

Paul, George F. "Welfare Work on a Delta Plantation." *Southern Workman* 54 (July 1925): 317–18.

Peek, George, with Samuel Crowther. *Why Quit Our Own?* New York, 1936.

Percy, William Alexander. *Lanterns on the Levee: Recollections of a Planter's Son*. New York, 1941, 1967; reprint, Baton Rouge, 1973.

Pereya, Lillian A. *James Lusk Alcorn: Persistent Whig*. Baton Rouge, 1966.

Perkins, Van L. *Crisis in Agriculture: The Agricultural Adjustment Administration and the New Deal*. Berkeley, 1969.

Phillips, U. B. "The Central Theme of Southern History." *American Historical Review* 34 (Oct. 1928): 30–43.

Proceedings of the Committee on Organization, National Cotton Council, Hotel Peabody, Memphis, Tenn., Nov. 21–22, 1938.

Prunty, Merle, Jr. "Changes in Settlements on the Deltapine Plantation, 1939–1954" (abstract of a paper presented at a meeting of the Association of American Geographers, Apr. 1955). *Annals of the American Association of American Geographers* 45 (Sept. 1955): 292.

———. "The Renaissance of the Southern Plantation" (abstract of a paper presented at a meeting of the Association of American Geographers, Apr. 1954). *Annals of the American Association of American Geographers* 44 (Sept. 1954): 254.

———. "The Renaissance of the Southern Plantation." *The Geographical Review* 45 (Oct. 1955): 459–91.

Ratcliff, J. D. "Revolution in Cotton." *Collier's,* July 21, 1945, 24, 40–42.

Reed, Nicholas. "The South—A Middle Way." *Carolina Magazine* 66 (Mar. 1937): 3–7.

Richards, Henry I. *Cotton and the AAA.* Brookings Institute Publication No. 66. Washington, 1936.

———. *Cotton Under the Agricultural Adjustment Administration, Developments Up to July 1934.* Brookings Institute Pamphlet No. 15. Washington, 1934.

Robinson, Sid, David Dill, J. W. Wilson, and Malus Nielsen. "Adaptations of White Men and Negroes to Prolonged Work in Humid Heat." *American Journal of Tropical Medicine* 21 (Mar. 1941): 261–87.

Robinson, Sid, David Dill, P. M. Harmon, F. G. Hall, and J. W. Wilson. "Adaptations to Exercise of Negro and White Sharecroppers in Comparison with Northern Whites." *Human Biology: A Record of Research* 13 (May 1941): 139–58.

Roller, David C., and Robert W. Twyman, eds. *The Encyclopedia of Southern History.* Baton Rouge, 1979.

Roseboom, Eugene. *A History of Presidential Elections.* New York, 1957, 1964.

Rosenman, Samuel, ed. *Public Papers and Addresses of Franklin D. Roosevelt.* Vol. 2. New York, 1938.

Rowland, Dunbar. *Courts, Judges, and Lawyers of Mississippi.* Jackson, Miss., 1935.

———. *History of Mississippi: The Heart of the South.* 2 vols. Chicago and Jackson, Miss., 1925.

———. *The Official and Statistical Register of the State of Mississippi.* Nashville, 1908; Nashville, 1912; Madison, Wisc., 1917; Centennial Edition, 1920–24; Jackson, Miss., 1923.

———, ed. *Mississippi, Comprising Sketches of Counties, Towns, Events, Institutions, and Persons, Arranged in Cyclopedic Form.* 3 vols. Atlanta, 1907.

Russell, Albert. "Activities of the Delta Council." *The [Oxford] Mississippian* (student newspaper), May 9, 1941, 6; copy in Delta and Providence Farms Papers.

Saloutos, Theodore. "The Southern Cotton Association, 1905–1908." *Journal of Southern History* 13 (Nov. 1947): 492–510.

———. *Farmer Movements in the South, 1865–1933.* Berkeley, 1960.

———. *The American Farmer and the New Deal.* Ames, Iowa, 1981.

Sayre, Charles R. "Cotton Mechanization Since World War II." *Agricultural History* 53 (Jan. 1979): 105–24.

Schlesinger, Arthur M., Jr. *The Coming of the New Deal.* Boston, 1958.

———. *The Crisis of the Old Order, 1919–1933.* Boston, 1957, 1964.

Schuyler, Michael W. "The Politics of Change: The Battle for the Agricultural Adjustment Act of 1938." *Prologue: The Journal of the National Archives* 15 (fall 1983): 164–78.

Shapsmeier, Edward L., and Frederick H. Shapsmeier. *Henry A. Wallace of Iowa: The Agrarian Years*. Ames, Iowa, 1968.

Shideler, James. *Farm Crisis, 1919–1923*. Berkeley and Los Angeles, 1957.

Shlomowitz, Ralph. "The Origins of Southern Sharecropping." *Agricultural History* 53 (July 1979): 557–75.

"Smith, Ellison DuRant." *Biographical Directory of the United States Congress, 1774–1989, Bicentennial Edition*. Washington, D.C., 1989.

*Statistical History of the United States from Colonial Times to the Present*. Stamford, Conn., 1965.

Sternsher, Bernard. *Rexford Tugwell and the New Deal*. New Brunswick, N.J., 1964.

Straus, Robert K. "Enter the Cotton Picker: The Story of the Rust Brothers' Invention." *Harper's* 173 (Sept. 1936): 386–95.

Swain, Martha. *Pat Harrison: The New Deal Years*. Jackson, Miss., 1978.

*Tennessee: A Guide of the State*. New York, 1939.

*Tennessee: The Volunteer State, 1769–1923*. 5 vols. Chicago and Nashville, 1923.

TRB. "Washington Notes." *New Republic*, Sept. 22, 1937, 186–87.

Thomas, Norman. *After the New Deal, What?* New York, 1936.

———. *The Plight of the Share-Cropper*. New York, 1934.

Thompkins, David. *Senator Arthur H. Vandenberg: The Evolution of a Modern Republican, 1884–1945*. East Lansing, Mich., 1970.

Thompson, Jon, with photographs by Cary Wolinsky. "King of Fibers." *National Geographic* 185 (June 1994): 60–86.

Tindall, George B. *The Emergence of the New South, 1913–1945*. Baton Rouge, 1967.

———. "Business Progressivism: Southern Politics in the Twenties." *South Atlantic Quarterly* 62 (winter 1963): 92–106.

Tugwell, Rexford G. *Roosevelt's Revolution: The First Year— A Personal Perspective*. New York, 1977.

Van Auken, Sheldon. "A Century of the Southern Plantation." *Virginia Magazine of History and Biography* 58 (July 1950): 356–87.

Venkataramni, M. S. "Norman Thomas, Arkansas Sharecroppers, and the Roosevelt Agricultural Policies, 1933–1937." *Mississippi Valley Historical Review* 47 (Sept. 1960): 225–46.

Wallace, Henry A. *New Frontiers*. New York, 1934.

———. "Cotton Control and Exports." *Cotton Digest*, Feb. 9, 1935, 6–8.

———. "The Cotton Program Carries On." *Cotton Digest*, Apr. 20, 1935, 7–10.

Wallace, Schuyler C. *The New Deal in Action*. New York, 1934.

*The War of the Rebellion: A Compilation of the Official Records of the Union and Confederate Armies*. 69 vols. in 128 books plus index. Washington, 1880–1901.

Weaver, Herbert C. *Mississippi Farmers, 1850–1960*. Chapel Hill, 1947.

Webber, Thomas L. *Deep Like the Rivers: Education in the Slave Quarter Community, 1831–1865*. New York, 1978.

Weeks, Linton. *Clarksdale and Coahoma County: A History*. Clarksdale, Miss., 1982.

Wenger, O. C. "A Wasserman Survey of the Negroes on a Cotton Plantation in Mississippi." *Venereal Disease Information* 10 (July 20, 1929): 281–88.

White, Mabelle, Mary Jane Whittington, and W. M. Garrard Jr. "William Mountjoy Garrard IV, 1881–1958." *Staple Cotton Review* 36 (Sept. 1958): 1.

Woodruff, Nan Elizabeth. "Mississippi Delta Planters and Debates Over Mechanization, Labor, and Civil Rights in the 1940s." *Journal of Southern History* 60 (May 1994): 263–94.

———. "Mississippi Delta Planters and Debates over Mechanization, Labor, and Civil Rights in the 1940s." *Journal of Southern History* 60 (May 1994): 263–84.

———. "Pick or Fight: The Emergency Farm Labor Program in the Arkansas and Mississippi Deltas During World War II." *Agricultural History* 64 (spring 1990): 74–85.

Woofter, T. J., Jr., and A. E. Fisher. *The Plantation South Today.* Works Projects Administration. Social Problems Series Number 5. Washington, 1940.

Woofter, T. J., Jr., William C. Holley, and Ellen Winston. *The Plantation South, 1934–1937.* Work Projects Administration. Research Monograph 5. Washington, 1940.

"The World's Largest Cotton Plantation." *Manufacturer's Record* 98 (Aug. 28, 1930):50.

Wright, Gavin. *Old South, New South: Revolutions in the Southern Economy Since the Civil War.* New York, 1986.

## Government Publications

*Agricultural Adjustment, 1939–1940, A Report of the Activities of the Agricultural Adjustment Administration, July 1, 1939 through June 30, 1940.* Washington, 1940.

*Agricultural Adjustment, A Report of Administration of the Agricultural Adjustment Act, May 1933 to February 1934.* Washington, 1934.

*Agricultural Adjustment in 1934, A Report of Administration of the Agricultural Adjustment Act, February 15, 1934, to December 31, 1934.* Washington, 1935.

Mississippi House of Representatives. *Journal of the House of Representatives of the State of Mississippi.* Nashville, 1912; Memphis, 1914; Memphis, 1916; Jackson, 1918.

National Emergency Council. *Report to the President on the Economic Conditions of the South.* Washington, 1938.

Rowland, Dunbar, comp. *The Official and Statistical Register of the State of Mississippi.* Nashville, 1908; Nashville, 1912; Madison, Wisc., 1917.

Sayre, Francis B. "What Trade Agreements Mean to the Cotton Grower." Address before the Delta Chamber of Commerce, Cleveland, Mississippi, June 15, 1938. *Department of State Commercial Policy Series 52.* Washington, 1938.

U.S. Congress. *Congressional Record.* 73d Cong., 2d sess., 1934. Vol. 78, pt. 4.

U.S. Dept. of Agriculture. Bureau of Agricultural Economics. "The Cotton Situation." Sept. 28, 1937 (first page). Courtesy to author by Dr. Gladys Baker, Historian, Agricultural History Group, National Economic Analysis Division, USDA, Washington.

———. *Yearbook of Agriculture, 1926.* Washington, 1927.

———. *Yearbook of Agriculture, 1927.* Washington, 1928.

———. *Yearbook of Agriculture, 1935.* Washington, 1936.

U.S. Senate. Senate Documents. Payments Made Under Agricultural Adjustment Program. 74th Cong., 2d sess., no. 274, ser. 10016. Washington, 1936.

## Unpublished Works Not in Manuscript Collections

Balsamo, Larry T. "Theodore G. Bilbo and Mississippi Politics, 1877–1932." Ph.D. diss., Univ. of Missouri–Columbia, 1967.

Brieger, James F., comp., "Hometown Mississippi." 4 parts. n.d.; copy in MDAH.

Foreman, Bill. "The History of the National Cotton Council." Typed manuscript draft, 1963. In author's possession.

Hamilton, Charles G. "Mississippi Politics During the Progressive Period, 1904–1920." Ph.D. diss., Vanderbilt Univ., 1958.

Helms, Douglas. "Just Lookin' for a Home: The Cotton Boll Weevil and the South." Ph.D. diss., Florida State Univ., 1977.

Steward, Dick. "In Search of Markets: The New Deal, Latin America, and Reciprocal Trade." Ph.D. diss., Univ. of Missouri–Columbia, 1969.

WPA Historical Research Project, Coahoma County, the Bar (project 2984, assignment 27), May 7, 1937 (including interview with Mary Flynn Johnston), CL.

# Index

*King Cotton's Advocate* was designed and composed on a Macintosh computer system using PageMaker software. The text is set in New Caledonia; the titles are set in Madrone. This book was designed and typeset by Sheila Hart and manufactured by Thomson-Shore, Inc. The recycled paper used in this book is designed for an effective life of at least three hundred years.